Passion, Craft,
and Method
in Comparative
Politics

Gerardo L. Munck and
Richard Snyder

Passion, Craft, and Method in Comparative Politics

INTERVIEWS WITH

Gabriel A. Almond

Robert H. Bates

David Collier

Robert A. Dahl

Samuel P. Huntington

David D. Laitin

Arend Lijphart

Juan J. Linz

Barrington Moore, Jr.

Guillermo O'Donnell

Adam Przeworski

Philippe C. Schmitter

James C. Scott

Theda Skocpol

Alfred Stepan

THE JOHNS HOPKINS UNIVERSITY PRESS

BALTIMORE

The Johns Hopkins University Press
2715 North Charles Street
Baltimore, Maryland 21218-4363
www.press.jhu.edu

Library of Congress Cataloging-in-Publication Data

Munck, Gerardo L. (Gerardo Luis), 1958–
    Passion, craft, and method in comparative politics / Gerardo L. Munck and
Richard Snyder ; Gabriel A. Almond . . . [et al.].
        p. cm.
    Includes bibliographical references and index.
    ISBN-13: 978-0-8018-8463-4 (hardcover : alk. paper)
    ISBN-13: 978-0-8018-8464-1 (pbk. : alk. paper)
    ISBN-10: 0-8018-8463-2 (hardcover : alk. paper)
    ISBN-10: 0-8018-8464-0 (pbk. : alk. paper)
    1. Comparative government—Study and teaching (Graduate)—United States.
2. Political scientists—United States—Interviews. I. Snyder, Richard (Richard
Owen) II. Title.
JF130.M86 2007
320.3—dc22   2006019755

A catalog record for this book is available from the British Library.

To the fifteen scholars we interviewed for this book,

for all the years they have inspired and taught,
reminding us and so many others
why we were first drawn
to the study of comparative politics,

and for the memorable hours they shared with us
talking about their ideas and lives

Contents

Preface

This book opens a unique window on some of the greatest minds in the field of comparative politics over the past fifty years. It consists of texts based on in-depth interviews with fifteen of the most influential and important scholars in modern comparative politics. The texts are broad in scope, rich in content, and organized around a common set of themes and questions. They span the entire career of each scholar, from graduate school to the present, addressing their formative experiences, intellectual influences, and mentors. They explore these scholars' major works and their perspectives on science, research strategies, and methodological tools. They also delve into relationships with colleagues and students. Finally, they present these scholars' views about the key theoretical and methodological issues being debated today in comparative politics.

To select the fifteen interviewees we first decided to focus on scholars based at U.S. universities during most of their careers. We then identified potential candidates through a survey of graduate syllabi in comparative politics; our goal was to identify the authors whose work is read most widely in graduate training.[1] This list included a larger number of names than we could realistically interview. Using 1950 as the latest date for year of birth, we narrowed the list to a set that (1) spans various generations and (2) encompasses senior scholars associated with a range of diverse approaches to comparative politics. The final list included Gabriel A. Almond, Robert H. Bates, David Collier, Robert A. Dahl, Samuel P. Huntington, David D. Laitin, Arend Lijphart, Juan J. Linz, Barrington Moore, Jr., Guillermo O'Donnell, Adam Przeworski, Philippe C. Schmitter, James C. Scott, Theda Skocpol, and Alfred Stepan.

The end result obviously was not a complete list of scholars who have made significant contributions to modern comparative politics. Some major contributors have passed away, and others, including sociologists and economists who have profoundly shaped how we think about politics around the world, also could not be included in the book. Thus we have no doubt that this book does not tell the full story of comparative politics in the United States, let alone in the world.[2] Still, it does tell an important and

---

1. We conducted our survey in 2000. For a subsequent effort to identify "canonical" works and their authors in comparative politics, see España-Nájera, Márquez, and Vasquez (2003).

2. On the work and contributions of many of these other scholars, see Skocpol (1984), Swedberg (1990), Lipset (1996), Daalder (1997a), Merritt, Russett, and Dahl (2001), *Rivista Italiana di Scienza Politica* (2003), Pasquino (2005), and Velasco Grajales (2004).

illuminating part of the story, because the fifteen scholars on which the book focuses are leading figures in the field.

In preparation for the interviews, we contacted each scholar and set up a time and place for our interview. We sent each the same questionnaire consisting of twenty-five broad questions organized under five headings: (1) intellectual formation and training; (2) major works and ideas; (3) the craft and tools of research; (4) colleagues, collaborators, and students; and (5) the past and future of comparative politics. Finally, prior to each interview, we prepared a more extensive and detailed set of questions by carefully reading each interviewee's corpus of publications and reviewing whatever biographical information we could find about him or her.

The interviews themselves, conducted between mid-2001 and mid-2003, were held at the homes and/or offices of the interviewees (see appendix). They ranged from three to twelve hours in length, and several were conducted over more than one day. The interviews were digitally recorded and later transcribed with the help of a research assistant. The daunting process of transforming a long conversation into a tight, well-organized, and readable document involved several key steps. First, we carefully edited each transcript word-by-word, conducted a thorough check of factual information, and reorganized the material into sections and subsections. We then added headings, references, annotation, and a set of follow-up questions to clarify items and fill in gaps. Next, we returned the edited text to each interviewee, inviting the person to revise the document and give written responses to our follow-up questions. Finally, we incorporated the revisions and additional responses of each interviewee into the final document. Our aim was to produce an accurate, complete, and polished text that, unlike standard academic writing, had the quality of a lively exchange and addressed issues raised through face-to-face dialogue.

The texts that resulted from this process track the evolution of comparative politics since the 1930s. They thus offer valuable oral histories in which scholars from different generations discuss what it was like to be part of the key universities and institutions where the field of comparative politics took shape, and how major projects that spawned seminal works were conceived and carried out. These documents also offer an engaging view of comparative politics in action, getting beyond the textbook discussion of how to do comparative politics by allowing a precious, rare glimpse of the working methods of some of the best scholars in the field.

In addition to the texts based on the interviews, the book also includes material that frames the issues discussed in the interviews and introduces the interviewees. Chapter 1, written by Richard Snyder, explores striking patterns that emerge across the interviews in the passions, skills, and habits of mind of the leading scholars. It thus sheds light on the human dimension of comparative politics, a crucial, yet rarely discussed aspect of the research process. In Chapter 2, Gerardo Munck offers an analytic overview of the origin and evolution of comparative politics in the United States, organized around three issues—the definition of the field's subject matter, the role of theory, and the use of methods—and draws some conclusions about the current state of the field. Each of the subsequent fifteen chapters begins with an introduction that gives an overview of the scholar's major contributions and career landmarks, thus highlighting why he or she is an important figure in modern comparative politics. The fifteen chapters are presented in chronological order according to the year of birth of the interviewees.

This book is a result of the collaborative effort of Gerardo Munck and Richard Snyder from start to finish. But a division of labor was employed. Munck interviewed, was the principal editor of the interviews with, and wrote the introductions on Almond, Collier, Laitin, Lijphart, O'Donnell, Przeworksi, and Schmitter. Snyder performed the same tasks with regard to Bates, Dahl, Huntington, Linz, Moore, Scott, Skocpol, and Stepan. In addition, Snyder, with the assistance of Matthew Lieber and Michael Findley, prepared a glossary that provides key information about the hundreds of social scientists mentioned in the interviews. The glossary serves a dual purpose: it makes it easier for those unfamiliar with the history of comparative politics to comprehend the interviews; it also helps situate the fifteen individuals on which this book focuses in the context of the broader communities of colleagues, students, mentors, and "invisible colleges" in which they live and work. The glossary is available online at www.brown.edu/polisci/people/snyder/.

Several institutions helped support our research. Funding for the transcription of most of the interviews was provided by the Campus Research Board of the University of Illinois, Urbana-Champaign. Richard Snyder acknowledges timely grants from the Humanities Research Fund at Brown University and from the Harvard Academy for International and Area Studies.

Our main debt is to our fifteen interviewees, both for agreeing to be interviewed and for the time they devoted to this project. As an expression of our appreciation and in recognition of their many contributions to comparative politics, we dedicate this book to them. We are saddened that two of our interviewees, Gabriel Almond and Barrington Moore, Jr., did not live to see the final product.

We are grateful to Robert Whiting, who completed the Herculean task of transcribing nearly all of the interviews. At the Johns Hopkins University Press, we enjoyed working with our editor, Henry Tom, and benefited from the suggestions of the Press's three anonymous reviewers. We also appreciate the editorial assistance of Claire McCabe Tamberino and the careful work of our copy editor, Maria denBoer. We acknowledge helpful comments on various aspects of this project from Robert Adcock, Peter Andreas, Jason Brownlee, Melani Cammett, Houchang Chehabi, Thad Dunning, Sean Elias, Robert Fishman, John Gerring, Angela Hawken, Evan Lieberman, James Mahoney, Scott Mainwaring, Dietrich Rueschemeyer, Daniel Slater, Timothy Snyder, Judith Tendler, Kurt Weyland, and Alan Zuckerman. We also thank Rocío de Terán for her help with the interview with Linz, Nancy Leys Stepan for her help with the interview with Stepan, and Sebastián Mazzuca for his participation in the interview with O'Donnell.

Finally, Gerardo Munck thanks the many friends who have enriched his life since early 2001, when the idea for this project crystallized in the course of long conversations back in Illinois. He is thankful for their reminding him that life is about more than ideas. Richard Snyder wishes to thank his wife, Margarita, and his parents, Margaret and Roger, for their love and support. He also hopes that Ellen Margarita Snyder, who was born as the book was nearing completion, will read it someday with interest and pleasure.

*Passion, Craft,
and Method
in Comparative
Politics*

The Human Dimension of Comparative Research

Richard Snyder

This book fills a void in comparative politics: the lack of a text that illuminates the human dimension of scholarship and the intricacies of the actual research process.[1] Social science research, as presented in professional publications, is cloaked by the "rhetoric of impersonality" that obscures the people who actually do the research.[2] When students read key works in the field, they seldom learn about the extra-scientific aims and motives that often drive scholars to tackle a research problem, how networks of colleagues, students, and collaborators, that is, the "invisible college," influence research, and, finally, the fits, starts, and surprises that inevitably characterize real, workaday research. We occasionally get a fleeting glimpse of such matters in the preface to a book, where the author may carefully draw back the curtain of impersonality and selectively disclose some of the twists and turns of the actual research process or the role played by his or her invisible college.[3] Still, by the time they finish their training, most students know nothing about the people who produced the books and articles they have spent years debating, admiring, and attacking. The authors of the leading works in the field are literally just names on the jackets of books and the title pages of articles.

Unless otherwise noted, all quoted material is drawn from the interviews presented in subsequent chapters of this book.

1. The lack of such a text characterizes political science, in general (though see Baer et al. 1991). Most textbooks focus on tools and methods; or, alternatively, are organized around distinct theoretical approaches and schools, often advocating one particular approach. Instead of focusing on "schools and tools," this book focuses on *people,* that is, individual scholars, drawn from across the range of approaches, schools, and generations. Along related lines, see Daalder (1997a) for a portrait of the field of comparative European politics based on intellectual autobiographies by leading figures in this area, including several of the fifteen scholars interviewed for this book.

2. The term *rhetoric of impersonality* is from Berger (1990, xix). On how interviews with scholars can serve to break through "workaday rhetoric," see Swedberg (1990, 18). See also Klamer (1984), McCloskey (1986), and Wolpert and Richards (1988).

3. Journal articles do not have prefaces and are thus even more impersonal than books.

What is wrong with this state of affairs? Is not science *supposed* to be impersonal? The value and importance of scientific research surely does not depend on who the scientist is. Students already have plenty to learn, and thus a focus on the human dimension of research, while perhaps titillating in a *People Magazine* way when juicy gossip surfaces, is arguably a waste of scarce time. Moreover, focusing on the people who produce research, especially on a small set of leading scholars, as this book does, may foster a pernicious cult of personality. Why, then, is the human dimension of comparative research something worth knowing?

First, a focus on the human dimension of scholarship helps puncture the intimidating façade that makes the authors of major works appear as "hallowed figures not easily imagined as flawed human beings" (Berger 1990, xvi). Biographical information can make the achievements of the best scholars seem attainable, which, in turn, elicits far more striving from students than a perspective that sets the leading lights atop an unreachable Mount Olympus.

Second, studying the human dimension exposes how the actual research process often diverges sharply from the stylized version presented in methodology textbooks and also in final, published products. Instead of proceeding in a linear, orderly fashion, real research, as practiced by the fifteen leading scholars on whom this book focuses, is actually laden with mistakes, false leads, and serendipitous breakthroughs. By getting beyond the rhetoric of impersonality that characterizes professional publications, a focus on the human dimension helps better align students' expectations about how research works with the realities of research.[4]

Third, a focus on the human dimension of scholarship highlights that a career in comparative politics involves far more than just mastering and applying techniques of research. A scholarly career encompasses a host of other key activities: teaching; participating in departmental and university communities as well as professional associations; interacting with colleagues, collaborators, and students; attending and organizing professional conferences and workshops; seeking funding for research; deciding whether and how to engage policy makers and other nonacademic audiences; and choosing the kinds of research projects to pursue at different stages of a career and a life. With the exception of teaching, students receive little, if any, systematic instruction about the various elements that comprise the "total package" of a modern scholarly career. Although some graduate programs offer a seminar on the professional aspect of the discipline, typically focused on publishing and job market strategies, most students learn about the non-technical elements of a scholarly career informally

4. For one scholar's effort to expose his "actual ways of working," see Mills (1959).

from their teachers. By showing how leading scholars structure their careers and balance the often competing demands of research, teaching, and service to their universities and profession, this book offers valuable insights about the range of diverse career pathways in modern political science.

The interviews presented illustrate these various advantages of exploring the human dimension of research. This introductory chapter emphasizes a further advantage: focusing on the human dimension sheds light on the skills, qualities, and habits of mind that lead to excellence in comparative research. Although the interviews with fifteen leading figures in comparative politics during the past half-century reveal no single path to excellence, no cookie-cutter template for how to become a top scholar, the best researchers share three key attributes: (1) rich life *experiences* that spark an interest in research topics and, more important, give scholars a compelling reason to care about the problems on which they work; (2) *passion* about research, often rooted in life experiences and normative commitments; and (3) a willingness to take intellectual and professional *risks*. Moreover, the scholars interviewed in this book voice a strong concern that these very qualities are in alarmingly short supply among students and professors today. Hence, a focus on experience, passion, and risk not only helps us better understand the achievements of the best researchers in comparative politics over the past fifty years, it also points to major current challenges facing the field as it advances into the twenty-first century.

It bears emphasis that experience, passion, and risk should not be seen as *sufficient* conditions for excellence in comparative research. The leading scholars have many other qualities that clearly contributed to their successes, including formidable intelligence, self-discipline, ambition, persistence, creativity, wide-ranging curiosity about politics and society, an extraordinary capacity for hard work, and maybe even luck.[5] As highlighted in the interviews, each scholar also has a distinct personality and intellectual style. Moreover, had a random sample of comparativists, rather than leading lights, been interviewed, passionate and experienced risk takers might have been found among the ranks of the less renowned or even the mediocre.[6] Still, the combination of experience, passion, and risk stands as a striking and important commonality across the fifteen scholars, and

5. Luck may be more important in determining the impact rather than the quality of research. When told that he had been lucky in his research, Louis Pasteur replied, "Fortune favors the prepared mind." See Wolpert and Richards (1988, 6).

6. Put in more technical terms, the "cases" were deliberately selected on one value of the dependent variable, because ordinary and below-average scholars were not interviewed. Also, had the N been increased by interviewing more top scholars, some might have been found to lack experience, passion, and risk taking. Although these three attributes may be neither necessary nor sufficient conditions for success in comparative research, they do characterize the fifteen leading scholars in the sample.

because the following chapters probe the specific characteristics of each scholar, this commonality is emphasized here.

The next three sections assess how a focus on experience, passion, and risk illuminates both the qualities that distinguish the best researchers and key challenges currently facing comparative politics. The fourth section discusses how exploring the human dimension of comparative research provides a stronger understanding of one of the most elusive aspects of scientific inquiry: the process of generating ideas. Finally, the chapter makes a plea against professional amnesia, arguing that the tendency of the field to dismiss older works as antiquated, even pre-scientific, robs us of powerful models of excellence and weakens our self-confidence about the achievements of comparative politics. We thus need to strengthen professional memory by knowing, teaching, and drawing inspiration from the history of our field.

Experience: Rich Lives

May you live in interesting times.—*Attributed to a Chinese curse*

The scholars on whom this book focuses draw a clear and explicit connection between their life experiences and the research problems they select. Some recount how their interest in studying politics was sparked by large-scale social trauma, for example, war, economic crisis, or political instability. Others tell how involvement in political organizing, military service, or foreign travel had a similar effect. The overall picture that emerges of the leading scholars in comparative politics is not of cloistered bookworms, but of engaged people with remarkably rich real-world experiences, especially during their formative years. This suggests a provocative hypothesis: *the quality of one's scholarship depends on the quality of one's life experiences.* Why does experience matter? How can the quality of experience affect the quality of research? First, experience infuses research with meaning and purpose. If one has lived under a repressive, non-democratic regime, as did several of the scholars interviewed in this book, then the challenge of explaining the rise and fall of these regimes is not an abstract mental puzzle, but a visceral matter of good and evil. Linkages between life experiences and research questions can thus foster the commitment and drive required to excel. Second, experience strengthens knowledge about the range of human behavior and about how the political and social worlds work. Knowledge grounded in experience serves both as a source of fresh ideas and as a basis for testing, and potentially challenging, generalizations. The interviews provide ample evidence of how life experiences generate passionate devotion to research problems as well as a reservoir of knowledge from which new ideas are drawn.

Table 1.1. Year and Country of Birth of Leading Scholars in Comparative Politics

Gabriel A. Almond	b. 1911	United States
Barrington Moore, Jr.	b. 1913	United States
Robert A. Dahl	b. 1915	United States
Juan J. Linz	b. 1926	Germany (raised in Spain)
Samuel P. Huntington	b. 1927	United States
Arend Lijphart	b. 1936	Netherlands
Guillermo O'Donnell	b. 1936	Argentina
Philippe C. Schmitter	b. 1936	United States (raised in Europe and United States)
James C. Scott	b. 1936	United States
Alfred Stepan	b. 1936	United States
Adam Przeworski	b. 1940	Poland
Robert H. Bates	b. 1942	United States
David Collier	b. 1942	United States
David D. Laitin	b. 1945	United States
Theda Skocpol	b. 1947	United States

The fifteen scholars can be fruitfully classified according to when and where they were born.[7] As seen in Table 1.1, these dimensions divide the scholars into three groups: (1) *older Americans* born during the 1910s and 1920s (Almond, Dahl, Huntington, Moore); (2) *foreigners* born during the 1920s and 1930s (Lijphart, Linz, O'Donnell, Przeworski);[8] and (3) *younger Americans* born during the 1930s and 1940s (Bates, Collier, Laitin, Schmitter, Scott, Skocpol, Stepan). The first and second groups converge in their common experience of large-scale societal trauma: the four Americans born during the 1910s and 1920s were young adults or adolescents during the Great Depression and World War II. Two (Almond, Dahl) served in the U.S. armed forces during the war, and a third (Moore) worked for a government intelligence agency (i.e., the Office of Strategic Services [OSS]).[9] The three European scholars born during the 1920s and 1930s (Linz, Lijphart, and Przeworski) experienced the dislocations caused by World War II,[10] whereas O'Donnell, who was born in Latin America, lived through the political and economic turmoil of Argentina during the 1950s and 1960s. By contrast, the seven American scholars born during the 1930s and 1940s did not directly experience large-scale social disruption. Still, they were young

7. The criteria used to select the fifteen scholars interviewed for this book are discussed in the preface.

8. Przeworski was born in 1940.

9. The OSS was the precursor to the CIA.

10. On how the traumatic events in Europe during the first half of the twentieth century affected a whole generation of older émigré social scientists, see Coser (1984), Bendix (1986), Hirschman (1995, Part II), Gay (1998), and Dawidoff (2003).

adults in the 1960s, during the political and societal upheavals associated with the civil rights movement and the Vietnam War. As the interviews reveal, these experiences often had a strong effect on their scholarship.

Older Americans and Foreigners: The Trauma of the Great Depression and World War II

The Great Depression and World War II had a major impact on the older Americans. Gabriel Almond draws an explicit link between his scholarship and his work at the Unemployment Relief Service in the Chicago Stock-yards during the Depression: "When I grew up, it was one problem after another, one disaster after another . . . I was moved by these unemployed Chicago workers who came and told you: 'My children don't have any shoes, and in the winter their feet get wet, and they get sick. Can I see my social worker so she can give me a certificate to take to a department store and they will give me some shoes?' That's what made me a kind of social scientist of Left politics at that time." As a result of these experiences and his later work in the U.S. army in Germany at the end of World War II, Almond says he "always thought of political science as dealing with very urgent and palpable evils, such as civil conflict, economic breakdown and poverty, and war" (Almond 2002, 2–3).[11]

Robert Dahl offers a gripping account of how his battlefield experiences in Europe during World War II had a decisive impact on his decision to become a scholar: "Sometime between November 1944 and May 1945, somewhere in France or Germany, it became clear to me that the things I liked to do most were read, write, and talk about ideas. So the light came on, and I decided that if I survived I would be an academic." Moreover, his wartime experiences made the topic on which his scholarship centered, democracy and its enemies, a compelling one laden with normative con-tent: "For people like me, the real threat during the 1930s and 1940s that democracy would end, that it would be destroyed, impressed on our gener-ation the importance of democracy. We realized that the alternatives to democracy were so much worse."

Barrington Moore, Jr.'s work as a government analyst in the OSS during World War II exposed him to an extraordinary group of German intellec-tuals who had fled Nazi Germany, including Herbert Marcuse, Otto Kirch-

11. In Chapter 3, Almond further discusses how the historical context of the 1930s and 1940s influenced his choice of research topics: "I have been concerned about the big problems, first the Depression, the New Deal, the war, National Socialism, fascism. Take Germany. Here's the country that invented higher education in the social sciences, where the first real social science journal was published, edited by Max Weber, going Nazi. It drove me crazy. I felt obliged to study these problems however I could."

heimer, and Franz Neumann.[12] Through his interaction with these émigré scholars, Moore learned how to use Marxist theory in historical analysis, a technique he later applied fruitfully in his most important work, *Social Origins of Dictatorship and Democracy* (Moore 1966). Moore thus concludes, "In many ways, that book was a product of my experiences at the OSS."

The research interests of the foreign scholars born during the 1920s and 1930s—Linz, Lijphart, O'Donnell, and Przeworski—were shaped deeply by the fear, uncertainty, and economic hardship they experienced during World War II and living under repressive authoritarian regimes. According to Juan Linz, who experienced the Spanish Civil War (1936–39) as a boy, "My interest first in social problems and then in politics is the result of living, practically since childhood . . . all the complex history of Europe in the interwar years from post–World War I to the Franco regime." Linz draws a connection between his Spanish background and the research questions that have commanded his interest:

> To ignore the [Spanish] Civil War and its origins, or the Franco regime, was not conceivable for a young Spaniard like me with an interest in political and social science. And who could live in the 1970s without looking at transitions to democracy? As soon as the transition started in Portugal in 1974, I quickly got my plane ticket and went several times so I could follow the democratization process by attending party meetings and rallies and by talking with politicians. What was happening in Portugal might be relevant to what was eventually going to happen in Spain, because Franco was not eternal. Because of your biography, you have a personal interest and involvement that motivate the selection of many research problems.

Arend Lijphart vividly describes the fear and deprivation he experienced as a child in the Netherlands during World War II, recalling dogfights in the sky above his town, food shortages, and a refugee from the Germans who hid in his house. In assessing the relationship between these events and his subsequent research, Lijphart concludes, "my experience during World War II made me unusually averse to violence and especially interested in questions of both peace and democracy."

Guillermo O'Donnell, who grew up in Argentina during the 1950s, was nearly arrested when the student group in which he participated ran afoul of the dictatorship of Juan Perón. Later, during the military dictatorships that ruled Argentina in the 1970s, O'Donnell was a target of threats from armed groups both on the Right and Left of the political spectrum. He sees a direct link between these terrifying experiences and his work as a social scientist: "I have done research on questions that originated in the fact that

---

12. See Coser (1984) for useful vignettes about Marcuse and Neumann.

we were governed by horrible regimes in Latin America and because I much preferred democracy." Adam Przeworski, who was raised in communist Poland in the 1940s and 1950s, recalls that "one's everyday life was permeated with international, macro-political events. Everything was political." Like O'Donnell, Przeworski, too, ran into trouble with the dictatorship that controlled his country, essentially forcing him into exile abroad.

As a result of their formative experiences, the core research questions on which these scholars focused—Why do democracies break down? How can stable democracy be achieved? What is the relationship between capitalism and democracy?—were not mere abstractions, but palpable, normatively charged problems.

Younger Americans: The Turmoil of the 1960s

Growing up in the United States during the 1950s and 1960s, the seven younger Americans (Bates, Collier, Laitin, Schmitter, Scott, Skocpol, and Stepan) were not exposed to the hardships of economic crisis, war, and repressive regimes experienced by their American elders and foreign-born contemporaries. They were too young to remember the Great Depression or to have served in World War II. Still, several of the younger Americans recount how the defining political events of the 1960s—the civil rights movement and the Vietnam War—sparked their interest in comparative politics. James Scott participated in the student rights movement and took part in numerous civil rights marches in his capacity as a leader of the National Student Association. Indeed, his political engagements proved a source of friction between him and the political science faculty at Yale, where he did his doctoral studies. According to Scott, "the first thing I did in graduate school was try to pass a student resolution against the Bay of Pigs, which the faculty went ape shit over and tried to stop, because they thought graduate students were professionals and should not take political positions." Skocpol describes herself as "a passionate supporter of the antiwar movement" and discusses how her undergraduate volunteer work teaching African American college students in Mississippi provided "a way to get involved in large-scale social change."

Among the younger American scholars, a wide range of extracurricular experiences—foreign travel and study, service in the Peace Corps, a summer internship in Washington, D.C., military duty—shaped both their initial decisions to become social scientists and their subsequent choices of research questions. Bates took a high school trip to Africa that marked the start of a lifelong enchantment with the region: "I decided that going to Africa was the most important thing I'd ever done in my life, and I wanted a career that would get me back to Africa as often as possible." A summer internship at the Department of State during college deepened his fascination with Africa. Schmitter's interest in Latin America was piqued by studying painting in Mexico. Stepan took a six-month trip around the world after college that exposed him to puzzling cross-national differences in the relationship between politics and religion, a theme that would figure prominently in his research decades later. Moreover, Stepan's decision to write his dissertation and first book on the military's role in politics in Brazil cannot be understood apart from his prior service in the U.S. Marine Corps and work as a journalist in Latin America (Stepan 1971). Laitin's stint as a Peace Corps volunteer in Somalia proved an "exhilarating" experience that informed his research on language and politics in Africa and beyond. By broadening their horizons and generating enthusiasm about substantive political issues, the extracurricular experiences of the younger Americans served as less traumatic surrogates for the shocks of war, repression, and socioeconomic dislocation experienced by their elders and foreign-born peers, who, as the purported Chinese curse puts it, lived in more "interesting" times.

Are You Experienced?

The scholars interviewed in this book are concerned that students today lack experience.[13] Linz observes that many students "typically go from a good high school to a good college, get good grades, and then go directly to graduate school, having already majored in college in the same field in which they do their graduate work. They have never done anything else except be in the university, and that may be a drawback." Dahl notes, "My impression is that graduate students today, although many are better educated coming out of high school than I was coming out of college, lack a depth of human experience with ordinary people who aren't involved in the academic framework." Przeworski voices a similar concern:

> The people who entered graduate school during the Vietnam era had gone through quite a lot in their lives. They had intense feelings about politics, culture, and society. They usually had done something else, often political organizing, and were going back to school to reflect on their experiences, often seen as failures. Very often they were not teachable, because they were mistrustful of "positivism" and hostile to rigorous method. . . . But they deeply

13. This section embraces the spirit of the "art of mentoring" series, published by Basic Books, which is based on Rainer Maria Rilke's *Letters to a Young Poet,* and invites leaders of the arts and professions to contribute a text "meant to shape the future of their disciplines and inspire the careers of the next generation and generations after that." See, for example, Dershowitz (2001).

cared about politics; they studied politics because they wanted to change the world. Today the situation is different. These kids, and they are kids, who are now in graduate school, by and large, have grown up in exceptionally peaceful, prosperous, and non-conflictive times. These students are smart, well educated, and eager to be taught. But they have no passions or interests. These kids absorb education and all the skills easily, but when the moment arrives when they are supposed to start asking questions, they have nothing to ask.

If, as the evidence from the interviews suggests, the quality of comparative research depends in part on the quality of the life experiences of the people who do it, then the experiential deficit noted by Linz, Dahl, and Przeworski among students today raises concerns about the future vitality of the field. What can be done about the experiential deficit? How can aspiring scholars who have not known economic crisis, war, or repressive political regimes, that is, who have had the good fortune to live in relatively *uninteresting* times, enrich their lives in ways that could enhance the quality of their work?[14]

One way to gain experience is to avoid going straight to graduate school after finishing the undergraduate degree. Taking time off after college to travel or work can help whet the appetite for comparative research. Regrettably, admissions committees for doctoral programs in the social sciences probably place insufficient emphasis on extracurricular experiences and are too eager to admit students directly from undergraduate programs. MBA programs routinely require students to spend several years acquiring hands-on business experience beforehand; social science doctoral programs might do well to adopt a similar standard. In sum, professors should strongly consider advising undergraduate students who are contemplating academic careers to "slow down!"

In addition to travel and nonacademic work, other ways to broaden one's horizons include learning languages and even reading literature. Both provide exposure to different ways of thinking, and reading literature helps attune us to variation in human behavior. Carrying out research in a foreign country provides a further way to surmount an experiential deficit, especially for students who go straight into doctoral programs after finishing their undergraduate degrees. As Bates bluntly puts it, "Fieldwork is the cure for bullshit. When you do fieldwork, you take your research problems from reality." Here, the recommendation to "slow down" merits repeating. Graduate students today often face heavy pressure to finish their doctoral degrees quickly, in five or at most six years. This pressure, which may stem largely from cost-management measures by university administra-

14. Of course, the post-9/11 period of global terrorist threat may turn out to be far from uninteresting.

tors, makes it harder to acquire experience through extended fieldwork or by spending time abroad as an exchange student. In light of the relationship this book reveals between life experiences and excellence in comparative research, efforts to shorten the length of doctoral training may prove quite costly if they cut the amount of time students with experiential deficits can spend in the field.

The process of seeking new experiences should not stop after graduate school. As Schmitter observes, "to be a good comparativist, you have to be comparative yourself. That is, you must habituate yourself to living in different cultures and being on the outside. You have to structure your life comparatively, seeking out opportunities to go to different countries." The quest for rich experiences that infuse our work with meaning and purpose, provide fresh ideas, and deepen knowledge about the range of human behavior is a lifelong endeavor.

Passion: The Emotional and Normative Aspects of Research

I am a brain, Watson. The rest of me is a mere appendix.
—*Sherlock Holmes (as quoted in Grann 2004, 62)*

Inspiration plays no less a role in science than it does in art.
—*Max Weber (1946a, 136)*

In his claim that he is just a brain, Sherlock Holmes evokes a common perception of scientific inquiry as a dispassionate endeavor carried out by brains in formaldehyde. From this perspective, emotion, feeling, and other "hot" aspects of human nature are contaminants that cloud "cool" rational judgment and thus block scientific progress. Passion has no place in science.

The interviews in this book challenge the view that scientific inquiry is a cold, heartless enterprise. Instead, the evidence from the interviews supports Weber's assertion that "inspiration plays no less a role in science than it does in art." The best scholars in comparative politics are very passionate about their work. Indeed, they often describe their research in patently emotional terms. O'Donnell sees himself as someone who "deal(s) with the kinds of real-world problems that deeply bother me when I'm shaving." He says that throughout his life he has been "obsessively concerned" with the political misadventures of his country, Argentina. Reflecting on what motivated him to continue doing research into his nineties, Almond remarks, "It's enjoyable to solve a problem. I get a thrill." Dahl observes that "for the best students the study of politics engages not just their intellects, but also their somatic systems. There is feeling, emotion." Finally, in reflecting on his experience doing ethnographic fieldwork for two years in a Malaysian village, Scott concludes, "It's very productive when you become so preoccupied with something intellectually that it occupies your waking and sleeping hours, and you're even daydreaming about it. That's a great thing for ideas."

Emotional engagement may even be *necessary* to produce excellent research (Zuckerman 1991, Ch. 6). Dahl proposes the intriguing hypothesis that the quality of our work depends on how much we enjoy it. The interviews provide evidence that pleasure matters in scientific research. Linz notes, "Each time I follow some hunch and it fits, it's interesting and pleasurable. I learn something, and, fortunately, society is paying me for having my fun." Asked what motivated him to keep working at the age of eighty-nine, Moore responded, "There's a certain amount of idealistic curiosity and intellectual pleasure that partly comes from problem solving." Stepan's description of his collaboration with Linz, which often involves late-night work sessions that, by 3:00 a.m., leave dozens of books, articles, and maps strewn like a field of debris across Linz's living room, evokes a childlike sense of play. Przeworski succinctly states, "I just like doing research."[15]

What drives the enthusiasm these scholars feel for their research? Their excitement stems partly from the pleasure they get from scholarship. Still, their passion for research is often rooted in something deeper: the conviction that the questions they study are normatively important and, hence, their work has implications for the "real world" of politics, policy, and public opinion. This conviction imbues the research enterprise with meaning, which, in turn, elicits passion.

But are normative motives and goals compatible with science? According to a currently influential school in political science, "positive political economy," the answer is "no." Indeed, this school partly stakes its scientific aspirations on the claim that it studies how things *are,* not how they *should be,* which it regards as a matter for nonscientific, "normative" theory (Alt and Shepsle 1990).[16] The interviews challenge the view that positive and normative theory should operate in separate spheres: some of the most influential scholars in comparative politics self-consciously straddle positive and normative research. Dahl describes himself "as comfortably combining the normative, ethical aspects of political science with the empirical, and thus the scientific, aspects of political science." He laments that "many political scientists today unfortunately feel uncomfortable linking normative political theory with empirically grounded social science, to the detriment of both sides . . . [because] it is very hard to ask important research

---

15. Research is not all "fun and games." Przeworksi even notes that he finds painful the process of getting up to speed with methodological advances. Overall, the leading scholars demonstrate a remarkable capacity for hard work.

16. The notion that science should be "value-free," of course, has a long pedigree.

questions unless you define them in terms of their human value, in terms of what difference it will make if you answer them." Lijphart describes his work in similar terms:

> I see my research as starting with a normatively important variable—something that can be described as good or bad, such as peace or violence. I then proceed to investigate what produces these different outcomes. Finally, I conclude by presenting prescriptions, that is, measures that would produce the desired outcome. I don't see a tension between normative concerns and an aspiration to do science. In fact, I think a normative, prescriptive conclusion can be drawn from most empirical relationships.

As these examples suggest, the belief that one is addressing normatively important problems with real-world implications makes research meaningful, which, in turn, helps generate and sustain enthusiasm for scholarship. Moreover, it is feasible to combine a focus on research questions that are meaningful in terms of our values and moral commitments with impartiality, rigor, and objectivity in the pursuit of answers to these questions (Weber 1949, 49–112).[17] Efforts to build a firewall between positive and normative theory are thus unnecessary to achieve scientific objectivity; and because such efforts run the risk of draining the passion from research, they should be avoided.

Passion Lost: The Iron Cage of Professionalism

The scholars interviewed in this book worry that both professors and students today lack passion for their work. Skocpol observes, "I talk to a lot of graduate students who say they feel very confined. They seem to choose research questions out of a sense of duty, working on a particular topic because it is what they are expected to do to reach the next career stage. I am not sure enough people are following their noses and trusting their curiosity to lead them to a question that matters." In a similar vein, Dahl states, "Sometimes when I look at what gets published in the *American Political Science Review* I ask myself, 'Is this person really excited by that?'" Scott is concerned that too many professors and students "think of scholarship as a career, as an 8-to-5 job."[18]

17. On Weber's "dual commitment to objectivity *and* subjectivity in the social science enterprise," see Fishman (2005). See also Schluchter (1979). On how leading social scientists, including Robert Dahl, combined their normative commitments to liberalism with objective empirical inquiry in the aftermath of World War II, see Katznelson (2003).

18. Concerns about the negative impact of professionalization on the social sciences are not new. See the review of previous work on this matter in Gunnell (2004, 264–66).

What can be done about the lack of passion these scholars observe? First, professors need to do better in communicating their enthusiasm for their work to students. If professors show little passion for research and signal that scholarship is a 9-to-5 job, then students cannot be blamed for behaving this way, too. Second, works can be assigned that give students models of first-rate research by scholars who care deeply about what they study. This strategy can be seen in Bates's use of Grant McConnell's *Private Power and American Democracy* (1966), which he regularly assigns in courses. McConnell's book palpably conveys his anger about the use of public power for private advantage, which gives the reader, as Bates puts it, "a reason to care, a reason to get pissed off and join the author in the joy of the chase."

Fostering interactive communities that break the confines of a 9-to-5 routine can also help generate and sustain enthusiasm among both professors and students. Schmitter describes how most of his colleagues at the University of Chicago lived in the same neighborhood, Hyde Park, and thus frequently saw each other outside the workplace. This interaction elicited nonstop, rolling conversations and arguments, even among colleagues with quite different views about how to study politics. These conversations helped keep the faculty challenged, engaged, and excited. Skocpol notes that the study groups she joined as a graduate student had a similar effect, as did the weekly faculty-student workshops in which she later participated as a faculty member at both the University of Chicago and Harvard. These examples suggest that igniting passion in comparative politics requires that we pay closer attention to organizing our communities of learning in ways that generate excitement about research.

Finally, sparking passion requires the recognition that emotional engagement, normative commitments, and excellence in research are by no means incompatible: some of the best scholars explicitly see themselves as driven by both normative and positive concerns. Not only is it feasible to study issues we care about, it is *desirable* to study such issues. Yet in the absence of rich life experiences and normative commitments, finding a topic we care about passionately can be a tall order.

Risk: Taking Chances

In addition to rich life experiences and passion, the scholars interviewed for this book share a third quality: audacity. The best researchers in comparative politics have taken professional, intellectual, and even personal risks across three key areas: (1) how they define their relationships to teachers; (2) how they position themselves in relation to mainstream research; and (3) the kinds of questions they study.

Teachers

Defining our relationship with mentors and advisors is often a tricky matter, as we seek to balance autonomy and independence against the impulse to emulate and even imitate an admired teacher. Moreover, many teachers expect allegiance, even obedience, from students, although they may not realize or admit it. Because the support of a mentor can play an indispensable role in getting a job and successfully launching a career, challenging one's advisors can be a frightening move fraught with hazard. Still, the interviews with leading scholars provide numerous examples of this kind of risk taking.

Skocpol's very first article (Skocpol 1973), published when she was a graduate student, was a critical review of her teacher, Barrington Moore's magnum opus, *Social Origins of Dictatorship and Democracy* (1966). Stepan chose not to heed his advisors' warnings against writing a dissertation on the Brazilian military (Stepan 1971), a topic they said would prove too difficult. And Schmitter and Laitin both had the audacity to disagree openly with their teachers at the University of California, Berkeley. While taking a class with Seymour Martin Lipset, Schmitter boldly told Lipset he was wrong in arguing that political parties were the main vehicles of representation in democracies. Likewise, when Ernst Haas, Laitin's mentor, poked fun in class at Karl Deutsch's efforts to devise objective measures of human emotions, Laitin defended Deutsch against Haas's criticisms. Bates and Przeworski took a different kind of risk: they chose not to have any mentor. At Northwestern University, where he received his Ph.D. in political science, Przeworski was nobody's student. Bates, who had a similar profile at the Massachusetts Institute of Technology (MIT), says, "I basically went away to Africa, did my thing, and dropped a lot of dissertation pages on people's desks near the end."

Still, not all the scholars in this study aimed to define an autonomous position in relation to their teachers. Moore and Scott describe how their dissertations and early publications mimicked the work of their doctoral advisors. In hindsight, both express regrets about the lack of originality in their early work. In discussing his dissertation and the book that resulted from it, Scott says he aimed to "follow in [the] footsteps" of his advisor, Robert Lane, by applying Lane's theoretical framework for studying political ideology to the case of Malaysia (Lane 1962; Scott 1968). Although his first book pleased his advisors, Scott regards it as a "cheap success," because it was sharply criticized by specialists on Malaysia who found the work empirically shallow. Scott thus concludes that his first book "is [not] much worth reading." Moore takes a similarly dim view of his first academic publication, a quantitative cross-national analysis of social stratification

(Moore 1942): "I was copying my teacher [George Peter] Murdock. I regard [that article] as kind of a joke now."

These examples are not meant to suggest that graduate students should rebel against their teachers and blithely dispense with mentors. Still, a willingness to disagree with and establish independence from teachers does characterize some of the best scholars.

The Mainstream

The best researchers are prone to risk taking in a second area: how they position themselves in relation to mainstream work. Several of the scholars interviewed in this book show relentless determination to pursue their interests and passions, even when they know they are risking professional marginalization. During the 1970s, Bates found himself at the edge of the field as a result of both his substantive focus on Africa and his use of rational choice theory at a time when non-choice approaches, such as dependency and modernization theory, dominated comparative politics.[19] As he describes it, "I felt I was on the margins of the profession, and I was happy being there. I mean, I was an Africanist. You don't become an Africanist to be mainstream." Similarly, Laitin spent much of the first decade of his career indulging his fascination with political culture in Somalia, despite his clear awareness that this topic commanded little interest. Laitin tartly observes, "I had zero impact on the profession. In fact, I did not even have a substantive footnote the first twelve or thirteen years of my career . . . The only citation to my work that anyone ever made was 'Somalia is on the east coast of Africa, see David Laitin.'" As a young assistant professor, Scott chose to cultivate his passion for Southeast Asia by taking a yearlong leave of absence to study the classic historical and anthropological works on the region. He recalls the withering criticism of a colleague who admonished, "You're a knucklehead, Scott. Becoming a Southeast Asianist is a stupid waste of time. This is not where political science is headed. It's the end of your career."

A further example of risk taking in relation to the mainstream involves how scholars package research. The scholars interviewed in this book do not always follow the dominant strategy of publishing books and articles in peer-reviewed journals. For example, Linz and Stepan both tend to write hundred-page manuscripts that are too long to publish as refereed journal articles, yet too short to publish as books. As a result, much of their work appears as chapters in edited volumes, a format conventionally seen as

19. Rational choice theory did not see widespread use in comparative politics until the 1990s.

commanding less attention than books and journal articles. Moreover, one of Linz's most influential papers, on presidential democracy, was available only in an unpublished *samizdat* form for years until an abbreviated version was finally published (Linz 1990a).[20]

Questions

Another area where leading scholars take risks concerns the research questions they address. Among the scholars in this study, numerous attempts can be observed to answer *big* questions whose scope requires huge investments of time and energy in the face of an uncertain payoff. Efforts can also be seen to move on to *new* questions from the standpoint of their prior research. Some of the best researchers have a restless curiosity that drives them to seek out new problems and topics, instead of clinging safely to old ones where they have a proven record of success.

BIG QUESTIONS. Several of the scholars display a striking willingness to tackle ambitious questions: Why are some countries democratic and others not? What are the causes of revolution? What explains economic development? Addressing such questions can require an extraordinary amount of energy and patience. ·

Reflecting on *Social Origins of Dictatorship and Democracy* (Moore 1966), which analyzes eight countries across several centuries and took more than ten years to write, Moore sheds light on the audacity that motivated him to undertake such a daunting project: "I actually started *Social Origins* with a much more ambitious plan—an overly ambitious plan. I was going to study a wider range of countries, not just ones with an agrarian class structure, but also ones with an industrial social structure, and maybe even a couple of others." About her decision to write a doctoral dissertation that compared three major revolutions, Skocpol observes, "It was unheard of at that time for a graduate student to write a thesis about a topic as vast as the French, Russian, and Chinese revolutions. We were expected to study statistics and find a focused, 'doable' project." Finally, David Collier, who, with Ruth Berins Collier, produced an 877-page book, *Shaping the Political Arena* (Collier and Collier 1991), that explores the historical roots of modern political systems across eight Latin American countries, highlights the stamina involved in tackling big questions when he explains why comparative historical research is so often published in long books: "Writing this book was a challenging undertaking, and it took much longer than we had intended. We worked on *Shaping the Political Arena* for ten years . . . It simply

20. The full paper was eventually published as Linz (1994).

takes a lot of space to nail down the arguments for particular countries. In our case, we covered a period spanning the first decade of the twentieth century to the 1980s. So we ended up doing a long, elaborate analysis . . . focused on the evolution of these countries through five or six historical phases."

NEW QUESTIONS. Instead of playing it safe by defending turf where they have already proven their credentials, many leading scholars challenge themselves by moving on to fresh research topics where their skills and talents have not yet been tested. This form of professional risk taking is exemplified by Huntington, who, over the past fifty years, has published widely across the three major empirical subfields of political science—American politics, international relations, and comparative politics. According to Huntington, "I wander around from field to field." To explain his peripatetic trajectory, he points to the central role of substantive problems, rather than methods, theory, or disciplinary boundaries, in driving his research: "I like to address what seem to me to be important questions—both for the real world and intellectually important issues. So I follow the trail where those kinds of questions and issues are, even if it requires moving from field to field." A similar urge to tackle new problems can be seen in the evolution of O'Donnell's research, which shifted from authoritarian regimes to transitions from authoritarianism and, most recently, to the quality of democracy. O'Donnell describes his compulsion to address new questions in the following terms: "I've had some colleagues get kind of angry and tell me that, after spending some time on some of my texts, I had already moved on to another topic. In some sense, I think this is a bad characteristic of mine. But that is something I have never been able to control. When a new theme captivates me, I abandon my children to their uncles, so to speak, and move on. That's the way my mind works." Skocpol offers another example of moving on. After producing a major book and many successful articles on the comparative study of revolutions, Skocpol shifted to a new and distinct issue: social policy in the United States. In explaining this shift, she remarks, "Soon after *States and Social Revolutions* (Skocpol 1979) appeared, I reached a point where I did not want to write about revolutions anymore. My strategy as a scholar is to define fruitful problems and use them to puzzle through theoretical issues, and I wanted to move on to new problems. I did not want to be an expert on revolutions." Finally, after spending the first decade of his career as a successful specialist on Russia, Moore transformed himself into a broadly comparative scholar. Asked what motivated him to make this move, Moore said, "I couldn't stand the idea of being a Russia specialist . . . I got interested in something else. My curiosities shifted to what emerged finally in *Social Origins* (Moore 1966): the roots of totalitarianism, liberalism, and radical revolution."

Still, not all top scholars take the risk of moving on to new research questions. Over the course of his career, Lijphart has focused steadfastly on the challenges of achieving stable democracy in plural and divided societies. Likewise, Laitin's research has centered consistently on the relationship between culture and politics. When asked to respond to the observation that most scholars in comparative politics focus narrowly on the same region or country, whereas his research spans multiple regions, Laitin offered,

> I'm the one who's very narrow. During all the years I've been doing political science research, I've largely focused on the same narrow set of questions, basically about the relationship between culture and politics, and the implications of cultural heterogeneity for politics . . . Whether my work was in Somalia, Nigeria, Catalonia, or the post-Soviet World, you can see the same questions asked repeatedly in several different ways. I've often said to other comparativists that they overestimate the costs of equipping themselves for going to a new place and underestimate the costs of studying a new issue in the same place.

The Risks of Risk Taking

Risks, by their very nature, do not always pay off. Although innovative research at the margins occasionally penetrates, and even transforms, the mainstream, the usual fate of work at the margins is to be marginalized. For example, Bates partly attributes the lack of widespread attention received by his book, *Rural Responses to Industrialization* (Bates 1976), to its reliance on rational choice theory, which set it outside the theoretical mainstream: "At that time, in the mid-1970s, comparative politics was focused on dependency theory and the Marxist critique of dependency theory. My book doesn't mention any of that and thus was far removed from the theory of the times. That's one reason the book was not taken up very strongly."

Other forms of risk taking can also be costly. Huntington notes that when one moves across fields, as he does, "the specialists in one field are generally unfamiliar with what you have done in another field. People in comparative politics think of me in terms of *Political Order in Changing Societies* (Huntington 1968) and *The Third Wave* (Huntington 1991). But they don't know anything about *The Soldier and the State* (Huntington 1957) or my book on American politics (Huntington 1981b)." Linz suggests that his penchant for writing lengthy pieces best-suited for publication as chapters in edited volumes may have lessened the visibility and impact of some of his work.[21] Finally, Schmitter recounts how his efforts to get beyond the case of Brazil, on which his research had previously focused, by doing substantial fieldwork in a new country, Argentina, generated no publications. He regards this outcome as one of his "great failures."

Even the best researchers experience disappointment and setbacks as a result of the risks they take, and the dustbin of comparative politics history is probably filled with the work of little-known and forgotten scholars who took risks that failed.

Playing It Safe: Are We Too Risk-Averse?

Although risk taking can be costly, the scholars interviewed in this book voice a concern that professors and students are too risk-averse. According to Przeworski,

> The entire structure of incentives of academia in the United States works against taking big intellectual and political risks. Graduate students and assistant professors learn to package their intellectual ambitions into articles publishable by a few journals and to shy away from anything that might look like a political stance. This professionalism does advance knowledge of narrowly formulated questions, but we do not have forums for spreading our knowledge outside academia; indeed, we do not talk about politics even among ourselves.

Linz echoes this point, arguing that the increasing use of standardized criteria for measuring professional success, such as the number of publications in refereed journals, reduces the likelihood of innovation: "There is more and more reliance on impersonal and mechanical criteria, like publications in peer review journals, for making decisions about who should be promoted and get positions. By becoming more impersonal and more bureaucratic, the field produces standard, predictable products, but this standardization allows little room for mavericks and innovators."[22] Huntington observes that graduate students are "often very hesitant about setting forth a broad proposition." This timidity, he finds, makes graduate students far less interesting to teach than undergraduates. O'Donnell laments the passing of an era of big, daring books: "I worry that in its current drive toward methodological sophistication, political science has lost the ambition and

21. See Linz's discussion of his paper, "From Primordialism to Nationalism" (Linz 1985a), in Chapter 6. Writing papers of unconventional length is likely to be a recipe for failure given the tenure requirements that exist today, and students and untenured faculty members are cautioned against such an approach.
22. Scott makes a similar point in discussing what he calls "hyper-professionalism." See Chapter 11.

hubris of writing great books that give an account of big issues. When Moore, Dahl, or Shmuel Eisenstadt produced their major books, for example, there was a sense of possibility that you could do both methodologically self-conscious and important work on great issues. I fear this sense of possibility is disappearing."

Despite these concerns, few, including the scholars interviewed in this book, would propose universal, perpetual imprudence: not everyone can or should do high-risk research. Fierce independence is not for all; and much solid and good research has been produced through emulating and even aping mentors. Moreover, a healthy discipline may actually require a large mass of researchers doing low-risk, "normal" science: too many mavericks swinging for the fences in the hope of hitting paradigmatic grand slams is probably a recipe for disaster.[23]

Still, self-conscious steps are necessary to prevent the dominance of a herd mentality that could lead the whole field to stampede over a cliff. The leading scholars offer practical recommendations to counter the hegemony of group think. Skocpol urges students to expose themselves to a variety of faculty: "Make space for yourself by diversifying; don't apprentice yourself to just one person or approach, but to several. Learning from several different people is a good way to create an original combination." Linz advises, "Don't limit yourself by saying, 'I am in political philosophy, so I am not going to take any courses in comparative politics,' or 'I am in comparative politics, and so I will not take anything on political philosophy.' Use the best resources of your department broadly." Scott stresses the importance of reading widely: "Just as the health food people say, 'You are what you eat,' you are as an intellectual what you read and whom you're talking with. And if you're just reading in political science and only talking with political scientists, it's like having a diet with only one food group. If that's all you do, then you're not going to produce anything new or original. You're just going to reproduce the mainstream. If you're doing political science right, then at least a third of what you're reading shouldn't be political science." Lijphart proposes that young scholars hedge their bets by keeping one foot anchored in the mainstream while stepping outside it with the other: "The trick is to build on existing research without being bound by it, to work within the paradigm but also to think outside it."

Finally, it may be more appropriate, and certainly more prudent, to take risks after tenure. As Moore wryly remarks, "Tenure is a great thing. It allows you to be as much of a damn fool as is humanly possible." Though a field dominated by damn fools is surely not desirable, greater effort to exploit

---

23. On the key role in generating scientific progress of "traditionalists" who, in contrast to self-conscious innovators, "enjoy playing intricate games by pre-established rules," see Kuhn (1977, 237).

the remarkable freedom tenure gives for taking intellectual risks will help keep comparative politics vibrant and exciting.

Stirring the Comparative Imagination: Creative Hypothesis Generating in Comparative Research

A focus on the human dimension sheds light on one of the most elusive aspects of scientific inquiry: the process of generating ideas. Textbooks and courses on methodology center mainly on the issue of *testing* ideas, yet usually offer little insight about the prior matter of how one *generates* ideas worth testing in the first place.[24] Likewise, professional publications rarely include discussions of how ideas emerge. Because the interview format allowed an exploration of how leading scholars actually do their research, the material presented in this book opens a valuable window on the process of formulating good ideas. As discussed above, the interviews show that rich life experiences provide fertile ground for generating new ideas. Yet experience is not the only path to insight in comparative research. Scholars spend a large share of their time reading; and books, journals, and newspapers all play an indispensable role in the development of ideas. Moreover, directly observing political and social interaction is also an important tool for creative hypothesis generating. The interviews highlight five methods that help spark the comparative imagination of the leading scholars: (1) "bibliographic sleuthing," that is, hunting for untapped sources in libraries and bookstores; (2) following current events; (3) critical engagement with contemporary works; (4) reading, and rereading, the classics of political and social theory; and (5) real-time observation of political action.[25]

Bibliographic sleuthing, which involves searching, even haphazardly, in libraries or bookstores, can lead to the serendipitous discovery of works that provide new insight.[26] For example, while rummaging in a used bookstore in Rio de Janeiro, Schmitter found an obscure book written in the 1930s that triggered his insight that the system of interest representation in Brazil could be conceptualized as "corporatist."[27] Similarly, Skocpol discovered an old, forgotten book on social insurance in the United States in the early 1900s, which argued that Civil War pensions were a major social policy that

24. This imbalanced focus on hypothesis testing, as opposed to hypothesis generating, is not unique to political science and sociology. See McGuire (1997). On "tricks of the trade" for doing creative social science research, see Becker (1998).

25. This is not an exhaustive list of strategies for stimulating the comparative imagination. Still, this list contains the main strategies discussed by the fifteen scholars on which this book focuses.

26. Bibliographic sleuthing can be done increasingly on the Internet.

27. Manoïlesco (1934). For Schmitter's account of this incident, see Schmitter (1997b, 289–90).

would soon lead the United States to surpass Europe in the public provision of social benefits.[28] According to Skocpol, "When I read this, it made me curious, because the mere empirical assertion that, in 1913, a lot of government social spending was going on that amounted to de facto old age pensions cut against the grain of the whole literature that saw the United States as a laggard in social provision. I was skeptical at first . . . but I decided to look into the matter, because I had a hunch it might lead to something." Skocpol's hunch proved correct, and her probing resulted in a novel argument: the United States was actually a precocious welfare state, not a laggard behind European countries. This argument, in turn, played a pivotal role in her book *Protecting Soldiers and Mothers* (Skocpol 1992).

Following current events by reading newspapers and magazines can also serve to stimulate new ideas. Huntington says that reading "about what's going on in the world" plays a fundamental role in his research. He recounts how his observation of chaos, anarchy, and corruption across developing countries in the 1960s, "when everybody was talking about modernization and development," led to the insight that "there [was] more political *decay* out there than political development. And so I wrote *Political Order in Changing Societies* (Huntington 1968)." Reading about current events can work in tandem with bibliographic sleuthing in the formation of new ideas. While reading the newspaper in Switzerland one day, Schmitter saw an article about the role of the Swiss Milk Producers' Association in the annual price-fixing mechanism for milk.[29] He noticed that this regulatory framework bore a remarkable resemblance to the corporatist systems of interest intermediation he had previously studied in Brazil and Portugal. This realization led him to the library in search of material on Swiss interest group politics, where he discovered an unpublished dissertation from the 1930s on Swiss corporatism. As a result of his newspaper-inspired trip to the library, Schmitter saw that the concept of corporatism could be applied not only to authoritarian countries, but also to democratic ones. This insight anchored his influential article, "Still the Century of Corporatism?" (Schmitter 1974), as well as subsequent works that further elaborated the corporatist model of interest group politics as an alternative to the pluralist model.

Critical engagement with contemporaries is a further way to generate new ideas. Laitin describes how research on the relationship between culture and politics by contemporary scholars like Harry Eckstein, Aaron Wildavsky, and Arend Lijphart provided a compelling foil against which he developed and refined his own ideas: "I was going after Harry Eckstein from

28. Rubinow (1968). Rubinow's book was originally published in 1913.
29. In addition to Chapter 10, see Schmitter (1997b, 291–92).

the very beginning. I was arguing against Eckstein's congruence theory, which posited a kind of direct mapping from one realm—culture—on to another—politics (Eckstein 1966). In contrast, I said that there was no necessary connection between the cultural and other realms, between say religion and politics . . . My views also went against Lijphart and also against almost everyone who had been writing on culture." Laitin's critical engagement with the work of these interlocutors helped him formulate his idea that culture both shapes and is in turn shaped by political choices. Similarly, Skocpol notes that arguing against "mistaken others" plays a key role in the process of developing her own ideas: "I have always worked out what I was thinking by critiquing work done by others. What gets me excited is seeing that someone else is partly right and partly wrong . . . My major projects have always been launched with a sense of argument against a received wisdom or an interlocutor, especially somebody important whose work I respect."

Another way to stir the comparative imagination concerns *classic works* of political and social theory.[30] These classics play an important role in the intellectual life of leading scholars in comparative politics. Dahl sees himself as having engaged throughout his career in what he calls an "imaginary dialogue" with Plato, Rousseau, and Marx. Przeworski observes, "Reading classics of political theory is extremely important to me. It is a source of hypotheses, historical information, and great ideas." Schmitter offers: "For me, engaging the classics is almost automatic. I start by thinking about the nature of the problem on which I want to work, and then I ask myself, 'Who's said something about this?' Sometimes it is simply a matter of having these classic works in your head, having read them . . . My first instinct is to go through my own memory of what I have read in political thought."

Finally, Linz notes, "Whenever I start working on something, I usually look to see whether Weber has anything to say on that theme." To show how he draws ideas and inspiration from the classics, Linz recounts his use of Weber's concept of sultanism to study personalistic dictatorships, such as those of Anastasio Somoza Debayle in Nicaragua and Rafael Leonidas Trujillo in the Dominican Republic.[31] Because the degree of cronyism, nepotism, and unbridled discretion enjoyed by the ruler was so extreme in these cases, Linz felt uncomfortable classifying them in the same category as

---

30. For an insightful essay on the role of classics in modern social science, see Merton (1996a). It bears emphasis that not all the scholars interviewed in this book gain inspiration from reading the classics. Indeed, several (e.g., Laitin and Lijphart) say that the classics have little influence on their research.

31. Linz's initial formulation of the sultanistic regime concept is in Linz (1975). See also Chehabi and Linz (1998a).

regimes like Francisco Franco's in Spain and Antonio Salazar's in Portugal. According to Linz,

> Weber makes a distinction between a traditional, legitimate form of patrimonialism, on one hand, and the corruption of patrimonialism into sultanism, on the other. When I reread Weber's section on patrimonialism, I thought, "That's exactly what I am looking for!" Then I reformulated Weber's concept in a modern way by specifying indicators of sultanism, like nepotism, cronyism, and the private appropriation of power and wealth.
>
> You have questions in your own mind that you want to address, and sometimes you read the classics and say, "Well, that's an interesting insight, it illustrates what I was groping for." So, the more you read and the more you know, the better.

Real-time observation of political action is a further technique for generating fresh ideas. Scott describes how living in a Malaysian village for two years enabled him to conduct rolling interviews with peasants that helped him see the "subterranean forms of resistance to hegemony, such as desertion and foot-dragging, underneath the placid surface of the village."[32] Scott also emphasizes that "politics is everywhere," not just in the distant and exotic setting of "the field," and he offers a fascinating example of observing political interaction among passengers while riding on a train from New York City to Washington, D.C. Schmitter also highlights the value of observation, noting that his efforts to form new concepts are often stimulated by talking to political actors and listening closely to the words they use to describe what they do. Laitin's discussion of watching a Catalan national dance, the Sardana, while doing fieldwork in Barcelona offers an especially vivid example of how observation can help trigger new ideas:

> When the people perform the Sardana they put their little bundles of possessions in the center and dance around them. So, they developed an urban dance that enabled them to protect their property the whole time they were dancing. And they have to count a fairly large number of steps . . . I saw them counting their steps with their lips, though trying to hide it because you're not supposed to show it.
>
> Thousands of tourists have seen the Sardana; it happens all the time, and the dance itself is relatively boring. But to me it was inspirational, and I asked myself a very simple question. "Here I am in the most bourgeois city I've ever lived in, with a commercial bourgeoisie that goes way, way back, which developed an urban form of culture in which they can protect their property while dancing. And they count! It's the fundamental commercial function to

---

32. The results of this research were published in Scott (1985).

count." Then I asked, "Why are people who are so rational and so calculating pushing a linguistic movement that would increase their communicative capabilities by zero? You would think the Catalans would be on this gigantic learn English campaign, which would be tremendously more useful for their commercial dealings. Why are they pushing this language, Catalan, which, if successfully promoted, will allow them to communicate with no more people than they presently communicate with, and which will have no communicative payoff whatsoever?" And I just walked through the town for the next two or three days, sort of like a zombie, asking and re-asking that question to myself.

Watching the Sardana made it easier for Laitin to see that the tools of game theory, especially the concept of coordination games, offered a powerful and fruitful way to explain why people participate in language movements that do not serve their material interests.[33] Laitin concludes, "this insight from Barcelona pushed my research program for quite a while, in utterly new directions. Fieldwork has that excitement for me."

Just as rich life experiences, passion, and risk taking are no guarantee of becoming a leading scholar, hunting for obscure books, perusing the newspaper, critically engaging contemporary authors, reading the classics, and making observations are, of course, not sufficient to formulate important ideas. After all, many social scientists read the newspaper and follow current events, yet few produce works with the impact of Huntington's *Political Order in Changing Societies* (1968) or Schmitter's "Still the Century of Corporatism?" (1974). And many people do fieldwork and make real-time observations, yet few achieve the level of insight seen in Scott's *Weapons of the Weak* (1985). Moreover, as Weber (1946a, 136) reminds us, "Ideas occur to us when they please, not when it pleases us."[34] Hard work, discipline, and perhaps a measure of luck are also necessary to develop good ideas, as is intelligence, especially the capacity to recognize an important question, puzzle, or lead when it arises.

Although factors like luck and intelligence are difficult, if not impossible, to control, there may still be ways to increase the probability of developing new ideas. The evidence from the interviews underscores the importance of openness to the possibility of surprise combined with the curiosity, confidence, and drive to follow a hunch. Moreover, by mastering the literature so that we have a firm grasp of the "conventional wisdom," we may be able to enhance our ability to notice puzzling new information. For exam-

33. On coordination games, see Schelling (1980).
34. Weber (1946a, 136) further notes, "ideas come when we do not expect them, and not when we are brooding and searching at our desks. Yet ideas would certainly not come to mind had we not brooded at our desks and searched for answers with passionate devotion."

ple, had Skocpol not understood that the standard view cast the United States as a welfare laggard, then she probably would not have seen that the book she serendipitously discovered through bibliographic sleuthing made an argument that cut sharply against the grain. And her fortuitous discovery of this book still might have led nowhere had she lacked either the curiosity to pursue the lead or the skepticism and confidence to question received wisdom.

While there is no magic formula for sparking the comparative imagination, the interviews in this book suggest that rich life experiences and the various methods of creative hypothesis formation discussed here are important aspects of the process of generating good ideas.

Against Professional Amnesia

Despite the important role that older works, especially the classics, play in inspiring some of the best scholars, the field of comparative politics has a feeble professional memory.[35] Few works have been written about the history of comparative politics, and students are rarely taught this history.[36] Indeed, graduate students are often discouraged from reading older works, which are routinely seen as passé and even "pre-scientific." Why is a weak professional memory a reason for concern? Does not scientific progress require amnesia? According to Weber (1946a, 138), "In science, each of us knows that what he has accomplished will be antiquated in ten, twenty, fifty, years. That is the fate to which science is subjected . . . Every scientific 'fulfillment' raises new 'questions'; it *asks* to be 'surpassed' and outdated." Claude Bernard asks pointedly, "What use can we find in exhuming worm-eaten theories or observations made without proper means of investigation?" And A. N. Whitehead offers the dictum, "A science which hesitates to forget its founders is lost."[37]

From this standpoint, the problem with comparative politics is too *much*, not too little, professional memory. The field has been too hesitant to

35. On the importance of professional memory—and its weakness in comparative politics—see Almond (1990, 23–29 and Part II).

36. A recent survey of graduate syllabi and reading lists for comprehensive exams revealed no items on the history of comparative politics among the canonical works of the field (i.e., works assigned by more than one-third of the thirty-two departments in the sample) (España-Nájera, Márquez, and Vasquez 2003). The virtual absence in comparative politics of works about the lives and contributions of leading scholars is a further sign of the field's weak professional memory. By contrast, sociology and economics have been more attuned to the biographies of their founders and leading lights.

37. The Bernard and Whitehead quotations are taken from Merton (1996a, 28 and 33). Similarly, Thomas Kuhn argues, "Science destroys its past." Quoted in Dryzek and Leonard (1988, 1249).

forget its founders, as seen by the large amount of time students spend reading antiquated "classics" from the 1960s, 1970s, and 1980s in pro-seminars and in preparation for comprehensive exams. Progress in the field requires that we purge these outdated works from the curriculum and re-place them with recent, cutting-edge research.[38] A book like this one, which focuses retrospectively on authors of many of these older works, is useful, at best, for a course in the history of science and, at worst, poses a barrier to the advancement of science. There are no classics in science.[39] Ignorance of the past of comparative politics is not just bliss, it is necessary for the health of the field.

This book disagrees strongly with the idea that professional amnesia is desirable. First, a fundamental principle of modern science is that scientists should know and acknowledge prior work on the topic of their research. According to Robert Merton (1996a, 27), the "rationale for this is as clear as it is familiar: ignorance of past work often condemns the scientist to dis-covering for himself what is already known." Hence, professional amnesia is antiscientific. Dahl offers a good example of the perils of professional amnesia when he notes his frustration with the lack of progress since the 1950s that he discerns in the study of what is arguably the central subject of political science—power. "Fifty years later, I see people use the word and concept *power* as if we were back where we started. Even elementary distinc-tions going back to Max Weber—such as the distinction between power and authority, or legitimate power—seem to have been forgotten. So perhaps we've not only failed to progress in the study of power, we've actually gone into reverse." Professional amnesia can also lead to the problem of *mis-specified ignorance,* that is, identifying false gaps in knowledge that would have been revealed as such had the researcher thoroughly reviewed prior work.[40] Professional amnesia poses a threat to progress in comparative re-search because it prevents us from benefiting from past accomplishments and increases the risk of both repeating past mistakes and reinventing the wheel (Almond 1990, 7–8).

Second, by expunging classic works from the curriculum, professional

38. An extreme variant of this position can be seen in Auguste Comte's "principle of cere-bral hygiene." As Merton (1996a, 29) puts it, "[Comte] washed his mind clean of everything but his own ideas by the simple tactic of not reading anything even remotely germane to his subject."

39. One study of the "half-life" of journal articles found that in physics and biomedical journals there were virtually no citations to works older than ten years (Baum et al. 1976). Of course, professional amnesia is not always driven by scientific aspirations. It often results from the efforts of new generations of scholars to assert their independence from previous ones.

40. On Merton's concept of "specified ignorance"—the recognition of "what is not yet known but needs to be known in order to advance the pursuit of knowledge"—see Sztompka (1996, 11).

amnesia robs us of inspiring models of intellectual excellence. Reading the classics allows us to watch great minds at work. O'Donnell's description of Weber illustrates the point: "To see [Weber] think through a problem, to see how his mind works, is very instructive . . . He is my model of intellectual power." Classic works are indispensable tools for cultivating standards of taste and good judgment (Merton 1996a, 31–32). Moreover, as highlighted in the interviews, reading the classics serves as an important way to generate new ideas.

Third, by producing ignorance about what comparative politics has accomplished, professional amnesia contributes to a crisis of confidence about the field. Laitin argues persuasively that political scientists should take greater pride in the many achievements of the discipline over the past fifty years.[41] This, of course, requires that we first *know* what the field has accomplished, which is obviously not possible without a strong professional memory.[42]

Finally, while "a serious student of physics . . . can safely ignore the original writings of Newton, Faraday, and Maxwell,"[43] and, likewise, a biologist does not need to read Darwin's *On the Origin of Species,* no serious student of political order can ignore Hobbes and Huntington, no serious student of democracy can ignore Aristotle, Schumpeter, Dahl, and Lijphart, and no serious student of revolutions can ignore Tocqueville, Moore, and Skocpol. Comparative politics is defined by a fundamental continuity in what is worth knowing; and this continuity differentiates the social from the natural sciences. This core of perennial questions and themes gives classic works an enduring vitality in the social sciences.[44]

The past holds the key to our field's identity. If professional amnesia severs our connection to the history of our field, then comparative politics will be soulless, condemned to perpetual envy and imitation of other fields and disciplines with a stronger sense of where they come from, and, hence, who they are.

Conclusion

Focusing on the human dimension sheds light on key aspects of comparative research. It reveals that the best researchers have rich life experiences, are passionate about scholarship, and take risks. It offers fresh insight about

41. See Chapter 16 and also Laitin (2004a).
42. On the inextricable link between professional history and identity, see Dryzek and Leonard (1988).
43. M. M. Kessler, as cited in Merton (1996a, 24).
44. The existence of an enduring core of themes and questions in comparative politics is emphasized especially in the Dahl and Laitin interviews in Chapters 5 and 16.

how to generate new ideas. Finally, it illuminates major challenges facing comparative politics. Because the quality of comparative research depends in good part on the quality of the life experiences of the people who do it, the experiential deficit observed by leading scholars among students today raises concerns about the future vitality of the field. *Steps should be taken to ensure that students and professors, too, find ways to enrich their lives by regularly stepping outside the academic framework.* Passion about research is in jeopardy because of the widespread tendency for professors and students alike to regard scholarship as just a 9-to-5 job. *To avoid this iron cage of professionalism, enthusiasm for research as a "calling" should be cultivated and rewarded, which requires acknowledging that emotional engagement and normative commitments are compatible with, and even necessary for, excellence in scientific research.* Professionalism threatens to squelch risk taking and creativity. *Incentives for innovation should thus be strengthened to prevent the hegemony of a herd mentality.* Finally, professional amnesia is depriving us of powerful models of intellectual excellence and weakening our self-confidence about the achievements of the field. *We need to improve professional memory by knowing, teaching, and drawing inspiration from the history of our field.*

To conclude, the following recommendations for aspiring scholars can be drawn from the examples offered by the fifteen leading comparativists interviewed in this book:

1. Get off the academic track and gain real-world experience by working or traveling before you go to graduate school. This will make you a better social scientist by helping infuse your research with meaning and purpose. It will also provide a stronger foundation of knowledge about the range of human behavior, which can serve both as a source of fresh ideas and as a basis for testing generalizations.
2. If circumstances do not permit you to take time off before graduate school, then doing a fieldwork-based dissertation is probably the next best way to gain experience. Consider extending the amount of time you spend in the field. Fieldwork provides an indispensable empirical grounding for comparative research, helps hone skills of observation, and should be seen as a lifelong investment that will inform your research over the course of your career, even if you never do fieldwork again.
3. Study with faculty who are enthusiastic and excited about their research and do not see scholarship as just a 9-to-5 career. Have fun doing your research, because the more enjoyment and pleasure you get from it, the better it will probably be.
4. Build strong, interactive communities with other students and with your professors that get beyond the confines of the classroom and for-

mal training. Interaction outside the classroom in study groups, workshops, and even social gatherings can help strengthen your enthusiasm for research.

5. Do not be afraid to let normative commitments shape your selection of research problems or to explore the normative implications of your work. This will nurture your passion for research. But do not let normative commitments blind you to "inconvenient facts" that do not support your position.

6. Take measured risks. Enroll in courses that excite you, even if they are offered by professors in other subfields and departments. Know and master mainstream research, yet try to stand with one foot outside the mainstream. Do not apprentice yourself to a single professor, but gain exposure to a variety of faculty with different perspectives. As you advance and get tenure, you can afford to take greater risks.

7. Look beyond professional fashions and fads by paying attention to classic and older works and also to the wisdom of senior scholars. See yourself as part of a field with a distinguished lineage reaching back to antiquity.

Combined with recent important advances in the methodological training of students, a stronger focus on experience, passion, risk, and professional memory holds the promise of new generations of comparativists whose achievements match, and even surpass, those of their most illustrious predecessors.

2

The Past and Present
of Comparative Politics

Gerardo L. Munck

Comparative politics emerged as a distinct field of political science in the United States in the late nineteenth century and the subsequent evolution of the field was driven largely by research associated with U.S. universities. The influence of U.S. academia certainly declined from its high point in the two decades following World War II. Indeed, by the late twentieth century, comparative politics was a truly international enterprise. Yet the sway of scholarship produced in the United States, by U.S.- and foreign-born scholars, and by U.S.-trained scholars around the world, remained undisputable. The standard for research in comparative politics was set basically in the United States. In sum, a large part of the story of comparative politics has been, and continues to be, written by those who work and have been trained within the walls of U.S. academia.[1]

This chapter focuses on the past and present of comparative politics in the United States. The discussion is organized around three issues: the definition of the field's subject matter, the role of theory, and the use of methods. These three issues are the basis for an identification of distinct periods in the history of comparative politics and for assessments of the state of the field. Attention is also given to the link between comparative politics, on the one hand, and other fields of political science and other social sciences,

---

1. Basic references on the history of political science in the United States by political scientists include Crick (1959), Somit and Tanenhaus (1967), Waldo (1975), Ricci (1984), Seidelman and Harpham (1985), Almond (1990, 1996, 2002), Farr and Seidelman (1993), Gunnell (1993, 2004), Easton, Gunnell, and Stein (1995), Adcock (2003, 2005), and Adcock, Bevir, and Stimson (2007). On the relationship between political science and its sister disciplines, see Lipset (1969), Ross (1991), and Doggan (1996). On political science in the United States relative to other countries, see Easton, Gunnell, and Graziano (1991); and for a discussion of convergences and divergences of practices in the most recent period in the United States and Western Europe, see Norris (1997), Schmitter (2002), and Moses, Rihoux, and Kittel (2005). For overviews of comparative politics written by U.S. scholars, see Eckstein (1963) and Apter (1996); for overviews of this field written by Europeans, see Daalder (1993), Mair (1996), and Blondel (1999).

on the other hand, and, more briefly, to political events and the values held by scholars of comparative politics.

The argument presented here is as follows. Since the institutionalization of political science as an autonomous discipline, a process initiated in the late nineteenth century, the evolution of comparative politics was punctuated by two revolutions: the behavioral revolution, which had its greatest impact on comparative politics during the immediate post–World War II years until the mid-1960s, and the second scientific revolution, which started around the end of the Cold War and is still ongoing. On both occasions, the impetus for change came from developments in the field of American politics and was justified in the name of science. However, the ideas advanced by, and the impact of, these two revolutions differed. The behavioral revolution drew heavily on sociology; in contrast, the second scientific revolution imported many ideas from economics and also put a heavier emphasis on methodology. Moreover, though each revolution centrally involved a tension between traditionalists and innovators, the current revolution is taking place in a more densely institutionalized field and is producing, through a process of adaptation, a relatively pluralistic landscape.

Beyond this characterization of the origin and evolution of comparative politics, this chapter draws some conclusions about the current state of the field and offers, by way of parting words, a suggestion regarding its future. Concerning the present, it stresses that scholars of comparative politics—comparativists for short—have accomplished a lot and produced a vast amount of knowledge about politics, but also have fallen short of fulfilling the field's mission to develop a global science of politics due to some serious shortcomings. Specifically, the lack of a general or unified theory of politics, and the failure to produce robust, broad empirical generalizations about world politics, are highlighted. Concerning the future of comparative politics, this chapter suggests that potentially paralyzing or distracting divisions among comparativists, which hamper progress in the field, will only be overcome when comparativists appreciate both the depth of the roots of comparative politics in a humanistic tradition and the vital importance of its scientific aspirations.

The Constitution of Political Science as a Discipline, 1880–1920

Political science, which had to be constituted as a discipline before the subfield of comparative politics could be formed, can trace its origin to a number of foundational texts written in many cases centuries ago. It can date its birth back to antiquity, and thus claim to be the oldest of the social science disciplines, in light of the work of Greek philosophers Plato (427–

Table 2.1. Classical Social Theory, 1776–1923

Country	Author	Some Major Works
Britain	Adam Smith (1723–90)	*The Wealth of Nations* (1776)
	David Ricardo (1772–1823)	*On the Principles of Political Economy and Taxation* (1817)
	John Stuart Mill (1806–73)	*The Principles of Political Economy* (1848)
		Considerations on Representative Government (1861)
France	Auguste Comte (1798–1857)	*Course in Positive Philosophy* (1830–42)
	Alex de Tocqueville (1805–59)	*Democracy in America* (1835)
		The Old Regime and the French Revolution (1856)
	Herbert Spencer (1820–1903)	*The Principles of Sociology* (1876–96)
	Emile Durkheim (1858–1917)	*The Division of Labor in Society* (1893)
		Rules of the Sociological Method (1895)
Germany	Karl Marx (1818–83)	*The Communist Manifesto* (1848)
		The Eighteenth Brumaire of Louis Bonaparte (1852)
		Capital (1867–94)
	Max Weber (1864–1920)	*The Protestant Ethic and the Spirit of Capitalism* (1905)
		Economy and Society (1914)
		General Economic History (1923)
Italy	Vilfredo Pareto (1848–1923)	*The Mind and Society: A Treatise on General Sociology* (1915–19)
	Gaetano Mosca (1858–1941)	*The Ruling Class* (1923)
	Robert Michels (1876–1936)*	*Political Parties: A Sociological Study of the Oligarchical Tendencies of Modern Democracy* (1915)

*Though German by birth, Michels is generally seen as an Italian thinker.

347 BC), author of *The Republic* (360 BC), and Aristotle (384–322 BC), author of *Politics* (c. 340 BC). In the modern era, important landmarks include the Italian Renaissance political philosopher Nicolo Machiavelli's (1469–1527) *The Prince* (1515) and French Enlightenment political thinker Baron de Montesquieu's (1689–1755) *On the Spirit of Laws* (1748). More recently, in the age of industrialism and nationalism, political analysis was further developed by European thinkers who penned the classics of social theory (see Table 2.1).

Political thought in the United States, a new nation, necessarily lacked the tradition and the breadth of European scholarship. Indeed, significant contributions, from *The Federalist Papers* (1787–88), written by Alexander Hamilton (1755–1804), James Madison (1751–1836), and John Jay (1745–1829), to the writings by German émigré Francis Lieber (1800–1872), the first professor of political science in the United States, did not match the broad corpus of European work. In addition, the relative backwardness of the United States was apparent in higher education. Many teaching colleges existed in the United States, the oldest being Harvard, founded in

1636. But the first research university, Johns Hopkins University, was not established until 1876, and a large number of Americans sought training in the social sciences in Europe, and especially in German universities, the most advanced in the world from 1870 to 1900. Yet, as a result of a series of innovations carried out in U.S. universities, the United States broke new ground by constituting political science as a discipline and hence opened the way for the emergence of comparative politics as a field of political science.

The clearest manifestations of the process pioneered by the United States were various institutional developments that gave an organizational basis to the autonomization of political science. One new trend was the growing number of independent Political Science departments. Also critical was the formation of graduate programs, the first one being Columbia University's School of Political Science founded by John W. Burgess in 1880—the event that opens this period in the history of political science—and hence the expansion of Ph.D.s trained as political scientists in the United States. Finally, a key event was the founding of the discipline's professional association, the American Political Science Association (APSA), in 1903. These were important steps that began to give the new discipline a distinctive profile.

This process of autonomization involved a differentiation between political science and history, the discipline most closely associated with U.S. political science in its early years.[2] Many of the departments in which political science was initially taught were joint Departments of Politics and History, and APSA itself emerged as a splinter group from the American Historical Association (AHA).[3] Moreover, the influence of history, but also the desire to establish a separate identity vis-à-vis history, was evident in the way political scientists defined their subject matter.

Many of the founders of political science had been trained in Germany, where they were exposed to German *Staatswissenschaft* (political science) and historically oriented *Geisteswissenschaft* (social sciences). Thus, it is hardly surprising that, much in line with German thinking at the time, the state would figure prominently in attempts to define the new discipline's subject matter. But since history, as an all-encompassing discipline, also addressed the state, they sought to differentiate political science from history in two ways. First, according to the motto of the time that "History is past Politics and Politics present History," political scientists would leave the past as the preserve of historians and focus on contemporary history. Second, they would eschew history's aspiration to address all the potential factors that went into the making of politics and focus instead on the more

2. On the relationship between political science and history during this period, see Ross (1991, 64–77 and Ch. 8) and Adcock (2003).

3. The AHA was founded in 1884.

delimited question of government and the formal political institutions associated with government.[4]

This way of defining the subject matter of political science bore some
instructive similarities and differences with the way two other sister disciplines—economics and sociology—established their identities during
roughly the same time.[5] The birth of economics as a discipline was associated with the marginalist revolution and the formation of neoclassical
economics, crystallized in Alfred Marshall's (1842–1924) *Principles of Economics* (1890), that is, with a narrowing of the subject matter of Smith's,
Ricardo's, and Mill's classical political economy. In contrast, sociologists
saw themselves establishing a discipline that explicitly represented a continuation of the classical social theory of Comte, Tocqueville, Spencer,
Durkheim, Marx, Weber, Pareto, Mosca, and Michels, and, proclaiming an
interest in society as a whole, defined sociology as the mother discipline,
the synthetic social science. Thus, like economists, and in contrast to sociologists, political scientists defined their discipline by betting on specialization and opting for a delimited subject matter.

But the way in which the subject matter of political science was defined
differed fundamentally from both economics and sociology in another key
way. These sister disciplines defined themselves through theory-driven
choices, economics introducing a reorientation of classical theory, sociology seeking an extension of classical theory. In contrast, the process of
differentiation of political science vis-à-vis history was largely a matter of
carving out an empirically distinct turf and involved a rejection, rather
than a reworking, of European grand theorizing and philosophies of history. In sum, political science was born out of history and as a result of
efforts to distinguish the study of politics from the study of history. But the
birth of this new discipline also entailed a break with, rather than a refor-
mulation of, the classical tradition.

The way in which political science was born had profound implications
for the research conducted during the early years of political science (see
Table 2.2). Most critically, the discipline was essentially bereft of theory,
whether in the sense of a metatheory, which sought to articulate how the
key aspects of politics worked together, or of mid-range theories, which
focused on just one or a few aspects of politics.[6] Indeed, the formal-legal

4. For formal definitions of the subject matter of political science, see Somit and Tanenhaus
(1967, 23–27 and 63–69).

5. Useful markers are the founding of the American Economic Association (AEA) in 1885 and
of the American Sociological Association (ASA) in 1905. On the birth of economics and sociology, and the way these two disciplines defined their subject matters, see Ross (1991, Chs. 6 and 7).

6. A metatheory is defined here as a scheme that logically connects and integrates partial
theories and thus is critical in the construction of general theory. A mid-range theory is defined,

approach that was common in the literature of this period was largely atheoretical, in that it did not propose general and testable hypotheses. Research also addressed a fairly narrow agenda. Political scientists studied the formal institutions of government and presented arguments, which largely reflected the prevailing consensus about the merits of limited democracy, on the institutional questions of the day, such as the reforms adopted in the United States after the Civil War and the constitutional changes in Europe in the late nineteenth and early twentieth centuries.[7]

In terms of methods, the U.S. reaction to what was seen as the excessively abstract and even metaphysical aspects of European philosophies of history had the positive effect of grounding discussion in observables, that is, in empirical facts. But most of this work consisted mainly of case studies that offered detailed information about legal aspects of the government, at best presented alongside, but not explicitly connected to, more abstract discussions of political theory.[8] Moreover, it tended to focus on a fairly small set of countries and not to provide systematic comparison across countries.

The limitations of the early research done by political scientists in the United States notwithstanding, the establishment of political science as an autonomous discipline was a critical development that prepared the ground for future growth. In Europe and elsewhere, the strength of sociology, an imperialist field by definition, worked against the establishment of a discipline focused on the study of politics.[9] Thus, in breaking with the more advanced European tradition by establishing political science as a distinct

---

following sociologist Merton (1968, 39–73), as a theory with a more limited scope than what he called grand theory.

7. To be sure, not all political scientists viewed their discipline as concerned with government and formal institutions. For example, Arthur Bentley's (1870–1957) *Process of Government* (Bentley 1908) went beyond formal political institutions and prefigured subsequent work on interest group politics. However, it is telling that this book was written by an outsider and ignored for four decades. For other exceptions to the dominant formal-legal work of the period, see Eckstein (1963, 13–16) on evolutionary theory and Ross (1991, Ch. 8) on research on extralegal institutions and social and economic factors. Moreover, exceptional works from this period, such as *Politics and Administration* by the first APSA president Frank Goodnow (1859–1939), display a concern with theory that begins to be systematic (Goodnow 1900; on Goodnow, see Adcock 2005).

8. This literature is generally characterized and criticized as "descriptive." Yet this label is not accurate in that description is one of the key goals of the social sciences and description requires theory and thus is not an antinomy of theory.

9. While the APSA was founded in 1903, most other national political science associations were not created until after World War II. For example, political science associations were founded in France in 1949, in Britain and the Netherlands in 1950, in Germany in 1951, in Greece in 1959, in Denmark in 1965, in Chile in 1966, in Austria in 1971, in Italy in 1973, and in Argentina in 1983. The International Political Science Association (IPSA) was founded in 1949.

Table 2.2. The Origins and Evolution of Comparative Politics in the United States

Dimensions		1. The Constitution of Political Science as a Discipline, 1880–1920	Period 2. The Behavioral Revolution, 1921–1966	3. The Post-Behavioral Period, 1967–1988	4. The Second Scientific Revolution, 1989–present
I. Subject matter		Government and formal political institutions	The political system Informal politics Political behavior	The state and state-society relations Formal political institutions Political behavior	The state and state-society relations Formal political institutions Political behavior
II. Theory	i. Metatheories	None	Structural functionalism	Theories of the state	Rational choice and game theory, rational choice institutionalism, historical institutionalism
	ii. Mid-range theories	None	On interest groups, political parties, political culture, bureaucracy, the military, democratization, and democratic stability	On state formation, revolutions, varieties of authoritarianism and democracy, democratic breakdowns and transitions, the military, political parties, democratic institutions, political culture, corporatism, social democracy, models of economic development, economic reform	On state collapse, civil conflict, ethnic conflict, varieties of democracy, electoral and other democratic institutions, political parties, electoral behavior, citizen attitudes, political culture, social movements, economic and policy making, varieties of capitalism
III. Methods		Case studies and some small-N comparisons	Case studies and small-N comparisons Cross-national, statistical analysis	Case studies and small-N comparisons Cross-national, statistical analysis	Case studies and small-N comparisons Cross-national, statistical analysis Within-country, statistical analysis Formal theorizing

IV. Assessment	i. Strengths theory	Establishment of a distinctive subject matter for the discipline	Attempt at metatheorizing Incorporation of a focus on societal actors	Theorizing grounded in case knowledge Growing attention to political processes and change	Emphasis on action (actors and choice) and institutions Recognition of the problem of endogeneity
	ii. Strengths empirics	Emphasis on empirical grounding in observables	More comparative analysis Broadening of empirical scope	More rigorous comparative analysis Long-term historical analysis	More comparative analysis and rigorous testing
	iii. Weaknesses theory	Formal legal approach as atheoretical and narrow	Lack of integration of mid-range theories The state as a black box and politics as an outcome of nonpolitical factors Overly structural and functionalist analysis	Lack of integration of mid-range theories	Lack of integration of mid-range theories
	iii. Weaknesses empirics	Lack systematic comparison Narrow empirical scope	Lack of testing of structural functionalism		Lack of testing of formal theories
V. Relationship to other disciplines and fields within political science, and to theories, schools, and approaches	i. Reaction against . . .	European grand theorizing and philosophies of history	History	Reductionism Evolutionism, the view that societies develop in a uniform and progressive manner Functionalism	Area studies
	ii. Borrowing from . . .	History: the German historical schoo[l] Legal studies	American Politics field Sociology: Parsonian Sociology Anthropology Psychology	Sociology: Historical Sociology Marxism: Western Marxism Latin American dependency	American Politics field Economics

Table 2.2. The Origins and Evolution of Comparative Politics in the United States

Dimensions		1. The Constitution of Political Science as a Discipline, 1880–1920	2. The Behavioral Revolution, 1921–1966	3. The Post-Behavioral Period, 1967–1988	4. The Second Scientific Revolution, 1989–present
				Period	
VI. Research context	i. Political events and trends	The "social question" in the U.S. Gilded Age, European democratization and constitutional reform, World War I, the Russian Revolution	Great Depression, the New Deal, fascism, World War II, independence of African and Asian countries, the Cold War, McCarthyism, the civil rights movement	The Vietnam War, 1969, European social democracy, authoritarian and totalitarian regimes in the South and East, global democratization, the fall of communist systems	Post–Cold War, globalization, market reforms, ethnic conflicts, 9/11, the Iraq wars
	ii. Values of comparativists	Consensus around Whig (antimajoritarian) tradition of limited democracy: conservatives and moderate liberals	Consensus around liberal values	Conflicting values: liberals, conservatives, and radicals	Consensus around democracy, but conflict over neo-liberalism and globalization

discipline with its own organizational basis, the United States opened a new path that would allow it to catch up and eventually overtake Europe.[10]

The Behavioral Revolution, 1921–1966

A first turning point in the evolution of U.S. political science can be conveniently dated to the 1921 publication of a manifesto for a new science of politics, which implied a departure from the historical approach embraced by many of the founders of political science in the United States, by the University of Chicago professor Charles Merriam (1874–1953) (Merriam 1921).[11] This publication was followed by a series of National Conferences on the Science of Politics, which were important events for the discipline, in 1923, 1924, and 1925. It was also followed by the formation of the Social Science Research Council (SSRC), the world's first national organization of all the social sciences, based largely on Merriam's proposal to develop the infrastructure for research in the social sciences. And it signaled the rise of the Chicago School of political science, an influential source of scholarship in the 1920s and 1930s.[12] However, the impact of Merriam's agenda on the study of comparative politics would not be felt in full force until the behavioral revolution swept through the field in the 1950s and 1960s.

One reason the impetus for a new approach to political science was temporarily muted was that it was centered in, but also restricted to, the study of American politics. Initially, political science was conceived as practically synonymous with the study of comparative politics or, as it was usu-

10. This break with the classical social theory tradition was not a uniquely U.S. phenomenon. Indeed, as Adcock (2005) shows, during the last quarter of the nineteenth century U.S. political scientists drew on the works of German, English, and French scholars who themselves departed from the tradition of classical social theory and sought to develop a more institutional approach. But it was in the United States that the push to carve out a distinct political subject matter gained the momentum needed to establish political science as a new discipline.

11. The emphasis on science could be seen as the working out on U.S. soil of the European *Methodenstreit* (methodological controversy), which had endured from 1883 through roughly 1910 and was eventually lost by the German historical school of Ranke. But it also reflected Merriam's concern with developing a political science that moved away from speculative thinking and that, by focusing on problem solving, had policy relevance. In this sense, the call for a new science of politics had its roots in American pragmatism and the work of James and Dewey (Farr 1999).

12. The Chicago School refers to Charles Merriam himself, Harold Gosnell (1896–1997), Harold Lasswell (1902–78), Leonard White (1891–1958) and Quincy Wright (1890–1970). The label is also extended to graduate students trained at Chicago, such as Gabriel Almond (1911–2002), V. O. Key Jr. (1908–63), David Truman (1913–2003), and Herbert Simon (1916–2001), who holds the distinction of being the only political scientist ever awarded a Nobel Prize, in economics. On the Chicago School and some of its key members, see Almond (1990, 309–28; 1996, 65–68; 2002, Chs. 3 and 4).

ally called in those days, comparative government.[13] Indeed, Burgess and other founders of political science were strong proponents of a "historical-comparative" method. But as the boundaries between political science and other disciplines were settled, another process of differentiation, leading to the formation of fields within political science, began to unfold. This secondary, internal process of differentiation reflected the increased weight of U.S-trained Ph.D.s and cemented the view that the study of American politics was a distinct enterprise within political science. In turn, more by default than by design, comparative politics was initially constituted as a field that covered what was not covered by American politics, that is, the study of government and formal political institutions outside the United States. This would be an extremely consequential development, whose effect was noted immediately. Even though Merriam's ideas were embraced by many in the field of American politics, the new structure of fields insulated comparativists from these new ideas.

Another reason the impact of Merriam's agenda was not felt at once had to do with timing and, specifically, the rise of the Nazis in Germany and the onset of World War II. On the one hand, due to these events, a considerable number of distinguished European and especially German thinkers immigrated to the United States and took jobs in U.S. universities.[14] And these émigrés reinserted, among other things, a greater emphasis on normative political theory in political science. On the other hand, many Americans who proposed a recasting of political science joined the U.S. government and participated in the war effort. This produced a general hiatus in political science research and put any revolution in the discipline on hold.

This transitional period came to a close with the end of World War II and the ushering in of the behavioral revolution.[15] As in the 1920s, the

13. This was the case even though the term *comparative politics* had been coined some time before, in 1873, by Oxford scholar Edward Freeman (1823–92) (Freeman 1873).

14. The list of German political scientists who came to the United States includes Theodore Adorno, Hanna Arendt, Karl Deutsch, Max Horkheimer, Otto Kirchheimer, Herbert Marcuse, Hans Morgenthau, Franz Neumann, Leo Strauss, Eric Vogelin, and Karl Wittfogel.

15. Eckstein (1963, 18–23) appropriately characterizes the most influential books in comparative politics of this period—*Theory and Practice of Modern Government* (1932), by British professor Herman Finer (1898–1969), and *Constitutional Government and Politics* (1937), by German-born Harvard professor Carl Friedrich (1901–84)—as "transitional" works between the prior formal-legal literature and the subsequent behavioral literature. The advances made in these works were significant. Thus, rather than offering country-by-country discussions, as was the case of British author and ambassador to the United States James Bryce's (1838–1922) *Modern Democracies* (1921), these two books presented institution-by-institution analyses and, going beyond a sole emphasis on formal-legal aspects, addressed political parties, interest groups, and the mass media. Yet, their approach to issues of theory and methods had changed little. That is, even though these texts made reference to political theory, they were characterized by a disjuncture between their theoretical and empirical aspects and they did not rely on rigorous

impetus for change came from the field of American politics and was led by various members of the Chicago School. But this time around the proponents of change had a more ambitious statement of their agenda and also controlled greater organizational resources, including the Committee on Political Behavior established within the SSRC in 1945.[16] Moreover, the calls for change were not limited, as before, to the field of American politics. Rather, through a number of key events—an SSRC conference at Northwestern University in 1952, several programmatic statements, and, most important, the creation of the SSRC's Committee on Comparative Politics chaired by Gabriel Almond during 1954–63—behavioralism spread to comparative politics.[17]

Behavioralism in comparative politics, as in other fields of political science, stood for two distinct ideas. One concerned the proper subject matter of comparative politics. In this regard, behavioralists reacted against a definition of the field that restricted its scope to the formal institutions of government and sought to include a range of informal procedures and behaviors—related to interest groups, political parties, mass communication, political culture, and political socialization—that were seen as key to the functioning of the political system. A second key idea was the need for a scientific approach to matters of theory and methods. Behavioralists were opposed to what they saw as vague, rarified theory and atheoretical empirics, and argued for systematic theory and empirical testing.[18] Thus, be-

---

methods. In sum, Finer's and Friedrich's texts represented a synthesis and maturation of traditional research that was relatively unaffected by calls for a new science of politics.

16. Three key books that gave momentum to the behavioral revolution were Lasswell and Kaplan (1950), Truman (1951), and Easton (1953). Though the influence of the Chicago School was quite patent in the launching and spread of behavioralism, in the 1950s and 1960s Yale University—where Almond, Dahl, Deutsch, Lane, Lasswell, and Lindblom taught—was the most exciting center for political science research. Also noteworthy as a site for the cross-fertilization of ideas was the Stanford Center for Advanced Study in the Behavioral Sciences in Palo Alto, established in 1954 as a result of a Ford Foundation initiative. On the early impact of behavioralism, see Truman (1955); and on the political science literature of the 1940s and 1950s more broadly, see Lindblom (1997). On the SSRC and its various committees, see Sibley (2001) and Worcester (2001); and on political science at Yale during 1955–70, see Merelman (2003).

17. The statements that launched the new agenda for comparative politics included the report on the SSRC's Interuniversity Research Seminar on Comparative Politics at Northwestern University (Macridis and Cox 1953) and the programmatic papers by Kahin et al. (1955) and Almond, Cole, and Macridis (1955). On the 1952 Northwestern University conference as the birthplace of "modern comparative politics," see Eckstein (1998, 506–10); and on the SSRC Committee on Comparative Politics, see Gilman (2003, Ch. 4).

18. As Dahl (1961b, 766), a leading figure in the behavioral revolution in political science, wrote, behavioralism was "a protest movement within political science" by scholars who questioned the "historical, philosophical, and the descriptive-institutional approaches . . . of conventional political science" and who subscribed to notions of systematic theory building and empirical testing.

havioralists sought to bring about major changes in the established practices of comparative politics. And their impact on the field would be high.

Behavioralism's broadening of the field's scope beyond the government
and its formal institutions opened comparative politics to a range of theoretical influences from other disciplines. The strongest influence was clearly
that of sociology. Indeed, Weberian-Parsonian concepts played a central
role in structural functionalism (Parsons 1951), the dominant metatheory
of the time, and some of the most influential contributions to comparative
politics were written by scholars trained as sociologists.[19] Moreover, anthropology had some influence on structural functionalism, as did social
psychology on the literature on political culture (Almond and Verba 1963).
Thus, behavioralists helped political science overcome its earlier isolation
from other social sciences and this reconnection to other disciplines was
associated with a salutary emphasis on theorizing.

The central role given to theory was counterbalanced, however, by
some shortcomings. The redefinition of the field's subject matter instigated
by the behavioralists led comparativists to focus on societal actors and
parties as intermediary agents between society and the state. Nonetheless,
to a large extent, behavioralists focused attention on processes outside of
the state and offered reductionist accounts of politics. The state was treated
as a black box and, eschewing the possibility that the constitution of actors
and the ways in which they interacted might be shaped by the state, politics
was cast as a reflection of how social actors performed certain functions or
how conflicts about economic interests were resolved politically. In other
words, politics was not seen as a causal factor and a sense of the distinctiveness of comparative politics as a field of political science was thus lost.

Another shortcoming of this literature concerned the approach to theorizing as opposed to the substance of theories. The most ambitious theorizing, well represented by Almond and James Coleman's edited volume
The Politics of the Developing Areas (1960), sought to develop a general theory of politics. Yet the key fruit of these efforts, structural functionalism,[20]
had serious limitations. In particular, for all the talk about science among
proponents of structural functionalism, much of the literature that used

19. This link with sociology was not unprecedented. For example, the influence of sociologists Pareto and Mosca is evident in Lasswell's *Politics: Who Gets What, When, How* (1936). But
the extent of the interplay between sociologists and comparativists was much greater in this
period. A prominent example of this interplay is Lipset, who wrote many influential texts on
political sociology (Lipset 1959, 1960a) and has the distinction of having served as president of
both the American Political Science Association (1979–80) and the American Sociological Association (1992–93).

20. Though structural functionalism was the dominant metatheory at the time, it was
not the only one. On the different metatheories of this period, see Holt and Richardson (1970,
29–45).

this metatheory fell short of providing testable propositions and testing hypotheses. Another strand in the literature, more concerned with mid-range theorizing, did generate testable hypotheses and conduct empirical testing. An example was Seymour Lipset's *Political Man* (1960a), which included his widely read *American Political Science Review* article on the link between economic development and democracy (Lipset 1959). But this mode of theorizing lacked precisely what structural functionalism aimed at providing: a framework that would offer a basis for connecting and integrating mid-range theories, that is, for showing how the various parts connected to form the whole. These mid-range theories tended to draw on metatheories other than structural functionalism; for example, a Marxist notion of conflict of interests played a fairly prominent role in the works of political sociologists. Yet these metatheories were less explicitly and fully elaborated than structural functionalism.[21] In sum, though these two literatures were parts of the same modernization school that sought to come to terms with the vast processes of socioeconomic and political change in the post–World War II years, their metatheories and mid-range theories were not linked together and hence the twin goals of generating general theory and testing hypotheses were not met.

In terms of methods, behavioralism also introduced notable changes. Though the dominant form of empirical analysis continued to be the case study and the small-N comparison, comparative analyses became more common and the scope of empirical research was expanded well beyond the traditional focus on big European countries. More attention was given to small European countries. Interest blossomed in the Third World, as comparativists turned their attention to the newly independent countries in Asia and Africa and the longstanding independent countries of Latin America.[22] Moreover, comparativists studied the United States and thus broke down the arbitrary exclusion of the United States from the scope of comparative politics.[23] Another key methodological novelty was the introduction of statistical research. Such research included fairly rudimentary cross-national statistical analyses, as offered in the pioneering survey-based study *The Civic Culture*, by Almond and Sidney Verba (1963).[24] And it was associated with efforts to develop large-N cross-national data sets on

21. On the lack of an explicit metatheory that would frame the research agenda of political sociology, see Lipset and Bendix (1966, 6–15).

22. On the political development literature on Third World politics, see Huntington and Dominguez (1975) and Almond (1990, Ch. 9).

23. The tradition of studying the United States in comparative perspective, pioneered by de Tocqueville, would be a feature of important works in comparative politics in the 1960s (Lipset 1960a, 1963; Moore 1966; Huntington 1968).

24. For an overview of cross-national survey research through the late 1960s, see Frey (1970).

institutional and macro-variables, a key input for quantitative research, through initiatives such as the Yale Political Data Program set up by Karl Deutsch (1912–92).[25] Comparativists could rightly claim to be engaged in an enterprise of truly global empirical scope.

All in all, the stature of U.S. comparative politics grew considerably in the two decades after World War II. Despite its shortcoming, the field had become more theoretically oriented and more methodologically sophisticated. Moreover, the identity and institutional basis of the field was bolstered by developments such as the expansion of SSRC support for fieldwork and research, the creation of an area studies infrastructure at many research universities,[26] and the launching of journals specializing in comparative politics and area studies.[27] Comparative politics in the United States was maturing rapidly. And its new stature was evident in the new relationship established between comparativists working in the United States and scholars in Europe. In the 1960s, comparativists in the United States began reconnecting with classical social theory[28] and collaborating with European scholars.[29] But now, unlike before, the United States had a model of comparative politics to export.

25. On the Yale Political Data Program, see Deutsch et al. (1966) and the quantitative data it generated, the *World Handbook of Political and Social Indicators* (Russett et al. 1964). Another new database was Banks and Textor's *Cross-Polity Survey* (1963).

26. The expansion of area studies centers was spurred by federal funding to U.S. universities through Title VI of the National Defense Education Act (NDEA) of 1958. The exchange of knowledge among area students was further fostered by the establishment of area studies associations. The Association for Asian Studies (AAS) was founded in 1941, the American Association for the Advancement of Slavic Studies (AAASS) in 1948, the African Studies Association in 1957, and the Latin American Studies Association (LASA) and Middle East Studies Association (MESA) in 1966.

27. Key journals for the field as a whole included *World Politics*, a journal geared to research in comparative politics and international relations that was first published in 1948, and *Comparative Politics* and *Comparative Political Studies*, both launched in 1968. Area-focused journals were usually created by area studies associations.

28. Key European classics became more accessible to U.S. scholars with their publication in English in the 1960s. For example, Robert Michels's *Political Parties* (1915) was published in English in 1962, Russian scholar Moisei Ostrogorski's (1854–1919) *Democracy and the Organization of Political Parties* (1902) in 1964, and Max Weber's *Economy and Society* (1914) in 1968.

29. During the behavioral period, the international links of U.S. universities were largely limited to Europe. As Almond (1997, 59) notes, of the 245 scholars associated with the SSRC's Committee on Comparative Politics since its creation in 1954 through the late 1960s, 199 were from the United States and most of the non-U.S. scholars were European. In exchanges with Europe, a key figure was Norwegian scholar Stein Rokkan, who played an important role in forums such as the Committee on Political Sociology (CPS) of the International Sociological Association (ISA), established in 1960, and in institutionalizing European social science through the creation of the European Consortium for Political Research (ECPR) in 1970. On the rebuilding and reorientation of European comparative politics after World War II, see the personal accounts in Daalder (1997a).

The Post-Behavioral Period, 1967–1988

The ascendancy of behavioralism in comparative politics came to an end in the mid-1960s or, more precisely, in 1966. Critiques of behavioralism had started earlier, in the mid-1950s, and behavioral work continued after 1966. Moreover, elaborate metatheoretical formulations by leading voices of the behavioral revolution were published in 1965 and 1966 (Easton 1965a, 1965b; Almond and Powell 1966). But these works signaled the culmination and decline of a research program rather than serving as a spur to further research. Indeed, the initiative quickly shifted away from the system-builders who had taken the lead in elaborating structural functionalism as a general theory of politics. The publication one year later of Lipset and Stein Rokkan's "Cleavage Structures, Party Systems, and Voter Alignments" (1967b) marked the onset of a new intellectual agenda.[30]

The authors who contributed to the new scholarship were diverse in many regards. Some were members of the generation, born in the 1910s and 1920s, which had brought behavioralism to comparative politics. Indeed, some of the most visible indications of change were publications authored by members of that generation, such as Lipset's collaborative work with Rokkan, Samuel Huntington's *Political Order in Changing Societies* (1968), and, later, Giovanni Sartori's *Parties and Party Systems* (1976).[31] But rapidly the early works of the next generation began to reshape the field with their analyses of consociationalism (Lijphart 1968a), corporatism (Schmitter 1971), the military (Stepan 1971), authoritarianism (O'Donnell 1973), and revolution (Scott 1976; Skocpol 1979). Thus, the new literature was spawned by both members of an established generation and a generation that was just entering the field.

These authors were also diverse in terms of their national origin and the values they held. The shapers of the new agenda included several foreign-born scholars working in the United States and, for the first time, these were not only Europeans primarily from Germany.[32] Moreover, the political

30. Sartori (1969, 87–94) makes a strong case for seeing Lipset and Rokkan's (1967b) work on party formation as a landmark study that departed in key ways from the previous literature.

31. The SSRC's Committee on Comparative Politics itself continued to operate until 1979 and published several works in the 1970s (Binder et al. 1971; Tilly 1975; Grew 1978) that reflected the new trends in the field. However, the intellectual agenda was not being set, as had been the case before, by this committee.

32. Among the scholars who made major contributions to comparative politics after 1967, some were born in the United States but had lived in Europe for many years (Schmitter), others were born in Europe (Linz, Sartori, Lijphart, Przeworski), and yet others had grown up in Latin America (O'Donnell). Thus, though this new group still primarily had European roots, it included for the first time voices from the Third World. In addition, this new group, unlike the group of European émigrés who came to the United States in the 1930s, had usually studied in the United States and received their Ph.D.s from U.S. universities.

values of many of these authors departed in a variety of ways from the broadly shared liberal outlook of the previous period.[33] The experience of fascism and World War II continued to weigh heavily on the minds of many scholars. But the U.S. civil rights movement (1955–65) and the Vietnam War (1959–75) had given rise to conservative and radical positions concerning democracy in the United States and U.S. foreign policy. Relatedly, outside the United States, the urgency of questions about political order and development made democracy seem like a luxury to some.

This diversity makes it hard to pinpoint the novelty and coherence of the new period in the evolution of comparative politics. On the one hand, though the emergence of a new generation was in part behind the move beyond behavioralism, the shift did not coincide solely with a generational change. Part of the new literature was authored by members of the generation born in the 1910s and 1920s and, in cases such as Lipset, these authors had even been closely associated with the behavioral literature. Moreover, many of the younger generation had been trained by behavioralists.[34] Thus, the new literature evolved out of, and through a dialogue with, the established literature, and not through a clean break. On the other hand, the decline in consensus around liberal values was not replaced by a new consensus but rather by the coexistence of liberal, conservative, and radical values. This lack of consensus did introduce an element of novelty, in that many of the key debates in the literature confronted authors with different values and in that the link between values and research thus became more apparent than it had been before. But these debates were not organized as a confrontation between a liberal and a new agenda. Indeed, the difference between conservatives and radicals was larger than between either of them and the liberals. Hence, the new literature cannot be characterized by a unified position regarding values.

Yet the novelty and coherence of the body of literature produced starting in 1967 can be identified in terms of the critique it made of the modernization school and the alternative it proposed. The most widely shared critique focused on the behavioralists' reductionism, that is, the idea that politics can be reduced to, and explained in terms of, more fundamental social or economic underpinnings. In turn, the alternative consisted of a revindication of politics as an autonomous practice and an emphasis on the importance of political determinants.[35] The new literature, it bears noting,

33. On the emergence of a consensus around a pluralist, liberal conception of democracy in the interwar years, see Gunnell (2004). On the conflict over values in the 1960s, see Ladd and Lipset (1975).

34. For example, Lijphart's dissertation committee was chaired by Almond and Schmitter's dissertation committee included Lipset.

35. Other important critiques concerned the evolutionism and functionalism of modern-

was not authored by system-builders but rather by scholars who rejected the work done by the system-builders of the behavioral period. Indeed, the new literature did not propose an equally elaborate and ambitious alternative framework for the study of comparative politics and hence it is most appropriate to label the new period in the evolution of field as "post-behavioral."[36] But the changes introduced by the new literature were extremely significant.

The centrality given to distinctly political questions implied a redefinition of the subject matter of comparative politics. This shift did not entail a rejection of standard concerns of behavioralists, such as the study of political behavior and interest groups. But issues such as interest groups were addressed, in the literature on corporatism, for example, from the perspective of the state.[37] What was new, as Theda Skocpol (1985a) put it, was the attempt to "bring the state back in" as an autonomous actor and thus to see state-society relations in a new light. The new literature also brought back the formal institutions that had been cast aside by behavioralists. After all, if politics was to be seen as a causal factor, it made sense to address the eminently manipulable instruments of politics, such as the rules regulating elections, the formation of parties, and the relationship among the branches of the government.[38] In short, the critique of behavioralism led to a refocusing of comparative politics on the state, state-society relations, and political institutions.

The approach to theorizing also underwent change. Theorizing during this period was less geared to building a new metatheory that would replace structural functionalism and more focused on developing mid-range theories. Metatheoretical questions were debated, and a large literature on theories of the state was produced. But the frustrations with the adaptation of Parsonian categories to the study of politics led to a certain aversion to top-

---

ization theory. The critics of evolutionism questioned the view that societies could be seen as developing in a uniform and progressive manner and, more specifically, that the end point of history was in evidence in the United States. These critics tended to argue, as an alternative, for a historicist approach. The work of Moore (1966) and O'Donnell (1973) emphasized these themes. The critique of functionalism was slower to come to a head, and was most clearly articulated as a question of what constituted an adequate explanation by Barry (1970, 168–73) and Elster (1982). The alternative to functionalism was an approach that put emphasis on choice and actors.

36. Some critics of the behavioralist literature, who drew on Western Marxism and Latin American dependency studies, did seek to offer a new alternative paradigm (Janos 1986, Ch. 3). And this literature had some impact in comparative politics. But it was never as strong in political science as in sociology and was criticized, or simply ignored, by the scholars who pioneered the new post-behavioral agenda.

37. On this shift in perspective in the study of interest groups, see Berger (1981).

38. The revalorization of formal institutions gained impetus from the seminal works on electoral laws by Duverger (1954), a French jurist and sociologist, and Rae (1967).

heavy grand theorizing that precluded the elaboration of ambitious and encompassing frameworks, and certainly no metatheory was as dominant as structural functionalism had been in the previous period.[39] Hence, efforts at theorizing were not seen as part of an attempt to generate an integrated, unified theory and thus produced unconnected "islands of theory" (Guetzkow 1950). But the freedom from what was seen, by many, as a theoretical straitjacket opened up a period of great fertility and creativity. Old questions, about interest groups, political culture, and the military, continued to be studied. New questions, on matters such as state formation and revolution, varieties of authoritarianism and democracy, democratic breakdowns and transitions, democratic institutions, social democracy, and models of economic development, garnered much attention. Moreover, research on these questions did much to advance theories and concepts that brought political processes to life and to address the question of political change, a feat particularly well attained in Juan Linz's *The Breakdown of Democratic Regimes* (1978) and Guillermo O'Donnell and Philippe Schmitter's *Transitions from Authoritarian Rule* (1986). In sum, the knowledge base of comparative politics was rapidly expanded and was increasingly shorn of reductionist connotations.[40]

The story regarding methods is more complicated. To a large extent, research during this period relied on case studies and small-N comparisons. These were the staples of area studies research, which sought to capitalize on in-depth country knowledge gained usually while conducting fieldwork. In addition, the use of statistics, introduced in the previous period, continued. As before, attention was given to survey research and the generation of data sets.[41] Moreover, a quantitative literature started to develop on

---

39. Alford and Friedland (1985) distinguish three perspectives—pluralist, managerial, and class—in the literature of these years. For a review and assessment of the theories of the state, that spans the Marxist literature, and things such as the Miliband-Poulantzas debate, as well as the literature by economists, including works by Tulloch and Buchanan and the public choice school that comparativists were barely reading in the 1980s, see Przeworski (1990).

40. Though the new literature can be read as offering an alternative to the reductionism of the modernization literature, it also filled a key gap: the analysis of political change. Structural functionalism was a theory of statics, that is, of the functioning of a system, and the discussion of change, that is, modernization, had centered on social and economic aspects. Indeed, there was very little in the literature prior to the late 1960s on political change per se. For an overview of some of the central works on comparative politics during this period, see Migdal (1983) and Rogowski (1993).

41. Two important contributions in the 1970s to the cross-national survey literature were Inglehart (1977) and Verba, Nie, and Kim (1978). Regarding data, some efforts focused on updating and improving data sets launched in the early 1960s. Banks, who had worked on the *Cross-Polity Survey* (Banks and Textor 1963), started publishing the widely used and regularly updated Cross-National Time-Series Data Archive in 1968. Two new versions of the *World Handbook of Political and Social Indicators* were also published during this period (Taylor and

issues such as electoral behavior, public opinion, and democracy.[42] Thus, even as structural functionalism as a metatheory was largely abandoned when the field of comparative politics altered course in the mid-1960s, the methodological dimension of behavioralism—its emphasis on systematic empirical testing—lived on.

But a methodological schism was also starting to take root. Indeed, during this period, quantitative research was not at the center of the agenda of comparative politics and, to a large extent, was ignored by scholars working within the dominant qualitative tradition. Hence, though comparativists began to take an interest in quantitative analysis in the 1960s, in tandem with political science as a whole, thereafter they started to fall behind other political scientists and especially Americanists in this regard. Precisely at a time when a concerted push to develop quantitative methods suitable for political science, and to expand training in these methods, was taking off,[43] comparativists followed a different path.

The relatively low impact of the quantitative literature that went by the label of "cross-national" research during this period was not due to a lack of emphasis on methods in comparative politics. In the first half of the 1970s, comparativists produced and discussed a series of methodological texts about case studies and small-N comparisons.[44] This was, relatively speaking, a period of heightened methodological awareness in comparative politics. Rather, the standing of quantitative research was due to certain limitations of this literature. As the debate on the political culture literature based on survey data shows, comparativists frequently had serious reservations about the theoretical underpinnings of much of the quantitative re-

Hudson 1972; Taylor and Jodice 1983). In addition, in the 1970s two new influential databases were created. Freedom House started to publish its annual indexes of political and civil rights in 1973 and the first version of Polity was released in 1978. For an overview of the broader, international data movement, see Scheuch (2003).

42. For an overview of the quantitative literature on electoral behavior and public opinion until the late 1980s, see Dalton (1991). On the quantitative literature on democracy, see Jackman (2001).

43. Earlier, in 1948, the Survey Research Center at the University of Michigan had begun summer training courses in quantitative methods. But it was the establishment of the Inter-university Consortium for Political and Social Research (ICPSR) at Michigan in 1962 that really provided the institutional infrastructure and the motor for a turn toward a scientific, quantitatively oriented political science. Another significant marker was the admittance of political science into the National Science Foundation (NSF) in 1965. The momentum continued and eventually quantitatively oriented political scientists launched a publication—*Political Methodology*, subsequently renamed *Political Analysis*—in 1975, began a tradition of annual summer methods conferences of the Society for Political Methodology in 1984, and constituted the APSA section on Political Methodology in 1985.

44. Key works published at the time on what was usually referred to as "the comparative method" include Smelser (1968, 1976), Przeworski and Teune (1970), Sartori (1970), Lijphart (1971), and Eckstein (1975). See also George (1979) and Skocpol and Somers (1980).

search.[45] In addition, the quantitative literature did not speak to some of the most pressing or theoretically relevant issues of the day. Largely due to the lack of data on many countries, quantitative research was most advanced in the study of functioning democracies, precisely at a time when most of the countries in the world were not democracies and issues such as elections, democratic institutions, and even citizen attitudes were simply not germane.[46]

The rationale for this segregation of quantitative research from the mainstream of the field notwithstanding, it had important consequences for the field's evolution. Within comparative politics, this situation led to the development of two quite distinct, quantitative and qualitative, research traditions that did not talk to each other.[47] In turn, within political science, it led to a growing divide between comparativists and Americanists. Comparativists were largely aloof of advances spurred primarily by scholars in the neighboring field of American politics, where the sophistication of quantitative methods was steadily developing (Achen 1983; King 1991; Bartels and Brady 1993). Indeed, comparativists were not only not contributing to this emerging literature on quantitative methodology; they hardly could be counted among its consumers. The question of common methodological standards across fields of political science was becoming a source of irrepressible tension.

The Second Scientific Revolution, 1989–Present

A new phase in the evolution of comparative politics began with a push to make the field more scientific, propelled in great part by the American Political Science Association (APSA) section on Comparative Politics, constituted in 1989 with the aim of counteracting the fragmentation of the field induced by the area studies focus of much research. This emphasis on science, of course, was reminiscent of the behavioral revolution and statements about the limitations of area studies research even echoed calls made by behavioralists.[48] Moreover, as had been the case with the behavioral

45. For a discussion of the theoretical critiques of the quantitative political culture literature, see Johnson (2003).

46. For example, Lijphart's *Democracies* (1984), a pioneering study in the revival of institutional analysis that relies extensively on quantitative analysis, had little to say to the student of authoritarian regimes.

47. For a sense of the fundamental differences in perspective, see the counter-posed views of Sartori (1970), an advocate of qualitative research, and Jackman (1985), an advocate of quantitative research.

48. In the very first paragraph of the preface to *The Politics of the Developing Areas*, Almond emphasized "the importance of moving from an 'area studies' approach . . . to a genuinely comparative and analytical one" (Almond and Coleman 1960, vii).

revolution, this second scientific revolution in comparative politics was not homegrown but, rather, was the product of the importation of ideas that had already been hatched and elaborated in the field of American politics. Nonetheless, there were some significant differences in terms of the content and impact of the behavioral revolution that swept through comparative politics in the 1950s and 1960s and the new revolution that began to alter the field in the 1990s.

The advocates of this new revolution shared the same ambition of the behavioralists who aspired to construct a general, unified theory. But they also diverged from earlier theoretical attempts to advance a science of politics in two basic ways. First, the proposed metatheories drew heavily on economics as opposed to sociology, which had been the main source of the old, structural-functionalist metatheory. This was the case of the game-theoretic version of rational choice theory, as well as of rational choice institutionalism, a related but distinct metatheory that introduced, in a highly consequential move, institutions as constraints.[49] Second, the new metatheories did not lead to a redefinition of the subject matter of comparative politics, as had been the case with behavioralism. That is, while behavioralists proposed a general theory of politics, which had direct implications for what should be studied by comparativists, rational choice theorists advanced what was, at its core, a general theory of action.[50] Indeed, rational choice theory offers certain elements to study decision making under constraints, but these elements do not identify what is distinctive about political action in contrast to economic or social action. In effect, rational choice theory is seen as a unifying theory, which can integrate theories about action in different domains, precisely because it is not held to apply to any specific domain of action.

49. This argument about economics and sociology deserves some clarification. During the previous period comparativists had drawn on the work of economists, but these tended to be historical or institutional economists in the tradition of Thorstein Veblen (1857–1929), such as Gerschenkron, or relatively unorthodox economists, such as Hirschman. In turn, some sociologists, including prominent scholars such as Coleman (1990a) and Goldthorpe (2000), have embraced rational choice theory. But even sociologists that focused on the economy and economic action tended to see the economy as part of society and rational action as a variable (Smelser and Swedberg 1994).

The popularity of rational choice theory in political science owed much to the work of William Riker (1920–93), of Rochester University. In turn, rational choice institutionalism owed much to the widely read book by the economist North (1990). For Riker's programmatic statements, see Riker (1977, 1990); on Riker and the Rochester school, see Amadae and Bueno de Mesquita (1999). For a discussion of the origins of rational choice theory, and the key role played by the RAND Corporation, see Amadae (2003). For an early though largely ignored call for political scientists to shift from theories drawn from sociology to economics, see Mitchell (1969).

50. On the sense in which rational choice theory might be considered a general theory, see Munck (2001).

In turn, with regard to methods, the drive to be more scientific took two forms. One, closely linked with rational choice theorizing, was the emphasis on logical rigor in theorizing, which was taken much farther than had been the case before with the advocacy of formal theorizing or formal modeling as a method of theorizing.[51] The other, much more of an outgrowth of the methodological aspirations of behavioralists and the maturation of political methodology, centered on the use of quantitative, statistical methods of empirical testing.[52]

The impact of this new agenda with three prongs—rational choice, formal theory, and quantitative methods—has been notable. Some rational choice analyses in comparative politics had been produced in earlier years.[53] But after 1989 the work gradually became more formalized and addressed a growing number of issues, such as democratization (Przeworski 1991, 2005), ethnic conflict and civil war (Fearon and Laitin 1996), voting (Cox 1997), government formation (Laver 1998), and economic policy (Bates 1997a). An even more formidable shift took place regarding quantitative research. Political events, especially the global wave of democratization, made the questions and methods that had been standard in the field of American politics more relevant to students of comparative politics. Moreover, there was a great expansion of available data sets. New cross-national time series were produced on various economic concepts, on broad political concepts such as democracy and governance, and on a variety of political institutions.[54] There was also a huge growth of survey data, whether of the type pioneered by Angus Campbell, Philip Converse, Warren Miller, and Donald Stokes's *The American Voter* (1960)—the national election studies

51. It bears clarifying that there is not a necessary link between rational choice theory and formal theorizing. There is rational choice theorizing that is advanced without formal methods, and formal methods can be linked to other theories.

52. Though these two forms of methods are in principle supplementary, their respective users have at times been critical of each other. For example, Green, an advocate of quantitative methods, strongly criticized the failure of formal theorists to produce empirical results (Green and Shapiro 1994); and the tendency of some quantitative researchers to engage in "mindless number crunching" has been criticized by formal theorists. Nonetheless, there has been a definite push to bridge the gap between formal theories and quantitative empirical methods (Morton 1999; Camerer and Morton 2002). One important NSF-supported initiative in this regard has been the summer institutes on Empirical Implications of Theoretical Models (EITM), running from 2002 to 2005.

53. Samuel Popkin's *The Rational Peasant* (1979), which was read as a rational choice response to James Scott's *The Moral Economy of the Peasant* (1976), was one of the first widely discussed applications of rational choice theory to a question of concern to comparativists. Another key early work was Bates's *Markets and States in Tropical Africa* (1981). For reviews that address this earlier literature, see Bates (1990) and Keech, Bates, and Lange (1991).

54. One important source of economic data was Penn World Tables (Summers and Heston 1991). For an overview of data sets on politics, see Munck and Verkuilen (2002) and Munck (2005).

model—or the broader and explicitly cross-national surveys such as the regional barometers and the World Values Survey.[55] And, as the infrastructure for quantitative research in comparative politics was strengthened, the number and the sophistication of statistical works increased rapidly.

Some of this statistical research, such as Adam Przeworski et al.'s *Democracy and Development* (2000), revisited old debates about the determinants and effects of democracy. Yet other works focused on electoral behavior and citizen attitudes, and the legislative and executive branches of government, issues that had long been concerns within American politics. Also, going beyond the kind of cross-national, statistical analysis familiar to comparativists since the 1960s, this quantitative research began to use within-country, statistical analysis, a standard practice in the field of American politics. Moreover, though much of this work was not linked or at best poorly linked with formal theorizing, even this gap was gradually overcome, especially in the work of economists who began to work on standard questions of comparative politics (Persson and Tabellini 2000, 2003).

However, in spite of the significant change brought about in the field of comparative politics by this new literature, the agenda of the second scientific revolution did not bring about as profound a transformation of comparative politics as the behavioral revolution did in the 1950s and early 1960s. The effect of this agenda was limited due to opposition from the Perestroika movement, a discipline-wide reaction to the renewed emphasis on scientific approaches to the study of politics.[56] But another key factor was the existence of other well-established approaches to theory and methods. Indeed, the post-1989 period has lacked anything as dominant as structural functionalism or the modernization school had been during the behavioral period, and is best characterized as a period of pluralism. In contrast, the new revolution in comparative politics triggered a heightened awareness about issues of theory and methods among a broad range of comparativists, which has led to real diversity and a relatively healthy interaction among scholars holding different views.

The most polarizing issue has been the status of rational choice theory. There is undeniably something to claims that many comparativists have blindly rejected the ideas of rational choice theorists and, likewise, there is a basis for the worries expressed by some regarding the hegemonic aspira-

55. The first regional barometer, the Eurobarometer, began operations in 1973. The other barometers started to track public opinion in post-communist nations in 1991, in Latin America in 1995, in Africa in 1999, and in Asia in 2001. The World Values Survey started collecting data in 1990–91. On these and other cross-national surveys, see Norris (2004).

56. The Perestroika movement started in October 2000 with an e-mail sent by an anonymous "Mr. Perestroika" to a number of political scientists, criticizing trends in the American Political Science Association (APSA) and the association's flagship journal, the *American Political Science Review*. On the Perestroika movement, see Monroe (2005).

tions of rational choice theorists (Lichbach 2003). But the polemics surrounding rational choice theory have actually diverted attention away
from a core problem. The introduction of rational choice theory in the
field has had a salutary effect, because it has forced scholars to sharpen
their proposals of alternative views and helped to structure theoretical debates. Indeed, the contrast between rational choice theory and structural
approaches, and between institutional and cultural approaches, has helped
to frame some of the thorniest theoretical issues faced in the field. Nonetheless, as rational choice theorists began to include institutions in their analysis, and as debate centered on rational choice institutionalism (Weingast
2002) and historical institutionalism (Thelen 1999; Pierson and Skocpol
2002) as the two main alternatives, it became hard to detect precisely what
was distinctive about these metatheories.[57]

The convergence on institutions has served to highlight that rational
choice institutionalism and historical institutionalism face a common issue, the fact that the institutions seen as constraints on politicians are
themselves routinely changed by politicians or, in other words, that institutions are endogenous to the political process. But these different metatheories have not proposed well-defined solutions to this core issue in the
analysis of political action, failing to distinguish clearly and to link theories
of statics and dynamics. Moreover, these metatheories fail even to differentiate appropriately among issues related to a general theory of action as
opposed to a general theory of politics. Hence, despite a lot of talk about
paradigms, the basis for either a debate among, or an attempt at synthesis
of, these different metatheories remains rather clouded.

A different situation developed concerning methodology. Along with
the increased use of quantitative methods, there was a reinvigoration
of qualitative methodology. This process was initiated practically single-
handedly by David Collier with a critical assessment of the state of the
literature (Collier 1991, 1993).[58] It was fueled by Gary King, Robert Keohane, and Sidney Verba's influential *Designing Social Inquiry* (1994) and
various critiques of small-N research.[59] And it was consolidated with important new statements about qualitative methodology (Brady and Collier
2004; George and Bennett 2005).[60] In addition, this revival of interest

57. On these and other metatheories commonly used in comparative politics in the 1990s,
see Hall and Taylor (1996) and Lichbach and Zuckerman (1997).

58. Collier is also the author, with Ruth Berins Collier, of *Shaping the Political Arena* (Collier
and Collier 1991), a book that was widely seen as an exemplar of rigorous qualitative research.

59. Important critiques of small-N research, which were important precursors of King,
Keohane, and Verba's (1994) implicit critique of standard practices, were authored by Geddes
(1991) and Lieberson (1991).

60. This process has also led to the institutionalization of research and training in qualita-

in qualitative methodology was associated with various efforts to build bridges among different methodologies, whether through an exploration of the link between statistical, large-N methods and qualitative, small-N research (Brady and Collier 2004); the use of case studies as a tool to test formal theories, a proposal advanced by advocates of "analytical narratives" (Bates et al. 1998; Rodrik 2003), and the possibility of "a tripartite methodology, including statistics, formalization, and narrative," an option articulated by David Laitin (2002, 630–31; 2003). Thus, the debate about methods, in contrast to the debate about theory, has led to a clear sense of the potential contributions of different methods and hence to the identification of a basis for synthesis.

Finally, in terms of substantive research, the influence of rational choice theory has no doubt increased the influence of ideas from economics in comparative politics and this has opened new avenues of research (Miller 1997). But unlike in the 1950s, the new scientific revolution of the 1990s did not bring a major shift in the focus of empirical research. Rather, there is a great degree of continuity with regard to the mid-range theorizing that had been done during the previous fifteen to twenty years. And it is noteworthy that, at this level of theorizing, the cross-fertilization among researchers coming from different traditions is not uncommon. Thus, though charges of economic imperialism have been made and in some instances might be justifiable, the relationship between economics and comparative politics has been a two-way street. Some economists have taken comparative politics seriously, drawing in particular on the insights about political institutions offered by comparativists. The work of economists has been used by comparativists to revitalize research on central issues such as the state and citizenship (Przeworski 2003). And economists have revisited debates launched by classics of comparative historical analysis, such as Barrington Moore's *Social Origins of Dictatorship and Democracy* (1966), and of area studies research, such as Fernando Cardoso and Enzo Faletto's *Dependency and Development in Latin America* (1979).[61] Indeed, when it comes to substantive research, the cleavage lines between rational choice theorists and the rest, between formal and verbal theorists, and between quantitative and qualitative researchers, lose a large degree of their force.

This disjuncture between the programmatic statements that, since 1989, have so often emphasized divisions regarding issues of theory and methods,

---

tive methods through the initiation of an annual training institute on qualitative research methods, run by the Consortium on Qualitative Research Methods (CQRM) in 2002, and the founding of the APSA section on Qualitative Methods in 2003.

61. This book was first published in Spanish in 1969. For the new research by economists, see Sokoloff and Engerman (2000) and Acemoglu and Robinson (2006). On the links between these classics of comparative politics and recent research by economists, see Przeworski (2004a).

and the actual practices of comparativists, is attributable to many factors. The lack of clarity regarding the differences among metatheories, and the fact that methods are after all only tools, are surely contributing factors. But this disjuncture is also probably associated with the values held by comparativists. After 1989, consensus among comparativists concerning democracy as a core value has been high enough to override divisions rooted in contentious issues such as neo-liberalism and globalization. And, given this consensus, passions usually flamed by conflicts over political values, a feature of the previous period in the history of comparative politics, have been channeled instead into debates about theory and methods. As a consequence, research in comparative politics has lost something, due to a relative lack of value-driven engagement of comparativists with politics. But the field has also gained something, as attested by the production of a rich and rigorous literature, many times drawing on different traditions, on big and pressing questions.[62]

Conclusion

This retrospective on comparative politics suggests that the field has made significant progress. Metatheories have come and gone. The relationship with other fields of political science and with sister disciplines has changed repeatedly. Yet, despite this instability, a focus on a distinctively political subject matter has become largely the norm, mid-range theorizing on a range of important questions has grown steadily, and the methods used in the field have become increasingly sophisticated. Comparativists have accomplished a lot and produced a vast amount of knowledge about politics around the world.

But there are a number of shortcomings. The first concerns theory. The proliferation of mid-range theorizing has yielded valuable insights about politics but also fragmentary knowledge. Yet, comparativists have largely abandoned the aspiration of the system-builders who sought to elaborate an explicit metatheory of politics in the 1950s and 1960s. In turn, despite some recent attempts to integrate theories of statics and dynamics, there is a strong tendency to segregate the study of statics, which takes key parameters of the analysis as given and fixed, from the study of dynamics, which is

---

62. For a broad overview of research in comparative politics during this period, see Laitin (2002). For overviews on more delimited research agendas, see the chapters by Barnes, McAdam et al., Hall and Migdal in Lichbach and Zuckerman (1997), and by Kohli, Alt, Gamm and Huber, Geddes, and Thelen in Katznelson and Milner (2002). On the contributions of the comparative historical tradition, see the chapters by Goldstone, Amenta, and Mahoney in Mahoney and Rueschemeyer (2003), and on area studies scholarship, see Szanton (2004). See also Wiarda (2002).

concerned precisely with the change of these parameters and thus does not take them as given. Thus, a key challenge facing comparativists is the development of a general or unified theory of politics, which integrates both mid-range theories of various substantive issues and theories of statics and dynamics.

The second shortcoming concerns empirics. Despite major advances in recent times, comparativists lack good measures for many of the concepts used in their theories. Likewise, despite significant improvements, comparativists still rarely use methods that would subject their hypotheses to rigorous testing. A telltale sign of the magnitude of the challenge concerning empirical analysis is that much research that is given the label of comparative politics is not even strictly speaking comparative, that is, it does not compare at the very least two political systems. Taken together, these limitations seriously weaken comparativists' ability to produce strong findings. Thus, another challenge facing comparativists is the establishment of robust, broad empirical generalizations about world politics.

How comparativists might fruitfully go about tackling these challenges is a complex question, which goes beyond the scope of this chapter. But some broad lessons can be drawn from the history of the field. Comparative politics has been and remains a diverse field and many times comparativists have shown that this diversity can be a source of strength. But comparativists have also shown a tendency to accentuate paralyzing or distracting divisions. Thus, if the field is going to further contribute to its mission to develop a global science of politics, it is imperative that comparativists work with a greater sense of common purpose. And this will only be possible when comparativists recognize two fundamental points. One is that the study of politics is inextricably linked with normative concerns and that, in the absence of an explicit consideration of the values involved in politics, the stakes and rationale of research will be obscured. A second point is that, to answer normatively important questions, researchers must not only be passionate about their subject matter. In addition, it is necessary that they use appropriate scientific methods.

What is required, in short, is an appreciation of both the depth of the roots of comparative politics in a humanistic tradition and the vital importance of its scientific aspirations. The souls of comparativists are not stirred solely by a substantive interest in global politics and, even less so, by the methods used to learn about this subject matter. Hence the future of comparative politics is likely to hinge on the ability of comparativists to overcome weakening divisions and to blend their concern with substance and method, politics and science.

THE INTERVIEWS

3

Gabriel A. Almond

Structural Functionalism and Political Development

Gabriel A. Almond was one of the most influential scholars in comparative politics during the 1950s and 1960s, when he chaired the Social Science Research Council's (SSRC) Committee on Comparative Politics. His work stood out as a pioneering attempt to achieve a truly comparative framework for the study of politics, one that encompassed non-Western countries and thus broke with the European focus of much prior research in comparative politics.

Almond's prolific academic career spanned seven decades. His initial research focused on U.S. domestic and foreign policy. His dissertation, recently published as *Plutocracy and Politics in New York City* (1998), analyzed elites and political power in New York City. His work on international relations included *The American People and Foreign Policy* (1950). In the early 1950s, he began working in comparative politics, focusing on political parties in Western Europe.

Almond's most important work consisted of a series of publications, starting in the mid-1950s, in which he formulated a structural-functional approach to the study of political development and political culture. He saw the political system as comprised of "structures," such as political parties, legislatures, and bureaucracies, which performed distinct "functions," such as articulating and aggregating the preferences of citizens, making and implementing public policy, and maintaining overall political stability. Drawing on the distinction between structures and functions, he developed a broad typology of varieties of democratic and non-democratic political systems. Almond's framework was applied to the many developing countries in Asia and Africa that achieved independence after World War II, as well as to Latin America. Early versions of the framework were presented in "Comparative Political Systems" (*Journal of Politics*, 1956) and in *The Poli-*

This interview was conducted by Gerardo Munck in Palo Alto, California, on March 20, 2002.

tics of the Developing Areas (1960). More sophisticated versions of the framework appeared in Almond's collaborative works with G. Bingham Powell, *Comparative Politics: A Developmental Approach* (1966) and *Comparative Politics: System, Process, Policy* (1978).

Almond's book with Sidney Verba, *The Civic Culture* (1963), was a pathbreaking work on political culture that demonstrated the potential of comparative studies using survey research. Almond and Verba employed comparative survey data to distinguish three kinds of citizen orientations toward politics: parochial, subject, and participant. A civic culture, composed of a balanced mixture in individuals of all three orientations, was seen as most conducive to democracy. In *Crisis, Choice and Change* (1973), Almond aimed to achieve an integrated theory of political change by combining his structural-functional approach with other approaches that put more emphasis on the role of political leaders. His later research included widely read works on the intellectual history of, and ongoing debates within, political science and comparative politics. These essays are collected in *A Discipline Divided* (1990) and *Ventures in Political Science* (2002).

Almond was born in Rock Island, Illinois, in 1911, and died in Pacific Grove, California, in 2002. He received his B.A. from the University of Chicago in 1932 and his Ph.D. in political science from the same institution in 1938. Almond taught at Brooklyn College (now part of the City University of New York) from 1939 to 1942, Yale University (1946–50, 1959–63), Princeton University (1950–59), and Stanford University (1963–76). He became a professor emeritus at Stanford in 1976. Almond was president of the American Political Science Association (APSA) in 1965–66. He was elected to the American Academy of Arts and Sciences in 1961 and to the National Academy of Sciences in 1977.

Intellectual Formation and Training: From Chicago to Germany

Q: How did you first become interested in political science?
A: I got into college at the University of Chicago in 1928, just before the crash, and at the time I was an aspiring journalist and writer. I had been editor of my high school newspaper, and I had contributed to the literary journals published by students at the University of Chicago in the 1920s. I had good reason to believe I might have some talent as a writer, because Thornton Wilder, one of our instructors in composition, told me I had a "natural wrist." Also, to put myself through college, I had a job on the side. I went to class in the mornings and in the afternoons I did the editorial work for an optometrists' journal. When the Depression hit, I lost that job and things got kind of tough. So I began to reconsider my romantic desire to

become a journalist and began to think seriously about what I was going to train for. I thought about becoming a teacher and, as I was wondering what I would teach, I was taking courses from Charles Merriam, Harold Lasswell, and Fred Schuman. I got good grades and this encouraged me to do something in political science. I also took a course in economics from the economist Frank Knight, and a course from George Herbert Mead, the social psychologist. So I had a feel for what the social sciences were like, and political science seemed to be something I could do. I applied to Chicago and was admitted. I started graduate work in political science at the University of Chicago in 1933, at the depth of the Depression.

Q: Did you consider other graduate programs besides Chicago?
A: I came from an immigrant family and we didn't think in terms of traveling far away, of going to Harvard, Yale, or Princeton. And in the Chicago area, the University of Chicago was the most serious academic institution; it was the Mecca. The question was if I could get into Chicago, and I did get into Chicago.

Q: The standard training at Chicago during those days was clearly interdisciplinary. Can you discuss the courses you took?
A: As an undergraduate, you really didn't have much of a sense of what the Political Science Department was like. You don't really make that kind of appraisal. I didn't know if it was interdisciplinary or not. When I took Lasswell's course on "Non-Rational Factors in Political Behavior" in my senior year, I knew it was an innovative course, that it was kind of far out. But I didn't know how it would stand in the discipline generally speaking. In other words, I didn't know what kind of a department I was getting into as an undergraduate, but I surely learned about it once I became a graduate student.

Early in my graduate days, in order to accumulate enough money to afford to go to school, I had to take a little time off and got a job as a complaint aide in the Unemployment Relief Service in the stockyard district in Chicago. The job involved me sitting at a desk and listening to the stories of unemployed men, mostly foreign-born—Mexican Americans, Italians, all kinds of Slavs, blacks—who were applying for emergency aid. Well, from the course I had taken with Lasswell, my head was full of all kinds of psychoanalysis and sociological interpretations of human behavior. And it occurred to me, while I was sitting there taking all these complaints, that this was social science data waiting to be analyzed. So I convinced Lasswell that we ought to do a study, and we decided to focus on the aggressive behavior of clients on public relief, our theory being that the aggressive ones might become revolutionary leaders. You have to remember, this was before the New Deal, things were really rough. It looked at the time that the United States might have a revolution.

Our study involved several thousand contacts, over a period of months, with three complaint aides, and men of various social backgrounds. We tried to distinguish between what we called aggressive and submissive individuals, and we had a control group. We then looked at their case records to see what factors distinguished the aggressive ones (Almond and Lasswell 1934). I was learning science in the process. In effect, this experience clinched not only my career in political science but also my methodological interests. I got hooked on science right off.

Q: Beyond this formative practical experience, were there any particular authors or books that influenced you, that really made a difference in how you thought about the social sciences?
A: Aristotle's *Politics* made a very big impact on me. Actually, the first thing I did when I was admitted to the graduate program was get a copy of Aristotle's *Politics*. I read it from cover to cover. Aristotle is very much an empirical comparativist. That was my model of political science, that somehow the important things about politics and institutions could be explained in that way. I never lost that perspective. I was also very much influenced by the psychoanalytical literature I came across in Lasswell's course.

Q: Did you read Max Weber in graduate school?
A: Most definitely. He was a very powerful influence on me, both scientific and moral. I encountered all of his works early on. I read German. My wife was German, and we had our honeymoon in 1937 in Germany visiting her parents. I gathered many of Weber's works in bookstores. The Nazis were in power but there were still bookstores in Cologne where you could find Max Weber's books. I came home with a collection of his writings. I was very influenced by his three-volume sociology of religion (Weber 1951, 1958a, 1967), and the general statement of his theory in *Wirtschaft and Gesellschaft* (Economy and Society) (Weber 1978). I had an early edition of the latter. I had Weber's *Gesammelte Politische Schriften* (Collected Political Miscellanies), his political writings (Weber 1921),[1] and read his *Politik als Beruf* (Politics as a Vocation) (Weber 1946b), the lecture he gave in 1918. I even translated this lecture as a way of getting experience to take my German exam. And I found his sociology of music (Weber 1958b) fascinating. So I was very much affected by him.

---

1. Weber's political writings have appeared, selectively, in various English publications, including Gerth and Mills (1946), the appendix of *Economy and Society* (Weber 1978), and more recently in Lassman and Speiers (1994).

Q: Your dissertation, however, had less to do with Weber than with Marx, and you also drew on a social-psychological perspective.
A: My doctoral dissertation really was an effort to get an empirical hold on Marxist theory. I had taken a couple of courses from Samuel Harper, one of the early scholars who wrote about Bolshevism, which was recent Russian history back in those days. You have to remember: this was the 1930s, before the purges and everything. Here in the United States there were strikes, sit-down strikes in plants not far from Chicago. And there were young Communists and socialists making lots of speeches on the campus. Serious people my age were discussing the collapse of the American economy we were living through and the future of the country. I picked my dissertation topic in that crisis period. The idea was to do a strictly empirical study looking at the economy and polity over time. And I decided to do it in New York, which had some history of wealth and politics to deal with. I tried to introduce psychoanalytic interpretations to address the question of why some capitalists were liberals, some were conservatives, and some were reactionaries. How could you account for a rich liberal, like Andrew Carnegie—at least he got to be a liberal in terms of the standards of those days—as contrasted with a reactionary like William Randolph Hearst? To address this question, I accumulated biographical material on New York businessmen, corporate executives, and entrepreneurs, people like J. P. Morgan and John D. Rockefeller who were on the margin between economic and political power. As I explain elsewhere (Almond 1990, 318–22), Merriam was not too happy with my dissertation because he was concerned I had done some psychologizing of John D. Rockefeller, who founded the University of Chicago and was the major source of its funding. I had also gathered personal material on Carnegie, and the Carnegie Corporation was becoming an important source of research funds. Merriam wanted me to eliminate the psychological chapters, which, on reflection, I believe he thought were based on inadequate evidence. At any rate, the dissertation was not published until 1998. Only a journal article was published in 1945 (Almond 1945).

Q: In terms of the current division of subfields within political science, people would say that you started your career studying American politics, as an Americanist.
A: But the model that I had and the courses I took at the graduate level were comparative. L. D. White gave a course in comparative public administration, in which the French, German, and British cases were discussed. Harold Gosnell gave a comparative course on political parties. Lasswell was very comparative. So, the curriculum was very modern, but what was not available was area studies in depth, as we have today. You could only get it with someone like Samuel Harper, a very fine scholar in Russian studies, or

L. D. White. We learned a lot about British politics, British administration, British bureaucracy.

Q: In terms of your research and writing, it seems as though the experience of World War II had a big impact on you, shifting your attention to European politics and, more specifically, to Germany and the Nazis.
A: I spent a lot of time in Germany doing interviews.[2] For example, I interrogated German Gestapo and security personnel in internment camps. In a way, I was already converted to a Europeanist. I was very interested in resistance movements in Europe and studied that topic comparatively, looking at Germany and France. My language skills were a very useful tool in this regard. German was the language I learned as an undergraduate. So when I got back to the United States after the war, I was retooled and thought of myself as a Europeanist.

Q: While you were in Europe, in the summer of 1945, you met Weber's widow, Marianne Weber. Why did you do that? How was the meeting?
A: We were headquartered in Bad Nauheim, not very far from Heidelberg, and I took a jeep ride on a Sunday to Heidelberg with a friend of mine, Wolfgang Stolper, an economist and the son of a very renowned German economist. We found Marianne Weber in her home. She was very elderly at the time and very frail. So we didn't burden her too long. We gave her some Lucky Strike cigarettes, the most precious coinage you could give anybody at the time—they could be traded in for coffee. We didn't really get much insight into Max. Nevertheless, we made our visit to the Weber house not so much to get information as to pay homage.

Comparative Research and Social Science: The SSRC Committee on Comparative Politics

Q: After the war, you moved to Yale in 1946.
A: I had tenure at Brooklyn College, but that was not a very exciting place intellectually. It had been an interesting place before I went into war service. Our department was innovative. We had a lot of young people who were able to have some influence. But when I got back, it had been reorganized. I wanted to give a course in comparative political parties and it wasn't possible. All I could do was continue teaching "Introduction to American Government." So I was on the lookout for other possibilities. There was a University of Chicago group in the Yale Institute of Inter-

2. During World War II, Almond worked for the U.S. Strategic Bombing Survey, studying the effects of Allied bombing on the German war effort.

national Studies, Bill Fox, Klaus Knorr, Bernard Brodie, and they knew me and brought me into that setting. I started out as a research associate, and after a couple of years, they gave me a chance to teach. I was given a regular, tenure track position, as an assistant, and then received tenure in 1949.

Q: A few years later, a very successful initiative—the formation of the Committee on Comparative Politics of the Social Science Research Council (SSRC)—was launched. Could you discuss how this committee was formed and how it was related to the SSRC Committee on Political Behavior?

A: The formation of the Committee on Comparative Politics was stimulated by the Committee on Political Behavior, which had already begun to put out manifestos of one kind or another. Most of the members of the Committee on Political Behavior were leading, original, young Americanists. They were working with Pendleton Herring, who was then the president of the SSRC. They were pioneering the study of pressure groups, the infrastructure of the political system, and trying to encourage in-depth study of politics by bringing in the study of parties and elections in a systematic, empirical way. This approach to the study of American politics was innovative and productive. In contrast, the comparative politics field was straightforward, structural, institutional, legal, and philosophical at best. The things being studied here in the United States at the time were not being examined at all in other contexts. Among the Europeanists, Marxism had contaminated the study of interest groups, which were analyzed either as part of capitalism or part of the proletariat. That really made it impossible to have an empirical investigation of the political infrastructure. So the first project undertaken by the Committee on Comparative Politics was the encouragement of interest group studies in European and non-European countries. Half a dozen young comparativists and political sociologists—Henry Ehrmann, Joseph LaPalombara, Juan Linz, Myron Weiner, Edward Banfield, Seymour Martin Lipset—made their reputation replicating in the European context the innovations that had been made in the 1920s and 1930s in the study of American politics.

Q: Shortly before the Committee on Comparative Politics was formed and you became its first chairman in 1954, there had been a meeting of scholars at Northwestern University in 1952—the SSRC's Interuniversity Research Seminar on Comparative Politics—that led to the publication of an important manifesto (Macridis and Cox 1953; Friedrich et al. 1953). What was the connection between this group and the Committee on Comparative Politics?

A: Early on, Roy Macridis wanted the SSRC to do something. But we had more of a focus than the Northwestern group had. That is, we definitely had a research design, and that's the reason why the SSRC moved in our direction. Macridis became a member of our committee, and so did Bob Ward. The Northwestern initiative was overtaken by the more professional political science that was being developed by the Committee on Political Behavior, which we sought to emulate.

Q: Besides focusing on interest groups and the political process, it seems you aimed to develop a more scientific approach to political science.

A: Yes. More empirical, rigorous, and involving the use of statistics. Also, with a richer collection of hypotheses coming out of the broader social sciences, including anthropology, sociology, and social psychology. If you look at the revolution that Merriam made in the 1920s, it was those two things; for him, professional political science would involve the rigor of quantification and the testing of hypotheses drawn from the social sciences.

Q: Was this project of a scientific political science modeled on the natural sciences?

A: No. There was a very clear recognition by Merriam—less so by Lasswell—that there was a very definite difference between the natural sciences and what he called the human sciences, the social sciences—he never used the term *behavioral sciences*, because it had a bad odor at that time. Merriam made a distinction between the sciences, as to what kind of science they could produce.

Q: What were the main accomplishments of the Committee on Comparative Politics? Do you think it achieved the goals and aspirations that it had when it formed in the 1950s?

A: Well, yes. And it's obvious that it did. In the first place, before the committee came into existence, the field of comparative government involved very little comparison. It was just a case-by-case study of the major European powers. You studied British government, you studied French government, you studied German government. Britain, France, Germany, maybe a little bit of Italy, in a rare case Japan, but that was about it. The non-Western world wasn't represented, and the small Western powers weren't represented. The first book put out by the committee, *The Politics of the Developing Areas* (Almond and Coleman 1960), brought all the world areas into a sharp focus. It got a great deal of attention. Despite the crudeness of the introductory essay that I wrote, the application of my framework in four or five different ways by the contributors really brought modern social science to bear on the field of comparative politics and broke with the prevailing parochialism. Doing those two things, even if to a limited extent, was a significant accomplishment. Furthermore, Lucian Pye, who assumed the committee's chairmanship in 1963, edited the nine-volume Studies in Political Development series published by Princeton University Press. So we left a strong record, one that involved a number of scholars, American and foreign.

Q: Is there anything the Committee on Comparative Politics left uncompleted?
A: We really had hoped our efforts would culminate in some sort of theory of political development, and my impression today is that we really took that about as far as it could go. Modernization theory with modifications has been rehabilitated. The idea that modernization, with its basic economic and social processes of change, produces a different set of political potentialities has undergone a revival. It is true that modernization mobilizes populations and opens up an option for democratization. That aspect of our work, you might say, stands. But we also thought we might have some kind of mathematical formulas or something. At the limit, I think we were smoking pot in a figurative sense. When I was writing the introductory essay for *The Politics of the Developing Areas* (Almond 1960), I let myself go. I don't think I seriously meant some of what I wrote, and I don't think today that we will ever have a serious "hard science" theory of comparative politics. That's an illusion. The study of comparative politics is a probabilistic thing.

The Broader Field of Comparative Politics

Q: Going beyond the work of the Committee on Comparative Politics, two very significant books appeared in the 1960s, neither of which was linked to the committee. One is Samuel Huntington's *Political Order in Changing Societies* (1968), which broke with the optimistic, liberal bent of much of the modernization literature. The other is Barrington Moore's *Social Origins of Dictatorship and Democracy* (1966), which was rooted in a more critical, Marxist perspective. Did you see yourself as engaged in a dialogue with these other authors? Did these works influence your research?
A: Moore's work was really very influential and important, but the book I like best by him is *Soviet Politics* (Moore 1950). *Social Origins of Dictatorship and Democracy* was really quite original in important ways, but I thought it was reductionist. It left out the role of uncertainty, leadership, and accident. It's a structural, a very heavily structural, interpretation, and because

of that I could never really accept it. At that point I was trying to bring in leadership and chance.

Q: What about Huntington?
A: Compared to Moore, Huntington puts greater emphasis on decisions and the state. He has a better grasp of the interaction of the economy and the polity. But Huntington is heavy-handed, he comes down with a very powerful chop. One sees this again in his *Clash of Civilizations* (Huntington 1996). Editorially, this tendency toward exaggeration is justifiable because it adds to debate and generates polemic. But it's not accurate. In contrast, what I was trying to do was be multi-causal and stay as close as possible to the actual historical events. For example, in *Crisis, Choice, and Change* (Almond, Flanagan, and Mundt 1973), I focused on crises and looked at them from every possible perspective. That was my role in the larger disciplinary debates.

Q: During this period, Robert Dahl published *Polyarchy* (Dahl 1971) and a couple of works on opposition politics (Dahl 1966a, 1973). What did you think of that research?
A: Bob Dahl and I were at Yale together, and I encouraged him to take this comparative route. In the 1950s, Dahl wrote *A Preface to Democratic Theory* (Dahl 1956) and later published his prize-winning study of New Haven, *Who Governs?* (Dahl 1961a). Dahl used the "oppositions" concept to organize his approach to comparison. His *Polyarchy* was one of his most important contributions. It provided a systematic and rigorous analysis of all the factors that impact democratization. It was a very important book, one of the most important in the postwar period.

Q: Another person also linked with Yale and known for his systematic approach to the study of politics was Stein Rokkan.
A: Rokkan was a sociologist who had a great impact on comparative political sociology, another significant tendency in the development of comparative politics. Stein was also very much under the influence of the Committee on Comparative Politics. He attended all our sessions and was one of the collaborators on the eighth volume in the Studies in Political Development series, the historical one edited by Charles Tilly (Rokkan 1975). We were very close. As I have written elsewhere, at the time the committee was forming, there were various centers of creativity in the comparative field (Almond 1997, 60). Dahl and Huntington were especially influential, as was Rokkan. And we cannot overlook Seymour M. Lipset, who was of major significance in the study of political modernization and democratization.

Q: It seems this was an exciting period to be in comparative politics, starting with the milieu in which you were trained at Chicago in the 1930s, to the people you were interacting with in the 1950s and 1960s at Yale, Princeton, and through the activities of the committee.

A: The broad point to be made is that the years right after World War II were a time of very rapid growth, of opportunity. The anomaly to explain in the history of political science is Merriam's innovativeness in the interwar period of the 1920s. That's what has to be explained, not the period after World War II when the United States was the only place with a functioning economy, which meant that we had resources. Also, the moment the Cold War began, we really had to tool up and invest in education. So the environment was an open and growing one. There was a reason to explain the creativity. And it was facilitated by the sudden expansion of the U.S. economy and all the opportunity that a growing education system provided to a generation of young people who came out of the military, who had lived through the experience of war.

Colleagues and Students

Q: You have interacted over the years with some of the very best people in the discipline. What have these interactions meant to you?

A: I was at Chicago from 1928 to 1938 and over this period came to know Merriam, Lasswell, Schuman, Gosnell—mostly as teachers and friends—and V. O. Key, Albert Sepawsky, Victor Jones, Bill Fox, David Truman, and many others—as fellow students and lifelong friends. I was at Yale twice, once between 1946 and 1950, and again from 1959 to 1963, with the interval of the 1950s at Princeton. Dahl, Charles Lindblom, and Robert Lane were lifelong close friends. In the last decades we added our many Stanford friends. Many of our Yale, Princeton, and Stanford graduate students became collaborators and friends—Bernie Cohen, Lucian Pye, Myron Weiner, Sidney Verba, Bing Powell, Bob Mundt, Scott Flanagan, Steve Genco, and many others. I have had a wonderful comradeship with these younger colleagues and many others over a long and rewarding career.

Pen Herring was my special mentor, and the SSRC was my cultural and intellectual home. What the Committee on Comparative Politics made possible during many years was a lot of extra-university contact. One of our biggest budget items for the committee was travel that allowed us to get together mainly in New York City. The Carnegie and Rockefeller foundations recognized the creative component of such gatherings and we benefited from the availability of resources. More recently, the growing information technology has enabled me to continue exchanging ideas with my colleagues. I have e-mail. Lots of e-mail. I'm still in touch with many scholars.

Q: When you finished your term as chairman of the Committee on Comparative Politics, you moved to Stanford University. Could you discuss this transition?

A: While I was chairing the Committee on Comparative Politics, it was important to be close to New York City. It wouldn't be today, because communication is so easy now. But eventually I had had enough of being chairman. As a matter of fact, that is when my heart problem began. I've had a heart condition since the 1960s. What keeps me going is that I've had every kind of surgery you can imagine. Without it, and the best kind of rehabilitation, I would not be here. At Yale, I was being pressured to take on administrative responsibilities, more than I could handle.

So I moved to Palo Alto, where I've lived ever since. I knew people here. I had been here in the 1950s at the Center for Advanced Study in the Behavioral Sciences, and they had asked me to stay, though I'd decided not to at the time. When I did join Stanford in 1963, I became the department chairman. If I was going to be a department chairman, I wanted to be in a department where there was going to be a lot of growth. And at Stanford there were possibilities of significant development. There was a lot of hiring. I brought in Alex George, Sidney Verba, John Lewis, David Abernathy, Bob Packenham. I built up the comparative field at Stanford.

Q: You have been at a number of great universities and must have had a lot of contact with graduate students. What kind of interaction have you had with graduate students?[3]

A: The association I've had with graduate students is one of the most gratifying parts of my life. I've had them from Yale, a generation or two from Yale, from Princeton, and from Stanford. Graduate students are one's best interlocutors. The relationship with a graduate student is the most closely creative interaction a person can have. I have had a series of such creative relationships. I've been very lucky to be associated with such people. These have been the most gratifying intellectual relationships that I have had. And I have maintained my relationships with them. Usually they become my adult, mature collaborators.

Q: One of the students with whom you have had an especially long collaborative relationship is Bingham Powell.

A: Bing Powell was my first graduate student at Stanford. He was a Ph.D. candidate who came from a small town in Oregon. And he was a treasure, productive and lucid. Within a couple of years, he was my collaborator. We

3. On Almond as a teacher, see the interviews with Arend Lijphart and James Scott in Chapters 8 and 11.

coauthored *Comparative Politics: A Developmental Approach,* in 1966, and the 1978 edition of this book, *Comparative Politics: Systems, Processes, and Policy.* And we have worked on multiple editions of *Comparative Politics Today,* now in its seventh edition (Almond et al. 2000). We're working on the eighth edition, but, over the year, Bing has essentially taken over the editorship; this is the last one where I will be a coeditor. Bing has had an independent scholarly career. He was editor of the *American Political Science Review.* He's respected for his own work, which is of a different genre than mine.

Q: What kind of training and advice did you give graduate students?
A: In terms of training, I was not among the modernists and behavioralists who pushed completely in the direction of statistics and mathematics. I gave much more of an emphasis to knowledge in depth of at least one case. I really felt that was important. Every one of my graduate students has had that kind of background, along with a good statistical training.

Q: Do you consider a background in political and social theory an essential part of graduate training?
A: You ought to have a good course in the history of political theory, in which you learn the classics. This is one of the problems with the people who come into political science from economics. They don't know who Aristotle and Plato were. And that shouldn't be: these thinkers are really central to the creative history of the field. I wouldn't give up such a course in political theory for a course in mathematics, as a lot of the modern people are prepared to do. I would push history and some specific area in depth, and the language tools that allow you to learn about cases. If you've got a mind for math, by all means do it. But I don't think mathematics is that important to the field.

Q: Have you encouraged students to do fieldwork and spend a year or so deeply immersed in a case?
A: Always. Sid Verba, Germany; Bing Powell, Austria; Lucian Pye, well, Lucian Pye, came from China and Southeast Asia; Myron Weiner, India; Scott Flanagan, Japan; Bob Mundt, Francophone Africa.

Research: Structural Functionalism, Historical Analysis, and Political Culture

Q: You have stated that your early work on structural functionalism can be understood as an effort to develop a theory of comparative statics, whereas your subsequent historical writings can be considered an attempt to offer a theory of dynamics (Almond 1997, 62–65). I would

like to start with the structural-functional model, before moving to your more historical work. How did you develop the basic categories of structural functionalism?

A: One insight was that sociology, anthropology, social psychology, psychiatry, and ultimately economics were alternative and complementary ways of explaining process. This way of thinking had been developed at the University of Chicago. If you read Merriam's *New Aspects of Politics* (Merriam 1925), he talks about this. He made this breakthrough, he did it for me, and I took it for granted. So I learned to treat politics as process, not as formal institutions, but as process. That is the beginning of formalism, really, because when you describe parties in terms of process, or interest groups in terms of process, or the media in terms of process, then you're beginning to make such processes visible and to distinguish different processual components that are essential.

Another key insight, which I discovered in the course of writing my introduction to *The Politics of the Developing Areas,* is that the same processes take place in developed societies and primitive, undifferentiated systems. For example, even in primitive systems, interest articulation was still going on, only it was tucked away in what seemed to be some other process. You just had to look for it. The anthropologists helped me figure this out. I participated in a little anthropological seminar with a wonderful group of anthropologists at the Center for Advanced Study in Palo Alto in 1956–57. And in between throwing darts at the dartboard, we cooked up this functional approach. Structural functionalism had its origins in that group.

So, process came from the work of political scientists like Odegard, Schattschneider, Herring, and David Truman. Functionalism came out of anthropological theory, from anthropologists like Kluckhohn.

Q: What effect did Talcott Parsons's effort at systematization have on you? Did it inspire you?

A: Very much, especially the Parsons and Shils (1951) formulation. Although "inspiring" is not the word to use with Talcott Parsons. His later work unfortunately became increasingly blown up and exaggerated. It also became very wordy and repetitious. But the formulation he offered with Shils and in his earlier theoretical work was extremely productive. He assimilated Weber. He did what he said he was doing, that is, codify the nineteenth-century sociological/historical theory. I found useful the way Parsons thought about the functions that had to be performed by any system.

Q: As you were working on your structural-functional model, you developed a typology of political systems. Why did you build a typology and what role did it play in your thinking?

A: The first job, from my point of view, in embarking on a new comparative politics was what I would call a primitive sorting operation. You're talking about phenomena that are out there, they're real, they're objective. You want to discover what their properties and dynamics are. So the first thing you need to do is sort them out. This is what I did in my *Journal of Politics* article (Almond 1956). That was a beginning of *The Politics of the Developing Areas,* and there was a need for it, a great need for it, to make it possible to compare the undeveloped societies with the developed ones.

I mentioned earlier that I always had a love affair with Aristotle. I should have had one with Plato and Herodotus, too. All of them had a typology, a political typology. I got the idea of the importance of typology from the Greek period. Now, to get an accurate typology you need a good structural functionalism, a good statics.

Q: But what about firsthand knowledge of the societies you place in your typology? One thing that struck me as curious in reading the introduction to your 1970 collection of essays, *Political Development*, is that you mentioned you had not had much direct contact with Third World societies until 1962–63, when you traveled through Japan, Southeast Asia, India, and Africa (Almond 1970, 21). Yet prior to that experience you'd written a key essay proposing a structural-functional theory applicable to the developing areas.
A: My father was a rabbi, and as Lasswell once told me, my exposure to biblical studies as a child had given me an outlook into another culture. In some sense, I had grown up in more than one culture.

Q: Still, it seems curious. You had done fieldwork in New York for your dissertation, and your writings on Europe drew on some direct experiences with these societies. Though you could obviously pick up a lot from anthropology when it came to the Third World, nonetheless you wrote your first major work about developing areas before traveling to these societies. Did your experiences traveling in Asia and Africa in 1962 and 1963 make you change some of your ideas?
A: I don't think so. Let me put it this way: the distinction between three different levels of functioning—system, process, and policy—came to me internally and logically, not through induction. It was the result of a process of logical development, elaboration, and differentiation of a more complicated system. So, the answer is "no." I've had the direct impact of an African village, an Indian slum or village, and the back streets of Tokyo. I've been in the Third World. But I don't think any of those experiences in the Third World significantly altered my ideas. I'm not saying this is a virtue, just telling you a fact. The theoretical development that I experienced in my

lifetime was the result of trial and error in dealing with political systems that were brought to my attention mostly by the writings of others.

Q: What impact do you think your structural-functional model has had on the field of comparative politics?
A: In a way it got assimilated. It's kind of the commonsense conceptual vocabulary. Nobody would do a study of a new nation without some discussion of an infrastructure and an infra-process. And they would use concepts such as interest articulation and aggregation, which I developed in my work. That kind of vocabulary would already be there. It isn't the only vocabulary, and there are alternative ways to formulate it. But, in a sense, the effort to develop a structural-functional approach was the first attempt to devise a systematic scheme for studying comparative politics globally, and much of it still survives.

Q: After working for a long time within a structural-functional framework, you started to move toward a more historical perspective. This can be seen especially in *Crisis, Choice, and Change* (Almond, Flanagan, and Mundt 1973). What was the driving force behind this new research? What theoretical issues were you grappling with?
A: We knew our structural functionalism had a role to play in a theory of political development or change. You needed statics for a system more or less at rest, or repeating. A system in equilibrium. But when it came to change, we saw shortcomings in a straightforward structural-functional approach. For example, we could make a study of, say, France, before and after the French Revolution. And we could do a comparative statics of France, before and after the Revolution. But we wouldn't find out, explain, how it got from A to B.

Q: So how did you tackle this theoretical challenge in *Crisis, Choice, and Change?*
A: We started by looking at the existing scholarly work that could help explain why systems were changing from A to B. We discovered four different schools out there, one being our own structural functionalism. Then we began to play around with these other approaches, even though they were in a sense counter-posed to structural functionalism.

One approach was social mobilization theory, as developed by Karl Deutsch, Seymour M. Lipset, and Daniel Lerner. We found that the social mobilization approach could explain the emergence of a situation in which the political system is under stress, as in the emergence of a new class, where there were basic, structural changes. So, the social mobilization approach could get you from A to B, to the extent that this was a structural course with no open potentialities, where a Napoleon, a Hitler, or something like that, could enter in. But there was a problem with the dozens of efforts to demonstrate this theory with statistical associations among structural variables.

When you look at actual historical cases, say, the forming of the French Third Republic, you couldn't really get to the Third Republic without the collapse of Napoleon III. Then you immediately see that leadership—the stupid errors of Napoleon III—was tremendously important. Napoleon III let Bismarck sucker him into the Franco-Prussian War. It was a stupid and untimely decision. And it turns out, he was in failing health, not in command of his whole powers. This is a case where you might say the physiological facts were of significance. As we studied more and more cases, we came to the conclusion that leadership had to be brought into the picture. In this context, we encountered rational choice theory. Before we could really develop a good leadership theory, we first needed a good game theory. Indeed, we needed game theory to demonstrate how, or in what kind of setting, leaders were able to accumulate the resources necessary to formulate and implement decisions.

Q: You had actually come in contact with rational choice and game theory quite early on.
A: I think I first became aware of it in 1956, when I spent a year at Stanford as a fellow at the Center for Advanced Study in the Behavioral Sciences. Kenneth Arrow was at Stanford, and Arrow was a fellow at the same time. And almost the first day he gave me a copy of Anthony Downs's dissertation *An Economic Theory of Democracy* (Downs 1957). I still have the copy of the manuscript he gave me. I read it and was impressed. I thought it was very powerful stuff. It brought to the theoretical level a model of politics that had been introduced and developed in political science by the people who worked on interest groups and political parties. The idea was one of seeing democratic politics as a bargaining process. If you look at the studies of pressure groups and political parties in the 1930s and 1940s, on the eve of the Downs book, the politician is no longer the great ideologist and hero. Rather, the view of the politician was one captured by a University of Chicago philosopher, who said that the secret of democratic stability is the capacity of people to form "sordid bargains." What Downs did, and his mentor Ken Arrow required of him, was to formalize, through mathematical calculations, this view. Of course, John von Neumann and Oskar Morgenstern were already developing game theory at the time (von Neumann and Morgenstern 1944).

Q: Your effort to develop a theory of political change could be characterized as eclectic.

A: Exactly. We drew on existing theories in an instrumental way rather than treating them as paradigms. We gradually found that to explain how you got from A to B we needed a combination of factors. It was a little bit like what the physicists are trying to do now to get the four forces in one mathematical system, one set of equations. In the same sense, we were trying to get these four approaches—structural functionalism, social mobilization, rational choice, and leadership—into a homogeneous theory. And we succeeded. In *Crisis, Choice, and Change* we had the beginnings of an analytical system for the study of political development. That has not, as yet, been appreciated in the field.

Q: Beyond the works we have just discussed, you have had an enduring interest in political culture. Your early work on this subject with Sidney Verba, *The Civic Culture* (Almond and Verba 1963), was clearly seminal.

A: *The Civic Culture* encouraged a lot of research on political culture. Scholars knew culture was a significant variable in explaining historical outcomes. If you looked at the Carl Friedrich (1937, 1963) or Herman Finer (1932) type of comparative politics, they referred to public opinion. They spoke about the media. You can't say they were pure institutionalists or legalists. But they didn't have a systematic way of addressing culture. I was born later than they, and I benefited from survey research, which was then beginning. I put this new tool that was already available together with a whole bunch of hypotheses about attitudes that helped explain why the French, German, British, and Italians did the kinds of things they did in politics. This was a major effort. We spent years perfecting the interview schedule. It drew on social-psychological theory, political theory, and Weberian and Parsonian sociology. It took us five years, and we needed all that time. If Sid Verba hadn't been as much of a genius as he was, it never would have been done in that amount of time. Again, like Bing Powell, we worked on this project together before he even finished his dissertation, which turned out to be a very fine monograph by itself.

The Civic Culture had an important impact on the history of the concept of political culture. But when Sid and I collaborated on that book, I had a set of interests that I knew were not going to let me settle in this part of the discipline for the rest of my professional life. I had other theoretical problems I was concerned with. And I knew Sid did it better. In effect, it was a simple and easy passing of the baton to Verba. And he has done incredibly.

I also think Ron Inglehart's work on political culture is excellent. Ron Inglehart is one of the great, neglected heroes of political science. He is the only one of us that made a forecast—arguing back in the 1970s that changing attitudes were going to produce structural changes—and it's been proven by events. I don't know why he's overlooked. He's never been made president of the American Political Science Association. I don't understand. I've complained about it, but not made a big issue of it.

Q: In terms of your own works, is there any one that stands out as your favorite? Are there any ideas you are especially proud about?
A: In *The Appeals of Communism* (Almond 1954), I think the use of content analysis as a way of depicting communism as a system of communication showed a lot of virtuosity. Comparing the mass publications geared to the worker with the theoretical publications and doing systematic content analysis was kind of tricky. Overall, the works I like are those in which I've done something empirical that I think is pretty elegant methodologically.

Do I have any favorites? The lecture I gave in Moscow in 1990, "Capitalism and Democracy" (Almond 1991), was pretty nifty. I did that in a hostile setting, dominated by Gary Becker, and all the other people were economists. They all took a hard approach to eliminating socialism, arguing for drastic change, no matter what the cost, with no need for safety nets. I argued against that approach. That was the principal conclusion of my lecture.

The Research Process

Q: Turning to the research process, how do you actually go about your projects?
A: If I think of my doctoral dissertation on plutocracy and politics, I had an earthy sense of the reality I was interested in explicating. I also kept my nose very close to the ground. I became familiar with a lot of libraries, where they hide directories that record the fate of individuals in print. When I was involved in projects for which the empirical data was not there, I created it. This is what Verba and I did through our instruments. We created the civic culture data. This process reveals one of the key problems of research. Until we have some theory of what's out there, we don't know what to put in our instruments. It's kind of a circular process. But I don't take seriously these debates about constructivism, about whether or not there is a reality out there. That's nonsense.

Q: To what extent is your work affected by big, real-world events?
A: When I grew up, it was one problem after another, one disaster after another. Things were in very bad shape. I was in Paris in 1937 and I remember the headline, during the Spanish Civil War, about the fall of Santander. It brings a lump in my throat again. I was moved by these unemployed

Chicago workers who came and told you: "My children don't have any shoes and in the winter their feet get wet, and they get sick. Can I see my social worker so she can give me a certificate to take to a department store and they will give me some shoes?" That's what made me a kind of social scientist of Left politics at that time. On the other hand, I didn't take anybody's word for it. If Marx said that the capitalist class had such and such powers, I asked myself, is it really so? And I'd go out and look. I'd invent ways to test whether or not it was that way. So, yes, I have been concerned about the big problems, first the Depression, the New Deal, the war, National Socialism, fascism. Take Germany. Here's the country that invented higher education in the social sciences, where the first real social science journal was published, edited by Max Weber, going Nazi. It drove me crazy. I felt obliged to study these problems however I could. I am not saying that elegance is not a virtue. But I wouldn't feel comfortable being too elegant, because I don't think political science is a discipline where elegance is the highest virtue.

Q: Does reading case studies play a role in your research?
A: I do a lot of case study reading. I like to. Once I've decided I'm interested in a particular problem, I like to soak myself in the literature on it, without any preconceptions. That is, I don't set up a bibliography and say I'll read only these works or ones that deal only with this specific angle. It's a more passive process. I let the problem master me before I try to master the problem. Take *Crisis, Choice, and Change* as an example. Rather than take one approach, say, social mobilization theory, I explored the literature and found there were various schools emerging around different modes of inquiry. Eventually, as I told you, I proposed a theory that combined various theoretical strands. So I used a creative mixture of passive and active aspects. I think the passive aspect is neglected. For example, Huntington is more on the active mastery side. I don't think he has enough of the passive side. He doesn't let reality master him.

The Future of the Field

Q: This discussion of problem-versus method-oriented approaches to research has obvious connections to current debates about the direction of comparative politics and the potential contribution of rational choice and game theory. What is your view of the proposal to bring an economic approach into comparative politics?
A: Every generation needs to establish its ground and argue that it has something to say. This is a structural given. They have to say, "Our fathers did it this way and what they overlooked is this," even though they may

not have overlooked it. So, the proponents of an economic approach to comparative politics are establishing a ground on which to stand, and I think there is an awful lot of that going on right now. Having said this, I think there is a place for rational choice theory, if it were used imaginatively and eclectically, and if the people using it were well grounded in the literature they are trying to improve on. But that has not been the agenda.

Take Barry Weingast. He came to me several years ago, when he first wanted to get into political science and asked me, "What should I read?" I gave him a whole bunch of books. That's what was done with graduate students, you gave them a bunch of books and told them to go read and then come back to talk about them. I don't know what he did with them, because they never show up in anything he writes. He failed to really respect the accomplishments in the field he was trying to master and make contributions to. Look, I think the field has really improved and has been quite creative. I don't think it's true that we have to start from scratch. The work that's been done on democratization is fascinating, and it continues the great tradition of constitutional theory that has its origins in Greece. The best work is in this great tradition of constitutional analysis, institutional analysis, which is the bread and butter of political science.

Or take John Ferejohn. He thinks we are going to end up with a kind of physics of politics, a real physics, an $E = MC^2$ state of the discipline. He really believes that. And to some extent all the rational choice people think they can make substantial progress in that direction. Philosophically speaking, there is a real ontological problem that rational choice theorists don't face up to. The data, the reality, that the different sciences examine are not the same. They don't lend themselves equally to analytic methods. It's as simple as that. It's like the clouds and clocks problem of Karl Popper.[4] Take the work of Ernst Mayr, the evolutionary biologist. He has a wonderful analysis in terms of Darwinian theory, which shows that the kind of rigor possible in the biological sciences is different from that of the physical sciences (Mayr 2001). This is because the physical sciences deal with the physical world, which is different from the biological world in the sense of being non-organic. And I would say that the social world, while being more similar to the biological world, is still different. These are separate ontologies. The kind of rigor one can aspire to, the kind of theory one can build, the kind of reductionism one can expect, the extent to which one can reduce phenomena to underlying elements, differs. This is the first philo-

---

4. The reference is to Karl Popper's "Of Clouds and Clocks" (Popper 1972). Popper's metaphor serves as the point of departure for Almond and Genco's "Clouds, Clocks, and the Study of Politics" (Almond and Genco 1977).

sophical problem the social scientist needs to confront. To assume political science is like physics is ridiculous.

Conclusion

Q: What advice would you give to a graduate student starting out in comparative politics?
A: The first thing is to go to some strange, foreign country. That has been the instinct of everybody, starting with Montesquieu, the father of comparative politics. He wrote about an imaginary Persia. He kind of invented Persia. He needed a Persia in order to be able to say things about France. The same can be said about Tocqueville. He said France never left his mind while he was describing America in *Democracy in America* (Tocqueville 1969). All the great political theorists over the generations have confronted the need for comparison.

Q: You are one of the oldest members of our field, and you have published across an astonishing eight decades. What keeps you going? How do you stay interested in your work?
A: I started graduate school in 1933 at the University of Chicago at the depth of the Depression, so we're covering roughly seventy years of professional life. This is something new in the field, the fact that people are staying around so long and still producing. You might say that in part it's a matter of habit. Also, the invention of information technology has helped make possible my longevity in the profession. Fortunately, I learned how to type in high school, and when personal computers were invented, I began to work at home on my computer. It's the easiest thing in the world. I get up in the morning. I'm an early riser. Hell, I wouldn't know what to do in the early morning if I didn't have some project to work on. Let me put it this way. If my mind didn't continue to cope with these issues and problems, I would cease to exist. So I quite selfishly exploit my ability to be creatively busy. It's enjoyable to solve a problem. I get a thrill. I'm not immune even at this late date from getting thrills from good work. And it can become very habitual. From very early boyhood I developed this habit, and that keeps me going.

I've had a very eventful medical history. I mean, I should be dead. But I've been part of a cardiac rehabilitation exercise program for almost thirty years, meeting with many of the same people three times a week. They're good friends of mine. We celebrate events together. That's kept me in shape. I'm relatively limber, though I do creak. I'm ninety years old, that's pretty old. I'm just grateful.

Q: What are you working on these days?
A: I have a book coming out in the fall on fundamentalism. I was involved in a study of fundamentalism that has five large volumes. And I was the principal author of four chapters in the last volume (Marty and Appleby 1995, Chs. 16–19). With my two collaborators, we have turned these chapters into a small paperback. It's called *Strong Religion,* and the University of Chicago Press is going to publish it in September (Almond, Appleby, and Sivan 2003). I'll be reading the proofs on that. I'm still active.

4

Barrington Moore, Jr.

The Critical Spirit and Comparative Historical Analysis

Barrington Moore, Jr. was a pioneering figure in comparative historical research. The ambitious scope of his work on the roots of modern democracy
and dictatorship has inspired generations of students since the 1960s.

Moore began his academic career as a specialist on Russian politics and
society. His first two books, *Soviet Politics* (1950) and *Terror and Progress*
(1954), addressed the question, what happens to a revolutionary movement when it takes power? *Soviet Politics* analyzed how the ideology of
Bolshevism was adapted to solve problems such as achieving rapid industrialization. *Terror and Progress* probed contradictions in the Soviet system and
made tentative predictions about sources of change in the Soviet regime.

During the 1960s, Moore published his most important work, *Social
Origins of Dictatorship and Democracy* (1966), which analyzed the contrasting routes taken by eight major countries as they were transformed from
agrarian to industrial societies. He identified three distinct paths: democracy, as in the United States, France, and England; communism, as in the
Soviet Union and China; and fascism, as in Germany and Japan. He used
the cases of Russia and China to challenge the view that industrialization
was the main cause of twentieth-century totalitarian dictatorships. Instead,
he focused on the role of the landed upper classes and the peasantry, showing that unless there was a violent revolution that weakened landed elites,
the democratic path to modernity was not a feasible option. Moore's historical analysis thus punctured the widely held view during the postwar period
that industrialization and democracy could be achieved together peacefully
in Africa, Asia, and Latin America.

Moore's research after *Social Origins* continued to address large moral
and political questions. *Injustice* (1978) explored why obedience is a far
more common response than rebellion in the face of social misery and

This interview was conducted by Richard Snyder in Cambridge, Massachusetts, on May 13,
2002.

repression. *Privacy* (1984) drew on anthropological and historical studies of different cultures, including Hebrew society, ancient Greece, and China, to examine variation in understandings of privacy. And *Moral Purity and Persecution in History* (2000) argued that monotheism has generated large-scale persecution and suffering throughout history.

Moore was born in Washington, D.C., in 1913, and died in Cambridge, Massachusetts, in 2005. He received his B.A. from Williams College in 1936 and his Ph.D. in sociology from Yale University in 1941. He taught as an instructor in the Social Science Division at the University of Chicago (1945–47) and then became a senior research fellow at Harvard University's Russian Research Center. In 1979 he became a lecturer emeritus at Harvard.

Intellectual Formation and Training

Q: How did you first become interested in the study of politics?
A: As a child I guess I had some interest in authority because I didn't like it as it was being applied to me! But I don't remember having any real interest in politics until I was about fourteen and went to boarding school at St. George's near Newport, Rhode Island. I detested my fellow students. They were rich bullies who picked on me because I was intelligent, and they weren't. It was mostly a clutch of rich boys who couldn't get into a better school. There was also a collection of kids from the navy, an entirely different kind. I rather liked them, and I got along alright with them. I had one very good friend at St. George's, and we ran a print shop together. We got hold of an old foot-peddler printing machine and published some leaflets for and about the school. But it was mostly a stationery store. It was known as the Hunt Stationery Company, named after my friend. The faculty at St. George's was first-rate. They taught me how to write simple English prose.

Q: Were you from a wealthy family?
A: Yes. My grandfather was J. P. Morgan's private lawyer. In a way, I knew my grandfather better than I knew my parents. My parents weren't getting on, and I was, so to speak, grabbed by my grandmother and dumped on my grandfather to keep me away from my parents' quarrels.

Q: After boarding school, you went to Williams College in 1932, where you majored in classics.[1] What was that like?
A: Going to Williams was my own choice. I wanted to go there mainly because it was one of the only colleges that still had a Latin requirement, four years of Latin. I had liked Latin in high school and wanted to get more

1. On Moore's instructors and coursework at Williams, see Jackall (2001).

of it. I had some very good Latin teachers at Williams. I also took courses in the natural sciences and was not very successful at them. There was quite a bit of history in the classics major—one course each year. I took an excellent modern history course by a splendid teacher who ran a little series of Berkshire histories, short little things. Years later he asked me to write a short book on Gandhi for his series, because I had discussed Gandhi in my *Social Origins* (Moore 1966). By that time I was tired of Gandhi and was doing something else. So I turned him down. Overall, at Williams I got a good education, learned about life, fell in love, got married, and all that.

Q: Not everyone gets a thrill from Latin. Why did you like Latin so much?
A: In part because I have a certain contrary streak in my makeup and tastes. Also, Latin was just difficult enough to be demanding, and the selections we had were extremely interesting. I didn't have Catullus in high school, but I had it in college, and it hit me right here. Catullus was full of beautiful emotional things. I also took ancient Greek, which was even better than Latin.

Q: How many languages did you learn altogether?
A: In college I learned Latin, Greek, French, and German. I also started Russian and had a command of it within a year of graduating. Russian is an interesting and tough language to study—the vocabulary is a long, slow slog. I love languages, and I would say that students don't learn enough languages. Languages open up an entirely different pattern of thought, a different way of putting together meaning. Learning languages is good for you, and it's also good professionally. It makes you a better social scientist and a better human being.

Q: How did you go from majoring in classics as an undergraduate at Williams to enrolling in a sociology Ph.D. program at Yale?
A: I took a year off after I finished my undergraduate studies. That was mainly when I learned Russian. I had told Albert Galloway Keller, with whom I hoped to work in the Yale Sociology Department, that I was going to take a year off, and I didn't want to waste that year completely. So I asked Keller if he had any suggestions about what I should do. He immediately told me to learn Russian. Being an obedient young man in some ways, I sat down and learned Russian. When I got to graduate school the next year, there was a certain amount of talk about whether or not this rich boy would be able to hack it. Well, I hacked it "right between the eyes," you might say. I did a good job, except when I got to the dissertation.

Q: Why did you choose to study at Yale? Did you consider other graduate programs?

A: At that time, during the mid-1930s, sociology was mostly the study of welfare relief rolls, as exemplified by the work of Robert Park and Ernest Burgess at the University of Chicago. I was totally alienated by that kind of work and didn't want to have anything to do with it. The Yale Sociology Department was different, because it was still 60 percent William Graham Sumner, even though Sumner had already passed away, and his main protégé, Keller, was about to retire. I took one course with Keller on his book with Sumner, *The Science of Society* (Sumner and Keller 1927), which was mostly anthropology. The Yale Sociology Department had other first-rate teachers and good scholars, younger people in their forties. George Peter Murdock, an anthropologist by training, later went on to make a very distinguished career, in a technical way, in anthropology. James G. Leyburn, a historian by training, was also in the Sociology Department. Leyburn came from the South and worked on the South. On the whole, I got a vastly better education at Yale than I would have at Chicago, which was really the only other established Sociology Department around at that time.

Q: Why did you choose sociology?

A: It had a very broad subject matter and a claim of being scientific, a claim I treated with some lack of respect. I remember getting a set of scales and weighing each volume of Keller and Sumner's big, four-volume thing, *The Science of Society* (1927). Well, I got the weight per generalization, and, as an in-house joke, I typed it up and sent it around to some of the faculty members. Leyburn was amused; he said this was "*les faculte.*" I'm not positive if Keller found out about what I'd done. Maybe he did.

Q: Do you recall the ratio of generalizations per pound?

A: It was about one book per generalization, which was about five pounds.

Q: What were some of the books you read in graduate school that had an important influence on you?

A: Certainly *The Science of Society* (Sumner and Keller 1927) and *Folkways* (Sumner 1959). There were some very bright remarks in *Folkways,* but it was the worst written book I've ever read. Sumner just fired shots from the hip. I also read a lot of social history. In particular, I remember reading an old French study, *The Ancient City* (Fustel de Coulanges 1882), which was beautifully pulled together. It was one of those lovely French books where every fact falls into its niche, forming an overall picture, which may of course be false, because, history being what it is, the next historian may prove it false.

Q: You mentioned that your dissertation did not turn out well. What happened?

A: I had absorbed most of *The Science of Society*. The subject matter of that was primarily anthropology, and I decided I'd had enough anthropology. So I wrote a comparative dissertation on class systems using whatever cases I could get some decent facts on. I had a chapter on the Tikopia of the Solomon Islands and a chapter on the Eskimos. I think I had a section on China. I even tried to make a world scatter plot.[2] But I didn't have any way of putting all this stuff together. It was close to a disaster. Later I realized I was trying to write *Social Origins* but didn't know how to do it yet. My teachers talked to me about the dissertation afterward. Murdock wanted to make me do the whole thing over again, and I'm glad he didn't succeed, because I really didn't know enough then to have significantly improved it. Keller said, "Look at the amount of work he's done, he's got generalizations and some things have come together." In the end they passed it. But it was a very rocky start.

Postdoctoral at the Department of Justice and the Office of Strategic Services (OSS)

Q: In 1941 you finished your Ph.D. What were your plans?

A: I hoped to get an academic job, but the war broke out. I was 4F because of my poor eyesight and various other things. I ended up with a very interesting group and job at the Department of Justice. I recall writing a long paper on the Communist Party of the USA and on other leftist and rightist groups.[3] I met the sociologist Morris Janowitz there, and he became a lifelong friend.

Q: You worked under Harold Lasswell at the Department of Justice.

A: Way under. One part of the flow of academics during the war—mainly social scientists with the emphasis on science—was pushed by Lasswell into various jobs, including at the Department of Justice. Another part of the flow was channeled by the historian William Langer, who handled the more historically oriented, young graduate students. Some of them had made-up military uniforms. I remember the head of our section, who was quite young, had a blue naval uniform covered with cigarette ashes. Quite sloppy-looking! The way it worked was you'd meet Lasswell who would size you up and say "Justice Department" or something like that. Lasswell sent

2. Moore's Yale doctoral dissertation was entitled, "Social Stratification: A Study in Cultural Sociology" (Moore 1941).

3. Moore later published an article stemming from this research (Moore 1945).

me to the Justice Department after making some nasty cracks about Bill Langer and the diplomatic historians.

I quit the Department of Justice after being asked to write up some well-known philosopher, I think it was John Dewey. After a long interval of private research, I landed a job at the Office of Strategic Services (OSS). The part of the OSS that I was in was not a cloak and dagger outfit, or anything of the sort. We didn't clip anything more dangerous than the *New York Times,* but it was research.[4] I wrote one longish essay on Austria for the occupation forces, on the general social structure and politics of the country. I also remember writing a historical study of German communism.

Q: At the OSS you met a remarkable group of German émigrés, including Herbert Marcuse, Otto Kirchheimer, and Franz Neumann. What was it like working with them?

A: It was quite nice. They were intelligent, not cynical, but *disabused,* you might say. I learned a lot from those people. It was a great education for me. I learned how to dissolve Marxism and use it in what I wrote. We were all in very tight quarters in the office. Marcuse, who was technically my boss, had his desk very close behind me. I remember after he looked at my paper on Austrian social structure, he leaned over me and said in his heavy German accent, "It has a Marxist odor." I had previously been exposed to Marxism by reading *The Communist Manifesto* and stuff like that, but I didn't know how to use it, how to get certain positive things out of it. If you look at my *Social Origins* you see a certain amount of Marxism in it. In many ways, that book was a product of my experiences at the OSS.

There was some fuss made about the presence of these German intellectuals at the OSS. The accusation I heard was that the German intellectual will not have an American outlook, which was true. But I didn't take that seriously at all because there really wasn't anything in the way of documents that should have been kept secret. And I figured these guys have prejudices like anybody else, but they're interesting and thoughtful ones. I remember Marcuse went on strike once and said, "I'm not going to write anything else for people who make remarks like this." And he didn't. Marcuse was a bit lazy anyway, so he found an excuse to quit.

Q: Working at the OSS sounds like going to graduate school a second time.

A: Yeah. If you're given the job of writing a paper on Austrian social structure, it's like going to graduate school a second time.

4. On the research aspects of the OSS, see Katz (1989).

one of the few permanent acquisitions of social science. He stated some generalizations and supported them effectively. Although he wasn't in the Social Relations Department, Albert Hirschman was also a good friend of mine for a while. He was another person I liked at Harvard.

Q: Were you afraid of the consequences of resigning from the Social Relations Department?
A: No, I wasn't afraid, I was bored. And I had tenure. If I hadn't had tenure by that time I would have been afraid. Tenure is a great thing. It allows you to be as much of a damn fool as is humanly possible.

Q: What was Harvard like for you after you withdrew from the Social Relations Department?
A: It was a place where you earned your living, as far as I was concerned. It has the most marvelous library in the world, which I still use and admire. What kept me here was the library, even more than the students. The library was the main thing.

Q: What about your invisible college in the Boston area? Your friends and collaborators like Marcuse and Robert Paul Wolff?
A: Well, they're all gone now.

Q: But they must have been important to you.
A: Important, but not decisive. As long as I had the library, I didn't care. My friendship with Marcuse was the longest and perhaps the closest. But he was at Brandeis, not Harvard. We mainly argued together, about the prospects for democracy and light subjects like that. I might have been a little more optimistic than Marcuse about the prospects for democracy. His general—cynicism is not the right word—but his disabused view had an important impact on me. When I would make some hopeful remark he would say, "Barry," and then point out something very wrong in the argument I was making. I learned from him not to use arguments that wouldn't work.

Q: What were the costs and benefits of your decision to resign from a regular academic department and become disengaged from the profession?
A: The costs are what some people consider the benefits. You don't have to go to meetings and listen to a lot of nonsense that you might disagree with but don't feel like arguing about. On the other hand, there is a loss in emotional support.

Q: When you publish something, how do you get feedback?

A: Reviews. My books have always been reviewed. They always get a complete fan of reviews, from stinky to marvelous. My most recent book, *Moral Purity* (Moore 2000), has been an exception to this. I've seen a review by some militant Catholic who sure didn't like it. I've also seen a couple of reviews that seize on the gaps between my cases to discredit the undertaking.[7] To fill in the gaps would of course set up an unreadable mass in which the book's polemical thesis about monotheism would vanish. I came to the thesis by my usual inductive route, realizing what the facts were telling me only when I was well along in writing. I am very proud of *Moral Purity*. I think it's a *Social Origins* with a much narrower compass and a very sharp point.

Research on Soviet Politics, Comparative History, and Moral Analysis

Q: You started your career as a specialist on Soviet politics, and your first two books were on this topic (Moore 1950, 1954).

A: I still think that *Soviet Politics* (Moore 1950) is a very good book. It raised a recurring and very interesting question, what happens to a revolution when it takes power? I spell that out in great detail. And the book is still used in teaching.

Q: *Soviet Politics* has a structural-functionalist flavor, as seen in the main argument that industrialization requires stratification and inequality.

A: Yes, I think that's correct.

Q: Did you get the structural functionalism from Parsons when you came to Harvard?

A: No, that came from Sumner.

Q: One interesting aspect of your second book, *Terror and Progress*, is that you make predictions about the Soviet Union's political development.

A: I'm not sure if the alternative scenarios I proposed were as well chosen as they could have been. I was as surprised as anybody else about the collapse of the Soviet Union, though I was no longer active in following Soviet affairs at that point. To try and predict was sort of an assignment to all of us who were working on the Soviet Union after the war. Some people

---

7. See, for example, Malia (2000) and McManners (2000). For a favorable review, see Bernhard (2002).

took it seriously, as I did, and others, like my Harvard colleague Alexander Gerschenkron, treated it as a huge joke.

Q: Was Gerschenkron a big influence on you?
A: He wrote a book about bread and democracy in Germany that highlighted the "iron and rye" business (Gerschenkron 1966).[8] I knew a good deal about that before I read his book. Gerschenkron was far from the first to make the connection; there's a lot in the German historical literature on the "iron and rye" coalition between industrialists and the Junker farmers. But he put it together quite nicely I thought. Gerschenkron's essays are very bright, especially his essays on economic growth (Gerschenkron 1962, 1968).

Q: I want to pose a thought experiment. If I could go back in time to 1956, ten years before the publication of *Social Origins* (Moore 1966), and I had to pick the scholar who was most likely to produce that book, I doubt I would have chosen you. In 1956, your publication profile was that of an area studies expert, not a broad comparativist. You'd written two successful books on the Soviet case. Why didn't you write a third book on Russia? Why did you shift away from the study of Soviet politics toward the broadly comparative project that became *Social Origins*?
A: I couldn't stand the idea of being a Russia specialist, especially after looking at some of the people who were becoming Russia specialists. Many were very narrow and simultaneously conceited. I didn't like them and didn't think much of them. I find that country specialists are often pretty unbearable. When I wrote my books on Russia, I never had any idea of becoming a semi-permanent Russia specialist. If I had wanted to be a specialist, France, Germany, England, and even the United States would have been more interesting. Not that Russia wasn't important, but I had said everything I wanted to say about it. I usually get good and tired of what I am working on and want to change to something else. I can't understand people who write the same thing over and over again.

Q: When did you realize it was time to get beyond working on Russia?
A: I got interested in something else. My curiosities shifted to what emerged finally in *Social Origins:* the roots of totalitarianism, liberalism, and radical revolution.

Q: Let's discuss *Social Origins*. How did you come to write such a broad and ambitious book covering eight countries? Did you start out intending to end up with such a product?

---

8. Gerschenkron's book was first published in 1943.

A: I actually started *Social Origins* with a much more ambitious plan—an overly ambitious plan. I was going to study a wider range of countries, not just ones with an agrarian class structure, but also ones with an industrial social structure, and maybe even a couple of others. I always tell my students— and I do it myself—that when you set up a study, set it up like an accordion so you can increase or shrink the size of it as you go along. It's only humanly possible to do some things, and do them well. If I had tried to write the *Social Origins* I had in mind when I started, it would have been too much for me, and I would have failed.

As to the question of where I got the ambition to take on such a daunting challenge in the first place, that's built into me. Even my dissertation, which may be wrong for the reasons the critics say, shows a very broad mind and a very broad curiosity. Some of that I got as an undergraduate at Williams, from good teachers and interesting subjects. Later on the experience of writing my first books on the Soviet Union taught me how to do certain things. But most of it I just had to figure out for myself.

Q: Could you discuss the intellectual milieu in which you wrote *Social Origins?* Who were the interlocutors you were engaging? In the book's preface you wrote that you were uncomfortable with arguments that industrialization was the cause of twentieth-century totalitarian regimes.
A: When I got through with *Social Origins* I was a lot more uncomfortable with those arguments. I would only buy part of the simple Marxist idea that industrialism will come and explode democracy.

Q: Hannah Arendt's work could be read as an argument about the industrial origins of totalitarianism (Arendt 1951). Were you engaged with her work while you were writing *Social Origins?*
A: I didn't like Hannah Arendt, though she was very favorable to me. I felt her book on totalitarianism was pretty junky. She only has Germany as a model, neither Russia nor China appears. I recall the opening paragraph of her book, and it struck me as nonsense. She's not worth taking seriously. I took Lenin, or Leninism and Stalinism, more seriously. All along those have been and still are my counter-models. People think of Lenin as a Marxist George Washington, but if you look at him closely at all, he's a repulsive dictator.

Q: What about Marcuse's argument about the origins of totalitarianism (Marcuse 1968)?[9] Did that influence you?

9. Marcuse (1968, 19) views totalitarianism as corresponding to the monopolistic stage of capitalism.

A: I've forgotten what it was. I'd have to look at it again. When I read his best book, the Freud book (Marcuse 1955), I remember telling him he had used Hegel to take the sting out of the death instinct and thereby save Marx. He laughed furiously and agreed.

Q: A Hegelian influence is evident in your work. For example, *Social Origins* analyzes the dialectical interplay of contradictory historical imperatives.
A: Hegel has a couple of good ideas. You can't write that many pages of nonsense without writing something intelligent. As a consequence of my friendship with Marcuse, I bought several volumes of Hegel and studied the stuff. I came to the conclusion that whatever makes sense in Hegel can be expressed much more simply and empirically. The dialectical flourish doesn't add any true value.

Q: Why did you choose to focus on agrarian class relations as the master explanatory variable in *Social Origins*?
A: I decided to stick to the agrarian side in part because, as I said, I got too tired to cover countries with an industrial social structure. So it was partly a personal thing. Also, there weren't many people who wrote comparative agrarian history, just a few specialists. There were some very good ones, of course, but their agrarian history was of a very special kind. They would tell you the difference between field A and field B in some area, which can of course be very important. R. H. Tawney was a different animal. He had a broad spectrum. Every scholar has a framework, and he had a diluted Marxist one. I used his book *The Agrarian Problem in the 16th Century* (Tawney 1967) quite a bit.[10] My argument about the impact of the commercialization of agriculture was certainly influenced by Tawney, whom I had read early on. I also remember reading all those rise and fall of the English gentry arguments (Tawney 1954). I had to read and judge that material while I was writing *Social Origins*.

Q: While you were writing *Social Origins*, a number of other broad comparative and historical studies on the origins of different types of political regimes were published, including Seymour Martin Lipset's *Political Man* (1960a), Reinhard Bendix's *Nation-Building and Citizenship* (1964), Karl de Schweinitz's *Industrialization and Democracy* (1964), and Samuel Huntington's *Political Order in Changing Societies* (1968). Were you aware of these other projects?

10. Tawney's book was first published in 1912.

A: I was aware of them, certainly. And I wanted to carefully avoid just doing a piece of product differentiation. I said to myself, "I'm working on an important problem here, and I'll do the best I can to resolve it. If it comes out exactly the same as Marty Lipset, that's fine." At least that was the idea. Underneath there was probably something else.

Q: What else? What was underneath?
A: Jealousy. Jealousy of somebody else doing a job well.

Q: Where did you come up with the method of comparative historical analysis employed in *Social Origins?*
A: It's a little hard to say. I remember a point when I was in the middle of writing *Social Origins* when I said to myself, there's not just one route to industrialization, there are three. That gave me the impetus for a comparative historical approach, and I've been using it in one form or another ever since.

Q: Which of the three routes did you start working on first?
A: I wrote them in approximately the order in which they appear, starting with the democratic path first, which includes the French Revolution and also the English Revolution, which some very distinguished books had failed to mention.

Q: What was the initial title for *Social Origins?* Did you have another title when you started out?
A: I don't remember any other title. I probably didn't have the title when I started out, because it was somewhere in the middle of writing that I realized there were three paths, not just one, and that meant considerable rewriting of some parts.

Q: How long did it take to write *Social Origins?*
A: My two big books—*Social Origins* (Moore 1966) and *Injustice* (Moore 1978)—each took about ten years.

Q: Is it true that you wrote most of *Social Origins* on a boat?
A: Yes. My wife and I lived on a boat. In Washington, during the war, we lived on a scow. After that, we lived on a boat a large number of summers. One time I had three hundred books on a boat! But I tried to do all the necessary reading, especially the books from Harvard's Widener library, during the spring and fall, so I could do all the writing on the boat itself. Writing on a boat is very refreshing. I did not put as long hours in, and

when the weather was attractive, I would knock off for a day or two and sail or cruise. When you get stiff from writing, you can stand up and look out the ports. Later, we had a powerboat, which was fine for living in. We also had a little sailboat, which gave you the fun of sailing. I think we spent thirteen years on the powerboat, which is an awful confession for a sailor. But it also made a very good place to write, because it had a little more room.

Q: Is it true that Harvard University Press turned down *Social Origins*?
A: Yeah. I still don't know who the jerk was who wrote a negative review of my book for that press. Everybody tells me I must know who it is, but I don't. I'm not that anxious about this—I've had my rewards, so to speak. I'm sure he's convinced he is right, though. I remember the sentence in his review that said "This is a book that will find its way onto many reading lists, but it's still a bad book." With that attitude, no matter what reputation the book got, he was going to be perfectly safe and happy, presumably.

Q: When did you first realize *Social Origins* was going to be a huge hit?
A: The review in the *New York Times* by J. H. Plumb (1966) was very enthusiastic, and I figured that's done it. I certainly remember that review, and lots of people talked to me about it, so I knew it hit the jaw, or something.

Q: Did you have a hunch the book would still be selling thirty-five years later?
A: No, I didn't think that was true of any book.

Q: Why do you think *Social Origins* has been such a big hit? Why does it still sell?
A: Well, I hear from people who teach it that there are no books like it yet in terms of the scope.

Q: Would you like to see someone write a sequel to *Social Origins*?
A: Yes. That's part of the whole ethic of scholarship—the good supposedly replaces the antiquated. There is certainly room for a similar and improved study.

Q: Is *Social Origins* your favorite book?
A: I suppose it's the most important. If I were to choose my best one, I suppose I would choose that, though *Moral Purity* is in some ways a more concise argument. It's a lot shorter, and that doesn't hurt. *Social Origins* has certainly been my most successful book.

Q: In terms of replying publicly to criticisms of *Social Origins*, you haven't done very much of that. The one exception is Stanley Rothman (1970a).
A: Given his position and the fact that he was coming out with his own book (Rothman 1970b), I felt he could fool people. So I disposed of him pretty quickly (Moore 1970). By and large I avoid replying to critics, but not completely.

Q: What is the legacy of *Social Origins* in terms of inspiring a research program in comparative historical analysis?
A: Frankly, I refuse to talk about that. Somebody else can figure that out. I've done my job, and people can make of it what they will.

Q: After *Social Origins*, your work reflected an increasing interest in moral concerns, as seen in books such as *Reflections on the Causes of Human Misery* (Moore 1972); *Injustice* (Moore 1978); *Privacy* (Moore 1984); and *Moral Aspects of Economic Growth* (Moore 1998). Since you regard *Injustice* as one of your two big books, could you discuss why you chose to work on that subject?
A: Injustice can be a great source of pain. Some people suffer very severely from the injustice of society. Of course, justice can also be a great source of pain, maybe even more a source of pain than injustice, though I'm not sure. A thoroughly unjust society, and we're getting plenty of those nowadays, though we have always had many of them, can really hurt. The neo-Islamic view of the world is going to cause a lot more pain—not just the suicides either. The injustice book, which is a good book, doesn't have the neatness that *Social Origins* has. There are more rough edges. I would maintain that that's the nature of the material, that it will not fall into as neat patterns as appear in *Social Origins*, and it's not my fault if it doesn't. *Injustice* did get quite a lot of favorable reviews, but then it was dropped.

Q: Why was *Injustice* dropped?
A: That's the wrong question to ask. Ask of a certain other book, why is it not forgotten? Why is it *not* dropped? The normal fate is to disappear, and that requires no special explanation.

Q: In the preface to *Privacy*, you write that it was the most fun book to write (Moore 1984, xii). Why?
A: I like privacy, and in part I felt I was writing a defense of it. Also, I found it enjoyable to stop trying to write something like *Social Origins* or *Injustice*. To keep the book manageable, I narrowed my study so that I wouldn't have to

go into the modern arguments about privacy. The final chapter of *Privacy* has caused problems. Someone at Johns Hopkins University Press recently wanted to reprint the book, but the editor there said no, because it was too dated, especially all the statistics and the last chapter on America. I figured out how to handle that problem by simply saying that the figures are dated but the theoretical thesis—that the evil in the world is not properly explained by American economics—was still valid. In the end, I did not pursue the matter because I was writing *Moral Purity* when I got the inquiry from Johns Hopkins, and I had enough going on.

The Research Process
Science and Normative Concerns

Q: Do you think of yourself as a scientist?
A: Yes, as a social scientist. If I have to define myself for somebody who doesn't know what I do, I say I'm a social scientist. My father was a forestry engineer, and a lot of biology and natural science rubbed off on me.

Q: What does science mean to you? You once wrote, "The essence of science is simply the refusal to believe on the basis of hope" (Moore 1965, 55).
A: I stand by that.

Q: Your work usually strives to address large, morally compelling questions. Can one be scientific in addressing those types of questions?
A: Sure. You can talk about morals without taking a moral position. You can talk about the connections between morals and various forms of behavior, consequences, lack of consequences, and so on. What are the consequences of theft? What are the consequences of bringing kids up in a society where there is no taboo on theft? That's what I try to do. I don't preach.

Q: But your work has clearly been guided by normative concerns.
A: In some of my work, like *Privacy,* for example, which is in part a defense of privacy, the normative concerns are obvious. But for the most part, my work is not driven by normative concerns in the sense of trying to make a better world. I am trying to get better answers to problems. I've always been highly skeptical of do-gooders, from Marxism to Christianity. Explicit and intellectually sloppy do-goodism gets on my nerves.

Q: Still, at certain junctures in your career you've been actively involved in politics. For example, you signed a critical open letter to

President Kennedy in 1961 after the Bay of Pigs invasion of Cuba, and you wrote a memo pronouncing the New Frontier a fraud.[11]
A: I don't do any more of that. I could see very quickly that pressure was being put on me to do things, particularly for the students, and it was pretty obvious I wasn't any good at it. So I decided to keep a very low profile.

Q: One critique of the social sciences—especially political science—is that we don't address humanly important questions, like injustice, anymore.
A: Well, that's always a complaint. Instead of complaining about it they should do something, like write about a particular form of happiness or un-happiness. Just sitting around drinking coffee and complaining is a waste of time and energy. It's an evasion, and there's too much of it. Sit down and work.

Social Theory

Q: What value does political and social theory have for comparative historical research? Has reading social theory had much influence on your work?
A: Used properly, social theory shows how to look for connections among facts. Vilfredo Pareto (1963) and especially Gaetano Mosca (1939) both influenced me greatly, certainly as much as Sumner. At the end of World War II, there was a considerable vogue for Pareto in the United States, then it completely disappeared because Talcott Parsons smothered it. Pareto is interesting, but too long. It's really only one volume, volume 3 on deriva-tions, which is worth reading, and that's quite enjoyable. I was talking once with the Harvard political theorist Judith Shklar about Pareto, and we in-stantly agreed that all there is to his work is French newspapers and classics. Mosca knew more and was more balanced. There's a good deal of Mosca in my *Social Origins*. It runs through the book, which has a rather ambivalent attitude about doing good.

Q: Did the work of Max Weber influence you much?
A: Oh, yeah. I was quite an admirer of Weber. However, if you're too critical, you can demolish him. *The Protestant Ethic* (Weber 1958c) won't stand up to an empirical evaluation. His big series on religion (Weber 1951, 1958a, 1967) is his best and most interesting work, though it's not very outstand-

11. See Schlesinger (1965, 285–86). The New Frontier was the slogan Kennedy used to refer to his policy agenda.

ing. As for all Weber's theoretical stuff, the things that Parsons liked, I think
that's worthless and just toss it away. That leaves you with his empirical
sociological work, and if you take *The Protestant Ethic* out, what are you left
with? But somehow I still respect and admire Weber. He was a very interesting man, and the biography by his wife (Weber 1975) is quite interesting.[12]

History

**Q: Could you comment on the role historical analysis has played in your
work? What do you find pleasurable about reading and doing history?**
A: It takes you out of yourself and into a strange world, and it's often just
plain exciting, too. It depends on the book, obviously. Works of history
provide an account of human behavior, usually evil, and an attempt to
explain it. If it's well done, it's very persuasive. People today, and I think it
was true earlier, don't read enough. They only read what's assigned to them.
They don't read for pleasure or for loose instruction. They miss out as human beings and they miss out in terms of becoming competent social scientists. My house is full of books.

Q: What works of history do you especially admire and enjoy?
A: E. P. Thompson's *Making of the English Working Class* (1964) is exciting. I
appreciate Marc Bloch's work, though some of the Annales School is just
textbooks. There's a book on the Calas affair that's exciting. The Calas affair
was a very brave feat by Voltaire. He was about to get it between the eyes.
Much later I read another book on it—the usual modern history, a debunk-
ing job—which showed that Voltaire was not such a hero after all. You can
practically write the book. It was by a good enough historian, from Princeton (Bien 1960). There's a book on ways of lying that I like (Zagorin 1990). I
also enjoy reading history about magic and witchcraft.

I am less interested in the one damn thing happens after another kind of
history, like Namier's *England in the Age of the American Revolution* (1930).
That book cuts the earlier radical interpretations. He's very much a conservative. In the *Times Literary Supplement* they are still arguing about him. My
feeling is they can argue all they want about whose interpretation is right,
but they don't get anywhere doing that. They've got to go back to the
sources.

**Q: You mentioned you enjoy reading about magic and witchcraft.
What interests you about this topic?**

12. For some of Moore's thoughts on Weber, see his "Strategy in Social Science" (Moore
1958).

A: Self-deception. It's also one form of adjustment to the environment. Magic is not exactly to be recommended today, although we are going back to it good and fast. Many Islamic kids and grownups certainly go for magic. Christianity got over that about five hundred years ago, which was for the better, at least for a while in the nineteenth century. My theory is that human society was bearable for a short time in one place, in England under the Edwardians. At least they had full free speech and a democratic, decent government.

Q: Is there good evidence that people were actually happier during that period?
A: Yes, a lot of it. But you have to be careful, because a lot of the evidence is just memoirs, but memoirs will certainly tell you something about some people. During the Edwardian period, a large mass of people was suffering economically, but that happens in all times. That kind of suffering can be escaped in small countries and in small units that are favorably placed. Switzerland is the key example and some Scandinavian countries. But I don't agree with someone like Robert Dahl who thinks the future is to be read in Norway or Sweden. That's just self-deception. I think Washington, D.C., is a more realistic guide to the future than Sweden or Denmark.

Q: In all your work, your rigor about the use of historical evidence is striking.
A: That's one thing that makes me a scientist.

Q: Why is it important to be rigorous about the use of evidence?
A: Well, why is truth important? That got banged into me as early as boarding school.

Q: What kind of skills are necessary to do first-rate historical analysis?
A: Languages. That's the main thing. Otherwise you're stuck. You can't write anything historical about the Orient now without knowing Chinese and Japanese. *Social Origins* may have been the last book written about the Orient without knowing the languages. You can't do that anymore. An eye for irony also helps because it keeps you from getting too many notions of grandeur, but if that's all you've got it's not enough. An eye for unintended consequences is excellent, too. That's another good antidote to intellectual arrogance. Other kinds of arrogance don't matter. So what if someone is arrogant at the dinner table? But if he's arrogant in his monograph on early Christianity that's more serious, because it affects more people.

Q: How about synthetic skills, like the ability to handle huge amounts of information without getting bogged down?

A: I don't know any recipe for that except for a certain amount of practice.

Fieldwork

Q: What are your thoughts on the role of fieldwork in social science analysis?

A: I have a lot of respect for it, though I never did much myself. I can tell good fieldwork from poor fieldwork, because it has inconsistencies, obvious bias, and lovie dovie. Too much lovie dovie is not good for any book. I had to do some fieldwork as part of getting my doctoral degree at Yale. And I've done other fieldwork of an informal sort by getting to know slightly odd types of people. For example, I learned to get along with people working in a shipyard, and I learned about the lives of good carpenters or mechanics, what their gripes were. I liked and respected them because of their skills. Because they knew I respected them, they talked to me about themselves. You might call that fieldwork. A similar thing happened with mountain guides when I was an alpinist. Curiously enough, the better guides I've had are the ones who have been killed in accidents. They had just a little touch more skill, and a little bit more daring, and it caught up with them.

Sometimes I try to talk to homeless people to see what makes them tick, although in many cases I will just step around them. At the entrance to Massachusetts Eye and Ear Clinic, which is also a parking spot for a boat, there was a woman with a huge sign saying she needed charity or something. She had picked a spot right at a traffic light, which allowed her to catch the traffic. I went up to her and asked how much she made, and she told me right away, "Sixty bucks a day." She had a completely matter of fact attitude about this big piece of cardboard. I guess you could call that fieldwork.

Q: There's an obvious tension between doing fieldwork and doing broadly comparative work. Are there any examples of broadly comparative scholars like yourself who have also done first-rate field research?

A: I don't think you can swing it. The Polish anthropologist Malinowski probably comes the closest to being both a broad theoretician and a fieldworker. He was certainly a good theorist, though his diaries (Malinowski 1967) are trivial and whiny. You wouldn't think from reading the diaries that this man could write some of the best things about human culture. He wrote the essay on culture for the *Encyclopaedia of the Social Sciences* (Malinowski 1931). I knew him a little bit when I was a student at Yale, and you could see he was a man of broad intellectual curiosity. What helped him with the fieldwork was simply being a gentleman. If you know how to behave like a gentleman in a strange culture, you can find things out.

Max Weber also did a bit of fieldwork when he was young, and during his visit to America he also did a lot of fieldwork, though I haven't read that.[13] Chicago's elevated street-car system fascinated him, especially the safety rules. There weren't any safety rules, and Weber attempted to explain this by arguing that it was cheaper to pay for an accident than to try to prevent it.

Collaboration

Q: What role has collaboration played in your research?
A: When I started working on *Social Origins* and Marcuse started working on *One-Dimensional Man* (Marcuse 1964), we both thought for a while, but not very long, that we would be collaborating and writing one book together. But we were both smart enough to see that wouldn't work. During that period, I somehow managed to wangle a Fulbright fellowship for a year's leave in Europe, and I managed to get it transferred to Herbert. He went to Paris for about a year of the work on *One-Dimensional Man*. He came back and said it was very hard to write an anti-American book in Paris, because the French were so sloppy and lousy that America's technological civilization started to look pretty good after a while in France.

Q: What do you think of *One-Dimensional Man*?
A: There were some perfectly brilliant passages in that book, others that were weak, and others that practically made me lose my temper, especially remnants of old, pro-Marxist socialist things. The whole crowd to which Marcuse belonged started as clubfooted Marxists. I made him take those passages out.

Q: What did Marcuse think of *Social Origins*?
A: He liked it. But I remember him liking *Injustice* more, though his reaction to it was partly comical. It was a fairly heavy book, and Marcuse said he first tried reading it while standing on his head, and then he tried several other comical positions.

Q: Which position worked best?
A: None of them were satisfactory, as I recall.

---

13. On Weber's empirical research, which includes surveys of agricultural and industrial workers, see Lazarsfeld and Oberschall (1965).

Q: Did you collaborate with your wife?
A: Oh, yes. I wrote four or five drafts of the section on enclosures in *Social Origins*, but I couldn't get it to make sense. I finally said, "Betty, you write it." And she wrote it and it stuck, it made sense. So there are about three printed pages by her on the enclosures. That's one case where I'm not sure my careful investigation of the facts worked, but at least it got me a piece by Betty.

Betty mostly did more of the technical editing—getting the damn fool misstatements out, the mistakes. She read what I was reading so she could edit what I wrote. She read French, German, and Russian. There were great difficulties. She might come across a passage I had written three or four years before and totally forgotten. She would hand it to me and say, "What does this mean?" I would be deeply engaged in some other part, and I'd have to stop and straighten the matter out. It was painful for both of us, very painful. All this romantic talk about husband-wife or girlfriend collaboration just didn't apply to our case at all. Fortunately, we had other outlets. She learned how to be a very good skier, was a very good crew on the boat, an excellent cook at all times, an attractive personality, and so on. So, these rough spots, though they were unpleasant, could be gotten over.

Funding

Q: Have grants and funding been necessary for your research?
A: Salaries and pension are enough, plus a bed of savings from the family, but the salary is really enough. I just need transportation to the library and transportation back home again, that's it.

Q: What about funding for traveling to archives?
A: I would like to be able to do that, but I just don't. And I happen to live next to one of the most accessible and biggest research libraries in the world.

Missed Opportunities

Q: Are there any projects you wish you had done but did not? Any missed opportunities?
A: I had a project in mind similar to *Social Origins*. I wanted to see the moral aspects in several different kinds of economic transformation and growth.[14] I decided that was too ambitious for my stage of life. I was just about to

14. The beginning of the longer study that Moore abandoned appears as "Moral Aspects of Economic Growth: Historical Notes on Business Morality in England" in Moore (1998).

retire, I think. That was the right decision because I would not have been pleased to have been halfway through something and given up. It's better to give up beforehand than to struggle and be defeated.

Teaching and Students

Q: What role has teaching played in your career?[15]
A: I love it. Teaching continuously stimulates your research. And it prevents a narrowing, because young people ask a lot of big questions. Teaching also gets you away from delusions of grandeur, because you are dealing with much simpler minds. And there is usually a pleasure of interchange and back-and-forth reaction. There may be only two or three students in your class with whom you can have back and forth interchanges, but that's enough if you can keep the others somewhat engaged. Teaching, even if you've done the same course two or three times, is always a delicate exercise in human manipulation. I never made any bones about that to the students.

I still remember the best teaching day I ever had, quite early in the game. It was a section on Mosca with about twenty students. I just walked into the room and kept quiet. One student asked a question, another student answered it, and there was a systematic discussion of Mosca corresponding almost exactly to the notes I had made on how this should go. There it was. I don't think I had to say a word during the whole forty-five minutes. It's the sort of thing one remembers because it was so unusual.

One year I got tired of the courses I had been giving. I was becoming far too popular and wanted to change. So, I cancelled my seminar and started a new one. Well, I certainly succeeded at becoming unpopular. I went from having had a hundred applicants for the seminar to having just three students. That was one of the best years I ever had teaching. There was one boy who was training to be a musician, and he mixed up some of the genders of the classical gods. There was also a charming, intelligent girl who was a graduate student in classics. It was a collection of very enthusiastic youngsters.

A few years ago, I volunteered to take a section of Harvard freshmen, about a dozen, to see what was on their minds and let them ask questions. I hadn't taught for a while. All the students were talking about "What I feel" and "What I want." So, I said, "Stop, you're going to listen to me. You all came here not to change the world, not to make a revolution, but to learn something. Now get out of here and learn." Apparently this created a favor-

15. On Moore's teaching as seen from a graduate student's perspective, see the discussion by Theda Skocpol in Chapter 17.

able excitement, because they were all seen coming out of the building talking and very happy. That surprised me. What they needed, and I didn't realize this until I did it accidentally, was a good firm hand. That's a teaching experience I have not forgotten.

Q: What are the hallmarks of the best teachers?
A: Clarity and order. Some scholars have the reputation of being awful teachers, but they are still good people to have around. Ben Schwartz at Harvard was one of those. Apparently he couldn't keep a straight line.

Q: What are the qualities of the best students?
A: Clarity and industry. Being a student requires a fair amount of work, and if you can't keep your head above water and give an ordered presentation, it's going to be a mess.

Q: Are you proud to have taught students like Charles Tilly and Theda Skocpol, who have become some of the most famous contemporary social scientists?
A: Chuck is a good man. I like his first book (Tilly 1964). It's the most readable. Some of the more general things he's done don't strike me as succeeding very well. I don't remember them clearly; they're just impressions left in my head.

I'm fond of Theda. She did a lot better when she got out from under me—too much trying to be the next Barry Moore. I don't think *States and Social Revolutions* (Skocpol 1979) is such a good book. It had one good point—on the importance of the foreign setting—that was missing in my *Social Origins*. That made the book, but there were other things missing, or wrong. The argument about the autonomy of the state is okay, but that's an old chestnut. Her work on the American soldier (Skocpol 1992) had a lot more feeling. She really did a very nice job there.

Q: In the early 1960s, you participated in founding Social Studies, the honors interdisciplinary major at Harvard that has trained many students who later went on to become leading social scientists. Could you discuss how this initiative emerged?
A: McGeorge Bundy, who was dean of Harvard's Faculty of Arts and Sciences, called about six of us in, including Stanley Hoffman and Robert Paul Wolff, while he was at Harvard. Gerschenkron, though he wasn't active in the social studies program, was a critical outsider. Bundy got us all together and said, "We need to do this kind of social science. Who does it?" I took what I'd taught years before at Chicago out of my pocket, and that served as

the basis for Social Studies 10, the core course in the major, until about a year ago. Every senior was required to give a presentation before the whole class on what his or her thesis would be, or at least what the problem would be, and how he or she would go about it. I usually went to those presentations, but I got a little tired of it after I started feeling like I was becoming an expert on everything. So I quit, just as they were about to give me a professorship I didn't want. But I'm glad I did that teaching.

Judy Vichniac, who later came in to run the social studies program, was my Ph.D. student. I was forced to retire before I finished with her. In those days it was the opposite of now, you were forced to retire at a certain age, and if you weren't a professor, which I wasn't because I had refused a professorship, that knocked three or four more years off. That didn't bother me, because I didn't want to stay on until my head dropped off onto the table. I wanted to have a somewhat free life after retirement, and I did.

Q: What advice can you offer a young scholar or student just starting out? What skills should they acquire? What questions should they ask?
A: The first thing I would ask is, what can this person do? What are his or her passions and skills? Otherwise you're just advising into a blank thing and sounding off with your own wisdom. I can advise a student that I've had in class all year without any difficulties. That's easy. "Go jump in a lake," maybe. But I can't advise a complete stranger, as if I were a wise man. I don't feel I can be honest with someone like that. Come with a specific problem, like, would I be a good teacher? Is there enough money in it? But I am very hesitant to speak about more general issues. The only general piece of advice I will offer is: finish the paper on time. That was the worst problem I had with students. Graduate students at Harvard were allowed to take incompletes. I finally announced no incompletes in my course—you either pass or fail.

Q: Would you recommend that students consider following your path of professional disengagement?
A: I have a certain shyness, not shyness, but I have hesitations about telling people how to live their lives. I don't like to preach, and I don't like to listen.

Conclusion

Q: What are you working on now?
A: I'm writing a biographical essay on my grandfather, the circle he moved in, and the bits I could see of it. It's called *Grandfather* and then his name, Lewis Cass Ledyard. He was actually a step-grandfather. When I was grow-

ing up I heard the family using the word *step*, but I didn't know what it meant. So he was just a grandfather to me. He died when I was nineteen, and I was perhaps closer to him than anyone else at that point in my life.

Q: Is *Grandfather* just a personal project, or does it have a larger objective?
A: I see him as a lackey of imperialism, but he was a pretty good lackey. He's one of the people who are hated now. His first big legal job was to take the American Tobacco Company, which had been split by the antitrust legislation, and put it back together as pieces, but so the pieces worked together. It was a very successful surgical operation. Today that would not exactly be popular.

Q: Your first professional article was published in 1942, and today you're working on a new book. You've been a productive scholar for more than sixty years. What keeps you going?
A: Good question. At this late stage, once you're in the habit of writing books and you stop, you're at loose ends. The only way to pull the ends together, for me at any rate, is to write something else. So, I kept on writing. Enough things are wrong with me now—eyes, guts—that I can't write anymore, but I console myself with saying it probably means I can't live very much more. So, to go back to your question, once you get the habit, you can't break it very easily.

Q: There has to be more than habit that keeps you going.
A: Habit is a very big part. There's also a certain amount of idealistic curiosity and intellectual pleasure that partly comes from problem solving. What is the origin of democracy? Is the standard explanation mostly wishful thinking? Recently I did a study of a whole series of medieval and late medieval cities to see if they contributed to democracy (Moore 2001). They certainly did not, and I showed how. That's a nice little retirement occupation.

Q: What about the wish to transcend? Has that motivated you?
A: The wish to transcend? I'm not that ambitious. And I certainly don't feel like transcending Talcott Parsons! That wish has got something wrong with it.

5

Robert A. Dahl

Normative Theory, Empirical Research, and Democracy

Robert A. Dahl's work focuses on the origins, characteristics, and consequences of democracy. Over the course of his sixty-year career, he has made major contributions to democratic theory, American politics, and comparative politics. He is widely regarded as one of the leading theorists on democracy in the second half of the twentieth century.

Dahl's early research focused on American politics and democratic theory. His first book, *Congress and Foreign Policy* (1950), analyzed the domestic political determinants of U.S. foreign policy. His first work on democratic theory, *A Preface to Democratic Theory* (1956), critiqued conceptions of direct democracy inspired by Rousseau and argued instead for a pluralist theory of democracy, which holds that power in liberal democracies is dispersed among interest groups, political parties, and citizens; hence, no single group controls the political arena (Isaac 2002). In subsequent research, he advanced his theory of democracy by challenging methodologically and empirically the work of "elite theorists," such as C. Wright Mills, who saw liberal democracies as dominated by a small power elite. Dahl wrote a series of articles on the concept of power that criticized elite theorists for failing to meet the conventional methodological standards of social science. He also provided an empirical critique of elite theory in *Who Governs?* (1961a), a work on New Haven, Connecticut, that showed that the city's politics were pluralistic in nature and that its government was not run by a narrow business elite.

Dahl played an important role in the late 1950s and 1960s as a leader of the behavioral revolution in political science. This movement was inspired by the work of positivist philosophers such as Carl Hempel, and it aimed to introduce into political science a greater appreciation for rigorous methods and scientific standards. The behavioral revolution resulted in the wide-

This interview was conducted by Richard Snyder in New Haven, Connecticut, on March 4, 2002.

spread adoption by political scientists of quantitative forms of analysis and survey-based research.

Dahl's work in comparative politics initially focused on the role and impact of political oppositions under democratic and non-democratic systems. His work on oppositions resulted in two influential edited volumes, *Political Oppositions in Western Democracies* (1966a) and *Regimes and Oppositions* (1973). His most important work in comparative politics is *Polyarchy* (1971), a landmark cross-national study of contemporary democracy that helped generate a wide-ranging consensus about how to conceptualize democracy. Because Dahl argued that democracy is an ideal that no empirical case can ever attain, he used the term *polyarchy* to refer to actual cases that could be studied empirically. His concept of polyarchy was distinguished by (1) its focus on the procedural aspects of democracy as opposed to substantive outcomes and (2) its definition of democracy in terms of two core dimensions, contestation and participation. Although the term *polyarchy* has not displaced the more popular term *democracy,* Dahl's conceptualization is an obligatory point of reference in the large comparative politics literature on democracy.

In the 1980s, Dahl published three widely read books on democratic theory, *Dilemmas of Pluralist Democracy* (1982), *A Preface to Economic Democracy* (1985), and *Democracy and Its Critics* (1989). These books focused on the past and present gap between democratic ideals and actual institutions. They also explored persistent challenges to democracy, such as the economic inequalities created by market capitalism. His most recent book, *How Democratic is the American Constitution?* (2001c), became a subject of public discussion in the wake of the discrepancy between the electoral and popular votes in the presidential election of 2000.

Dahl was born in Inwood, Iowa, in 1915. He received his B.A. from the University of Washington in 1936 and his Ph.D. in political science from Yale University in 1940. He taught at Yale (1946–86), becoming a professor emeritus in 1986. He was president of the American Political Science Association (APSA) in 1966–67. He was elected to the American Academy of Arts and Sciences in 1960 and to the National Academy of Sciences in 1972.

Intellectual Formation and Training

Q: You grew up in small-town America in the 1920s and started graduate school in political science at Yale in 1936.[1] I understand you went to graduate school hoping to have a career in government.

1. Dahl was born in a town in Iowa with a population of less than a thousand. He moved to Alaska with his family when he was ten and grew up in Skagway, a town with a population of

A: My ambition as an undergraduate, and certainly as a graduate student,was to go into public life. After my first year in Yale's Ph.D. program in political science, I went to work in Washington, D.C. This was in 1937, at the height of the New Deal. I had a very influential year-long experience as an intern in the Division of Economic Research at the National Labor Relations Board (NLRB) in Washington. Several things about that internship had a very powerful and lasting impact on my life.

First, I met the woman who would later become my wife. She was a student at Wellesley College who was interning at the NLRB. Also, I got to know Jewish people for the first time. In the little town in Alaska where I grew up, there was one nominally Jewish family, and I had some Jewish acquaintances at the University of Washington, where I did my undergraduate studies. But until my NLRB internship I hadn't really gotten to know Jewish people. Luckily for me most of the staff of the Division of Economic Research was Jewish. They came from New York, from Brooklyn or the Bronx, and were mostly second-generation immigrants whose parents had migrated from Poland or Russia. And they were all radicals of one stripe or another. There were Trotskyites, Norman Thomas socialists, social democrats, and probably a Stalinist or two. This was new to me, and it had a very powerful impact. Although my Jewish colleagues weren't much older than I, I admired the quality of their judgment, and primarily under the influence of some of these people I joined the Socialist Party at the end of that year in Washington. When I came back to Yale to continue my graduate studies, I chose to write my doctoral dissertation on the topic of socialist programs and democratic politics (Dahl 1940a).

Q: What was the graduate training in political science like at Yale during the 1930s?

A: It was a very tiny, and not particularly distinguished, department. Francis Coker, who was my mentor more than anyone else, had recently been president of the American Political Science Association, and he was the best known member of the department. He had written a book called *Recent Political Thought* (Coker 1934) that traced the development of socialism from the utopian socialists to the Guild Socialists and Marxism. There was a young faculty member, Harvey Mansfield, not to be confused with his son, who currently teaches at Harvard. Harvey was a dry person, but I came to like him a great deal. He taught American government and administration, and I learned whatever I did learn about that subject from him.

Besides Coker and Mansfield, there was Cecil Driver, an Englishman

about five hundred. On Dahl's early formative experiences, see Dahl (2005). See also Dahl (1997a, 1997b).

who had gotten his Ph.D. at the London School of Economics. He was a fine scholar, though he never published very much and was barely known outside New Haven. He published one book about a nineteenth-century British Tory who was in some sense a Radical (Driver 1946). Driver taught comparative government. In those days, Herman Finer's book (Finer 1932) was the main text in comparative government courses at Yale and elsewhere. If I remember correctly, that text concentrated on the United States, Britain, France, with perhaps a little bit on fascism and the Soviet Union. At that time, comparative government was a very narrow field with a primarily historical, descriptive, and institutional content. There was a lot of valuable information, but the study of comparative government was not theoretical, at least not in the sense of theory as we mean it today. Fortunately, we could take courses in the Law School, and I took courses in constitutional and labor law, as well as on business law and regulation. Those law courses helped round out what was not offered in the Government Department.

Q: You mentioned that comparative government during the 1930s had a very heavy institutional content. What did institutional analysis mean then?
A: It meant a focus on constitutions, whether it was the British unwritten constitution, the constitution of the French Third Republic, or the American Constitution. Political parties were also extremely important, as were the judiciary and the executive. I don't remember much emphasis on the significance of federalism. Overall, the field was very Eurocentric. There was no study of Japan or China, for example.

Q: Did people recognize this parochialism? Did they scratch their heads and say, "This is too narrow, where are Japan and China?"
A: I don't think we did. There may have been some people who wanted to study the Soviet Union. But until the outbreak of World War II, our horizons were really quite limited. The big thing going on in the world was the New Deal. Very few people had mastered the languages, even Russian, that were required to understand non-European countries. Even Latin America —a rich treasure house of experience nearby—was not within our ambit. I don't think we studied Canada. It was all very parochial.

Q: What books and authors had the most influence on you during graduate school?
A: I would say the classics of political science. Looking back, the writers who had the most impact on my thinking were people with whom I disagreed, but who were more than worthy political opponents. They were giants, and because they were giants they set down a challenge I could struggle with my

entire life. They include Plato, for example. *The Republic* (Plato 1946), as you can see from my writing, has had a tremendous impact on me, not because I accept Plato's version of the good life, but because I challenge and reject it. I read Plato in graduate school and later assigned *The Republic* in my early teaching. Another major figure whom I first encountered in graduate school and who played a similar role in my intellectual development is Rousseau, especially his work on the social contract. I saw Rousseau as another adversary like Plato, because he set down a challenge to the Greek notion of democracy based on small, intimate groups. Rousseau posed the question, how can you have a democracy on a grand scale? How can you enlarge democracy yet still retain the quality of representation that is potentially attainable in the smaller demos? That's something I've been fascinated by my whole life.

I also studied a lot of Marx as a graduate student. It may seem less so today, but Marx was a powerful and worthy adversary in the political and ideological culture of the 1930s and 1940s, and even into the 1950s and 1960s. By the end of my graduate studies and in the course of writing my dissertation, I decided that Marx as a theorist was totally unsatisfactory, that none of his theory, from the labor theory of value to his class theory, was satisfactory. To some extent, this put me out of phase with many of my contemporaries. I've never been a Marxist, though I'm indebted to him. Marx was an amazing scholar, and the logic and reasoning of his argument in *Capital* (Marx 1930) are very powerful.

Schumpeter was another major thinker with whom I disagreed early on, especially his reduction of the democratic process to a competition between elites. I did not encounter Schumpeter until about 1950, after his *Capitalism, Socialism, and Democracy* (Schumpeter 1942) had appeared. C. E. Lindblom and I assigned that book in a graduate seminar we jointly taught for some years and that led in turn to our *Politics, Economics and Welfare* (Dahl and Lindblom 1953). Elite theory was very important in my formation, and I appreciated Schumpeter's insight that competition among elites could produce desirable results in the taming of power, but I felt this was incomplete. He did not adequately explore the institutional requirements and the elements of popular participation on which the elite depends. In fairness to Schumpeter, I should go back and reread him to make sure I'm right.

Q: Mosca and Pareto were also important elite theorists. Were you influenced by them?
A: Yes, I read Pareto and was influenced by him. I don't know whether I read Mosca in graduate school or later on. Mosca and Pareto provide the classic formulation of ruling elite theory. These are powerful voices from the socio-

logical tradition of elite studies. A more important early influence on me
was the legal pluralist Léon Duguit. His work was assigned in an undergraduate course on jurisprudence by a teacher whom I much admired at the
University of Washington. And Coker's book, *Recent Political Thought,* had a
chapter on the legal pluralists. Duguit posed a challenge to the standard
notions of legal sovereignty by focusing on divisions within the state. He
argued that there is no single, unified source of sovereignty. Another early
influence on me was Harold Laski, who, with his wife, translated Duguit
from French into English (Duguit 1919). Laski became a legal pluralist and
wrote a lot about that. This was before his Marxist stage. I met Laski a
few times but wouldn't say I knew him. He was a younger friend of Coker,
and he visited Yale from time to time. Laski was a significant figure back
then, but I don't suppose any graduate student today knows about him. He
doesn't seem to have left any great legacy.

**Q: How did this early exposure to the work of the legal pluralists influ-
ence you?**
A: The more complex vision of political reality of the legal pluralists, as
opposed to an excessively simple monistic vision, appealed to me in some
latent way. But I want to make clear that I myself never developed a theory
of pluralism, though I've been said to have developed such a theory. I have
a theory of *democracy* in which organizational pluralism plays a part, but I
never tried to advance a theory of pluralism.

**Q: Did Weber and Tocqueville have much of a formative influence on
you?**
A: I didn't read Weber or Tocqueville until after graduate school. I don't
remember having ever made extensive use of Weber, though I was of course
influenced by his work, as everybody was. His notion of ideal types sub-
liminally had a great deal of influence on me. This can be seen in the
distinction I later drew between democracy as an ideal system and polyarchy as an imperfect approximation of that ideal (Dahl 1971, 9).

Tocqueville plays a very interesting part in my intellectual life, and I've
had a wonderful, slightly adversarial dialogue with him. I did not encounter Tocqueville until after I became a faculty member, when I read both
volumes of *Democracy in America* (Tocqueville 1969). I never read his other
work about the ancien régime (Tocqueville 1955), I mean, I read it, but not
with equal care. But *Democracy in America,* especially the first volume, had a
very important influence on my thinking. Like everybody else, the two
aspects of the first volume that caught my attention were, first, Tocqueville's emphasis on equality among Americans and the idea that equality
had almost a divine source and would keep on rolling indefinitely, and,

second, his focus on the importance of associational life. Very recently I've come to disagree with Tocqueville. In the second volume of *Democracy in America*, the more pessimistic volume, you can interpret Tocqueville as saying there was a high likelihood democracy would decline into petty tyrannies that encroach on basic rights. I think he is mistaken with that projection. If you look at the history of democratic countries, what you see is an *expansion* of rights, not Tocqueville's gloomy projection of a decrease of rights. The more I think about that, the more I believe democracy is an open-ended system of rights, opportunities, obligations, and, more radically, resources, because if you don't have the resources to enjoy rights, then they are meaningless. In democratic countries there is usually an unfolding and expansion of these rights, in both depth and breadth, to more people. The history of the democracies that have existed for more than fifty years shows that the idea of democracy is open-ended. Tocqueville's pessimistic view of the future of democracies does not fit what has happened.

Q: It is quite extraordinary that a young graduate student in his twenties would regard giants like Plato, Rousseau, and Marx, as adversaries and intellectual opponents.
A: I think of it more as an imaginary dialogue. The most productive dialogues are not adversarial in the sense of trying to win points, like in a tennis game. I think of it as dialectical in the Platonic and Hegelian sense. I start here, my adversary is over there. I move over a little bit, then they move to a new position, and so forth. Conversations like that are rare. When you have one, you come out of it feeling great. Of course, the classics are static in a sense—they're not going to change—but I like to think of my use of them as moving in a dialectical way.

Q: Did you really see it that way when you were a graduate student?
A: I doubt it. It was probably more tennis-like adversarial.

Q: You wrote your dissertation on the compatibility between socialist programs and democratic politics. What did you learn from the dissertation experience?
A: In the course of writing my dissertation I came more firmly to the conclusion that the theoretical foundations of Marx were wrong. I also came to two other conclusions that remained with me. One was that nationalization of industry was not the way to go, even though European social democrats generally thought it was the way to go. I also began to reach the conclusion that a modern economy required a market system, and I became interested in market socialism. If you had market socialism, you might need some form of collective ownership, but simply nationalizing an industry

and turning it into something like the U.S. Post Office was not enough. There had to be a market; you had to have competition. In fact, the first article I ever published, which appeared in 1940 in a journal called *Plan Age* (Dahl 1940b), made this point about the need for markets. That article came right out of my dissertation. I don't think I modified a word of it. I don't know if it was cause and effect or not, but that journal disappeared with the issue in which my article appeared! I didn't publish anything again for seven years.

Q: Is this because you went back to work in Washington, D.C., after you finished your dissertation?
A: As I said at the outset, my ambition in graduate school was to go into public life. In 1940, I moved to Washington and spent about three years there. I worked first in the Department of Agriculture, in the secretary's office. Then I moved to several government bureaus engaged in economic mobilization for the war effort. I became very dissatisfied with that kind of life and was increasingly dubious about my ability to make a contribution as a bureaucrat. I felt I just didn't fit in. I found myself in the branch of the Office of Civilian Supply that recommended allocations of steel. It was an extraordinary instance of a highly successful central planning system in a wartime economy. But, to give an example of why I was increasingly dissatisfied, I'd be allocating the amount of steel for safety pins for diapers. Back then you had to have safety pins for diapers.

I found myself drawn more and more not to the struggles to manage the bureaucracy, but to research, which was neither very interesting nor very important research. For example, you might need to determine the amount of steel used over the past ten years to make safety pins. I just felt this was not something I wanted to do. Nor did I have the skill or ambition to become the head of a government bureaucracy. If you're going to thrive in Washington, you want to acquire power. I didn't have that kind of drive.

Q: Why not?
A: I don't know. It's just an element of my personality. I really don't have a good answer for that. I've written so much about power, yet I never had a strong desire for it. Maybe that's why I can write about it.

Q: So you left the bureaucracy and enlisted in the army.
A: For a variety of reasons and in a foolish, even irresponsible, way, because I was married and had a child, I wrote my draft board and said, "Take me." And they did. I ended up in the 44th Infantry Division and, probably because I had a Ph.D., was assigned to the intelligence and reconnaissance

platoon of the 71st Infantry. I suppose I was the only one in the whole division with a Ph.D. and probably one of the few with a college degree. We arrived in Europe in September 1944 and went into combat in late November. We went out on patrols between our lines and theirs, typically at night, thank heavens.

Q: That sounds extremely dangerous.
A: It was very dangerous. But if you have well-trained men, and we were very well trained, we were good, it's less risky compared to what the guys in the rifle companies experienced. One of the good things about being in a reconnaissance platoon is that part of your job is to *get back* with the information. You're no good if you're dead. So you don't have to stay out there. If you're getting flares overhead, and the enemy is beginning to shoot at you, you can move out. It was very dangerous, and I felt it was quite possible I would not survive. But, dangerous as it was, there were people in much more dangerous positions.

The third day in combat in November 1944, I became a fatalist. However, I decided I would be prudent and not do anything foolish. I realized there was an element of chance and luck beyond my control, but within that, I would be prudent. So I became a prudent fatalist. But I also gained clarity about my future. Sometime between November 1944 and May 1945, somewhere in France or Germany, it became clear to me that the things I liked to do most were read, write, and talk about ideas. So the light came on, and I decided that if I survived I would be an academic.

The Behavioral Revolution

Q: When World War II ended, you took a job as an instructor back at Yale in 1946. In the 1950s you became associated with the behavioral revolution launched in political science during that period. Could you discuss how you got involved in the behavioral movement?
A: In the 1950s, I served on the Committee on Political Behavior, a brand-new committee of the Social Science Research Council (SSRC). V. O. Key was on it, as was David Truman. Important developments in public opinion research and election studies were beginning to happen at places like Columbia and Michigan, and I knew little about the methodologies being used in this work. I began to feel that I needed to know more about statistics and methodology in general. When I first came to Yale as a graduate student in the 1930s, there was no course on statistics and no course on methodology. I felt both I and the Yale department could benefit very much by hiring people like Robert Lane who were engaged in statistical, empirical,

scientific research. During this period I also read Carl Hempel's work with keen interest and was very influenced by his positivist ideas about the importance of empirical verification. I participated in innumerable discussions with Hempel at that time, because we were neighbors and friends as well as members of the same daily carpool.

Q: What attracted you to positivism?
A: Although much of this has become conventional wisdom by now, the notion that you needed to be able to formulate a hypothesis and then test it, if you were talking about the empirical world, was not widely accepted in political science back then. With regard to testing hypotheses, I was aware from an early time that the experimental method had limited application in political science, and always would. This meant that in political science statistical techniques were the appropriate methodology for testing hypotheses. By the late 1950s, a wide range of new data was opening up, data that were unimaginable when I was in graduate school. In American politics, a great amount of new data was generated by surveys and other means. I felt that a department that was not up to speed methodologically was going to fall behind.

Q: And you thought Yale's Government Department was not up to speed?
A: We definitely were not. A rivalry in the department had blocked progress. The rivalry was between Cecil Driver, a strong personality and powerful teacher who attracted many students, and a political theorist named Wilmoore Kendall. Kendall was a brilliant guy with misspent intellectual and personal potential. The rivalry between Driver and Kendall was hard on the graduate students, who often had to choose sides. The rivalry also made it uncomfortable for the chairman of the department V. O. Key. It was a bad time that was only resolved when Kendall resigned. Then James Fesler came in as chair, and he was a healer.[2] Driver eventually retired, and the department became highly harmonious, almost the opposite of what it had been. Fesler decided that the Government Department was out of the mainstream of American political science, and one way of putting it into the mainstream was to change its name to the Department of Political Science. As much as I admired what my dear friend Jim Fesler accomplished here, I've always regretted that he changed the name. I preferred "government" as a title for the department, like the Government Department at Harvard or the Politics Department at Princeton. It's kind of snobbish, I suppose.

2. Key left Yale for Harvard because of the Kendall-Driver unpleasantness, and Fesler was brought in as his successor from North Carolina. Personal communication from Nelson W. Polsby, December 31, 2003.

Q: During the mid-1950s you spent an important year in Palo Alto at the Center for Advanced Study in the Behavioral Sciences, where you were exposed to game theory and social choice theory. In fact, you have written that you may have been the first American political scientist to use "Arrow's Theorem" about the instability of collective preferences (Arrow 1951; Dahl 1997b, 77).[3] Moreover, you used some formal notation in *A Preface to Democratic Theory* (Dahl 1956). In some ways, therefore, you were a precocious mathematical modeler. Could you discuss the year you spent at the center?

A: That year—1955–56—the center was packed with econometricians and game theorists. R. Duncan Luce and Howard Raiffa were both there.[4] They were very interesting and likable people. I sat in on their seminars and realized how little I knew. That year I also met and became close friends with Ken Arrow, a marvelous man. My friend, neighbor, and collaborator at Yale, Charles Lindblom, had told me about Arrow beforehand, because he had recently learned of Arrow's work at a seminar on mathematics and the social sciences.

Q: Did you sense something exciting and attractive about the new tools of game theory and mathematical modeling?

A: Yes, I did. Mathematical modeling seemed to hold the promise of providing fruitful insights into the complex realities of politics. I know that's very general, but after reading Ken Arrow's little book (1951), you sometimes look at voting patterns and alternatives in a different way. When I came back to Yale from the center, I felt I was so lacking in mathematical preparation that I actually sat in on an undergraduate mathematics course. When I got more adept at math, I also took a very good graduate statistics course by a close friend of mine, the economist James Tobin. I started to get up to speed with these methods. But I soon realized I would never be top-notch in statistics.

Q: Why not? Because of the limitations of your own skill set?

A: Yeah, and because of the kinds of problems I wanted to address. I also felt I could readily find collaborators who had better training in behavioral methods than I. The survey research in *Who Governs?* (Dahl 1961a) is the product of such a collaboration.

Q: Still, you wrote that you were somewhat skeptical at the time about the contribution game theory could make (Dahl 1997b, 72).

3. See Dahl (1956, 42–43), where he writes that "[Arrow's] brilliantly developed and quite startling argument has, unfortunately, so far been totally ignored by political scientists."

4. Luce and Raiffa wrote one of the earliest books on game theory (Luce and Raiffa 1957).

A: I was skeptical because the assumption of rational actors narrowed, and in a great many cases narrowed too much, the ability to develop a complex description, if I can use this word, of what I would regard as reality. Reducing reality to rational actors and how they would behave in a particular situation seemed to restrict the scope of analysis to a point where it might become irrelevant. Years later my colleagues at Yale, Don Green and Ian Shapiro, wrote a book, *Pathologies of Rational Choice Theory* (Green and Shapiro 1994), that essentially argued just this point. I do think that placing too much emphasis on rational choice is a worrisome trend in political science, though I also think rational choice theory has a place. My intuition tells me there will be situations where the assumption of rational actors may lead to answers that are relevant. I'd hate to be pushed to describe what those situations are, I don't think I can. So I don't want to see rational choice theory ruled out or abandoned, but I don't want to see it take over the field either. I don't think rational choice theory will take over the field, though it may take over some departments. I also think it may have expanded to the detriment of other parts of political science.

Q: Does the recent advocacy of rational choice theory in political science remind you of the behavioral revolution of the 1950s?
A: It has something of that same quality. As I said, I served on the SSRC Committee on Political Behavior. And I thought it did a lot of good work. The people on the committee were a pretty broad group, and we subsidized a lot of good scholars and good research. But I eventually came to the conclusion that there were lots of questions, especially historical questions, that the behavioral movement could not deal with very well (Dahl 1961b). Rational choice theory does not deal with historical developments very well either.

Q: What were the lasting contributions of the behavioral revolution?
A: Behavioralism contributed to revolutionizing the field methodologically by establishing the importance and desirability of quantitative analysis, good empirical data, and hypothesis testing. Those notions were elementary from the point of view of behavioral scientists, and they are now standard in political science. There are very few people today who would deny them. So, in a sense we are all behavioralists now. And even those who are not behavioralists in any sense—for example, somebody whose interest is in the history of political ideas—would not fight against behavioralism and say, "You can't have people like that in our department." The behavioral revolution also made lasting contributions in survey research. It also made substantive contributions that will stay. We know a lot more than we did.

I'm biased here, but I think the lasting methodological and substantive contributions of the behavioral revolution may be greater than those of rational choice. The notion that we should limit our models to ones that can be based on rational action restricts the potentiality of rational choice theory. Overall, the basic assumptions of rational choice theory seem far more self-limiting than those of behavioralism.

Research on Political Oppositions, Polyarchy, and Democratic Theory
Entry into Comparative Politics

Q: You started out as an Americanist, writing your first book on American foreign policy (Dahl 1950), and by the mid-1950s you had moved into political theory with *A Preface to Democratic Theory* (Dahl 1956). You did not begin working in comparative politics until later, during the early 1960s. What motivated your entry into comparative politics?
A: In the late 1950s, I began to realize that my comparative knowledge was very limited. I had not been outside the United States since World War II, when I was a soldier in France, Germany, and briefly in Austria. But that was probably not the best way to learn about a foreign country. I started to get this feeling that I was just focusing on the United States, lacked a good comparative background, and needed to know more about other systems. I think the first time I went abroad after the war, unless you count Canada, was an International Political Science Association meeting in Rome in 1959. Like 99 percent of the people who go to Rome for the first time, I was entranced by it. A couple of years later, when I had a sabbatical and was beginning to write my textbook on American government (Dahl 1967), I decided if I was going to write about the United States, I was going to go abroad and get an outside perspective. I was directly influenced by Tocqueville when I made that decision—Tocqueville came from the outside to write about the United States. So I went to Rome in 1962 with my wife and two youngest children and spent a year there.

During that year in Rome two comparative projects began to come together. One was my project on oppositions. The role of oppositions in political systems struck me as an obvious question that needed to be addressed. Work had been done on political parties, but the role of oppositions seemed totally unexplored. Second, I began a comparative project on the smaller European democracies, such as the Netherlands, Norway, Sweden, and Austria. I think it was Hans Daalder who said to me, "The smaller European democracies have not been adequately studied; even within those countries themselves there are no studies of their political systems." Stein Rokkan was an obvious choice to join a working group on this topic. Then I added an old friend, Val Lorwin, who knew a lot about Belgium. He had lived in France, was fluent in French, and had become interested in Belgium. Together we set up the smaller European democracies project.

Q: Of the two comparative projects that started during your sabbatical year in Rome, one succeeded and one failed. The oppositions project resulted in the influential 1966 volume on political oppositions and the follow-up 1973 volume on this topic (Dahl 1966a, 1973), whereas the smaller democracies project never really took off, at least in terms of resulting in visible publications.[5] Could you comment on this?
A: Though the results are not visible in a volume, the smaller democracies project was really enormously successful. We recruited scholars from each of the small European democracies to write a chapter in a single volume, and we got together often at the Villa Serbelloni in Belagio, Italy. Then, primarily under the impulse of Stein Rokkan, the goal expanded from a chapter to an entire book on each of the dozen or so countries. Although we never produced the books or the volume, the people we had recruited to do the books were, like Rokkan himself, very active in the study of political science in their countries. So an important spin-off from the smaller de-mocracies project—and I don't want to claim too much—was to stimulate research within and on these countries. Today there is a rich body of writing about the political systems of the smaller European democracies. The impe-tus for this work partly came from the group that participated in the smaller democracies project. So, I don't think of that project as a failure, except that we didn't produce the books.

Q: Why didn't you produce the books?
A: I think that when we expanded the project from a series of essays to whole books, we overloaded the participants. Many, including Stein Rok-kan himself, had gotten involved in setting up the European Data Infor-mation Service of the European Consortium for Political Research (ECPR), and they were all writing about their countries, but not in the format we had proposed. My book *Size and Democracy,* with Ed Tufte (Dahl and Tufte 1973), in a sense came out of the smaller democracies project. That book was very much a product of thinking about small democracies.

Q: What explains the contrasting success of your other comparative project, on political oppositions, in terms of actually producing the proposed volumes?

5. Chubb's book on Ireland (1970) was the only country study to result directly from the project on smaller democracies.

A: I very carefully formulated the theoretical framework from the get go and then refined it in the initial discussions with the participants in the project. Without that framework as the basis for the volume, it could easily have dispersed into unrelated essays about opposition politics in various countries. Having good people involved was also essential.

Q: How do you pick good people?
A: By reputation. Obviously I couldn't know everyone or read all their works. Stein Rokkan was an enormous resource, because he knew all the European universities and scholars in a way I never did. Likewise, Hans Daalder knew so much about this.

Polyarchy

Q: Your most influential work in comparative politics is *Polyarchy* (Dahl 1971). Polyarchy is a concept with staying power—thirty years later, your formulation of the concept in terms of the two dimensions, contestation and participation, endures. Could you discuss how you went about forming this concept?
A: Let me first say something about the word *polyarchy*. Lindblom and I used the term in our book, *Politics, Economics, and Welfare* (Dahl and Lindblom 1953), though we did not pull out those two dimensions, contestation and participation. We did not want to use the word *democracy*, because it blurred the distinction between democratic ideals and democratic realities. So we called a friend of mine in the Classics Department at Yale, Ed Silk, and he actually came up with the term *polyarchy*. It was only years later that I discovered the term had been used in the early seventeenth century by Johannes Althusius (1964, 200).

Q: You could have chosen many attributes to analyze democratic political regimes. Why did you choose those particular dimensions—contestation and participation (Dahl 1971, 4–6)?
A: Those dimensions seemed to be two things that were fundamental parts of a democratic system. I thought the tensions between them would help focus attention on the relevant theoretical and empirical aspects of democratic systems.

Q: But there are other essential parts of democratic systems. Around the time you were writing *Polyarchy*, Stein Rokkan developed his own scheme with four dimensions: the same two you used—contestation and participation—plus two more: representation and executive ac-

countability to the legislature (Rokkan et al. 1970). Why did you stick to just two dimensions?

A: I suppose I stuck to two dimensions because I felt the drastically simplified theoretical structure provided by those two dimensions would be fruitful, especially for seeking and finding historical relationships and patterns. That was my intuition. If that simplified structure had not provided fruitful questions and inquiries, I would have abandoned it. I would have gone back and done more. In general, I was not comfortable with Rokkan's more complex formulations.

Q: In the end, your formulation is the one that got picked up, not Rokkan's.

A: That may have been because of the simple, easy-to-grasp tension between the two dimensions I chose.

Q: During the late 1960s, when you were working on *Polyarchy*, a number of major works appeared in comparative politics. For example, Samuel Huntington's *Political Order in Changing Societies* was published in 1968. Did that have an impact on you?

A: I read Sam's stuff, and I came to know and respect him. But I was never close to him. I often felt his take on political systems and political change was different from mine, especially in his earlier work. He was rather more sympathetic toward military regimes than I felt myself to be. I always learned from his work, but we were viewing the world and democracy in somewhat different ways.

Q: Another major work from this period is Barrington Moore's *Social Origins of Dictatorship and Democracy* (1966).

A: I certainly knew the book, but I don't know that it had the deep impact on me that it probably deserved.

Q: Why not? I imagine Moore's book was more normatively appealing to you than Huntington's.

A: Yes, it was. But I didn't spend a lot of time thinking about and pondering Moore's book. Its impact may have been more indirect.

Q: Gabriel Almond and Sidney Verba's *The Civic Culture* (1963) was another important work in comparative politics published in the 1960s. Did that influence you?

A: Almond and Verba's book had a big influence on me, both substantively and as part of my methodological education. I remember reading it carefully. Almond and Verba helped me see the potential for comparative stud-ies using survey research. They were pioneers in this area.

Q: Did you know that *Polyarchy* was going to be such a big hit? Did you have a hunch people would still be reading it thirty years later?
A: No, I never have had a very good judgment about how people are going to receive what I've written. Books are a little bit like children, you love them all, but for different reasons. I didn't have any expectations that *Poly-archy* would be read after thirty years. Hopes, yes, but expectations, no.

Works on Democratic Theory after *Polyarchy*

Q: Since the publication of *Polyarchy*, you have written a series of widely read books—*Dilemmas of Pluralist Democracy* (1982), *A Preface to Economic Democracy* (1985), *Democracy and Its Critics* (1989), and *On Democracy* (1998)—that have greatly influenced scholarly thinking about democracy. Could you discuss the common intellectual thread that runs through these works, the core ideas you have sought to de-velop in these books, and the key conclusions about democracy you reached as a result of your thinking and research on the topic?
A: The more I thought about democratic theory, the more I became aware of several things. First, after more than two millennia of theory and practice, I thought we still lacked an adequate contemporary exposition. Second, a lot of what one would need in order to formulate work along these lines was already lying around in scattered and unrelated bits and pieces.

However, I don't think I ever explicitly thought to myself, "Now, I'm going to try to create a coherent body of democratic theory." Even *A Preface to Democratic Theory* was just that, a preface, and a very incomplete preface, too. Instead, I was stimulated by questions that I thought were impor-tant and relevant, and they generally turned out to be questions about democratic theory and practice. Most of my books begin with a question or a problem, and these deal more often than not with some aspect of democracy.

For many years I taught an undergraduate course and sometimes a grad-uate seminar called, guess what, "Democracy and Its Critics." Some of what I wrote was a by-product of my explorations there, including, of course, *Democracy and Its Critics*.

The central elements of the views that evolved bit by bit are my effort to treat democracy in a way that is consistent with its origins and history; distinguishes ideal and actual; allows for the past, present, and future evo-lution of both democratic ideals and actual institutions, particularly the development of large-scale democracy or polyarchy; recognizes the enormous gap between ideal and reality; presents some persistent challenges; and offers some views on future possibilities. It was only in *Democracy and Its Critics*, though, that I tried pretty much to touch on all these matters—and perhaps, in a much more concise way, in *On Democracy*.

An important aspect of my thinking about democracy that has become increasingly prominent, I believe, is my emphasis on the fundamental moral principles that in my view justify democracy—and no alternative to it. This is the principle of political equality, and the two basic principles on which it is in turn justified. These are a moral judgment that the interests, or good, of each human being are entitled to equal consideration in making government decisions, and a prudential judgment that in making governmental decisions, among adults no person or group is better qualified, with only extremely rare exceptions, to judge what those interests are and thus to substitute their judgment for that of the person whose interests are affected. The claim of one group to possess superior knowledge of the interests of another group of persons, and also to possess a reliable commitment to protect those interests, seems to me utterly falsified by historical experience. To see how hollow that claim is we need only recall the denial of full political rights to the working class, the unpropertied, women, and nonwhites.

Missed Opportunities

Q: Are there any projects that in hindsight you wish you had done but did not?
A: In a lifetime we can only do so many things. I wish I had taken the subject of size and democracy further. The whole issue of scale has fascinated me from the beginning and continues to fascinate me. My book with Ed Tufte, *Size and Democracy* (Dahl and Tufte 1973), opens up the problem of scale. But I regret that I have not had and won't have more time to think that through. If I were twenty years younger, I would mine the problem of scale. I have this intuition that in human relations, and specifically in the domain of political life, there are thresholds where relationships change in important ways: the threshold from 2 to 3, from 10 to 50, from 100 to 1,000, and so on. I don't know where the thresholds are and they probably are not exact, but we all know they are very critical. That needs to be explored in some better way, though I'm not sure what methodology would be appropriate, maybe experimentation.

Yesterday I attended a "deliberative polling" session organized by the political scientist Jim Fishkin. The idea behind a deliberative poll is to get a sample that is large enough to make statistical inferences but also representative when checked against census data. You bring a relatively large group of 150 to 250 people together and randomly form them into small groups of, say, fifteen. The small groups are led by a moderator, and they discuss a problem, in this case how to expand our dinky little New Haven airport in a way that will not damage the wetlands. The groups also discussed the problem of how the different local jurisdictions involved should share the new tax revenues that an airport expansion would generate. I sat in as an observer, and it was very heartening to hear these people discuss the issue with one another. People changed their minds through the process, not drastically, but they were learning. That can be done on a small scale, with a group of fifteen, in a way that cannot be done through the Internet or through a meeting with thousands and thousands of people. I have said for years that I would like to see something that combines small- and larger-scale deliberation institutionalized in American life for all sorts of issues.

I also probably should have written one more article on defining democracy, on my use of democracy as an ideal type in two senses. The first way I use democracy as an ideal type is simply as an abstract definition of what democracy would be given certain assumptions. This way of using democracy resembles Galileo's use of the vacuum to determine the rate of a falling body. Galileo did not actually have a vacuum, he assumed it, and then he defined the rate of a falling body as if it were in a vacuum. The second way I use democracy as an ideal type, and I have often confused the two, is in the sense of something to be aspired to. Now, you could propose democracy as an ideal type in the first sense and reject it, in principle, as a desirable state of affairs.

The Future of Democracy

Q: You have been studying democracy for more than fifty years. What are the major contemporary problems and trends students of democracy should be working on today?
A: That's a huge question. There are a number of serious problems on the horizon that worry me. One problem, which I've been very interested in my entire academic life going back to my dissertation, concerns the relationship between democracy and market capitalism. Later in life, I have regrettably come to the conclusion that there is no feasible alternative to market capitalism on the horizon. Throughout the nineteenth century and during most of my lifetime, it was possible to believe there was a structural alternative to market capitalism, but unfortunately that's just not plausible anymore. On the other hand, there are structural alternatives to democracy,

which is unfortunate for those of us who want democracy to survive and expand. Powerful tensions exist between market capitalism and democracy. A fundamental and inescapable quality of market capitalism, and even of a socialist market economy if it could exist, is that it unavoidably creates inequalities in resources, not just in wealth, but also in status, prestige, communication, and access to information. These inequalities are all convertible into political resources and can thus undermine political equality. The danger market capitalism poses for political equality is as serious now as it has ever been, both in our own country and in countries with weaker democratic traditions. That tension will have to be managed, and I don't think this can be done with the simplistic doctrines currently out there—that the market is so great you always have to bow to it, or, alternatively, that you can constantly take care of the inequalities created by the market by regulating it. I don't feel at all confident that we have solved this very old problem, and I worry that a kind of ratchet effect may be emerging that makes it impossible to reduce economic inequalities after they arise (Dahl 1993, 2001a).

There are also some relatively new problems facing democracies today. One involves the somewhat meaningless word *globalization* and its consequences. The extreme view is that the process of globalization will empty the democratic content from the nation-state. I don't believe that's true. My view is that the nation-state—I actually prefer the term *country,* because so many countries are not nations—will in some ways become more necessary as a means of dealing with the impacts of globalization. Still, lots of decisions are going to be made increasingly by international organizations, and I am skeptical about the possibilities of democracy in international organizations. A lot of the preconditions that most people think are necessary for democracy don't exist in international organizations, probably not even in the European Union (EU), though I think the EU is the most promising case for eventually becoming a democratic international organization. The last time I looked at the University of Michigan website, I counted about ninety international organizations, and a lot of them are damn important.[6] I've come up with three assumptions, or axioms: (1) international organizations are extremely important; (2) international organizations are likely to increase their influence and importance; and (3) international organizations are unlikely to be democratic (Dahl 1999, 2001b). If all three axioms prove correct, then we have a problem that will not go away. It's absolutely imperative that we come up with a system to make international decisions in an accountable and acceptable way, but it

6. www.lib.umich.edu/govdocs/intl.html.

won't be what we know as democracy. That's an extraordinary challenge, and your generation has to find answers to that problem. I certainly don't have them.

Q: But your generation has lived with international organizations like the International Monetary Fund (IMF), the United Nations (UN), and the World Bank for more than fifty years.
A: That's right, and the IMF and World Bank are examples of what I'm talking about. They impose decisions on countries that are not always in the best interest of the people of those countries. But these kinds of organizations are essential. We have to have something like them.

Let me turn to a third problem facing democracies today. I gave a talk in Seoul, South Korea, about ten years ago that called attention to the problem of immigration. I said that immigration would become a major issue in all the European countries and that the American model of assimilation would not work in those countries for various reasons. That talk was published as an English article in Korea (Dahl 1997c). I don't think anybody has read or paid attention to it, and probably for good reason. But meanwhile, what I argued has come true. For many of the European countries, especially the homogeneous ones like the Scandinavian countries, coping with the challenges posed by immigration and cultural diversity has been difficult. Amazingly, the country that seems to have dealt with these challenges in the most humane way so far is Germany. In the past fifteen to twenty years, we've lived through so many cases of—I don't want to use the old word *genocide*—enormous death and destruction of people who have different views of the world and how to act in the world. The daunting challenge of how to cope with immigration and cultural diversity is not going to go away.

Terrorism poses a fourth challenge to contemporary democracies. In the United States, we've already seen the erosion of our civil liberties after September 11. It hasn't gone far, but the weakening of civil liberties could go much farther if there were another highly destructive terrorist event, or a series of them. The erosion of civil liberties would not necessarily require that citizens agree with these restrictions, because the political momentum by itself could drive the process. In the making of foreign and military policy in this country, and this goes back to my first book on foreign policy (Dahl 1950), there is an inherent tendency during times of crisis to shift power to the executive at the expense of civil liberties. This shift to the executive may even be inescapable.

I am an optimist by nature, while still a prudent fatalist, so I won't say these problems cannot be solved. But these are the kinds of challenges and real problems on the horizon that political scientists and others should be tackling. The consequences are so great.

The Research Process
The Study of Politics as a Science

Q: Do you think of yourself as a scientist?
A: In part, yes. I think of myself as comfortably combining the normative, ethical aspects of political science with the empirical, and thus the scientific, aspects of politic science. Many political scientists today unfortunately feel uncomfortable linking normative political theory with empirically grounded social science, to the detriment of both sides.

Q: Why is this unfortunate?
A: Because it is very hard to ask important research questions unless you define them in terms of their human value, in terms of what difference it will make if you answer them. Normative political theory, including the history of political ideas, is very useful for identifying relevant and important questions that are worth asking. Identifying a question that is important is a moral and normative issue, not a scientific issue. I thus worry about the consequences of a sharp separation between normative theory and empirical research. At the same time, I don't think everybody should try to bridge normative theory and empirical research. It's always important to be clear about which of the two domains one is writing about. I have sometimes been frustrated and disappointed when what I meant as empirical statements were mistakenly taken as normative ones. For example, I saw *Who Governs?* as a wholly empirical work, and I had a footnote saying that nothing in the book should be interpreted as endorsing "the program" of New Haven's mayor, Richard Lee, and I meant that (Dahl 1961a, 115). But many people have misread the book as a normative justification for Mayor Lee's policies.

Q: Why did so many readers see *Who Governs?* as a normative statement in favor of Mayor Lee's program?
A: That's a good question, and I'm not sure I entirely know the answer to it. One reason, but certainly not the only reason, was that my pluralistic interpretation challenged the influential, though not dominant, view that New Haven was being run by a small business elite. This quasi-Marxist, or Marxoid, interpretation was widely pervasive then in understanding local and national politics. I did not set out to challenge that interpretation in *Who Governs?* Rather, I tried to design a methodology that would be open-ended in the sense that if there were a tiny group of businessmen, or any other tiny

group, running things, the methodology would show that. If it turned out not to be that way, I wanted the methodology to show that too. And the book shows the latter. It is true that I had a lot of sympathy for Mayor Lee's attempts, maybe more than I should have. But I was never fully convinced that everything his administration was trying to do was good for New Haven, nor was I convinced it was bad for New Haven. I was trying to be neutral about the whole situation.

Q: This example highlights the fundamental tension between normative theory and value-free, or, as you put it, neutral, empirical research.
A: There is a tension, but it's a productive tension. Take someone like Machiavelli. He was a keen observer, and his writings are full of empirical propositions. But his data are quite inadequate. That's why the more hardnosed empiricists don't like it. With regard to moral propositions, the problem is how to verify them. Although the logical positivists in the most extreme form say moral propositions are nonsense, I've never believed moral propositions are meaningless, even under the strongest influence of my positivist friend Carl Hempel. Moral propositions may have a different way of guiding your life than do empirically verifiable propositions, but they're not meaningless.

Q: Scholars such as William Riker have argued that the lack of a unifying paradigm prevents political science from becoming a genuine science (Riker 1990). Should political science have a paradigm?
A: One first has to ask, *can* political science have a paradigm? It would be desirable if it were possible, but it may be impossible. Politics is one of the most complex activities that human beings engage in, and one reason for its complexity is that political life and political behavior is not static, it's not fixed. Politics is historically dependent at the atomistic level of individual humans and also at the big level of countries and international systems. The units involved in politics change over time. It's not like physics, where an atom or proton a million years ago presumably behaved the same way an atom or proton does today. That's not true of political life and political systems.

Q: Yet there are certainly regularities in political life, even if they are not universal and timeless.
A: There are regularities, and that is where the science of political science comes in. One needs to search for repetitive elements that can be observed; at the same time one also has to stay aware of changes and contingency. One may observe repetitive phenomena in political life that indicate a trend. And you can learn from that. Still, it's always important to keep in mind that in politics, as opposed to physics, the units change over time.

Just the other day I was thinking about playing a little game with a friend. Think of the different types of relationships that could exist in politics—dyadic, triadic, or multi-relational—and then think of the number of different types of possible combinations among those relationships. You quickly get a degree of complexity that is like the human nervous system or brain, with 5 billion connections or something like that. Just as with the brain, in spite of the overwhelming complexity, there are regularities in politics we are learning to identify. So you don't abandon the search for regularities, but complexity makes it very difficult for political science ever to be a hard science like physics, which reduces the physical world to very simple systems.

Q: I am struck by your deep appreciation for the complexity of politics given that one of your great skills is simplification, as illustrated by your reduction of democratic systems to two dimensions in *Polyarchy* (Dahl 1971).
A: Without simplification you cannot deal with complexity. You need some kind of map that simplifies reality. If you tried to make a map that charted everything out there, you'd be lost. You have to simplify in order to act in the world. We do that automatically. The problem is how to simplify so that the gains outweigh the losses.

Questions

Q: This leads us to the issue of how we go about studying this complex reality. You say it is important to justify our research questions by reference to normative political theory. But you also seem to take care to craft your research questions in a way that focuses your empirical investigations. Indeed, a hallmark of your intellectual style is that you often use a question in the titles of your books and begin them with a question.
A: I have always tried to formulate what I'm doing in an article or a book in the form of a question. Most of my books open with a question in the first paragraph. For example, *Who Governs?* starts with the question, how is democracy possible with economic inequality? My most recent book, *How Democratic is the American Constitution?* (Dahl 2001c), opens with the question, why should we obey the American Constitution? This technique so focuses the mind on what's to follow that I'm astounded when other people don't use it.

Q: Should a question be posed in a single sentence?
A: Not necessarily, though it helps if it can be. Usually what happens is that you ask the question and it unfolds into other questions. Although the

original question may continue to unfold into more questions throughout the book, it gives a framework for your research. Starting with a question also helps you select your methodology. It seems absolutely backward to start with methodology. If you have a question first, then you can decide what methods will help answer it.

Q: But where do the questions come from?

A: They come from a whole combination of things: a mixture of formal learning, engaging with the great minds, your personal experiences, and the experiences of your time. The times thrust questions at you. You don't have to invent them, they are presented to you. For example, the questions I raised about democracy and its survival in *Democracy and Its Critics* (Dahl 1989) reflect the concern that people of my generation had about democracy and the alternatives to it. We were concerned about whether democracy could survive in the face of threatening and appealing alternative systems, both theoretical and real alternatives.

Q: So your interest in addressing critics of democracy, like Plato, was not motivated purely by a philosophical objection to Plato's argument that democracy was not desirable. Rather, your life experiences had attuned you to real-world threats to democracy.

A: Very much so. And they're interconnected—the experience of the world around you and the possibilities and dangers it poses for democracy animates your interest in the philosophers.

Q: How do you actually go about "experiencing the world around you"? Do you read the newspaper, travel, talk to interesting people who visit Yale?

A: It's all those things. The personal experiences I had growing up in small towns and meeting people in small towns and later in the war were important. Encountering the world indirectly through newspapers and other media is also important, as are discussions with people around you. To some extent, and this is more common today than when I started, you encounter the world in foreign travel.

Q: Have you done a lot of foreign traveling?

A: I have, but not early on. Except for Canada, I had not been outside the United States until I went overseas as a soldier in 1944. That was typical of my generation. During the war, I greatly improved my reading capacity in both French and German. I never became highly fluent in either language, but my reading capacity in French became excellent. I could read novels. I think my greatest language fluency, speaking, but also reading, is in Italian.

Later, in preparation for a trip to Chile, I studied Spanish, and, as with French, my reading is excellent.

Q: Your point about how the times one lives in generate research questions raises a broader issue. I am reminded of the supposed Chinese curse, "May you live in interesting times." Is living in "interesting times" a blessing, not a curse, for social scientists? In your case, the traumatic experience of fighting in World War II helps explain your lifelong passion about studying democracy. What effect did living through the Great Depression, the New Deal, and World War II have on you?

A: Such experiences do tend to focus the mind. For people like me, the real threat during the 1930s and 1940s that democracy would end, that it would be destroyed, impressed on our generation the importance of democracy. We realized that the alternatives to democracy were so much worse. I don't think these experiences clouded our view of democracy's defects, because we understood that we had to commit ourselves not just to preserving democracy but also to removing the defects and the dangers to it. Living through World War II and the events leading up to it was a very powerful influence for all of us.

As for the New Deal, that influenced my conviction that change is possible. And because we lived through the Great Depression, many people of my generation do not have the consumerist psyche of my children's and grandchildren's generations, where a wonderful toy from a month or two ago is no longer worth anything. If you grew up with a toy made from a broom handle, you had some appreciation for the fundamental aspects of things.

These powerful early experiences live on in your memory, and some feelings and judgments formed early in life become a very important part of how you see and judge the world. This reminds me of a cartoon I saw in *The New Yorker* magazine a few years ago. It shows two characters, the proverbial Vikings wearing the horned hats that the Vikings never wore, standing under a tree, and one is saying to the other, "Is the world really going to hell, or are we just getting older?" This speaks to the danger of seeing changes in the world as not quite like the "good old days." But the good old days were the bad old days, in many, many ways. The world is really better off because of many of the changes that have happened since the New Deal.

Q: What can a young scholar growing up in the "good new days" do to find a surrogate for the rich, if traumatic, life experiences that helped focus the minds of many scholars of your generation?

A: That's a tough question. I can't think of a surrogate, though I can think of several things your generation has that mine did not. First, you travel a lot.

You come into contact with parts of the world that are different and challenging. You spend two months in a different world, like India or Africa, it doesn't really matter where. This puts you into contact with differences and helps cultivate an openness to diversity. My generation was much more parochial. Second, a lot of young people, and I'm thinking of undergraduates at Yale, but it's a fairly wide movement, spend time doing work in the community. Believe me, they are not the same when they finish their six or eight months doing something out in the community. That's a transformative experience. Finally, I think literature is very important, because it takes you into worlds you would not otherwise experience, whether it's *War and Peace, The Brothers Karamazov,* or whatever. Literature can help enlarge your sensitivity to differences.

Fieldwork

Q: Fieldwork would seem to be another way for young scholars today to gain experience. What role has fieldwork played in your research?
A: In writing my first book, *Congress and Foreign Policy* (Dahl 1950), I went to Washington regularly during the course of a year and interviewed people on Capitol Hill. There was a tradition in political science, rooted in parts of the Chicago School, where you went out and talked to people. I figured if I was going to write about Congress, I needed to know about it, and that required talking to some people. I did a lot of interviews, and that was quite enlightening. In fact, Dean Acheson asked me to come to Washington and do some research for his autobiography. I turned him down because I had been away from my family enough when I was in the army, and I didn't want an obligation that would have required me to spend more time away from them. I've never regretted that decision.

Who Governs? also involved extensive fieldwork, here in New Haven. For that I had the resource of graduate students, like Nelson Polsby and Raymond Wolfinger, who each got their dissertations out of the project. A lot of other graduate students were also involved in that study. We did a preliminary test of the methodology in Branford with a group of students in a graduate seminar of mine. I was fully involved in all the major interviews for *Who Governs?* I don't want to say there weren't any interviews where I wasn't present, but I participated in all the major interviews with all the major actors in business and politics.

Later, in the mid-1960s, I spent two months in Santiago, Chile, when Eduardo Frei was president. I was much taken with the Chilenos I met, especially with the quality of their public life. I was shocked when the country later became extremely polarized and the democratic regime collapsed. Looking back, I can see the seeds of that polarization, but I never would have predicted it, which might say something about how shallow my knowledge of Chile was. I developed an attachment to both the people and the country, and I went back two or three times under the military dictatorship at the invitation of the Christian Democratic opposition. Some socialists were at those meetings, too. I observed that, within certain limits, discussion was actually pretty free, though people had to know what the limits were. If they ventured outside those limits, they were in trouble.

Colleagues, Collaborators, and Students
Colleagues

Q: Over the years, you have interacted closely with many of the top people in the field. Which colleagues have had the greatest influence on your comparative work?
A: Stein Rokkan, certainly. He was a marvelous person and a marvelous scholar who combined the hallmarks of the European scholar, enormous erudition and historical knowledge, with a finely developed sense of the need for data and the methodology to handle them. I met Rokkan and Giovanni Sartori during the sabbatical year I spent in Rome in 1962–63. And they were both here at Yale as what we called rotating visiting professors. Rokkan and Sartori were about as different as a Norwegian and an Italian can be at the extremes. I remember walks and dinners with them, especially with Rokkan and his wife. I also took a number of trips to Norway when Rokkan was at Bergen, and I stayed over with him there. We had so many conversations.

Q: In the mid-1960s Rokkan was involved in an influential collaboration with the political sociologist, Seymour Martin Lipset (Lipset and Rokkan 1967a). Did you interact with Lipset?
A: I met Marty Lipset in California in 1955–56, when we were together at the Center for Advanced Study in the Behavioral Sciences. He had a young research assistant with him named Juan Linz whom I also met, though I did not get to know Juan terribly well then. I remember going with the Lipsets and with Herb McClosky and his wife to San Francisco to see one of the first performances of Arthur Miller's play, *The Crucible*. Marty had quite an acerbic view of some of the political interpretations being made of *The Crucible*. Elements of the Left were interpreting the play as a veiled reference to McCarthy witch-hunting, or something like that. Marty and I kept in touch after that year, and I felt close to him.

Q: Karl Deutsch, who was more a scholar of international relations, was your colleague at Yale during the 1960s. Did you have much contact with him?

A: Deutsch came to Yale while I was chairman of the department.[7] His hiring was part of the process where I, supported by others, including Bob Lane, who was a junior member of the faculty then, sought to recruit more scholars using behavioral methodologies and approaches. Karl became a very good friend, both socially and intellectually. He had an enormously creative and stimulating mind, with a wealth of knowledge. You could have lunch with Karl, and he would spin off twenty interesting ideas, nineteen of which might be absolutely wrong, but they were all creative and insightful. He was a powerful teacher, too powerful for some students who were suspicious of all these ideas and could not sort them out.

Deutsch and his students gathered cross-national data. This influenced me in thinking that quantitative cross-national research on democracies was not a hopeless undertaking because data to carry out such research would be available (Russett et al. 1964). Of course, I did not use quantitative data to the extent that Karl or his student, Bruce Russett, did in their work.

Q: Harold Lasswell was also at Yale during this period. Did he influence you?

A: Lasswell was an important influence. He and Deutsch got along well, and the three of us would go to lunch together. Lasswell was different in many ways from Deutsch, but, like Karl, he was full of interesting ideas. Lasswell was devoted to psychoanalytical approaches and also to the precision of language. He spoke very precisely and seemed to choose his words quite carefully. Many people found his vocabulary very daunting, and in some cases incomprehensible. But once you got used to the vocabulary, it was quite clear, I think. Lasswell's work was very important to me in the 1950s, when I was starting to get into the study of power, because he was the one person, along with Abraham Kaplan, who was trying to parse out and make sense of what power could mean (Lasswell and Kaplan 1950). I don't think they succeeded, though they strongly influenced people like me. I don't think anyone today really knows who Harold Lasswell was. It's a shame his *Power and Society* is not read anymore. It's an impenetrable book in many ways, but worth the struggle because it sharpens you up. It sensitizes you to the need to be precise about basic terms.

Q: Gabriel Almond was at Yale on two occasions, during the late 1940s and again in the early 1960s. Did you have much contact with him?

A: I knew Almond well when he was first at Yale during the 1940s. He was a very good friend and has remained so in the many years after he left Yale to go to Princeton and then Stanford.

---

7. Dahl was the chairman of Yale's Political Science Department from 1957 to 1962.

Q: With colleagues like these, Yale was obviously a very stimulating and exciting place to be.[8] However, most of the other leading scholars interviewed for this project moved around a bit. Do you have any regrets about having stayed put at Yale since graduate school?

A: I have a few regrets, though they don't overcome my feelings that, on balance, Yale was the right place to have been. I think it would have been helpful to have spent time at other institutions and to have come into contact with other people. But the three years I spent moving around in the army made me want to stay in one place. My friends were here at Yale, and we were happy here. The only time I seriously considered moving—and it's an amusing story in a way—was in the early 1960s, after I had been chairman of the department and served on a number of time-consuming university committees. For much the same reason that I knew I didn't want to be a government bureaucrat after I worked in Washington, I knew I didn't want to be an academic bureaucrat either. I wanted to spend the rest of my time without heavy administrative duties, doing the things that I came into the university to do. So I decided to take a year of leave in Rome and let it be known that I was considering other options.

I had some very nice offers at distinguished universities. My colleagues at Yale knew about this, and while I was in Rome I got a call from Kingman Brewster, the provost and soon to be president of Yale. We were good friends, and I much admired him. He said, "Bob, I know you don't want any more administrative duties, but your department would like you to come back here." And he said he would put a letter in my personnel file saying that as long as he was president, I would not be asked to take on any major university administrative duties. I came back to Yale of course. After that, Brewster would call and say, "Bob, I know there is that letter from me in your file, but would you chair such and such committee?"! Sometimes I said yes, sometimes no. I didn't feel a civic obligation to serve. I would do it because I thought it was something important and that I ought to do it. Brewster and I would often chuckle about that letter in my file.

So, on balance I'm happy I stayed here at Yale. Still, there is a part of me that would have liked to have been on the West Coast, at Stanford or Berkeley. Those would have been really good places for me. But I don't profoundly regret that I never went there.

Collaboration

Q: You have been involved in a number of collaborative projects, starting with your book, *Politics, Economics, and Welfare,* with Charles

8. For an in-depth study of Yale's Department of Political Science during the 1955–70 period, see Merelman (2003).

Lindblom (Dahl and Lindblom 1953). Could you discuss your various collaborative projects?
A: Lindblom and I lived two houses apart when we collaborated on that book. He lived there with his wife until recently, when they moved to New Mexico. We agreed which chapters would be written by whom. After a draft of each chapter was written, we would talk about it at either his house or mine. The book is almost seamless. I don't think you can pick out which chapters were written by him and which ones by me, except by guessing from the subject of each chapter.

Later I collaborated with Paul Lazarsfeld on a volume on business and the social sciences (Dahl, Haire, and Lazarsfeld 1959). The book was commissioned by Pendelton Herring at the Social Science Research Council, I think. I first got to know Lazarsfeld in 1955–56, when we were both in Palo Alto at the Center for Advanced Study in the Behavioral Sciences. He was a European scholar of great range and depth and was a much finer methodologist than I. Lazarsfeld also had a much better mathematical background. I have a feeling he had been exposed to mathematics early in his career.

I also collaborated with one of my students, Ed Tufte. He came out to the Center for Advanced Study at Stanford in 1967, the second time I was there. Hans Daalder, Stein Rokkan, and my other colleagues involved in the project on smaller European democracies were also at the center that year. Ed came out as my research assistant, and during the course of the year we began to work on the question of size and democracy. Ed was a much better statistician and methodologist than I, and by the end of that project it became clear that he was not just a research assistant, but a coauthor (Dahl and Tufte 1973). Although I did the bulk of the writing, you can see the important role he played in some of those chapters. Ed has since moved on to a very creative period in his life with his work on the visual presentation of data, which reflects his aesthetic side. He even began to do sculpture.

Students

Q: What role has teaching and interaction with students played in your career?[9]
A: Teaching has been a very rewarding and important part of my life. I enjoy undergraduate teaching because undergraduates, especially freshmen, are unfamiliar with the state-of-the-art and thus ask innocent but very important questions. As for graduate students, a lot of my graduate students in due time became friends and colleagues. Nelson Polsby, Raymond Wolf-

9. For two students' perspectives on Dahl as a teacher, see the interviews with Guillermo O'Donnell and James Scott in Chapters 9 and 11.

inger, and Fred Greenstein are all examples. Although we didn't collaborate on research after they had finished their graduate work, we continued to exchange ideas. Talking about Latin America with students like Guillermo O'Donnell often gave me insights. I've often wondered if I was wrong about these insights, or if I had misinterpreted them, but students like Guillermo gave me ideas I would not have otherwise gotten. Graduate students push you constantly, if you're open to it, with more and more advanced questions. Several of my books grew out of graduate seminars. *Democracy and Its Critics,* as I say in the introduction, was a seminar for years. Graduate students were also a very important part of *Who Governs?* both as research assistants and participants in seminars. When I was working on *Polyarchy,* I was running into foreign students with a variety of backgrounds, from South Korea, Argentina, Brazil, and this helped me gain some insight about their countries. This insight may often have been a little superficial, but even that opens up horizons.

Q: What are the hallmarks of the best students?
A: Obviously they have to be smart. But intelligence is a characteristic of a great many students, so by itself that does not distinguish the best students. Curiosity is important. And they have to be driven, not languid. Also, for the best students the study of politics engages not just their intellects, but also their somatic systems. There is feeling, emotion.

Q: Passion!
A: Passion, absolutely. That's a quality of all the best students. Finally, my best students—and this wouldn't necessarily be true of the best students of others—have some connection with the real world and real people in it. Their interest in the study of politics is more than library- or mathematics-driven. There is some understanding, almost at the gut level, of what the world outside is.

Achievements and Shortcomings of Comparative Politics

Q: What have been the main achievements of comparative politics over the past fifty years?
A: Over the past fifty years, there has been an enormous gain in the quality and quantity of knowledge in the field of comparative politics. This is a very positive and impressive change. I don't know that it's a bigger change than has occurred in other branches of political science, but it might well be, especially since comparative politics started with the rather narrow base that I mentioned earlier, the Herman Finer base (Finer 1932).

The expansion outward of the study of comparative politics beyond a handful of European cases and the development, thanks to the growth of often quite good worldwide data, of methodologies and analytical techniques have fundamentally altered the field in a positive way. We know a lot more about political parties, constitutions, and about broader things like regime breakdowns and transitions. Fifty years ago we knew almost nothing about these things. We know so much more about electoral systems, their consequences, and how they function than we did only a few years ago. The growth of knowledge about these important issues is heartening and positive. I don't want to exaggerate and say we are anywhere near achieving a final, conclusive body of knowledge, we never will be, but we know so much more. The study of comparative politics and comparative democracies, specifically, might be the most promising part of political science today.

One of the extraordinary changes over the past fifty years, one that I can't exaggerate, is the emergence of political science as a worldwide enterprise. When I first got involved in the discipline, political science only existed in the United States, Britain, and France, though in France it was just starting. Political science as a discipline did not exist in places like Italy or Japan. Today political science exists everywhere. Even in China there is some good political science going on despite the rather repressive regime.

The problem now is an excess of information, especially qualitative information. Theoretical frameworks are crucial for dealing with all this information, because information that can't be tied to a theoretical framework just becomes a book of facts, or random knowledge.

Q: What are your major disappointments with the field of comparative politics?
A: It's appalling that at this late date we are still struggling with how to conceptualize and measure democracy. I find the continuing debates about what we mean by democracy—I mean this and he means that—depressing.

Q: Why has it been so difficult to achieve a satisfactory definition of democracy?
A: Part of the reason is that a satisfactory definition has to respect the history of the term. You don't want a definition of democracy that makes the Greek city-state undemocratic. You have to accommodate to that. At the same time that a satisfactory definition of democracy has to respect the history of the term, it also has to be able to accommodate the evolution in its meaning. And a satisfactory definition also has to be formulated in a way that allows you to measure it. This requires judgment and rankings based on judgments. For example, you need to judge how free speech is in Peru. This is not like reading a scale on a thermometer, but with a large degree of

observer agreement on such judgments, you can put some trust in them. These are all demanding requirements that are rarely met.

Q: Do you have other disappointments with the field?
A: I am enormously disappointed that the study of power and the conceptualization of power has made no progress that I can detect since Laswell and Kaplan (1950), Jim March's work (1955, 1956, 1957), and my early efforts (Dahl 1957, 1968). Power is such a central concept, and Jim March and I had hoped a vocabulary would evolve that would allow for observation, comparison, and the accumulation of information. We also hoped a precise and discriminating language for studying power would evolve, along the lines of what Lasswell had tried to develop and what I tried to develop for political analysis (Dahl 1957; 1963, 39–54). These expectations turned out to be highly optimistic. Today, fifty years later, I see people use the word and concept *power* as if we were back where we started. Even elementary distinctions going back to Max Weber—such as the distinction between power and authority, or legitimate power—seem to have been forgotten. So perhaps we've not only failed to progress in the study of power, we've actually gone into reverse.

Very few people study power today. I don't know what explains this. Perhaps the requirements for studying power in a way that we would now regard as methodologically sound and reasonable outstrip our capacities for definition and measurement. Maybe the problem is we don't have good ways of measuring power, so the people who would be likely to study it know that the methodological requirements are too daunting.

The Future of the Field

Q: In some Political Science departments today there is a strong feeling that political theory is not a necessary component of graduate training. Indeed, there is even discussion of eliminating political theory as a subfield. What do you think about that?
A: I'm sure that in some corners this will sound reactionary, but I think that eliminating political theory as part of graduate training in political science would be a profound mistake. Reading political theory and political philosophy is important because it is the only way I know to get at the enduring questions, the ones that are always around. Political theory raises fundamental questions about the nature of alternative political systems: Why are they valued? Why do we want them? Why do we make sacrifices for them? Political theory also addresses enduring questions about authority and the good society: Why should we obey laws? Why should we prefer one consti-

tutional system over another? Those are the kinds of issues that seem to be around for a long time.

Reading political theory also helps broaden one's horizons and increase the range of questions that come into one's purview, and I don't know a full substitute for it. I worry about the narrowness of contemporary political science. Through publications and promotions the profession tends to reward specialization, and I think there is a great risk of getting questions that are so specialized they cease to matter. Human beings are not going to be any better off if such questions get answered. The opposite danger of course is superficiality, that you answer questions that are so broad the answer is almost meaningless. But that's a risk that needs to be taken.

Q: Earlier, in discussing the behavioral revolution, we touched on the rational choice movement that has emerged as an important force in political science over the past two decades. What is your view of the future of rational choice theory in political science?
A: Rational choice may have peaked. Its limitations are becoming clearer after an initial period of acceptance by people who did not really understand the limits of rational choice. As important as rational choice theory may be in dealing with some types of problems, it's not a satisfactory way of dealing with the most important problems. So, you get things like the Green and Shapiro (1994) critique of rational choice, and I don't think that's going to go away. Also, I sense that in some of the departments where rational choice had been seen as heading in the direction of definite dominance, such as the Harvard Government Department, a growing opposition has emerged to the imperial tendencies of the rational choice groups. I would guess this opposition is not likely to reverse, but to gain strength. As I said before, it would be a grave mistake to drum rational choice out of the field. But I don't think that's going to happen either.

Q: If rational choice has peaked, where do you see the discipline heading?
A: The most likely possibility—and this may prove totally wrong ten years down the road—is that the discipline will be eclectic and there won't be a single model. There are lots of teasing possibilities, but none is going to do the job as far as providing a single model for political science. For example, there is a powerful reductionist attraction in genetics and brain research, but reductionism cannot take us very far.

Q: Why not?
A: Because of the problem of complexity. I just wrote an article for Fred Greenstein's festschrift that critiques the reductionism of research in ge-

netics. It's called "Reflections on Human Nature and Politics: From Genes to Political Institutions" (Dahl 2006), and the general idea is that you can't get from genes to human rights because, for one thing, you need institutions, and you can't explain institutions with genes. Genes may say something about tendencies and possibilities, but they don't explain institutions.

Q: So you predict pluralism for the discipline.
A: Yes. This may reflect my biases, but I just can't see anything out there that can deal with the overarching complexities of the field.

Q: A frequent criticism of political science today is that it is too disconnected from the real world and has little impact beyond the Ivory Tower. By contrast, your work seems to offer a striking example of normatively driven research that aims to have a real-world impact. Have you in fact aspired to have such an impact?
A: I have. I believe that what I write has value only to the degree that it affects the welfare of human beings. That goal is reflected in the title of one of my first books, written with Ed Lindblom, *Politics, Economics, and Welfare* (Dahl and Lindblom 1953). Back then, welfare meant human well-being, not being "on welfare," as it does today. The wish to have an influence on people and the way they think about things explains why I've always tried to write in a clear way that makes my work more accessible. I'm somewhat gratified to know that my books have been translated into other languages and that people around the world have read them. I think *On Democracy* (Dahl 1998) has been translated into twenty-eight different languages.

Q: Given your desire to have an influence in the real world, have you served as a consultant for democratic opposition groups or for foreign governments concerning issues of constitutional design?
A: Not really.

Q: People must ask you to offer advice about such matters.
A: They do, from time to time. And I've served on some committees, but I think the effective answer to that is "No."

Q: Why not?
A: I think it's because my Washington experience taught me early on that I didn't want to spend my time that way. I want to leave that to other people who are probably more competent.

Conclusion

Q: For political science to continue thriving as a field, it has to attract new recruits. Successful recruitment is likely to depend on the discipline's capacity to convey to young scholars a sense of fun and excitement about studying politics. Do you regard "having fun" as an important aspect of the scholarly enterprise?

A: Yes, that's a very good point. I'm going to make an empirical statement for which I have absolutely no validation whatsoever: if you are not enjoying your work, it is not going to be very good. I think that is true whether it's painting, writing, or research. I don't mean that every minute of it has to be enjoyable. There is going to be some drudgery, but there has to be something more, there has to be enjoyment and intellectual gratification, perhaps from seeing a piece of work coming together or getting a sense that things fit. If you don't get that kind of gratification, then I don't know why you're doing it. Sometimes when I look at what gets published in the *American Political Science Review* I ask myself, "Is this person really excited by that?"

Q: What is your advice to young scholars starting out in comparative politics today?

A: I would encourage them—without leaving the academic track—to get some experience in the world outside. I don't want to say the "real" world, because ours is real, too, but I would encourage them to get out and interact with people other than academics, to get to know a world beyond the academic track from kindergarten to Ph.D. My impression is that graduate students today, although many are better educated coming out of high school than I was coming out of college, lack a depth of human experience with ordinary people who aren't involved in the academic framework. One of the reasons I'm a big believer in democracy is that I had the chance to interact with ordinary people early in life, and I found them to be pretty smart if given the opportunity.[10] Getting to know ordinary people has always been heartening to me. So, I would encourage graduate students to get to know a world of experience outside academics. There are lots of ways to do that.

Q: Do you have any further advice?

A: I don't know that this is worthwhile advice, because I don't know that you can control it, but don't ever lose your curiosity, or, I like the word you used, passion. That's terribly important. If you have that, it will keep you going forever.

10. See Dahl (2005).

6

Juan J. Linz

Political Regimes and the Quest for Knowledge

Juan J. Linz is one of the preeminent political sociologists of the second half of the twentieth century. He is widely recognized for his seminal work on authoritarian political regimes and democratization.

Linz's early research on non-democratic regimes questioned the dichotomy of totalitarianism and democracy that prevailed after World War II in the comparative study of political regimes. Drawing on his in-depth knowledge of General Francisco Franco's Spain, he wrote a widely cited paper, "An Authoritarian Regime: Spain" (1964), in which he formulated the concept of the authoritarian regime, an intermediate category that provided a better understanding of the many countries across the world that had neither totalitarian nor democratic regimes. In "Totalitarian and Authoritarian Regimes" (1975), he expanded the scope of his analysis by developing a full-blown typology of regimes that encompassed virtually every country in the world. His typology stands as perhaps the most comprehensive effort in modern social science to map the variety of political regimes. *Sultanistic Regimes* (1998b), coedited with Houchang Chehabi, extended Linz's conceptual work on non-democratic regimes by focusing on the origins, dynamics, and breakdown of personalistic dictatorships.

A second strand of Linz's work focused on regime change. In his introductory volume to *The Breakdown of Democratic Regimes* (1978), coedited with Alfred Stepan, he focused on how the people in power in a democratic regime, not just the opponents, played a decisive role in the overthrow of democracy. This perspective, combined with the emphasis Linz placed on the contingent, non-inevitable nature of regime breakdowns, challenged Marxist theories, which highlighted economic causes, as well as other approaches that focused on opposition groups to explain why democratic regimes collapse. The next phase of his work on regime change focused on

This interview was conducted by Richard Snyder in Hamden, Connecticut, on April 25–26, 2001.

the institutions of presidential democracy, arguing that presidential democracies were more prone to collapse than parliamentary democracies. His paper on presidentialism (1985b), eventually published in the two-volume collection he coedited with Arturo Valenzuela, *The Failure of Presidential Democracy* (1994), launched a debate in comparative politics about the vulnerabilities of presidential regimes. Linz also contributed to the study of democratization, publishing *Democracy in Developing Countries* (1988–89), coedited with Larry Diamond and Seymour Martin Lipset, and *Problems of Democratic Transition and Consolidation* (1996), a coauthored book with Alfred Stepan that offered an ambitious cross-regional comparison of thirteen countries in South America, Southern Europe, and post-communist Europe. *Problems of Democratic Transition and Consolidation* made an empirical contribution by incorporating post-communist European cases into a systematic framework alongside the South American and Southern European cases that had been the focus of previous research on democratization. The book made important theoretical contributions by (1) introducing into the study of democratization a novel focus on "stateness" problems stemming from nationalist conflicts and (2) highlighting how the type of old non-democratic regime affected subsequent trajectories of democratization. Linz's current research, in collaboration with Alfred Stepan, on federalism, democracy, and multinationalism explores further the issue of "stateness" problems.

A final dimension of Linz's research concerned a broad set of questions at the intersection of society and politics, including business and local elites in Spain, nationalist conflict in the Basque region, Spanish social history, and the sociology of fascist movements.

Linz was born in Bonn, Germany, in 1926. He received his undergraduate degree in 1947 from the University of Madrid and his Ph.D. in sociology from Columbia University in 1959. He taught at Columbia University (1961–68) and Yale University (1968–99), becoming a professor emeritus at Yale in 1999. He served as chairman of the Committee on Political Sociology of the International Sociological Association (ISA) and the International Political Science Association (IPSA) (1971–79) and as president of the World Association for Public Opinion Research (WAPOR) (1974–76). He was elected to the American Academy of Arts and Sciences in 1976.

Intellectual Formation and Training

Q: Can you discuss how your Spanish background relates to your intellectual development?
A: The years before 1950, when I came to study sociology at Columbia, decisively shaped my interests and academic training. Born in Bonn in

1926 in a German-Spanish family at the time that my father's business went bankrupt with the inflation, I spent my childhood in the Bavarian Forest. In 1932, with the Depression in Germany and the advent of the Republic in Spain, my mother accepted a position in the Center for Historical Research and the National Library in Madrid. My father stayed in Germany and soon he was killed by a drunken driver. In Madrid, I went to the German School until the Civil War in 1936.

My interest first in social problems and then in politics is the result of living, practically since childhood, directly or through what my mother told me, all the complex history of Europe in the interwar years from post–World War I to the Franco regime. Even the Russian Revolution and Baltic and Northern European culture became familiar to me through my relation to Alexander Kesküla, an Estonian revolutionary nationalist exiled in Switzerland who had been involved in Lenin's trip to the Finland station and Estonian independence, and who took care of my homework when I was a kid. But to tell that story and the story of my journey to Germany with my mother in October 1936, when the Civil War reached the outskirts of Madrid, a trip that left some memories of Nazi Germany, my return to Spain in February 1937, the Civil War of 1936–39, my contact with the poverty and the persecuted in Salamanca, the capital of Franco's Spain, through the work of my mother in the Falangist welfare organization, and a large "et cetera," would take many pages. The same would be true for my identification with Spain, when I could have been German. My *verstehen* of so many themes in my work[1]—the breakdown of Spanish democracy, the limited pluralism of the Franco regime, Nazism and fascism, nationalism—owes much to the experience that starts when I was less than ten years old. This is not the place to tell that story (Linz 1997a, 101–14; see also Linz 1997b, 141–52).

After finishing secondary education (*bachillerato*) in 1943, I enrolled in the Law School and also in the newly created Facultad de Ciencias Políticas y Económicas (Faculty of Political Science and Economics) of the University of Madrid. The five years of law studies covered civil, commercial, criminal, international, public and private, and political law, including comparative constitutional law. The political science curriculum covered a wide range of subjects from political economy, public administration, local government, labor relations and social security law, international relations, church and state relations, modern history, to the history of political theory. In both faculties some teachers were excellent, others were mediocre, but when I

---

1. Max Weber used the German term *verstehen* (to understand) to refer to the social scientist's attempt to understand the context and meaning of human action from the actor's point of view.

graduated respectively in 1948 and 1947 as *licenciado* with honors, I had a broad legal and social science background that would have allowed me— after competitive entrance examinations—a career in the higher civil service. Much of what I learned then has always been useful in my scholarly work.

The Franco regime was in power then, and we law students formed a small, more or less illegal, discussion group on Spanish society and politics. One issue we discussed was how Franco could be ousted within the Franco constitution, and we analyzed the constitutional texts of the Franco legislation. Later, in the 1970s, some people did the same thing before the transition to democracy in Spain: they studied how to make the transition within the constitutional framework of the Franco regime. And some of those people actually carried out the transition to democracy.

Q: How did you turn to sociology?

A: I was exposed very early on to the classics of social theory. Professor Javier Conde was trained in Germany in the 1930s and had absorbed the tradition of German political science and sociology. I was interested in social problems, labor relations, and social security legislation, and when I talked to Conde about my interests, he said, "Look, that's all very pedestrian and intellectually uninteresting stuff. Read this." And he gave me Karl Mannheim's *Ideology and Utopia* (1936). He also gave me books by Hans Freyer and Max Weber. As Conde's assistant, I helped him prepare a reader for a seminar we were planning on sociological theory. I read practically all of Auguste Comte, Vilfredo Pareto, Weber, and Georg Simmel, whose *Soziologie* (Simmel 1908) was available in Spanish by that time.[2] I worked on all those classics because I had to teach them. One of the lectures was on Ferdinand Toennies and his distinction between community (*Gemeinschaft*) and society (*Gesellschaft*), another was on Weber's distinction between class and status, and another compared Marx's and Weber's concepts of class. Later, when I came to Columbia, there was a course on the history of sociological theory taught by Theodore Abel, a Polish sociologist who did very good work on the Nazis. I got the reading list and attended two or three lectures, but I quickly realized that I already knew what he was teaching. So, my interest in the classics of social theory comes from German-Spanish intellectual culture. You learn to pay attention to classics.

When Javier Conde was appointed director of the Instituto de Estudios Políticos in 1948, I went to work with him, participating in seminars, the editorial board of journals, decisions about publications, and pre-legislative reports. I also participated in the translation of a book by Günther Holstein

2. The English translation of part of this work is found in Simmel (1950).

on the history of political theory, a contribution to a German *Handbuch der Philosophie* (Holstein 1950). As a teaching assistant, I read and taught not only sociologists like Weber, Toennies, and Freyer, but German political scientists like Hermann Heller and Hans Kelsen. In 1950, at a summer seminar of students of political science from all over Europe, organized in the south of France by a group from Sciences Po,[3] I made a presentation on democracy based fundamentally on Kelsen's *Wesen und Wert der Demokratie* (1929) and an article he published in *Ethics*. Kelsen and Heller—and the experience of France in 1949 and 1950—were central in my intellectual development.

It was my work in Spain, reviews of French "electoral geography," Rudolf Heberle's work on the Nazi vote in Schleswig-Holstein (Heberle 1945), and the preparation of a bibliography of electoral sociology that later landed me the coauthorship with Paul Lazarsfeld, Seymour Martin Lipset, and Allen Barton of a chapter on the psychology of voting (Lipset et al. 1954).[4]

Q: In 1950 you started graduate school in sociology at Columbia. How did you come to the United States?
A: At the Instituto de Estudios Políticos I organized an extensive journal exchange and we bought American social science books. Research monographs, like Richard Centers's *Psychology of Social Classes* (1949), stimulated an interest in empirical research and the urge to learn research methods. Conde obtained for me a fellowship from the Spanish Ministry of Foreign Affairs, and a German sociologist, Rene König, who was very active in the International Sociological Association (ISA), on a visit to Spain suggested I go to Chicago, Columbia, or Harvard, although initially I was to go to the New School for Social Research, intending to work on civil-military relations with Hans Speier. The Spanish embassy in Washington objected to the New School, so I applied to the three other universities, and Columbia accepted me as a "non-matriculated" student.

I came to the States in 1950 as a student, not as an exile or immigrant, as had many of my elders. My experience was different from the experience of those who were in their adolescence in the 1930s. Remember, I was only nine years old when the Spanish Civil War started. My social science training would be American but on the basis of a Spanish university education, a German cultural background, and the European social and political experience. I do not think that my intellectual work can be understood without reference to that background. I was on the cross-cutting edge of disciplines and countries like few of my generation.

3. Sciences Po refers to the French National Foundation of Political Science (FNSP).
4. Lipset (1995, 7) jokingly refers to this as the "law firm" article.

Q: Columbia's Sociology Department in the 1950s, when you were a graduate student, was one of the most exciting departments in the social sciences.[5] What was it like studying in that environment?
A: The decisive thing at Columbia was that there was a fairly heterogeneous faculty with several towering figures. Robert Merton was a magician with theory and concepts. I use the word *magician* deliberately.[6] He taught you how to work with concepts by showing how to move up and down the ladder of abstraction. Drawing to some extent on Durkheim's method-ological classic, *Suicide* (Durkheim 1951), Merton also showed you how to transform a concept into indicators and indicators into concepts. That was something very unique to learn, as was the logic of structural functional-ism, which Merton also taught.

Paul Lazarsfeld, a great innovator in methodology, was another power-ful figure. Though not a good teacher, Lazarsfeld was a very good researcher and a most stimulating person to work with. I worked on a project for the *Handbook of Social Psychology* with him, Seymour Martin Lipset, and Allen Barton (Lipset et al. 1954). Lazarsfeld was always prodding and encouraging us. In a sense, Merton was discouraging people because of his perfection-ism, whereas Lazarsfeld was pragmatic, saying, "Okay, finish it and get it ready." Lazarsfeld and Merton taught a very stimulating joint seminar on general methods and theory—it was basically a conversation between them in front of the students. Although Lazarsfeld was a methodologist, he had a broader intellectual framework and could communicate with a larger au-dience. He was a cultivated man with a good humanistic training who read the great classics of literature and had learned history, Greek, and Latin, I imagine at the Austrian *gymnasium*. One indicator of his breadth was a course he gave together with Ernest Nagel in Columbia's Philosophy De-partment, which I attended as an auditor. Lazarsfeld was a psychologist by training, and his thinking was grounded in questions about motivations and in a theory of action—he has a beautiful paper on that. Lazarsfeld's grounding in psychology was evident in his decision to study the most ele-mentary, least complex actions—not voting for a party, which, as a young social democrat, was his obvious interest, but an action as simple as buying soap. Lazarsfeld saw a simple decision like that as the molecular level of human behavior, and he realized it was something that could be studied

5. See Coleman (1990a).
6. As an adolescent, Merton had worked as a magician, and had even changed his last name to Merlin. As Merton himself describes it, "Just as Ehrich Weiss, the son of Rabbi Mayer Samuel Weiss, had become Harry Houdini, naming himself after the celebrated French magician, Rob-ert Houdin, the fourteen-year-old Meyer R. Schkolnick fleetingly became Robert K. Merlin, after the far more celebrated magician of Arthurian legend. Merlin, in turn, soon became Merton." See Merton (1996b, 347).

easily. So, Lazarsfeld pursued the idea of using market research as a way to study fundamental dimensions of human behavior, something that the anti-Lazarsfeld students saw as a rationalization for his decision to work with business. But I don't think it was a rationalization at all; it was a very conscious decision.

I was amazed the other day when I attended a dinner talk by Bob Dahl on the history of political science at Yale and his participation in it. In the 1950s, methodology, research techniques, and statistics were completely absent from political science at Yale. Dahl discovered these techniques at least ten years later than I, largely because at Columbia we were at the forefront of methodological training with Paul Lazarsfeld. Graduate students were required to take a basic two-semester statistics course, which I passed, though not with flying colors. I learned how to do survey research from Lazarsfeld.

Another influence at Columbia was Kingsley Davis who, like Merton, also did structural functionalism, but with a focus on developing countries, demography, and the family. He had a very interesting seminar on development in which we dealt with urbanization, illiteracy, and social structures in developing countries. Finally, there was the team of Robert Lynd and Seymour Martin Lipset. Lynd had an "American Progressive," slightly Marxist, outlook, and he was centrally concerned with Mannheim's questions about social justice and "knowledge for what." Lipset had recently completed his research in Canada on agrarian socialism, and he was working on his project on union democracy (Lipset 1950; Lipset, Trow, and Coleman 1956). So, these individuals—well, in the case of Lipset and Lynd, a team—were very different. Many students did not benefit from this heterogeneity because they took sides. Some said, "I hate Lazarsfeld because he is working for business," and were only Lynd-Lipset oriented. Others did not like Kingsley Davis because they thought he was authoritarian and practically a fascist. So, students did not benefit as much as they could have. Fortunately, I decided to take courses and learn from all of them. That was my great luck.

Q: Why, unlike many other students, did you have this posture of openness to these various teachers?
A: Probably because I came from the Spanish university, where we had to take all the courses because they were all required. I also came to graduate school a bit more mature than most students because I had a law degree and had already worked as a research assistant in Spain. Finally, the heterogeneity of faculty did not disturb me because I wanted to learn as much as I could about different things, and each of these professors had something to offer me. So, I said "Let's see what I can grab from these people." And I learned different things from all of them.

Q: Toward the end of your graduate studies, you spent a year with Lipset as his research assistant at the Center for Advanced Study in Palo Alto in 1956–57. Was he your main mentor in graduate school?
A: Yes. I worked with Marty Lipset as a research assistant for more than a year and a half on a big project on the social bases of political diversity, which resulted in a coauthored book that we never published (Linz and Lipset 1956). Our unpublished book was very important for the development of Marty's *Political Man* (Lipset 1960a). Marty also supervised my dissertation.[7] Originally it was going to be a sociological study of the Italian and German electorates using survey data in order to learn about two new democracies. Finally, I limited myself to an exhaustive analysis of public opinion data on the 1953 Adenauer election in Germany that Elizabeth Noelle-Neumann of the Institut für Demoskopie had made available for "secondary analysis" (Linz 1959).[8] Out of that came a lifelong friendship with her and later my collaboration in the European Values Study.

My dissertation was inspired by the work I had been doing with Marty Lipset on political behavior, my wish to dominate the survey research methodology to use it in the future in Spain, and the desire to better understand democratic politics. Certainly my knowledge of German and German society also contributed to the dissertation.

Q: During your stay in California in the late 1950s you also worked as a research assistant for Reinhard Bendix at Berkeley.
A: Bendix had a project on the history of entrepreneurship in Germany in the nineteenth century. He was especially interested in how the business elite of imperial Germany interacted with the bureaucracy and the politicians. My job was to read hundreds of biographies, autobiographies, and correspondences of leading businessmen of imperial Germany, like Siemens and Rathenau. The work was fairly simple. I just told Bendix what was in those books and documents, marked relevant pages, and had them microfilmed. But this experience sparked my own interest in entrepreneurship. It also led to a funny incident many years later, in Berlin. The German sociologist Claus Offe told me he was living in the Ballin House. I said, "Oh, Ballin; he founded a big shipping company and was a good friend of the Kaiser." Offe was very surprised because nobody had any idea who Ballin was.

Q: Your experiences working closely as a research assistant with Lazarsfeld, Lipset, and Bendix clearly had a major impact on your intellectual development.

7. For Lipset's reflections on Linz as a student, see Lipset (1995).
8. Linz's dissertation was never published as a book, though part of it appeared as Linz (1967). See also Nolle-Neumann (1995).

A: Immense. Today it is far less common for students to start their professional lives as research assistants collaborating with a senior scholar. We were not paid very much in those days, but the experience working on a theme that someone very important was working on was invaluable. The close contact this allowed made it easy to establish a human and personal relationship that formed the basis for a lifelong friendship, like the one I have with Marty Lipset. That is much less likely today. One reason is the pressure the university administration puts on students to finish fast, another is that students today have much better funding than we did and thus do not need side income and summer work to supplement their fellowships. The Spanish students who came to the United States in the 1950s, when I did, and even those who came in the 1960s and early 1970s, did not go home for Christmas because they could not afford to. Now they all go. Students today are economically more independent than they have ever been. This creates autonomy, which can be good if it is used well, though I'm not sure that working on one's own without a mentor is such a good idea, because no faculty member is going to be particularly interested in your project. If you work with somebody on a topic in which that person has a direct interest, then you will obviously get more advice and more integration into a research community.

Q: Overall, Columbia seems to have been an incredibly rich and stimulating place to study sociology in the 1950s.
A: It was an environment that contributed to real creativity. It is hard to explain why there is such a burst of creativity in some places and times, but not others. Take the New York school of abstract expressionists, a group of people who knew each other and exchanged ideas. They were ultimately lone wolves who did their own things, but they operated in a certain milieu, a supportive environment. In the social sciences, too, we have certain schools, certain contexts that emerge historically and generate all kinds of productive things. And you are lucky if you are a part of that.

Q: You defended your thesis at Columbia in 1958. How did you come to teach there in 1961?
A: After the defense, I went to Spain to work on interest groups and politics with a research grant from the Social Science Research Council (SSRC) Committee on Comparative Politics led by Gabriel Almond. I went via France, which was in the midst of the transition from the Fourth to the Fifth Republic, which I followed closely. Since I could not find a permanent position in Spain and did not think it was the best place to work on the Franco regime, I welcomed the offer from Columbia to start teaching as an assistant professor in 1961, after completing my research in Spain.

On Structural Functionalism

Q: Regarding the theoretical side of your training at Columbia, structural functionalism was emphasized strongly, especially by Merton and Davis. Today structural functionalism has largely disappeared from the map in the social sciences. What do you think about this development?

A: In a sense, we are all structural functionalists. We are always analyzing political and social structures. Whether we are talking about the presidency, political parties, or trade unions, they are all structures. When we study what parties do—they recruit elites, support a government, articulate issues—we are analyzing the functions they perform. And you might say that when we claim "parties cannot do certain things that social movements can," we are comparing the functions of parties and social movements. Even if we never actually use the language of functions and structures, we are always dealing with them. In one of his papers, Merton shows how all of Marxist analysis, at least the classical Marx, not the Marx of the youthful writings, is a kind of structural-functional analysis (Merton 1968, 93–95, 160–61, 516ff.). Structural functionalism is so much a part of what we do that we don't remember it anymore.

Q: Does structural functionalism have a negative side?

A: It can be misused, especially if one assumes that everything has a function. By the 1930s, anthropologists had already recognized this potential for the misuse of functionalism, and they began to identify certain human activities as "survivals," that is, as things that persist yet have no function. The classic example is a freshly painted army bench, which has a guard assigned to it so that nobody spoils the paint. After the paint dries, new commanders maintain the post at the bench, and every day a soldier stands guard there, an activity with no function whatsoever. You might argue that, even if they have no visible function, certain things in society are maintained because they have "latent functions." Using this logic, you could see the posting of a guard at a bench as a way to keep discipline and order in the daily routine of an army unit. But if you try to find functions for everything, you can easily push the idea of a function to the level of the absurd. Approaches and concepts can be used in a stupid way, and if you're stupid, well?

Q: Despite your observation that in some ways we are all latent structural functionalists, the fact remains that structural functionalism as a theoretical school has lost the prestige and preeminence it enjoyed when you were in graduate school. What explains the decline of structural functionalism?

A: The critiques of and the hostility toward Talcott Parsons played an important role in this decline. Part of this critique involved the silly argument that Parsons cannot be understood, because he is so opaque and writes so poorly. I do not think that is true. Parsons's *The Social System* (1951) was a major work that ambitiously attempted to organize the whole field of the social sciences, and to some extent it succeeded. But, in the end, this effort at systematization was not very fruitful. Nevertheless, Parsons's pattern variables—particularism-universalism, ascription-achievement, diffusion-specificity, and so on—were extremely useful. I used them in some of my research in Spain, operationalizing them somewhat in survey questions. The pattern variables fit perfectly well within a long tradition of social thought on matters such as the distinction between law and custom, *Gemeinschaft* (community) and *Gesellschaft* (society), and property rights and contracts. Parsons's pattern variables have a long intellectual history grounded, for example, in Roman law. Most people did not realize how much was behind some of Parsons's ideas.

Parsons made a mistake by defining his pattern variables in terms of absolute dichotomies instead of continuums. For example, there is no necessary radical trade-off between ascription and achievement: you can have a kind of "ascriptive achievement." Take a person who becomes a finance inspector or gets accepted to the École Nationale d'Administration in France. He has achieved these things, yet after he gets the position or the degree, these achievements become ascriptive and diffuse, because as soon as he presents his card with the title *finance inspector,* people respect him regardless of what he does. You can play with these kinds of hybrid combinations among the pattern variables much more than Parsons does.

Parsons's A-G-I-L model had an enormous influence on Lipset and Stein Rokkan.[9] Lipset became interested in this Parsonian material in part because I had used it in papers I wrote for him, although he did not like it very much. In *Party Systems and Voter Alignments,* Lipset and Rokkan's (1967b) explanation for how distinct party systems emerged from different societal cleavages was partly developed out of the Parsonian scheme, although *forced* into the Parsonian scheme might be a better way of putting it. I don't know which way to interpret it, even though I was close to both Lipset and Rokkan when they were working on that book. So, there is a lot you can get from *The Social System,* and it is too bad no one reads it anymore, because it is quite a stimulating book in many aspects. For example, Parsons's application, despite all the simplification it involves, of the pattern variables to American, German, and Latin American societies is very interesting.

9. The A-G-I-L model was Parsons's fourfold scheme for classifying the functions of a social system: adaptation, goal attainment, integration, and latency.

Why was Parsons rejected? First, his notion that society is an interlocking system in equilibrium, which in some ways comes from Pareto, was criticized because it supposedly could not account for social transformation and change. In this respect, I think Parsons's ideas were largely misunderstood, because systems can be disrupted and can break down. It is true that, like Pareto, Parsons was mainly interested in the conditions under which social systems become relatively stable, and, to the degree that he focused on social change, he emphasized incremental change within the system. This approach did not provide much room for a theory of revolution. In the 1960s, Ralf Dahrendorf and others started arguing that conflict was more important than consensus, and there is no theory of conflict in Parsons. Parsons actually does have some writings that deal with conflict, for example, his work on the rise of fascism. But those works are not very good.

Another reason Parsons was rejected was the anticonservative "revolution" in the social sciences during the 1970s. Parsons became the symbol of conservatism, and everything that he represented was thrown out. This is somewhat ironic, because Parsons himself was a liberal democrat, not politically conservative in any way.

Research: Authoritarian Regimes, the Breakdown of Democracy, and Democratization
Authoritarian Regimes

Q: Your 1963 paper entitled "Spain: An Authoritarian Regime," which you presented at a meeting of the International Sociological Association's (ISA) Committee on Comparative Political Sociology in Tampere, Finland, was the foundation for much of your subsequent work on political regimes.[10] It also proved a seminal work in the field. What motivated you to write that piece? What was your contribution?
A: I was interested in non-democratic regimes partly because, as a Spaniard, I had grown up under one. When I wrote the piece on authoritarian regimes, the literature on non-democratic regimes, which consisted of work by people like Carl Friedrich and Zbigniew Brzezinski (1956; see also Brzezinski 1962), Hannah Arendt (1951), Sigmund Neumann (1942), and Franz Neumann (1957), was confused by its limited focus on the distinction between democracy and totalitarianism. On one hand, that literature practically did not make any references to non-democratic regimes other than Nazi Germany and the Soviet Union. The prevailing view was that non-democratic

10. The paper was published as Linz (1964). Further elaborations include Linz (1970, 1973a). See also Linz (1975), which was reprinted with a new introduction as Linz (2000).

regimes that did not fit into the category of totalitarianism were the result of a failure to reach the totalitarian stage due either to administrative inefficiency, economic underdevelopment, or external pressures. On the other hand, the hope for the expansion of democracy to the newly decolonized countries of Asia and Africa was being disappointed, and scholars writing on those countries turned to the idea that single-party regimes and later military dictators were only a stage in the process of modernization. The term *tutelary democracies* was frequently used to indicate the supposedly transitional character of these regimes. For me, Spain did not fit into this continuum. It was clear that from the very beginning Franco had not conceived the regime he was creating as totalitarian. Despite some of his rhetoric, the totalitarian model did not fit his way of thinking about politics. And, from the start, the political and social realities of Spain had led to a different type of regime. Also, it was obvious to me that there was no intention on the part of the rulers to prepare Spain for a transition to democracy.

In general, I felt that analyzing the political reality of most of the world in terms of the polar dichotomy of totalitarianism and democracy did not make sense. Many regimes around the world were neither on the way toward totalitarianism nor democracy. Nor did their rulers aim at either of these two models, despite the mimicry they may have used in their pronouncements, constitutions, laws, and institutions. So, on the basis of the case of Spain, which I knew well, I set out to question the polar dichotomy of totalitarianism and democracy by formulating my own concept of authoritarian regime. Other people, like Raymond Aron (1968) and Lewis Coser were moving in a similar direction. But my contribution was to systematically articulate the notion of an authoritarian regime, and it had a certain success.[11]

Q: What were the main weaknesses of your paper on authoritarian regimes?

A: I tended to put too little emphasis on the leadership dimension. My study of the authoritarian regime in Spain reads a little bit like an authoritarian regime without Franco. In downplaying the personal leadership dimension, I was partly reacting against the emphasis that previous work gave to charismatic leadership. I felt that some of the literature on totalitarianism had fallen into the trap of overemphasizing the charismatic element of Hitler or Stalin, and I wanted to avoid making a similar mistake. When I wrote my paper there just was not much to tell about Franco, a gray personality. The biographies, even the hagiographic ones, were very bad and did not give

11. For Linz's reflection on how he came up with his formulation of authoritarian regime and its subsequent use and reception, see Linz (1997b).

much of a sense of the person. Those close to the regime obviously did not feel free to tell much about Franco, and those who were opposed tended to have uninformed, simplistic, and negative views—they could not say much except that Franco was a dictator. The way in which he made decisions or responded to crises could only be known later, after the end of the regime. A certain passing of time is necessary for some types of information to become available. So, we knew very little about Franco when I wrote my paper, and that is another reason why he does not appear as central to the authoritarian regime as he probably was. In a sense, I had to underplay the role of Franco.

Q: The distinction between "mentalities," which characterize authoritarian regimes, and "ideologies," which characterize totalitarian regimes, is a key component of your work on non-democratic regimes. Yet that distinction has proven difficult to operationalize.

A: This is partly because ideologies and mentalities are both the product of minds—they are both ways of thinking. But mentalities are not codified intellectually in the same way that ideological formulations are codified. Mentalities do not play the same role as ideologies. It is a relatively easy matter to see where ideologies exist. If you went to Moscow during the Soviet period and asked for a copy of the history of the Communist Party of the Soviet Union, you would find it all over, even in the schools. In Nazi Germany, when you got married you would get a copy of Hitler's *Mein Kampf* as a wedding present from the City Council. But if you went to a bookstore in Spain under Franco and asked for Franco's writings, most bookstores would not have them. They would send you to the Editora Nacional (National Publishing House) that published them, and you might find copies in a used book fair because free copies were given away by some Francoist organizations, and people quickly sold their copies at the used book fairs. Few people, if any, read Franco's writings. This does not mean that an authoritarian regime like Franco's has no ideological formulations, yet the system does not operate by reference to the ideology, but by reference to the mentalities of the people in power. Operationalizing that distinction, as I have tried to do with these little anecdotes, is difficult, especially a posteriori.

The Breakdown of Democratic Regimes

Q: When did you start to envision the project that led to the 1978 volume that you coedited with Alfred Stepan on the breakdown of democratic regimes?[12] How did you put together the group of contributors to the volume?

12. See Chapter 12 for Stepan's perspective on this project.

A: To a European, like me, the experience of the breakdown of democracy in the 1920s and 1930s was something close. Intellectually, the work of the great German historian Karl Dietrich Bracher on Weimar (1952) was the most important stimulus for this project. Teaching a seminar at Columbia on the subject led to early formulations. The chance to organize a session at the Varna, Bulgaria Congress of the International Sociological Association (ISA) in 1970 allowed me to bring together a number of scholars—students and colleagues—who presented papers that eventually became contributions to the volume on the European and Latin American cases. Their work and my reading on many cases, particularly the work of Renzo De Felice on Italy, enriched my thinking.

Q: What were the driving theoretical concerns behind this project on the breakdown of democratic regimes? Were you arguing against any particular views or authors, as was the case with your conceptualization of Spain as an authoritarian regime? For example, was Barrington Moore's work on the social origins of dictatorship and democracy (1966) a point of reference?
A: I was not arguing against any specific theory or approach but trying to understand what happened, how, and why. I started by immersing myself in the wealth of historical research, and, at the same time, I was rereading the classics. For example, the notion of re-equilibration comes from Pareto (Linz 1978). My analysis has no relation with the work of Barrington Moore on the origins of democracy. It was articulated before the publication of his book and deals with a different problem. I find Moore's analysis of fascism, really of German fascism, unsatisfactory and misleading.

Q: A hallmark of your intellectual style, something that is especially evident in the volume on the breakdown of democratic regimes, is your focus on human agency, in particular, the actions of leaders and elites (Linz 1978). Why have you adopted such a focus in your work?
A: All society is ultimately based on the actions of individuals, though not only on the actions of elites and leaders. What is an army? An army is generals, colonels, lieutenant colonels, captains, sergeants, and ultimately soldiers. These individuals interact with one another and obey for various reasons. And the aggregation of all those behaviors—of a hundred thousand or fifty thousand people—is what makes an army. The general alone is not an army; an army without soldiers is inconceivable. So, ultimately there are individuals.

Q: One of the main criticisms of your work on the breakdown of democratic regimes is that it is overly voluntaristic. It focuses too much on

actors and their choices, neglecting the structural constraints on these actors. How do you respond to this criticism?
A: The fact is that when some of the actors involved in the breakdown of democratic regimes made different choices, different outcomes resulted. The impact of choices is especially clear in cases like Norway and the Netherlands, which had similar structural situations, similar levels of unemployment, yet the outcomes were different because leaders made different choices. I do not believe things are predetermined that much. Ultimately, people make choices—good ones, bad ones—which have consequences.

Obviously, the range of choice gets narrower and narrower in a crisis situation, and the number of actors who are important probably becomes smaller and smaller. Daniel Bell captured this narrowing with his notion of the "small c's": conspiracies, complots, clubs, committees, confabulations. Bell invented that term in a seminar we gave together at Columbia. You can see how the number of important actors becomes smaller in a book like Henry Ashby Turner's (1996) on the thirty days before Hitler came to power. The people who had an influence on Hindenburg's decisions—we have a record, almost hour by hour, of who had access to and influenced him— became an incredibly small group. And this small group of people was not acting as a representative of larger social forces; but, to some extent, these people were acting out of miserably petty nastiness. Of course, they were operating in a context provided by the Nazi movement, the economic crisis, the prior abdication by the democratic parties of an active role because they wanted to avoid having to make unpopular decisions and preferred to let the cabinet deal with the problems. Still, it was an incredibly small group that mattered in the end.

Q: Why did your focus on the choices of leaders to explain the breakdown of democracy elicit so much hostility and criticism?
A: To start with, it did not fit with a Marxist view in which the economic factor of the Great Depression was the explanation of everything. Also, I introduced an emphasis on the people in power in the democratic system, not just the opponents, making decisions and, by implication, bearing some responsibility for the breakdown of the regime. I argued that the overthrow of democracy was not only the result of the actions of the opponents, but also of the actions of those who tried to maintain the system and keep democracy working. But if you have a devil interpretation of history in which there are the "goodies" and the "badies"—the good ones are the democrats and the bad ones are the antidemocrats who want to overthrow democracy—then nothing the people in power do has anything to do with the breakdown of democracy. From that perspective, only the ones who attacked the system bear responsibility for its collapse. I find that too simple.

Q: The concept of legitimacy plays a central role in *The Breakdown of Democratic Regimes*. That concept has fallen into disfavor in contemporary political science, partly because legitimacy, like mentalities and ideology, is seen as difficult to operationalize in empirical analysis. How would you reply to this criticism?

A: The funny thing is that during the Florida controversy surrounding the presidential elections of 2000, everyone was talking about the legitimacy or non-legitimacy of the Bush presidency. The word came into general use, and people knew what you were talking about when you used it. Weber provides a very complex treatment of legitimacy (Weber 1978). The way I define legitimacy is relatively simple: people believe that the existing political system is the best possible one for their country; they don't see an alternative kind of system as more desirable. That's a minimum. Legitimacy also entails that people are ready to obey decisions made by those who govern regardless of whether obedience is in their self-interest. The National Guard in Oxford, Mississippi, obeyed President Kennedy's orders when it was federalized, even though the Mississippi guardsmen were just as racist as the next person.[13] They believed the commander-in-chief had the authority to make them enforce the decisions of the courts. It is particularly important to understand when people obey not out of self-interest. That is essential for any military organization, because it is never in your self-interest to die, you are not a beneficiary of an action that costs you your life. You need some other motivation besides self-interest.

Q: Your volume on the breakdown of democratic regimes contains a brief, three-page excursus on the special vulnerabilities to breakdown of presidential, as opposed to parliamentary, democracy (Linz 1978, 71–74). You picked this theme up in the 1980s, and it eventually resulted in the publication of a widely cited paper on presidentialism as well as an edited volume on this topic (Linz 1990a, 1994; Linz and Valenzuela 1994). How did you develop your insights about presidentialism?

A: In many pieces I have written there is a reference, at least a footnote, to the next big problem that has to be covered. That was the case with the excursus on presidentialism. I wrote that excursus at the last minute, just as the breakdown volume was about to go to press, that's why that section of the volume does not have any footnotes. In fact, I wrote it in the basement of Alfred Stepan's home in New Haven, where I was correcting the galley

13. In the fall of 1962, President John F. Kennedy federalized the National Guard in Mississippi to restore order in the wake of rioting that erupted at the University of Mississippi in Oxford. The protestors were angered over the admission of James Meredith, a black American, to the university.

proofs for the breakdown volume. I was staying at Al's home because I was on leave from Yale at the time and had come to New Haven for some conference.

Q: But you must have done some thinking beforehand about the vulnerabilities of presidential systems to breakdowns.
A: I was reacting to Guillermo O'Donnell's "impossible game" kind of model, which he used to explain the breakdown of democracy in Argentina in the 1950s (O'Donnell 1973, 1978a). In postwar Italy, which unlike Argentina, had a parliamentary system, the "game" was not impossible. Democracy did not break down in Italy, despite the presence of the Communist Party, which was a powerful anti-system force similar to the Peronists in Argentina. So, I posed the question, "Does presidentialism have something to do with the political instability of Latin American democracies?"

Q: What were the core ideas of your subsequent work on presidentialism?
A: I tried to highlight in a simple way the problems for democratic stability that derive from two elements of presidentialism: (1) the fixed term and zero-sum, winner-take-all nature of such systems, and (2) the "dual legitimacy" of the Congress and presidency. It is basically a very simple idea, but the implications of it that I worked out have generated some discussion.

Q: Your work on presidentialism did indeed launch a lively debate on the comparative merits and demerits of parliamentary and presidential systems.[14] Could you comment on this debate?
A: Some people try to defend presidentialism by arguing that there are presidential systems that work better than others. Certainly, some presidential regimes work, and you could probably improve them by doing away with midterm elections, vice-presidents, and who knows what. That's all interesting stuff, but I don't think it challenges some of my basic assumptions. In general, I don't have much more to say on the topic, unless I were to write an in-depth monograph on the crisis of presidential regimes. But I am not that interested in doing an in-depth study of Latin American, East European, or Russian politics. Other people will do that. Once you have said your piece, you move on.

Q: Another hallmark of your research is your focus on political institutions. This can be seen in your work on political regimes, and perhaps

---

14. See, for example, Horowitz (1990), Lipset (1990), Shugart and Carey (1992), and Mainwaring and Shugart (1997). For Linz's response to Horowitz and Lipset, see Linz (1990b).

most clearly, in your work on presidentialism. Where does this interest in institutions come from? None of your teachers at Columbia worked much on political institutions.

A: Well, Weber deals with institutions all the time, when he talks about sects, churches, political parties, and the types of authority. Those are all institutions. Besides, my legal training in Spain gave me a good sense for institutions and for how to read through a constitution and make comments on it. In fact, many of the important European scholars who were of the generation of my mentors—people like Franz Neumann, Otto Kirchheimer, Henry Ehrmann, and Carl Friedrich—were trained as lawyers. Some of them, when they came to the United States, since they could not be politicians or labor lawyers, became political scientists. In their seminars, they would have students write papers on topics like the conflict between the Senate and the National Assembly in France and how that conflict was managed by the rules of the Fifth Republic's constitution. Kirchheimer, who was in the Political Science Department at Columbia, not in the Law School, had students write case studies of constitutional law. We don't teach students to do that kind of legal institutional analysis anymore, and I think that is a big weakness of contemporary American political science.

My interest in institutions also stems from the analysis of historical cases. Institutions are central, partly because authority in our modern society is legal-rational, in the Weberian sense. People believe that decisions made by the rules should be binding. To give a contemporary example, the public and many politicians in America generally felt that the decision made by the Supreme Court regarding the presidential elections of 2000 was totally partisan, technically incorrect. Still, no one was ready to challenge the Supreme Court. Those five judges rendered their decision, and that was the end of the story. In a country where the institutions work according to a different principle, for example, in many Latin American countries, the people would have said "This is a travesty," General X would have dismissed the Supreme Court, and Mister Gore, who had the popular majority, would have become president.

So, institutions matter. I don't know why you have to prove something like that. You just have to read the newspaper every day to know that institutions make a difference in politics. You don't have to do any research to be aware of that.

Fascism

Q: Fascism is another topic on which your research has focused (Linz 1976, 1980, 2003a). What drew you to this question and what contributions have you made in this area of research?

A: My childhood in Salamanca during the Civil War and the identification at the time with the Falange in the context of the different political currents in the Franco coalition, my knowledge of German politics, and my work on the breakdown of democracy inevitably led to an interest in fascism. Karl Dietrich Bracher, the great German historian, whom I got to know at the Center for Advanced Studies in the Behavioral Sciences (CASBS), suggested my name to the publisher Fischer for a little book on comparative fascism, which finally was done by Ernst Nolte. This, however, led me to teach a seminar on fascism at Columbia. Later I contributed a long essay to Walter Laqueur's *Fascism: A Reader's Guide* (Linz 1976) and participated in a number of meetings on fascism. I have dealt with the subject in at least five publications, including a book published in Italy (Linz 2003b). I also helped the historian Stanley Payne, who is now the major authority on the comparative study of fascist movements, with his dissertation on the Falange.

I think I contributed much to break with the dominant Marxist interpretation and formulate a typological definition by a comparative study of all fascist movements and leaders.

Democratization, Nationalism, and Federalism

Q: Your work since the 1980s has focused on three major themes: democratization, nationalism, and federalism. Let's start with your 1996 volume with Alfred Stepan, *Problems of Democratic Transition and Consolidation*.[15] What were the principal contributions of that book?
A: We made several important contributions. We developed the idea that the type of previous non-democratic regime shapes the different paths of transition to democracy by conditioning what you can do and how you can do it. We also analyzed the conditions for successful democratic transitions in terms of political society, civil society, economic society, the bureaucracy, and the rule of law, and we provided dimensions for analyzing the consolidation of new democracies. I believe our analysis of the "stateness" problem in multinational societies was another important contribution. Those things are all relatively accepted by and diffused among many people.

Q: Why had the vast amount of prior research on democratic transitions overlooked the importance of the old, non-democratic regime for conditioning processes of democratization?
A: This question raises again the normative bias that democracy should be the result of the will and actions of "the people," and therefore there can be nothing good in the previous regime. But the fact of the matter is that, for a

15. See Chapter 12 for Stepan's view of this project.

variety of reasons, people who are part of the old non-democratic regime sometimes make the transition possible and thus contribute to a good result. Some of them, like Adolfo Suárez in Spain and Lee Teng-hui in Taiwan, even become the leaders of the democratization process. That is disappointing for some people—that the "good guys" did not achieve democracy and the "bad guys" played a positive role.

Q: Turning to your interest in nationalism and the problem of achieving stable democracy in multinational societies, how did you become interested in this topic and what contributions have you made to that area of research?
A: As a Spaniard, I always had a latent interest in the problem of Spanish peripheral nationalisms. Who could not be interested in Catalan and Basque nationalism? I wrote my first major paper on nationalism in the 1970s for a conference Stein Rokkan organized (Linz 1973b), later I wrote a book on the Basque problem (Linz 1986), and I am now working with Al Stepan on multinationalism in federal states (Stepan, Linz, and Yadav, forthcoming; Linz and Stepan, forthcoming). My interest in nationalism was initially stimulated by conversations at the CASBS with Joshua Fishman on language policies and with Karl Deutsch.

Q: What are your best ideas on the topic of nationalism?
A: You never know. Sometimes you write a paper, which you don't have a particular interest in, but you articulate something quite original that you did not expect. My contribution to the book edited by Edward Tiryakian on the transition from a primordial to a territorial conception of nation turned out that way (Linz 1985a). It is a very complicated paper that draws on a question we asked in a survey about how the members of a nation defined the boundaries of their national community. The sample for the survey was taken from different parts of Spain—Catalonia, the Basque Country, and Galicia—and also from the French Basque Country. We did not know what we would get from that question, and I was not even sure it would be a useful question to ask. But it turned out to offer some very strange insights about how a nationalist movement based on a shared cultural-linguistic identity manages the challenge of integrating non-native populations into the new nation. The surprising finding was that the most radicalized supporters of the ETA (Euskadi Ta Askatasuna—Basque Fatherland and Liberty), the Basque separatist movement, actually held a *non-primordial* notion of nationalism—they felt that anyone who lived and worked in the territory and identified with the Basque nation, whether or not they were natives, should be considered part of the Basque nation. That seems contradictory until you see the logic of it: defining all those who live in the territory as

Basques makes it easier to integrate the non-native population into the emerging nation and the hoped-for new state. This non-primordial understanding of nation at first seems quite tolerant and integrative, but, in a curious way, it is a very intolerant idea, because it provides a basis for demanding that everyone who lives in the territory should identify with the emerging nation. So, that paper turned out to be very fruitful for me and also quite interesting for developing a theory of nationalism. But nobody has paid much attention to it.

Q: Why not?
A: First, the edited volume in which the paper appeared may not have had many readers. Second, nationalists of every stripe want to see things in terms of "us and them." This means they cannot see the complexity of national identity, that people have dual identities, and that nations are constructed and not based only on primordial characteristics. My paper was too complicated for many students of nationalism.

Q: Are there other ideas of yours about nationalism that you feel especially proud about?
A: I think my ongoing work on the distinction between a nation-state and a state-nation has been fruitful. In a state-nation citizens identify with and feel loyalty to the institutions of the same state, yet they retain different national identities. The Swiss case is the classic example of a state-nation. Belgium is another example. Every time I go there, people tell me it will be the last time, because the next time I visit, Belgium will be gone. But the years passed and Belgium is still there. This raises the question, "What is Belgium?" We have interesting data, which I have to analyze in greater depth, that show that, although Flemish and Waloon identities are very strong, there is also a fairly strong Belgian identity. Citizens retain different national identities but share a common identity with the Belgian state. This idea of a state-nation has slowly been evolving in more and more of my papers, and it will probably be a major theme in the book on federalism (Linz and Stepan, forthcoming).

Q: What motivated your current project on federalism? Why did you choose to write a big book on that topic?
A: My interest in Spanish peripheral nationalism and, more generally, in the "stateness" problem facing multinational countries as they underwent democratic transitions led me to be interested in federalism. Also, "the problem" today is to study different types of democracies comparatively, and my interest in federalism falls in line with that—democracies are not all the same, and the distinction between federal and unitary democracy is an

interesting way of getting at those differences. Besides, the existing work on federalism is pretty disappointing. Books on federalism do not deal much with democracy. Books on nationalism don't deal with federalism or democracy. The challenge of bringing the three themes together—nationalism, democracy, and federalism—was tempting.

Q: How is the work on the federalism book coming along?
A: Oh, too slow. Al Stepan and I have both been doing too many other things. But we have most of the theoretical part, and the themes are pretty clear. We still have to finish working on all the countries. I know some of them, like Spain and Germany, quite well. Al already knew Brazil well, and he has recently gone to Russia and India several times. He has also been to Canada. Writing the country chapters provokes modifications and rethinking in the more theoretical chapters, and vice versa. So, it will take a while.

Q: Besides the federalism book, are there any other projects on which you are currently working?
A: I just finished a think piece on political parties and why they are so disliked and mistrusted (Linz 2002). That piece has survey data because I managed to get some questions into a Spanish national survey. The survey has people who say, "Parties create unnecessary divisions," and people who say, "Parties are all the same." Curiously, a significant proportion of the respondents say both things. If I had the resources to go deeper into that I would explore why some respondents choose these and other seemingly contradictory answers. But I don't have the data, and I don't have a research project on how people perceive political parties. I would love to see somebody do it.

The Craft and Tools of Research
Social Science as Science

Q: Do you consider yourself a scientist?
A: If you mean a *natural* scientist, obviously not. If you define science the way biologists, physicists, or chemists do, you assume there are invariant relationships among elements that, if you discover them, would be valid five centuries ago and presumably would be equally valid for the same elements in the future. Natural scientists also assume that these relationships are valid across space: the atomic structure will be the same across all countries, and what is discovered in a lab in Moscow or in New Haven is valid everywhere.

Social phenomena are different, because they are bound by time and space. The kinds of political and economic systems we study may exist for a century or two, but that's all. Nationalist movements and nation-states are important phenomena only after the eighteenth century, because what we call a nation-state basically did not exist in 98 percent of the world before the French Revolution and maybe even the nineteenth century. Similarly, modern capitalism did not exist until the nineteenth century. And economic phenomena are constantly changing. I studied Spanish business enterprises in the 1960s. Many of the enterprises I studied—probably 60 percent of them—no longer exist; they have either disappeared or been absorbed by other companies. Others have become multinationals: the Banco de Bilbao-Vizcaya has fused with a Mexican bank and is now the largest bank in Mexico. It is no longer the kind of bank it was in the 1960s, and its relationship with business is totally different. Even at the most micro-level, patterns of human interaction are bound by time and space. An American family today is very different from what it was a hundred years ago in terms of husband-wife and parent-children relationships. If you are a young Hindu man in India, you may take it for granted that you will have an arranged marriage, whereas most young men elsewhere do not make this assumption. So, whatever we do as social scientists is historical in the sense that everything we study is bound by time and to some extent space. What you discover about the way democracy works in Sweden may be important for understanding how democracy works in India, but no one would say that Indian and Swedish democracy are the same. They are in the same genus, democracy, but that is all.

What some people are looking for—and it is a legitimate desire—is elementary building blocks of society. George Homans's book, *The Human Group* (1950), tries to do that. Durkheim tries to do something similar in *Elementary Forms of Religious Life* (Durkheim 1995), which partly explains why I am not Durkheimian. To some extent, Simmel does the same thing, which is why his work is not very relevant for political sociology, though it may be relevant for the study of small groups like the family and friendship cliques. These works aim to find the most elementary components of human interaction on the borderline of psychology, though Durkheim makes an interesting and complicated argument about why sociology is not psychology. When you get to the more simple components of social interaction, you might actually discover some "universal" elements that exist in very different societies across time. For example, the problem of a triad— that is, the conflicts and instability that can emerge when three people share power and decision making—can help us understand why the various historical forms of triumvirates have always been politically unstable and why, for example, the sharing of power in the Roman Empire among Octavian, Mark Antony, and Lepidus failed. You can even build an elementary theory of triumvirates. Yet things quickly become much more complicated when you try to extend these insights into a theory of political coalitions.

When some people in the coalition are anti-system and others are pro-system, coalition formation becomes much more complex. Coalition making in a polarized party system is not the same as coalition making in a moderate party system, and a coalition that includes the Nazis is distinct from a coalition among democratic parties. So, in order to understand coalition formation, you have to look at the actual content of the coalition, that is, the positions of the partners, the ideological distance among them. And you have to consider what an anti-system party is, what a semi-loyal party is, and whether or not it is legitimate to form coalitions with an anti-system party. All of this complexity involves matters that are much more historically bounded.

A related issue that also sets limits to our ability to make generalizations is the problem of limited cases. Take, for example, federal states (Stepan, Linz, and Yadav, forthcoming; Linz and Stepan, forthcoming). According to our definition, the number of democratic federal states is between twelve and fourteen, depending on whether you include Nigeria and South Africa. This is a very small universe of cases to begin with. Yet some people would say that Spain is not really a federal state. Others would argue that Germany is not really federal either, but is a "disguised" unitary state, which I think is nonsense, although Germany is certainly quite different from the United States and Switzerland. Moreover, each of the twelve cases has its specific history and phases, which makes it difficult to generalize across the full universe. And once you make a few distinctions among the twelve cases, as we do between "coming together" and "holding together" as contrasting motivations for choosing federalism, then the twelve cases are reduced into sets of three and four. You want to avoid dealing with a single case in isolation, but a complete, meaningful, and insightful analysis ends up being on a single case. This does not satisfy those who want generalizations.

Another example of how the nature of our subject matter limits our ability to generalize can be seen in the study of democratic transitions. We simply cannot understand the Spanish transition if we ignore the problems posed by the peripheral nationalism in the Basque Country and Catalonia. But those kinds of problems were absolutely irrelevant to the transition process in places like Portugal, Greece, and the Latin American countries. In fact, until the Eastern European transitions began in 1989, the Spanish case was the only transition where nationality conflicts played an important role. Other cases also have distinctive features that cannot be ignored. For example, the shaping of society by totalitarian rule for seven decades in the Soviet Union has no parallel. This means that the transition there is taking place in a societal context that is fundamentally different from that in other cases.

We have to add variables for some cases and ignore variables for other cases. That's the nature of the beast, it's the way the world is, and there is nothing we can do about it. If we don't emphasize different variables across cases, we end up with truisms, which are not very interesting. At best, we have generalizations that are valid for maybe four or five cases, but generalizations that are valid for all times and places probably do not exist for the phenomena we are studying.

Q: What should we aspire to if generalizations about politics and society are so difficult to achieve?
A: To *know* something. We should aspire only to know something about how a phenomenon came about, how it works, what its consequences are for people's lives, and how it is changing. The fact of the matter is that we know miserably little about political and social phenomena, and we will never know very much—in part, because the number of people working in our field is so limited. In many countries, nobody, or just a few people, is working on particular themes, and so those themes are not covered adequately. If you do good physics in Chicago, your work will be valid for anyone who wants to do physics in Jakarta. But if you know a lot about the presidency in the United States, that does not help you very much if you want to understand how the presidency works in Indonesia. You have to study the Indonesian context and do work on Indonesia. So, the cumulation of knowledge about politics and society is hindered partly by the limited number of people involved. We also face the problem of limited resources, which makes it difficult to repeat the same study every few years, as we would need to do if we wished to achieve something like an epidemiological study.

Q: Should we be repeating and replicating studies?
A: All the time. We should replicate all kinds of studies, although that work might be for "lesser lights." Nowadays, any bright, capable political scientist with a basic methodological training knows how to construct a questionnaire and do a study of who votes for whom in a national election. Because each election is different from the previous one, we very much need repeat election studies. It is essential to have time series data, but we don't have them for most countries. In the natural sciences, repeating an experiment when something changes is the normal way of working. By contrast, we social scientists have an emphasis, perhaps derived from the humanities, on originality and creativity. That is a nonscientific dimension of our work, the idea that each study has to be original.

Q: Should we do away, then, with the notion that originality is important in the social sciences?

A: No, I think there is much room for that. But the world we want to understand and study is so complex and changing that anything we do is good, and, at the same time, anything we do is insufficient. It's like the story of St. Augustine on the beach with the angel trying to empty the water out of the sea with a conch shell—it's ridiculous in a sense. We simply cannot do what we want and need to do, and there is no way around it. First, the total amount of resources available to the social sciences is woefully insufficient. Just compare the amount of money spent on natural science training and experiments with what we spend. Any student of physics learning how to handle the linear accelerator at Stanford—I had a friend who was a physicist —spent in five minutes of training the amount of electricity the whole city consumed in a day! But how many national sample surveys, not to mention worldwide surveys, do we have the money to do? The Latinobarometer is done once a year, but half the questionnaire focuses on one specific issue or another, so the total richness and representativeness of that survey is a problem.[16] And that's just to monitor democracy in the Americas. There is a disjunction between the resources society provides us, on one hand, and what we want to understand and know, on the other.

Something that makes social science simultaneously easier and more difficult than natural science is the fact that any intelligent person can achieve some knowledge about our subject matter without doing research or getting specialized training. We are all members of society, and therefore we all know how some things work. Consequently, people see our books and say, "Well, I knew that already," or "How can you say that when I know it is not so?" Social scientists are always challenging the knowledge that the actors in the society already have. And these actors are the ones who decide if we should do our job, because they decide whether we get funding or can work as advisors. It's as if the bacteria under the microscope were capable of saying, "Look, you're doing the experiment the wrong way." We cannot force people under the microscope and hold them there so we can repeat the experiment fifty times. If we are lucky we can interview an elite once, but they may not be available the next time. And the actors we want to study can simply refuse to be studied, or they can keep things confidential, which means that our knowledge is shaped by what the society wants us to know, except when the historical archives are opened. Now that the Soviet archives are open, we are learning lots of things we could not know before about the relationship between the Communist Party and the Soviet leadership. The first thing anyone who wants to engage in social science needs is awareness that the social world is different from other worlds.

16. Latinobarometer is a public opinion survey that covers seventeen countries in Latin America. See www.latinobarometro.org/.

People who want the social sciences to be more scientific often have a misconception of what science is, a conception that scientists would not agree with. Take geological prospecting. Geologists have reasonable expectations that in certain places you are likely to find petroleum, and companies spend millions of dollars prospecting based on such expectations. Still, you don't always find petroleum, even though you may have wasted millions of dollars on the assumption that there was a reasonable probability oil could be found. So, despite their use of sophisticated experimental models and measurement techniques, geologists retain a healthy appreciation for how unique and contingent combinations of factors can determine outcomes. Forecasting the weather has a similar contingent quality. In certain parts of the world the weather can be forecasted with great accuracy, in other parts, a week ahead. But here, in the northeastern United States, despite the vast amount of information available from all the weather stations, forecasts are subject to error. If we social scientists attempt to forecast elections or a coup, we are not that different. Given the small amount of resources we have—the limited number of stations for observing the weather, so to speak—we are doing quite well.

Social scientists are often criticized for not being able to provide results that avert disasters and help solve the world's problems. Well, sometimes the best we can do is say that this is an incurable situation with no solutions. When a Spanish politician asks me, "What is your solution for the situation in the Basque Country and the elections there next month?" all I can say is that I don't have a solution, but things will probably not improve overnight, and there is no miracle that can solve the problem.

Q: No one is going to pay millions of dollars to hear that kind of advice.
A: No. But you pay a doctor who tells you that you have a terminal illness, and nobody questions whether he knows his oncology.

Q: If social science is indeed so limited in its capacity to help solve human problems, then why do you do it?
A: I have fun. That's a cynical answer, I guess, but what else can I say? Each time I follow some hunch and it fits, it's interesting and pleasurable. I learn something, and, fortunately, society is paying me for having my fun. Now, why is it fun? Because knowledge is something worth having, and it may even be useful some times. It is not always clear who will use the knowledge we generate. Someone who reads my book on the breakdown of democracies might learn something about how to avoid a breakdown (Linz 1978). But somebody else might read it and learn something about how to exploit a crisis and cause a breakdown. You never know who might try to use your work or for what purposes. When Columbia University had its big crisis in

1968 during the student strikes, one of the students in my course on the breakdown of democracies said, "Don't you think what is happening at Columbia—the way the president and administrators are dealing with the problem—fits very well your model of democratic breakdowns?" I said, "Well, if you see things that way, then maybe what I am teaching you is not so irrelevant."

Problem Selection

Q: You say that our main aspiration as social scientists should be to know something. Yet this begs the fundamental question of *what* is worth knowing. Which problems are worth studying? What criteria should we use to select research problems?

A: That's central. Problem selection in the social sciences, as Weber (1949) says, is ultimately driven by extra-scientific motivations. You are interested in certain questions because you live in this world, because you are a citizen of a country that has a specific problem, or because you live in a particular historical period. There are personal, experiential, generational, and historical contexts that influence what one studies. Nobody could think about politics in the 1930s and 1940s without considering the Nazi experience, totalitarianism, the Soviet Union, Stalin, and everything that these phenomena meant. To ignore the Civil War and its origins, or the Franco regime, was not conceivable for a young Spaniard like me with an interest in political and social science. And who could live in the 1970s without looking at transitions to democracy? As soon as the transition started in Portugal in 1974, I quickly got my plane ticket and went several times so I could follow the democratization process by attending party meetings and rallies and by talking with politicians. What was happening in Portugal might be relevant to what was eventually going to happen in Spain, because Franco was not eternal. Because of your biography, you have a personal interest and involvement that motivate the selection of many research problems. This is why some of the best people in our field have been individuals with rich personal experiences, such as World War II, exile, political turmoil, or working in a factory. People like Albert Hirschman and Reinhard Bendix, for example, lived through so many traumatic things.[17] They had more complex and problematic lives than many of our graduate students today, who typically go from a good high school to a good college, get good grades, and then go directly to graduate school, having already majored in college in the same field in which they do their graduate work. They have never done anything else except be in the university, and that may be a drawback.

17. See Hirschman (1995, Part II) and Bendix (1986, 1990).

Obviously, problem selection is not always driven purely by personal and intellectual interests; it often results from a mixture of interests and opportunity. In 1958, after I defended my thesis at Columbia, I went to Spain with a grant from the SSRC (Social Science Research Council) Committee on Comparative Politics—the Almond Committee—to work on interest groups and politics. So, I started collecting data on Spanish interest groups. I took a trip to California, and on the way back to Spain to continue my research, I stopped in Washington, D.C., where I called an old friend, who was working as the economic attaché at the Spanish embassy. We met for lunch, and were joined by another Spaniard, who happened to be the director of the School of Industrial Management, a business school inspired by the Harvard and Pittsburgh models. Well, the School of Industrial Management was about to celebrate its fifth anniversary, and I saw this as a nice opportunity to link my study of interest groups with the study of businessmen. It turned out money was available to support my project, so I set to work designing a study. First, I went back to Schumpeter, whose work is fundamental if you want to study entrepreneurs (Schumpeter 1942). Then I looked at Hoselitz's (1960) work on the role of entrepreneurship in economic development and read the main books on business elites, including those of C. Wright Mills (1956) and Suzanne Keller (1963). So, I had an initial interest in the role of interest groups in the Franco system—trade unions, banks, and so on. Then, by chance, I got an opportunity to do a study of business elites. And, finally, I got the intellectual stimulus of going back to Schumpeter. All those elements came together. Opportunity is a key part of problem selection.

Q: Is there a method to problem selection? This example of how you came to work on Spanish business elites makes problem selection seem like a matter of chance and luck.
A: To a significant extent, it is chance and luck, or even accident. I have done work that did not fit into any broader research program of mine. The best example is probably a paper I wrote for a conference on intellectuals that Shmuel Eisenstadt organized in Jerusalem. I was inclined to write a paper on the role of intellectuals in the Spanish crises of the nineteenth and twentieth centuries, during the Republic and the Civil War, but Eisenstadt preferred something more historical, "Something on intellectuals in sixteenth- and seventeenth-century Spain." Since I wanted to visit Jerusalem and stop in Istanbul on the way, I said, "Okay," and I wrote a piece purely for the occasion (Linz 1972). Writing that paper turned out to be a fascinating experience. I learned a lot of things, some even relevant for other areas of my research. For example, it turns out that to have an intellectual elite in the sixteenth and seventeenth centuries, you needed a

certain population density from which to draw that elite, because the proportion of really creative minds was small relative to the size of the masses. An excellent bio-bibliographic work by the seventeenth-century Spanish scholar, Nicolás Antonio, *Bibliotheca Hispana Nova sive Hispanorum Scriptorum qui ab anno MD add MDCLXXIV floreure notitia,* had data on the number of members of different religious orders. I had the same information on the outstanding writers and scholars of the sixteenth and seventeenth centuries whose work is still considered relevant today—so to say, the intellectual elite of the period. It turns out that the proportions of members of different religious orders among the "elite" and among the "mass" were almost parallel. It seems, therefore, that an elite presence presupposes a mass pool. This finding certainly would be relevant for the study of the political elite today.

Another example of how accidents are involved in problem selection concerns my work on nationalism. I had a latent interest in the problem of Spanish peripheral nationalisms, but I did not write anything on this topic until Stein Rokkan organized a conference in France on state and nation building and invited me to give a paper. So, in the 1970s, I wrote my first major paper on nationalism—"Early State-Building and Late Peripheral Nationalisms against the State" (Linz 1973b). Since then the topic of nationalism has been a central focus of my research. The fact that Stein Rokkan had an interest in the problem of nationalism, combined with my latent interest in it, led me to write my first major paper on this topic.

Q: In addition to underscoring the role of chance and contingency in problem selection, these examples also highlight how one's professional networks structure research opportunities.
A: Very much so. That is the "invisible college." Academic communities shape research in part by linking individuals with funding or entrepreneurship to others who potentially have an interest in a problem or who can contribute something to a meeting. These connections force people to do more research on a topic and produce a paper. Some of the papers you give at a meeting may never be picked up by you or by anybody. But sometimes a paper becomes important. For example, Abe Lowenthal and his collaborator Lou Goodman at the Woodrow Wilson Center organized a conference on Latin American parties and democracy. I did not have much to say on Latin American parties, but I had written something on parliamentarism and presidentialism in my book on the breakdown of democratic regimes (Linz 1978, 71–74), which I decided to expand and develop, and my paper became the first version of my work on presidentialism-parliamentarism (Linz 1985b). The paper started circulating, I presented it at various meetings, several people published it, it was even called an "underground classic," and

finally Arturo Valenzuela and I organized a meeting at Georgetown University that resulted in a book with an expanded version of the paper (Linz 1994). I recently wrote an essay on presidentialism for the *International Encyclopedia of the Social and Behavioral Sciences* (Linz 2001a), so I have become an authority on presidentialism. This was not totally an accident, because I had already dealt with the theme in my book on the breakdown of democracy, but the fact that I wrote a paper that became the basis for subsequent debate was partly a result of that meeting on Latin American parties.

Classics

Q: You were exposed early on to the classics of social theory. How has your grounding in classical social theory influenced your empirical work?
A: My exposure to social theory has had a fundamental impact on my research. For instance, the notion of re-equilibration that I use in the book on the breakdown of democratic regimes comes clearly from Pareto (Linz 1978, 122; Pareto 1963). The constant references throughout my work to the state reflect my early exposure to Weber. I never had to "bring the state back in" or rediscover the state,[18] because the state was there from the very beginning through my familiarity with the work of Weber and also with the *Staatslehre* work of Hermann Heller, a social democrat who wrote a classic political science book, very much influenced by Weber (Heller 1934). The Weberian mixture of material interests and ideas—the notion that ideas and values have their own weight apart from material interests—has also been very important in my work. And the Weberian concept of legitimacy basically formed the core of my book on the breakdown of democratic regimes.

Q: What is it about Weber that is so special? Why is he your lodestar?
A: I deal with the problem of authority and legitimacy, which is basic for understanding the breakdown of democratic regimes, basic for understanding non-democratic regimes, and basic for understanding transitions to democracy. I also study political parties, and Weber and his junior friend and collaborator, Robert Michels, is the core for any questions you want to ask about democracy and parties (Linz 1966, 2006a). You cannot deal with religion and politics without Weberian concepts like church versus sect, ethical prophecy and exemplary prophecy, Caesaropapism, and the distinctions among Eastern Christianity, Western Catholicism, and Lutheranism. The course I taught for many years on religion and politics had to start with Weber. Even Weber's few pages on nationalism are key (Weber 1978,

18. The reference is to Evans, Rueschemeyer, and Skocpol (1985).

343–98, 921–26). I recently used them in developing my notion of the distinctions among a nation-state, a state-nation, and a multinational state. In a sense, this insight comes from one page of Weber, when he asks, "How can you call Switzerland and Luxembourg nation-states?"

Whenever I start working on something, I usually look to see whether Weber has anything to say on that theme. I also use some of Mannheim—especially his English period—in a similar way. Nothing organized in Mannheim's thought is very fruitful, but he has all kinds of little insights that are worth looking up. When I spent time at the Humboldt University in Berlin as the Georg Simmel Visiting Professor, I felt a moral obligation to see what I could do with Simmel. I reread some of his works and read some new ones and because I was teaching political sociology, I looked for something relevant to topics such as transitions to democracy and the conditions for stable democracy. There is not that much in Simmel, but he does have an essay on competition with a very insightful analysis of the harmful consequences of negative campaigning (Simmel 1995, 222–26). Although Simmel doesn't talk specifically about election campaigns, he says that if two competitors make their appeals by deriding the product of the other, neither gains. This happens because nobody is making a positive appeal that would convince the buyer that his product is the best; they are only making negative appeals to convince the buyer that the other's product is no good. And that does not create any identification with a product.

You have questions in your own mind that you want to address, and sometimes you read the classics and say, "Well, that's an interesting insight, it illustrates what I was groping for." So, the more you read and the more you know, the better.

Concept Formation

Q: You have generated numerous concepts with remarkable staying power, for example, the concepts of authoritarian and sultanistic regimes. What is your approach to concept formation?
A: First of all, I want to describe reality. There is a world out there, and I want to describe it in some way, just as a journalist or a historian does. But I want to describe the reality with a conceptualization more abstract than just telling a story. So, I try to describe reality, and then to conceptualize it.

I was interested in non-democratic regimes, so I read the work of Friedrich and Brzezinski (1956; see also Brzezinski 1962), Arendt (1951), Sigmund Neumann (1942), and Franz Neumann (1957). They all used the concept of totalitarianism. I asked myself, "Does this concept help me understand the Franco regime?" And I saw it did not fit and started working on my own formulation of the concept of authoritarian regime (Linz 1964).

In a similar way, I was dissatisfied with putting the regimes of Anastasio Somoza Debayle in Nicaragua and Rafael Leonidas Trujillo in the Dominican Republic into the same box as the regimes of Franco in Spain and Antonio Salazar in Portugal. The Somoza and Trujillo regimes were cases of non-democratic, non-totalitarian systems, but classifying them as authoritarian regimes would have diluted the concept and thus did not make much sense. I had a good understanding of how Trujillo's regime was distinct from Franco's, because I had a friend at Columbia, Jesús de Galíndez, who was opposed to both regimes, and talked much about it.[19] I picked up the concept of sultanistic regimes from Weber's sociology of power and typology of domination, which I taught every other year. Weber makes a distinction between a traditional, legitimate form of patrimonialism, on one hand, and the corruption of patrimonialism into sultanism, on the other. When I reread Weber's section on patrimonialism, I thought, "That's exactly what I am looking for!" Then I reformulated Weber's concept in a modern way by specifying indicators of sultanism, like nepotism, cronyism, and the private appropriation of power and wealth.[20] Specifying indicators helps you see the dimensions of the phenomenon. The next step is to identify clear cases of the phenomenon. Then you find cases that are a mixture, like Nicolae Ceauşescu's regime in Romania, which had elements of sultanism combined with very strong elements of totalitarianism.

I move back and forth between observations and concepts. In the case of sultanism, the evidence pushed me toward a certain conceptualization: observations of the Somoza and Trujillo regimes first led me to see the need for a new concept, and then the concept helped me organize observations of other cases. Sometimes, however, conceptualization precedes observations and data. In my paper in the festschrift for Hans-Jürgen Puhle, I wrote about the concept of state-nation as distinct from a multinational state (Linz 2001b). I referred to the Swiss case and said that Belgium also seemed to have the characteristics of a state-nation, though I did not have any empirical data to support this assertion. Just after I sent out the final version of the paper, I found a survey done in Belgium in 1996 that has questions about Belgian identity. The survey provides evidence supporting my idea that Belgium is in fact closer to a state-nation than a multinational

19. Galíndez was an exiled representative of the Basque government, who had taught international law in the Dominican Republic. "When he wrote a doctoral dissertation at Columbia University revealing some of the inside workings of the Trujillo regime, he confided to Juan Linz in 1955 that he feared for his life, and that he had deposited his manuscript in a safe place in case something happened to him. Soon afterward the dictator had Galíndez abducted in New York and taken to the Dominican Republic, where he was tortured to death." See Chehabi and Linz (1998a, 4–5).

20. Linz's initial formulation of the concept of a sultanistic regime is in Linz (1975). See also Chehabi and Linz (1998a).

state. So the discovery of evidence sometimes comes after the formulation of the concept.

After you have described and conceptualized reality, you move on to explanation. This requires asking "Why is this or that so?" and "Why are these things different?" Such questions cannot always be answered. Description is not easy, but it is relatively viable. People can agree—if they are in good faith—that the Nazi system was different from Franco's Spain. That's an empirical question. Explaining why these systems were different is more difficult. When you try to explain, to see which variables account for differences across systems, disagreements are much more likely. Since most phenomena that we deal with are multi-causal, you give primacy to some variables rather than others, but somebody else would give primacy to the others. How do you decide how much weight to give economic factors, ideological factors, or the personality of leaders? So, agreement becomes more difficult. Still, by making comparisons and controlling for different factors you can reach some conclusions.

Historical Analysis

Q: What role does historical analysis play in your research?

A: It's central. From the standpoint of existing explanations for federalism—for example, William Riker's (1964, 1975) theory of federalism, or the argument that federalism is needed to govern large, extended countries—the fact that Germany is federal poses a puzzle. A related puzzle involves the peculiar form that German federalism takes. Why does Germany have an institution like the Bundesrat, which is so different from the American Senate that it provides an alternative model of how to organize a federal upper chamber? To explain why Germany is federal and the form of German federalism you have to go back to the history of Germany, to the Holy Roman Empire, the Rheinbund, the 1848 convention in Frankfurt. This historical analysis immediately raises the question of why Italy, which, like Germany, also underwent a process of unification into a nation-state, ended up with a unitary, fairly centralized state. Why did Germany and Italy have such different institutional histories? To answer this question, I am reading books on the history of Germany during the period of unification and I have also started reading on the Italian unification. I have to go back to history—there is no way of escaping it if you want to account for these institutional outcomes.

Q: Do you ever wish you had been a historian?

A: I actually was a visiting associate professor of history at Stanford for a semester in 1966. And I have been on the board of some historical journals, including the *Journal of Interdisciplinary History, Comparative Studies in So-*

ciety and History, and an Austrian journal of social history. I have also written an unpublished social history of Spain during the Franco period.

Q: What distinguishes your work from the work of a historian?
A: A historian would spend much more time working in archives and with
primary sources than I can afford to, though I wouldn't mind doing it.
A historian would also dwell much more on concrete events and details,
whereas I deal more with conceptual problems and also do much more
comparative analysis. Take the outstanding book on fascism by the historian Stanley Payne (1995). Payne would never have a table—as I would—on
the vote for fascist parties in different countries or on the social background
of fascist leaders in different countries. Nor would he deal systematically
with comparisons between fascisms, although he does compare fascism to
other non-democratic movements. He would also pay less attention than I
to the social bases of fascist movements. And he would have separate chapters telling the story of fascism in Latvia, fascism in Finland, and so on,
yet Latvia and Finland would not appear in the other chapters. By contrast, I would be moving all the time from one case to the other (Linz 1976,
1980, 2003a).

Survey Research

**Q: Survey research has played an important role in much of your work.
How have you used this methodology?**
A: Public opinion research has always been one of my pet interests. I
learned how to do survey research from Paul Lazarsfeld when I was in
graduate school. My dissertation analyzed public opinion data for the 1953
election in Germany, and I later used public opinion research in my studies
of Spanish youths and entrepreneurs (Linz and de Miguel 1966, 1974). In
the late 1970s, I used survey methods to study elections and public opinion
during the Spanish transition (Linz et al. 1982). I also used surveys to
study nationalism; my book on Basque nationalism is a public opinion
study (Linz 1986). I helped found a private survey research organization
in Spain, which analyzed data for me. I have not done much work with
surveys recently, in part because I have not learned to handle the new
computers.

**Q: What is the value of survey research as a methodology? What kinds
of issues and research questions is it uniquely suited to?**
A: Public opinion research is the only instrument with which we can study
the opinions of the common man, as opposed to leaders and elites. That's
fundamental. Also, studies of elites based on surveys can be an important
way of getting at their more private opinions. If you want to understand

what Catalan politicians think about linguistic policies, you can look at their public statements, but they also have private opinions that are interesting. And it may be possible to get at these private opinions using a survey instrument.

Q: What is the trick to designing an effective survey instrument?

A: First you need to have an interesting problem, and you have to know something about it. Then you have to use what Max Weber would call *verstehen*—putting yourself in the skin of the people you are studying. If you are designing a survey with questions about nationalism, and the respondents are likely to range from extreme separatist nationalists to people who dislike nationalism, you have to put yourself into the minds of the different types of potential respondents. This helps you formulate a question that allows them to express their opinions. You also need a balanced question that takes care of all the nuances without revealing your own preferences, so that you don't bias the responses. This process of formulating a question actually helps you think more deeply about the research problem, because it requires that you define and put yourself in the place of the different actors you are studying. The next step is to develop a whole set of questions, some of them standard questions used in other research. Then you might ask the same question to the elites and the general population so you can compare the two groups in terms of what they support and don't support.

Fieldwork

Q: What role has fieldwork played in your research?

A: Fieldwork is very important and fruitful because it gives you a feel for the context and for how people understand the questions you are studying. In my study of Spanish entrepreneurs, fieldwork gave me a sense of what the businessman was like, what he thought, and how he reacted to the environment in which he worked. Fieldwork can also be a source of new ideas. In the mid-1960s, when I did a study of Andalusian villages, I visited eight villages and even spent time living in one or two of them (Linz 1971). I learned that a village that looks poor and dirty may actually be a wealthy village without many social problems, whereas a village that looks very neat, with clean streets and a nice town square, may actually be a poor, miserable place. The reason is simple: in places with rural unemployment there may be government money going into employment-generating public works to beautify the village. In a rich and agriculturally productive area, the streets may be full of mud, but they are also full of trucks transporting the produce. So, through fieldwork you discover that social policies and public works programs can, in a sense, cover up social problems. By bringing you closer to contexts, fieldwork allows you to acquire a different sensitivity. It is also exciting because you really get to talk with people.

Q: As we move on in our lives and careers, it often gets harder to do fieldwork because we accumulate personal and professional obligations that make it difficult to spend a lot of time in the field. As a result, the typical pattern is to do fieldwork for the dissertation and first book and then shift away from fieldwork in subsequent research. What do you think about this tendency?

A: My experience was actually the opposite of what you describe. My dissertation was based on secondary analysis of survey data and library work on the German party systems and German social history. My fieldwork was a bit later in my career, for my studies of Spanish youth and entrepreneurs. And in 1976 and 1977, I did a year-and-a-half of fieldwork in Spain on the democratic transition. I think you can and should do fieldwork later in your career. It is not a good idea to give up fieldwork because you are an established academic.

Q: You mentioned the fieldwork you did on various occasions in Spain. Have you done fieldwork in other countries? For example, did you do fieldwork in Brazil for your 1973 article on what you called the "authoritarian situation" (Linz 1973c)?

A: No. I had read things about Brazil and had talked many times with Al Stepan. I also attended a meeting in Brazil on the future of the authoritarian situation, but, overall, I did not spend very much time there. There is actually a funny story about that article. *Veja*, the well-known Brazilian magazine, wanted to publish a translation of my paper on the authoritarian situation. They interviewed me in connection with the article and wanted to know how long I had been in Brazil and how many politicians I had met. I said I had been there for just four or five days and had not seen any politician.

Q: That does not sound like the answer they were looking for.

A: I told them I had been to Brazil on another occasion and that the total time I had spent in the country was at most twelve or thirteen days. They asked if it would be alright if they said I had spent three weeks in Brazil doing the research for my article. I told them "Fine."

Q: If you had spent more time in Brazil, would you have arrived at the same insights? In other words, might keeping a kind of distance from the case have helped you analyze it better?

A: No. If I had been able to spend more time in Brazil, I would probably have documented my argument better.

Q: What advice do you offer students who want to do fieldwork?
A: I suggest that they take notes during interviews, because taping interviews and later transcribing them is an expensive and hopeless task. Taking notes also makes it easier to capture the gist of what the person says. I am also in favor of fairly closed questionnaires; otherwise people talk and talk without saying anything. This is particularly true of politicians.

Normative Biases

Q: Are you aware of any normative biases in your research?
A: There is clearly a bias in favor of a democratic political system, which I understand as one in which everyone who accepts the rules of the game, whatever his past—unless it's a criminal past—has a place and can participate. I do not see a total purge of the bureaucracy, or the army, as a requirement for a successful transition to democracy. And I believe that even people who were non-democrats under the old regime should be allowed to participate as democrats in a new democracy. I am against the idea that only the people who were *for* something have a right to participate in it, which you might say is a democratic bias of mine. I also have a bias against violence. I see democracy as a type of political system where you try to exclude the use of violence, to either gain or retain power, and I disagree with those who think that only violence can create a good society because it is the only way to break and destroy whatever you don't like, whether it is a class structure, a state in which you are a minority nation, or who knows what. I prefer nonviolent forms of handling problems. Another bias is my preference for a kind of democratic order based on a search for majority consensus and not on the decisions of a minority that supposedly "knows" what is right and wrong. The alternative bias is that somebody actually knows what a good society is and should fight for and impose their vision. History is full of tragedies that resulted from that kind of bias.

Q: Does the package of normative biases you have just described create any analytic blind spots? Are there certain aspects of political regimes and processes of regime change that your biases have led you to neglect?
A: Perhaps I do not give enough credit to the people who fought and used violence to achieve the overthrow of non-democratic regimes. Some people

who study the Spanish transition say that the decisive event was the murder of prime minister Carrero Blanco by ETA.[21] I don't think this assassination produced a positive change. Franco continued in power and died in his bed. In that sense, the murder of Carrero Blanco was not the factor that caused the transition. Those who see the killing as a decisive factor assume that should Carrero Blanco have lived, the authoritarian regime would have lasted longer. If Carrero Blanco had lived, it is true that he might have been the prime minister at the start of the transition and that he might have put greater obstacles to democratic change. But it is not clear that Carrero Blanco would have had the allegiance of everybody in the system; even people close to him were not as rigid as he might have been. So, if Carrero Blanco had lived, the transition process might have been delayed, but I don't think it would have changed radically. On the other hand, the assassination of Carrero Blanco left a harmful legacy of romantic legitimation of violence for political purposes that Spanish democracy is still suffering from three decades later. Certainly, the violent dimensions of the overthrow of Fulgencio Batista or the Shah of Iran have not been very constructive for democracy in Cuba and Iran. Successful transitions to democracy—for example, in Poland with Jaruzelksi—have been nonviolent. This does not mean that those who fought or died in opposition to a non-democratic regime do not deserve respect and even admiration in some cases. Still, if one wishes to understand why successful transitions to democracy occur, it is a mistake to give greater weight or value to actors who use violence, although perhaps one could give them a little more value than I tended to.

One chooses to emphasize some things more than others. In my analysis of non-democratic regimes, I have tended—except in the paper on human rights and types of regimes—to pay less attention to the repression aspect (Linz 1992). There are two reasons: First, I do not think those regimes —not even the worst of them—stayed in power simply by repression. Second, emphasizing the repression dimension blurs the distinctions among different types of regimes. The totalitarian regime in Italy was very unrepressive, whereas Franco was very repressive, but not particularly totalitarian in his conception of society. Some authoritarian regimes have a more or less "reasonable" and "humane" form of repression—no repression is humane, of course—whereas others are really outrageous. So, repression is not a variable that helps very much for understanding the nature of regimes.

21. Admiral Luis Carrero Blanco, who was seen as Franco's most likely successor, was assassinated in December 1973.

Time and Scholarship

Q: You tend to have many projects going on simultaneously. Is this juggling of different projects deliberate?
A: It is not deliberate, and it may not be the most desirable way of working. It happens because I am moving in different circles, which generates lots of different commitments. I am asked to give a paper at a meeting on a certain subject and sometime later I am asked to give a paper somewhere else on a different subject. For instance, I participated in a meeting on totalitarianism in Hamburg and was asked to write a paper on the intellectual history of theories of totalitarianism. The paper was written very quickly, a sort of draft. Later, when the person who organized the conference wanted to publish it, even though I was working on something totally different at the time, I had to shift my focus to the totalitarianism paper, edit it, and add footnotes and references in order to make it a real paper. So, working simultaneously on multiple things is partly a scheduling problem.

There is another way of working, I suppose. Take Pareto, who was independently wealthy because of his earlier business activities as an engineer and manager. Pareto was able to spend twelve years in his villa with his cats, he had lots of cats, with nothing else to do but write his two-tome *Sociology* (Pareto 1963). He did not have to make a living or publish articles to get tenure. And because he was not very sociable, he probably did not go to many meetings. We forget that many of the classical social scientists were rentiers who did not have the distractions of students, classes, or much else. Simmel was largely subsidized by his uncle, who had a chocolate factory. Weber must have had quite a fortune, judging by the size of his house in Heidelberg. He spent many years doing just his research. And Karl Marx, if you put it bluntly, was living as a capitalist rentier from the exploitation of the workers in the factories owned by his friend, Engels. So, these scholars were able to center their work on one piece and spend a long period of time on it, which leads to a certain type of product. I have never had the chance to do that, and maybe it would not have suited me because I really enjoyed teaching.

No matter which way we work, though, there is only time to do so much. Time is the most constraining thing in life. You can stretch it by working more hours, taking fewer vacations, and doing fewer things that you like to do, but in the end the constraints of time make us all "one-dimensional," to use Marcuse's (1964) language. It is not society or the capitalist system that makes us one-dimensional, as Marcuse argued in that horrible little book, it is the fact that we have to make choices with the limited time we have. This means that for every paper I write or have to finish in the next week or two, I am not able to go to New York to see some art exhibit I would love to see. And that's frustrating. The fundamental limitation of time always forces you to narrow down and exclude things, thus becoming "one-dimensional." Time is the one thing you cannot beat. It is the ultimate boundary of everything, and there is no way around it.

Q: Do you wish you had used your time differently? In hindsight, are there projects you did not do that you wish you had? Conversely, are there projects you did do that you wish you had not?
A: You can make better or worse use of time, and I may use it less efficiently than some of my colleagues who seem to get things done in much less time than I. There are some types of work in which there is a disproportionate relationship between the time you put into it and what it produces. Checking references, quotations, footnotes, or data is a time-consuming activity that is not that fruitful, though it is important to check facts and quotes in order to have adequate documentation for what you say. Sometimes I write that Weber said something, because I remember Weber saying it. But when I check the original source and page, what I remembered turns out not to be exactly what Weber said. So, you have to check things, and that takes time.

Looking back, I probably should have been more careful about not wasting time on projects in which I invested a lot of energy but ultimately did not pursue. I put a lot of work into the European Values Study when it was launched, but the meetings required flying often to Europe for a weekend, which proved too exhausting. So, I ended up dropping out of the project. I put so much work into that without getting anything out of it in a sense. That happened with other collective projects of various types. Maybe I should have been more careful, though I learned something even from those unsuccessful projects.

I also have several major studies that I started and did not finish for one reason or another. I never got around to publishing my dissertation, even though I had a contract and a friend had started to do some editing. But I never got around to cutting and editing it. It would have been one of the best books on the sociology of partisan elections in Germany. Another unfinished project is the big study on Spanish entrepreneurs that Amando de Miguel and I worked on. It ended up being a collection of fifteen or twenty articles, which constitute a book, but were never summarized and pulled together into a book (Linz and de Miguel 1966, 1974). Something similar happened with a major study on economic mentalities in Spain, which I did for the Instituto de Estudios Económicos (Institute for Economic Studies). That study resulted in a two-volume manuscript, and in my basement I still have piles of tables prepared for it. But there was a change in leadership at the Instituto, and the new leaders decided not to support the publication of my book, in part because the findings were not to their liking. I did not have enough freedom perhaps to publish it on my own, and, besides, I was already doing many other things.

My work on the transition to democracy in Spain provides another example. I spent a year-and-a-half in the field and collected an enormous amount of material for a study of the Spanish transition—tapes of interviews, surveys, newspaper clippings, party propaganda, and all kinds of things. But I never wrote the book on the Spanish transition that I could have written. I wrote a lot on the transition, and I used some of the material I collected in other projects.[22] But writing a book would have required sitting down at my desk and doing nothing else for two or three years, and that was not possible after I came back from Spain, because I had to start teaching again. All the material I collected is being shipped to a research library in Spain.[23]

I also have a long manuscript on the social history of Spain, a very short version of which has been published in a collective book (Linz with de Terán 1995). If I had time, I would publish that as a book, especially since I had a contract that I never paid any attention to. But I may never get around to finishing that since I am working now on the federalism book with Al Stepan.

So, there are lots of things I could have done and wish I had done. I wish I had extended my study of Spanish intellectuals of the sixteenth and seventeenth centuries to the eighteenth, nineteenth, and twentieth centuries (Linz 1972). And I probably should have written a book on religion and politics. But between teaching, directing dissertations, attending professional meetings, and what not, certain things fall by the wayside.

Colleagues, Collaborators, and Students
Professional and Extraprofessional Engagement

Q: You have been actively involved in professional organizations, most notably the Committee on Political Sociology (CPS) of the International Sociological Association (ISA). What role did you play in the committee and what did you get from your involvement in it?
A: With my seniors, I was a founding member of the CPS at the International Sociological Association's Congress in Stresa in 1959, and years later I succeeded Stein Rokkan as president, at which time I enjoyed the collaboration with the committee's secretary Richard Rose. It was a very active group. We would meet regularly between the triennial Congresses of

22. See, for example, Linz (1993).
23. The Juan Linz Archive of the Spanish Transition to Democracy, 1975–89, is housed at the Center for Advanced Studies in the Social Sciences at the Juan March Institute in Madrid. See www.march.es/ceacs/ingles/biblioteca/proyectos/linz.asp.

the ISA, and the committee would organize sessions at the Congresses.[24] In 1963, we had a meeting in Tampere, an industrial city in Finland, where I first presented my paper on authoritarian regimes.[25] After the meetings we all went together to the lake. You could have taken a picture of the whole crew—Giovanni Sartori, Lipset, Erik Allardt, Richard Rose—in the sauna. Jerzy Wiatr, who would later become Poland's minister of education after the democratic transition, was also there. Wiatr and I had a long, long evening of walking and discussion. I remember standing on a bridge over the waterfall talking with him for hours about how the Polish system fit more closely the authoritarian than the totalitarian model. The CPS also had meetings in Bellagio at the Villa Serbelloni. Those were reasonably small meetings that proved very fruitful. Indeed, some of the most productive meetings I have attended have been small, with ten or twelve people alone and talking among themselves for three days without a tight agenda. That provided time for real in-depth discussions. Conferences and meetings today are often much larger, with too many people and papers, and this is less fruitful.

Q: Some funders prefer big, high-visibility events and do not want to support small, intimate meetings.
A: That happens abroad much more than in the States, because many meetings are organized with the participation of politicians or bankers. I organized a conference with Norberto Bobbio to encourage collaboration between Spanish and Italian social scientists. The idea was to have a Spaniard write a paper on the military in Spain, an Italian write on the military in Italy, and so on. We had a two- or three-day conference in Madrid, which was paid for by an Italian bank. There was a luncheon that the mayor of Madrid gave in a very nice restaurant in a park. Then there was a reception in a castle on the city outskirts organized by the head of regional government. Next, there was a dinner organized by the Spanish minister of education where the ambassadors of Italy and Spain gave speeches. Well, when you add all that time up, the amount actually devoted to the meeting was drastically reduced. Not much really came out of that meeting.

Q: Have you participated in the European Consortium for Political Research (ECPR), which Stein Rokkan founded?
A: I think I was at the founding meeting of the ECPR in Mannheim. The ECPR has been very decisive for the development of comparative politics in Europe, but the problem is that its annual meeting has been during Easter

24. On the history of the Committee on Political Sociology, see Rokkan (1970).
25. The paper was published as Linz (1964).

Week, a vacation in the European universities but not in America. So, the ECPR has tended to fragment the European and American comparative politics community. The old kind of interaction of Americans with Europeans has been reduced, whereas the interaction among the Europeans has increased appreciably.

Q: Over the course of your career you have also been involved in numerous extraprofessional engagements, such as participating in a working group with politicians on constitutional reforms in Bolivia in the mid-1990s. Also, I understand that you were considered for an appointment as a royal senator in Spain during the transition to democracy. Did you ever aspire to be a politician?

A: From early on I had a vocation for politics, I have been close to politicians, and, if circumstances had been different, I might have become a politician. My generation in Spain, for complex reasons, has been relatively absent from the politics of the transition to democracy. You are right that my name appeared in a newspaper as one of the royal senators to be appointed on election night in 1977. When my name did not appear on the final list, I felt both sad—not to participate in the constitution-making process—and relieved because I was spared from interruption and probably abandoning my quiet scholarly life at Yale.

Collaboration

Q: Can you discuss the role that collaboration has played in your career?

A: There is no time here to recount my collaboration with many colleagues resulting in coauthored publications: Amando de Miguel, Jesús de Miguel, Yossi Shain, Larry Diamond, Arturo Valenzuela, the team at Data: Francisco Andrés Orizo, Manuel Gómez Reino, Darío Vila, and, most recently, José Ramón Montero and Miguel Jerez. Houchang Chehabi, with his Iranian experience, picked up my theme of sultanistic regimes and organized a conference on such regimes that resulted in a book of essays for which he and I wrote the theoretical introduction (Chehabi and Linz 1998b). Collaboration is essential to my work. I have always been part of groups of people who invited me to contribute papers to conferences and edited volumes. This solved the whole problem of getting my work published, because I never had to worry about sending an article to journals for peer review or negotiating with a publisher. My papers were always assured publication in a volume that somebody else took the trouble to organize. Besides this sort of group collaboration, I have also collaborated with coauthors. I tend not to finish things and often leave texts hanging around and loose, so to speak.[26] A coauthor who does some editing helps me get my ideas into shape for publication. With a coauthor, a text certainly turns out more organized, clearer, better written, and more systematic. The constant exchange of ideas with a coauthor is also key. You write one version and your collaborator reads it and says, "No, I'm not convinced." Then you spend hours and nights talking and talking, and a new version comes out of both of you. My coauthor gives me whatever he writes, I give him whatever I write, and, in the end, it's not possible to say who contributed which idea. I had this kind of very intimate collaboration with Amando de Miguel in our study of entrepreneurs (Linz and de Miguel 1966, 1968, 1974), and for some time now with Al Stepan, with whom I collaborated on the breakdown volume and, especially, on *Problems of Democratic Transition and Consolidation,* which is a book from both of us (Linz and Stepan 1978, 1996).[27] Now we are working together on our new book on federalism (Stepan, Linz and Yadav, forthcoming; Linz and Stepan, forthcoming). Not only have Al Stepan and I been coauthors and coeditors, but we have also co-directed dissertations and co-taught joint seminars. Working together over more than thirty years has been a unique intellectual and personal experience, leading to genuine friendship. Then there has been the constant collaboration of my wife Rocío. Without it much of my work would never have been completed.

Teaching and Students

Q: How has teaching and interaction with students shaped your work?
A: I always enjoyed teaching. Teaching forces you to broaden your intellectual interests and work on subjects that you would not work on otherwise. Giving courses requires you to have a broader focus than you would have if you only did research. If you teach a course on religion and politics, you cannot focus on just one country, as you might in your own research, but you have to deal with a wide range of countries. And if you teach a course on nationalism, you cannot limit yourself to peripheral nationalism in Spain, but you have to deal with nationalism in general. It is a bad idea not to teach. The Centre National de la Recherche Scientifique (CNRS) in France has some

26. Two of Linz's previously unpublished essays, "Tradition and Modernity in Spain" and "Freedom and Autonomy of Intellectuals and Artists," as well as two essays that were not previously accessible in English are now available in Linz (2006b). This volume includes a comprehensive bibliography of the more than three hundred chapters, articles, books, and edited volumes that Linz has published since 1949.

27. For de Miguel's personal reflections on Linz as a teacher and colleague, see de Miguel (1993). On the dynamics of the Linz-Stepan collaboration, see Stepan's account in Chapter 12.

of the best people, but they don't do any teaching and have gotten narrow in their research interests, which I don't think would have happened if they had been teaching. And you learn from students, too—sometimes.

Q. How would you characterize your teaching style?[28]
A: Basically, I lecture a lot, even in seminars. I don't like passive seminars, where you assign students papers, make each of them responsible for leading a discussion or two, and then sit there listening to them, maybe making an occasional comment. I have been fortunate not to have taught large undergraduate courses, although I had fairly large graduate courses at Columbia with 25 to 30 students. Directing dissertations has been a major activity for me. I have directed some 60 or 70 dissertations of which 35 to 40 have been published, covering 30 countries. That's quite a lot of work. This has been one of the most satisfying parts of my scholarly life.

I have had some students, fewer than I wished, whose work built on the types of themes that I have worked on. For example, several students worked on entrepreneurs. And I have had students doing work on democratic transitions in Taiwan, Korea, Uruguay, Greece, and the GDR. One student wrote a dissertation on the French working class that somewhat resembled my dissertation work on the German voters in the 1953 election. I currently have two students working on peripheral nationalism in Spain. So, some students have worked along the same lines as me. But other students have done different things, though they may have a certain common outlook that they derived from my work. I think it should be up to the students to decide what they want to do—you have to let them do their own thing. In this sense, my approach differs from that of someone like Harry Eckstein, who funded a number of his students to do dissertation work that applied his ideas about congruency.[29] But it did not succeed. Eckstein's scheme was much too simple and rigid, and people got frustrated trying to apply it. To some extent he insisted that they apply it, and, as a result, some of his students never finished.

Q: Do you modify your mentoring style depending on the type of student? What are your mentoring strategies?
A: I think there are phases. When students first start working on a problem and are designing their research and questionnaires, you work very intensely with them. Then they go out and collect the data. During this phase, you keep in touch, but the interaction is less frequent. After the students have analyzed the data and have written some draft chapters, you

28. For perspectives on Linz as a teacher, see the interviews with Guillermo O'Donnell and Alfred Stepan in Chapters 9 and 12. See also Mainwaring (1998, 19–21).
29. Eckstein's theory of congruency is developed in Eckstein (1966).

start working intensively with them again. So, you don't continuously give the same kind of attention. And some students need more attention than others. Some work well on their own, whereas others need pressure to get anything done. It also matters whether or not the student is physically close. Sometimes they write a dissertation hundreds of miles away, which makes it difficult to sit down and talk with them for days and days about their work.

Q: What traits and qualities distinguish the successful from the unsuccessful students?

A: It is not good when students feel from the outset that they know what they want to do and are not ready to listen to your advice. These students usually come back with a dissertation that is not very well conceived, but, by then, you cannot do much about it. You accept it, and they get their union card, but it is not a successful relationship. Sometimes it's just that they aren't that smart, or sometimes they have chosen the wrong person to advise them. Occasionally, students start working with somebody else, run into problems, and then come to you to help them save things.

Q: And the success stories?

A: The success stories are bright people who find an interesting problem that fits their personal styles and attitudes. There has to be some congruence between the person and the research. For example, take two students who were friends and worked in Spain at the same time: Robert Fishman, who did a study of Spanish unions, would have found it more difficult to do a study of business elites, whereas even his appearance fit well with the union leaders he was interviewing; and Robert Martínez, who did a study of business elites, would have been quite out of place interviewing trade unionists.[30] He later worked for a Republican administration and ended up being a business executive. So, the successful students find the study that fits their personality, and even their dress.

Unfortunately, there are some very, very good students who, because of personal circumstances, have not done as well as they could and should have. Both at Columbia and Yale I have had students who were selected by the graduate admissions committee as the most brilliant prospects and were very good in seminars, yet never finished, or took ages to finish, because of problems with their personal lives, divorces. Other students, who were far from brilliant, worked hard, did solid work, and went on to become very successful and competent scholars.

30. Fishman's and Martínez's dissertations were published as Fishman (1990) and Martínez (1993).

Q: What sets the stars apart?
A: A certain commitment and capacity for work—a passion for what you do—is important to succeed in scholarship. The very best students of mine had a certain ambition and enthusiasm, which motivated them to put all their time and energy into their work. I worry that some of the training we give students today provides less room for this kind of enthusiasm. We put so much emphasis on methodological tools and on getting students to start with a hypothesis and theory that they can go out and test. Instead, we should encourage them to go out with a problem and remain open to whatever theories and methodologies turn out to be most appropriate for studying the problem. If we give students too much direction about how to go about their research and, at the same time, do not make them enthusiastic about problems, that will result in solid work, but not exciting work.

Q: Is it our duty as teachers to make students enthusiastic about problems?
A: Yes, I think that's obvious.

Q: But how can we do it?
A: By showing your enthusiasm for problems. If students see how you get excited and interested in what you are doing, then they might say, "Well, this must be worth doing."

Q: Did somebody show you that?
A: Yes. All the good teachers I had had their own enthusiasms. They were excited about their work, and it showed.

Q: What advice can you offer students who are just starting out in the profession? What kind of training should they get?
A: First, read as much as possible and get to know some of the classics in the field. Read a lot of good monographs, books like Bendix's *Work and Authority* (1956) or Lipset's *Union Democracy* (Lipset, Trow, and Coleman 1956). Monographic works like those will give you a good idea of how to do an in-depth study of a problem. In terms of methodological training, try to develop a little bit more knowledge about how to do survey research than you will get in the regular curriculum of graduate departments. I always face the problem of students starting to work on a dissertation and wanting to put together a questionnaire, but lacking the training and experience to do it. You also need to learn modern methodology, like advanced statistics, which is required to read certain papers and works. And languages are essential if you want to work on certain areas. It is also important to take some courses in fields that are not your own. Don't limit yourself by saying,

"I am in political philosophy, so I am not going to take any courses in comparative politics," or "I am in comparative politics, and so I will not take anything on political philosophy." Use the best resources of your department broadly.

When it comes to the dissertation, do one that could result in an important book—and get it published. Try to write the dissertation already thinking about the form it would have to take to be published. That way you won't have too much work rewriting it. And you have to conform to the patterns of the times. Nowadays, this means you have to start publishing refereed journal articles as soon as you can, and you need to get as many as you can before you apply for a job. I don't think that is always the best way to do it, because it leads to a waste of resources. But that's how the game is played today.

Then just struggle and try to get a job wherever you can. And you don't necessarily have to start out at one of the leading places. It would be nice, but that's not always possible. There are also interesting jobs outside of academia, in government, for instance, though it is not easy to go back from those jobs to academia.

Q: In terms of deciding where to study and with whom to work, is it important that students try to work with leading, stellar scholars?
A: Some scholars—because of their research, experience, and maybe something up there in the brain—really are more creative than others. And those scholars are obviously the best influence that students can have. At the same time, some stellar people may not be good mentors. They may try to impose their own way of thinking and doing things. Or they may set ideal standards that people cannot satisfy, and, as a result, students get discouraged. For example, I think Merton did not have the number of students that he could and should have had because he was a sort of "King-God," and people felt they could never meet his expectations. Even though Merton always encouraged students by saying how promising their ideas were, they felt they had to improve so much that sometimes they never showed up again. Also, sometimes a stellar person is not that effective at influencing students. I'm not sure, but I have the impression that while he was in the United States, Sartori did not have much impact on the people who worked with him compared to his great impact on a whole generation of Italian scholars.

In terms of choosing a dissertation advisor, it is probably not a good idea if the person with whom you want to work has no interest, no knowledge, and no preparation to deal with the project you want to work on. In that case, you should go to somebody else. I have discouraged people from working with me because I had no particular interest in what they were doing. I often ended up helping them with advice and suggestions, but I could not direct their work. Occasionally students started working with me and later realized that I had ideas about what they should do that they were not able to accept. So they went to work with somebody else. Sometimes they didn't finish with the other person either, so I'm not sure it was a relationship with me that explains those cases.

The Past and Future of Comparative Politics
Achievements of the Field

Q: A recent criticism of comparative politics is that it has failed to generate cumulative knowledge. Hence, we have learned nothing, or very little, from all the research of the past fifty years.[31] What do you think of this critique?
A: There are several areas of research where we have quite a lot of learning and cumulative work. One example of learning can be seen in the research on consociational democracies by Arend Lijphart (1968a, 1977) and others. That work persuasively challenged the old prevailing notion that a majoritarian, two-party model of democratic politics worked far better than a multiparty system. Now we know that a number of democracies with multiparty systems have actually worked very well. That's an insight we did not have when some of the literature on political parties started. Similarly, the research on corporatism, starting with Schmitter and Lehmbruch (Schmitter and Lehmbruch 1979; Lehmbruch and Schmitter 1982), taught us that a close integration of interest group politics and political parties was not necessarily bad for democracy. I think the comparative literature on transitions to democracy has taught us something about how to make a transition possible. In particular, we have learned that transitions take place within the institutional framework of the previous regime, can be negotiated, and are not necessarily violent breaks with the past. That is a pretty solid body of research and thinking. Work by people like Sartori (1997), Rein Taagapera, and Matthew Shugart (1989) on the consequences of different electoral laws has also generated lots of solid knowledge. Finally, comparative work on elections using survey research has produced a lot of cumulative knowledge about the relationship between social variables, like class and religion, and voting behavior.

The problem is that our knowledge about issues like voting behavior is cumulative only until you have a political earthquake. Then some of the relationships among the variables no longer hold. The library I have in my basement on Italian politics and voting was very cumulative from

31. Lindblom (1997); Geddes (2003).

1948 to the 1990s. But then the Christian Democratic Party disintegrated, Berlusconi and the Northern League emerged, and the whole party system changed. This means that to understand Italian elections you have to start not from scratch, but you have to start anew. Previous research cannot be the only basis for analysis. By creating these discontinuities, Italian politicians were being unfair in a sense to the social scientists who had spent decades working on Italian parties and elections.

More generally, all the knowledge generated by research on voting behavior in advanced industrial democracies is getting dated. This is partly because the industrial working class, which used to represent some 30 to 40 percent of the population, has shrunk dramatically in many places. The old linkages among variables like working-class identification, trade union membership, and participation in labor, social democratic, or communist parties have been weakened. And you increasingly find a much more homogenized "middle-class society" in these countries. As a result, the old loyalties to parties have eroded. A worker who, in the past, would have said, "I am a worker, therefore I am a union member, and therefore I have to vote social democratic or communist" today might say, "I am a worker, but I have a summer home on the Mediterranean coast which I rent to tourists, and the social democrats propose to raise taxes on my second house." So, that person, even though he is still a worker, may vote against the party he would have voted for in the past. And voters today are much freer in some ways. For a long time, the Italian voter who saw the Christian Democrats as his protectors against the threat of the Communists coming to power, voted Christian Democrat despite his other misgivings about the party and the corruption that characterized its governments. Today, no parties are seen as serious threats, and Italian voters feel much freer to vote for whichever party they think best fits their interests, which makes it infinitely more difficult to predict voting behavior. Decades ago, whenever I met a Dutchman, I only had to ask two or three questions: Are you a Catholic, a Calvinist, or a nonbeliever? What is your occupation? and I knew how he would be voting, because 90 percent of the voters with certain social characteristics voted for a particular party. That is not the case anymore, which obviously makes the study of political parties more difficult. All these types of changes set limits on our ability to generate cumulative knowledge about politics.

Q: You have mentioned areas where you think comparative politics has generated a solid body of knowledge. What are some of the areas of research where our knowledge is especially limited and needs improvement?
A: We know much too little about political leadership and the quality of political elites. We know that political elites usually have higher education,

come from a certain background, know foreign languages, have studied abroad, and so on. But we do not know why some leaders are more creative and more committed than others, and why some leaders are real crooks. As Schumpeter notes at the very beginning of his theory of democracy, in order to have a working democracy you need a pool of qualified people who are committed to public service (Schumpeter 1942, Ch. 23). Why do some societies have these people but others do not? And why do some countries produce creative business elites? In today's *New York Times* there is a story about the Hyundai Empire. Why did the Hyundai Empire emerge in Korea and not in Argentina or somewhere else? These are things we do not know. The number of things we know so little about is startling. There is so much work to be done.

Area Studies

Q: An ongoing debate in comparative politics, one that has generated much controversy recently, involves the status of area studies. Some argue that area studies are a hindrance to progress in the discipline because they generate parochial, atheoretical research. Others argue that area-based knowledge is indispensable for building and testing theory. What is your take on this debate?
A: I am very much in favor of area studies. I think it is a disaster to discourage or eliminate them, to tell students they don't need any area specialty, that their work should be purely theoretical. That's nonsense.

On the other hand, research can become quite sterile if people only know about one area and have never done any thinking, reading, or work on other parts of the world. That was a great limitation of Latin American studies when it started in the 1950s. Back then, there was an important Center for Latin American Studies at Stanford with lots of students and some money. They collected clippings from all the Latin American newspapers, and the Stanford students knew everything, more than you ever wanted to know, about every military coup. Ironically, Stanford did not produce leading Latin Americanists then, but Columbia, which was much weaker in terms of devoting detailed attention to Latin America, did. At Columbia in the 1960s, we had an anthropologist, a geographer who worked on Brazil, and a few Latin Americanists in the History Department. The administration wanted me to give a course on Latin America, but since I did not know a thing about it, I weaseled out of the obligation by teaching a course on "Authoritarian Regimes in Hispanic Societies" in order to cover Spain and maybe a bit of Portugal. I taught methodology, conceptualization, and the comparative perspective. The students who took that seminar included Peter Smith, Al Stepan, Susan Eckstein, Alex Wilde, and Arturo and Samuel Valenzuela. Columbia's contingent of Latin Americanists went on to become quite important.[32] In some ways, having a broader perspective can enhance work in a specific area. However, you cannot do good work, let's be very clear about that, without knowing at least some cases, some area, or some theme in depth, with all its historical and cultural richness and complexity.

Q: Why is depth so important? Isn't too much depth a hindrance to achieving broader generalizations and powerful theory? After all, theory requires abstraction.
A: Depth is never a hindrance. It allows you to understand and know your subject matter, which constantly makes you aware of why you cannot simplify. You cannot stay at an abstract, superficial level. You have to face some facts, inconvenient facts, which are disturbing, make you think further, lead you to introduce more variables, and become more sophisticated.

Rational Choice and the Economic Turn in Political Science

Q: Rational choice theory has become an increasingly important force in political science over the past two decades. What is your assessment of how the rise of rational choice theory has affected the discipline?
A: Rational choice would be perfectly fine if it were accepted as just one way of looking at things and doing work; everyone ought to choose the approach that best suits their way of thinking, and then we can see who ends up where. But I am disturbed by the hegemonic ambition and self-righteousness of rational choice scholars who think that other ways of doing work are undesirable because they are not scientific. I also find that most of the time the sophisticated way of handling the problem with statistics and mathematics is very much out of proportion with the conclusions. Sometimes I am left wondering and asking, "So what?" So much technical effort seems to be expended to come up with something that is generally stated very much at the beginning of the whole exercise. I am also skeptical of the method of having an interlocking set of propositions that logically hang together in some way and then saying that you have "proven" the propositions by logical analysis. Moreover, the assumptions about reality are so simplified most of the time that you wonder, "What can I do with that? What situation really fits this model?" Finally, some of the people who do this sort of work have no knowledge of any political reality; they are economists and mathematicians who work purely deductively.

32. On this contingent of students and, more generally, on Linz's contributions to the study of Latin America, see Mainwaring and Valenzuela (1998).

Another problem is that if you define rationality in terms of actors pursuing the goals they set for themselves, then everything is rational. Palestinian suicide-bombers who blow themselves up in Israel are acting rationally if they really believe that sacrificing themselves in jihad means that you go to heaven. What could be more rational than to assure that you go to heaven? And the whole monstrosity of the gas chambers in Nazi Germany was an extremely rational action if the goal was to have a world free of Jews and you wanted to kill them in the most efficient way. My God, it was all perfectly rational. But who would want to use the word *rational* to describe madness like that?

There are some interesting rational choice pieces. For example, Josep Colomer's book (1995), which provides a game-theoretic analysis of the transition to democracy in Spain, is wonderful. In fact, I recommended to Colomer that he send a paper to the *American Political Science Review,* and he got it published there (Colomer 1991). But I don't think we have the data to test some of the models he constructs, for example, the game of the coup. It is an interesting mental exercise, but we don't know if it explains what happened, or even if it adequately describes what happened. Also, without Albert Hirschman's earlier work on reform in the face of a threat of revolution (1963), neither Colomer, nor I, would have worked on transitions the way we did. The whole idea of a four-player game—with extremists on both sides of the ideological spectrum, moderates in the middle, and a convergence of the moderates in response to the threat from the extremists— was already in Hirschman. I think it is appropriate to apply that game to the case of Spain, and Colomer succeeds in fitting it into a relatively neat model. But, to apply that game to a transition from the Taliban makes little sense. The four players are not there, and if the players are missing, the game is not possible. Try to apply the model to Sierra Leone. Who are the moderates? Who are the radicals on both sides? What is the spectrum of actors who can reach a compromise in the middle? So, the four-player game is nice for places where you have the four types of actors. But no actors, no game. Knowledge of cases is necessary to judge what kind of model makes sense.

Q: Does the rational choice revolution remind you of any earlier episodes in the history of the discipline?
A: In its effort to displace the work of previous generations, the rational choice movement of today somewhat resembles dependency theory in Latin American studies during the 1970s. The rational choice revolution also resembles Marxism to some extent. Marxism never became that dominant for a variety of reasons, but, in fields like the study of fascism, it prevented serious work for a while. By contrast, I don't think the behavioral

revolution attempted to displace the preceding generation so much. The people who made the behavioral revolution had great respect for the cohort that preceded them. For example, Bob Dahl, who became the symbol of the behavioral revolution, respected the older generation of scholars, people like Ehrmann, Kirchheimer, and Franz and Sigmund Neumann. The behavioralists were not claiming to supplant other work. They were more modest and saw themselves as adding another dimension, a new perspective.

Q: Why do many rational choice scholars claim to be displacing, rather than building on, the work of earlier generations?
A: They have this odd feeling that what other people are doing is not scientific—it's journalism or maybe history, but it's not political science. And I think they feel we are not on a par with real scientists, so there must be something wrong with the way we have been doing our work. My Yale colleague Charles Lindblom, who is not a rational choice person, in an article in *Daedalus,* has highlighted how far the discipline is from achieving its "scientific" ambition (Lindblom 1997). I do not think this kind of pessimistic attitude is justified. Instead of asking why our discipline hasn't achieved the kind of coherent structure that some of the hard sciences have, we should recognize that the nature of the subject matter we are studying is different, which means we cannot—and perhaps should not—be like the hard sciences.

Q: The model for many rational choice scholars is economics. What does economics offer to comparative politics?
A: Neoclassical economics provides an enormously powerful instrument for understanding pure, reasonably functioning market economies. The market as it works on Wall Street, or the monetary system of the U.S. Federal Reserve, may fit the models of economists reasonably well. But these models do not work if we want to understand the Russian or Sierra Leonean market economies. In this regard, one important limitation of economics is that the basic tools of the discipline—the theory of prices, supply and demand, indifference curves—are all based on the assumption that you are dealing with relatively simple monetary units and that all commodities can be reduced to dollars and cents. Although votes are similar in some ways to monetary units, there is an obvious and fundamental difference between money, which is divisible and fungible, and many of the things we want to study, such as power. Another limitation of neoclassical economics is that it does not explain economic development. It has no mechanism to explain why dynamic capitalist entrepreneurs emerged in Korea and Taiwan, but not in Argentina. That's where Schumpeter comes in. Curiously enough, Schumpeter was president of the Econometrics Society and one of the

founders of econometrics, but his major work is historical and sociological.[33] Hirschman is another example of a very interesting economist who dealt mainly with problems that interest sociologists. And Pareto, one of the founders of neoclassical economics in many ways, wrote in one of his personal letters that economics had become something that anyone with the skills could do and handle. He felt that the more difficult and interesting problems—the problems on which he wanted to work—involved the non-rational, non-"means-end" aspects of social life, which economics was ill-equipped to handle.[34] So Pareto left economics and became a sociologist.

The curious thing is that when something does not fit into their powerful and interesting models, the economists are readily able to admit what they cannot do. They say, "This is a very relevant and very interesting dimension of the problem, but we are not qualified to deal with it; that's something the political scientists or sociologists should deal with." But instead of dealing with those things in our way, we say that we have to do it the way the economists would. I find that a little bit paradoxical.

Q: Reflecting on the future of the field, how will comparative politics evolve in light of this "economic turn"?
A: I think there will be excess production, so to speak, in the mainstream, and therefore competition for survival will be very great in the future. And as more and more people are doing similar things and competing for the field's limited resources, it will become harder for them to help and support each other, which could make it difficult for a movement like rational choice to sustain its momentum. Also, unless economics-inspired research delivers interesting findings, people may get more bored and critical, which is what happened to research on voting behavior—people found it to be too much of the same repeated over and over again. So, like worms in a bag of flour, overpopulation may cause a crisis.

On the other hand, there are mechanisms that are encouraging a hegemonic pattern of dominance by whichever group conquers the academic market. There is more and more reliance on impersonal and mechanical criteria, like publications in peer review journals, for making decisions about who should be promoted and get positions. By becoming more impersonal and more bureaucratic, the field produces standard, predictable products, but this standardization allows little room for mavericks and innovators. Also, the increasing reliance on impersonal criteria allows less room for someone who is bright, has lots of potential, but lacks articles in refereed journals. In my own case, Merton, Lipset, and Sartori were able to

33. See Swedberg (1991).
34. Pareto in his letters quoted by Eisermann (1987, 22 and 24).

support me early in my career even though I had not published much. They believed I would end up doing interesting things. This is less likely today. When you rely on objective indicators like the number of publications, you lose the feel for the person and his qualities, and the whole process becomes more bureaucratic. To me, this is a negative trend.

Q: But personal connections still seem very important in shaping academic careers. Everyone, including rational choice scholars, pushes their own.
A: Yes, and the rational choice scholars have an important advantage in this because they can apply some fairly objective standards of quality. Does he know his mathematics or his logic? Does he handle the tools competently? Instead of getting into how important or interesting the findings and research problem are, they can focus on relatively straightforward issues of technical proficiency. It is easier to reach consensus about these matters. To illustrate my point, if I am asked by the university administration to give my opinion about hiring someone like Adam Przeworski, I can say, "I like some of his work very much, he is a brilliant man, and I would love to have him as a colleague. But I think he is totally wrong about this and that." If a committee with a physicist or mathematician on it reads that, they will ask, "How can they say he is so good if they say that he is wrong?" The disagreements among us about our work are very great, whereas there is much more consensus among people who have a more standardized way of dealing with things

Q: Your outlook combines a kind of Malthusian analysis of demographic crisis with a Weberian, Iron Cage analysis of the deadening effects of bureaucratization on creativity and innovation. If you are right, what does this Malthusian-Weberian perspective bode for the future of comparative politics?
A: Who knows? A crisis, perhaps. Look at what has happened with some departments dominated by a particular group or tendency. Sometimes an outsider—the university administration—intervenes and says, "This is too inbred and limited, and something has to be done about it." I guess some people of my generation sound pretty pessimistic. Maybe it's just because we are getting older.

Conclusion

Q: You have been an emeritus professor for several years, and I wonder how you keep up with what is happening in the discipline. Do you still read the journals?

A: Some of them, but not the mainstream journals. And I have given up on most of the sociology journals. When you get older you realize you cannot keep up-to-date and informed about everything in the field, even in a limited field. You try to keep up on certain themes on which you have been working. I read some of the new work on the great breakdowns of democracy and on the comparative study of fascism. But there are other problems —for example, transitions to democracy—on which I have done my share of work and don't want to get into more deeply. Lots of new work is coming out on democratic transitions, on the transition in Russia, but since I am not going to write about that, I don't follow the literature closely. You also develop new areas of interest and have to focus your reading on those themes. I am working now on federalism, and I have to read about Belgium, Switzerland, the history of the Australian Federation, and the origins of German federalism. There are many things that may be important, influential, and command lots of attention in the field, but you don't follow them because they are not essential for what you are working on.

It is different if you are teaching, because you have to stay up-to-date, at least on the broader themes of your course. If I were still teaching a course on non-democratic regimes, I might want to read some new books that may have appeared on Marxism. But if you don't have to teach and you are not doing research on a particular topic, you don't do much reading on those topics anymore. So, in a sense, you become narrower and narrower until you know almost everything about a limited number of subjects. Yesterday I received a book from Estonia. A historian there sent me a book on the Estonian fascist movement of the 1930s, and I spent two or three hours leafing through and reading it. I would not have gone to the library to look at that book, but I read it since I had it. The French political scientist Guy Hermet recently sent me a very good book on populism (Hermet 2001). People send me things because I have worked on a particular topic. I get a lot of books and papers from different people, and just reading that material keeps me busy.

Q: Do you still attend professional meetings?
A: I have been going less to meetings, partly because they have gotten so big, with so many people and sessions. You have to go from one end of the building to the other to get to a session that interests you, and by the time you get there, the paper you wanted to see has already been presented. So, you rush to another session, and the same thing happens. And each session has so many papers that there is no time left at the end for questions. Decades ago, there were fewer people and meetings were much more manageable, particularly when they took place in smaller or isolated places. The

location matters, because if the meeting is in a big city, everybody escapes to see a museum or to meet friends.

Q: Given the many changes in the profession since you were a student— the greater emphasis on refereed journal articles and the use of increasingly sophisticated methodological techniques—would you have succeeded if you were a young scholar starting out today?
A: Today you have to produce a lot of small articles to succeed, but my style is to write fairly lengthy pieces, which are hard to sell as journal articles. And I tend to collect data with a broad net, rather than using precise measurements of specific little things. My work might not have been methodologically satisfactory in terms of some of the standards used today, although I could have learned to use the new methodologies. Furthermore, my work would be too descriptive and too historical for people who prefer very neat arguments based on a simple premise. The whole style of thinking that underlies rational choice is not my style, you see. So, I don't know. I would have done what would have been expected, but I don't think it would have been as productive, and I would not have enjoyed it as much.

7

Samuel P. Huntington

Order and Conflict in Global Perspective

Samuel P. Huntington has made influential and enduring contributions to three fields of political science—American politics, comparative politics, and international relations—by emphasizing the themes of order, authority, and conflict.

In his first book, *The Soldier and the State* (1957), Huntington argued that professionalization of the military was necessary to achieve both national defense and civilian control over the armed forces. The book had a large impact on the nascent field of civil-military relations. In *The Common Defense* (1961) and his first work in comparative politics, *Political Power: USA/USSR* (1964), coauthored with Zbigniew Brzezinski, he focused on issues of national security raised by the Cold War.

Huntington's attention turned in the mid-1960s to the problems facing the newly independent countries of Africa and Asia. This research culminated in *Political Order in Changing Societies* (1968), widely seen as a classic of modern comparative politics. With empirical evidence drawn from across the globe, he challenged the prevailing optimism that economic modernization would produce stable democracies, arguing that, in the absence of strong political institutions, modernization led instead to violence and political decay. Achieving political development in poor countries thus required building effective political institutions, especially political parties.

Huntington continued his work on comparative politics and political development in the 1970s, coediting *Authoritarian Politics in Modern Society* (1970) with Clement Henry Moore and coauthoring *No Easy Choice* (1976) with Joan M. Nelson. During the second half of the 1970s, Huntington's focus returned to the United States, resulting in *American Politics: The Promise of Disharmony* (1981). He argued that the anti-governmental element of

This interview was conducted by Richard Snyder in Cambridge, Massachusetts, on May 31 and June 11, 2001.

America's liberal tradition had generated recurrent episodes of conflict and instability throughout the country's history.

With the global expansion of democracy in the 1980s, Huntington's interests shifted to democratization. His key work on this issue, *The Third Wave* (1991), aimed to explain the many transitions to democracy that occurred during the 1970s and 1980s. A distinctive aspect of *The Third Wave* was its broad global scope and novel conceptualization of democratization as a transnational wave.

Since the early 1990s, Huntington has focused on the threats posed by the post–Cold War world, especially cultural conflict. *The Clash of Civilizations and the Remaking of World Order* (1996) challenged the idea that the end of the Cold War meant the triumph of Western ideas and values, arguing instead that Western influence would increasingly be rejected, often violently, by non-Western societies. Conflict in the post–Cold War World would thus occur mainly along cultural and civilizational lines. Huntington's most recent book, *Who Are We?* (2004), argued that immigration, especially from Latin America, posed threats to America's national identity. His provocative ideas about cultural discord, at both the global and domestic levels, have made Huntington one of the most visible and controversial political scientists of the contemporary era.[1]

Huntington was born in New York City in 1927. He received his B.A. from Yale University in 1946 and his Ph.D. in government from Harvard University in 1951. He has taught at Harvard University (1950–58, 1962–present) and Columbia University (1959–62). He served at the White House as coordinator of security planning for the National Security Council (1977–78). He was president of the American Political Science Association (APSA) during 1986–87, and he was elected to the American Academy of Arts and Sciences in 1965.

Training and Intellectual Influences

Q: Who were your most important teachers?
A: As an undergraduate at Yale in the field of international relations, Arnold Wolfers, William T. R. Fox, and Nicholas Spykman were certainly very impressive. Apart from a historian, Walter Johnson, the people at the University of Chicago, where I got a master's degree in the late 1940s, did not have a tremendous impact on me. The late 1940s was the low point in the history of the Chicago Political Science Department. During the 1930s, it was *the* department, with Harold Lasswell, Charles Merriam, Harold Gos-

1. See Kaplan (2001).

nell, Quincy Wright, and a variety of other people. By the time I arrived, they had mostly left, except for Merriam. I took his last course at Chicago, which was an interesting experience—anecdotes about presidents he had known. I think I was also in Hans Morgenthau's first course at Chicago; it was certainly his first year there.

Q: Why did you choose to go to the University of Chicago if the political science program there was in decline?
A: I didn't have any clear idea as to what was good and what was bad. Having grown up on the East Coast, gone to Yale, and then served in the army for a while, also on the East Coast, I wanted to see the Midwest. That was the principal reason, and Chicago was clearly the best university there. So I went for a year.

Q: You entered the Ph.D. program in government at Harvard in the fall of 1948. Whom did you learn from at Harvard?
A: The most impressive person was Louis Hartz, who was a very young professor then. He was just extraordinary, and had an impact on all the graduate students. Dynamic, charismatic, brilliant are the words that come to mind. Hartz was a brilliant lecturer. Many of us took his graduate lecture course on political theory, and at the end of the lectures we would just sit there exhausted. We wanted to give him a round of applause, but we were too exhausted after the workout he had put us through.

Q: Did you take any courses with Hartz besides political theory?
A: Somehow he was dragooned into teaching a seminar on American politics, which I took. I wrote a paper for this course that subsequently became my first publication in the *American Political Science Review,* with the title "A Revised Theory of American Party Politics" (Huntington 1950).

Q: A modest title.
A: Yes, indeed, especially for a paper by a graduate student.

Q: Whom else did you study with?
A: William Yandell Elliott, Robert McCloskey, and Arthur Holcombe. Holcombe was the grand old man of the department. I think he was in the department when it was established, whenever that was, in 1905 or so. He was a grand old gentleman who wrote books on a wide variety of different topics—American politics, the Chinese Revolution, ethics and international relations (Holcombe 1930, 1940, 1948). He was somewhat starchy in appearance. There was a tradition in the department that every spring we would have a big departmental softball game, usually at Elliott's place in

Belmont. Holcombe would divide people into two teams and be the leader of one. He would make a *great* concession this May day out there playing softball—he would take off his suit jacket, but not his vest.

Q: What did you learn from Elliott?
A: Elliott was in political theory. His book, *The Pragmatic Revolt in Politics* (Elliott 1928), had quite an impact on me. He had been a Rhodes scholar at Oxford and was very much involved in American foreign policy. Until he retired, he commuted nearly every week to Washington. That was before there was a shuttle, so he went back and forth on the overnight train. He had a farm in Virginia, as well as his home in Belmont. He was a very impressive person.

Q: What about Samuel Beer and Carl Friedrich? Did you interact with them?
A: Certainly. The department at that point was divided between the Elliott people and the Friedrich people. I was very much in the Elliott camp. Friedrich was a tremendously impressive scholar, much more of a scholar than Elliott, but he lacked the personality of Elliott.

Q: What was the cleavage about?
A: Elliott and Friedrich were two terribly forceful people. I guess there were ideological differences between them. Elliott was more conservative than Friedrich, not that Friedrich was necessarily a flaming liberal. It was mostly a competition for influence in the department, and they were the dominant figures.

Q: Did this rivalry involve any methodological issues?
A: I don't think so. People didn't worry about methodology back then.

Q: Your teachers at Harvard all seem to have been wide-ranging scholars.
A: That was certainly true for all these people because they wrote books on all sorts of different things. Hartz, after all, did theory, but also wrote a book on the founding of new societies (Hartz 1964).

Q: Was anyone on the Harvard faculty narrowly focused?
A: Not really. Even Merle Fainsod, whom one thinks of as a Soviet specialist, taught public administration for the Graduate School of Public Administration, the forerunner of the John F. Kennedy School of Government. He wrote a big book on the role of government in the economy that was mostly about the United States (Fainsod and Gordon 1941). Fainsod was

not a narrow specialist at all. Others clearly were specialists to a greater degree. V. O. Key would be the most outstanding example. His specialty was American politics, and, as far as I know, V. O. did not do anything but American politics. I don't think he did anything comparative.

Q: Your training appears to have involved quite a bit of exposure to political theory.
A: That was the department—it still is the Harvard department. We have five or six people teaching political theory now. Back then, everybody got into political theory in one way or another. Sam Beer, who taught comparative government and British government, was also in political theory.

Q: It is interesting to hear about these various teachers whom you learned from as a graduate student at Harvard. But you were, in fact, a graduate student for only a very short time. You got your Ph.D. in just two years!
A: I did one year at the University of Chicago, where I got a master's degree, and then did two years of graduate work here at Harvard.

Q: Is it true that you wrote your dissertation in only four months?
A: Well, sort of. In my second year, after I'd passed my general exams, I was thinking about writing a thesis, and in January, Bob McCloskey, the chairman of the department, called me in and said, "We've voted to offer you a teaching appointment here provided you finish your Ph.D. by the end of the academic year." I said, "Well, I guess I've got to write a dissertation in four months."

Q: Did you ever publish your dissertation?
A: No, but a large part of it was published as an article in the *Yale Law Journal* called "The Marasmus of the ICC" (Huntington 1952). It was a very simple thesis—that regulatory commissions get taken over by the industries they are created to regulate (Huntington 1951).

Q: Had that thesis been articulated before?
A: Ideas had been floating around a bit, but I think my thesis was the first to do a fairly extensive, systematic study of it, looking at the Interstate Commerce Commission (ICC), the Civil Aeronautics Board (CAB), and the U.S. Maritime Commission. I focused on the transportation regulatory commissions, and I made the point that if you create commissions that are limited to a particular industry, then capture is almost inevitable. If you create commissions with a broader span—like the Federal Trade Com-

mission, which regulates all sorts of industries—the problem of capture is less likely. Capture certainly happened with the three transportation commissions.

Q: How did you become interested in the topic of regulatory policy?
A: It was an idea that struck me after doing some reading, perhaps after taking Fainsod's course on government and the economy, which I may have audited.

Colleagues

Q: Although you started your career as a professor at Harvard, you were denied tenure there. Do you know who was opposed to giving you tenure and why they were opposed?
A: Carl Friedrich led the opposition to my being promoted to tenure at Harvard. The Government Department had to ask for an extra year from the dean to decide my fate, and, at one point during Harvard's lengthy consideration, Friedrich invited me to lunch and explained all the reasons— well, the principal reasons—why he was opposing my promotion. He said that, as a refugee from Nazi Germany, he was disturbed by my book, *The Soldier and the State* (Huntington 1957), because he felt it was basically an argument for authoritarianism. I said, "No, it was not an argument for authoritarianism, it could, however, be interpreted as an argument for *authority,* and there is a difference between authority and authoritarianism." We had a long discussion about this. Needless to say, neither one convinced the other. I think the primary reason for his opposition was basically that I was a protégé of his big rival in the department, Elliott.

Q: Why was *The Soldier and the State* misinterpreted as an argument in favor of authoritarianism?
A: Because it said there was something to the military ethic—authority, discipline, emphasis on community. Many people called my book an argument for militarism, which it certainly was not, but it was even less an argument for totalitarianism.

Q: I have heard that people reacted especially strongly to the concluding vignette contrasting the adjacent civilian community, Highland Falls, with the U.S. Military Academy at West Point, which you described as "ordered serenity" and "a bit of Sparta in the midst of Babylon" (Huntington 1957, 464–65).
A: Yes, that was rather dramatic.

Q: After you were denied tenure at Harvard, you moved to Columbia, where you started teaching in 1959. Did you meet interesting people there?

A: Reinhold Niebuhr in particular stands out. Immediately after graduate school in the early 1950s, my general outlook on politics was influenced profoundly by Niebuhr. I read most of his books, though not all of them, because he was tremendously prolific. He seemed to have the proper approach to the question of the interrelations of politics and morals. He was a big intellectual figure at that time. Somebody—I think it was Arthur Schlesinger—said, "He is the father of us all," and that was true in a sense. I got to know him reasonably well when I taught at Columbia, because he was at Union Theological Seminary. I saw a fair amount of him.

Q: Your teaching days at Columbia were quite short, however. Indeed, you returned to Harvard after only four years.

A: Yes. The story again involved Friedrich, who, as I said, had led the opposition to my being promoted to tenure at Harvard. Four years later I got a phone call from Friedrich's secretary saying he was coming to Columbia to give a talk and would very much like to get together with me. We arranged to have drinks at the faculty club and had an interesting conversation. At one point he said, "Sam, as you probably have heard, we have reconsidered our decision on you and want to invite you back to Harvard. All of us who so strongly supported your promotion now feel vindicated."

Q: That's bizarre.

A: He was firmly convinced he had strongly supported my promotion, while, in fact, he had been the most influential opponent, because he was probably the most distinguished scholar in the department.

Q: How did you feel about that incident?

A: I did not know what to say. My mouth dropped open, and I did not say anything. I let it pass. What I would have said was, "Professor Friedrich, don't you remember that you opposed my appointment? I greatly respected you because you invited me out for lunch to explain why you were opposing my promotion, and nobody else did that." But I didn't say that. I just let it pass.

Research: Core Ideas and Their Reception

Q: One of the most striking aspects of your research is that it spans all three of the main fields of political science. You began in the 1950s as

an Americanist, then you moved into international relations (IR) in the late 1950s and early 1960s with your work on national security issues, and finally you turned to comparative politics with the publication of *Political Power: USA/USSR* (Brzezinski and Huntington 1964). Since then, you have continued to publish across these three fields.

A: I've wandered around. I majored in international relations as an undergraduate at Yale. As a graduate student at both the University of Chicago and Harvard, I worked primarily in American politics. Then I shifted to civil-military relations and security issues (Huntington 1957, 1961, 1962). I got into comparative politics when Brzezinski and I did our book together (Brzezinski and Huntington 1964), and then I got into political development (Huntington 1968). Currently, I teach a course each year in American government, in comparative politics, and in international relations.

Q: Do you recommend this kind of wide-ranging approach?

A: Not necessarily. People differ and, as I say, I wander around from field to field. But other people carve out a field and become learned specialists in it. I don't have any really deep specialty.

Q: What are the disadvantages of wandering around and not settling in one field?

A: You don't belong in any deep way to a particular grouping or club. And you don't become *the* expert on a particular subject. If you publish things in different fields, the specialists in one field are generally unfamiliar with what you have done in another field. People in comparative politics think of me in terms of *Political Order in Changing Societies* (Huntington 1968) and *The Third Wave* (Huntington 1991). But they don't know anything about *The Soldier and the State* (Huntington 1957) or my book on American politics (Huntington 1981b). That's an interesting phenomenon in its own right that reflects how divided and specialized political science is. I like to address what seem to me to be important questions—both for the real world and intellectually important issues. So I follow the trail where those kinds of questions and issues are, even if it requires moving from field to field.

Q: What do you consider your best ideas?

A: Forty-five years later, the arguments in my first book, *The Soldier and the State* (Huntington 1957), about the nature of the military profession—objective and subjective civilian control—are still being debated, questioned, and used. Obviously, the ideas in *Political Order in Changing Societies* (Huntington 1968) had a tremendous impact, especially the argument about how social and economic change can lead to political decay if it is not accompanied by the development of political institutions. That certainly stirred up tremendous interest, and there have been dozens and dozens of studies testing those propositions in various circumstances.

Q: Why do think those ideas from *Political Order* caught on?
A: I laid out propositions in a fairly clear and undoubtedly rather simple fashion. This provided a series of hypotheses people could get hold of and try to apply.

Q: What is the relationship between *Political Order in Changing Societies* and modernization theory? This book has been described as "closet modernizationism" (Domínguez 2001, 229), because it criticizes the assumption in modernization theory that socioeconomic development leads to stable democracy, yet it also draws heavily on modernization theory by treating socioeconomic forces as the fundamental cause of political change.
A: What does "closet modernizationism" mean? Modernization theory is about the processes of economic and social change and development. My book is obviously concerned with that. The whole argument is that these processes can have a political downside. In the 1950s and early 1960s, the implicit, and often explicit, assumption was that modernization was all of one piece: all good things went together and therefore improvements in economic well-being would necessarily bring political democracy and stability.

Q: Are there any other ideas of which you are especially proud?
A: I think *American Politics: The Promise of Disharmony* (Huntington 1981b) made a useful contribution to debates about the nature of American politics. It started from the basic Tocquevillian thesis, later elaborated by Louis Hartz (1955), about the huge consensus in American society on values and said, "Yes, that is true, but this consensus actually explains why we have a lot of instability and conflict in our society at times." I think that was a useful contribution to understanding the dynamics of American politics.

Q: Which of your ideas or works did not get the attention they deserved or were misinterpreted?
A: All of them have been misinterpreted.

Q: You suggested that you try to state things clearly in your work. So, why are your ideas misinterpreted?
A: My clarity could be part of the problem. Also, people often project into a work what they think it should be saying. For instance, somebody I more or

less consider a friend, Carl Gershman, the head of the National Endowment of Democracy, wrote a review of *The Clash of Civilizations* (Huntington 1996) that referred a couple of times to my alleged view of Islam as a "monolithic entity" (Gershman 1997). I don't know how he can say that. The book emphasizes again and again the *divisions* in Islam. Islam is treated in several parts of the book, but the biggest section on Islam has the title: "Islam, Consciousness without Cohesion." Somehow one gets the idea that Huntington is thinking about civilizations, and he thinks civilizations are all single, monolithic entities, which simply is not the case. But that is one of the criticisms that lots and lots of people have made of that book.

Q: And you think those types of criticisms are driven by projections?
A: Yes. People think, "Huntington is talking about civilizations and the conflict among civilizations, so he assumes they all are unitary and have no divisions within them," which clearly is not the case.

Q: This view of your work makes it sounds like billiard ball realism.
A: Yes. In fact some people have explicitly said that *The Clash of Civilizations* is the latest version of billiard ball realism, except that it talks about civilizations rather than nation-states.

Q: Do you regard *The Clash of Civilizations* as a realist work?
A: I don't know what you mean by realism, but it certainly is not billiard ball realism.

Q: In contrast to *The Clash of Civilizations*, which some interpret as a pessimistic work, *The Third Wave*, because of its focus on the expansion of democracy across the globe, is sometimes seen as a hopeful, optimistic book.
A: I object when people do that. These two books deal with different subjects. *The Third Wave* has a whole chapter on possible reverse waves and problems of democratic consolidation (Huntington 1991, Ch. 6). It is essentially a study of how and why thirty or so democratizations occurred in the 1970s and 1980s, but there is certainly no wild optimism in the book about democratization continuing indefinitely. I very carefully point out the limits—cultural, economic, and otherwise—on further democratization. And I discuss the problems the new democracies face consolidating their democratic systems.

Q: Is the Third Wave over?
A: In considerable measure, yes, it is over. Now, that does not mean there will not be more democratization, but the series of changes that began

in the mid-1970s toward democracy occurred in countries that economically and culturally had conditions favorable to democratization, and, third, in addition to culture and level of economic development, were subject to the influence of either the United States or Western European countries. The category of countries where those three factors exist has been pretty much exhausted. That is why democratization has slowed down. It is also why a gap exists, as Larry Diamond (1999), Fareed Zakaria (2003), and others have shown, between, on the one hand, the introduction of democratic procedures in the form of elections and, on the other hand, the development of liberal democracy. If you look at the Freedom House ratings, about thirty-five countries are classified as democratic yet only partly free.[2] This is a new development. In the remaining countries that are not democratic—China and a few other Asian countries, most of the Muslim countries, and the African countries—one or more of the three factors I mentioned—culture, level of economic development, and the influence of existing democracies—is deficient. That does not necessarily mean these countries won't become democratic. People argue, and I would agree, that if China continues to develop economically and becomes increasingly involved in the world economy, the prospects of political change in China are pretty good. I am not sure whether that will be in the direction of a Western-style democracy, much less liberal democracy. But certainly some opening up and a greater degree of pluralism, internal discussion, debate, and competition are very likely to happen in China in the coming decades.

Q: Are there any works you feel were neglected or did not get the attention they deserved?
A: I wish *The Promise of Disharmony* (Huntington 1981b) had received more attention. It got extraordinarily favorable reviews—I don't know of any unfavorable review, though there probably were some. Still, somehow it did not generate the overall attention that some of my other books did. There are probably several reasons for that. First, there was a lot of competition. A book aiming to explain American politics comes out every few weeks, and everybody is in the game of trying to do a more or less definitive interpretation of the American political experience. So, there is a lot of competition. Second, I think the timing was a factor. The book was published in 1981, and the theme of disharmony in American politics was not grabbing people's attention then. If I had not gone to work in the Carter administration and had published the book back in 1977 or 1978 instead, I think it would have gotten a lot more attention.

2. See www.freedomhouse.org/ratings/.

The Research Process
Problem Selection

Q: Public problems and contemporary events obviously influence your choice of what to study. How do you identify a problem that merits research?

A: It may not be a *public* problem in the sense that governments or public agencies are focused on it, but I want to look at things going on in the real world, interesting problems that are in the real world of government and politics. For example, I got interested in civil-military relations because Truman fired MacArthur. So, civil-military relations seemed important. I looked around and found there was not much of a literature on that topic—maybe two or three modestly serious books had been published in fifteen or twenty years. So I said, "This is an interesting area with important, unanswered questions on the relationship between the military and society" (Huntington 1957, 1962). Then in the 1960s, when everybody was talking about modernization and development, when I looked out at the developing countries I saw chaos and anarchy and corruption. So, I thought, "Let's look at this a little bit more carefully—there is more political *decay* out there than political development." And so I wrote *Political Order in Changing Societies* (Huntington 1968).

Q: You were not just being contrary?

A: No. But there isn't much point in repeating what other people have said. If you don't have a different viewpoint, a different thesis to advance, not necessarily a contrary one, there isn't much point.

Q: When you wrote *Political Order in Changing Societies*, you say you looked out at the world and saw violence, instability, decay, and disorder. Why hadn't anyone else seen what you did?

A: It is a natural tendency for people to assume that the things they would like to have happen *are* happening. Still, other people besides me were beginning to take a more realistic attitude toward what was going on in the Third World—Shmuel Eisenstadt (1966), Lucian Pye (1966), and others were moving in that direction.

Q: What does it mean to "look out at the world"? How, concretely, do you do that?

A: You read about what's going on in the world.

Q: Is it just reading? Or do you go to talks and interact with people? Interesting visitors obviously come to Harvard all the time.

A: Sure. But I would say it's mostly reading.

Q: What is the next step after you choose a research problem?
A: I try to learn more about it, think about it, develop ideas on it, and devise a theoretical approach or a theoretical framework. You read material, see what other people have said, try to learn more about it, and think about it.

Methods

Q: How do methodological tools figure into your research?
A: I don't think much about method. I don't consciously try to pursue or define a method. Basically I'm trying to study a topic and come up with what I would call "empirical generalizations" concerning it. That obviously involves trying to draw comparisons.

Q: You are not a "small-N" comparativist, someone who wrestles with three or four cases and gets deeply into them. You tend instead to be a medium or "large-N" comparativist. Do you agree?
A: I guess so. However, in *Political Order in Changing Societies* I certainly did discuss a number of cases of revolutions in some depth—Mexico and Bolivia—but I used cases to illustrate general points. When you say "large-N," it brings to mind elaborate quantitative statistical studies with 130 cases. I have nothing against that kind of work, but I have not done much in that line.

Q: You did large-N analysis in *No Easy Choice* (Huntington and Nelson 1976).
A: If that kind of data is available I try to make use of it. I did something comparable in *Political Order in Changing Societies.*

Q: Some argue that the best comparativists know how politics works in one country, because knowing one country well provides a firm foundation for making broader generalizations. Do you agree?
A: I am dubious about that. The only country whose politics I know reasonably well is the United States. But I don't think that knowledge is of great use in making broader generalizations.

Q: What role has historical analysis played in your research?
A: You have to draw on history, because you are studying experience. History *is* human experience. You have to work with historical materials and look at what has happened in history. The function of political scientists is, as I said, to try to make generalizations about historical processes. Of course, you can do that in a variety of ways. Theda Skocpol (1979) and Bar-

rington Moore (1966) looked at three or four revolutions, though Moore really doesn't make much in the way of generalizations. That's one approach. As you pointed out, I don't really go in for doing three or four detailed case studies.

Q: What trade-offs are involved in covering a lot of ground less deeply, as you prefer to do?
A: Both types of approaches are useful. If you are trying to make generalizations, you want to look at a wide variety of cases and instances, and then make comparisons. I have nothing against the other approach.

Q: What do you think about fieldwork?
A: I don't believe in it!

Q: Why not?
A: I am being facetious, obviously. But there is a potential problem with fieldwork: people go off to study a particular problem in a particular country, and that experience often dominates their subsequent work in one way or another. I don't like to feel captured, to become the prisoner of a particular experience. If you spend two years doing fieldwork in a country, that is obviously going to have an impact on you. For what I am interested in doing—making empirical generalizations—that impact, while it might produce positive benefits, could also have negative consequences.

Q: Still, you travel a lot. Has your extensive travel abroad influenced your scholarship?
A: I'm sure it has, but I have never spent a prolonged period of time in any one place doing research. If you travel and are only in a place for a couple of weeks, you may get a very biased view, because you only talk to a selected number of people and see a selected number of things. The only place where I did what might be called relatively sustained fieldwork, for a period of two months, was in South Vietnam in 1967 when I was working for the State Department at the height of the Vietnam War. It was fascinating. I learned a lot about South Vietnam and a lot about how stupid our policies were at that point.

Q: You also spent time in South Africa and Brazil during their democratization processes.
A: I was marginally involved in the political transition in South Africa, because I wrote something that had a certain impact and was widely discussed in South Africa during the 1980s (Huntington 1982). I was more

actively involved in the transition from military rule in Brazil, where I made a number of trips at the request of the generals to advise them on how to move to a more open and pluralistic regime.

Normative Concerns and Science

Q: Is your work guided by normative concerns?
A: Almost everybody's work has a normative starting point. People are concerned about a particular issue or problem: inequality, injustice, the desirability of promoting democracy. In most cases, I think this is the incentive that leads scholars to look into particular topics.

Q: Yet, according to some understandings of science, researchers should not allow normative agendas to affect their work.
A: What do scientists study? In the physical and biological sciences, they often do simply try to understand the universe better. But a lot of scientific work is driven by the notion that if we could solve this problem it would help humanity in some way.

Q: Do you think of yourself as a scientist?
A: Nope. The word *scientist* implies physical sciences and biological sciences. I consider myself a scholar, not a scientist.

Q: Yet our discipline is called political science.
A: I know, and that is unfortunate.

Q: What would be a better name?
A: I suppose the counterpart to economics would be "politics." But how do you describe a person who is working academically in that field? You have economics and economists. If the field is politics, then what do you call someone in that field? You can't call them "politicians." I guess you could say "politicist" . . .

Q: Pushing the proposition that we should call everything "politics," instead of "political science," would probably stir up a lot of dissent.
A: Fine. What's wrong with that?

Q: Do you see yourself as a public intellectual?
A: I resist and object to being called an intellectual, because it connotes somebody who spouts off on public issues and engages in esoteric intellectual controversies. I don't view it as a compliment.

Q: Some of your works, for example, *The Third Wave* (Huntington 1991), make explicit policy recommendations. Indeed, Zbigniew Brzezinski's blurb on the jacket of *The Third Wave* describes you as a "democratic Machiavelli." Do you self-consciously strive to produce work that is relevant for policy makers?

A: Any serious study of real-world problems has implicit policy implications. That's true of virtually all of my books. My first book, *The Soldier and the State* (Huntington 1957), certainly had implicit—in fact, fairly explicit—ideas on how civil-military relations should be ordered. There isn't a policy section in that book, but I think the policy implications certainly come through loud and clear. As I say in the preface to *Political Order in Changing Societies,* I wrote it in part because I was concerned about political order and the conditions under which political order is realized in modernizing societies (Huntington 1968). But if somebody wants to create disorder or revolution, they can read the book and learn from it too.

Political Theory

Q: In discussing your teachers at Harvard, you mentioned that virtually all had a strong connection to political theory. What is the value of being exposed to political theory?

A: In the Harvard Government Department today, all students have to take a general exam in the field of political theory. I think this is a good thing. Having a grounding in basic political theory, political concepts, and the great political theorists—from Plato on down—is essential because the most important issues political scientists study have been around throughout human history. These issues have been thought about by very distinguished theorists. One can accept or not accept their arguments, but Plato, Aristotle, Machiavelli, and Hobbes were all dealing with central issues that political scientists are still wrestling with.

Q: Do you go back to the classics frequently in your own work?

A: Sure. Look at *Political Order in Changing Societies* (Huntington 1968). I quote Aristotle, Burke, and various other people from time to time, and they certainly influenced my thinking.

Q: How is it helpful to go back to classical political theory if you are working, for example, on a book on problems of political development in the 1960s?

A: Plato and Aristotle had a theory of political development, political decay, and the evolution of types of political systems (Plato 1946; Aristotle 1946).

That's not a bad place to start. It may not turn out to be relevant, but it is worth going back and thinking about what they said about the evolution of political forms and about why every type of political system tends to decay.

Teaching and Students

Q: What role has interaction with students played in stimulating your research?
A: All my books have grown out of courses. I taught courses on political development when I was working on *Political Order in Changing Societies* (Huntington 1968), and I taught a course on democratization for almost a decade before *The Third Wave* (Huntington 1991) came out. If I get interested in a particular topic and start thinking about it and reading on it, I will want to teach a course on it. That's a tremendous stimulus: whether it is an undergraduate course where you have to lecture before fifty or a hundred undergraduates the next day, or a graduate seminar where you confront very skeptical graduate students who know a lot about the subject. I find teaching almost indispensable to the early work on a book.

Q: Does collaboration with students and research assistants play a role in your research?
A: I certainly work with students, but normally on the things they are writing, not what I am writing. Obviously, if you do a big empirical project you need research assistants to dig up stuff, because you'd never be able to do it yourself. The assistants go through data and investigate particular topics to let you know what's there.

Q: What are the hallmarks of the best students?
A: They think for themselves and develop their own ideas. That's the most important thing.

Q: How does one inspire students to focus on important questions?
A: You don't have to do much to inspire undergraduates, at least the undergraduates at Harvard. They are interested in big questions: What are the causes of war? Why are some countries democratic and others not? What is the relationship between politics and economic development? Graduate students, because they are confronted with making a career in the discipline, and the discipline is not exactly favorable to wrestling with these big questions, tend to be more circumspect and to focus on more concrete issues. In my experience, this often makes graduate students nowhere near as interesting to teach as undergraduates. Graduate students obviously know more and can talk in a more sophisticated fashion, but they are often

very hesitant about setting forth a broad proposition. That is certainly truer in my observation of graduate students in political science at Harvard now than it was thirty years ago.

The Achievements, Shortcomings, and Future of Comparative Politics

Q: **What are the most significant achievements of comparative politics?**
A: If you go back to the 1950s, scholars in comparative politics performed a very useful service in rapidly studying the politics of developing countries. Through World War II, comparative politics was nothing more than the study of the major European powers and the United States. Any textbook of comparative politics back then had just five chapters: one on the United States, one on Germany, one on France, one on Britain, and so forth—that was it. With all its shortcomings, the literature on political development that emerged in the 1950s, 1960s, and 1970s was very broadening and constructive. Also, comparative politics has become more sophisticated in its methods of analysis, and I am in favor of sophistication and methodology when it is useful, and in many cases it is useful. We now have increasing quantitative data on political developments, political variables, and non-political variables relevant to politics. For example, back in the 1960s, Karl Deutsch put together the very useful *World Handbook of Political and Social Indicators* (Russett et al. 1964). Today more data are available, and Ronald Inglehart (2003), with the World Values Survey, which has limitations stemming from the fact that he has to rely on some not terribly sophisticated polling outfits in Third World countries, has compiled a very useful source of quantitative information on the values of people around the world.

Q: **I am struck that you have not mentioned any big theoretical contributions or breakthroughs as major achievements of comparative politics.**
A: Theories come and go. The field has gone through phases. Back in the 1950s structural functionalism was the big thing—Almond and Coleman's *The Politics of the Developing Areas* (1960), for example. Theoretical frameworks come and go. In responding to your question about the major accomplishments of comparative politics, I was trying to think of things that made a more lasting improvement. There have certainly been a wide range of propositions—empirical generalizations—which have stood the test of time. One example is the positive relationship between economic development and democracy. Marty Lipset set it forth in a rather crude form in the 1950s (Lipset 1959). It has been refined, and dozens of scholars have built on his initial article. Overall, Lipset's proposition holds up. Propositions

about the impact of social and economic change on social and economic equality have also endured. In my own work, I showed, and other people have supported the same conclusion, that political instability is not a product of poverty, it is a product of people getting *out* of poverty (Huntington 1968). The work of Donald Horowitz (1985, 2001) on ethnic conflict is also a very considerable contribution. At the conjuncture between comparative politics and international relations, the so-called "democratic peace" proposition was a major contribution that, despite all the debate about it, holds up pretty well.[3]

Q: What are the major shortcomings of comparative politics?

A: Political science, including the study of comparative politics, is heavily influenced by other disciplines. The principal external disciplinary influences change from time to time. During the past several years, economics has certainly been dominant. Before that, it was sociology; certainly Almond and others were heavily influenced by Talcott Parsons. And before sociology, it was psychology. For example, Harold Lasswell in the 1930s and 1940s tried to look at politics in terms of its psychological dimensions. It would be useful to go back and revisit that earlier work on psychological approaches to politics, partly because there is always a tendency, in the laudable desire to produce generalizations, for people to study issues where a large number of variables can be compared and quantified. This tends to omit the decisive role played by political leaders. In Harvard's comparative politics field seminar, which I have taught regularly during the past several years, I have an ongoing battle with the other people involved in teaching the seminar. We spend a week each on political development, revolution, regimes and democracy, political culture, bureaucracy and states, political parties, political participation, and so on. I am always fighting to include a session on political leadership, a subject that has been seriously ignored in recent decades. One of the arguments my colleagues make back to me is that there is no real literature on political leadership—and they are right! I consider this unfortunate. Over twenty years ago Bob Putnam (1976) wrote a superb book that synthesized all the relevant knowledge to that point on political leadership. Since then, very little serious work has been done on political leadership. What do you assign? We assign Putnam's book and try to pull together a few other things. The serious study of political leadership has been a great deficiency in recent political science.

Thirty or forty years ago, a lot of work was being done on political

---

3. The "democratic peace" proposition is the idea that democratic countries rarely go to war against one another.

socialization. That topic also has dropped by the wayside. It might be time to go back and study political socialization, which basically means how people's political values develop. A lot of the literature thirty or forty years ago looked at children, asking where do they get their ideas about politics, political leaders, the presidency? We live in a very different era now, and it would be useful to look at political socialization in the present context and also to focus on how political values change. I've been involved in a project with Larry Harrison on culture and development (Harrison and Huntington 2000). If culture is important and there are some cultural systems—systems of beliefs and attitudes—that are conducive to economic and political development and others that are not, the next question is, how do you change a culture? How do you change people's political and social attitudes, beliefs, and assumptions? That's a very important question on which little relevant work has been done. One can think of examples of things that change values. A traumatic event will change people's values. For example, Germany and Japan in the 1930s were the two most militaristic countries in the world, but the trauma they suffered in World War II turned them into two of the most pacifist countries. Economic development changes people's values. That can be seen clearly in Inglehart's work on the development of materialist values and the shift to post-materialist values (1990, 1997). But if you want to change values in order to *produce* economic development, that work is not much help. A propos of the day on which we are conducting this discussion, attitudes in the United States on the death penalty are slowly changing.[4] The churches and other religious groups have played a central role in making Americans less enthusiastic about the death penalty.

Q: Why has there been such resistance in comparative politics since the late 1960s to the study of culture and attitudes?
A: I don't think there has been. Again, things come and go. If you go back to the 1950s and early 1960s, political culture was a big thing: you had Almond and Verba (1963), Pye (Pye and Verba 1965), and all sorts of people doing very important work on political culture. There were very serious cultural studies by sociologists, too—David McClelland's research on "achievement motivation" (1961), for example. In the late 1960s, the study of culture faded from the scene, as happens with most approaches in our discipline. Then it began to come back in the 1980s, and we have had a great renaissance of work in political culture.

---

4. The interview was conducted on the day of Timothy McVeigh's execution for his role in the bombing of a federal government building in Oklahoma City in 1995.

Q: Still, people argue that political culture is not amenable to scientific study.
A: Yes, it is difficult. What do we mean by culture? There are various definitions. A certain amount of confusion exists because the concept of political
culture that is most prevalent in political science is very different from
that in anthropology. Anthropologists like to think of culture as *their*
thing—power may be our thing, but culture is theirs. They define culture
as an entire way of life of a society; Clifford Geertz (1973), among others,
has advanced this idea. We political scientists mostly think of political
culture in terms of values, attitudes, orientations, and concepts. It's something subjective, and we want to understand it in order to explain behavior.
So, we're looking at culture as an explanatory variable in most cases. Why
are some countries democratic and others not? You may want to look at
culture as an explanation. Why do you have economic development here
and not there? Maybe culture explains it. Or why, as I argued in *The Clash of
Civilizations* (Huntington 1996), are new patterns of alliance and conflict
developing in the post–Cold War world? I said culture explains at least
some of it.

**Q: A common criticism of comparative politics today is that there has
been a lack of cumulation of knowledge. What do you think of this
critique?**
A: Certainly the body of knowledge about political systems, political behavior, political institutions, and so forth has expanded tremendously. If
this critique simply means we have not reached any definitive answers to
many of the recurring important problems of politics, then it is true. We are
never going to come up with definitive answers. One has to recognize that
our subject matter changes from time to time, and political scientists very
appropriately focus on things that seem important in the era in which they
live. We were talking earlier about Carl Friedrich. Well, one of Friedrich's
great contributions was his work on totalitarianism (Friedrich and Brzezinski 1956). That was a very useful concept—people debated it—but it was
certainly a very relevant concept back in the 1930s, 1940s, and 1950s. The
usefulness of that concept has faded today, and we focus on different issues
because the situation has changed.

**Q: Another criticism is that progress has been hindered in comparative
politics by the tendency to focus on "big questions."[5] Instead of looking at large-scale, macro-outcomes, which are difficult to study scientifically, we should analyze smaller aspects of events.**

5. See, for example, Geddes (2003, Ch. 2).

A: I obviously do not agree with that argument. You want to focus on the big questions, at least I certainly do. Why should one spend one's time dealing with trivia? You may not answer the big questions. In fact, you *won't* answer them in any permanent way, and you certainly won't answer them in a way that will convince lots and lots of people. Still, it is very worthwhile to wrestle with big questions, and it's particularly worthwhile to challenge students by asking these questions. Unfortunately, the trend in the profession has been to focus on more specific issues where you can apply very sophisticated methodology. This makes the results of work by political scientists irrelevant to the concerns of the public and unreadable by everybody who is not trained in those methods. As a result, political science becomes a very limited discourse, a theological discourse, among a very few.

Q: Looking ahead, what is your assessment of the future of comparative politics?

A: The time has come to rethink the conventional subdiscipline categories in political science. First, there is a practical reason, but no logical reason, for separating out the field of American politics. If one is going to study comparative politics, you obviously have to include the United States. You may want to just study American government by itself—American political parties, elections, and so on—but clearly comparative politics has to include the United States in comparisons. So there is no real basis for the distinction between American politics and comparative politics. Also, any basis that might have existed for a distinction between international relations (IR) and comparative politics seems to be fading fast. According to the classic realist stereotype, and this is obviously a gross oversimplification, the study of international relations was about billiard balls bouncing around and impacting each other in various ways, with states conceived as unified, single actors. By contrast, comparative politics was about what went on *within* the states, and students of comparative politics compared the politics inside one billiard ball with the politics inside another billiard ball. Now, comparative politics people and international relations people, too, although they are somewhat reluctant, have learned that international politics is heavily influenced by what goes on within states, and what goes on within states is heavily influenced by international forces, the actions of external states, transnational movements, international institutions, the diffusion of ideas and technology, and so on. I do not see how a distinction between IR and comparative politics can be maintained any longer, although this distinction obviously exists in people's thinking and in course catalogues. We are moving into a phase of what you might call "transnational politics" or "global politics," where these distinctions will become less and less meaningful.

Q: Your argument that the boundaries between the fields are outmoded will probably appeal to those who believe comparative politics should become more like American politics, that it should adopt the same sophisticated statistical and mathematical methods that are increasingly prominent in the American politics field.

A: I am talking about the nature of the subject, not the nature of the techniques. You are probably right that the techniques you refer to have been used more in American politics, but they certainly are used in comparative politics. It is appropriate to use those techniques—in either American or comparative politics—where they serve useful purposes. What I'm concerned about is that the techniques will become an end in themselves, and people will think they have made a great advance in learning when they reproduce what is common sense in pages of equations. I don't think that's much of a contribution.

Q: Do you see a lot of that going on?

A: Yes. People like to become more and more methodologically sophisticated, and if you can "one up" somebody else and say, "Your form of regression analysis is not as good as mine, mine is more sophisticated," you have scored a point. Also, the more sophisticated you make your techniques, the more difficult it is for anybody to challenge you.

Q: If you extrapolate this tendency forward, where do we end up?

A: We end up with a lousy profession, because the obsession with technique drives good people out of the profession. I can name many graduate students—very bright students with superlative records here at Harvard—who could easily have become very accomplished scholars, yet decided they did not want to put up with this and went off into doing other things.

Conclusion

Q: What advice can you offer students about the training and skills they need to become successful scholars?

A: There may be a difference between what you should do to become a successful member of the political science discipline and what you should do to become an important scholar. Those are not two entirely different things, but if you want to get ahead in the discipline you have to pay attention to the prevailing doctrines and methodological emphases. I have had many students who have written first-rate theses, including several that won prizes, and who felt they had to couch part of their argument in terms of rational choice theory. That's an unfortunate necessity. To make a real contribution to scholarship, you have to focus on an issue you think is important and on which you have something original and significant to say.

Q: The theme of a gap between the political science discipline and important scholarship has arisen several times in our conversation. Do you feel alienated from the discipline?
A: Disappointed in many of the trends that have developed in the discipline.

8

Arend Lijphart

*Political Institutions, Divided Societies,
and Consociational Democracy*

Arend Lijphart is a leading empirical democratic theorist who reintroduced the study of political institutions into comparative politics in the wake of the behavioral revolution, which had deemphasized institutional factors in favor of attitudinal and sociological ones. He is best known for his career-long dedication to a research program centered on the concept of consociational democracy, which he used to advance a novel theory of the conditions for stable democracy. He argued that in societies divided into religious, ethnic, racial, or regional segments, democracy is possible when elites craft institutions that allow, on the one hand, for shared decision making by representatives of all significant segments of society with regard to matters of common concern and, on the other hand, for autonomous decision making by each segment on all other matters.

Lijphart began to develop this research program in *The Politics of Accommodation* (1968a), a study based on the Netherlands that challenged the conventional view that democracy was unlikely in plural societies. Thereafter, he elaborated and refined the distinctiveness of consociational democracy and the contrast between consociational and majoritarian democracy in a number of works of increasingly broader empirical scope: *Democracy in Plural Societies* (1977), *Democracies* (1984), and *Patterns of Democracy* (1999a). This last book, an updated and expanded version of *Democracies*, stands as the most elaborate statement of Lijphart's oeuvre. He showed how ten institutional variables (effective number of parties, minimal winning one-party cabinets, executive dominance, electoral disproportionality, interest group pluralism, federalism-decentralization, bicameralism, constitutional rigidity, judicial review, and central bank independence) cluster into two dimensions: the executives-parties and federal-unitary dimensions. He also showed how consociational democracies outperform majoritarian democr-

This interview was conducted by Gerardo Munck in San Diego, California, on August 5, 2003.

racies across important outcomes, such as political equality, women's representation, and citizen participation.

Lijphart made a significant contribution to the study of the relationship between electoral rules and various other aspects of party systems. In *Electoral Systems and Party Systems* (1994), he classified electoral systems and studied the effect of the electoral formula, the number of representatives elected per district, electoral thresholds, and other key features of electoral systems on the proportionality of the election outcome, the degree of multipartisanism, and the creation of majority parties. He also had an impact on debates about qualitative methods, through his classic article on the comparative method and case studies, "Comparative Politics and the Comparative Method" (1971), and through *The Politics of Accommodation* (1968a), widely seen as a key exemplar of deviant case analysis.

Lijphart was born in Apeldoorn, the Netherlands, in 1936. He received his B.A. from Principia College in 1958 and his Ph.D. in political science from Yale University in 1963. He taught at Elmira College (1961–63), the University of California, Berkeley (1963–68), the University of Leiden (1968–78), and the University of California, San Diego (UCSD) (1978–2000). He became a professor emeritus at UCSD in 2000. He was president of the American Political Science Association (APSA) in 1995–96, and was elected to the American Academy of Arts and Sciences in 1989.

Formative Experiences: Family, the Netherlands, and World War II

Q: You grew up in a small town in the Netherlands during World War II. What was it like growing up in that context?
A: My very first memory is of the outbreak of the war. The feeble attempt of the Dutch to repel the German invasion included a plan to flood large parts of the country. My family lived in an area that was going to be flooded, so we had to move. We didn't have to go far, only to the other side of town, which was on higher ground, where we stayed with distant relatives. The fighting was over in five days. Afterward, the situation was typical of an occupied country: most people saw the occupier as the enemy. I wasn't even four years old at the time. Though nothing really terrible happened to my family, or myself, the adults communicated an atmosphere of fear to us children.

During the course of the war, there wasn't any real fighting on the ground in the area where I grew up. But I lived on the flight path to the Ruhr area in Germany, and twice every day a large group of bomber planes flew overhead. It was the British during the day and the Americans at night, or it might have been the other way around. Just the noise of the planes was something frightening. And the German fighters were trying to intercept the bombers. A lot of dogfights took place over Holland, in fact, right over my house. We would often go into the cellar to be safe. If I took you to this area now, I could point out where some planes fell down.

I also remember very vividly two specific incidents. In one case, near the end of the war, a group of German soldiers came through with an officer and they needed a place to stay. We had a big house in the countryside, but it was full of people, some who had fled Arnhem, where a big battle took place in the fall of 1944. The German officer was considerate and did not requisition the whole house. Rather, he said they just needed one room, for himself and his adjutant. So we actually had German officers living in the house with us for a short while. In the other case, two German soldiers walked up to the house and told my father that he had to take a shovel and go to work for them. They were rounding up men and taking them away. The great fear was that we would not see my father again. During that time, there were always rumors of people who had been arrested and shot. Well, my father did come back in two or three days. Apparently what they had to do was dig ditches along the nearby river. So nothing terrible happened. But you never knew what was going to happen next. This climate of fear and insecurity is what I remember most. At one point, we had a refugee, the son of friends of my parents, hiding in our house. He had been called to work in a Germany factory, but had escaped. This situation heightened the overall climate of fear, because we were hiding somebody who was being sought by the Germans.

Toward the end of the war there was also the problem of food. We lived in the part of Holland where there were farmers, and my parents knew lots of them. So we could get enough food. But it wasn't plentiful, and I remember being hungry. It wasn't famine, but there was not enough to eat.

Mine is not a story of enormous deprivation or of an extreme situation like living in a concentration camp. Nothing like that happened to me. Still, it was the kind of childhood you really do remember. These experiences are vivid memories for me.

Q: How did things change after the war?
A: Things got much better immediately. The occupation ended, and all the insecurities brought by the occupation were gone. The food situation improved a great deal. But there was still a lot of tension and friction. The Korean War began in 1950. The Dutch became involved in a colonial war in the Dutch East Indies, and this was a huge enterprise. At the height of the colonial war, there were one hundred thousand Dutch soldiers in Indonesia, which was roughly one percent of the total population. So, war and the fear of war were around for a long time. I'll never forget my mother telling me she would not live through another war like World War II. She said she would commit suicide instead, because she was not going to take

that again. For her, the five years of the war had been such a terrible time because she had five young children. I had a younger sister and brother and an older sister and brother. At the end of the war, my younger sister died. She might not have died if there had not been a war, if the proper medicines had been available. My sister's death made a big impression on me. I was very close in age to her, and she was my best friend.

Q: What lasting impact did World War II have on you?
A: When I think back to these times, I realize that my experience during World War II made me unusually averse to violence and especially interested in questions of both peace and democracy.

Q: Do you also see some specific influences of your father and mother?
A: The Dutch population was divided into subcultures, and my family belonged to the secular, non-Calvinist, and non-Catholic subculture. My father was a businessman, a part owner and manager of a factory. So we were well off. Indeed, before the war, we actually had two cars, which was somewhat unusual. My father was also very much a community activist. He was engaged in lots of work for civic organizations. I think that has had an effect on me. Though I have never worked much for civic organizations myself, I did get from him the idea that you should put to good purposes whatever knowledge and abilities you have. Thus, in my research, I have sought to focus on outcomes with a clear normative content, things that can be described as good or bad. And I have tried to offer prescriptions, too. Perhaps I got this impulse from my father.

My mother was quite independent and she loved to travel. The only time she was settled in one place was during the period she was married to my father. Before that, she had moved around the world a great deal—she was born in Suriname in South America and, before her marriage, she lived in Switzerland and the Dutch East Indies. After my father died, she resumed that pattern of moving around. She was really a citizen of the world. I think I got my interest in international relations and foreign countries from my mother.

Intellectual Formation and Training:
From the Netherlands to the United States

Q: In 1955, when you were nineteen years old, you went to the United States to study at Principia College in Illinois. Why did you choose to study abroad?
A: Neither of my parents had gone to university. But there was no doubt in my parents' minds that their children should go to university. My older

brother went to a Dutch university in the postwar reconstruction phase, a time when there were no opportunities to go abroad. By the 1950s, the situation had changed. Lots of scholarship opportunities were available for students wanting to study in the United States. Since I wasn't sure what I wanted to study, the option of studying abroad had an added appeal. In Holland, you had to decide right away what your major was going to be, whether you wanted to study chemistry, physics, sociology, or English literature. I didn't know what I wanted to do. Studying law was one option I considered, and this might have had something to do with an interest in the social sciences. But law was also a fallback option considered by many students who did not know what they wanted to do. Indeed, since I was so uncertain about what I wanted to study, I thought I should postpone that decision, and the perfect solution to my quandary seemed to be go to the United States for one year to get international experience and become more fluent in English—I had had lots of English in high school already. After that, I would return to Holland and do my two years of obligatory military service. My plan was to have a three-year period to think about what I wanted to do.

Q: Why did you choose to study at Principia College, a small Christian Science institution?
A: My mother's special interest in the United States, even though she had never been there, played a role in my seeking this opportunity in the United States. And the fact that my mother was a committed Christian Scientist—all her children were brought up as Christian Scientists, attending Sunday School and so on—influenced my choice of Principia College. Looking at this choice in hindsight, I was really pretty ignorant about colleges and universities in the United States. I should have given more thought to what college I was going to attend and what impact that would have on my future chances. But I was just thinking about things one year at a time.

Q: Things did not work out exactly as planned, because you ended up staying on in the United States instead of going back to Holland after one year.
A: I had an opportunity to add one year to my stay at Principia College. Then I had the opportunity to add a third year, which allowed me to graduate and get a B.A. I was still thinking of going back to Holland. So it was a step-by-step process. At the end of each year, I decided what I was going to do the next year.

Q: What was it like living in the United States?
A: Principia College was a small college, with about five hundred students, located in Elsah, a village north of St. Louis on the Illinois side of the

Mississippi River. It was not the most exciting place. Still, I did get to see other parts of the United States. On my way from Europe, I visited New York. Over the first winter break I drove to California with three friends. I spent about a week in Pacific Palisades, near Los Angeles, with distant relatives of my mother, and a week in San Francisco, with my father's distant relatives. This was an eye-opener, because I had led a rather sheltered life until then. I had not really traveled outside Holland before I went to the United States. I had only gone to Switzerland and driven to Italy. I had spent so much time in the periphery that any contact with the center was exciting.[1]

Being in the States, I felt far away from Europe. Back then, communication was not as easy as today. During the entire three years I was in college, I only went back to Holland during the summer, traveling nine days by ship between New York and Rotterdam. I did not even think about going by plane, because it was very expensive. Also, I never talked by phone with my parents, because it was so expensive. We communicated by letters. The very first time I called to Europe was the first year I was in graduate school. I spoke with my brother and mother on the phone, because my father had died rather suddenly.

Q: When you reached your final year of college, what plans did you have for the future?
A: By the last year of college, my interest in political science had become clear. I was majoring in international relations, which was basically political science with an emphasis on international relations and comparative politics. So, I started to explore the option of graduate studies in political science.

By that time, you could study political science in Holland. The first political scientists in Holland were actually not political scientists, but lawyers and sociologists who transformed themselves into political scientists. They founded political science at three universities, which correspond to Holland's division into three subcultures, starting at the secular University of Amsterdam in 1947, and at about the same time at the Calvinist Free University in Amsterdam and also at the Catholic University in Nijmegen. I belonged to the secular subculture, so I was considering the University in Amsterdam.

I was also contemplating other options. If I went back to the Netherlands, I probably would have had to do my military service then. Also, I realized that political science was much more developed in the United States than in Holland or anywhere else in Europe. So, even as I was still

---

1. Lijphart develops this center/periphery theme further in Lijphart (1997).

thinking I would probably go back to Holland, I explored the option of going to graduate school in the United States. Now, I took a gamble, because even though I needed a scholarship—at that time the United States was very expensive compared to Europe—I only applied to big-name universities. As it turned out, Yale University admitted me and gave me a scholarship. This decision by Yale changed my life considerably. If that had not happened, I probably would have gone back to Holland.

Q: You arrived at Yale in 1958. Could you discuss your experience there?
A: My experience at Yale was unusual. I was in more of a hurry than other graduate students, because the Dutch military draft was hanging over me. The Dutch Ministry of Defense asked Yale for a statement about how long I would need to complete my studies, and Yale gave them the minimum time in which one could possibly finish a Ph.D.: just three years! So I was caught in a bind. I basically had two years for coursework and one year for my dissertation, which was really a ridiculously tight schedule. At that time, if you took the required full load, you could finish the coursework in two years. Still, most students took the summer after these two years and even part of the following fall to prepare for the comprehensive exam, whereas I had to do that at the end of the second year. And this was indeed a pretty comprehensive exam, which you had to pass in three fields. I did that, and it put a lot of pressure on me. But I was not able to do my dissertation in one year. Even so, I probably finished my Ph.D. faster than anyone else at the time.

My experience at Yale was also unusual, because after I finished my coursework and exams, I went to Holland to do fieldwork and then never really came back to Yale. After a year in Holland doing my dissertation research, I escaped the Dutch draft by taking a job in the United States, at Elmira College, in the Finger Lakes region of New York. I wrote my dissertation while teaching at Elmira College. I only went back to Yale to defend my dissertation and perhaps twice more.

Q: What was your overall impression of Yale and its Political Science Department?
A: Yale was a real revelation. I had gone from a small, not very well known college to one of the main centers of political science at the time. It was very exciting. I also felt a little intimidated when I arrived. But then I noticed that my preparation wasn't really any worse than that of other students. The Yale Political Science Department was a very congenial place. I felt lucky.

Yale also had lots of interesting speakers come to campus. For example, I remember a speech by Senator Prescott Bush, the grandfather of our current president. New Haven was a small town, but it had interesting theater, kind of a tryout for Broadway. I enjoyed that a great deal. The Boston Symphony would travel down to New Haven maybe twice a year. And it was close to New York City, even though I didn't go there often. So, suddenly I had access to lots of cultural life and excitement.

Q: Which members of Yale's Political Science Department most impressed you?
A: Gabriel Almond, who was only at Yale for a relatively short interlude, was doing very interesting work. I took his seminar, and he was a great inspiration. Karl Deutsch was also there. I found him so original and creative. He could speak on just about any subject and have something original to say. He had it all thought out in his mind. It was a joy to go to his seminars, even though they were very disorganized. I don't think he spent much time thinking about how to organize his ideas. But whenever he would speak, give a presentation, or offer comments, it was a fantastic experience. To have known Deutsch and to have seen him in action so many times was a real treat. Both he and Almond were a real inspiration.

Q: You eventually picked Almond to supervise your dissertation.
A: I had good relations with both Deutsch and Almond, and either could have supervised my dissertation. But Deutsch had a reputation of riding roughshod over people. There is a novel called *Tell the Time to None,* by Helen Hudson, the wife of Robert Lane, who was a faculty member at Yale (Hudson 1966). This fictional novel has characters who are clearly members of the Political Science Department at Yale. You can easily tell which is Robert Dahl, which is Karl Deutsch, and so on. Deutsch is portrayed as a professor who neglects his students and lacks feelings for them. He is not described as an appealing character. This novel caused a big scandal in the department, and I think it is one of the reasons Deutsch left Yale and moved to Harvard.[2] I never had a bad experience with Deutsch, but he was obviously a very busy man who didn't always have time for his students. So, though Deutsch was on my dissertation committee, I thought it was wiser to have Gabriel Almond as the supervisor.

Q: Did you have a chance to take a seminar with Robert Dahl?
A: No. At Yale we had to choose three fields, and I chose comparative politics, international relations, and, mainly because I had taken some courses as an undergraduate in the area, political theory. I did not choose American

---

2. Deutsch was at Yale from 1957 until 1967. See Merelman (2003, 43–45).

politics, which was Bob Dahl's field at the time. He became a comparativist later in his career, and it was in that connection that I met him again and got to know him better. But I certainly knew of him when I was a student at Yale, and he is one of the people for whom I have a really great admiration.

Q: What sort of training in methods was required of graduate students at Yale?

A: One of the new things I learned at Yale, and I believe it was a requirement for all graduate students, was statistics. This had a big influence on me, not so much because of any technique I learned, but because studying statistics introduced me to probabilistic thinking and forced me to consider what it meant to offer a generalization. I also took a course on scope and methods with Bob Lane. Lane was a very good teacher, and his course was an eye-opener too. This was in 1958–59, and I doubt many graduate programs in political science offered this kind of training then. Yale was at the forefront of the behavioral revolution, an attempt to get away from ad hoc, descriptive work and make political science into a real science.

Q: Are there any fellow graduate students from your class whom you were close to and with whom you have kept in touch?

A: In part, because I was at Yale for quite a short time, I did not get to know a lot of people. Two graduate students who were working pretty closely with Deutsch were Bruce Russett, whom I got to know quite well, and Richard Merritt. I also knew Edward Dew, who got an M.A. from Yale and then went on to get a Ph.D. from UCLA. I lost touch with him for a good while, but then we crossed paths again in Holland. He married a Dutch woman and was interested in the politics of Suriname, which I had also written about. I should also mention R. William Liddle, an expert on Indonesia. I've kept in touch with him over the years,

Q: Turning to your dissertation, could you discuss how you picked your topic?

A: My dissertation was on the response of the Dutch political system to decolonization. The real reason I chose this topic was that I had just spent three years at Principia College and two years at Yale, and I was looking for an opportunity to get back to Holland. If I was going to do field research, I figured I might as well do it in Holland. Decolonization in West New Guinea happened to be a big issue in Dutch politics at that time. I had written a paper on the topic for Deutsch's seminar, where I concluded that there was a puzzle to be solved: Why were the Dutch trying to hold on to West New Guinea? I felt I had found an issue in Dutch domestic politics that would be interesting to study.

The official reason I chose this topic went as follows. Key Marxist and non-Marxist theorists of imperialism, such as Lenin and Hobson, argued that, in the final analysis, economic interests dictate colonialism. But in the case of West New Guinea, it seemed obvious there were no strong economic motives for Dutch colonialism. Indeed, Dutch economic interests arguably pointed in the opposite direction—*not* to be involved in West New Guinea, to withdraw. Dutch economic interests in Indonesia were far greater than any present or potential future interest in West New Guinea, and the Dutch were jeopardizing their economic interests in Indonesia by hanging on to West New Guinea.[3] So, I argued that from the perspective of existing theories of imperialism, Dutch involvement in West New Guinea was a deviant case, one that provided a crucial instance, or crucial experiment, that was particularly interesting to study. Even though this was an ex-post facto rationale, I was still able to justify my choice of case in theoretical terms.

Q: You mentioned that you did not write your dissertation while in residence at Yale, but while teaching at Elmira College.
A: When I went back to the United States from Holland, I arrived at Elmira College and started teaching. I faced a tough situation, because I had come back from the field with lots of notes but nothing written. Elmira was a small college, and I had a three course per semester teaching load. I had not taught at all before, so teaching took quite a bit of time. I wrote the dissertation during whatever free time I had. I wrote every evening and on weekends. It took me about a year-and-a-half to finish the dissertation.

Q: The topic of your dissertation suggests you were straddling the fields of comparative politics and international relations.
A: Not really. I approached decolonization more as a domestic politics issue than an international relations issue. Except in a background chapter, I didn't deal with diplomatic relations between Holland and Indonesia or what went on in Indonesia. I was mainly interested in understanding how the Dutch political system worked, and I just happened to be focusing on a

3. Though Indonesia gained independence from the Netherlands in 1949, the Dutch retained control over the western half of the island of New Guinea. Hence, by holding on to West New Guinea, the Dutch were antagonizing the leaders of the newly independent Indonesia and thus jeopardizing the properties their citizens owned in Indonesia. During the 1950s, the Dutch government began to prepare West New Guinea for full independence and allowed elections in 1959. An elected Papuan Council took office in 1961 and decided on the name of West Papua, a national emblem, a flag, and a national anthem. These were adopted and the flag was first raised, next to the Dutch flag, on December 1, 1961. However, Indonesia invaded on December 18, 1961, and annexed the fledgling nation. After armed conflict in December 1961 and early 1962, West New Guinea was briefly placed under United Nations administration before being transferred to Indonesian administration in 1963 and becoming a province in 1969.

case of foreign policy decision making: Dutch reluctance to give up their colony. Indeed, the title of my dissertation was "West New Guinea as an Issue in Dutch Domestic Politics." When I turned the dissertation into my first book, I selected a fancier title, *The Trauma of Decolonization* (Lijphart 1966). Still, the title of my dissertation shows that it was a comparative politics dissertation.

Q: Why were the Dutch so reluctant to give up this colony?
A: I concluded that psychological and emotional reasons explain this reluctance. World War II was a huge event that shook up the country, and after the war, people wanted things to return to normal. The normal situation for the Dutch was being a colonial power and lording over a number of colonies. For a small country with a self-image of being more than a small country because it was a colonial power, decolonization required an adjustment. At the same time, being pushed out of the colonies by armed independence movements was also quite a shock. Indeed, the anti-colonial revolt in Indonesia in the late 1940s had such a strong emotional impact because the Dutch had regarded themselves as benevolent rulers of the grateful Indonesian masses. Dutch politics regarding West New Guinea in the 1950s was not rational. Dutch politicians were pursuing goals that just did not make any sense. In most other instances, cooler heads prevailed. But the decision to hold on to West New Guinea was a deviant case in Dutch politics.

Research on Consociational Democracy
Launching a Research Program

Q: In your second book, *The Politics of Accommodation* (Lijphart 1968a), you continued to focus on politics in the Netherlands. But you also used this book, as well as a couple of articles published at about the same time (Lijphart 1968b, 1969), to launch a research program on consociationalism, or consensus democracy. Could you discuss how you developed the ideas at the heart of this research program?
A: When I was writing *The Politics of Accommodation*, I was influenced by the classification of countries Almond presented in his wonderful 1956 article. He had drawn a distinction between Anglo-American political systems, characterized by a homogeneous, secular political culture, and continental European political systems, characterized by a fragmented political culture. And he argued that stable democracy was harder to achieve in fragmented political cultures, as found in France, Germany, and Italy. Now, Almond classified the Netherlands, Belgium, and the Scandinavian countries as standing somewhere between homogeneous and fragmented political cul-

tures; and I seized on that. If you look at its political culture, the Netherlands is actually just as fragmented as France, Germany, or Italy, yet it seemed to have a stable democracy, which Almond argued was characteristic of the Anglo-American homogeneous political cultures. So here was another beautiful deviant case that cried out for analysis.

I suggested that a distinction should be made between mass and elite culture. This distinction, in turn, made it possible to consider how cooperation at the elite level can counteract cleavages at the mass level. Thus, in my book on Dutch politics (1968a), I refer to this pattern as the "politics of accommodation." In my 1968 (b) and 1969 articles, I used the term *consociational* for the first time. I was looking for a term that seemed to fit, and I got *consociational* from a book by David Apter (1961, 24–25) called *The Political Kingdom in Uganda*. The term can actually be traced back to the German political thinker Johannes Althusius, who was very much influenced by the Confederacy of the Dutch United Provinces, a highly decentralized state, and who wrote in 1603 about a *consociatio*.

A second source of inspiration was Seymour Martin Lipset's argument that crosscutting affiliations are necessary for stable democracy (1960a, 88–89). In this respect, too, Dutch politics presented a deviant case: stable democracy in spite of mutually reinforcing affiliations within each of the subcultures instead of affiliations cutting across the subcultural divisions.

Q: You have acknowledged that other authors were working on similar ideas during this period. But, maybe in part because you framed your study of the Netherlands as a deviant case analysis, you were more successful in reaching a broad audience and shaping a new research agenda. For example, *The Politics of Accommodation* has been described by Hans Daalder (1997b, 236) as "the cornerstone of the 'consociational democracy' school."

A: My name is frequently mentioned as the greatest proponent of the concept of consociationalism. But I have always felt I was just one of a whole group of people working on the idea of power sharing, that I was part of a broad consociational school. We all knew each other, corresponded, and got quite a bit of inspiration from each other. Hans Daalder was part of this group, as was Gerhard Lehmbruch, whose work was especially important. Lehmbruch published a book in 1967 called *Proporzdemokratie*, which was never translated into English. He was a considerable source of inspiration, and I learned quite a bit from him.

A few things perhaps distinguish me from the other contributors to the literature on consociational democracy. First, I made more of an attempt to put things in terms of broader theory. Second, I pursued the idea of power sharing more tenaciously. I stuck with it and worked to improve it. Third, I have been more interested in seeing how this idea can be used as a prescription for solving problems of divided societies. Fourth, I think I did more to find generalizations; and the big prize usually goes to generalizers.

Generalizing the Idea of Power Sharing

Q: Though your first two books were on the Netherlands, your next two books—*Democracy in Plural Societies* (Lijphart 1977) and *Democracies* (Lijphart 1984)—sought to offer generalizations anchored in a much broader comparative analysis. Could you discuss the progression from the deviant case analysis at the heart of your two books on the Netherlands to the explicitly comparative analysis in these two subsequent books?

A: As we discussed, I finished my dissertation while teaching at Elmira College. I then took a job at Berkeley in 1963. My first priority at Berkeley, in terms of research, was to turn my dissertation into a book. I spent quite a bit of my time revising my dissertation, and it was published in 1966 as *The Trauma of Decolonization*. This was obviously a very specialized topic, not of great interest to a lot of people. Indeed, many people think my 1968 (a) book, *The Politics of Accommodation,* is my first book. Both books were on Dutch politics, and though most of the heavy field research was associated with my dissertation, I did additional fieldwork and interviewing for *The Politics of Accommodation.* I was drawn to studying Holland because of my own Dutch background. But the fact that I was in the United States, not Holland, when I was writing these books meant I had some distance from Dutch politics, which made it easier not to get sidetracked by day-to-day events, think in theoretical terms, and see broader patterns.

I also had started working on more general statements of my ideas about consociational democracy. During 1966 and 1967, I worked on a paper for the International Political Science Association (IPSA) Congress in Brussels in 1967 that became the lead article in the first issue of *Comparative Political Studies* (Lijphart 1968b). This shift toward more generalized, comparative analysis was further reinforced by a conversation I had with Aaron Wildavsky, who was the chair of political science at Berkeley. I told him about my publications—my first book was out, my second book would be published shortly, and I had some articles—and I asked what it would take for me to get tenure. He said, "What the department wants from you is a real comparative piece. That is what we are looking for." I replied, "Sounds good, that is what I am already working on"—although I regarded it as a pretty steep price for tenure. In any event, the point is that already in those early years, while I was an assistant professor at Berkeley, I was moving in a comparative direction.

I did get tenure at Berkeley in 1968, but, by that time, I had decided to return to Holland to take a job at the University of Leiden. Now, my appointment at the University of Leiden was actually as a chair of international relations. And my agreement was that, even though I was free to do the research I wanted, I would be responsible for teaching international relations at Leiden. As a result, the focus of my thinking shifted away from the comparative research I had begun at Berkeley toward theories of international relations. In my inaugural lecture at Leiden, I discussed how theory develops in international relations. I eventually transformed this lecture into a piece for the *International Studies Quarterly* (Lijphart 1974a). Still, I realized I could do better work in comparative politics than international relations. I found international relations too fluid. I could not get a grip on it the way I could with comparative politics. One lesson I drew from this was that the next time I moved, when I was hired by the University of California, San Diego (UCSD) in 1978, I made it clear I was not going to touch IR.

Q: This detour through IR notwithstanding, you did continue working on the ideas about consociationalism you had initially formulated in your work on the Netherlands.
A: The question I addressed in my comparative research was whether the process of peacefully managing societal conflict through political power-sharing arrangements I had detected in the Netherlands might be found in other countries. I first sensed that the idea of power sharing could be generalized when I studied cases such as Belgium, Switzerland, and Austria. Then I began to look beyond these four countries, and the best examples of power sharing I could find elsewhere were Lebanon, Malaysia, and Cyprus. These cases took on considerable importance in my 1977 book *Democracy in Plural Societies,* where I focused on the problems of plural societies and showed how they can have stable democracies if they devise mechanisms of power sharing. I used the term *consociational democracy* to capture this situation.

This research got me thinking about ways to generalize further, not to look just at a set of cases with some strong intrinsic interest, but to classify *all* democracies. This is how I got working on *Democracies,* which was published in 1984.

Q: Could you discuss the origins of *Democracies* (Lijphart 1984)?
A: At about the time I had finished writing *Democracy in Plural Societies,* in 1976, and while I was still at Leiden, Bob Dahl wrote to me and asked if I would prepare a volume for the Prentice-Hall Foundations of Modern Political Science series. Dahl had published his *Modern Political Analysis* (Dahl 1963) in this series, and Karl Deutsch had written a volume on inter-

national relations for it (Deutsch 1968). Dankwart Rustow was going to write the volume on comparative politics, but he decided that either he didn't have time for it or he couldn't cover the field in the allotted space—these were short books, around 150 pages long. So, Dahl was thinking of dividing the treatment of comparative politics into two volumes, one on democratic politics, the other on non-democratic, authoritarian politics, and he wanted to know if I would be interested in doing the volume on democratic politics. This proposal fit my interest in writing something broadly comparative, and I figured I could use the idea of consociationalism as the basic organizing device. So I agreed to do it.

I did not get around to working on this project immediately. Then, in 1978, I moved to San Diego. Moving takes time away from scholarly pursuits. Also, the early period at San Diego was a turbulent time in my personal life, because I got divorced. That took a toll, too. Finally, after I had been working on the book for a while, there was one last change. Bob Dahl wrote to tell me that Prentice-Hall was no longer interested in publishing the book! They thought there was no market for it. From my perspective, this was actually a fortuitous turn of events, because it gave me more freedom to write the book I wanted to write. When I eventually finished the manuscript, I submitted it to Yale University Press and they published it. I still get satisfaction from the fact that Prentice-Hall was wrong; it turned out there was, indeed, a market for this kind of book.

Q: *Democracies* is an ambitious book that analyzes numerous institutions across twenty-one countries yet also has a strong organizing argument. Could you discuss how you went about writing such a book?

A: *Democracies,* more than any other book I have written, unfolded chapter by chapter. For example, as I was writing Chapter 3, I didn't know exactly what was going to be in Chapter 4. I was thinking step by step. Still, I did have a clear working hypothesis about how the institutions I was studying worked together. I started with the broad contrast between consociational and majoritarian democracies I had developed in my previous work. I then proceeded, in what I would describe as a loose deductive process, to spell out what each type of democracy meant in terms of political institutions, from the cabinet, executive-legislative relations, and the number of legislative chambers, to the party system, the electoral system, the division of power, and constitutional guarantees of minority rights. My hypothesis, which was influenced by what I knew about pure majoritarian democracies, such as the United Kingdom and New Zealand, and pure consociational democracies, such as Switzerland and Belgium, was that certain institutional features would go together. I therefore expected countries to either have those institutional features that were associated with a consociational democracy or the opposite features that were associated with a majoritarian democracy.

As I worked chapter by chapter on different institutions, I found that this hypothesis worked quite well but that not all cases lined up as I expected. Then, in the final chapter, I considered how the nine institutional features I studied held together.[4] Using factor analysis, I found they worked together not as a single dimension, but as two distinct dimensions that were not correlated with each other: the executives-parties dimension and the federal-unitary dimension.[5] A related finding was that in the property space formed by these two dimensions, the countries fall all over the property space rather than being neatly aligned on an axis linking the bottom left to the top right corner (Lijphart 1984, 219). So, my hypothesis worked pretty well, but things ended up being a little more complicated than I had expected. I thought these results were interesting and also that the analysis was new enough that I should distinguish it from my previous research on consociational democracy by coining a new term, *consensus democracy.*

Q: You eventually returned to the issues addressed in *Democracies* in your book, *Patterns of Democracy* (Lijphart 1999a), which might be considered an updated and expanded version of *Democracies*.
A: I regarded *Democracies* as a work in progress, and I have been more critical of that book myself than have most of my readers. There were a lot of really loose ends in it. Almost as soon as I had written it, I knew I wanted to follow up on that effort. My original thinking was that since *Democracies* covered the period from 1945 to 1980, I would wait until 1990 to write an updated volume that would add the 1980s. Also, *Democracies* included twenty-one countries, and I wanted to increase the number of countries. Well, I did this and even more, though it took me longer than I had anticipated, because I was working on other projects in the meantime, including a book entitled *Electoral Systems and Party Systems* (Lijphart 1994). In the end, *Patterns of Democracy* examined thirty-six countries during the 1945–96 period. Besides covering more countries, *Patterns of Democracy* was also more ambitious than *Democracies* in terms of the range of political institu-

4. These nine features are minimal winning cabinets, executive dominance, effective number of parties, number of issue dimensions, electoral disproportionality, unicameralism, centralization, constitutional flexibility, and referendums.

5. Factor analysis is a statistical technique used to discover simple patterns in the relationships among variables and to discover if the observed variables can be explained largely or entirely in terms of a much smaller number of variables called "factors." The executives-parties dimension is determined by the following features: minimal winning cabinets, executive dominance, effective number of parties, number of issue dimensions and, to a lesser extent, electoral disproportionality. The federal-unitary dimension is determined by the features of unicameralism, centralization, and constitutional flexibility.

tions it analyzed and the questions it addressed. I added a focus on interest groups in order to get at the difference between corporatist and pluralist accounts of interest group politics, and I also considered central banks. All in all, I addressed ten institutional features. Finally, I focused more explicitly on the "So what?" question by assessing how the type of democracy affects government effectiveness and public policy.

Two further features of *Patterns of Democracy* should be highlighted. First, the book makes a real effort to integrate a large literature. When I wrote *Democracies,* there was not a great deal of existing research with regard to some institutions, and in those instances I had to improvise. For instance, I devised somewhat more sensitive measures than the crude dichotomies of bicameralism versus unicameralism and rigid versus flexible constitutions. By the mid-1990s, however, there was a substantial literature on the various institutions I address, for example, on executives and cabinets, legislatures, parties and interest groups, and so on. So one thing I offer is a summary and synthesis of the research in the field. A second noteworthy feature of *Patterns of Democracy* concerns the operationalizations of concepts. For some concepts, all I was able to do was offer pretty basic, four- or five-fold, impressionist classifications: better and more sophisticated measures of the degree of "cameralism" and constitutional flexibility than I had used before, and also of degrees of federalism and decentralization, but far from ideal. This leaves lots of improvements for future researchers to make! But for most of the other variables, I have very sophisticated indicators. Gathering data on some of these variables took an enormous amount of time and effort.

Q: What are the main findings of *Patterns of Democracy?*
A: *Patterns of Democracy* reinforced the findings in *Democracies.* I found that the ten institutional variables in the new study could be summarized in terms of the same two dimensions and that countries fall throughout the property space formed by these two dimensions. I went further, however, in justifying why we have these two dimensions (Lijphart 1999a, Ch. 14).

With regard to the "So what?" question, I expected to confirm the conventional wisdom that majoritarian democracies are at least slightly more effective than consensus democracies in terms of decision making and therefore in terms of policy. Instead, using quantitative indicators of economic policy making, I found it was the other way around: consensus democracies do slightly better. But the differences are not large enough to be statistically significant. On the question of quality of democracy, I expected consensus democracy would come out a little better. Instead, I ended up with very strong and significant statistical results that point to the superiority of consensus democracies. These democracies have higher participation in elections and do quite well with regard to civil rights. They are also quite flexible in terms of making policy adjustments and in terms of responsiveness. Indeed, the idea of power sharing has overwhelming empirical support.

Core Ideas and Their Reception

Q: Your career has been characterized by a great degree of coherence. In your early publications you proposed the idea of power sharing as a mechanism for achieving stable democracy in culturally divided societies, then you fine-tuned and increasingly generalized this core idea in subsequent works.
A: If you consider all my publications over the years, you will see I have written on a range of subjects. But you are right: the main thing I have done is study comparatively the stability of democracy, the quality of democracy, and how to achieve both peace and democracy. These are the big questions that engage me. My interest in these issues was prompted partly by the experiences in my youth that we discussed earlier. But I have also been driven by the desire to do good political science by generalizing. Thus, my first works focused on the Netherlands. But I gradually expanded the scope of my analysis by first becoming a specialist on West Europe and then venturing out into other regions in search of cases of divided societies where stable democracy has developed, cases such as South Africa, Lebanon, India, Malaysia, and Colombia. Over time, I became a worldwide comparativist.

Q: Your work has had a major impact on comparative politics and political science. When did you start to sense that your ideas about consociationalism were catching on? Did you expect your work to have such an impact?
A: The response my work has received has been very gratifying to me. I think the recognition given to my work happened gradually. Many ideas did not catch on immediately. Though *The Politics of Accommodation* appeared in 1968 (a), and I published a couple of articles on the consociational model of democracy in 1968 (b) and 1969, it wasn't until quite a few years later that people really started to pay attention. Indeed, Brian Barry's two critiques of the consociational model came out seven years later, in 1975 (Barry 1975a, 1975b). Or take the Dutch edition of *The Politics of Accommodation*. The first Dutch edition, which I translated myself and adapted for a Dutch audience, was published in 1968. The second edition wasn't published until 1976. But after that eight-year gap, new editions were printed in 1979, 1982, 1984, 1986, 1988, 1990, and 1992. Basically, it looked like the book was dead before people started paying attention to it. I

honestly have to say that it was not until I became president of the American Political Science Association (APSA) in 1995 that I sensed I had attained a certain degree of prominence as a political scientist. Did I expect this success? No. When I started my career, I wanted to do good work, but I did not have the ambition to become a leading political scientist.

Q: Which of your books is your favorite?
A: *Democracies* used to be my favorite book, but now *Patterns of Democracy* is my favorite. *Patterns of Democracy* is a better, more systematic, and more comprehensive successor to *Democracies*. Of all my works, it has the broadest scope, in terms of both the issues it deals with and the cases it covers. And I think it is my most systematic book. I would also describe *Electoral Systems and Party Systems* as a very systematic book, which comes to some important conclusions. Electoral systems strongly influence the proportionality of election outcomes; in fact, I found that they explain about two-thirds of the variance in the degree of proportionality. Their influence on the degree of multipartism and other aspects of party systems is weaker but still significant. But *Electoral Systems and Party Systems* focuses on a much narrower subject matter than *Patterns of Democracy*, and in many ways is quite technical. *Patterns of Democracy* really dealt with very broad and important themes, and it is a finished, pretty polished work.

Q: How would you compare your contributions to democratic theory to those of Robert Dahl (1956, 1971, 1989) and Giovanni Sartori (1987a, 1987b)?
A: Both Dahl and Sartori dedicate more time than I to addressing questions of definitions and the normative aspects of democratic theory. Indeed, one of Dahl's big contributions concerns how to define democracy. I find more parallels between my work and Dahl's than between my work and Sartori's. When you think of Sartori, you think of his book on democratic theory (Sartori 1987a, 1987b). But I have been inspired less by this work than by his work on political parties and the question of polarized pluralism (Sartori 1976). Even though I think polarized pluralism is not as dangerous as Sartori makes it out to be, I have been very much interested in the kind of generalizations he provides.

With regard to Dahl, I find clear parallels among our works. For example, Dahl's *A Preface to Democratic Theory* (1956) contrasts Madisonian and populistic versions of democracy in a way that resembles my distinction between consensus and majoritarian democracy. When I came up with this distinction, I found that other people, including Dahl, had already made similar distinctions. When I was working on the idea of consociational democracy, I also learned a lot from Dahl's edited volume *Political Opposition in Western Democracies* (1966a). In addition to the important chapters on the Netherlands, Belgium, and Austria, Dahl has three concluding chapters where he discusses subcultural fragmentation.[6] I gladly recognize that parts of Dahl's writing have had a direct impact on my work. Still, I think I have done more than Dahl with regard to making systematic comparisons and testing theories.

Q: When you started your career you made your mark by identifying the shortcomings of Almond's and Lipset's influential ideas about the conditions of stable democracy and offering ways to modify their theories (Lijphart 1968a, Ch. 1). Gradually, your alternative ideas, which posited the viability of democracy in divided societies that adopted the institutional arrangements you labeled as consociational, themselves became the conventional wisdom and the target of criticisms. One of the most comprehensive critiques is the article in *World Politics* by Ian Lustick (1997).[7] What is your response to your critics?
A: Lots of critics, starting with Brian Barry (1975a, 1975b), have sought to chip away at various aspects of my work on consociationalism. So, in Chapter 4 of my 1985 book, *Power-Sharing in South Africa*, I tried to answer all the critiques of my work that had been published through 1983. I answer their criticisms one by one and say why I disagree with them. I did this because I was arguing for power sharing as a solution for South Africa, and I thus felt it was important to deal with all the critiques of the theory. In some cases, I have found critics to be constructive and sought to adopt points they have made. These are the criticisms from within the consociational school, so to speak, by people who are basically sympathetic to the idea of power sharing.

With regard to Ian Lustick's 1997 *World Politics* article, I must say that when I read it I couldn't believe my eyes. I had considered Lustick one of my constructive critics, and I had incorporated some of his previous critiques in my work. But I really disagreed with his 1997 article. Lustick makes fun of the fact that the number of conditions I identify as favorable for consociational democracy has varied over time. What's so wrong with that? As I analyzed additional empirical cases, I learned new things and thus sought to fine-tune the theory of power sharing. As it currently stands, I identify nine conditions of stable democracy in divided societies. My final word on

6. Dahl (1966b, 357) stressed the difficulty of managing conflicts involving subcultures because they involve conflicts regarding a whole "way of life" and cannot be confined to single, discrete issues.

7. Other critiques are presented in Barry (1975a, 1975b), Van Schendelen (1984), and Bogaards (2000).

the matter, which I have stuck with since, is in *Power-Sharing in South Africa* (Lijphart 1985, 119–26).[8]

Q: One fundamental critique of your work is that consociational democracy is actually not democratic, because vigorous political oppositions are lacking in such regimes.
A: This is a critique made by Samuel Huntington (1981a, 14), who refers to consociational democracy as "consociational oligarchy," and Pierre Van Den Berghe (1981, 82), who argues that consociational democracy is really façade democracy. In the abstract, these arguments may sound reasonable, but if you look at actual cases, such as the Netherlands, Belgium, Switzerland, or Austria, it is clear these are democracies that work quite well. How can you say these countries are lacking in democraticness? In fact, these countries are among the most decent and humane of all the democracies in the world today. I disagree with the view that you can only have a vibrant democracy if there is a vigorous partisan opposition. As I argue in my book on South Africa (Lijphart 1985, 108–12), the critics who say consociational democracy is not democratic mistakenly equate democracy with majoritarian democracy.

Q: Has your decision to pursue a research program focused so heavily on consociationalism caused you to miss opportunities to address other questions and follow other potentially fruitful avenues of research?
A: I don't think so. There is nothing I really wish I had done but didn't have the time to do. What I wanted to do, I did. But maybe there is one exception. One thing I started to work on, but never got around to doing, concerns the development of theory in international relations. I wrote one major article on the topic, published in the *International Studies Quarterly (ISQ)* (Lijphart 1974a), which tried to organize theoretical approaches in international relations around Hobbesian versus Grotian approaches or, in terms of modern authors, around the contrast between Hans Morgenthau and Hedley Bull, on the one hand, and Karl Deutsch, on the other hand. I thought that contrast captured a lot. I drew on Thomas Kuhn's discussion of paradigms in scientific revolutions (1962), and I saw Deutsch as a revolutionary in the field of international relations, because he broke with the old, Hobbesian paradigm. For years, I gathered bibliographic information on things I was going to look at when I finally wrote a book on this issue. But I've never written that book. The initial reason I never wrote it was that I never got much positive feedback on the *ISQ* article (Lijphart 1974a) or on a

8. These nine conditions are no majority segment, segments of equal size, small number of segments, small population size, external threats, overarching loyalties, socioeconomic equality, geographic concentration of segments, and traditions of accommodation.

couple of subsequent pieces I published (Lijphart 1974b, 1981). Basically, this series of articles was met by deafening silence, which dampened my enthusiasm. Still, for about twenty years after my 1974 *ISQ* article, I thought I would eventually come back to this project. Then, in the mid-1990s, I decided the time for such a project had simply passed. There had been many new developments in the field of international relations, and I did not want to spend my time reading up on this literature. So, I stopped making bibliographic notes, and I think I just threw all my files away. I do not consider this a missed opportunity. Had I written this book right away, it might have been useful, but it probably wouldn't have been all that important. My time was probably better spent doing the other things I did.

Q: Is there anything else you regret not having written or, alternatively, having written?
A: I have one regret. I was asked to contribute to a festschrift for Gabriel Almond (Verba and Pye 1978), and I declined because I really didn't have anything in the pipeline to contribute. Perhaps I should have made a greater effort to think of something to do, to honor him. I partly made up for that omission by contributing to Almond and Verba's *The Civic Culture Revisited* (Lijphart 1980). I also know that Almond regarded it as an honor for himself, and rightly so, that two of his former students, Sidney Verba and I, served as presidents of the APSA consecutively from 1994 to 1996.

The Research Process and Goals
Science and Normative Concerns

Q: Do you see yourself as a scientist?
A: My conception of science is that it is a generalizing enterprise, and, taking your question in that sense, I see myself as a scientist. I try to formulate general propositions about classes of objects. And I find this very gratifying. Thus, in my most recent book, *Patterns of Democracy* (Lijphart 1999a), I started out with a contrast between consensus and majoritarian democracies, which I thought was a solid way to begin. But, when I first started working on the book, I was not yet aware of how powerful this distinction really was, of how much the different characteristics of consensus and majoritarian democracies tend to form a pattern, and the extent to which these different types of democracy affect policy making and policy results. When you come across these sorts of patterns, you get a great deal of satisfaction.

Q: What role do values and normative concerns play in your research?
A: I see my research as starting with a normatively important variable—something that can be described as good or bad, such as peace or violence. I

then proceed to investigate what produces these different outcomes. Finally, I conclude by presenting prescriptions, that is, measures that would produce the desired outcome. I don't see a tension between normative concerns and an aspiration to do science. In fact, I think a normative, prescriptive conclusion can be drawn from most empirical relationships. I am somewhat surprised that so many social scientists are reluctant to offer prescriptions. I guess there is an attitude on the part of some scholars that they should just be scholars and not engage in politics. Hence, they should refrain from making policy recommendations. That is not my attitude.

I have not been very successful with my policy recommendations, especially in the United States. But I am much better known in Holland than in the United States, even though I have been outside of Holland for so many years. For decades, all Dutch social scientists and many journalists read my book, *The Politics of Accommodation* (Lijphart 1968a). My ideas about power sharing as a solution to the problems of divided societies have been discussed in Holland quite a bit.

Q: You have advised politicians in a range of countries, most notably in South Africa, but also in Israel, New Zealand, Lebanon, Chile, Angola, and Fiji. Do politicians listen to the advice that you, as an academic, have to offer?
A: One can offer advice in different forms. Sometimes it is formal, and other times it is informal, as may happen at a conference where the government is not necessarily seeking recommendations. Politicians do listen, but they don't necessarily act on the advice. In some cases, they ask for advice simply as a means of stalling. If they don't know what to do or don't want to make a decision, they appoint a commission to study the issue. Their intent is not really to produce useful recommendations that will be implemented. I've seen some of that. In any case, I think one has, at best, a modest impact.

The one case where I would say I have had a real influence is South Africa.[9] I was so convinced of what power sharing might be able to accomplish in South Africa that I made a concerted effort to get involved in the debate about how South Africa might democratize, and I accepted any opportunity to push my views. I first visited South Africa in 1971, under the

9. An apartheid regime was established in South Africa after the National Party came to power in 1948. Under this regime, racial discrimination that denied blacks the right to vote, among other things, was institutionalized. This regime was opposed by the African National Congress (ANC), which turned to guerrilla strategies, and the government used repressive measures to control the ANC and other opposition movements. Change began when Frederik Willem de Klerk became the leader of the National Party in 1989 and was elected president of South Africa that same year. As president, De Klerk lifted the ban on the African National Congress (ANC), released Nelson Mandela from prison, and conducted negotiations that opened the way for the end of the apartheid regime and the election of Mandela as president in 1994.

auspices of a cultural exchange program between South Africa and the Netherlands. I went for six weeks and traveled to different universities, lecturing and meeting politicians and civil servants. I introduced the idea of consociational democracy to South Africa, and, as a result, some people started thinking about how political power sharing could help solve some of the country's problems. After that, I returned to South Africa many times. I probably went there ten times between 1971 and 1991. So, not only did I write a lot about South Africa, including a book, *Power-Sharing in South Africa* (Lijphart 1985), I was also busy talking to people in the country. Over the years, I had lots of conversations with members of the ruling party— including F. W. de Klerk when he was a cabinet member in 1985—and a number of civil servants who supported the ruling party. When I talked about power sharing, they showed interest and were very polite, even deferential, to this professor who came from abroad to meet with them. They would say, "This is a very interesting idea, but it seems like a risky thing to do." To this, my standard answer was, "It seems risky because you are thinking in terms of a choice between maintaining exclusive white power and sharing power with leaders of the nonwhite opposition. But think ahead a little bit. The choice you are eventually going to face will be between sharing power and losing power. When you think about it in those terms, doesn't sharing power seem more attractive?" They would admit that it did. And though they did not take action immediately, I think the eventual decision to initiate the process toward sharing power was taken when people like De Klerk accepted this way of framing the choice.

During the 1980s, I also served twice on an advisory committee, the Buthelezi Commission, which was set up by the KwaZulu Legislative Assembly.[10] The commission's official report, which advocated a form of power sharing, was submitted to the legislature of the KwaZulu homeland and also to the government of South Africa. Now, let me be clear. I was asked to join the Buthelezi Commission because the people organizing this commission had *already* decided they wanted to recommend power sharing. That is why they wanted me on the commission. The government of South Africa rejected the commission's report. Still, this formal proposal had an impact because it was circulated and discussed widely. As a result, the idea of power sharing became much better known.

So, I think I did have some influence. It took quite a bit of time and energy on my part. I relentlessly pursued every opportunity to go to South Africa and push the idea of power sharing. But it has given me great satisfaction. I think I really made an important contribution to politics, especially

10. KwaZulu was a black "homeland" that was granted internal self-rule by the government of South Africa in 1977.

by giving the idea of power sharing its initial impetus in the South Africa context. I am prouder of that achievement than of any particular piece of writing I have done. In fact, I am prouder about my involvement in South Africa than about any other aspect of my entire career.

From Case Studies to Statistical Analysis

Q: Turning to the strategies you have used to generate and test ideas, your second book, *The Politics of Accommodation* **(Lijphart 1968a), is widely seen as one of the most influential case studies in comparative politics.[11] What is the secret to writing such an influential case study?**
A: Case studies have the greatest impact when they are embedded in a broader theory. In *The Politics of Accommodation,* I framed the Dutch case as a deviant case in relation to influential theories at the time, those of Almond and Lipset.

Q: Another way of putting this is that although your early work focused on a single case, the Netherlands, you were interested in generalization.
A: You can classify social scientists into two groups: those whose main inclination is to generalize and those whose main inclination is to particularize. Though both approaches have their value, I like to generalize.

Q: After your first two books, your interest in generalization seems to have led you to move beyond the Netherlands and eventually to use statistical analysis.
A: I learned correlation and regression analysis in graduate school. But I did not use these methods in my early publications, which were based on small-N research. Later, however, my research spanned more and more cases, and I also began quantifying my variables. That allowed me to use statistical analysis. In *Democracies* (Lijphart 1984), I still relied mainly on cross classifications, but in the final chapter I used factor analysis to get at the correlation among my nine institutional variables. *Electoral Systems and Party Systems* (Lijphart 1994) is the book in which I most consistently use statistical analysis. In that book, I also very explicitly use the comparative method, considering, for example, electoral systems before and after a change in the electoral law. On the whole, I think the results of that part of the study were stronger than the results of the statistical analysis. Finally, in *Patterns of Democracy* (Lijphart 1999a), I relied again on cross classifications and factor analysis. But I also showed scattergrams that included regression

11. See, for example, Rogowski (1995).

lines, and I used regression analysis to assess the effect of different types of democracy. So, I have used statistical tools when I covered more cases, but also relied on other tools as well.

Q: As you moved toward statistical analysis, did you sense you had lost a feel for the cases you were studying?
A: In *Patterns of Democracy* (Lijphart 1999a), which covers thirty-six countries, I was close to reaching the point where I would have lost a feel for the countries in my study, but I still think I knew my cases. Obviously, I am not an expert on all thirty-six countries, but I have read a lot of case studies that offer very valuable descriptive information. I have also visited most of these thirty-six countries, in fact, thirty-two of them. I had enough of a sense of the cases to tell you a story about each one, enough so that I felt I had more than just a collection of statistics.

Q: Even as you turned to worldwide comparisons, you continued writing articles that addressed a particular country, for example, Northern Ireland, South Africa, India, Australia, and France (Lijphart 1996a, 1996b, 1998, 1999b, 2003). What were you trying to achieve with these studies?
A: I would call some of those pieces "occasional articles," which were written because I was invited to some conference or wanted to address a specific question. Still, these papers usually have something to do with my broad theoretical concerns. For example, I have written on the extent to which various proposals for institutional reform in Northern Ireland, such as the Good Friday agreement, constitute a consociational solution.[12] On South Africa, I have written papers that explore what kind of power sharing would be most suitable to that country. I have been interested in India because it looks like the one deviant case in terms of consociational democracy. When you take a closer look at India, it turns out not to be a deviant case and instead fits my definition of consociational democracy almost completely. Similarly, my work on Australia dealt with an issue I had ignored in my prior classification of Australia—because I had ignored upper houses—and my new research lets me show that Australia is really more of a consensus democracy than I had thought. Finally, I recently published a paper showing that France, a case I classify as a majoritarian democracy, performs quite poorly in comparison with other continental European countries. So, these

12. The Good Friday Agreement, signed in 1998, sought to address relationships within Northern Ireland; between Northern Ireland and the Republic; and between both parts of Ireland and England, Scotland, and Wales. The agreement was put to a referendum in May 1998 and was overwhelmingly approved.

pieces are all quite closely connected with my broader theoretical and comparative studies.

Q: One important characteristic of your work is its focus on political institutions. Indeed, you analyzed the origins and effects of institutions long before it became fashionable to be an institutionalist. Could you describe how you approach the study of institutions and compare your approach to other approaches to institutions?
A: My approach to institutions differs from the current new institutionalism favored by rational choice theorists. As I see it, there is an element of deductive logic to my work. For instance, I developed the distinction between consensus and majoritarian democracies by thinking about what it means to have a majoritarian democracy and then deducing a number of characteristics from the principle of majoritarian democracy. Still, I am mainly an inductive empirical generalizer, not a deductive thinker. In contrast, rational choice institutionalists are more elaborate and formal in their deductive thinking. I am not saying deductive analysis is a bad thing, but I put more emphasis on the empirical study of real-world problems and phenomena.

Fieldwork, Languages, and Library Research

Q: In the early years of your career, you carried out a fair amount of fieldwork. What kind of research did you do in the field?
A: My main experience with field research was in Holland and was linked to my dissertation and first book, *The Trauma of Decolonization* (Lijphart 1966). I looked through a large amount of documents—parliamentary debates, commission reports, party platforms, interest group publications, and so on. I also did a lot of elite interviews with politicians, high civil servants, scholars, and journalists. The year 1960–61 was full of arduous research, which left me no time to do any writing. I needed all the time for research. I went back to Holland in 1964, when I was working on *The Politics of Accommodation* (Lijphart 1968a), but I only spent a few months there. For *Democracy in Plural Societies* (Lijphart 1977), I did similar documentary research, especially in Belgium and Switzerland. I also did some elite interviewing, particularly in Suriname and the Netherlands Antilles. I spent only a bit more than a week in each of these last two places; these tiny countries are really wonderful, because in about a week you can talk to everybody who really matters.

Q: Did you continue doing fieldwork after these three books?
A: Not really. As my career has progressed, I have done less and less field research. The last serious field research I did was in 1991, when I was in

Berlin on a four-month leave. Eastern Europe had just opened up, and I took the opportunity to travel to several East European countries. I did some elite interviewing in Prague, Budapest, and Warsaw. Like my previous elite interviews, these were unstructured, free-flowing conversations. My objective was partly to discover factual information and partly my respondents' views and interpretations of particular political developments and circumstances. I used this material in an article on constitutional choices in Czechoslovakia, Hungary, and Poland (Lijphart 1992).

Q: How important is language training for doing good comparative research?
A: Through my education in the Netherlands, I received training in English, French, and German, as well as Latin and Greek. Later in life I learned some Swedish and Spanish. These language skills have come in handy. Having Dutch as my mother tongue made a big difference in my initial fieldwork in the Netherlands. In my work on South Africa, my knowledge of Dutch helped me understand some Afrikaans. Also, I've certainly found it useful to be able to read in other languages. For example, Lehmbruch's *Proporzdemokratie* (1967) appeared only in German. It was an important book, and I would not have been able to read it had I not known German.

More and more, you can get by with just English. Things are increasingly available in English, and when you travel you find many people who can communicate in English. Still, to do detailed, intensive research, you need more. For example, as I was doing research in Eastern Europe in 1991, I realized I simply did not have the language facilities to do more in-depth research on the region. For any in-depth case study, a minimum knowledge of the country's language is required.

Q: Since you are not gathering much information through fieldwork at this stage of your career, how would you characterize your current mode of research?
A: I rely mainly on written material and statistics on the countries I study. What I have really needed for my work is a good research library, which we have here at UCSD. The quantity and quality of information available on the Internet has improved. Still, in the mid-1990s, when I was working on *Patterns of Democracy*, I found the Internet somewhat disappointing. A book like the yearly *Political Handbook of the World* proved much more useful to me than surfing the web.

Besides these sources, I count on personal advice from people in the field. In this regard, I am fortunate. Over the years, I have gotten to know country experts who do research on almost all the countries covered in

Patterns of Democracy (Lijphart 1999a). When I have a question, I contact them through e-mail. This is an important resource.

Q: Do research assistants help you in the task of gathering information?
A: I have had money for research assistants many times, and that has been useful. But I am the kind of person who wants to have his hands on everything and make his own judgments. So, when I have sought research grants, I have mainly sought funds to buy out my teaching time. I've had grants from the Guggenheim Foundation and the German Marshall Fund that simply allowed me not to teach for a number of quarters. At one point, I had a whole year off. That is really all I have needed.

Q: Even as you have put greater emphasis on library research, you have continued to travel a lot. I assume your trips abroad feed into your thought process.
A: Yes, such experiences are very important. Even brief visits to a country can be enlightening. You can learn a great deal, even if you go somewhere in a superficial way, for example, as a tourist. You can still get a feel for a country. Now, obviously, when you get to meet politicians and members of the political elite, you learn a great deal more.

Let me give examples of how traveling has stimulated my thinking. I went to Costa Rica in 1990 with my wife to take a three-week language course. We lived with a local family that spoke almost no English. So we had to try and communicate in Spanish with them. I read the local newspaper every day and met a couple of political scientists as well as a member of the electoral tribunal. And we also traveled around. Obviously, this is not what an anthropologist would do, but having this knowledge is better than nothing. And when you deal with a large number of countries, as I do, you cannot spend much time visiting each one.

I had another, very different, experience when I visited Lebanon for a conference in 1984. It was not safe to be in Lebanon then, because kidnappings were very common. We went to Beirut and it was a really chaotic, anarchic situation. There was no established authority, and bands of men with guns were roaming around, so you never knew who was who and what was what. When I was on the plane heading back to San Diego, I felt glad to be getting out of there. Still, it was a wonderful experience. I met with lots of interesting people, for example, the members of the Constitutional Commission of the Lebanese Parliament. I learned a great deal in just a week. In fact, it was one of the most exciting weeks of my life. Traveling in different countries, especially when you have contact with the local people, benefits you as a comparativist.

Political Theory

Q: Do you find it useful for your research to go back to the classics of political theory?
A: I really have not done that, though I think it would be interesting. But time is limited, and other things have a higher priority. In my work, I have quoted some passages, say, from J. S. Mill's *Considerations on Representative Government*. But these are things I remembered from my undergraduate and graduate student days, and I just quoted a specific passage without reread- ing the whole work thoroughly. Still, a basic knowledge of theorists such as Locke, Hobbes, Rousseau, and so on, is a good thing. Knowing these classic works gives political scientists a common language that allows them to talk to each other.

On Methodology

Q: As you started to shift from focusing on the case of the Nether- lands to more explicitly comparative work in the 1970s, you wrote two widely read articles on the methodology of comparative research (Lijphart 1971, 1975). What was the purpose of these publications?
A: I started to do really comparative work while I was at Berkeley, in the mid-1960s. I wanted to make more general statements of the ideas I had developed in my research on the Netherlands. I was trying to figure out how I could generalize on the basis of a few cases. I had some ideas about this matter that were reinforced by a seminar that Neil Smelser gave and a conference paper he wrote.[13] I thought it would be worth seeing if I could systematically put these ideas into writing, just for my own purposes.

The first of my two methodological articles, the one published in the *American Political Science Review* (Lijphart 1971), is the more useful. It is pretty basic, but many people thought it clarified both what exactly the comparative method has to offer as well as its limitations. The article also has a short discussion about case studies, which calls attention to the im- portance of deviant case analysis. That material has been well received.

Q: Since those two articles, you have not published anything else on methodology.
A: After I wrote those two pieces, I never had the urge to write anything more on methodology. First, there is nothing I would really want to add to what I had already said. At most, I would want to make clear that I consider the comparative approach more a research strategy than a method. Second,

---

13. This paper was subsequently published as Smelser (1968).

I see a tendency for people to study methods just for the sake of studying methods, and I wonder how productive that is.

Q: You have written about the drawbacks of "methodological perfectionism" and "unrealistically high standards of empirical research" (Lijphart 1985, 87–88). What is your view of the proper role of methodology?
A: The methods used today in political science have become very sophisticated. I confess that I read some articles and don't understand their methods. But one thing is clear: the quality of our data is still primitive. So it would seem to make sense to work on improving the quality of the data we analyze before we worry about sophisticated methodological techniques. I am not sure we gain much from these techniques, and these methods are making it quite difficult for us, as political scientists, to communicate with each other. In my own research, I have used quite basic correlation and regression analysis, that is, the method I was taught in my first course in statistics at Yale. I have not really progressed beyond that, because I feel I have not needed more sophisticated tools. I do not deny that more advanced techniques might be needed for some kinds of substantive problems. But I worry we are putting more premium on the methods we use than on our ultimate aim of contributing to substantive knowledge and being able to offer policy recommendations.

Institutions, Colleagues, and Students
Berkeley

Q: After a brief stint teaching at Elmira College during 1961–63 while you were writing your dissertation, you joined the political science faculty at Berkeley in 1963. What was your experience at Berkeley like?
A: It was exciting to be at Berkeley. The most useful interactions I had were with Ernie Haas. He had a wonderful theoretical mind, which reminded me in some ways of Karl Deutsch's. He helped you think through things, even on topics that were not his specialty. I was also influenced by David Apter, who was a real comparativist as well as a regional specialist on Africa. I was inspired by what he had written, especially the reader on comparative politics that he edited with Harry Eckstein (Eckstein and Apter 1963). This was a wonderful book that drew together a really important literature. I used it in my comparative politics seminar right away.

Seymour Lipset and Neil Smelser were at Berkeley, then, though they taught in the Sociology Department. I met Lipset, though we didn't interact on a regular basis. I was quite inspired by his writings, such as *Political Man*

(Lipset 1960a). Smelser was an important influence. He was a very obvious source of inspiration for my work on the comparative method.

Berkeley was a good place to meet people in general. There were lots of visitors, and it had the advantage of being close to the Center for Advanced Studies in the Behavioral Sciences at Stanford, where Hans Daalder, Robert Dahl, Val Lorwin, and Stein Rokkan—the main promoters of the Smaller European Democracies project—spent a year in 1966–67. I was in touch with them, which was very stimulating.

The one drawback was that the problems on campus associated with the free speech movement overshadowed the sense of intellectual excitement. During my second year, the Berkeley Political Science Department became very contentious, a situation that persisted the whole time I was there. The key issues were divergent views of student radicalism and the place of political theory in the discipline, which was dominated then by behaviorist concerns and by the search for systematic theorizing. Watching the free speech movement develop was exciting. You were seeing a revolution in the making. But it also meant there was constant turmoil and a lot of internal conflict in the department. In this atmosphere of crisis, I found it difficult to concentrate on the things I wanted to do, and I felt my scholarly work was being negatively affected. This is one of the main reasons I left Berkeley in 1968, even though I had been granted tenure that year. But there were also certain incentives that drew me back to the Netherlands.

Back in the Netherlands

Q: What were these incentives?
A: In 1964, I had met Hans Daalder, a professor at the University of Leiden, and he was plotting to get me back to Holland. This interest in me in Holland eventually led to three offers of full professorships, one from the University of Leiden, a second from Tilburg University, and a third from the Institute of Social Studies in The Hague. Of these institutions, the University of Leiden was the most prestigious—Leiden is like the Harvard of Holland—and Daalder was there. That seemed attractive. So I was both repelled a little bit by Berkeley and drawn to Holland.

Q: Was returning to the Netherlands what you expected it would be?
A: No. I did not find it easy to readjust to life in Holland. I had not lived there on a permanent basis since I had left when I was nineteen. I had spent my twenties in the United States and, without being aware of it, I had become American. Moreover, the same crisis I had tried to escape by leaving Berkeley emerged in European universities, and, in 1969, the student revolution broke out in Holland. In fact, the students occupied the very hall

where I was supposed to give my inaugural lecture at Leiden! Though the situation at Leiden itself was not too bad, I had to deal with the conflict triggered by student radicalism as chair of the national consultation group for all Political Science departments in Holland. Essentially, my job was to prevent a takeover by the radicals. I thought this was a waste of my time, that it was not why I had become a political scientist. Practically from the very moment I got back to Holland, the idea of returning to the United States was constantly on my mind.

Q: Still, you stayed at Leiden for ten years, until 1978. This was a period of important changes in comparative politics and political science in Europe. For example, in 1970, the European Consortium of Political Research (ECPR) was established.
A: Before the ECPR was founded, there wasn't much contact among European political scientists in different countries. Most collaborative research was between American and European scholars, but not among European scholars themselves. The people who created the ECPR changed that. My Leiden colleague, Hans Daalder, was very important in this initiative, as was Stein Rokkan, who became the ECPR's first president, and Jean Blondel, the ECPR's first executive director, who was an excellent and very energetic leader. They all recognized that the European countries should be compared with each other, and this comparative enterprise would be facilitated by increasing contacts among European scholars. That was one of the goals of the ECPR, and it was spectacularly successful in meeting this goal.

Q: How would you compare the way comparative politics developed in the United States and Europe during your years at Leiden?
A: Comparative politics, everywhere, was becoming more systematically comparative. Above all, this meant the comparative analysis of European countries improved greatly. The Europeans caught up quickly with what was going on in the United States during this period. But American comparativists retained an edge with regard to making wider comparisons that went beyond Europe.

Q: What is your overall evaluation of the ten-year period you spent at Leiden?
A: Going back to Europe was a good idea in terms of my intellectual development. I got to travel around Europe, got to know European countries better, and made contacts with European political scientists. I participated actively in the ECPR, most important, as the founding editor of its journal, the *European Journal of Political Research*. I was editor for four years, from 1971 to 1975, and that also gave me a lot of contacts. I was also on the

executive committee of the ECPR from 1976 to 1978, and I went to nearly all the annual meetings of the ECPR. This activity was very important, and the ten years I spent in Europe were worthwhile.

Back in the United States

Q: You returned to the United States in 1978, taking a job at the University of California, San Diego (UCSD).
A: I wanted to come back to the United States, and I had various offers, from Vanderbilt, Notre Dame, UCLA, UC Irvine, and UCSD. I chose UCSD because of the attractiveness of San Diego as a place to live and the opportunity to participate in building a new department. UCSD was a relatively new university—it had been founded in 1960—and the Department of Political Science was not started until 1974. It was a welcome challenge to help build an entirely new department. So, I felt lucky to move to San Diego.

The Political Science Department at UCSD grew from fewer than ten faculty in 1978 to close to forty now. As the department became larger, it lost some of its close personal atmosphere, but it has continued to offer a very supportive scholarly environment and congenial personal relationships. My closest colleague was David Laitin, but unfortunately he left San Diego to join the University of Chicago—one of only a few of my senior colleagues to be lured away by outside offers. The scholars with whom I have had the closest intellectual interaction have not been at UCSD but at nearby UC Irvine: Bernie Grofman and Rein Taagepera. I have also been very close to Matthew Shugart, one of Taagepera's students at UC Irvine, who joined the UCSD faculty in 1989. His primary appointment is not in political science, however, but in the Graduate School of International Relations and Pacific Studies.

Q: You must have really enjoyed San Diego. You are still here twenty-five years later!
A: I have had offers from other universities that I considered carefully. The most serious came from New York University (NYU) in 1994. They offered more money than I have ever earned at UCSD, and I could have taken early retirement here and gotten a pension from UCSD and a new income from NYU. So I certainly would have been rich. Also, the idea of living in New York was appealing, because you can hop over to Kennedy airport and get to Europe easily. In the end, my wife and I decided we really liked living in California. So I stayed here and took early retirement in 1994 to reduce my teaching load. I fully retired in 2000, though I am still involved in dissertations and advising.

Q: After all these years, even though you have described yourself as becoming American, you still seem to carry within you a longing to be close to Europe.
A: After I went back to live in Holland in 1968, I somehow never felt comfortable anymore in Europe. As I said, the idea of returning to the United States was constantly on my mind. Today I am well settled in the United States. I have children and grandchildren in California, and all of my wife's children—she is German—also live in California. Still, in the last few years, with the Bush presidency, I have felt strange. I am disenchanted with what is going on in politics in this country. I have never felt this way before since I first came to America in 1955. Now I increasingly have the feeling that I am more European than American after all—but hopefully this will just be a temporary phase.

Collaborators

Q: You have collaborated with different people throughout your career. Can you discuss your experience with collaborative work?
A: I have coauthored or coedited various works with some two dozen collaborators. Still, most of my work has been single-authored. Collaboration has obvious advantages: there is a division of labor, you can draw on the expertise of the different coauthors, and so on. The drawback is the need to coordinate and, when different people work at different paces, there is a potential for some frustration. But that is a problem mainly with multi-authored edited volumes, which involve different issues than coauthored work.

My most regular collaborator has been Bernie Grofman. I have coedited four books with him (Grofman et al. 1982; Lijphart and Grofman 1984; Grofman and Lijphart 1986, 2002). He is a wonderful, versatile, and very innovative scholar, who is also full of energy. He is constantly doing about twelve projects at the same time, and surprisingly he manages to finish all of them. He is an ideal collaborator. I am currently involved in a project with him, which is probably going to be the final book I write. The working title of this joint book is *A Different Democracy: American Democracy in Comparative Perspective*. Bernie and I thought it would be a good idea to have an extra collaborator, so we have drafted my colleague Matt Shugart to write some of the chapters. We have decided to divide up the chapters, and we will each take the ones we like, draft them, and go from there.

The rest of my collaborations are more occasional. I have not really had any other regular collaborators besides Bernie. Some of my coauthors have been students, who may have served as my research assistants, or former students. This is the case with Markus Crepaz (Lijphart and Crepaz 1991; Crepaz and Lijphart 1995). I have also coauthored many articles or book chapters with scholars who are country experts or have certain methodological skills. Sometimes these collaborations happen simply as a result of being brought together at a conference and figuring out that it makes sense to write something together. There is no general pattern.

Students

Q: What is your approach to training graduate students? What advice do you give them?
A: I am not a heavy-handed advisor, who says you should do this and that. In terms of general training, I do not give advice that differs from the department's requirements. And in terms of a dissertation, I tell students they should choose a topic they are excited about and that is also doable. Though I strongly endorse comparative studies, I advise my students that such a design can be hard to pull off in a dissertation. I tell them it might be better to do a case study, one that is theoretically based and poses clear questions to be answered and puzzles to be solved. Apart from that, I tell them to do what they like best. I have supervised dissertations covering a variety of topics, from political parties in Britain and Germany; to consociationalism and corporatism in Austria; to electoral systems in Southern Africa; to term limits in the United States, Costa Rica, and Venezuela; to interest groups and environmental policy in consensus and majoritarian democracies.

The Achievements and Future of Comparative Politics

Q: A current debate in the field concerns whether or not comparative politics has produced cumulative knowledge over the past several decades. What is your assessment of this issue?
A: I think a great deal of progress has been made. Today we have so much more work that is consciously and systematically comparative. The best comparative work is still very much focused on Europe and the OECD countries. With regard to case studies, the ones produced today in comparative politics are far more theoretically informed than they used to be. There are not many case studies anymore that are just descriptive.

The difference this progress makes is readily apparent. Back when I started my career in the early 1960s, I was influenced by the classification of countries Almond presented in his wonderful 1956 article. But, in terms of today's standards, Almond's analysis offered a very crude generalization.

Nowadays, nobody would say, as had Almond, that the United Kingdom, a multinational country with Welshmen, Scotsmen, and the Ireland problem, has a homogeneous political culture. Let me go further. I have not kept up with the entire field of comparative politics, so I cannot comment on the state of knowledge about authoritarian regimes, for instance. Still, I see definite progress in those areas where my research has focused. We have a much more sophisticated analysis of the functioning of democracies and democratic institutions, of cabinets, electoral systems, voter turnout, and so on. There is a lot of evidence, which gives us a pretty good, complete picture. In addition to all this information, we also have theory, theory based on evidence. As a result, when a student chooses a dissertation topic, he or she can draw on various theoretical frameworks. This does not mean there are no gaps in our knowledge or that no work remains to be done. We have a long way to go before we know as much about the politics of the other 150-plus countries in the world as we know about American politics. And even in American politics, scholars keep finding new and interesting topics to study. But I have no doubt that real progress has been made since I was a graduate student.

Q: One of the important changes within comparative politics over the past decades has been the increased centrality of the study of institutions, something many behavioralists in the 1950s and 1960s tended to ignore. What are your thoughts about this growing emphasis on institutional analysis?
A: The behavioral revolution meant many things. First, it meant political science should become more systematic and scientific. Second, the behavioral revolution implied a shift away from the old, formal institutionalism to things like political culture, attitudes, sociological factors, and so on. These aspects of the behavioral revolution were linked, because the old institutionalism was criticized for not generalizing, for not being sufficiently scientific, and also for being legalistic and focusing too much on institutions. But the potential for the field to come back to the study of institutions was always there.

A third aspect of the behavioral revolution was a reaction to the old institutionalism's emphasis on the developed countries: the United States and Western Europe. So, there was a shift to the study of developing areas in the 1960s, spurred by works such as Almond and Coleman's *The Politics of the Developing Areas* (1960) and Lucian Pye's analysis of non-Western political processes (1958). In the developing world, there were not many stable institutions to study. This changed with the process of democratization that started in the 1970s and the resulting emergence of democratic systems in more and more countries. Now there are institutions to study in developing countries, because, in democracies, rules and institutions are not just window dressing. This partly explains why we have come back to the study of institutions.

Q: Focusing on this large institutional literature, has it been successful in generating usable knowledge, that is, information that can be acted on by policy makers?
A: On the one hand, yes, we are in a position to offer usable recommendations. Some scholars are very reluctant to make policy recommendations, because they want every last bit of evidence to support their view. But I think we really do have quite a bit of knowledge about how democratic institutions should be organized. For example, Larry Diamond, in his book *Developing Democracy,* says that for divided societies, there is no longer any doubt that some form of proportional representation should be used (Diamond 1999, 99–105). We have made a lot of progress in finding out which institutions work and which do not. There is good evidence for making this kind of prescriptive statement.

On the other hand, we may have reached the point where we have too much information about all sorts of institutional features. This makes it hard to give useful advice. Indeed, a lot of political scientists talk about all the possibilities faced by institutional designers, how there are many compromises that can be made, and how they might try to achieve the best of both worlds. This is a problem, because it makes matters too complex. I recently wrote an article entitled "Constitutional Design for Divided Societies" (Lijphart 2004). It does not have a subtitle, but a suitable subtitle would have been "Specific Recommendations Instead of a Menu of Choices." Basically, I say, "Here is my best judgment. If you have a plural society, adopt a parliamentary form of government with proportional representation. Don't fool around with all the other stuff." I also give specific recommendations on how to set up a power-sharing executive, how to select the head of state, and how to achieve cabinet stability.

Q: Turning to the future, what are the most important challenges for the research agenda on consensus democracy?
A: I would like to see tests of the policy consequences of consensus versus majoritarian democracies in more areas. To do this, we first need more indicators of the quality of democracy and the effectiveness of government policies. For instance, I mainly rely on indicators of macroeconomic performance—economic growth, inflation, unemployment, strike activity, and budget deficits—to measure the effectiveness of governments. These are excellent indicators because they are not only valid reflections of how well governments perform but also available in precise, quantitative form.

But governments do much more than make economic policy; it is for these other policy areas that we need to develop accurate measures of performance. Similarly, to measure the quality of democracy, I used every quantitative indicator I could find—a total of seventeen—to measure, for instance, voter turnout, women's representation in parliaments and cabinets, and degrees of economic inequality. Nobody has criticized me for missing an important indicator that was available. But my seventeen indicators are obviously not an exhaustive list of what could, in principle, be measured. This is a challenge I hope other, younger scholars will take up.

Q: What about challenges for the field of comparative politics more broadly?
A: Here I can only offer some general comments. I have the most faith in the approach I have used over the years, that is, to search for patterns and try to generalize by using the most systematic, comparative data possible. I have misgivings about the way rational choice approaches are used. Rational choice work can provide very important insights, and I offer many examples of such contributions in a piece on voter turnout that I wrote for Richard Rose's *International Encyclopedia of Elections* (Lijphart 2000). Still, I come across many journal articles where the author simply presents a model without testing it, and I find that annoying. However you arrive at your hypotheses, you have to test them. If that is not done, then I don't see the use of beautiful deductive models. You need to test things in the real world.

Conclusion

Q: To conclude, what is your advice to graduate students starting out in comparative politics?
A: Science is a cumulative enterprise, in the Kuhnian sense (Kuhn 1962). Hence, you should try to build on what is already there. In terms of professional development, start by writing a good dissertation, try to be as innovative as possible. Then, later in your career, try to make as big a splash as possible. The trick is to build on existing research without being bound by it, to work within the paradigm but also to think outside it. Be skeptical, don't take the conventional, received wisdom for granted, and be original.

9

Guillermo O'Donnell

Democratization, Political Engagement,
and Agenda-Setting Research

Guillermo O'Donnell is a leading theorist of authoritarianism and de-mocratization and one of the most distinguished Latin American political scientists.

O'Donnell's *Modernization and Bureaucratic Authoritarianism* (1973) of-fered a pioneering analysis of the breakdown of democracies in South Amer-ica in the 1960s. He argued that the form of authoritarianism experienced by South America starting in the 1960s was novel because it was based on modern technocrats and a professionalized military organization, instead of populist politicians or traditional military strongmen. To capture this distinctiveness, he coined the term *bureaucratic authoritarianism.* O'Donnell argued that this new form of authoritarianism emerged as the result of political conflict generated by an import-substitution model of industrial-ization. He cast his argument as an alternative to the thesis, advanced most notably by Seymour Martin Lipset, that industrialization produced democ-racy. In South America, O'Donnell argued, industrialization generated not democracy, but bureaucratic authoritarianism. This work, along with a se-ries of subsequent articles, triggered an important debate in comparative politics and Latin American Studies about the political consequences of economic development. The central contributions to this debate were pub-lished in a volume edited by David Collier, *The New Authoritarianism in Latin America* (1979), which assessed and critiqued O'Donnell's thesis.

The next phase of O'Donnell's research focused on the demise of au-thoritarianism and transitions to democracy. His coauthored book with Philippe C. Schmitter, *Transitions from Authoritarian Rule: Tentative Conclu-sions about Uncertain Democracies* (1986), was one of the most widely read and influential works in comparative politics during the 1980s and 1990s. O'Donnell and Schmitter proposed a strategic choice approach to transi-

This interview was conducted by Gerardo Munck in Palo Alto, California, on March 23, 2002.

tions to democracy that highlighted how they were driven by the decisions of different actors in response to a core set of dilemmas. The analysis centered on the interaction among four actors: the hard-liners and soft-liners who belonged to the incumbent authoritarian regime, and the moderate and radical oppositions against the regime. This book not only became the point of reference for a burgeoning academic literature on democratic transitions, it was also read widely by political activists engaged in actual struggles to achieve democracy.

O'Donnell's research since the early 1990s has explored the question of the quality of democracy. His work warns against teleological thinking, that is, the tendency to see countries that democratized in the 1970s and 1980s as following in the tracks, though several steps behind, of the long-standing democratic countries of the West. To highlight the specificity of contemporary Latin American countries and the deficiencies of their democracies, he proposed the concept of "delegative democracy," by which he meant a form of democratic rule that concentrated power in the hands of elected presidents. His recent work centers on the current problems faced by most Latin American democracies as a result of deficiencies in the rule of law and the social capabilities of citizens. His key articles on the quality of democracy have been published in *Counterpoints* (1999b) and *The Quality of Democracy* (2004).

O'Donnell was born in Buenos Aires, Argentina, in 1936. He received a law degree from the University of Buenos Aires in 1958 and a Ph.D. in political science from Yale University in 1988. He taught at the University of Buenos Aires (1958–66), the Argentine Catholic University (1966–68), and the University of El Salvador (1971–75), all in Buenos Aires. He was a founding member of CEDES (Centro de Estudios de Estado y Sociedad) in Buenos Aires (1975–79), and a researcher at IUPERJ (Instituto Universitário de Pesquisas do Río de Janeiro) (1980–82) and CEBRAP (Centro Brasileiro de Análise e Planejamento) in São Paulo (1982–91). Since 1983 he has taught at the University of Notre Dame, where he was academic director of the Helen Kellogg Institute for International Studies from 1983 until 1998. He was president of the International Political Science Association (IPSA) in 1988–91, was vice-president of the American Political Science Association (APSA) in 1999–2000, and was elected to the American Academy of Arts and Sciences in 1995.

Early Interests and Training: From Law to Political Science

Q: How did you first become interested in the study of politics?
A: My interest developed through my engagement with politics in Argentina. I entered the university quite young, at just sixteen. By then I was

already an avid reader of history and philosophy. Because of the problem with my leg, I had more time to read than other kids.[1] When I was a child, my mother practically fed me history books. So my leg gave me a comparative advantage, or disadvantage, depending how you look at it. I became involved in politics at the University of Buenos Aires, where I was a student leader. I joined the Humanist Party in the Law School and, as a representative of this party, I was a member of FUBA (Buenos Aires University Federation). In 1954 we got into deep trouble with Perón's government, and the president, vice-president, and secretary general of FUBA were put in jail. In spite of my visibility, I was one of the very few who was not caught in the late night raid. So I became the acting president of the whole thing, in hiding. I had the strange experience of seeing my photograph posted as a dangerous person who had to be caught. When Perón was overthrown by a coup in 1955, I was a well recognized leader, and I thought I was beginning a successful political career. But it didn't take me long to discover that being deeply interested in politics didn't mean I was a good politician. So I jumped ship after some unfortunate experiences.

Q: You did not initially study political science. Indeed, in 1958 you received a law degree from the University of Buenos Aires.
A: I studied law, not because I particularly wanted to study law, but because in these times it was the closest thing to studying politics. In the 1950s and 1960s there were no Political Science departments in Argentina. In the Law School, there was something called political law and constitutional law, which was the closest I could get to political science. Also, being a lawyer offered me the opportunity to make a living. That's why I got into law.

I found law school immensely boring. In those days, half the scholars working in political theory and constitutional theory thought everything had already been said by Saint Thomas Aquinas, and the other half—the modernists—thought everything had already been said by Hans Kelsen. Everything else was nothing. It was really very, very boring.

Q: Why did you decide to leave Argentina in 1968 and go to Yale to study political science at the graduate level?
A: I got married, I had children, and to support my family I practiced law for a number of years. But I kept my interest in studying politics, and began teaching history of political ideas in the Catholic University of Buenos Aires. But I soon felt I wanted to become more empirically oriented. I was reading some North American books, for example, Lasswell and Kaplan's *Power and Society* (1950) and Lasswell's *Politics: Who Gets What, When, How*

---

1. O'Donnell had polio as a child, which damaged one of his legs.

(1936). These books did not influence me particularly. But they gave me a glimpse of a different way of thinking. And they made me want to get acquainted with the more empirically oriented Anglo-Saxon type of political science. Also, at that time North American political science had a behavioralist manifesto against legal formalism. Part of this critique was directed against precisely the kind of comparative studies of constitutions I had suffered through in law school. I agreed with these criticisms that formalism was barren and boring. Much later, I discovered that I had to go back to my legal side, although I don't think legal theory ends at all with Aquinas or Kelsen. But back in the 1960s I was looking for something that would allow me to break with my legal background. So I decided to apply to graduate school in political science in the United States.

I applied to several places. Harvard turned me down, but I was accepted at Michigan, Princeton, MIT, and Yale. And I chose Yale. My parents, who were traditional in their ways, were horrified. Here I was, with no personal fortune, taking my wife and three children away to starve. They thought that trying to make a living as a political scientist was a crazy idea.

Q: What did you know about Yale?
A: I had read things by Yale faculty, I asked around, and it became clear that in terms of what I was looking for, Yale was the place to be. It had an incredible constellation of great political scientists. I was fortunate to be accepted.

Q: You were at Yale from 1968 to 1971.
A: Exactly. That was a great period. People like Charles Lindblom and Robert Dahl were at their best. Harold Laswell was still around. The year after I arrived, David Apter joined the Yale faculty, followed the next year by Juan Linz. Alfred Stepan was a very young assistant professor. David Mayhew was also there. Those people were at the top of their game. I was a graduate student, so it was also nice that these guys got along well with each other. And they were very helpful and open. Those three years were wonderful. I remember sitting in the Yale library, thinking this is paradise: here I am, I have the privilege of being paid a reasonable scholarship to do research and study full-time. I had a great time.

Q: Which professors at Yale had the most influence on you?
A: I was very much in awe of Dahl. He gave a seminar while he was writing *Polyarchy* (Dahl 1971). We discussed his chapters, and it was wonderful to see a great mind working through problems and writing an important book. I also recall a superb course by Linz on Durkheim, Weber, and Pareto. That course strengthened the knowledge of Weber I had acquired in my

courses in Buenos Aries and greatly interested me in this author. But the biggest influence, someone to whom I will always be grateful, is David Apter. He was a wonderful and generous mentor. David is an extremely learned person. He is also very opinionated and provocative. David devoted a lot of time to me, including editing my dreadful English with incredible patience. He was so generous and supportive; here you had an important professor take his time to correct the crummy English of a graduate student.

Q: What books had a strong impact on you during your graduate school years?
A: Samuel Huntington's *Political Order in Changing Societies* (1968) was very important. I did not like the book's praise of Lenin, but I thought Huntington's depiction of institutions, power politics, and praetorianism was very good. An even better book was Barrington Moore's *Social Origins of Dictatorship and Democracy* (1966). It was a discovery to read Moore, and I was fascinated. Dahl assigned the book and was critical of it, because he thought it was too structuralist and Marxist. But I recall opining that Moore was a great scholar.

Q: At Yale, you prepared a draft of what would become your first book, *Modernization and Bureaucratic Authoritarianism* (O'Donnell 1973). But that did not become your doctoral thesis. Could you explain why this was not the case?
A: There is a long story related to my dissertation and my getting a Ph.D. that has to do with the peculiarities of my life trajectory. In 1971, I was done with all the degree requirements, and I had drafts of what later became chapters in *Modernization and Bureaucratic Authoritarianism*. I guess I had some prestige at that point, because I was offered a position at Harvard. So I was faced with a choice: go to Harvard or go back to Argentina. It was a tough decision. But 1971 was the year when the bureaucratic authoritarian regime had crumbled, and it was a moment when all of us had hopes for democracy in Argentina. So I decided to go back to Argentina.

The problem was there were practically no job possibilities in Argentina then, and I had a family to maintain. I would have to work as a lawyer, which meant I would have wasted all those years at Yale. But I was fortunate to be offered a Danforth fellowship, a three-year fellowship that paid $600 a month, a lot of money at that time, and, in Argentina, it was excellent money. The Danforth fellowship gave me a chance to go to Argentina and continue working as a political scientist. But the fellowship was for writing a dissertation.

I talked to my advisors at Yale, and to the amazement of some of them I decided to turn down Harvard. So I went back to Argentina and did not submit the manuscript that became *Modernization and Bureaucratic Authoritarianism* as my dissertation but published it instead as a book. Now, taking the Danforth fellowship allowed me to survive for three years, but it also meant that I didn't have a Ph.D. This became unimportant in terms of my career. It didn't prevent me from doing anything. I had publications, and I could have cared less about having a Ph.D. But, later, when I was working in Brazil in 1984, my lack of a Ph.D. became an issue. Brazil is very bureaucratic, and when Vilmar Faría and I decided to present a project to FINEP (Financiadora de Estudos e Projetos), a state funding agency in Brazil, my proposal was turned down because I didn't have a doctorate. To solve the problem they proposed a typical *jeito:*[2] somebody else would sign instead of me and I would get the funding. But I said I wouldn't do that, and I decided at that point that I needed a Ph.D. after all. So I wrote Apter, Dahl, and Stepan, and asked if they would accept as my dissertation a long manuscript I had written on Argentina's bureaucratic authoritarian regime of 1966–73. They finally accepted this work, which was subsequently published in 1988 as *Bureaucratic Authoritarianism* (O'Donnell 1988). So that's the story of my dissertation and my Ph.D.

Research and Institution Building in Diverse Contexts: From Argentina to Brazil to the United States

Q: Much like the story of your dissertation, your career path has been anything but linear. Could you discuss the various places where you worked, starting with your return from Yale to Argentina in 1971?
A: In 1971, the year the first Argentine bureaucratic authoritarian regime was disintegrating, I entered a research center that was part of the Di Tella Institute—the CIAP (Centro de Investigaciones en Administración Pública). It was formed by young scholars who had returned to Argentina with Ford Foundation fellowships—Marcelo Cavarozzi, Oscar Oszlak, Horacio Boneo —and a group of French-trained colleagues, like Dante Caputo and Jorge Sábato. It was a very nice group, and we had a great time, until 1975, when the Di Tella Institute got worried about two of its affiliated centers that were perceived to be leftist: the CIAP and particularly the CEUR (Centro de Estudios Urbanos y Regionales), led by Jorge Hardoy. Some of the people in the Di Tella Institute were close to the military who eventually carried out the coup in 1976.[3] They expelled CEUR. And we at CIAP were also thrown out, but in a more negotiated way. So in the end we became independent.

2. A *jeito* is a creative, informal, and frequently illegal means to accomplish one's purpose by manipulating the system.
3. Argentina was governed by military regimes from 1966 until 1973, and again from 1976 until 1983.

Q: Is this how CEDES (Centro de Estudios de Estado y Sociedad) was created?

A: Yes. I went to see Kalman Silvert, of the Ford Foundation, at a Congress in Campinas, Brazil. I also had a contact in Sweden's development cooperation agency, SAREC (Swedish International Development Cooperation Agency). I told them about our group of young researchers, about how despite the dangerous situation in the country we were trying to stay in Argentina, to preserve a space for academic freedom and reflection. I asked for their support, and the Ford Foundation and the Swedes immediately said yes. So we got two generous grants with which we created CEDES in June 1975.

Q: Did you think about looking for a job in the United States during this period?

A: No. I was stubbornly committed to staying in Argentina, I wanted to fight there, from the inside. I received several formal offers and many more informal expressions of interest from very good places in the United States. I even had a second offer from Harvard, from the Kennedy School of Government. And I visited the United States on numerous occasions and kept up my contacts there. For example, I spent time as a visiting professor at the University of California, Berkeley, and at the University of Michigan in Ann Arbor; I was a fellow at the Institute for Advanced Study at Princeton; and I was a member of the Joint Committee on Latin American Studies of the SSRC (Social Science Research Council). I did this partly out of intellectual interest and vanity. But it was also strategic. My colleagues in Argentina and I felt that having these institutional connections outside the country decreased the likelihood we would be smashed by the violence that surrounded us.

Q: What was the intellectual life at CEDES like during those years?

A: They were crazy years. Being associated with CEDES was risky from the inception in June 1975, and it became even more risky after the March 1976 coup. Moreover, because I was the director and kind of the founding father of CEDES, I tended to be the target of the threats. And these threats came from both sides: from the military, the paramilitary, and others on the Right; but also from the Montoneros, the guerrilla group linked to the Peronist movement. I knew from friends that CEDES and I were closely watched. This was an odd situation, being targeted by both sides. We made the black humor joke that at least we deserved one important human right: the right to know which group killed you! But this was a serious matter. Some of the people who were at CEDES had to leave the country very fast.

I will always remember the day, after the coup, when somebody who is a well known person today, came to tell me he was the financial officer of the Montoneros, and we were agents of imperialism, because we received all this money from foreign foundations. He said we had to pay a tax to them, and the tax was three or four times more than all the monies we had received! So I laughed. I laughed, of course, because I was so nervous. And this guy was insulted because I was laughing. But I said, "No way." And he said, "Well, you'll have to live with the consequences."

This was also a very creative period for us. We spent our full time and energy trying to understand what had happened and what could happen in Argentina. It was a period of intense discussion. Some unique work came out of those years. All of us traveled a lot in order to feed ourselves intellectually and to increase our protection. And we brought in good friends: the Brazilians Fernando Henrique Cardoso and Francisco Weffort; the Chileans Manuel Antonio Garretón, Ricardo Lagos, and Norbert Lechner; the Peruvian Julio Cotler; and others. In fact, at that time we Latinamericanized ourselves. Of course, other solidary friends came from outside Latin America. But the discussion was mainly among Brazilians, Chileans, and Argentineans. We saw each other a lot and supported each other, personally and institutionally.

We had a common moral and political language. We wanted to get rid of these authoritarian monsters and have democracy, good-old political democracy. There was strong agreement on these moral and political goals. And we had a fairly common, quite eclectic theoretical language. The Brazilians were coming down from their Marxism to a more Weberian position. The Chileans were already there—none of them had been hard Marxists. And, as you can see in my first book (O'Donnell 1973), I had an essentially Weberian bent, with some neo-Marxism, of course. These discussions with the Latin Americans, particularly the Chileans and the Brazilians, were incredibly enriching.

Q: Did this group see itself as explicitly attempting to formulate a perspective on the region that might serve as an alternative to the way Latin America was being studied in the United States?
A: Not really. In those times, we were very much absorbed by the concerns of life in a context of violence and fear. None of us sat down and said, "I'm going to write an alternative theory."

Q: Did this group undertake any joint projects?
A: We undertook several projects together. The most important culminated in a meeting at Cardoso's place in the interior of São Paulo, where we had a wonderful three-day discussion among Brazilians, Chileans, and Argentineans. It was a project on economic stabilization financed by the Ford Foun-

dation, and we were arguing against the free market, neo-liberal policies being followed at the time by Martínez de Hoz in Argentina, Pinochet in Chile, and, in a less orthodox fashion, by Delfim Neto in Brazil. This meeting was perceived by the government intelligence agencies as involving a possible leftist Latin American conspiracy. We learned later on that we had been closely watched by the Brazilian Intelligence agency.

Q: What came out of this project?
A: Well, this is one of my regrets. The economists José Serra, Roberto Frenkel, and Alejandro Foxley were going to write economic analyses. The political scientists and sociologists Garretón, Enzo Faletto, Cardoso, Weffort, and I were going to offer political analyses. In the end, we were left with only a few papers, which were published separately. I wrote a piece with Frenkel, which was published (Frenkel and O'Donnell 1979). But we never published a volume that would have been a critique of the orthodox neo-liberal adjustment of the times. We had some useful things to say, things not that different from the criticisms made today about the failings of neo-liberalism. It would have been a testimonial, an achievement. We should have been able to produce that book. That would have been nice. But we failed.

Q: Eventually you left Argentina in late 1979.
A: I left partly for family reasons. But there was another reason. By 1979, the period of high risk in Argentina was already past or, at least, the risk was clearly decreasing. Before this point, during the more risky years, I had a macho posture of not being scared, of not paying attention to threats. Out of a mix of vanity and guts I actually lived through the risk. But after the period of high risk was over, I eventually began to feel I couldn't take it anymore, that I had to take off. I was resentful about the number of Argentineans whom I saw supporting, or at least condoning, what the military rulers were doing. So I decided to take off and go abroad for a time.

I was very interested in Brazil and in Brazilian intellectuals. I had long-standing links with several Brazilians. Cándido Mendes offered me the chairmanship of the program committee of the World Congress of the International Political Science Association (IPSA) to be held in 1982 in Rio de Janeiro. This would require much work before the Congress, and I would get a good salary. I took the job and relocated to Rio, where I worked at IUPERJ (Instituto Universitário de Pesquisas do Rio de Janeiro). The next year I got a Guggenheim fellowship, which helped me financially. The idea, however, was still to be in Rio for about two years and then go back to Argentina. But then Cardoso left CEBRAP (Centro Brasileiro de Análise e Planejamento) because he had become active as a senator, and CEBRAP offered me Cardoso's slot. I took the job and went to CEBRAP, in São Paulo, in 1982. The next year, in 1983, I took a job at the University of Notre Dame, where I've been ever since. After 1979, I never went back to live in Argentina.

Q: You had several offers before you accepted the Notre Dame job? What was it about Notre Dame that finally convinced you to move to the United States?
A: All the other offers I had received in the United States were for normal appointments, which required me to live full-time there. But I never felt ready. I always had the hope or thought that things would get better in Brazil or Argentina. I felt comfortable in Brazil. It was wonderful for foreigners; the life of an intellectual in Brazil was like being part of a mandarinate, which is quite pleasant. But then came Notre Dame. Father Theodore Hesburgh and Father Ernest Bartell made Alejandro Foxley and me a very different kind of offer, a challenge. Mrs. Helen Kellogg had made a big donation, $10 million, to create an Institute for International Studies. Hesburgh offered Foxley and me the opportunity to build a program focused on Latin America, with no academic interference or preconditions whatsoever. The chance to work with Foxley was attractive to me. He was a brilliant economist, a judicious leader, and we had known each other for years and were good friends. We assumed we would be good partners. In addition, I would not have to spend the entire year in South Bend, Indiana, but only had to be there four months a year, from September until December, and again in April. So I could keep living in Brazil or Argentina if I wanted to.

This was, of course, tempting: to have these important resources and a partner whom I respected. I also got along very well with Father Bartell, who was the executive director of the institute. It was an enticing possibility to lead this institute and impress upon it an agenda on Latin America, made by Latin Americans, and focused on the kind of problems we had been devoting our lives to. So Foxley and I said, "Yes."

Q: The next major change in your work situation came in 1997, when you began to work full-time at Notre Dame.
A: Yes. In the course of the fifteen years after accepting the offer from Notre Dame, my life changed again. I got divorced and remarried. I also got older. The fact that every time I wanted a book from my own collection it was in some other place was a never-ending annoyance. Not having a permanent home became too hectic. So, in 1996 I renegotiated my contract with Notre Dame. I had long been meaning to end my tenure as academic director of the Kellogg Institute. I stepped down and took an appointment that requires that I teach two courses a year. I can't complain. They treat me very well at Notre Dame. Michigan, where I bought a house, is my home now.

Q: Given that you have lived and worked extensively in both Latin America and the United States, how would you compare the experience of building academic institutions in the two places?
A: The first years at the Kellogg Institute were extremely productive. Then, of course, everything gets institutionalized and somewhat bureaucratized. But I think those years were very, very valuable intellectually. As I told you earlier, my experience at CEDES was also vital, but it involved more daring circumstances than was the case at the Kellogg Institute. I am very proud of both institutions. Like every child you father, when they grow up, they become creatures of their own. You do not necessarily approve of everything they do, but you still keep a strong emotional link.

Q: And how would you compare the role of political scientists in Latin America and the United States? What are some of the key differences?
A: The main difference is that the boundary between academics and politics is much more blurred in Latin America than in the United States. This means the social and political definition of your role in each society is different. In Latin America, you are supposed to be some kind of political actor. What you say is potentially a political event. It's risky at times, as we discussed earlier, but it's also more challenging and interesting. In the United States, in contrast, I sometimes feel the lack of the excitement that comes from being closely in touch with real-world events. In the United States, you have all the advantages of being an observer who is well protected. But this has a cost, which is that you can become so disengaged from social reality that your work loses some touch, some vigor, some élan. And these are important components of political science.

Money, of course, is another factor. In Argentina you have to live more modestly, on a lower income than in the United States, and it is often difficult, if not impossible, to obtain support for research. But the main issue is the uncertainty. You never know if your grant will be renewed the following year or if your institution will survive. So there's a real trade-off. In terms of access to consumer goodies and the peace of everyday life, the United States has real advantages. But in terms of other factors, I find Latin America more invigorating for my intellectual life.

Research on Political Regimes and Democracy
Bureaucratic Authoritarianism

Q: Turning to your research, I'd like to start with your work on bureaucratic authoritarianism and the genesis of your first book, *Modernization and Bureaucratic Authoritarianism* (O'Donnell 1973).
A: This book grew out of papers I wrote for seminars at Yale and in dialogue

with some of my professors. The introduction grew out of a paper I wrote for David Apter in which I criticized the modernization theorists we discussed in his course. David's work was on modernization, but he was very critical of modernization theories. So we had some interesting discussions. Overall, David Apter was very, very helpful in the development of my book, including giving me a lot of help with my poor English. The more historical chapter developed from a paper I wrote for Dahl's course on polyarchy—that's where the footnote in *Polyarchy* comes in (Dahl 1971, 132). And the chapter on the impossible game originated as a paper I wrote for a seminar that Douglas Rae taught on rational choice approaches.

Q: What were the driving concerns behind this book and your subsequent publications on bureaucratic authoritarianism?
A: I was grappling with the emergence of the bureaucratic authoritarianism regimes that had come to power first in Brazil in 1964 and then in Argentina in 1966. I saw myself battling on two fronts. One front was academic, where the discussion revolved around how to characterize these regimes. I argued that these regimes were of a new type and that the models we had of *caudillismo,* populism, or totalitarianism did not fit the cases of Brazil and Argentina. I proposed to see these regimes as bureaucratic authoritarian, a new type of authoritarianism. But there was another front, a political one. This front had to do with a Latin American discussion, a hard discussion, which hinged on the use of the label *fascist* or *neo-fascist* by the radical Left to characterize the Brazilian and Argentine regimes. This characterization had a direct political implication, as Theotônio Dos Santos (1968, 1977) and others articulated well. The implication was that against these "neo"-fascisms the goal should be a socialist revolution. In contrast, I was interested in studying these regimes and understanding their internal workings and tensions as a step toward getting rid of them by nonviolent means and with the goal of achieving political democracy. The rightists who supported these regimes—and one has to remember that the Brazilian and Argentine regimes had a lot of support among very powerful sectors of society—thought I was a subversive leftist. On the other hand, the radical Left thought people like me were at best "reformists" and at worst accomplices of the authoritarian regimes.

So I was not just elaborating an academically interesting regime type. There was a lot at stake politically in characterizing these regimes and in saying this was a new political animal, which had such and such distinguishing traits. And in all this, the prospective question—how can these regimes change and in what way?—was very important. That really was the most engaging issue, that's where my passions and interests lay. As I said earlier, in Latin America the boundary between academics and politics is quite blurred. My work was intellectual and academic, but it was also very political. I guess this has been typical in my life.

Q: Beyond this debate mainly among Latin Americans, your work on bureaucratic authoritarianism was read as arguing against scholarship on Latin America produced in the United States. You were seen as explicitly arguing against the teleological view in the work of many modernization theorists.

A: I was opposed to and critical of theories that posited universal trends and had a teleological bent. This tendency is typical of the imperial center. The British did it, the Soviets did it, and U.S. intellectuals have been doing it. The core idea is that because you are at the center you can see some universal trends in history, and these trends are or should be occurring everywhere. I resisted this view, because I was keenly aware of the circumstances in Latin America, and because it denies the historical specificities of different regions. In this sense, I thought modernization theories were flawed.

Also, while studying at Yale, I reacted strongly against culturalist theories about why Latin America was doing so badly. I was especially politically opposed to right-wing culturalist theories that saw the Brazilian and Argentine bureaucratic authoritarian regimes as natural outgrowths of Latin American culture. These theories were not politically innocent; they had very real political consequences. For example the Onganía regime in Argentina and the Brazilian military invoked such views to justify their rule. So, I was searching for tools with which to criticize and falsify such theories. One of these tools was game theory, which I tried to use in parts of my first book, although I never became sufficiently literate in mathematics to get to the point of formalization. I found the assumption of rationality—that people usually pursue goals they believe are good for them—appealing in part because of my training as a lawyer.

Q: We have focused so far on your adversaries, on works you were arguing against. What about works you were drawing on or emulating, that is, positive influences on your work on bureaucratic authoritarianism?

A: I would point to three main positive influences on *Modernization and Bureaucratic Authoritarianism*. There is a heavy influence of Cardoso and Faletto (1979)[4] and also Celso Furtado (1970); there is the influence of Weber; and, finally, there is an Anglo-Saxon accent. So there were these three main influences, with some neo-Marxism, of course.

Cardoso and Faletto's *Dependency and Development in Latin America*

---

4. The Spanish version of Cardoso and Faletto's *Dependency and Development in Latin America* was published in 1969.

(1979) had an enormous impact on my thinking. It's a great book, and it provided an example of good social science with a macro-perspective that was an unusual combination of Weberian and neo-Marxian themes. I had an affinity for that way of thinking. Moreover, I was drawn to their emphasis on taking a historical view and appreciating the specificity of the historical roots of what you're studying. I saw these elements coming together in what Cardoso and Faletto called a "historical structural" approach, which says you have to take into account, historically, some large structures: states, classes, and the international context. It is within these encompassing parameters that you understand the rationality of actors.

Though you can find traces of neo-Marxism in my thinking, I was never a Marxist. For my generation, Marx was everywhere and was an influence by osmosis, in the language, in the discussions. Also, I began to reread Marx when I went back to Argentina after graduate school. So it's an influence. But I was much more attracted to the young, Hegelian Marx than the Marx of *Capital*. In contrast, my entire Weberian bent was essential, which, as I already mentioned, I owe to a large extent to Juan Linz.

Q: What do you think about the reception of your work on bureaucratic authoritarianism? Was there some aspect of it that was misinterpreted or criticized unfairly?
A: I am fortunate to have been widely read. One of the worst things that can happen is to be ignored. If they pay attention, and especially if they pay a lot of attention, it's rewarding. It's gratifying when people read and cite you. In this sense, I have no complaints. My one grudge is that some people said that because I argued that bureaucratic authoritarian regimes might foster economic growth, my work praised these regimes. Several authors said this, and they were very wrong. I found these distortions, which so clearly went against my writings and intentions, really annoying.

Q: One critique of *Modernization and Bureaucratic Authoritarianism* was that it provided an account of the breakdown of democracy that was overly structural and economically driven, that it did not account for the role of political actors and their choices, factors later highlighted in Linz and Stepan's *The Breakdown of Democratic Regimes* (1978) and especially in Linz's (1978) contribution to that volume. How do you respond to this critique?
A: In fact, I contributed a chapter to the Linz and Stepan volume (O'Donnell 1978a), which is a rewriting of the political chapter in my *Modernization and Bureaucratic Authoritarianism* that flows out of the analysis of the structural context developed in the previous two chapters. So I didn't see that as inconsistent. As I said in discussing the influence of Cardoso and

Faletto on my work, to understand actors as making rational decisions, you first need to grasp the parameters within which they act. I focused initially on these macro-parameters and then inserted the actors and analyzed how they engaged in rational behavior.

I did write an article, "Reflections on the Patterns of Change" (O'Donnell 1978b), which I think is too structuralist, too economistic. It's probably one of the worst things I ever wrote in my life, but, ironically, it's one of my writings that got the most attention. I realized that the article was too economistic, and in my next two pieces—the "State and Alliances" article (O'Donnell 1978c) and the chapter I wrote for the Collier volume (O'Donnell 1979a)—I tried to correct this by rebalancing my thinking to allow more interaction between the structure or economy, on the one hand, and politics, on the other. The "State and Alliances" article, which I wrote in Argentina during moments of great anger and fear immediately after the military coup in 1976, is my favorite piece.

Q: A more recent critique of *Modernization and Bureaucratic Authoritarianism,* made by Adam Przeworski et al. (2000, 99–101), is that the case on which you based much of your theorizing, Argentina, was an outlier. What do you think of this argument?

A: Well, that Argentina was an outlier is exactly the argument I made in 1973 in *Modernization and Bureaucratic Authoritarianism!* I am gratified, albeit not necessarily for Argentina, that Przeworski et al. recently made this finding, too.

Q: Your contribution to David Collier's *New Authoritarianism* (O'Donnell 1979a) volume is quite telling of your approach to research.[5] Rather than looking back to reassess the state of the debate you had helped launch, you looked forward and focused instead on the next topic, the question of transitions from authoritarian regimes.

A: David Collier's volume made a huge contribution in putting together, basically for an English reading audience, work that was already done, or being prepared. David convened an excellent group, organized a couple of very good meetings, and cajoled authors to develop their arguments, to look at each other. David made a great contribution in terms of crystallizing these exchanges and writing his own very useful chapters.

Actually, my chapter in the Collier volume is not a reflection on the main topic of the volume or even on the literature. I don't find in myself the drive to go back and assess debates on issues I have already raised. I find that kind of work much less interesting than facing some new questions. In the

5. On *The New Authoritarianism* project, see the interview with David Collier in Chapter 15.

late 1970s, when we were working on the volume, it was clear to me that the Argentine regime was not going to endure, because there were too many tensions and contradictions. Moreover, the transitions in Spain, Greece, and Portugal were underway. So I had already moved on to something else. I was beginning to get passionately interested in the next topic, transitions from authoritarianism.

I've had some colleagues get kind of angry and tell me that, after spending some time on some of my texts, I had already moved on to another topic. In some sense, I think this is a bad characteristic of mine. But that is something I have never been able to control. When a new theme capTivates me, I abandon my children to their uncles, so to speak, and move on. That's the way my mind works.

Q: Why do you think *Modernization and Bureaucratic Authoritarianism* made such a big splash?
A: I really do not know. My best hunch is almost Kuhnian (Kuhn 1962): there was the spectacular rise of these "new authoritarianisms," it seemed increasingly clear that existing theories and typologies could not account for them, and my book, with all its flaws, offered a new, surely more cogent interpretation that, in addition, raised new research questions.

Transitions from Authoritarian Rule to Democracy

Q: Could you discuss the origins of the Woodrow Wilson Center project that led to your 1986 volume on regime transitions with Philippe Schmitter and Laurence Whitehead?[6]
A: This project has an interesting origin. Abe Lowenthal had created the Latin American Program of the Woodrow Wilson Center for International Studies, and set up a wonderful board, chaired by Albert Hirschman, of which I was a member. The board met twice a year, and in 1978 we met to discuss new ideas about what to do with the program.

I was still in Argentina at the time, and I hooked up with Fernando Henrique Cardoso, also a member of the board, in São Paulo so we could travel together to the United States. Over drinks and during the trip, we discussed options for our meeting, and I told him I thought it was time to look at transitions. I was convinced—we were both convinced—that the days of the military rulers in Brazil and Argentina were numbered. Actually, I had elaborated the reasons for this belief in my chapter in the Collier volume, the title of which is indicative by itself, "Tensions in the Bureaucratic-

6. See the interview with Schmitter in Chapter 10 for his perspective on the project on regime transitions.

Authoritarian State and the Question of Democracy" (O'Donnell 1979a). I told Fernando Henrique, "Maybe it's time to study transitions to democracies." And we spent two or three hours brainstorming on the airplane about whether to propose this idea to the Wilson Center.

When we arrived in the United States, we conspired to talk first to Philippe Schmitter, another member of the board. Philippe and I had taught an SSRC seminar in Argentina—the day Perón died in 1974 we were teaching that seminar. He was also a good friend of Fernando Henrique and had been active coordinating the human rights movement for protection of Brazilians. When we told Schmitter about the idea of studying transitions, it turned out that he had had the same idea! So we decided to present this suggestion to the Wilson Center, and Lowenthal, Hirschman, and the whole board immediately thought it was an excellent idea.

We had a great meeting, and we began thinking about how to take the project forward. That's when Abe Lowenthal—who throughout the project was a superb coordinator and promoter—invented the expression of "thoughtful wishing," as opposed to wishful thinking, to describe our shared hopes for the demise of the authoritarian regimes. It's a great sound bite. Still, we faced deep skepticism from many people in Washington, including James Billington, the director of the Wilson Center. Fortunately, Abe overcame these doubts. We also had a lot of support from Hirschman and the rest of the board. So Abe got the first grant, and the project got rolling.

Later, Fernando Henrique became a replacement federal senator for the state of São Paulo, so he couldn't participate as one of the project directors. At that point, we invited Laurence Whitehead to be one of the editors, and we were fortunate he accepted. That's why the editors of the volume are, in alphabetical order, O'Donnell, Schmitter, and Whitehead.

Q: This project involved a number of conferences.
A: We held three conferences, in 1979, 1980, and 1981. The initial discussion focused on two papers. One was a paper Philippe wrote about Machiavelli's writings and their lessons for transitions (Schmitter 1979b). The other was a paper I wrote. It was published separately, originally in Spanish in 1979 and only recently in English.[7] I am proud of it. It presents the scheme about the hard-liners and soft-liners, two different kinds of oppositions, the resurrection of civil society, and other themes that later on became current in the literature.

Lots of people participated in these meetings, including several—Ales-

---

7. This paper was originally published as O'Donnell (1979b) and subsequently as O'Donnell (1982). The English version is O'Donnell (1999a).

sandro Pizzorno, Arturo Valenzuela, Linz, Dahl—who for various reasons did not write papers for the eventual volumes. All the participants were very interesting, intelligent people. I learned much from them and they added a lot to the project. For example, Alfred Stepan's (1986) paper presented a model of different paths of transition, which was very useful and offered a more complex, richer view than Philippe and I did. In his chapter, Adam Przeworski (1986) basically put in rational choice language the scheme that Philippe and I had created.[8] Laurence Whitehead's (1986) analysis of the international context was an important addition. And there are some superb case studies.

Q: I want to ask about your collaboration with Schmitter that eventually led to the core statement of that project, *Tentative Conclusions about Uncertain Democracies* (O'Donnell and Schmitter 1986). You are not known for doing much coauthored work. How was the experience? What steps did you go through before coming up with the final manuscript?

A: I am a lonely artisan. This makes me a bad source of employment because I seldom hire research assistants. I actually find it surprising that anyone would hire a student to read and summarize books for him. I could never do that. But I have collaborated a few times, the most important of which was with Philippe. There are a few reasons why the collaboration worked. First, we were and are good friends. Second, we truly respected each other intellectually. This is a necessary condition for a successful collaboration. Lastly, we only physically got together twice during the writing, which probably helps explain why we did not kill each other.

In terms of the steps involved in writing our book, I wrote the first draft based on the paper I prepared for the 1979 conference at the Wilson Center (O'Donnell 1979b). Then Philippe came to the Kellogg Institute, spent some time there, and wrote a new version in which he introduced several important changes and additions. Our first draft retained the basic scheme I had developed in my initial paper. But Philippe added some distinctive themes. For example, he brought in something that was completely absent from my draft: political parties. In my paper there were no political parties, which, of course, was a serious problem. Philippe also insisted on the importance of pacted transitions. As Juan Linz (1981) argued in his work on Spain, there seemed to be clear advantages to a pacted transition. But I was less convinced than Philippe about the convenience of pacted transitions, and we had to negotiate over this issue. In the end, I think it was a welcome

8. See the interviews with Przeworski and Stepan in Chapters 13 and 12 for their perspectives on the project on regime transitions.

addition to our text. In particular, Philippe brought a much better view than existed in the literature of the trade-offs involved in pacted transitions. But our text is still ambivalent about pacted transitions, because it reflects a negotiation in which we never really fully agreed.

Finally, we got together in Florence, where we worked jointly with Whitehead making adjustments and final revisions, in a wonderful milieu, with beautiful vineyards, olive groves, and great food and wine. We spent about ten days there. When we finished, we planned on dining out at a place where Machiavelli had lived. But before dinner I went to take a shower and broke my leg. It was a catastrophe. Instead of going to dinner we ended up in the hospital. And the next day Philippe's mother died. We had a sort of cataclysmic end to this thing.

Q: You must have been extremely pleased with the reception of the 1986 volume with Schmitter. It was a very successful work and ranked as one of the most cited books in comparative politics for several years.
A: It clearly made a splash. Journalists and politicians, not just academics, picked it up. It was widely read in South Africa, Poland, Hungary, South Korea, China, and the Soviet Union, in most cases as a translated *samizdat,* an underground publication. Even today I encounter someone from some country who will tell me how useful the book was. Part of its impact was probably due to the hope it apparently gave many people; it had a tonic value that went beyond the intellectual. That was very, very nice. It's the sort of thing you dream might happen, that you write something of value to people. It is one of the greatest satisfactions of my life.

Q: In addition to receiving wide acclaim, the book you wrote with Schmitter was also criticized along a number of lines. Two frequent criticisms were that the analysis was elitist and that it overlooked the international dimension.
A: I find the criticism that we offered only an elite-level model unwarranted. It must be something about how we wrote this piece. Actually, we insisted on the importance of the popular upsurge, the resurrection of civil society. We argued that these mass mobilizations are a critical element that allows democratizers to push for a transition, for taking the process of liberalization beyond where the authoritarian soft-liners want to leave it. So the dynamic of the transition is shaped by a dialectical relationship between mass mobilization, popular demands, and political leadership. We emphasized that without a bottom-up, popular component, most transitions would stall because a pure elite-level process would not lead to a transition to democracy. Of course, one possible criticism is that our model wrongly specified the interaction among elites and masses. But I frankly

don't understand the broader criticism that we ignored the popular side and offered an exclusively elite-level model. We insisted that mass mobilization plays a key role in transitions.

Concerning the international dimension, I agree that my work with Schmitter ignored it. The international dimension did not operate the same in all cases. For example, it played a role in the case of Spain but not in Argentina in 1971. But in terms of conceptualizing transitions, I think international factors should be incorporated fully into one's theoretical framework, which we failed to do in our text. On the other hand, the Whitehead (1986) chapter started to address this challenge nicely.

Q: Another line of criticism, which is ironic because your previous work on bureaucratic authoritarianism was criticized for the very opposite reason, is that your book with Schmitter is excessively voluntaristic, that it neglects the role of structural variables.
A: My book with Schmitter is a politicist text. I agree that we ignored structural factors to a large extent. Moreover, it seems inconsistent with what I wrote before and afterward. But I have a partly psychological and partly theoretical explanation for this apparent inconsistency. Existing theories told us that until you reached a certain level of economic development or maturation of political culture, it was hopeless to expect political democratization. We found this perspective rather dismal, so we sought to emphasize political factors, purposive political action, and show how politics could counteract or activate these slowly moving structural factors. We also had the notion, and I still stand by it, that the impact of structural variables on behavior is not a constant, but is itself a variable. Specifically, Philippe and I argued that since in transitions there are not established rules to the political game, the impact of the whole set of structural variables diminishes at those times of generalized uncertainty. But I agree, we put an exaggerated emphasis on politics, and we should have been more nuanced.

The key point is that this was a very political work. We were writing politics, not just an academic treatise. We were writing for intellectuals, journalists, and political leaders. If you look at who wrote the chapters— Cardoso, Luciano Martins, Manuel Antonio Garretón, Marcelo Cavarozzi, Julio Cotler, José María Maravall—all these guys were actually involved in antiauthoritarian politics in their countries. For Przeworski, the future of Poland was an obsession. I was also a political actor. We were all very visible intellectuals who were not just writing political science, but were writing in and about the politics of our countries. And we were sending a message, too: don't despair! There are deep tensions within authoritarian regimes and between them and society, and even though the rulers try to hide these weaknesses behind an impressive façade of coercion, opposition strategies do exist that are helpful for exploiting such tensions. So, yes, there was a great emphasis on political factors. But this was not by chance. The whole project was a very political thing.

Q: Despite these differences between your research on bureaucratic authoritarianism and transitions, one element remained constant: your desire to move on to new questions. In contrast, Schmitter took your joint work as a starting point for trying to create a field of "transitology," exploring the possibilities for generalizing the basic insights of this work to Eastern Europe, South Africa, and East Asia. What are your thoughts on this effort to extend theorizing on transitions beyond Latin America and Southern Europe?

A: The first time I heard the term *transitology* was when somebody said it tongue in cheek, because it sounded funny. But then it became an established word. I have carefully avoided it in my own work. Later, when I heard about *consolidology*, I almost had a heart attack. Consolidology makes me nervous and ready to deny any paternity to the whole monster. In this regard, Philippe and I are different; we have distinct personal and intellectual styles. I admire Philippe's intellectual power. As I told you, I have always been concerned not to neglect the specificities of the cases. For example, I have been careful to say that bureaucratic authoritarianism was a useful concept for the southern cone of Latin America, but that I did not think it fit Mexico. And if somebody says South Korea was bureaucratic authoritarian, God bless them, but it is not what I am saying because I don't know enough about that case.

The model of transitions that Philippe and I elaborated does have some pretensions of generality. But I never thought I had the knowledge or authority to say whether our model should apply to cases that I did not know well. In general, I feel I should leave such judgments to people who know other countries in depth. If they agree with our scheme, wonderful. And if it doesn't work, we can still learn by asking why it doesn't work. Let me be clear. I am not renouncing general concepts. But beyond a few cases about which I can claim reasonably detailed knowledge, I don't think I know enough to say that concepts I have found useful should be applied more generally. That is my self-restrained methodological position.

Let me add something on this issue that has nothing to do with Philippe's work—quite the contrary. I've frequently been annoyed by individuals from the North—not just North Americans but also Europeans—who come to Argentina, stay for two weeks in the center of Buenos Aires, and dispense, as their fellow economists do, ready-made prescriptions about what to do with the judiciary, congress, or political parties, or how to extend the rule of law, reform the police, or whatever, to poor natives whose language they barely speak. These transitologists and consolidologists operate like a well-paid touring company, telling you that if you want consolidated, stable, or whatever democracy, you should begin by reforming the institution or policy area on which they happen to claim expertise. I find this behavior so improper that I abstain, almost moralistically, from anything that might look like it. In this sense, you might call me an abstentionist transitologist and a militant anti-consolidologist.

The Quality of Democracy

Q: After focusing briefly on issues of democratic consolidation (Mainwaring, O'Donnell, and Valenzuela 1992), your research since the early 1990s turned to questions concerning the quality of democracy.[9] Could you discuss the driving problems and ideas in this ongoing research program?

A: Going back to the transitions project, part of the reason all of us got involved was that we shared a basic optimism about what democracy would bring. We thought that with successful transitions we would get not only political democracy, but also many other good things. We thought that in Latin America at least, these new democracies would be much better than the flawed democracies we had had before, because this time political democracy could work for social justice. We knew that the Spanish were already encountering what they called *desencanto* (disenchantment) with democracy, so we expected there would be a dose of that. Still, we thought the return to normal politics would result in decently functioning democracies. Of course, with the advantage of hindsight, we can now say that although things turned out reasonably well in some cases, like Spain, Portugal, and perhaps Chile and Uruguay, in most cases things turned out very disappointing.

I see a significant bifurcation of intellectual responses to the problematic situation of democracy in Latin America and elsewhere. One response is to see countries as deviating from some kind of "normal" path or pattern, as having not followed the prescribed route or the best possible route. This view, much like earlier modernization theories, posits universal trends, has a teleological bent, and has been adopted by quite a few authors. A different response, which I favor, is not to adopt this perspective, which assumes cases are moving along a preset path, and to look instead at a series of regional and time-bound specificities.

This critique of the literature on democratic consolidation, which I pre-

9. Some of the most significant articles from this period are collected in O'Donnell (1999b, Part IV) and O'Donnell (2001, 2004).

sented in an article in the *Journal of Democracy* (O'Donnell 1996), opens up a whole new research program with a strong normative component and an ambitious intellectual agenda. Concerning the normative component, I confess to having mixed feelings. Even flawed democracies are very different from authoritarian regimes. Things were very clear back then, before the transitions from authoritarianism. I hated those regimes and was happy to see them brought down. However, these days, even as I remember how horrible things were when the military was in charge, I get anguished and, at times, angry with Argentina, with what's going on there, and in general with the situation of many present Latin American democracies. I do not accept the injunction of some of my friends and the powers-that-be to just shut up and not criticize, because this might jeopardize the survival of these democracies. What I am trying to do is help provide a democratic critique of Latin America democracies.

From an intellectual perspective, what is needed, as I have begun to outline in recent publications (O'Donnell 2001, 2004), is a rethinking of democratic theory. It is incorrect to believe there is something called "democratic theory" that can be easily "exported," with only minor adjustments, to settings like Latin America.

Q: What is the problem with existing democratic theory?

A: Mainstream contemporary political science, particularly Anglo-Saxon political science, offers a kind of post-Schumpeterian theory of democracy. Dahl's work provides the most visible and intelligent manifestation of these views. I find this theory very useful in one sense. It places emphasis on things like elections, the freedom of association, and so on, which are very important. Still, I am more and more convinced there is a basic problem with this theory, in that it focuses exclusively on the political regime. In my view, this is very limiting, because I see democracy as going beyond the regime to include various aspects of the state and the society. Now, there are good historical and theoretical reasons why in the highly developed countries you may study the regime without taking into consideration factors that go beyond it. I don't think it's entirely right, but it's understandable. But if you go to Latin America, that posture becomes manifestly insufficient. Even if you are interested in understanding the regime itself, you need to understand some factors that are not strictly part of the regime.

Q: Yet you are surely well aware of the dangers involved in attempting to expand the notion of democracy.

A: Yes. I feel as if I have embarked on a risky trip, a trip in which I face the danger of falling into an abyss of conceptual confusion. I am sensitive to the fact that by attempting to expand the meaning of the concept *democ-*

racy, democracy could come to mean everything one likes, which, of course, would cause the death of the concept. So I am proceeding with care. I do this, to continue with the image of a risky trip, by taking a good rope and tying it to the only solid piece of the theory we have, which is the regime. Then, anchored to the regime, I descend to other areas, looking at other dimensions—the state, society—but always holding on to the rope and often going back to the regime to find solid grounding for further explorations. I am aware of the dangers you mention. But, I am convinced that in studying democracy in Latin America, it is necessary but not sufficient to understand the regime.

Q: In addition to conceptual innovation and theory building, your current research program on the quality of democracy also seems to require new data. What kind of information do we need to understand how democracy works in Latin America today?

A: This is probably a Herculean task. I would first like to know much more about the actual workings of state institutions, about how crucial decisions are really made. Second, I would like to have survey and anthropological data about how state institutions relate to ordinary people. What are citizens' perceptions of how they are treated by government agencies? This is a crucial component of everyday life in democracies about which we know too little. Third, I would like to know how people understand the functioning of the state, for example, if they think it governs for everyone or just a few sectors of society. I am also interested in the extent to which gaps exist in the implementation and adjudication of the law. We know too little about these mechanisms of power and domination and about how they are translated into the everyday perceptions and behavior of citizens. But once you convince yourself that democracy is more than just the regime, you realize this is precisely the kind of information we need. My hope is that these data will help us reach the other side of the moon, so to speak.[10]

The Research Process
Political Engagement and Science

Q: It is striking that your various research projects have always been driven by a strong normative component and that you are keenly aware, from the very outset, of the political dimension of your research. What is the proper link between social science and normative concerns?

---

10. O'Donnell's main work on the quality of democracy is O'Donnell (2004). This work has been a key input in a UNDP report on *Democracy in Latin America* (UNDP 2004).

A: Values determine your research questions, that is, questions come from your moral concerns and political engagements. I am a Weberian in this sense (Weber 1949). I have done research on questions that originated in the fact that we were governed by horrible regimes in Latin America and because I much preferred democracy. My questions still come from broad political and moral concerns. And, throughout my life, I have been obsessively concerned about the political misadventures of my country, Argentina. Now, once you get into your conceptual and empirical work, you have to be as clean and clear as possible in separating your values from the conclusions derived from your research and data. Inasmuch as you do good social science, you can serve your values better.

Q: Does theory serve as a source of research questions?
A: I have never tried to do theory per se. I never sat down and said, "Today I want to write a theory about something." Rather, I've tried to deal with the kinds of real-world problems that deeply bother me when I'm shaving—and for this purpose I have chosen theoretical frameworks that seemed to me adequate.

Q: You have mentioned that in Latin America the boundary between academics and politics is blurred, and that you and your collaborators on the transition project were "writing politics." Does this mean you would not characterize what you do as science?
A: I don't really see it as science. I am a person who gets troubled by certain problems and tries to understand them by doing whatever research seems needed, as well as by reading and listening a lot so I can get help from others. Then I sit down and write. I always felt more comfortable seeing myself as an intellectual, someone who, in contrast to a sheer professional, is moved by questions that are deeply and closely connected with one's values and life. It's like a painter: you paint because you have to express something, and that's it. So, I don't think I am a scientist. Sure, in the sense of checking that what I say is empirically sound, I do science. But that's just a basic rule of the art. If you're not doing that, you're painting junk.

Cases and Concepts

Q: You have repeatedly emphasized the need to address the specificities of cases and the dangers of generalizing beyond cases one knows quite well. Could you discuss the role case-based knowledge plays in your thinking?
A: It is absolutely indispensable. Detailed knowledge and the updating of knowledge of specific cases is something without which I would not be

able to think. It's as simple as that. The best work in comparative politics, with possibly very few exceptions, has been done by scholars writing about their home countries and countries they have spent a lot of time studying. Indeed, any roster of distinguished, influential comparativists would include a very large percentage of people who have spent an enormous amount of energy getting to know one, or a few, cases very well. This certainly holds for our most illustrious ancestors, Aristotle, Montesquieu, and Tocqueville.

Q: A related hallmark of your thinking has been your ability to craft new concepts that capture the specifics of the cases you study. Can you discuss the thought process involved in forming these concepts?
A: What is involved, at the core, is recognizing something as new, not in the sense that it is ontologically new, but in the sense that it has not been recognized before as something that has a claim to a new concept to be identified by a name. It is a very primitive and elementary moment of knowledge, saying, "This is something different." It's like having a newborn daughter; you give her a name and then the real world begins.

Take the example of bureaucratic authoritarianism. My aim in coining this term was to say that this was a new animal, it was different, and it was important, intellectually and politically, to recognize this. Because I thought it was important to recognize the specificity of this animal, it had to have a name. *Bureaucratic authoritarianism* is an ugly term to distinguish a type of authoritarian rule that was then confused with fascism, populism, and other regimes with which it had some family resemblance. By adding *bureaucratic* to *authoritarianism,* I was saying this was a type of authoritarianism that was built on large, complex organizations and professionalized military and technocratic agencies, not on the old caudillos or masses in the street of populist regimes, nor on the mobilizing mass parties of fascist regimes.

The term *bureaucratic authoritarianism* draws on terms used by Apter (1965), who was working on bureaucratic systems, and by Linz (1964), who was working on authoritarian regimes. I thought they combined nicely, because I was picking elements of both and adding some of my own. I also felt it was a nice tribute to two of my mentors to add the two names and build on them. But the term itself is not important. I could have named it anything, à la Humpty Dumpty. What is important is to persuade others that this thing has some specificity that deserves to be recognized, that it deserves a name, and, more important, that the concept itself elicits interesting questions.

To take another example, I chose the term *brown areas* because I wanted to distinguish regions of a country where the rule of law was weak (O'Donnell 1993). My first thought was *black*, but then I would have been accused of being racist, so I picked *brown*, which is the color of my skin.

Classics

Q: In addition to emphasizing knowledge of cases, you also seem to have been influenced considerably by various classic authors. Whom do you read and what do you get from reading the classics?
A: I have my own sanctuary, which I return to cyclically. I go back to Hegelian Marx. I go back to Weber. I've studied with great benefit some legal authors, especially Bruce Ackerman, Ernesto Garzón Valdés, Joseph Raz, and Jeremy Waldron. And there is always room for my fascination with Hobbes. He is my haunting ancestor—I try to get rid of Hobbes by turning to Locke, but I go back to being attracted by this incredible talent of Hobbes. Not so much Machiavelli. I've never been very attracted to Machiavelli. I've been rediscovering Durkheim, but I read him quite selectively. That is my personal sanctuary.

Q: Of all these authors, it seems you feel closest to Weber.
A: I have always had great affection for Weber. He was a politically nasty German nationalist, and I am a very antinationalistic person, so that element disturbs me. Still, I am fascinated by his intellectual style, his way of posing questions, the way he masters his material. To see him think through a problem, to see how his mind works, is very instructive. I get an aesthetic pleasure from watching his mind working. He was very self-conscious and disciplined, and he knew so much. But he is not overwhelmed by his knowledge, he manages his knowledge analytically, and then puts it in movement. To do this is so bloody difficult, and to do it clearly is even more difficult. He is my model of intellectual power. In this sense, Weber is my patron saint.

Unfortunately, Weber is often completely misread. For example, in *The Protestant Ethic and the Spirit of Capitalism,* he spends pages and pages saying he is not proposing a monocausal explanation of capitalism—the Protestant ethic is just one factor (Weber 1958c). But some readers try to oppose Weber to Marx linearly, saying that Weber explains capitalism not in terms of material factors but in terms of the Protestant ethic. Lazy people who don't actually read Weber repeat that idiocy again and again.

Of course, if you look at the intellectual milieu in which Weber worked, he was not really inventing something totally new. There were many contemporary works that addressed the question, "What is capitalism, and where is it going?" This was the problem of the times, and many authors had dealt with it. Weber drew on these works, often without citing them; he was a rather nasty colleague in this sense. But he did achieve a new synthesis. Weber was also writing politics in the sense of being immersed in political discussions in his country. The romantic Right was saying capitalism was destroying culture, whereas the socialists and Marxists saw capitalism as just a fleeting stage of history. Weber was by no means a pure academic working in a void and thinking, "I will explain capitalism" just for the sake of writing a better theory.

Q: You mentioned Hegelian Marxism. Have you read much Marx recently? What's the relevance of Marxism and Marxist literature in looking at current politics?
A: I've been rereading some Marx and a few Marxists lately, though not the Marx of *Capital*. The contemporary times have forgotten something I believe Stuart Hampshire called the "strategy of suspicion." Most contemporary theory—rational choice, various institutionalisms—assumes the transparency of society. Yet, as Marx and Freud, too, said, you will not grasp the realities by taking a naïve view of what is apparent. Rather, if you really want to understand what is going on, to understand change, you have to look deeper. To do this, you don't need to be a Marxist in any orthodox sense. But I think Marx had a powerful message in this regard. I am also interested in Marx's view of the state, which he sees not as a neutral thing administering the public good, but as a condensation, or crystallization, of power and social forces. Marx, jointly with Weber, also gives a healthy reminder that politics is fundamentally about struggle and conflict.

The Achievements, Shortcomings, and Future of Comparative Politics

Q: An ongoing debate in comparative politics concerns whether or not the field has produced cumulative knowledge over the past decades. What is your assessment of this issue?
A: I think we've learned an awful lot. When I compare what we know today to what we knew when I was a graduate student, I would say we have learned an enormous amount about the immense diversity of political forms and histories. This is a great contribution of comparative politics, one that benefits anyone who wants to educate himself or herself about the world. Still, I am mistrustful of efforts at synthesis, because I think they involve a false, simplifying thrust and a tendency to subordinate knowledge under the umbrella of one single theory. This is a misguided act of

intellectual hubris. It is instructive to recall that Aristotle wrote about some-thing like eighty different constitutions, and even in the Peloponnesus there was a large variety of political forms. So, we should live happily with diversity, accepting that different theories may be appropriate for different problems and circumstances. The study of politics is basically a humanistic discipline that should gladly accept diversity and avoid reductionism.

Q: What are the main shortcomings of comparative politics as it has been practiced over the past decades?
A: I would point to two main issues. One is the attempt to reduce compara-tive politics to a single theoretical view. My resistance to theoretical imperi-alism is not atheoretical. I think it is our duty to work theoretically. Thus, I agree with critiques against a lot of works in comparative politics that are essentially journalistic accounts without any theoretical questions. For ex-ample, I read studies on democratization that just tell stories which, if you had read the newspapers of the time, you would have known three years before. But I insist we need diversity when it comes to theory.

A second issue involves the loss of a sense of history. The historical dimension of phenomena is very important. Yet, with some important exceptions, mainstream comparative politics has become too separated from historical research, and our awareness of the historical roots of our object of study has been diminished.

Q: Over the past decade and a half, the field of comparative politics has looked far less toward sociology, its main companion discipline in the 1960s and 1970s, and far more toward economics. What do you think about this trend?
A: Political processes or phenomena have social, cultural, historical, and economic aspects. Thus, to study them properly, it is necessary to transgress disciplinary boundaries. Every good political work has looked at adjacent factors, not just political ones, though I don't think there is anything that ontologically determines whether you should look first at sociology, his-tory, economics, or psychology. Of course, academic vogues and power relations tend to bias where we look. If your career is fostered by the fact that you study economic factors rather than sociological ones, then you will likely know more about economics than sociology and put more em-phasis on economic than sociological factors. What would concern me is if institutionalized power relations were to turn these choices into dominant career paths. I would be worried if students felt pressured to look at eco-nomics and dogmatically viewed politics from an economic perspective, and I would be even more worried if an economic perspective were reduced

to one particular conception of this discipline. I mention this because, especially in the United States, these are worrying trends.

Q: Relatedly, you seem to have abandoned the interest in political economy, really classical political economy, which characterized some of your early work, including *Modernization and Bureaucratic Authoritarianism* (O'Donnell 1973). How would you re-create the field of classical political economy today?
A: Actually, I keep a keen interest in political economy. My problem is that nowadays in order to do decent work in political economy you need to handle at least some of the highly sophisticated tools that have been developed in mainstream economics. I don't have the mathematical skills to do this, and it is too late, or I have become too lazy, to acquire those skills now. Fortunately, some talented and adventurous young scholars are doing this; hopefully some of them will apply their skills to the great problems of history, economics, exploitation, and power that obsessed the classical political economists and that are still so much among us.

Q: Looking back again, is there anything you would rescue from dependency theory, especially as formulated in Cardoso and Faletto's book (1979)?
A: I have always thought that asymmetric power relationships are constitutive of most social realities. Unfortunately, the analysis of these power relationships has been erased somewhat from academic concerns. The fact that ideas about dependency were taken up by some true believers and exaggerated to the point of caricature did not help. But I don't think the Cardoso and Faletto book or, for that matter, my work on bureaucratic authoritarianism can be blamed for the gross exaggerations that some people committed on their behalf. Also, the mood of the times since the 1980s, which emphasizes markets and globalization as something that happens more or less homogeneously across the globe, has suppressed the *problématique* concerning how asymmetric power relationships are constitutive of Latin America and the rest of the world today. Of course, to address this *problématique* you have to find a way to clearly conceptualize and reasonably operationalize power relationships, and this is very hard to do. Indeed, how to conceptualize and measure power is one of the most vexing problems in political science. But I do not think this justifies throwing out the problem.

There were attempts in the 1970s to measure transnational power relationships through trade and investment patterns. But these were not very valid indicators, and those studies led to inconclusive results. I have become persuaded that one way dependency reveals itself—and this could perhaps be operationalized—is through how the public agendas of governments are formed. A gross indicator of dependency is that external actors impose most items on the public agenda. For example, Argentina today is a case where there is very low autonomy of the government to develop its own public agenda independently of external actors. By contrast, in less dependent countries, the governments have much more leeway in putting domestically generated topics on the agenda. If you look at the United States or at European countries, there are a series of issues on the public agenda that are domestically generated and have little to do with international constraints. So, you could approach the problem of dependency in terms of the relative autonomy of states to develop their own public agenda vis-à-vis external actors. That might be one way to bring a badly needed focus on inter- and transnational asymmetrical power relationships back into political science.

Of course, the political Right and the winners will always deny that these are power relationships. That's what the winners always do. Part of their natural ideology is to tell you that the way we relate is not the result of power, but of cooperation or interdependency. It's not easy to argue against that. But that's what political science should do.

Q: Another important recent trend in comparative politics is a push for greater sophistication in the use of empirical methodologies, both quantitative and qualitative. What do you think about this trend?
A: In this regard, I am a Maoist. I say, "Let a hundred flowers bloom." Different types of questions call for different kinds of methods, and the problems we study are so complex that we need many approaches. Let's see what can be done with this approach and that one, and let's live together joyfully and peacefully without preventing others from doing what they want. As I said before, I have always considered myself an artisan, and I think you need different tools and instruments, depending whether you are working on wood or marble. I do not claim any great methodological sophistication, and I find pure methodological discussions boring. But I am convinced that claims that any single methodology may offer the answer to everything are preposterous.

I also worry that in its current drive toward methodological sophistication, political science has lost the ambition and hubris of writing great books that give an account of big issues. When Moore, Dahl, or Shmuel Eisenstadt produced their major books, for example, there was a sense of possibility that you could do both methodologically self-conscious and important work on great issues. I fear this sense of possibility is disappearing. But maybe this feeling that the best books are in the past is just a symptom of my aging.

Conclusion

Q: What's your advice to people entering the field of comparative politics today?

A: First, ask yourself if you have a real interest in the world outside your country, a real human interest about other people and other places, how they live, how they survive. That is the first necessary, crucial condition. Second, know very well at least one country that isn't yours. That means learning the language, talking to all sorts of people, spending time in all sorts of places, and getting to know people who don't live in the capital city. Then you can write something good. But if you want to write comparative politics without ever leaving your own country, physically or mentally, then you had better go into another field. That's my basic advice.

10

Philippe C. Schmitter

Corporatism, Democracy, and Conceptual Traveling

Philippe C. Schmitter is widely regarded as the most influential analyst of corporatism—a pattern of interest group politics in which the state plays a significant role in the formation and activities of interest groups—a leading theorist of democratization, and an important contributor to the study of regional integration and the European Union (EU). His research has spanned many regions of the world. He established himself first as a Latin Americanist and Europeanist, and then authored numerous cross-regional studies in which he avidly sought to extend insights drawn from cases in one region to cases in other regions.

At the outset of his career, Schmitter challenged the then dominant pluralist approach to interest groups, criticizing it for seeing these groups as springing autonomously from civil society and thus failing to recognize how their formation and functioning are shaped largely by the actions of the state. He proposed the concept of corporatism as an alternative to pluralist conceptions of interest group politics. The first formulations of Schmitter's thinking on pluralism and corporatism were published in *Interest Conflict and Political Change in Brazil* (1971) and his widely read article "Still the Century of Corporatism?" (*Review of Politics* 1974). Thereafter, his research focused on Portugal, which he analyzed, like Brazil, as a case of "state corporatism," and then shifted to multiple Western European countries, which were understood as instances of "societal corporatism."[1] His research on societal corporatism addressed questions such as, What role does the state have in setting up and maintaining corporatist arrange-

This interview was conducted by Gerardo Munck in Notre Dame, Indiana, on December 4–5, 2002.

1. According to Schmitter (1974, 102–3), in "societal corporatism" the legitimacy and functioning of the state are primarily or exclusively dependent on the activity of singular, noncompetitive, hierarchically ordered representative corporations, whereas in "state corporatism" similarly structured "corporations" are created by and kept as auxiliary and dependent organs of the state.

ments? Who benefits from corporatism? What is the relationship between corporatism and democracy? How viable is corporatism in a changing international economic context?

The study of democratization has been a second key concern in Schmitter's career. His coauthored book with Guillermo O'Donnell, *Transitions from Authoritarian Rule: Tentative Conclusions about Uncertain Democracies* (1986), was one of the most widely read and influential works in comparative politics during the 1980s and 1990s. It also initiated a debate, in which Schmitter actively participated, concerning the possibility of extending ideas about transitions from authoritarianism developed through an analysis of the Southern European and Latin American experiences to Eastern Europe and the Soviet Union, as well as to the case of South Africa. He has also contributed to the literature on the international dimension of democratization, emphasizing international efforts at democracy promotion and protection, and he has written seminal articles on democratic consolidation and the quality of democracy.

Finally, Schmitter has published extensively on regional integration in Europe and the political characteristics of the EU. This research, published in *How to Democratize the EU . . . and Why Bother?* (2000a) and various articles, considers the possibility of democracy at a level above the nation-state, the unit of governance assumed by classic democratic theory.

Schmitter was born in Washington, D.C., in 1936. He received his B.A. from Dartmouth College in 1957 and his Ph.D. in political science from the University of California, Berkeley, in 1967. Schmitter taught at the University of Chicago (1967–82), Stanford University (1986–96), and the European University Institute (EUI) (1982–86, 1996–2004). He became a professor emeritus at Stanford University in 1999 and was named Professorial Fellow at the EUI in 2004. He was vice-president of the American Political Science Association (APSA) in 1983–84.

Intellectual Formation, Training, and Dissertation Research

Q: How did you get interested in studying politics and comparative politics in particular?
A: I lived in a somewhat political family, and I grew up in an environment where comparison was a daily event. My mother was French, and my father was American with Swiss origins. Though I was born in the United States, my family lived initially in Switzerland. My father was working for the League of Nations in the International Labor Organization (ILO). When the war broke out, we moved to the United States. So I spent the war years in the United States. My father worked for the International Organization section of the State Department during the war. So I came in contact with

people from all over the place, most of them refugees. After the war, we moved briefly back to France and I went to school there.

I was forced to live a comparative life. I lived in a milieu where you never knew the nationality, religion, or even the ethnicity of the next person walking into the house. I regarded this as quite normal. I never thought of the comparative part as a choice. I also never thought about political science or social science in general until much, much later. Let's put it this way: I did not choose comparison; comparison chose me. And I eventually chose political science.

Q: How did you come to study politics?
A: I got a B.A. in international relations at Dartmouth College and, after taking a break to study art in Mexico, I went to Geneva to pursue graduate work. I studied international relations, international public law, and international political economy. I found these most uninteresting subjects, and I found Switzerland a most uninteresting place. I was bored to death with academic matters and didn't know what to do, when Stanley Hoffman, a Harvard professor, showed up and gave a semester course on French politics. Stanley was a very French-thinking person, and it was a very French course—basically organized around a comparison between the Fourth and the Fifth Republics. Stanley was an outrageous Gaullist at the time, whereas I came from a socialist and anti-Gaullist family. I remember arguing a lot with Stanley. This was about 1959, around the time the Fifth Republic had been set up. Stanley was full of great man theories about how De Gaulle had providentially saved France. I thought what De Gaulle had done was a big mistake. Still, this was my first real exposure to comparative politics, and I learned two things.

First, I realized domestic politics was a lot more interesting than international politics. International politics was very boring, and the theory of international politics did not appeal to me. That reaction may have stemmed from my formation, because my family was Quaker, pacifist, and very much oriented toward international organizations. Indeed, my father had devoted his life to them. Therefore, I had an idealistic vision of what international relations could be like. And, of course, the world wasn't like that.

Second, my contact with Stanley Hoffman led me to think about going to graduate school in the United States. As a student in Geneva, I had briefly worked for the ILO and found it the most stifling environment imaginable. Even though I had gone to Geneva to prepare myself for a career as an international civil servant, I was discovering that I was not constitutionally capable of becoming one. Yet I had never thought of an academic career at all up to this point. Rather, the alternative I had considered was to be a painter. I still wanted to be a painter. In fact, I had a long beard and was a sort of beatnik, which was not your typical college appearance back then. So, I looked, and probably acted, a bit weird for the times. In any case, I took this seminar from Hoffman. What I liked about Hoffman was that you could disagree with him, and he actually seemed to like it. Now, if you went to university in Europe then, that was not normal. I had had a bunch of pontificating, non-dialogical professors. Here comes this illustrious Harvard professor, whom you could argue with, and he gave me some important advice. I'll never forget the day I went to his office at the end of his seminar. I said, "I'm about to get my degree, and I don't know what I'm going to do. I may stay here and do a doctorate in Switzerland." He looked at me and said, "You don't want to do that." He somehow had learned enough about me from my behavior in his classroom to realize I wasn't going to do well in the Swiss environment. "You should go back to the United States. You have to get a doctorate in the United States. That's the only place." Then he said, "You should go to Berkeley and you should study with Ernst Haas." I had read some of Ernst B. Haas's work in another course, and I had liked it. Somehow Stanley Hoffman made that connection.

Q: Did you follow this advice?

A: Yes. Hoffman explained that you had to apply to four or five U.S. graduate schools, because you never know where you were going to get admitted. I applied to Berkeley, Harvard, Columbia, and probably Princeton. I don't remember if I applied to Yale. I didn't know much about these schools or the American system in general. As it turned out, Berkeley was the only school that took me.

I had actually lived in Berkeley before, as a painter. I had studied painting at an academy in Mexico City. From Mexico I went to San Francisco and then Berkeley. I was painting there and sort of knew the Bay Area scene. I had started a friendship with a man named Judd Boyton, an architect who was building houses up on Panoramic Way above the campus. Now, I used to build houses during the summers before I became a painter. I had been a carpenter, a bricklayer, a cement worker/hod carrier, and a rod buster/welder. I liked physical work. So, while I was painting in Berkeley, I made money on the side building a house with Judd. I had no money at all when I applied to graduate school, but I knew that if I went back to Berkeley, I would somehow survive on the meager assistantship they offered me and working, if need be, on the side with Judd. So I went off to Berkeley.

Just before moving to Berkeley, I had an accidental experience that turned out to be quite important. When I was preparing for my final exams in Geneva, I went to Venice to visit a friend. She had a beautiful apartment on one of the side canals. My visit happened to coincide with the Biennale.

Every year they picked one country as the centerpiece of the exhibit, and that year it was Brazil. I simply fell in love with Brazilian art. They also had Brazilian music playing in the background. I decided that Brazil must be an absolutely fascinating place. I didn't know anything about Brazilian politics, nothing, but I formed a powerful image of the country as a syncretic mixture of all types of different cultures and as a place capable of producing astonishingly lively and beautiful art. I decided I wanted to live in Brazil at some point. I went to Berkeley in 1961 with the objective of working with Ernst Haas and figuring out some way to go to Brazil.

Q: What are your recollections about your studies at Berkeley?
A: When I arrived at Berkeley, I had only vaguely heard of political science. While studying in Geneva, I'd been a periodic visitor to Paris and sat in on courses at the Sorbonne. There, *science politique* was quite formalistic and strongly linked with the study of law. This was very different from what I encountered at Berkeley. At that time, Berkeley had perhaps the best combination of Sociology and Political Science departments in the States. I took advantage of this by enrolling in as many courses in sociology as political science, which turned out to be a good thing. I learned a lot from people like Seymour Martin Lipset, Reinhard Bendix, David Apter, and, of course, Ernst Haas.

Early on I started talking to Haas. I would never have called him Ernie in those days, about what I really wanted to do. I told him I knew Spanish—I had learned it while painting in Mexico—and that I wanted to work on Latin America and international relations. He suggested I try to apply European integration theory to Central America and Latin America. At that time, in the early 1960s, the most successful Third World integration organization was the Central American Common Market (Mercado Común Centro Americano). There was also a promising thing called ALALC,[2] that nobody had studied. So, I worked with Haas as a research assistant on Central America. I also went there and to Mexico to conduct interviews. The first paper I published was on the Mexican decision to enter ALALC (Schmitter and Haas 1964), which was a bit of a puzzle, because Mexico had virtually zero trade with the rest of its member countries.

Q: Though you were working initially on international relations, you eventually shifted to comparative politics.
A: In the process of doing research on integration in Latin America, I got more and more interested in domestic politics. Haas recognized that I really

2. Asociación Latinoamericana de Libre Comercio—Latin American Association of Free Trade.

wanted to do comparative politics, and he supported me. Haas was a maverick within the international relations field, because he approached European integration not as an international relations issue, but as a problem at the intersection between domestic politics and international relations. His book, *The Uniting of Europe* (Haas 1958), was not only about diplomatic, country-to-country relations, but also about what was happening to internal political structures, especially the domestic and transnational interest groups that were forming around the European Coal and Steel Community.[3] In the 1950s, Haas was already breaking the artificial boundary between international relations and comparative politics. He did not mind at all when I defected from international relations to comparative politics.

There is something else I should explain about Haas. During the period I was at Berkeley, we graduate students were in the middle of the anti–Vietnam War movement and he, like many other European academic refugees in the United States, was very strongly pro-government and anticommunist. I was on the opposite side, but this did not ruin our relationship.[4] Despite the fact that on a day-to-day political basis we were absolutely opposed, we were still able to work together.

Q: What comparative politics courses did you take at Berkeley?
A: The first course I took in comparative politics was from David Apter. Apter really got me excited about comparative politics. He taught from a political anthropology and systems theory perspective, which I didn't really take to. But David is very charismatic. He also allowed you to disagree with him, which I have always appreciated. The most important course I took, as far as comparative politics was concerned, was a seminar on political sociology with Seymour Martin Lipset. After Haas, Lipset was the second biggest influence on me at Berkeley.

Q: What other courses did you take?
A: I took several courses with Sheldon Wolin, who was also a major influence. He taught a two-quarter obligatory sequence on the history of political thought that began with Aristotle and Plato and ended with Marxism. It also covered some existential political thought, because Sheldon was very much into that. I also took a seminar with Hanna Pitkin, who had just finished a book on representation (Pitkin 1967), and her course got me very much centered on that concept. In the Sociology Department, I took a seminar with Neal Smelser on the theory of revolution, which I took at the

3. The European Steel and Coal Community, established in 1952 by the Treaty of Paris, is the precursor treaty organization of what has become the European Union (EU).

4. Schmitter's first publications were coauthored with Haas: Schmitter and Haas (1964) and Haas and Schmitter (1964).

same time as a formally identical one with Chalmers Johnson. Now, that was a contrast! I also took a sociology course on "The Politics of Mass Society," or something like that, from William Kornhauser and one from Reinhard Bendix on historical sociology.

Q: Lijphart was at Berkeley at that point. Did you take any courses with him?
A: Lijphart was there, but I didn't take any courses with him. In those days, Lijphart was very Eurocentric. The last thing I wanted to study was Europe. Even though I knew several European languages and had a European background, I was thoroughly bored with Europe.

Q: In terms of methodology, what training did you receive at Berkeley?
A: I arrived with zero knowledge of methodology. I had never taken a course on statistics, least of all, research design. I'd had some background in mathematics and had enjoyed it. At one point, early in my undergraduate career, I was even thinking of majoring in physics, but I completely let go all of the "hard" sciences. There was no obligatory course on statistics at Berkeley that I can remember. So, in terms of methods, I didn't have any training when I arrived, and I never took a course in it at Berkeley. But I was reading a lot of American social science, and I knew I would want to use statistics in my research, because you couldn't just interview people, and you certainly couldn't just use secondary sources and documents to tell a story. The notion of "qualitative methods"—for example, of compiling a so-called analytical narrative—never occurred to me. I suppose, in retrospect, you could label me a "mixed method" scholar. Moreover, I considered most of what I read about Latin American politics as "substandard" and saw no reason why it had to remain so (Schmitter 1969). So, I learned statistics by reading how other political scientists, mostly students of American politics, used them.

Q: Did you take any courses on Latin America?
A: I sat in on a course on Latin America, but the person who taught it didn't excite me, so I left. However, in the process of doing research on economic integration in the region, I had come across Raul Prebisch's work, and I got interested in CEPAL and their work.[5] Albert Hirschman was another very important influence. I read his *Journeys Toward Progress* (Hirschman 1963).

5. CEPAL (Comisión Económica para América Latina y el Caribe—Economic Commission for Latin America and the Caribbean) is the economic think tank established by the UN in 1948 and known for its unorthodox approach to economic development.

Q: Were you reading the classics in social theory, such as Marx and Weber?

A: Absolutely. I read Weber mostly through Reinhard Bendix, who both inspired and frightened me. I suppose he was the most erudite professor in both the political science and sociology faculties that I came in contact with. Behind that mild-mannered and soft-spoken façade, there was this immense fount of knowledge. He, along with Sheldon Wolin, is responsible for my deep-seated conviction that social science has to be historical. This posed a problem since I may have had a better than average knowledge of European history—thanks to my studies in France and Switzerland—but I had absolutely no grasp of the history of Latin America and, most specifically, of Brazil, where I knew I was going to do my doctoral research.

Interestingly, it was mainly through Lipset's courses that I engaged Marx. I had already acquired some knowledge of Marx's writings while studying in Europe and, of course, a superficial version of him was very much a part of the antiwar movement. What Lipset did was convert my existing political interest in class relations into an academic interest in class self-organization. So I got very deeply into Marx. The critical thing, for me, was that I saw Marx and Weber as contemporaries. I didn't think of them as remote historical figures.

Q: Do you have any other recollections about your studies at Berkeley?

A: Yes, and it concerns the most unpleasant part of my graduate career. My biggest problem was political parties, and the problem had a name: Herb McClosky. He was the "parties person" at Berkeley, even though he worked exclusively on the United States. One of the obligatory exams at Berkeley was on political parties. I resisted this, partly for intellectual reasons, because I was rebelling against the centrality accorded to the study of political parties and elections in the discipline of political science. But the core of the problem was that McClosky's course on political parties was essentially a prerequisite for passing the exam. It wasn't a formal requisite, but everybody knew you had to take this course. Anyway, I refused to take it and was the only one taking the exam that year who had not done so. I got an A on my exam from David Apter and a C from McClosky. It was pretty clear that McClosky was punishing me because I didn't take his course. The case had to be adjudicated by a third person and I believe he or she gave me an A−. So, I passed. I'd been lucky until then at Berkeley. All the people I had worked with were sure enough of themselves that they could afford to let students disagree with them. But McClosky wasn't that way. He expected you to regurgitate the material in the way he understood it. I'd had plenty of that in Europe, and I wasn't about to do it again.

Q: Were there any fellow graduate students you were close to?
A: There was a group of students around Haas and also a group working on Latin America. But I didn't have much to do with the latter, probably because Berkeley didn't have a real program on Latin America at that time. Moreover, as I mentioned above, I was "under-impressed" by the quality and methodological sophistication of the studies being done on that area. There was also a group of people working in comparative politics, including Ken Jowitt, Sid Tarrow, and Clement Moore, who was then a young assistant professor. But Ken was working on Romania and communist studies; Sid was working on Southern Italy; and Clem was a Middle Eastern specialist working on Tunisia, Egypt, and so on. Given my interests in Brazil, I was quite alone. I like to point out to my students that not a single member of my dissertation committee knew anything about the country I was studying, and this may have been an advantage since it forced me to think and write in generic terms—in lowercase rather than uppercase terms, to use the expression of Adam Przeworksi and Henry Teune (1970, 7 and 26–30).

Q: Turning to your dissertation (Schmitter 1968), how did you decide to work on interest representation in Brazil?
A: I can remember the exact moment when I decided on my dissertation topic. It came during my second year at Berkeley, in Lipset's class on political sociology, where, for some reason, I was picked to present a critique of an article by him (Lipset 1960b). There is a sentence in the article that says something I think 99 percent of political scientists would have agreed with at that time, namely, that political parties are *the* mechanism for the representation of social interests in democracies. They virtually alone provide the link between citizens and their rulers. Now, this was the period of the maximum influence of systems theory, à la Gabriel Almond, which held that, even if a country had associations and movements articulating interests and passions, what counted was the aggregation of their claims by political parties. *Ergo,* political scientists had to study political parties and, of course, the elections in which they competed. In my critique of Lipset's article, I said in effect: "You are wrong; political parties are not necessarily the main channel of social representation." This is one of the rare instances where I had learned something from Switzerland. I knew that in Switzerland interest groups were much more important than political parties, which were at best façades for interest groups. I knew this because I had done some research and learned that 75 percent of Swiss deputies were actually paid functionaries of interest groups. Although they ostensibly sat in parliament as members of the Liberal, Radical, or Populist parties, all

were, in fact, sitting there as representatives of interest groups. This was due largely to the simple fact that, in Switzerland, deputies did not earn a salary, just a per diem. If you wanted to make a living as a politician, you had to earn your salary elsewhere. So Swiss deputies were lawyers, administrators, or spokesmen for interest groups. I knew this, and I brought it up in Lipset's class.

I argued that it is incorrect to say that political parties are the exclusive or even the most important mechanism for the representation of social interests. This should be regarded as a hypothesis, which may fit some cases, but it is not valid as an a priori conclusion. Then, I remember making the outrageous further assertion that the role of political parties as mechanisms of representation would decrease in the future, because there was a tendency away from reliance on party channels toward more reliance on interest associations and social movements. Frankly, I don't know why I said that. To this day, I can't figure out the empirical basis I was drawing on to make this assertion. Maybe I said this because I was peripherally involved in the movement against the Vietnam War. So, it might have been pure wishful thinking. Or it could have been the result of having spent so much time in Europe, where interest groups were very well organized and entrenched within the state apparatus. In any case, we had a little bit of a debate in class, and when I went home that evening, I knew I had my dissertation topic.

Q: How did your ideas evolve thereafter?
A: I read American pluralist theory, which I had been exposed to in Lipset's and Kornhauser's seminars. I read Lewis Coser (1956). And, of course, I also read de Tocqueville. I had read de Tocqueville before in Switzerland, where I discovered his famous hypothesis that as societies become more developed they acquire more complex and pluralistic interest group structures. I realized this was a perfect topic to study in Brazil. At that time, Brazil had one of the fastest-growing economies and was clearly experiencing a major, sustained transformation. Brazil also had a very diverse population, ethnically, religiously, and regionally. I didn't know about the concept of a "critical case" then, but later I discovered that is exactly what Brazil was. If there was any country in the Third World where you would expect to see a pluralist interest group system emerging, it should have been Brazil. So, I decided to go to Brazil to study the emergence of organized interests.

Q: How did you get to Brazil?
A: It was not a straightforward matter. At Berkeley, I did not take any courses in Spanish, because I already knew it. And I decided not to take any courses in Portuguese. I figured, why waste my time learning Portuguese

when I could learn it when I got to Brazil? This created a problem. The Ford Foundation, which was the main source of funding for doctoral research in Latin America at the time, refused to give me a grant. Nobody considered me a bona fide Latin Americanist because I hadn't passed through the standard hoops. In fact, there was not a single course—graduate or undergraduate—in either Latin American history or politics in my curriculum vita and no visible indication that I knew anything about Brazil. I do not blame them for rejecting me, although at the time, I was devastated. So, there I was in Berkeley, with no money to get to Brazil. But then somebody —I don't know who, but it probably was Haas—said, "Wait a minute, we have money from the Rockefeller Foundation to send young professors abroad for one year. If we name you an assistant professor at Berkeley, we can send you immediately." So they made certain arrangements—I would have to teach in Brazil—that entitled me to go.

I went to Brazil in 1966 ostensibly not to do doctoral research but to teach political science at the Instituto de Ciências Sociais da Universidade do Brasil (Social Sciences Institute, University of Brazil) in Rio de Janeiro. This arrangement turned out to be great for several reasons. It gave me a higher status and a better salary than I would have had if I had just been a graduate student poking around on a fellowship. It also put me in the middle of a contentious and interesting intellectual milieu. I taught the very first course ever in political science as such in Brazil, and I had about eighteen lively students, five or six of whom later became professors of political science. Finally, teaching in Brazil helped me learn Portuguese fast. Indeed, one week after arriving I had to give a lecture in Portuguese, a language I had never even studied. I would speak in French, Spanish, or whatever came into my head, and the students would correct me in Portuguese.

Q: How did the dissertation research go? You certainly did not find a pluralist pattern of interest representation in Brazil. How did your views shift?
A: I quickly realized my main expectations were not working out. It was clear that Brazil had a state-recognized, state-subsidized, monopolistic, and hierarchical system of interest representation going back at least to 1943. The puzzling thing was that the period of democratic politics from 1946 to 1964 had done nothing to do away with this system; you would have at least expected strong tensions or pressures to have emerged during that period. Even after the military came to power in 1964 it seemed, at least at that moment, they were not doing anything to change the system of interest representation. In short, the system or, as they themselves called it, *o sistema,* had started earlier, more or less formally in 1943, and was still in

effect. It didn't take me long to figure that out and say, "Wait a minute, this doesn't fit."

I started by interviewing trade unionists, and they were quite happy with this arrangement. They did complain a lot about the dictatorial regime; nevertheless, the system of interest representation assured their formal importance and guaranteed them certain financial benefits. That's when I discovered the concept of corporatism when, looking through a used bookstore in Rio de Janeiro, I came across a copy of Mihaïl Manoïlesco's *Le Siècle du Corporatisme* (1934). After that discovery, I started reading everything I could get my hands on about corporatism.

For my dissertation I gathered a great amount of data on associability of various kinds, including membership in labor unions, which I used in my analysis. One of the main parts of the study was to try to use Brazil as a comparative setting. So I took the twenty-six Brazilian states and ran regressions to answer a variety of questions. That was my first exercise working with aggregate data, and I was basically self-taught.

In broad terms, I came to several conclusions. It was clear that interest representation in Brazil was inextricably shaped by the state. Moreover, interest representation was also closely associated with a peculiar dynamic of capitalist development.

Research on Corporatism

Q: You transformed your dissertation into a book, *Interest Conflict and Political Change in Brazil*, which was published in 1971. That same year you went to do research in Portugal. But before that, in 1969, you had actually done a good deal of research in Argentina, though you never published anything on Argentina. Why did you decide to go to Argentina and why didn't your research there result in any publications?

A: I wanted to see how corporatism in Argentina was different from corporatism in Brazil. I went to Argentina in 1969, and, for a change, I had a nice fat grant from the Social Science Research Council (SSRC) and the American Council of Learned Societies (ACLS). I got time off from the University of Chicago and spent around six months in Argentina. I found it a wonderful place to live, much like being back in Europe. I interviewed more people than I had interviewed in Brazil. I did seventy-five or eighty interviews. Working in Argentina was easier because everything was in Buenos Aries, though I did go to Córdoba, Rosario, and Mendoza. By that time, I had developed the idea that different sectors of capitalists are organized differently. So, I interviewed business leaders in addition to trade union leaders. Interviewing business elites was easier than interviewing trade unionists, because at that time the latter were killing each other. I think four of the trade unionists I interviewed were killed while I was still there. I started to wonder whether someone had my interview schedule and was knocking them off. I did a lot of work and gathered a huge amount of data. My data on Argentina were actually better in many ways than my data on Brazil. It was easier to work there at that time, despite the dictatorship. But not a thing came out of that research. That's one of my great failures.

The fundamental problem was that I didn't understand Argentina. When I finished my research in Brazil, I felt confident about my analysis. I really thought I had Brazil nailed down. But after I finished my work on Argentina, I looked at all these data and said, "I still don't understand this country." That was, for me, a crisis.

Q: What was the reason your research project on Argentina did not work out?

A: By the time I went to Argentina, I was already a reasonably well-practiced Latin Americanist. I knew half of the social scientists in Argentina, and they were very helpful to me. So I can't blame the failure of my project on the resistance of the environment. And, as I just said, I had great data. So I certainly cannot blame it on a lack of data. I had everything going for me; it should have been easy. But I just couldn't use the same methods and the same way of thinking that had worked so well for me in Brazil. To this day, I still don't know what I missed.

One of the reasons my project failed—and this just popped into my head—was the perversity of the Argentine party system. In Brazil, I didn't pay any attention to parties at all. I could not have cared less about them. I quickly decided that parties were an unimportant part of the picture in Brazil. It was immediately apparent from all my interviews that parties were largely irrelevant for class and sectoral leaders. They worked directly with the bureaucracy or the offices of the president. In Argentina, by contrast, parties were somehow important, yet important in a way that was hard to see. Brazil had no party system, but things still worked. Capitalists weren't threatened by the party system, because it was incapable of articulating the interests of the working class or any other subordinate group. The problem with Argentina, as Torcuato Di Tella (1971–72) argues, is that it's a conservative nation without a conservative party. There was no business-oriented, liberal, or, for that matter, traditional conservative party. Hence, Argentine capitalists were threatened by the party system. That's why it is harder to understand interest group politics in Argentina, because it is shaped by something that is not there, namely, a conservative party. It's like a dog that's not barking.

I think my problem with Argentina—and this is the first time I've ever thought about this in these terms—may have been that I didn't understand the party system, and I couldn't understand the interest group system without first understanding the party system. So, there is a pretty important lesson here. When you are a rebel against the orthodoxy, you may find yourself in trouble because there may be more truth in that orthodoxy than you're willing to concede. In my case, I was so fixed on putting an argument together that focused on the direct relationship between interest groups and the state apparatus, that I missed the importance of parties.

Q: After this experience in Argentina, you focused next on the Portuguese case. How did Portugal affect your thinking?
A: The failure to understand Argentina led me to go to Portugal. I saw it as a living remnant of corporatism, as an item of "political archeology." I wanted to go there because it was my only chance to look back into the 1930s. And I understood Portugal perfectly well. When I went to Portugal, the first thing I learned was that the Portuguese had a so-called dominant party that didn't really exist. It was a totally fraudulent organization. It sent people to parliament, and that was all. The party was totally unimportant in terms of policy making.

The nice thing about Portugal also was that it was an easy place to do research. There were very few Portuguese social scientists. I met them all, and I could have done it in an afternoon. In the early 1970s, Portugal was a country without sociology, let alone political science. I had talked to the few Portuguese living in exile, in Geneva or Paris, who had some knowledge, albeit not very direct, about the country. But, precisely because nobody was doing any social science research, I faced few obstacles gaining access to information. The funny thing about Portugal was that people were enormously helpful, because they were flattered that someone who had worked on a really important country like Brazil wanted to work on a country like Portugal. This allowed me to gain access to mountains of data and documents that no one had looked at. I also did some interviews with officials in the extensive formal system of *gremios, casas do povo, sindicatos,* and *confederacies.* I wanted to know what their activities were, how they gained access to public officials and, of course, what their sources of finance were. In very little time, I understood exactly what was going on in Portugal. And the most important thing going on was what was *not* going on. I concluded that the Portuguese corporatist system was extremely important for understanding the perpetuation of authoritarian rule in Portugal, not for what it accomplished, but for what it prevented from happening. The corporatist institutions occupied this space of representation, which made it easy to deny any others entry into that space. I wrote several articles on Portugal based on this research (Schmitter 1975, 1978, 1979a, 1980).

Portugal also put me back in Europe. If it hadn't been for Portugal, I probably wouldn't have returned to Europe. Well, I would have been going back to Europe for family reasons, because I married a German woman. Also, my mother's family was in Southern France. So I would have been going back and forth, but not for academic reasons. Indeed, while doing my research on Portugal I realized I had an important theme for future research on Europe.

I was reading a book by Sedes Nunes, virtually the only sociologist in Portugal then tolerated by the government. He was an apologist, but no fool. He made the interesting point that while it was true that Portugal had a corporatist system with its origins firmly rooted in an authoritarian regime, though he did not use this expression, this was also true of other European countries, including some of the very ones that most criticized "fascist" Portugal. He was essentially saying that Portugal's corporatist system was a feature of modern societies. It's what the Swedes are doing; it's what the Finns and Norwegians are doing. I read that and thought, "That's kind of funny. He's absolutely right when you look at the organizational structure of interest representation in Sweden." I didn't know at the time that the main difference was that the Swedish system worked and the Portuguese system didn't. That insight came later.

So, I had this idea in the back of my mind, and one day, when I was a visiting professor at the University of Geneva, I was reading the *Tribune de Genève* and it described the workings of the interest system in Switzerland, specifically the arrangements for determining the price and quantity of milk. I thought, "This is really interesting." I then remembered Manoïlesco's (1934) distinction between state and societal corporatism. I'd forgotten that, because every country I had studied—Brazil, Argentina, and Portugal—had been characterized exclusively by state corporatism. I didn't have any research materials with me, so, when I remembered Manoïlesco, I ran across the street to the Bibliothèque Publique et Universitaire, where I found a whole section of cards on "corporatisme, Suisse" and, there, an unpublished dissertation on corporatism in Switzerland during the 1930s. I don't remember the author's name, but this dissertation described Swiss corporatism and drew a contrast that was strikingly similar to the one Manoïlesco had developed in the 1930s to distinguish the Mussolini version of state corporatism from the societal corporatism of other countries.

The idea that the concept of corporatism could be applied to contemporary Western European cases was a core insight I developed in my 1974 article, "Still the Century of Corporatism?" (Schmitter 1974), and it helped launch my research on societal corporatism. This insight also helped me develop corporatism as an alternative model to pluralism. Based on my research in Brazil, I saw *state* corporatism as an alternative model to pluralism in developing societies. I thought that capitalist development under different conditions produced different forms of class conflict, which, in turn, produced different configurations of organized interests. In making this argument, I drew on works by Alexander Gershenkron (1962), Albert Hirschman (1963), Guillermo O'Donnell (1973), CEPAL (Prebisch 1963), as well as Manoïlesco (1934). So, I was aware that corporatism gave me an alternative model for the Third World, that is, for countries that were "late dependent developers," such as Romania in the 1920s, Brazil in the 1950s and 1960s, and, for that matter, Argentina and Mexico. This framework also seemed to work well enough in Portugal. Still, I had not realized that corporatism, in its *societal* variant, could also provide a model for advanced industrial European countries. Thus, the key shift was to move from peripheral and historical cases, where I found corporatism in its statist variety, to consider the applicability of corporatism in its societal form to contemporary Western European cases.

Q: Your explanation of corporatism in Latin America differed from that of other authors who provided a cultural explanation.
A: After I did my research on Brazil, I discovered there existed a literature on corporatism in Latin America that offered a cultural explanation. It said that corporatism was somehow produced by or, at least, consistent with Iberian culture. This argument was proposed by political scientists like Howard Wiarda (1974) and historians like Ronald Newton (1974). I just couldn't believe it. I didn't understand how anybody could possibly study corporatism without recognizing it was a state-imposed arrangement. I also disagreed with the notion of an overarching "Iberian" political culture. I had had enough experience living in Mexico before I went to Brazil that I could immediately recognize that, in cultural terms, Brazil was not Mexico. The day-to-day life experience was different, and conceptions about politics were very different. To say that these countries had the same political culture was ludicrous. It was clear to me that corporatism in Brazil had absolutely nothing to do with Brazilian political culture.

Q: Your article "Still the Century of Corporatism?" (Schmitter 1974) had a large impact. Why do you think this was so?
A: The article was published in a completely obscure journal. So I didn't think it was going to have any impact whatsoever. But I can tell you both the cause and the intermediate, triggering mechanism of its impact. The real cause was that the study of interest groups had been monopolized by the pluralist paradigm, and this American perspective was being transferred from the United States to Europe. The work of Joseph LaPalombara (1964) is a good example. He studied Italian institutions as if they were pluralistic.

Even though he does a good descriptive job, there was something fundamentally wrong with his approach. There were many single country monographs on interest politics in Europe which, lacking an alternative conceptual model, described things as "imperfect" pluralism. Hence, I think the corporatism framework filled a yawning analytical gap.

The triggering mechanism that explains the success of my 1974 article was that I was not alone. Other people in European countries were starting to think about alternatives to pluralism, even if they often didn't call it corporatism. Gerhard Lehmbruch, who had studied Switzerland and Austria and was beginning to talk about "liberal" corporatism, was especially important in this regard. The combination of offering an alternative model with the fact that others were beginning to work along similar lines helps explain the impact of my article.

A final factor that explains why my work on corporatism was picked up is that, for once in my life, I was entrepreneurial. Lehmbruch and I discovered each other, and we started organizing successive meetings over several years at the ECPR (European Consortium for Political Research). That made a big difference, because many young people were interested in the topic, and the corporatist model helped people organize their thinking in a way that moved beyond the notion of degrees of pluralism.

Q: Starting most visibly with the two volumes you coedited with Gerhard Lehmbruch (Schmitter and Lehmbruch 1979; Lehmbruch and Schmitter 1982), you published a large number of articles on corporatism in Europe. What were the main issues you sought to address, and what are the main conclusions you drew from this research?
A: This research had several strands. One focused on the question, what difference does corporatism make? I'd been busy simply trying to understand how interest groups were organized, how they emerged, and how they interacted with state agencies. But I hadn't really thought about their impact. Lehmbruch was interested in this issue, and we started focusing on the impact of corporatism on political outcomes, such as governability (Schmitter 1981), and on macroeconomic outcomes, such as fiscal deficits, inflation, employment, and wages.

One of the most salient challenges to corporatism came from Marxists, who saw it as some sort of capitalist trick. So, I also addressed the consequences of corporatism at the level of classes and sought to see who benefited. That led me to the question of whether the state had a class bias (Schmitter 1985). Marxists thought the state intervened to fashion corporatism because corporatism subordinates the working class and keeps it from achieving its true revolutionary goals. I reached exactly the opposite conclusion: the problem with corporatism is that it benefits the working class, and, therefore, is vulnerable to defection by capitalists. The big challenge is for the state to keep capitalists in the game.

This research also pointed to other important conclusions. One thing that kept capitalists in the game was the presence of a Social Democratic Party in power. As a result of my longstanding blindness toward political parties, I didn't pay much attention to the interweaving between parties and interest associations. But Lehmbruch always insisted on this point. I learned from him to think not only in terms of the state/interest group nexus but also in terms of the state/party nexus. What emerged was a more triangular way of thinking that incorporated the three-way relationship among the state, interest groups, and parties.

Beyond this, I would point to two other issues addressed in my research on corporatism. The most important conclusion regarding the viability of corporatism was: be careful about capitalists. As soon as I realized that, I said, "No one is thinking about capitalists." This insight led to an independent project on the organization of business interests. With Wolfgang Streeck, I sought to understand how capitalists organize and why they organize differently in different countries and sectors, that is, why capitalists in some countries have very strong peak organizations, why they bargain at different levels across sectors, and so on. That was a whole new line of work that came out of my research on corporatism (Streeck and Schmitter 1985; Lanzalaco and Schmitter 1989; Schmitter 1990; Hollingsworth, Schmitter, and Streeck 1994).

One other, much less developed, line of research concerned the relationship between corporatism and democratic theory (Schmitter 1983). The problem, as I saw it, was that definitions of democracy assumed a pluralist component. I started thinking about this question but didn't get very far, because I was getting increasingly involved in research on democratization. So I tried to drop corporatism. I wrote a last article, "Corporatism is Dead! Long Live Corporatism!" where I said that corporatism may be momentarily declining in importance, but it will come back, and I explained why I thought so (Schmitter 1989). I dropped corporatism with that article and started working on democratization almost full-time.

Research on Democratization

Q: How did your interest in democratization evolve?
A: With the Portuguese revolution in 1974 and then with the beginning of the political transformation in Spain after the death of Franco in 1975, I started to invest more in learning about the regime-level changes in these two countries. I also began an ongoing interaction with Juan Linz in 1974,

1975, and even 1976. I don't know how important our interaction was to him, but it was very important to me. I had known Linz for a long time already. In fact, I'd met him in the 1960s when he came to a conference in Rio while I was a graduate student working on Brazil. I remember sitting for two hours with him in a little restaurant—I could still find it now just off the Copacabana Beach—talking about his concept of an "authoritarian regime" (Linz 1964). That meeting established our relationship. We were interested in very similar things, and with the events in Portugal and Spain in the 1970s, we suddenly found ourselves together on the conference circuit.

It's an experience sitting down with Linz. He has encyclopedic knowledge, and because I'd known him for a long time, we both had a lot of confidence in each other. So we spent a lot of time going back and forth with ideas, trying to figure out the different processes occurring in Portugal and Spain. Grappling with these two cases sensitized me to the idea of modes of transition, of distinct paths to democracy. Still, I was very convinced, right from the start—I never wavered on this point—that, despite their different modes of transition, Portugal and Spain would end up in the same place. I was much more convinced than Linz that Spain would become a perfectly normal, even rather boring, country. I was also convinced that Portugal, too, was going to make it and become an even more boring polity in ten years. So, even though the process of getting there was different—Spain was obviously having a much more controlled, pacted transition than Portugal—I was convinced they were both going to end up becoming routine European democracies.

Q: You started a project with Guillermo O'Donnell that involved a series of conferences at the Woodrow Wilson Center in Washington during 1979–81. These conferences later resulted in the publication in 1986 of an influential collaborative volume on transitions from authoritarianism (O'Donnell, Schmitter, and Whitehead 1986). How did your collaboration with O'Donnell alter the way you were studying democratization?[6]
A: Until the opportunity to work with O'Donnell arose, I was moving exclusively within a circle of Southern European scholars. Above all, the experience of repeated interactions with Linz, trying to explain to each other what was happening in Spain and Portugal, was critical to shaping my thinking. Indeed, I see these interactions as an important prelude to the Woodrow Wilson Center project I did with O'Donnell. Then O'Donnell and I met at a conference at Yale. We had become friends before and had

6. See the interview with O'Donnell in Chapter 9 for his perspective on the project on regime transitions.

seen each other fairly often. We discussed the idea of bringing together the Southern Europeans and Latin Americans. Now, at that point in time, you had the Portuguese, Spanish, and Greek cases of democratization. But things weren't changing much in Latin America. One famous effort at political reform had been made in Brazil in 1974, with President Ernesto Geisel's proposal for a policy of *distensão* (distension). But none of us took it seriously. At least when we started our project, we had no particular reason to be optimistic about democratization in Latin America.

My collaboration with O'Donnell made me think about studying democratization through much broader comparisons. I was the Southern European part, and he was the Latin American part. Still, this forced me to learn more about Spain and also Greece, about which I knew a lot less. Also, I was interested in both the European and Latin American sides.

Working with the large, interregional working group that O'Donnell and I put together was a real experience. I was the only person at these meetings who initially knew everybody in the room. I knew the Southern Europeans, and I had also worked with almost all the Latin Americans. O'Donnell obviously knew all the Latin Americans but only one or two of the Southern Europeans. Few of the rest of the group knew each other. Still, we were able to develop a capacity to understand each other, even when someone was using a different language. For one, we had all read each other's work. Moreover, from the very start, we all shared the view that we had a very big problem before us, because according to the orthodoxy of that time, the countries we were interested in should *not* be successful at democratizing. Actually, our assumption was that, in light of existing theories about the prerequisites of democracy and the big problems these Southern European and Latin American countries faced, most were going to fail, and, at best, one in three would succeed in becoming democracies. This is where Albert Hirschman's (1992) concept of possibilism came in. We agreed to think possibilistically, not probabilistically, about what could work to achieve democracy in the countries we were studying.

Q: Could you elaborate on how you understood the literature on democratization at the time and the innovations you sought to introduce?
A: We were facing two literatures. One, to which I just alluded, emphasized the social structural and cultural "prerequisites" countries needed to fulfill before becoming democratic (Lipset 1959; Moore 1966). We responded to this literature by emphasizing possibilism. The second body of literature stressed the implications of the model of democratization fashioned in Britain, the Low Countries, and Scandinavia (Rustow 1970). One implication of this model was that democratization was a long, slow process based

on the gradual enfranchisement of citizens and the progressive widening of political liberties. A second implication was that, in order for democratization to occur, the previously dominant group in a country had to tolerate, for an extensive period of time, the mobilization of excluded groups. A third implication, which I was not aware of at the time, concerned the international context. A common argument in this literature, for example, is that the process of democratization in Britain was shaped by what had occurred before in France, especially the French Revolution. In this regard, this literature emphasized the antirevolutionary, reformist aspect of democratization, drawing attention to the recomposition of the old ruling elites alongside the mobilization of excluded groups from below.

We responded to this second body of literature by trying to find an alternative model, or set of models, for regime change that were neither reformist nor revolutionary, and which could work even if a country lacked a national bourgeoisie and an organized working class. Terry Karl's (1986) work was very important in this regard, because she had been working on Venezuela and had already developed an alternative model of pacted transitions. Her model fit nicely with the democratization experience the Spanish were going through at the time.

Q: Your own efforts to develop a model of democratization strongly reflect the influence of Machiavelli (Schmitter 1979b).
A: It suddenly occurred to me that Machiavelli was *the* theorist of regime change. I don't know why this came to me—maybe because I was teaching at the European University Institute and living in Florence at the time. I plunged into Machiavelli and read everything by him I could find, including his letters. And I came up with a pure Machiavellian interpretation of regime transitions. Quite self-consciously, Machiavelli did not consider himself a theorist of normal politics. He calls transitions "female times," that is, extraordinary contexts in which you can't trust anyone and when there are no agreed-upon rules. To study such moments, he said, you need a new political science. What I got from Machiavelli was that a distinctive set of assumptions about politics is required to study transitions.

Q: Your working assumption circa 1980 that only one in three of the cases you and your collaborators in the regime transitions project were studying would become democracies turned out to have been overly pessimistic.
A: Democratizing turned out to be much easier than I thought. At the time, I certainly expected most of these countries were not going to make it, and I was clearly wrong in thinking only one in three would have a successful transition to democracy. We all misunderstood the change in context that

made democratization a much more likely outcome of attempted regime change. We have since learned that democratizing is easier, yet also much less consequential in socioeconomic terms, than we used to think. Today, the non-elite groups that historically struggled for democracy make compromises where they accept a great deal less than they would have in the past, perhaps because of previous failures and a process of collective learning. As a result, inequitable systems of property rights survive many transitions to democracy without a scratch. And in some cases, for example, in Eastern Europe, income inequality has even gotten worse—deliberately worse—after democratization. So, democratizing is easier today precisely because it's less consequential. This is not terribly heartening. It's not what the people who struggled for democracy had expected. They compromised and accepted maybe even their third best alternative, because they had learned that going for the first best option by pushing immediately for socioeconomic redistribution can bring disaster.

Q: Adam Przeworski was brought into the transitions project and wrote a chapter for *Transitions from Authoritarian Rule* (Przeworski 1986). What do you see as his contribution to the analysis of transitions?[7]
A: Przeworski made fundamental contributions. One of the things he is most responsible for is the argument that legitimacy is neither the problem nor the solution of democratization. Many people were arguing that the reason authoritarian regimes collapsed was their lack of legitimacy. Later, people argued that a democracy requires legitimacy to become consolidated. Well, that argument is completely circular. One implication of his argument was that attitudinal variables, legitimacy-oriented ones, do not tell us much about the consolidation of democracy. Przeworski was very clear in his critique of these assumptions. O'Donnell and I were probably thinking along these lines already, but Przeworski has a nice way of capturing these insights and getting them into apodictic, declarative form. That was a very important contribution.

The other thing Adam did was emphasize the fundamental role of uncertainty in democratic regimes, a point he continued to develop afterward and summarized nicely in the phrase that "democracy is a system in which parties lose elections" (Przeworski 1991, 10). My view of the idea of "contingent consent" is something quite similar (O'Donnell and Schmitter 1986, 59–61). Essentially, you consent contingently to let your opponents rule, because you think the rules are fair and that you will get the chance under those same rules to come to power in the future. But I also see this

---

7. See the interview with Przeworksi in Chapter 13 for his view of the project on transitions from authoritarian rule.

uncertainty as more bounded than does Przeworski. The way to guarantee that uncertainty is tolerated is by making sure it's not very consequential, that is, by putting limits around it that restrict the range of choices facing politicians to a very narrow set of options.

One of the nice things about working with scholars like Przeworski and O'Donnell is that in many cases I cannot honestly tell you who is responsible for which ideas. This was especially the case with O'Donnell. There are a few parts of our book, *Transitions from Authoritarian Rule* (O'Donnell and Schmitter 1986), which I know he wrote and which I know I wrote. But I couldn't tell you who was really responsible for 80 percent of the book. We produced it through a process of going back and forth and arguing with each other. That kind of genuine collaborative work, that yields a final product in which you can't identify specifically where the ideas came from, is great. Terry Karl and I achieve that when we write together.[8] We don't know afterward who had an idea first. We simply know that the idea was generated by both of us. With Przeworski, the interaction has been much less intense, but I also feel sometimes that I do not know where a certain idea originated. He and I have different ways of expressing things, and we use different concepts, but many of our ideas are the same.

Q: But you and Przeworski also have different views on many issues.
A: Yes. Still, we both characterize transitions as periods of uncertainty, and we both emphasize the choices of the actors involved in transitions. Przeworski and I differ in that he uses the concepts and accepts the prior assumptions of rational choice theory, whereas I don't. I believe that this theory is inappropriate for analyzing transition situations, because certain of its assumptions, especially the proposition that actors fully understand the consequences of their actions and those of their opponents, simply do not hold in such instances.

I also differ from Przeworski on another matter: whether the mode of regime transition has a lasting effect on the outcome of transitions.[9] He thinks the mode of transition does not have a lasting effect, whereas I think it does. Let's take a good example, Spain and Portugal. These countries had very different modes of transition. Both are now stable, Western, liberal democracies, but they are nevertheless different types of democracy, especially in terms of institutionalized power relations. For example, in Portugal 35 to 40 percent of the workers, a relatively large share of the working force, are members of the trade union movement, whereas in Spain the corresponding figure is only 5 to 8 percent. Remarkably, the situation was ex-

8. Schmitter's collaborative work with Terry Karl includes Karl and Schmitter (1991) and Schmitter and Karl (1991, 1994).

9. Compare Przeworski (1991, 95–99) and Karl and Schmitter (1991, 1992).

actly the opposite before the transition, when the Spanish trade unions were larger proportionately than the Portuguese. There are some serious continuing differences across the two cases that, I believe, can be explained by the contrasting mode of transition.

Q: Did you expect *Transitions from Authoritarian Rule,* and, in particular, your volume with O'Donnell (O'Donnell and Schmitter 1986), would have a huge impact?
A: No. The project was cross-regional, which was rather novel, and I guess we assumed it would have an impact in research on the two regions on which the project focused, Southern Europe and Latin America. But we didn't have the faintest idea that studying regime transitions would become the growth industry of political science in the subsequent decades. There is not a word in our book that predicted that transitions from authoritarian regimes would happen elsewhere. We had no reason even to believe that large parts of Central America and Latin America would democratize. Moreover, the collapse of authoritarian regimes in Eastern Europe came as a total surprise to me, as it was to the people in that region. I and, I suspect, Guillermo, too, never imagined the sheer scope and extent of the emerging wave of democratization.

Now, I do not think the fact that all these other democratizations occurred is the only thing that explains the book's success. I also think we put something back into political science that Machiavelli knew a lot about, but had been lost. The "Little Green Book" sought to capture something about a crucial political moment as seen from the point of view of politicians, not from the point of view of academics.[10] O'Donnell and I tried to think like politicians and put ourselves in their shoes. This allowed us to reach a wide audience beyond academia. I have heard that many politicians have read the book and recognized in it the situations and choices they were making. This made the book part of the political process, not just something external to it. Our book may even have helped some countries get through their transitions. I was told that the book became a sort of bible to the South Africans and made a direct contribution to their process of regime change. I was told the same thing in Hungary, where the elite on both sides seem to have read it. And Nelson Mandela told somebody to tell somebody to tell me that he had read the book when he was in prison, and it inspired him to hope a transition could happen in South Africa. That's when I thought, "Yeah, I guess we did a good job."

Still, whether the book makes a lasting contribution to political science

10. The "Little Green Book" refers to O'Donnell and Schmitter's *Transitions from Authoritarian Rule* (1986), which had a green jacket.

will depend a great deal on whether these moments of regime change make a significant difference in the long run. If, as Adam Przeworski suggests, the mode of transition does not have a lasting effect, and structural/cultural variables such as the level and rate of development or the prevailing religion are determinant instead, then our ideas about transitions will not prove that important.

Q: In the wake of your 1986 book with O'Donnell, you have explored whether the model, or parts of the model, presented in that book can be extended to new cases and regions beyond Southern Europe and Latin America.

A: I have been trying to see how much I can extend those arguments to determine what sticks and what doesn't, what travels and what doesn't. I have done this in several articles with Terry Karl (Karl and Schmitter 1991; Schmitter and Karl 1991, 1994). I started this exercise as I came in touch with people from all over the world who were becoming interested and involved in the process of democratization.

There is a lot of interest in these kinds of broad comparisons. But there is resistance, too, of course. The idea of including the central European countries and the former republics of the Soviet Union in the same universe is difficult for some people to swallow. Resistance comes especially from those who believe these cases differ in terms of their historical point of departure or have radical cultural differences. For example, most of the literature on the Middle East begins with the presumption that Islam is so different that the Middle East cannot be fruitfully compared with other regions. I don't believe this (Schmitter and Hutchinson 1999). More important, my approach is to include these cases in my overall sample, so I can then partition my data and see whether relationships vary from region to region. The important thing is to start with a large N if you can get good data, which is not easy to come by. Generating these data is very time-consuming and expensive.

Q: Is this work part of a book-length project on democratization?

A: Yes, but so far, all I have is bits and pieces. I've been trying to finish this project for a very long time and get it off my desk. But I keep coming up with different things I feel I should include. For example, someone once mentioned to me, "You can't possibly write a book on this topic without including women." Then, by coincidence, somebody invited me to a conference on women and democratization. So I wrote a paper and that became another chapter. Then, of course, there is the international dimension, which I never paid enough attention to earlier on. I do not think O'Donnell and I were mistaken when we said that the processes of democratization we were analyzing were fundamentally driven by domestic, not international, forces. The situation is different now. Today, when a country democratizes, it gets invaded, not just by NGOs, but also by the European Union, the United States Agency for International Development (US AID), and all these different democracy promotion programs. They commit substantial resources, and they meddle in the internal politics of democratizing countries in ways that were unthinkable in the late 1970s and early 1980s, when we were studying the Southern European and Latin American cases. So now I am working on the international dimension of democratization (Schmitter and Brouwer 2000; Offe and Schmitter 1998).

Q: This emphasis on the international dimension of democratization dovetails nicely with your research on the European Union (EU).
A: The driving edge of my research now concerns issues of democratization in the context of the EU, a question about which I have recently written a book (Schmitter 2000a).[11] This continues my personal effort to promote democratization wherever it rears its benevolent head. I am treating the EU as a transitional polity, a polity in formation, which has not reached an institutional equilibrium. The question is whether democracy can be inserted into this process of producing an entity composed of previously sovereign states. That's absolutely the top political issue in Europe today. I may not think the EU should constitutionalize itself, but I do think the transitional mechanisms that should be applied in the EU are exactly the opposite of the ones that are desirable in national-level transitions. I am firmly convinced that the earlier a country constitutionalizes its politics, through a Spanish-style process of genuine consensus building and popular ratification, the better. But I argue just the opposite at the EU level. The EU should not constitutionalize itself right away; rather, it should do so gradually and only after public opinion has manifested its support for such a process. I think the EU should take fifteen years to get itself a constitution and become a democracy.[12] Only after Europe has actually felt the impact of a large-scale transfer of authority to supranational institutions and only after controversies about this have created a distinctively "European" public sphere should the EU make the effort to define its *finalité politique*.

Q: To summarize, what do you see as your main contributions over the past twenty-five years to the study of democratization?
A: I am not sure I can answer this question, certainly not objectively. Moreover, I have been repeatedly surprised by how other scholars have re-

11. Schmitter's writings on the European Union also include Schmitter (1997a, 2000b, 2003).
12. Subsequent to this interview, the proposed EU constitution was rejected by French and Dutch voters in mid-2005.

sponded to my work on this subject. Some of this must be due to my convoluted style of writing, my uncontrollable inclusion of foreign words and even invention of new ones, and my insistence on stretching comparisons across rather than confining them within regions. Hence, what I see as my major contributions probably does not track with what others would judge them to be, positively or negatively.

This is what I hope to have accomplished:

1. To have helped convert the study of democracy from a static to a dynamic enterprise.
2. To have undermined the myth that democracy is a luxury that only rich countries with an Anglo-Saxon "civic" political culture can afford.
3. To have tried to convince scholars that democracy is not always produced by democratic means and that it is possible for non-democrats to make a positive contribution to democratization.
4. In a similar line, to have pointed out that elites acting "from above" can be just as important, if not more important, than citizens acting "from below" to the success of transitions from autocracy.
5. To have shifted the discipline of political science from its obsession with political parties, territorial representation, and competitive elections toward increased attention to interest associations, functional representation, and policy making by pressure and/or concertation.
6. To have encouraged political scientists to think in *inter*regional, rather than *intra*regional, terms and to consider democratization as a generic process, despite its obvious national and subnational peculiarities.
7. Finally, following Machiavelli, to have defended the notion that there can be no one science of politics or even of democratic politics, but that its core assumptions, concepts, hypotheses, and methods must vary according to the context in which politics is practiced. At a minimum, this means one science for orderly situations in which actors know and more or less accept the rules of the game, and another for those in which the actors do not even know who they and their allies are, even less what the rules are. Machiavelli called these "male" and "female" times. Political science still pretends that this is what separates its subdisciplines of comparative politics and international relations.

Core Ideas and Their Reception

Q: Your research has had three major strands: one focused on corporatism, a second on regimes and democratization, and a third on EU integration. How are these research strands related? Do you connect them in your mind and have a way of synthesizing them?

A: I've been asked this question a few times before. I once met someone who thought I was three different "Schmitters," because she didn't understand how I could make these topics fit together. I do see a common thread to my research: interests, politics understood as the pursuit of interests, and the emergence and resolution of conflicts related to the pursuit of interests, at multiple levels of aggregation.

In this sense, I'm an old-fashioned social scientist who does not follow recent trends. I really believe you have to study capital and labor, and I see class, sectoral, and professional associations as the core of civil society. So, for example, when students tell me they want to study social movements and "the grass roots"—and I have had many such students—I say, first study capitalists, because they are the anchors of civil society, then study workers. Maybe I'm wrong, but I have never been a social movements person. I don't care about bowling clubs and even less about "bowling alone."[13] I've never given much credence to the idea of movement-based democracy. I always regarded that notion as an illusion. I can imagine having a corporatist-based democracy, with very little significant political party activity. But the core of democracy is missing unless the bargaining relationship between capital and labor is nailed down and somehow institutionalized.

Q: What do you think are your best ideas?
A: In a sense, I don't have any new ideas. My best ideas are ones I get from somebody else, often by disinterring them from an obscure source. I really mean that. Everything there is to say about politics has already been said, somewhere. I can't think of anything I have said that I would call genuinely original, though maybe I am using too high a standard. I may have brought things together in an original way or introduced preexisting ideas into a different context. Your question reminds me of my frustrated career as a painter. I didn't do anything original with painting, but there, at least, I knew what originality was, and I wanted to produce something that no-body had done before. I failed. In the social sciences, by contrast, it's very hard to do anything really original. You can combine old things in new ways or take something and put it in a different place. You can say things in a way people haven't heard before. But real originality . . . there isn't much.

Q: Still, your work on corporatism did alter the way interest groups were studied by providing an alternative to the dominant pluralist paradigm. Your contribution in this area could be seen as part of the influential literature that "brought the state back in" (Evans, Rueschemeyer, and Skocpol 1985).

13. The allusion here is to Putnam's *Bowling Alone* (2000).

A: Let me give a two-part answer to this question. First, the literature on corporatism critiqued pluralism and did introduce some new elements into the discussion. Gabriel Almond, in a piece in *World Politics,* stated that many of the ideas in the literature on corporatism were already developed in the work of pluralists (Almond 1983). I disagree. Maybe it's my own failing, but when I was working on my dissertation, I read the pluralists and did not come across the ideas that were later associated with a corporatist approach to interest groups. For example, Harry Eckstein went to Norway, one of the most corporatist nations in Europe, and yet did not find corporatism (Eckstein 1966). Instead, he came back from Norway with his congruence theory, a cultural theory positing that stable democracy is based on the congruence between cultural norms and authority patterns. Eckstein completely overlooked the fact that democracy in Norway was based on a well-organized system of capital-labor relations that had operated since the 1930s. Eckstein went to Norway to study interest groups, yet he failed even to mention this basic fact! This omission is quite incredible. So, yes, the pluralists did have an interest in interest groups, but they did not conceptualize interest groups in a corporatist way at all.

Second, I find exaggerated the claims of works such as Theda Skocpol et al.'s *Bringing the State Back In* (Evans, Rueschemeyer, and Skocpol 1985; Skocpol 1985a). You could say I was a member of that movement without knowing it. Obviously, the state was part of what I was addressing when I talked about corporatism as opposed to pluralism. Even societal corporatism has an extremely important state component. Those institutional configurations were not possible without the coercive power of the state. But I remember my first reaction when I saw the title, "bringing the state back in." I thought, "What do you mean? The state has been there all along. Who needs to bring it back in?" Only an American could write something like that. Anybody working on Europe or Latin America, almost without exception, didn't need to be told to bring the state back in.

Q: Do you have regrets about anything you wrote or did not write?
A: Let me mention two regrets, both related to my work on corporatism. One concerns the term *corporatism* itself. I once met Norberto Bobbio, the dean of Italian political thought, and a marvelous man. He was eighty-five years old at the time, and he came up to me, grabbed me by the lapels of my jacket, and said, "Ah, you're Schmitter. I find your work very interesting. But why did you have to call it corporatism?" Bobbio had lived through and struggled against an earlier version of corporatism during Mussolini's time. To apply the term *corporatism* to contemporary, democratic polities must have seemed to him to be stretching the concept beyond recognition. He had a point. One has to be careful about choosing one's terms, and it would

have been much better if I had been more imaginative in coming up with a new label instead of borrowing a normatively loaded, previously existing term. The use of the suffix *neo-* in front of *corporatism,* a practice adopted by several people, probably helped, though I didn't think of that. Instead, I used the terms *state coporatism* and *societal corporatism.*

The other side of this issue is that the use of the term *corporatism* was a great merchandising tool, because it annoyed people. The term did not have this effect in Brazil or Argentina, because a literature existed in those countries that talked about it. But, when the term *corporatism* was applied to developed European countries, it became provocative. That effect was positive, because it forced people to pay attention to aspects of interest group systems in Europe that simply could not be dismissed.

My second regret concerns how I conceptualized corporatism. I included a very large number of variables in my definition.[14] That seems excessive now, and I think it was a mistake. It probably would have been better if I had not been so elaborate, if I had focused instead on a smaller number of dimensions, say, four or five, rather than the nineteen I have been told are there. This would have been an improvement from an operational standpoint. At the time, I thought I could use my elaborate definition in a narrative, descriptive, "ideal-typical" way and that it would be self-evident whether, say, Austria, Finland, or the Netherlands was corporatist. But, later on, when I started to study corporatism quantitatively, I realized my definition was difficult to operationalize.

Q: After working on corporatism in Brazil, you shifted to Europe, but you never carried out an explicitly cross-regional comparison focused on corporatism. Indeed, the literatures on corporatism in Europe and Latin America are somewhat divorced. Did you ever attempt to launch a cross-regional project on corporatism?
A: No, and I have a twofold explanation for this. First, in 1974, the Portuguese revolution happened, and my interests shifted from corporatism to democratization. Second, in Europe, I worked with Gerhard Lehmbruch and all sorts of other people in the European Consortium of Political Research (ECPR). Though the ECPR was very effective both at organizing workshops to discuss different aspects of corporatism and at spurring the writing of monographs on different countries, we did not have the money

14. Schmitter's (1974, 93–94) definition is as follows: "Corporatism can be defined as a system of interest representation in which the constituent units are organized into a limited number of singular, compulsory, noncompetitive, hierarchically ordered and functionally differentiated categories, recognized or licensed (if not created) by the state and granted a deliberate representational monopoly within their respective categories in exchange for observing certain controls on their selection of leaders and articulation of demands and supports."

to organize something like the Woodrow Wilson project, which brought together the Southern Europeans and Latin Americans to address regime transitions. Remember, initially corporatism was not a fashionable topic. Besides, our ECPR group did not have an entrepreneur like Abe Lowenthal, who got the money for the Woodrow Wilson project. I must confess that I am very lazy when it comes to fund-raising. I don't like to spend my time writing proposals and administering projects. So, I didn't even try to put together an interregional working group on corporatism. Still, the main reason I never tried to launch a cross-regional project on corporatism was that I got completely swept up in the Portuguese revolution, and then the Woodrow Wilson project on transitions enticed me into focusing on a topic that I thought was at least as important as corporatism, maybe more.

Q: Do you think any of your ideas have been misinterpreted?
A: One constantly experiences frustration with the way others use one's writings. But the only matter I truly worry about is a misinterpretation of my work with O'Donnell on transitions (O'Donnell and Schmitter 1986). Some people mistakenly think we were proposing a permanent shift to an actor-centered, strategic perspective as a new vision of politics for all times. What we said, in fact, is that an emphasis on actors' strategies is justified during a regime transition, a particular and very important moment of time. This emphasis does not apply to normal politics. Indeed, under these circumstances, I generally take a rather determinist historical-institutional view and don't pay much attention to the strategies followed by individual actors.

One other thing that annoys me is many people said O'Donnell and I were writing about transitions *to* democracy, when the title of our book explicitly states that we were studying transitions *from* authoritarian rule. This seems to be a persistent misunderstanding. Yet we very consciously sought to avoid a teleological view. Indeed, this was one of the first things on which O'Donnell and I agreed. We genuinely did not know whether the authoritarian regimes we were studying would end up as democracies, or, if they did become democracies, how long they might survive. I can't speak for O'Donnell, but I am genuinely surprised both by how long the democracies that emerged during the past thirty years in Southern Europe and Latin America have survived and by how well they have done.

Q: How have you responded to your critics?
A: I have received a lot of criticism from both the Left and the Right, but I only answered critiques that made me think again about what I had originally written. If I did not agree with an insubstantial part of the criticism, or if the critique seemed clearly unfounded, I would not bother to reply. I used

to worry: "I'm not responding enough to my critics." Also, I thought that if I replied to more of them, it would help me clarify my own thoughts. But if I had responded to more critics, I simply would have had no time to do anything else.

The Process and Goals of Research
Classics

Q: What role do the classics of political and social theory play in your thinking?
A: For me, engaging the classics is almost automatic. I start by thinking about the nature of the problem on which I want to work, and then I ask myself, "Who's said something about this?" Sometimes it is simply a matter of having these classic works in your head, having read them. For example, with the issue of regime transitions, I almost immediately hit upon Machiavelli. It just made sense. My first instinct is to go through my own memory of what I have read in political thought. Another way to start thinking through a problem is to identify an analogous moment, situation, or structure in the past. For example, many people who study the breakdown of democracy start by thinking back to the Weimar Republic, a historic failure of democracy.

Cases and Concepts

Q: What role does knowledge of cases play in your thinking?
A: I get the most out of a case when I'm facing it initially and trying to figure it out. I'm a puzzle solver. As we discussed, I couldn't figure out the Argentine puzzle, but I did figure out other ones. I get the maximum return from that initial encounter.

Q: Once you get to know a country, do you keep up with events there?
A: Only to a certain extent. Take Portugal. I do not read regularly and systematically on Portugal. I would even forget about it for a while, but then something interesting would happen in Portugal, or an opportunity would arise, and I would catch up. Also, you can't just walk away from a country after you have done research there. You make friends and have a commitment to it. You may even write pieces that prove useful to people in that country. As a matter of fact, not long ago I collected all the things I had written about Portugal and ended up with an eight hundred-page book (Schmitter 1999). Still, there are diminishing marginal returns after the first encounter.

I try to dissuade students from working on a single country or region. You need to move around, even though working on a single country may have benefits from a purely professional point of view, because you can build a reputation as the best person working on, say, Argentina. I tell students, "Get the hell out of Argentina and go to Italy, Mongolia, wherever." The potential downside of this strategy is that some people will say, "He moves around too much. He does not know as much as he should about the country he is working on." But that is not an inexorable problem. In my own case, once I get a hold of a country, I work pretty hard to get into it, both historically and linguistically. I usually start with the secondary literature written by "native" social scientists, if it exists. And I read novels or even travelers' accounts, if I suspect I will have to go farther back in time. Since I started out with autocracies—Brazil, Argentina, and Portugal—I paid relatively little attention to newspapers. But now that I work virtually exclusively on countries with a free and competitive press, I find reading them very important.

Q: One obstacle to pursuing a strategy of moving from country to country is the difficulty of doing fieldwork—an ideal way to get a feel for a new country—as one advances in one's career.
A: When it comes to fieldwork, I don't think it's a matter of diminishing returns. Fieldwork continues to be both the most productive and exciting part of what we do. It is also a humanly interesting aspect of the work of a comparativist. I certainly feel that way, even though I get very frustrated when I'm in the field. Everything takes so much more time and the exact data one wants are almost never available. Also, fieldwork does become increasingly difficult to do, either because of family and professional obligations or the enormous amount of energy it requires. I'm not sure I could do it again at my age. I do fieldwork vicariously now, through my students. I get them to talk to me about their interviews, and I try to get a feel for that experience. Now that I have a certain standing inside the European Union, I do meet many illustrious people, including presidents and prime ministers. I learn more about politics by talking to people who have to make political choices than from anything else. But this kind of interaction is different from field research. It is not as much fun as doing interviews, as getting over the resistance of people to talk and tell you about things.

Q: Throughout your career you have played an important role shaping and clarifying concepts such as corporatism and democracy, which have been pivotal to large literatures (Schmitter 1974; Schmitter and Karl 1991). Could you discuss your approach to concept formation? Is there a trick to successful concept formation?
A: I wish I knew more about this matter. Somebody like Max Weber knew how to form complex, multifaceted concepts, that is, so-called ideal types.

In terms of myself, it's something that comes easily but unself-consciously. What I try to do is detect an underlying pattern, to discern the common element that lies beneath all the surface variation in particular cases. For example, in my piece with Terry Karl on democracy, we try to develop a generic, institution-free definition of democracy. That's why we focused on accountability and the reciprocal roles of citizens and rulers. We don't say that representatives have to be elected, that you need parliamentary sovereignty, or even that you need a parliament at all. Rather, we emphasize the need for regular, reliable mechanisms of mutual accountability.

In most instances, I am not inventing things *ex novo*. In the case of corporatism, the concept was lying around in older writings by authors such as Manoïlesco. It hadn't been used in a while, but it was there. I didn't have to invent it, though I did have to define it in a new way.

One thing I find useful in forming concepts is always to consider the antonym. If you are trying to develop a theory of integration, you must also have a theory of disintegration. You must understand both together. If you seek to define an integrated Europe, you must also imagine a disintegrated Europe. Thinking in terms of polarities is a useful means of concept formation. That's what I did with corporatism and pluralism. I put them in the same box, which nobody had done before, and then defined them in an antonymic way. This exercise helps nail down the "ideal-typical" ends, the extremes. Of course, everything in the real world is located somewhere in between, and it's an important and difficult challenge to imagine stable intermediary patterns. Still, nailing down the ends is a very useful device in forming a concept. The trick is to find an underlying pattern, imagine its opposite, and then nail down the ends.

I should add, however, that a lot of my conceptualizations derive simply from talking to real people, including politicians and interest group leaders. I listen closely to the words political actors themselves use in talking and describing what they do. For example, I've recently become a big enthusiast of so-called Euro-speak, the new language the European Union is inventing to talk about its politics, which are so different that they require a whole new vocabulary. Also, I have been lucky to have worked and lived in Brazil and Italy, two countries with marvelously imaginative political vocabularies. I am currently the editor of the Italian section of *Les Intraduisibles: The Dictionary of Untranslatable Political Terms,* and have identified eighty-seven untranslatable Italian terms.[15] I discovered a new one just the other day, *un pianista.* Do you know what a *pianista* is? Literally, it means a piano player, but the term also refers to the deputies in parliament who vote for

15. This dictionary can be accessed at www.concepts-methods.org/dictionary_intraduisi bles.php.

their neighbor when he or she is absent. The Italian parliament has electronic voting, and each deputy punches a code and a key to vote. There are pictures of deputies with their arms extended to either side punching in the votes of their absent colleagues as if they were playing a piano. *Pianista* is a perfect term for this; as soon as you hear it, you know exactly what it means. This aside is meant to suggest that one way of stimulating concept formation is to work or live in countries where politics is a lively matter and people are constantly inventing political terms. If you're lucky, people will use expressions you do not know, but when they explain them, you will discover that these expressions disguise important relationships that cannot be confessed openly or that they convey something distinctive for which no generic word exists. Listening closely to the words actors use to talk about their politics is an important way to study it.

Work Modes and Collaborators

Q: Since your book on Brazil (Schmitter 1971), you have mainly written articles and book chapters. Is there a reason why you have published mostly articles, not books?
A: I move too fast. I am impatient and like being challenged by new things. As soon as I feel something is old or settled, I lose interest and move on. That way of working does not lend itself to writing book-length manuscripts. So I have mainly produced articles.

Q: You have also done a fair amount of collaborative work.
A: Over the years I have collaborated with Gerhard Lehmbruch, Wolfgang Streeck, Guillermo O'Donnell, Terry Karl, and now Claus Offe.[16]

Q: Why do you collaborate, and how do you pick your collaborators?
A: The goal of collaborative work is to end up with a product that is better than what can be produced individually. Several factors make this outcome more likely. I have sought to work with people who have a background different from my own. This means my coauthors are usually foreigners, and they often have a different academic background, though not always in the sense of being trained in a different discipline.

I always collaborate with people whom I consider my intellectual equals. And I collaborate with people with whom I share many assumptions about

16. See Schmitter and Lehmbruch (1979), Lehmbruch and Schmitter (1982), Streeck and Schmitter (1985), Hollingsworth, Schmitter, and Streeck (1994), O'Donnell, Schmitter, and Whitehead (1986), Karl and Schmitter (1991), Schmitter and Karl (1991, 1994), and Offe and Schmitter (1998).

politics, which means people with "left of center" values. When you co-author, you have to share many views, but you also should disagree. You want to make sure you will discuss your disagreements in a productive way, rather than fighting over stupid or minor things. With all my collaborators, there is a huge number of things about which we initially seem to totally disagree. But we work on those disagreements and try to resolve them creatively. Let me give you an example. O'Donnell and I disagreed a lot when we started working on the transitions project. We had many fundamental agreements, but we also thought we had fundamental differences. Yet, in writing *Tentative Conclusions about Uncertain Democracies* (O'Donnell and Schmitter 1986), we never resolved our differences by resorting to bland compromises. We always tried to resolve them by coming up with a better solution than either of us started out with. That's the right kind of collaborator.

I've been very lucky. I've had incredibly good collaborators, and all have remained close personal friends of mine afterward. I know of collaborations where this was not the case. I am still very close to all the people with whom I have collaborated, and I would work with them again if the opportunity arose.

Science, History, and Political Engagement

Q: How would you describe the goals of your research? Do you see yourself as a scientist?
A: I seek to produce generalizations. Yet, I also see my work as always bounded by time and space. I am usually very explicit about the time period and range of countries on which I am working at a given moment. I never talk about politics in general. I do not buy into the universalistic aspirations of behavioralism and rational choice theory. That's just not the way I think about science and about what I do. I think the human sciences are fundamentally historical. Thus, you must specify the temporal and geographical context within which the generalizations you are working toward are valid. As Aristotle says, one of the first things you should understand about a science is that it must be true to its subject matter. This means there are many kinds of science, not just one kind. For me, the subject matter of politics is historical. If political science is to become a science, it will be a historical science.

Q: How do you see the link between your academic work and the world of politics?
A: I have never been a regular party person, partly because I've always been on the run and never lived much in any one place. I feel a little bit

more grounded now in Italy. I have a relationship to the democratic *centro-sinistra* (Center-Left). But it's still as an outsider.

The first and only time in my life that I agreed to advise a government—I now occasionally advise the European Commission, but I don't think of it as advising a government—was in 1974–75, when it was rumored that Henry Kissinger thought it would be a good idea if Portugal went communist. He thought this would inoculate other Western European countries from communism and help destroy all the domestic communist parties in the region. Well, the State Department was about to send Frank Carlucci as U.S. ambassador to Portugal. Carlucci was a notorious CIA type who, as a matter of fact, had denounced me in Brazil as "an enemy of the Pan-American system." I was asked to go to Washington to brief Carlucci on Portuguese politics. It was my view, and it still is, that my job is to produce works that are public. Indeed, I believe very much in the public nature of the social sciences, and I am opposed to having social scientists whispering things in the ears of rulers. But I did it this one time. I went to Washington and talked with Carlucci.

Seeking to counter the perspective that aimed to foment a red scare and thus trigger a U.S. intervention, I told Carlucci that Portugal was one of the most conservative countries in Europe, it was not going to go communist, and the Portuguese could take care of things themselves. Soon thereafter, Carlucci went to Portugal and did the exact opposite of what I expected. He made sure we didn't force the Portuguese into anything, and he essentially became the architect of the alliance among the United States, Germany, and Britain in support of the Portuguese Socialist Party. Carlucci deserves a lot of credit. He went into a situation where there was every reason to believe he would interpret things in a viscerally anticommunist way. Instead, he saw that Portugal was basically a conservative country and concluded that all the United States had to do was support the Socialist Party and wait. He was right.

Colleagues and Students

Q: You have basically worked at three institutions, the University of Chicago (1967–82), Stanford University (1986–96), and the European University Institute (1982–86, 1996–present). What was your experience like at these three places?

A: They are very different institutions. Chicago was by far the best from an academic perspective. It was a most stimulating department for three reasons. First, it was a very nonhierarchical department, despite having some very notable types like David Easton, Morton Kaplan, and Hans Morgenthau in it. Junior people had the same rights as seniors, and could teach the courses they wanted to. We were all equal in most regards, except for obvious things, like the ability to vote on tenure decisions. Second, Chicago had an unusually communicative department. This was due partly to an ecological factor: most of the faculty lived in the same neighborhood. As a result, we saw each other all the time and met in coffeehouses as well as in the classroom. We often ended up as best friends. Third, even though we were a very egocentric, strong-minded bunch of people, who liked to argue with each other, the lines of cleavage never became polarized. This had been the case at Chicago in the recent past, when a sharp divide existed between Straussians and others.[17] But that cleavage had been overcome by the time I arrived. At Chicago, you constantly found yourself agreeing and disagreeing with different people. Though arguments were strong, they never developed into an "Us versus Them" situation. That extended down to the graduate students, who felt free to put together committees with different kinds of people and even benefit from our disagreements. Chicago was a place where the whole was greater than the sum of its parts.

Q: Who were your closest colleagues at Chicago?
A: Almost the entire department. But I would mention in particular Aristide Zolberg, Leonard Binder, Ira Katznelson, and Brian Barry. I should add John Coatsworth and Friedrich Katz, two Latin Americanists in the History Department, to this list. After a time, however, lots of us left. It started with Barry, then Katznelson, and then I left for the European University Institute.

Q: You overlapped at Chicago with Adam Przeworski.
A: I was instrumental in bringing him to Chicago. He became very much a part of the mix and stayed on many years after I left. We do things differently, which sometimes translated into a prickly relationship that would occasionally manifest itself in the way we worked with graduate students. Przeworski likes to work with graduate students who do what he does, which usually has a rational choice bent. In contrast, I work with students who are interested in doing a wide range of things. We have admiration for each other, and he was a very good colleague. We have a longstanding personal relationship that transcends our academic differences. That is why, as I said earlier, Przeworski was brought into the project on transitions from authoritarian regimes at the Woodrow Wilson Center right from the beginning, even though at that time he was neither a specialist in Latin America nor Southern Europe. I wanted to make sure he was part of that project, because I knew he would make an important contribution.

17. *Straussians* refers to the followers of Leo Strauss (1899–1973), a German Jewish émigré political theorist who taught at Chicago from 1949 until 1968.

Q: After a few years in the 1980s at the European University Institute in Italy, you moved back to the United States and took a job at Stanford in 1986.
A: I was happy in Italy, and I would have stayed there for as long as possible. But I had a personal relationship with Terry Karl, and she had a job at Stanford. I moved to Stanford because of her, and I guess it looked perfect on paper. Stanford supposedly had a very good department. But I soon realized I was in the wrong place for me.

Q: What was the problem with Stanford?
A: Stanford was exactly the opposite of Chicago. Stanford was a place where no two people talked to each other, even if they were on the same side of an issue. It had no social or intellectual life whatsoever. People came to campus to work, if they came, at 9:00 a.m. and left at 5:00 p.m. Some people played tennis together. But if you were not one of them, you were not a member of anything. Moreover, at Stanford most of the department members were not very intellectual people; they were just professional academics doing their job. At Chicago, by contrast, we were not doing a job. Political science was our vocation, and we were thinking and arguing about politics all the time. At Stanford, they were more like businessmen than intellectuals. There was no interaction; the department was completely dead.

A growing rift developed in the department at Stanford, as a coalition led by rational choice theorists pushed for the Americanization of comparative politics and simply left no room for people who knew languages, did field research, and brought in-depth knowledge of countries to bear on their research. Things became very polarized. Many of the people who did comparative politics ended up spending more of their time in various area studies and international centers. In general, these people were attacked and marginalized. It became a very closed environment. An overwhelmingly compact group became dominant, and this group always voted together. As a result, department meetings were very uninteresting. I eventually stopped going. Stanford was a tremendously negative experience. There was just no payoff from being there, except for the intellectual and personal company of Terry Karl.

Q: In 1996 you moved back to Italy and rejoined the European University Institute (EUI).
A: The EUI has been wonderful. The location, in Florence, is obviously an attraction. We have wonderful students. And the faculty is top-notch. At the EUI, all the faculty have temporary appointments with a maximum stay of eight years. So, it's a constantly revolving door, which means you are always in the business of finding new colleagues, and you have a lot of say

in who they are. I am convinced we now have the best department in Europe in political science and sociology. It has become *the* place to go for graduate work in these fields. The EUI is also very stimulating because the student body is so diverse. It is a university with no dominant ethnic or national group. There is no other place on earth like it. We have the same number of Germans as Italians, French, British, and so on. That's exciting and challenging. I am exactly where I want to be, and I can't imagine a better job. I feel very lucky.

Q: Turning to teaching, what is your approach to training graduate students?[18]
A: As a matter of principle, I do not tell any graduate student what to work on. This is very unusual in Europe, because professors there usually tell their students what they should work on. Thus, students are surprised when I say they have to find a research topic themselves and decide whether that topic is sufficiently important to them. I tell them, "You should not worry about whether I think your topic is important. Also, forget about what the discipline might think. Make sure it's important to you." You have to care, very deeply, about the subject matter of your dissertation. Now, once a student has picked a dissertation topic, then I become very intrusive.

I place a lot of attention on theory, and I expect students to really know what they want to do from a conceptual point of view. I read literally every word they write, criticize it, and ask, "Why didn't you do this or that?" I really grill them, especially on that critical first chapter. I expect a dissertation to go through several drafts. On the other hand, I'm not at all insistent about the kinds of methods or data they should use. I have supervised everything from survey and aggregate data studies to interview- and documentary-based research. I'm very eclectic when it comes to methods and data. That's my basic philosophy. I imagine I am pretty difficult to work with. I am very demanding of students.

The Achievements, Shortcomings, and Future of Comparative Politics

Q: What has comparative politics accomplished? What do we know now that we did not know when you were in graduate school in the mid-1960s?[19]

18. For a graduate student's perspective on Schmitter as a teacher, see the interview with David Collier in Chapter 15.
19. For Schmitter's overall assessments of the field, see Schmitter (1993, 2002). Schmitter's efforts at synthesizing the literature on democratization include Schmitter (1995) and Schmitter and Guilhot (2000).

A: The field has made important gains. The most obvious ones concern what I would label the spatial dimension. Today, as opposed to forty years ago, you no longer feel you have knowledge about politics if you have knowledge about just one country. This is a big accomplishment, one that has helped transform comparative politics into a political science, though this transformation has perhaps gone less far in the United States than in Europe. We also study politics in a broader, more integrated way. For example, instead of studying elections or political parties in isolation, as was previously the case, we now look at the entire field of political interests and consider how they relate to political parties and different modes of public policy making. I am very proud to have been part of the efforts to reshape the field in this way. But these changes are also unintended byproducts of structural functionalism. This approach got it wrong in the way it went about doing things. It postulated a highly abstract set of functions, derived largely from Talcott Parsons, that had to be performed for a polity to become and remain stable. The static bias was obvious, as was the strong assumption of systemic interdependence. Needless to say, to someone like myself, who was more concerned with change in regime, and in changing regimes, this was rather daunting. But the real bias in this apparently "universalistic" theory came when specific institutions or institutional complexes were assigned a privileged status in performing specific functions. At this point, for me, structural functionalism looked suspiciously like an abstract and crude description of the American political system. It would have been much more useful to have started with historical, "real-existing" institutions in different polities and then tried to discover what functions they performed and whether or not their interdependence with other institutions actually led to non-coercive stability. In short, the whole approach lacked both historicity and stateness, precisely what I was looking for. Still, structural functionalism pushed us to take a broader, more holistic view of the political process. This is a new aspect of the discipline, and there are a number of generalizations that are linked to this broad-gauged research that we did not have in the decades before. For example, we now know that, *pace* Duverger, electoral systems do not alone produce party systems. Or, as I gradually and reluctantly discovered, that an understanding of different configurations of interest associations cannot be separated from the nature of partisan competition and the party or parties in power.

On some topics, there is no single received wisdom. There may be two or three alternative views, which we haven't quite unraveled yet and which stand as rival hypotheses. But this is much better than the approximate kind of knowledge we had before. It is wrong when people say there has been no accumulation of knowledge in comparative politics. Indeed, there would have been even more accumulation of knowledge by political science in the United States if it weren't for this business of fads—behavioralism, structural functionalism, and now rational choice theory. Because of fads, academics seek to prove themselves by denying that the generation that preceded them produced anything of value. This tendency can be seen among those who pretend they are starting political science from scratch with rational choice theory or whatever it is they have just picked up. They even go so far as to say that everything written before them about a certain topic is junk. I disagree. We stand at a different place today than where we stood before. By and large, it's a better place, a place with a wider and more discerning perspective from which to observe politics.

Q: Your remarks remind me of Gabriel Almond's emphasis on the need for better professional memory (Almond 1990, Part II).
A: Almond certainly argues that there is not enough cross-referencing across generations and across time. Indeed, as we discussed earlier, he even made this point with regard to the corporatism literature (Almond 1983). I think I actually go out of my way to reference previous sources. If I'm guilty of anything, it is that I haven't paid enough attention to American political science. I'm not denigrating this literature. But if I am going to work on, say, Brazil, I am probably going to work with monographs and articles written by Brazilians, not Americans. Maybe once in a while I'll find something useful written outside Brazil. But I confess that I have not paid much attention to what has been written by Latin Americanists except, of course, by my colleague and companion, Terry Karl. I say this with a certain amount of reserve, because I, too, write about other people's politics, and what I am saying here about Latin Americanists could certainly be said about my own work. Still, I find I learn more by entering into relationships with local social scientists.

Area Studies

Q: Do you see any notable failures of comparative politics?
A: The most obvious one was the enormous failure to understand the nature of communist systems. This failure illustrates the fundamental mistake of allowing students of Soviet systems to form a cyst inside comparative politics. They did not read what comparativists were writing, and they simply did not pay attention to matters as basic as Euro-communism. I didn't read any of their work either, with a few exceptions, because they weren't speaking my language. The separation of Sovietologists from the rest of the field was quite stark.

This episode provides an important lesson for area studies. Area studies have some very important payoffs, but they have to remain open. Students of particular areas have to read what other people are writing, and they have to be prepared to jump out of their respective regions to find points of comparison elsewhere. This is exactly what Sovietologists were unable to do. Their model held that communism was simply different, and, hence, communist systems were not to be compared with anything except each other. Indeed, there is still a group that says since communism was different, post-communism will also have to be different. I have argued strongly against this perspective.[20]

Students of Latin America—I was one of them—were never so insular. We were always interested in other areas. Latin America had an ambiguous intellectual position between the United States and Europe. There was always an implicit comparison being drawn between Latin American countries and these external reference points. This openness to other regions and areas explains why the literature on Latin America did a much better job of analyzing regime change. O'Donnell, and I, as well, had a lively sense of how vulnerable authoritarian regimes were in Latin America. We didn't predict exactly when democratization would occur, but we were not surprised by it, because our models of authoritarian rule gave us an understanding of the inherent contradictions of these systems. We were not locked into anything as hermetic as the totalitarian model that dominated the study of communist systems. It is a fundamentally misguided strategy to develop a different language and separate assumptions for a subset of countries.

The Future of Comparative Politics and the U.S. Model of Political Science

Q: In light of this assessment, what do you think about the future of comparative politics?
A: I wrote about this question in a paper published recently in *European Political Science* (Schmitter 2002). Many people—certainly Americans, British, and perhaps even a few Scandinavians—think this is an easy question to answer. In their view, the future of comparative politics and political science is already on display in the United States. The United States sets the standards, because of the number of political scientists in the United States, their high level of professionalization, the prestige and quantity of their journals, and so on. As a result, it is only a matter of time before political scientists in other countries converge on the American model. My article challenges the thesis that the United States provides "the face of the future" for comparativists.

Q: What problems do you see with the way political science is practiced in the United States?

---

20. See Schmitter and Karl (1994) and Karl and Schmitter (1995).

A: One key problem is that too much of U.S. political science is based on the study of the United States, and the United States is a peculiar case because of its non-feudal past, the absence of hostile neighbors, the presence of multiple and overlapping cleavages in an immigrant society, and so on. Therefore, the kind of political science generated on the basis of the American case, an exceptional political situation, cannot possibly be a universal political science. Findings based on the United States are simply not likely to travel well. Americanists in the profession find themselves in a peculiarly paradoxical position: they insist that "their" polity is exceptional and that whatever they discover must be universally applicable.

It would be another matter if U.S. political science were to treat the United States as a case, one just like any other. But this probably will not happen, because Americanists are very resistant to this suggestion. The situation is different in Europe. Nobody in Europe would resist the idea that Italy or Spain is just a case. In fact, in Europe, it is increasingly unclear whether Italy and Spain are still cases in the traditional sense, because the politics of these countries have become so intertwined with that of the European Union. European countries can no longer be seen as involving clearly independent units.

Another problem with American political science, to which I have already alluded, is that it is so prone to generating fads, something I see as a consequence of the vastly more competitive nature of the profession in the United States and the resulting tendency to exaggerate the importance of one's approach and methods. Competitiveness is both the worst and best aspect of American political science. On one hand, it leads to a negative cycle of fads and the overvaluation of what a new approach, method, or theory has to offer. On the other hand, the competitive nature of the profession in the United States destroys the very fads it produces; a competing group inevitably forms whose main business is to poke its fingers in the dominant tradition. In Europe, by contrast, the political science profession is more intrinsically conservative and anticompetitive, partly because of the highly bureaucratized nature of the universities. As a result, European political science is much more resistant to innovation, but once an innovation manages to penetrate, it sticks and gets absorbed more thoroughly. Perhaps this is what produces a stronger sense in European political science that accumulation of knowledge is occurring.

Q: With regard to the dominant approaches in American political science during the past fifty years—behavioralism, structural functionalism, and rational choice—do you draw any distinctions in terms of their impact?

A: In one sense they are exactly the same. Take the advocates of rational choice. They have been telling graduate students that they need to learn rational choice theory, they have exclusively promoted these students, and they have effectively formed a "club" within the discipline. That's precisely what the behavioralists did. And it's exactly what the structural functionalists did through the Social Science Research Council's (SSRC) Committee on Comparative Politics. They all formed their self-admiring clique, and then everyone promoted each other.

Still, I do see a difference among these approaches. Behavioralists, and to a certain extent the structural functionalists, helped produce a wealth of studies on the Third World. As a result, we have lots of people who became experts on various obscure parts of the world. They produced useful knowledge, for which there was a demand both inside and outside the academy. In contrast, I do not see rational choice scholars producing much of any practical utility, because the basic assumptions of rational choice theory about politics tend to be quite unrealistic. To be sure, there are some very interesting aspects of rational choice theory, or at least there could be, inasmuch as the limits of these assumptions are acknowledged and the theory is not applied to situations where it is completely inappropriate. But I perceive little willingness to understand and confront the limits of rational choice theory.

Q: What do you see, then, as the future of rational choice in political science?
A: I do not think it is dominant now, and I do not think it will become dominant, even in the United States, precisely because of the competitive nature of the profession there. I am very confident that the rational choice bubble will burst. As with previous fads, rational choice theory will leave some residue. After it passes, each successive fad leaves a little bit more diversity in departments.

Research Agendas

Q: Where do you think the big developments in comparative politics are likely to be in the next decade or so?
A: The problem with trying to answer such a question is that one tends to focus on the things on which one is working. At least I do, I have to admit. With this caveat, let me suggest two things that will be important. The first concerns transnational political processes that cannot be subsumed under international relations in the classic sense of processes driven by national interests and involving diplomatic bargaining, relative advantage, "self-

help," naked power struggles, and so on. The processes might be regional or global. A lot of this is already happening in Europe, because of the EU, but I also see such trends elsewhere, for example, in Latin America with Mercosur.[21]

The second thing I would highlight involves the quality of democracy and the possibility of developing a new normative democratic theory. The study of democratization has more or less run its course. Still, we need a new type of democratic theory that can grasp the fundamental changes that democracy itself is undergoing. Robert Dahl (1989, Chs. 1, 2, 15, 22, and 23) develops the wonderful insight that democracy has already undergone several revolutions. I think we are currently in the middle of another of those democratic revolutions. The nature of the actors is changing. The real citizens today are organizations, not individuals. Indeed, individuals act effectively in modern democracies, to the extent that they do at all, only through organizations. The types of organizations that are relevant have also shifted, as political parties become less important and interest associations and social movements more so. Thus, we need a more "organizational" theory of democracy. Moreover, the unit of government is shifting. We are now talking about supranational democracy and also paying more attention to subnational democracy. So we are going above and below the nation-state as the unit of analysis. This requires a different democratic theory, because 99 percent of democratic theory assumes the prior and consensual existence of a nation-state.

Conclusion

Q: To conclude, what's your advice to graduate students entering the profession?
A: Comparative politics is the most challenging and difficult, but also the most fun and rewarding, field of political science. To be a good comparativist, you have to be comparative yourself. That is, you must habituate yourself to living in different cultures and being on the outside. You have to structure your life comparatively, seeking out opportunities to go to different countries. This is not easy to do, especially if you have a family and other "fixed assets." I've been lucky. I've had children who didn't mind me moving around. Well, to tell you the truth, I'm not sure about that, because I forced my kids to live in eight different countries before they went to college. So they may tell a different story. In a nutshell, if you really wish to be a comparativist, you must be prepared to live a comparative life.[22]

21. Mercosur (Mercado Común del Sur—Southern Common Market) is a trading zone founded in 1991 by Argentina, Brazil, Paraguay, and Uruguay.
22. For further suggestions, see Schmitter (1997b, 295–97).

11

James C. Scott

Peasants, Power, and the Art of Resistance

James C. Scott, a Southeast Asianist by training, has made seminal contributions to the study of culture and politics and is widely known for his original ideas about how subaltern groups, especially peasants in developing countries, resist domination. He played a leading role in the Perestroika movement in American political science.[1]

Scott's early research focused on the ideology of political elites, the subject of his first book, *Political Ideology in Malaysia* (1968), and on corruption and clientelism, which he addressed in *Comparative Political Corruption* (1972a) and in several influential articles. His subsequent research on peasants and agrarian class relations, published in *The Moral Economy of the Peasant* (1976), explained peasant rebellion as a consequence of risk-averse behavior by peasants in the face of the breakdown of patron-client relationships. This book was widely read together with Samuel Popkin's *The Rational Peasant* (1979), giving rise to the so-called Scott-Popkin debate that pitted Scott's emphasis on "moral economy" against Popkin's "rational choice/political economy" perspective.

Scott deepened his knowledge about peasants by doing two years of ethnographic fieldwork on class relations in a Malaysian village. The result of this research, *Weapons of the Weak* (1985), demonstrated that subordinate groups engaged in what Scott called "everyday resistance" to authority. This finding challenged the idea, associated with Gramsci, that these groups were incapable of resistance because they were in the grips of "hegemony" that blocked them from even perceiving their subjugation. *Domination and the Arts of Resistance* (1990) broadened the focus of Scott's research

This interview was conducted by Richard Snyder in Durham, Connecticut, on July 20 and 28, 2001.

1. The Perestroika movement, which erupted in 2000, aimed to reform the governing structure of the American Political Science Association (APSA) and open the *American Political Science Review* (*APSR*) to a more diverse array of methodological and theoretical approaches.

by encompassing subordinate groups beyond peasants and drawing on cases from outside Asia.

Scott's research took a new direction in *Seeing Like a State* (1998), a broadly comparative and historical study of why state interventions putatively intended to improve the human condition instead produced widespread misery. Ranging across seemingly disparate cases, such as the *ujamaa* compulsory villagization scheme in Tanzania in the 1970s and scientific forestry in eighteenth-century Prussia, he showed how "high modernism," an ideology that ignored local, practical knowledge, led to catastrophic outcomes. His current research focuses on state-society interactions by exploring why states are hostile to groups that are physically mobile.

Scott was born in Mount Holly, New Jersey, in 1936. He received his B.A. from Williams College in 1958 and his Ph.D. in political science from Yale University in 1967. He has taught at the University of Wisconsin, Madison (1967–76) and at Yale University (1976–present), where he co-founded the Program in Agrarian Studies in 1991. He was president of the Association of Asian Studies (1997–98) and was elected to the American Academy of Arts and Sciences in 1992.

Intellectual Formation and Training

Q: Where did you grow up and what did your parents do? Do you recall any formative events that triggered an interest in politics?

A: I was raised in Beverly, New Jersey, a small industrial town along the Delaware River, halfway between Camden and Trenton. My father was the town doctor. He died suddenly of a stroke at age forty-six. I was nine years old at the time. Having been raised and educated in West Virginia, my father was an avid Democrat and FDR supporter. I had a cold and was at home the day FDR died. I heard the announcement on the radio first and told my mother who told my father; he had his offices in the other half of our large house. He immediately closed the office, and they and their close friends spent the next few hours weeping in grief.

I was imprinted with "Democrat" as a party affiliation very early, and it was, of course, a way to honor my dead father. I was the only Democrat in my class at Moorestown Friends' School; although it was a Quaker school, the kids were from well-to-do families and all Republicans. It was not lost on me that the teachers, who were all Democrats or socialists, were rather fond of my politics. They encouraged me. I had a special relationship to the school inasmuch as, after my father's death, I became its first scholarship student, working weekends and summers in exchange for tuition. Friends' School exposed me, especially through weekend and weeklong work-camps in Philadelphia and Washington, to a far wider range of experiences than I would have ever had in any other type of school. We visited prisons, settlement houses, dock-worker meetings, mental institutions, worked with slum families on repair, and visited the Soviet embassy at the height of the Cold War. And of course I met lots of Quakers who were conscientious objectors during World War II. In sum, I met a lot of people who had the courage to stand up in a crowd of a hundred and be a minority of one, and I became far less parochial than I would otherwise have been.

Q: You got your undergraduate degree at Williams College in 1958. What did you learn at Williams?
A: I was very badly prepared for Williams, both socially and intellectually. In fact, I was convinced I did not belong there and that I was going to flunk out. The first day I arrived at Williams there were freshmen talking about authors and poets whom I'd never even heard of, let alone formed an opinion about. I thought, "I don't know anything," and I called my mother and said, "You know I'll do my best, Mom, but I'll probably be home before Christmas because I don't think I'm going to make it here." Because of my self-doubt, I worked really hard at Williams.

Q: You majored in economics. What was the training like?
A: My Williams training gave me a pretty good grounding in political economy. We read Karl Polanyi, Jan Tinbergen on welfare economics, and all the stuff on planning, like Barbara Ward and Friedrich von Hayek. We read Anthony Downs, too. In fact, *An Economic Theory of Democracy* (Downs 1957) was one of the last things I read before I graduated. The one thing Williams did for me, something my subsequent graduate training at Yale did not undo, is give me a kind of intellectual ambition. It's not as if Williams educated me all that well, but it did give me a map of what it would take to be a real intellectual. At Williams, I also picked up a lifelong habit of spending an hour or two each day reading novels and poetry—something completely outside of political science.

The fact that I'm a Southeast Asianist, which is a complete oddity in many ways, also stems from my experiences at Williams. I was doing my senior honors thesis on German wartime mobilization during World War II. It turned out that the Germans did not have double or triple factory shifts early in the war, even though they had sufficient manpower to have had these shifts. No one had ever figured that out, and I'm not sure anyone has even today. I never got very far into the research, though, because I fell in love in the fall. I had a great professor, Emile Desprès, who called me into his office in December to see what I had done. I tried to fake it, and he saw right through me. He told me, "Get out! You're not doing an honors thesis with me, you haven't done anything . . . Get out!" Well, I was ambitious enough that I still wanted to graduate with honors. I went one by one to all the other professors in economics to see if any would adopt me. There was a guy named William Hollinger who had worked on Indonesia, and he said, "I have always wanted to know something about the economic development of Burma. If you work on Burma, I'll adopt you." I said, "Fine, where's Burma?" I didn't know where Burma was. Then, toward the end of senior year, I applied for a Rotary fellowship to go to Burma. My plan was actually to go to Harvard Law School, but, lo and behold, I got the Rotary fellowship. I said to myself, "You can always go to Harvard Law School, but when are you going to have another chance to go to Burma?" So, I spent a year in Burma in 1958–59 and never looked back.

Q: What was your year in Burma like? What did you do there?
A: The civilian government of U Nu was in power when I first arrived, but the military soon took over. I got quite involved in student politics, working in Rangoon for the national students' association. Then I received a death threat from left-wing students who did not like the idea of an American student activist, though God knows I was pretty left-wing back then. My friends said, "They are not fooling around, it's not a prank." I was scared enough that I left Rangoon and moved to Mandalay, where I just worked on Burmese. I learned to speak Burmese tolerably well, though I have forgotten all of it now.

Q: I am curious whether this early trip to Burma stimulated your subsequent interest in peasants and rural issues. Did you spend any time in the countryside in Burma?
A: Not really, though I did some traveling in Burma. I had a 1940 Triumph motorcycle that I resuscitated from a Burmese backyard. This old motorcycle was in such bad condition that the Burmese were not even operating it—the shock absorbers were up in the handle bars rather than going down to the front wheel.

Q: When you got back from Burma, why did you change your plans and go to graduate school in political science at Yale instead of attending Harvard Law School?
A: I switched initially from Harvard Law to Yale economics, because Burma and a year in Paris at the Institut des Etudes Politiques convinced me there were more important things in the world than legal codes, and Yale had a fine reputation in economic development. I then decided that politics was more important than economics and simply asked the Economics Department to send my application over to the Political Science Department to see if they would have me. I don't recall applying elsewhere.

Q: When you started your graduate studies in 1961, Yale was probably the leading Political Science Department in the country.[2]
A: I came at the height of the behavioral revolution. Positivism was the rage, and we all read Popper (1959) and Hempel (1965, 1966). Professors who themselves wouldn't have known a Chi Squared from a Pearson's R were teaching statistical methods like it was the true gospel. Robert Lane taught scope and method, and even though he didn't actually use many of the tools he covered, he was teaching that stuff as if it were the true shroud. It was like going to a Jesuit school. This was great in the sense that the faculty members seemed to have a sense of purpose: they felt they were going to revolutionize political science. But, like me, most of my graduate student cohort was pretty skeptical.

I remember the very first class meeting with Gabriel Almond, when he used the term *eufunctional*. Almond had just done his book on structural functionalism, *The Politics of Developing Areas* (Almond and Coleman 1960), and he was treating that like it was the biblical book of Genesis. Almond was using all these terms that I did not understand. I had had a very traditional training at Williams, so I did not know anything about the behavioral revolution. This was all a complete revelation to me. I made a list on 3 by 5 index cards of all the words I didn't know, and I was naïve enough that when I had accumulated six or seven of these words, I raised my hand and said, "Professor Almond, I don't understand these words. Could you please explain to me what they mean?" All the second-year students gasped, "Oh god, how embarrassing."

Q: How did Almond respond?
A: I noticed he had trouble providing the definition of at least some of these things. In any case, I tell the story not to say what a smart ass I was, because I didn't intend to be a smart ass. I tell the story to indicate how naïve I was when I arrived at Yale. This was all new stuff to me. For example, I'd never heard of Karl Popper. I was starting at zero. I had come to graduate school at Yale because I was interested in Southeast Asian politics, Burma, and economic development. I wanted to learn about the Third World.

This anecdote about Almond's class points to a pattern I recognize, something that I repeated at Williams, at Yale, and later at Wisconsin, where I got my first job teaching. I always arrive at a place thinking I don't belong and that I have to prove to these people, and to myself, that I'm good enough to be there. So, for the first year or two I am a good little boy and hold back all my misgivings. I guess I decide that I have to succeed on

2. For an in-depth study of Yale's Department of Political Science during 1955–70, see Merelman (2003).

their terms so that I'm accepted. But as soon as I feel secure, then I make trouble and rebel.

Q: Were there other courses at Yale that you found more stimulating than Almond's?

A: Robert Dahl taught wonderful courses. I remember one with a fabulous premise: How do stupid things happen in politics, things that everyone agrees in retrospect were dumb? Dahl had us write a paper explaining how and why a political decision that we all knew to be a bad decision got made. I took the agreement Churchill and Roosevelt signed at Quebec to de-industrialize Germany after the war, flood the mines, and take away all the industrial plants so that Germany could never make war again. Henry Morganthau Jr. was behind this idea of imposing a Carthaginian peace on Germany. This bad decision was undone in about a year-and-a-half, as soon as people realized that de-industrialization was going to create a large mass of surplus Germans who would have nowhere to go. What were they going to do, send them all to North Africa?

At Yale I was in the company of super-bright teachers like Dahl, Charles Lindblom, Lane, and Harry Benda, a historian who worked on Southeast Asia and was also very important for me. I read the classics of political science. I got a certain amount of Southeast Asian training. And I had a lot of very fast graduate students around me making me brighter. So, I am kind of grateful for the Jesuit behavioralist training I got at Yale. My political science professors believed in what they were doing, and they were trying to convey something they thought was important. They certainly did not have a "Get off the bus here, kid" attitude. I got training from people who had their hearts in it, and that's the first thing a student can tell. I also got some of the tools with which to make trouble later.

Q: What specific tools are you referring to?

A: Three tools, really. The first was a fairly serious training, for the time, in philosophy of science, which our mentors thought was the intellectual foundation of the revolution in political science they had launched. I was skeptical of what I read and its application to politics, and I did not fail to notice that the scholars I admired—Lane, Dahl, Lindblom—didn't practice what they preached! The second tool was a better grasp of the intellectual basis of socialism. All three of the scholars just mentioned were asking "socialist" questions, if you will: what is the relation between wealth and power, how is equality fostered, how are political beliefs formed and what is their relationship to class? Third, I acquired, through my work on language and Southeast Asia, an abiding respect for what is today contemptuously, and incorrectly, called "orientalism"—namely, a profound knowledge of the culture, literature, history, and language of the area studied. That's part of the reason why more people think of me as an anthropologist than a political scientist, though I maintain that what I do is, or ought to be, right at the center of political science.

Q: What books and authors had the greatest impact on you in graduate school?
A: The most important book I read—and I read it the summer before I started graduate work—was Karl Polanyi's *The Great Transformation* (1957). I still think it's an amazing and classic account of the origin and social consequences of laissez-faire capitalism.

Q: What was the topic of your dissertation?
A: I was a student of Bob Lane's, and I liked the work he had done on political ideology (Lane 1962). So, for my dissertation, I decided to follow in his footsteps by doing intensive interviews with elites in Malaysia to find out how they understood the world.

Q: Your first book, *Political Ideology in Malaysia* (Scott 1968), came directly out of your dissertation.
A: Yes, that's right. I'd like to forget that book.

Q: Why?
A: The book was a big success with my advisors at Yale: Bob Lane, Joseph Lapalombara, Robert Tilman, and Carl Landé. It was gracefully written, and they thought it was a good book. So it got published by Yale University Press. I can't complain, because the book probably helped me get my first job at the University of Wisconsin. Still, it was torn apart by people who knew a lot about Malaysia and Malaysian history. They thought it was pretty shallow, and I think they were right, actually. I hadn't really done my homework.

I regard my first book as a good example of writing for a telephone booth full of political scientists. I used the "right" techniques and methods, and I achieved a mastery of the sort of synthetic idea of ideology that impressed my advisors. So I had a cheap success. My reference group was a small, tiny telephone booth full of people, which is something that has happened a lot in political science today. And that's what happened to me. My first book pleased a subgroup of political scientists, but it was unsuccessful for people who knew a lot about Malaysia. I don't think the book is much worth reading. Eventually I did work that was more worth reading.

Research on Peasants, Everyday Resistance, and States
Peasants and Moral Economy

Q: After your dissertation and first book on elites and political ideology, the focus of your research shifted to corruption, patron-client relations, and, eventually, to peasant societies. How did your interests evolve?

A: In 1970, after I had been teaching at Wisconsin for three years, I got a postdoctoral fellowship to come back to Yale through Bob Lane's program in psychology and politics. Knowing the fate of my first book, I conceived the idea of spending my time at Yale becoming a real Southeast Asianist. I had already done a lot of Southeast Asian work, but, given my political science training, I didn't feel I had become a true Southeast Asianist. So, I went back to Yale explicitly to read all the classics on Southeast Asia. I remember a colleague at Wisconsin, Ira Sharkansky, a sharp, hard-working Americanist, "the Shark," as we called him, saying, "You're a knucklehead, Scott. Becoming a Southeast Asianist is a stupid waste of time. This is not where political science is headed. It's the end of your career." And it worried me actually.

Q: Why were you worried?

A: I wanted to have a good career. But I did it anyway, and it turned out fine. In any case, the linear progression of my research goes like this. After finishing my dissertation on political ideology, I became interested in corruption and machine politics (Scott 1969a, 1969b, 1972a). I even had a couple of students working on observing interactions between ordinary people and bureaucrats, though I never published that work. My interest in corruption led to my work on patron-client relationships (Scott 1972b; Schmidt et al. 1977), and my work on patron-client relations led me to the study of peasants. This was, of course, the period of the Vietnam War, and wars of national liberation were the zeitgeist. I realized that much of the literature on patron-client relations had to do with structures of feudal authority, and the breakdown of patron-client relations seemed to play an important role in generating the peasant-based revolutions that were happening at the time. This gave me the idea that understanding how vertical chains of authority break down might help explain how class consciousness emerges and how class-based social movements form. So, I started reading all the anthropological and historical literature about peasant societies that I could read—this literature was so exciting to me. With my friend, Ed Friedman, I started to teach a course on peasant revolutions at Wisconsin. My reading on peasants and my effort to make myself a real Southeast Asianist came together in *The Moral Economy of the Peasant* (Scott 1976).

Q: Could you say more about what excited you so much about peasants? After all, your first book was on urban elites, not peasants.
A: First of all, the Vietnam War was going on. I can't say that too often. Everyone was thinking about the National Liberation Front and about Mao. Peasants were on everybody's mind. Second, the best works on peasants and agrarian issues, books like Eric Wolf's *Peasant Wars of the Twentieth Century* (1969) and Barrington Moore's *Social Origins of Dictatorship and Democracy* (1966), were coming out at about that time. Finally, reading Chayanov (1966) on peasant economy, the great Chinese anthropologist, Fei Xiaotong (1953), on the Chinese gentry, or Marc Bloch (1961) on feudalism, took the formal abstractions of political science, brought them down to earth, and connected them with real people. The best of the anthropological literature on peasants is so exciting and has such texture.

Q: Turning to your book, *The Moral Economy of the Peasant*, what was the main contribution of that work?
A: The core of the book was the simple idea of risk-averse behavior by peasants. Once you understand risk-averseness, you are then poised to understand why certain kinds of oppression are worse than others and why certain kinds of extraction are more onerous, and thus more likely to provoke resistance, than others. It's a pretty simple point. In fact, most of my books have a simple argument.

Q: Did you anticipate the book would have such a big impact?
A: No. I thought it was good, but I also thought it was a specialized book that would only be of interest to the handful of people who worked on Southeast Asia. After all, it was about peasant rebellions in the 1930s, it was not about the Viet Cong. And I wasn't trying to write a contemporary book. So I was surprised it had such a big effect and became popular as a work of social science. It gives me great pleasure that *The Moral Economy of the Peasant,* first published in 1976, is still in print and still being read. I don't pay much attention to these things, but I don't imagine many books published in 1976 on comparative politics and Southeast Asia are still in print twenty-five years later. My book was local, arcane, and not meant for a big audience, but it has had a steady life for such a long time. I think Yale University Press was also surprised.

Q: Why did *The Moral Economy of the Peasant* attract so much attention?
A: I think people wanted something a little deeper about how peasant revolutions happen. Also, I have my competitor, Sam Popkin, to thank for the

fact that he produced an anti-moral economy book that provided a natural teaching vehicle by allowing people to stage a debate (Popkin 1979).

Q: The so-called Scott-Popkin debate on "moral peasants" versus "rational peasants" generated a lot of interest, especially during the 1980s. What are your reflections on that debate?
A: When Popkin wrote his book, he sent me the manuscript, and I sent him back fifteen or sixteen pages of criticism. He revised the manuscript to some extent in light of what I had to say and then sent back a second version. I started to read it, got four pages into writing my criticism, and then asked myself, "Why am I doing this? This is basically an attempt to attack my book, and it's going to remain an attack on my work. Why am I making it better?" So I tore up those four pages and sent Popkin a letter saying, "Sam, you're on your own. I'm not going to help you sharpen your sword to cut me up."

Popkin actually misrepresented my argument. Part of my exchange with him while he was writing his book was to say, "No, no, no. I'm not talking about irrational peasants. I'm talking about peasants whose behavior satisfies all the conditions of rationality in neoclassical economics, provided that you understand the particular constraints under which they operate. Namely, they have a limited food supply and thus have to minimize the maximum loss or they're dead." I was not writing about altruistic, irrational peasants. I made it clear enough, and, in fact, if I had to rewrite my book, I would hammer home even more that these were not dewy-eyed, altruistic peasants. These were people behaving rationally. I did argue that certain social arrangements that emerged to protect peasant subsistence acquired a moral quality and were seen as sacred, in part because they provided important social insurance. But I did not have a theory of irrational peasants. My whole argument could have been done in a completely rational choice format.

So, I thought Sam took a cheap shot by misrepresenting my argument. I guess I made a strategic mistake when I chose the title for the book. "The Ethics of Rebellion in Southeast Asia" was my first title. Then I read E. P. Thompson's article, "The Moral Economy of the English Crowd in the Eighteenth Century" (1971), and I thought "moral economy" would be a better title, because I was talking about the same kind of thing as Thompson, though not in the market, but in the fields. So, I decided to use the term *moral economy*. If you don't read the book carefully and you only know that it's about moral economy, then you might erroneously infer that I am talking about people who are doing moral reasoning and not trying to minimize losses in order to subsist. The title of my book gave Sam the running room he wanted.

I actually wrote forty pages of point-by-point refutation of Sam's argument and then realized that it would be more interesting to write a broadside against rational choice foundations, taking several examples besides Popkin. I accumulated a lot of notes in a folder toward this project but never returned to it. By now, most of the points I would have made have been made by others. The whole debate with Popkin became a series of defensive exchanges: you say I say this, here is what I say, and you say I say this, here is what I say. I think I was right, but I also think the whole thing was a colossal waste of time.

Q: Do you have any further comments on *The Moral Economy of the Peasant?*
A: Actually, in terms of intellectual history, I wrote a kind of reply to myself that critiqued *The Moral Economy of the Peasant* for not paying enough attention to the moral, spiritual, and religious worlds of peasants. This was a criticism I got from anthropologists, and I wrote a very long, two-part article in an effort to make amends for that big shortcoming of my book (Scott 1977a, 1977b). The idea that you can discount religious motives and magic in explaining peasant rebellions overlooks facts that are as plain as the nose on your face. Before the French Revolution, all revolutions had a religious core. And how the hell can you explain millennial rebellions with a rational choice framework? Writing that long article, which forced me to do a whole year's work on peasant religion, was penance for having neglected the role of religion in my book.

Q: This is ironic in light of the Scott-Popkin debate, because, in a way, you were criticizing yourself for having made too *rational* an interpretation of peasants! It would be nice to reprint that article, because it is not very well known.
A: I would reprint it if I ever thought of collecting a few of my articles. But pulling together one's essays seems like a retirement thing. I'll do that when I'm senile.

Weapons of the Weak

Q: After *The Moral Economy of the Peasant,* your next book was *Weapons of the Weak* (Scott 1985). This book was a departure from your previous research because it was an ethnographic work based on an extended period living in a peasant village. How did you make this transition?
A: By the time I finished *The Moral Economy of the Peasant,* I had spent five or six years working on peasants. I thought, "Most of the people in the world

are peasants, so why not make a career studying peasants?" I also thought that if I wanted to be serious about peasants, if I were going make this my life's work, I had to do actual fieldwork in a village. I admired anthropological methods, and I thought that every time I got tempted to do a fourth-order abstraction, it would help if I had a real peasant society that I knew like the back of my hand. So, I conceived the idea of living a couple of years in a Malay village. *Weapons of the Weak* was a real shot in the dark. People told me I was wasting my time, and I went off to Malaysia thinking I was making the stupidest professional move of my life. But *Weapons of the Weak* turned out to be the work I am proudest of. I also think it's my best work, because it's richer and deeper. It was the hardest thing I had ever done. *Weapons of the Weak* has more of my blood, sweat, and tears in it than anything else. Living in that village was a real investment in becoming a peasantist. I worked so hard. As an anthropologist, you're working from the moment you open your eyes in the morning until you close them at night, and I was learning faster than at any other time in my life in terms of sheer observations. I was there for the better part of two years, and, by the time I finished, I had over four thousand pages of handwritten notes. I would write my notes up every night, a process that usually generated further questions to explore the next day. The great thing about this kind of fieldwork is that it's like a rolling interview. If I realized I had more questions for a person, I would meet him or her out on the village path the next day. It's not like interviewing elites, where you just have an hour or two. Living in the village gave me a lot of time to observe and cogitate. It's very productive when you become so preoccupied with something intellectually that it occupies your waking and sleeping hours, and you're even daydreaming about it. That's a great thing for ideas.

Q: Unless you get so exhausted you can't think straight.
A: Right. That's why I had to get away from the village every two weeks to clear my head. I also brought things to read that would clear my mind of this village, because it was so totally preoccupying. I would write up my field notes at night, working by a kerosene lamp and bitten to death by the bugs, often finishing at midnight or one o'clock, long after everyone else had gone to sleep. Then, when I finally got into bed under my mosquito netting on the floor, I would put a flashlight on my shoulder and read Jane Austen, Zola, or Balzac, good literature with a strong plot that would just take me away. I had done something similar when I finished my dissertation and first started teaching at the University of Wisconsin. I used to get up at 5:00 in the morning and read novels for two hours to recover my sanity. I think I did that for two years before I couldn't get up at 5:00 a.m. anymore. But it was a noble effort. I've always found that a steady diet of

pure political science bores me to tears. So, as a way to entertain myself and also as part of a desire to become educated that my wife instilled in me—she was educated, I wasn't, when I met her—I have always aspired to read as much good literature as I can.

Q: Besides becoming a bona fide peasantist, what else did you set out to achieve in *Weapons of the Weak?* What else motivated your study?
A: I wanted to study class relations. Ironically, instead of ending up in a place where a revolution was in the making, which obviously would have made me quite happy, I ended up in a village where basically nothing was happening. There was some technological change going on, for example, the introduction of combine harvesters, and I latched on to that. But on the whole, not much else was happening, at least not on the surface. I eventually came to see that there were all these subterranean forms of resistance to hegemony, such as desertion and foot-dragging, underneath the placid surface of the village. These forms of resistance are important because they do bring down large structures. For example, the desertion of the hill whites in the American South had an important impact on the outcome of the Civil War. Still, as someone who shall remain nameless said, "Having found nothing going on in this village, you gave it the name 'everyday resistance,'" and the idea of studying "everyday resistance" sort of took off.[3]

Q: Why didn't *Weapons of the Weak* turn out to be just a narrow study of a village? You expected *The Moral Economy of the Peasant* to command a small audience limited to specialists, but *Weapons of the Weak* should have had an even smaller audience because it was about just one Malay village. How were you able to connect what was going on in a small place, a village, to big questions of broad interest to social scientists?
A: I like to flatter myself by thinking that what I do is independent of where the profession is headed and that I don't pay much attention to mainstream disciplinary signals. But, let's face it, when I was working on *Weapons of the Weak,* everybody and their brother was reading Gramsci and Althusser. Questions of class consciousness, hegemony, and resistance were being talked about, especially in the literary field. What I did was take what would have been a village study and connect it to larger themes about ideology and hegemony that people were generally thinking about at the time.

Q: Did you bring Gramsci and Althusser with you to the village when you did your fieldwork?

---

3. The subtitle of *Weapons of the Weak* is "everyday forms of peasant resistance." See also Scott and Kerkvliet (1986).

A: No. I'd read Gramsci's *Prison Notebooks* (1991), but I don't think I took it to the village. When I started, I didn't think I was writing a book about hegemony, I thought it was a book about class relations. Most of the stuff I took to the village was local studies on Malaysia. I was focused on just trying to understand this stupid little village. During the first six months, I was learning the local dialect, and I was learning from my Malay colleagues who had already done fieldwork. They understood so much more than I, and, in a sense, what I did was take a lot of their material plus my own fieldwork and put it in a theoretical bent that was interesting to North Americans. For what it's worth, the book did well in Malaysia, too. And I just came back from a trip to Thailand, where I learned that *Weapons of the Weak* had meant something to radical students and intellectuals there. The book was published about five years after these intellectuals had come out of the jungle, where they had gone in the mid-1970s in a failed effort to make a revolution. For them, *Weapons of the Weak* was important because it showed that the extremes of revolution, on the one hand, and abject quiescence, on the other, were not the only options. There was a lot of life in the middle, in what used to be called the "long march through the institutions."

Q: You seem pleased that your book resonated with this group.
A: It was interesting to me that my work meant something to the radicals. And since I am on their side politically, that was nice.

Domination, Resistance, and States

Q: Your next book, *Domination and the Arts of Resistance* (Scott 1990), builds on the theme of the behavior of subordinate groups addressed in *Weapons of the Weak*. What did you set out to achieve in that book?
A: *Domination and the Arts of Resistance* is about what is said behind the back of power. The book makes one simple point: the public transcript between the powerful and weak can never tell you everything you need to know about power relationships. There is a hidden transcript, a privileged window on political thought and action, that also has to be considered. *Domination and the Arts of Resistance* is the only one of my books that has really had an audience outside political science. It is assigned in literary studies because some people think it helps them read against the grain. By writing that book, I was paying my dues to the Quakers and speaking truth to power, too. So, I feel good about it.

Q: Let's turn to your most recent book, *Seeing Like a State* (Scott 1998). In its broadly comparative scope and lack of fieldwork, this book was a departure from *Weapons of the Weak*.

A: *Seeing Like a State* is about forms of state knowledge. It's about how state officials have to domesticate and simplify the world in order to get the information they need to govern. The book grew out of my involvement in the Program in Agrarian Studies at Yale, which I started in 1991 with some colleagues. I was interested in the question of why the state is the enemy of people who move around, for example, gypsies. Through the Program in Agrarian Studies, I began educating myself about this issue by inviting people to give talks and by co-teaching an interdisciplinary course on the comparative study of agrarian societies. I was reading about ecology and development, and I was co-teaching with anthropologists, historians, political scientists, and people from forestry. It was a real education. So, I regard *Seeing Like a State* as a seminar that the Program in Agrarian Studies gave to me. I suppose most people think *Seeing Like a State* is the most ambitious book I've done, and I guess that's true. But writing a broadly comparative book has actually driven me back to want to do fieldwork again and focus on small places and things.

Q: One criticism of *Seeing Like a State* is that it lacks methodological rigor and, as a result, does not provide an argument susceptible to testing and falsification.[4] In short, the book does not meet the methodological standards of modern political science. How do you respond to this line of criticism?
A: The snotty reply is, Too bad for political science if it ends up excluding a lot of insight about politics that does not come in a certain package or format. But the real question is, does the book say something about power and the state? If it does and it's presented in an easy-to-swallow way, then so much the better. I don't mind that criticism. Take Barrington Moore's *Social Origins of Dictatorship and Democracy* (1966). It is not a very scientific book in a rigorous sense of the word *science*. But it is one of the smartest and most creative books we have, and it addresses interesting and important questions. This reminds me of something my colleague Charles Lindblom once said about a student's thesis, "It's a failure, but it addresses big questions that are formulated in a brilliant way. Even though the student failed to answer these questions, the thesis still advances political insight further than lots of things that are rigorous but address trivial and banal questions."

I read David Laitin's review (1999a) of *Seeing Like a State*, and it's a rather interesting review. He says, "The book is good, it will last forever, and it will become a classic." But he also says, "It ain't social science, because methodologically it's a mess; Scott selected cases on the dependent variable and so on." A colleague of mine actually ran into Robert Bates and David Laitin at a

---

4. See the reviews by Laitin (1999a) and Bates (2003).

political science meeting shortly after *Seeing Like a State* came out, and he asked them what they thought of the book. I think it was Laitin who said, "What an artist, he's a real artist." At one level it was a compliment, but at another level it was meant as a put down, because he was saying my work was not scientific. Well, I am happy to be called an artist because I don't believe political science is a natural science in the first place. I like Laitin's work, and I think he's an interesting intellectual. But I also think he is less of a social scientist than he believes himself to be, and I think the interesting ideas that Laitin has had don't really add up to anything particularly "scientific."

Q: This discussion raises the broader issue of how one responds to critics. What has been your approach to critics?
A: I don't reply to critics because it seems to me that such replies can't help but sound defensive. Also, by the time the criticism appears, it's usually a year-and-a-half after the book was published. I don't want to go back over my own stuff—I get repetitive. I read critical reviews carefully, and when they make some sense they get incorporated into the way I look at the world. It's not as if all my critics are full of shit. There are a lot of good critics out there. I've done enough now, so that if I decided to just defend my little turf, I could spend all my time writing replies to critics. But why should I defend turf?

Q: Continuing with the theme of critics, you mentioned earlier that Samuel Popkin misrepresented your argument about peasant behavior in his book *The Rational Peasant* (Popkin 1979). Are there other ideas of yours that have been misinterpreted?
A: I suppose that if intellectuals were thinking at all straight, we would never complain about our ideas being misinterpreted as opposed to being ignored. If you have an idea that is remotely rich and that people find useful in other contexts, they are usually going to take a simplified version of it and run in their own direction with it. Sometimes they take the idea and show you bright, inventive, and clever aspects that you yourself never realized. In other cases, they have criticisms that you recognize as just or unjust. And, yes, some people have grossly misinterpreted and misapplied my work, which irritates me because it makes my ideas seem even stupider than they are. But I suppose that anybody who complains about that deserves to have their wrist slapped. Was it Mae West who said, "Just spell my name right"? There's no such thing as bad publicity. At the risk of sounding maudlin, I am extremely lucky that so much of my work has been picked up. I'm the last person to complain about being ignored.

My dear friend at Wisconsin, Murray Edelman, who died not long ago, had a very healthy attitude about scholarship. He said, "It's all a compost heap. You just put down a layer of humus that helps other stuff grow. Your work will all be forgotten, but it will help stuff grow." When you see people using your ideas, that's part of the compost heap.

Q: Are there any ideas you feel proud about that did not become part of the compost heap, ideas that were not picked up by other scholars?
A: There's a little idea in my article "Protest and Profanation" that I find myself repeating in lots of contexts because nobody knows that article (Scott 1977a, 1977b). The argument is pretty simple: if you want to understand folk communism and folk nationalism, as opposed to elite communism and elite nationalism, then you have to understand how doctrines and ideas are transformed as they move from elite to folk practitioners. I guess that idea has not been picked up because it's buried in an old article in the journal *Theory and Society*. Perhaps that's a good reason for writing books instead of journal articles.

Current Research

Q: What are you working on now?
A: I'm working on why the state is the enemy of people who move around, which is what I thought I was doing when I was working on *Seeing Like a State*. I want to do my next book on hill and valley relations in Southeast Asia, which is the age-old and most important cleavage in that part of the world. I hope to illuminate this cleavage so that everyone who knows about hill and valley relations in Southeast Asia will say, "Ah, this is interesting." I also hope the book will say something about why the state has always been the enemy of people who move around and why there is something about a state that wants to fix people in a space.

I'm going to focus on Burma, so I'm studying Burmese. I am proud of myself because I just finished reading a 623-page book, *The Gazetteer of Upper Burma*, written in 1890. It's part of a six-volume collection the British put together in an effort to gather all the information they could on Upper Burma, which had just come into their possession after the Anglo-Burman War of 1885. This was the first effort by the British colonial state to bring order to their new possession by identifying the different ethnic groups living in it. If I do this right, I will eventually have read all the classical chronicles of the traditional, pre-colonial kingdoms of Southeast Asia. I'm also reading about Gypsies, Cossacks, and theoretical stuff on tribes and ethnicity.

I'm in no hurry. Nobody cares if Jim Scott writes a book next year, but it better be a good book when he does. I'm going to take my time and do it right.

3

3334

333334

Q: Your project focuses on the relationship between states and people who move around. But there are also many historical examples of *states* that move around.
A: In fact, the earliest states moved around because people got tired of feeding them. So, the English and French courts in the fourteenth century had to move from place to place. They were itinerant states. Nomadic states, like those of Kubla and Genghis Kahn, obviously moved around, too. There's a Chinese proverb that says "You can conquer a kingdom on horseback, but you have to get off the horse to govern it." The Mongols and the Manchus eventually had to get off their horses and settle down. The same thing happened to the Ottomans. Osman, the founder of the Ottoman Empire, was a nomad. But eventually the Ottomans settled down, became a sedentary, urban ruling class, and started beating up the nomads themselves.

Q: It sounds as if you will mainly be doing historical work for this project.
A: No. I want to go back to fieldwork. To keep you honest, you have to know something about a particular place. I'd like to do fieldwork in Burma, and I want to go to villages. It would be good for me to be in a place where nobody knows Jim Scott and where I have to learn like crazy. It's not clear that I'll be allowed into Burma, though, because I've signed every petition the Burmese military government would hate me for.

Q: Why did you choose Burma?
A: It's the first Southeast Asian place I went to. I love the place. And I once spoke Burmese and would like to recover that. Also, nobody is working on it. Lots of people are working on Vietnam and even Cambodia, but Burma has been forgotten. It's one of the parts of Southeast Asia that could really stand a careful, analytical look. So, I'm partly doing this as a public service.

Q: Do you have fears about doing village fieldwork at this stage of your life?
A: It will be a challenge. I'm sixty-four, and there are not many people doing fieldwork at my age. It's been more than twenty years since I've done real village fieldwork. Also, Burma is not Malaysia. The Malay village where I did my fieldwork for *Weapons of the Weak* was a pretty civilized place. It wasn't more than an hour from a decent hospital. I'm in pretty good health, and I take good care of myself. So I think I can do this. It'll be fun trying anyway.

Q: Do you have a title for the book yet?
A: No. I usually don't have a title until much later. My title for *Weapons of the Weak* was originally *Losing Ground*. But just as I was about to publish it,

Charles Murray published a book by that title trashing the welfare state
(Murray 1984). He used the title "losing ground" for something I disre-
spected, so I had to find another title for my book. *Weapons of the Weak* is a
fine title, although some people thought it sounded too much like a self-
help book. You know, "Monday's weapon, Tuesday's weapon . . ." And even
though I worked hard on a title, Yale University Press didn't like *Seeing Like a
State* because it was grammatically incorrect. It should be "seeing *as* a state."
Like a state is bad grammar. I found that quite funny.

The Craft of Research
Stories

**Q: One hallmark of your work is your frequent use of literary refer-
ences. *Weapons of the Weak* and *Domination and the Arts of Resistance*
contain many references to the novels of Balzac and George Eliot, for
example. How has your exposure to novels informed your work as a
social scientist?**
A: Now that's a question. As Donald/Dierdre McCloskey shows in his work
on the rhetoric of economics, strong stories are a very important part
of how people make arguments in the social sciences (McCloskey 1983,
1990).[5] There are different ways to be persuasive. In the social sciences,
there is a tendency to present results as a report on an experiment, as if
the study were an actual scientific experiment: here's the hypothesis, here's
the relevant data, and so on. But this presentation usually does not re-
capitulate at all the actual mental process by which the work was really
produced.

One of the ways I have tried to be persuasive in the presentation of my
work is to start with a story. I don't always do this, but *Weapons of the Weak,
Domination and the Arts of Resistance,* and *Seeing Like a State* all start with a
story. In *Weapons of the Weak,* the story is about the rich Haji and the poor
person.[6] The idea was to somehow bring the reader to the village by presenting real people moving about and by capturing some of the major
themes of the book. If the book had started with the second, theoretical
chapter, a lot fewer people would have finished it. In *Domination and the
Arts of Resistance* there are several stories at the beginning of the book,
including something from George Eliot. The book has a leisurely first chapter. *Seeing Like a State* begins with a vignette about scientific forestry in
Saxony and Prussia in the late eighteenth century. This vignette is a condensed story about how states reformulate the natural world according

5. McCloskey is a famous transsexual now known as "Dierdre."
6. The term *Haji* refers to a Muslim who has made the pilgrimage to Mecca.

to an abstract system, and I used it repeatedly throughout the book as I worked out this story in different contexts.

Each of these stories tries to capture the argument of the book in a concrete way. In *Weapons of the Weak* it's personal stories, whereas in *Seeing Like a State* it's a vignette that captures the whole argument. You could say that I have given readers a little sugar at the beginning that gets them to open the book and say, "Aha, this is fun reading." This technique can be used at the expense of seriousness, but I don't think I use it that way.

Q: You would not accept the view that "it can't be good social science if it's not painful reading."
A: No, I don't accept that view. Now, that doesn't mean there can't be good social science that *is* painful reading. For example, some of Bourdieu is a pain in the ass to read, but there is a lot you get out of it. But is that necessary? Even though I admire Bourdieu's work, I still ask myself, "Did he have to make it so difficult? Couldn't he have said it in a different way?"

Q: One implication of this discussion is that political scientists should read more novels.
A: I would not put a pistol at people's temples and make them read good literature. They either want to or they don't, and reading literature should not be treated like taking vitamin pills. But I do believe that the observations of Tolstoy, Gogol, or George Eliot have much political insight that could be put into disciplinary political science terms. Just as the health food people say, "You are what you eat," you are as an intellectual what you read and who you're talking with. And if you're just reading in political science and only talking with political scientists, it's like having a diet with only one food group. If that's all you do, then you're not going to produce anything new or original. You're just going to reproduce the mainstream. If you're doing political science right, then at least a third of what you're reading shouldn't be political science. It should be from somewhere else.

Writing

Q: You have a reputation for being a good writer. What is your approach to writing?
A: It takes me a long, long time to start writing, because I never start until I have an elaborate outline. I use big sheets of butcher paper and write down a number of big ideas. For example, if I am doing hill and valley relations, which is the most important historical cleavage in Southeast Asia, I'll make a little category on valley stereotypes of hills. Then I go through all my

notes and find all the references to valley ideas about the hills. I take notes on everything I read, so I always have a pile of electronic and paper notes. Also, whenever I have an idea I write it down and file it away. This whole process generates a set of intermediate ideas about a couple of big ideas. For *Seeing Like a State* I had about 150 ideas, most of which ended up on the cutting room floor. In the end, I have huge pieces of butcher paper, and then I use big highlighters to draw connections among all the ideas. Sometimes I do a completely new outline from that before I start writing.

I know many people who are able to write even when they are still in a semi-confused state about what it is that they are writing. Sometimes a lot of the problems disappear or resolve themselves in the process of writing. That's a technique I wish I had cultivated more.

I write very slowly. If I write three pages in a day, I feel like sending up Roman candles because that's an exceptional day. Normally, I write about one page a day when I'm in a full writing mood.

Q: Your first drafts must be very polished and good.
A: Yes. I write by hand and use a Staedtler eraser. Every sentence is drafted at least twice because I don't like going back later to revise. I make a big effort to get it the way I like the first time. That includes finding a felicitous way of saying and expressing it. I actually don't think of myself as an exceptionally good writer, but I had great teachers in grammar school who told me to start each sentence with a different particle of speech. If you start one with a subject, start the next one with a gerund, the next one with a subordinate clause, and so on. I was taught to vary the sentence structure and to write short sentences. Here I should mention George Orwell's essay, "Politics and the English Language" (Orwell 1950, 77–92). That's the best little thing you can read on the issue of how to write clearly. Orwell wrote it in the 1940s and has examples of egregious social science writing, although some of it looks pretty good to us now.

Q: A lot of cumbersome social science terms were not even invented yet in the 1940s.
A: That's right. One of the things I do for my graduate students if they are writing very badly is take two pages of their work and rewrite everything. Chances are the two pages will wind up being a page and a quarter when I get done with it. There is a standard social science way of writing that is longwinded and that we usually don't think a second about. But if McCloskey (1983, 1990) is right that everything is a story at some level, and if you've gone to the trouble of having an idea, then why not present that idea in the most powerful and convincing way possible?

Q: Regarding the form your written work takes, you seem to have a clear preference for writing books over articles.
A: I generally don't do articles anymore. If I do one, it means I am writing a book on that subject. And if somebody asks me to write a paper for a conference or volume, I tell them what I am doing, and if something fits the conference, fine. But my contribution has to be related directly to what I am doing. Some scholars live by being hostage to the interests of other people and taking assignments from people who ask them to write something. As a result, they may end up learning things they never thought they would learn. By contrast, I have a little path I have marked out, and if what I am working on coincides with what other people are interested in, that's fine, I'm flattered. But if not, too bad, because that's where I'm headed.

Theory

Q: Much of your work is informed by political and social theory. We discussed the influence of Gramsci's ideas about hegemony on *Weapons of the Weak,* and *Seeing Like a State* draws on the work of anarchist theorists like Kropotkin. Do you consider yourself a theorist?
A: No. To be frank, I actually think of myself as bad at theory. And I'm not being coy or overly modest. One of the reasons I did fieldwork was that I was lost whenever I had a discussion with anybody about, say, hegemony, and we put four or five fourth-order abstractions together. I am capable of quasi-abstract thought, but only if I can see something walk around on the ground on its own two feet. So, I can't tell you a lot that would be interesting to hear about hegemony, but I can show you how it might work in a particular context. There are lots of people who can think in pure abstractions, whom I can understand, and whose work I admire and use, people like Stuart Hall. But that's a style of thought that I am not very good at. If I have any theoretical and conceptual contribution to make, it comes from setting abstractions in a particular context and seeing how they work.

Fieldwork

Q: Can you describe your fieldwork techniques? For example, what kind of information do your field notes contain?
A: I was never trained as an anthropologist. I followed, pretty scrupulously, the advice given to first-time fieldworkers in anthropology in a series of never published, mimeographed, lectures given by F. G. Bailey at Sussex. The advice was exceptionally practical. For example, "Okay, you've gotten off the bus to your village. What do you do next?" He recommended that

you use your eyes as well as your ears and record everything as carefully as possible, under the theory that you don't know what might turn out later to be relevant and important. I did this while I was working on *Weapons of the Weak* and had over four thousand pages of field notes. Bailey also recommended that one keep a separate set of notebooks that record the fieldworker's intellectual efforts to make sense of the material, a kind of intellectual diary. I did this, too, and am grateful that I spent roughly one-third of my time recording notes. The temptation to accumulate undigested information is so seductive that stopping to reflect on it seems a waste of time, but it's not. I discovered that the most important information I had came from real events and disputes in the village and not from my quasi-structured interviews themselves. Since there were only seventy-nine households in the village, I got to know everyone reasonably well and many very well, as these things go. I would always have further questions after I read my notes, and I knew I'd encounter them on the village path in the next day or two and could follow up. This is not an opportunity those who study elites often have!

Q: How did you select the village you studied in *Weapons of the Weak?*
A: I chose the village because it was representative of the major rice growing area, because a Japanese scholar had spent three months there a decade before and was willing to share his information with me, which gave me a little time-series information, and because I liked looking at the mountain, Gunong Jerai, lying directly to the south of the village.

Q: How does fieldwork help you generate and fine-tune ideas?
A: I actually *cannot*, I repeat *cannot,* think in terms of fourth-order abstractions. Once you get three or four of them dancing around I may sound smart enough, but I really don't know what I'm talking about. I have always found that I *can* work out abstractions like class, ideology, property, and resistance by watching them work themselves out in a concrete situation. Then, it's possible for me to go back to the abstractions and write carefully about them. This, I think, is the essence of E. P. Thompson's intellectual position in *The Making of the English Working Class* (Thompson 1964) so far as understanding "class-consciousness" is concerned.

Collaboration

Q: You rarely collaborate on articles or books. Why is this so?
A: I regard it as a kind of failure of mine not to have written more things with others. I am something of a "control freak" when it comes to how an

argument is made and presented, and, frankly, it is easier for me to collaborate when my collaborators defer to me. I have learned a great deal through the intellectual give-and-take in the Program in Agrarian Studies, but when it comes to actual writing, I'm something of a loner. I would sometimes like to think that it makes for a more cohesive, single authorial voice but, in fact, it is something of a temperamental matter.

Colleagues, Students, and Institutions
Wisconsin during the Vietnam War

Q: Your first job was at the University of Wisconsin, Madison, where you were a young assistant professor in the late 1960s, a turbulent and interesting time. What was it like?

A: I arrived at Wisconsin in the fall of 1967, and we were right in the middle of the Vietnam War. The student demonstrations against Dow Chemical, which made Napalm, were going on at Wisconsin. In October or November of my first year, the whole faculty of the university was having its regular meeting. Although these events were supposed to be an exercise in direct democracy, like a big town meeting, they were poorly attended, with just the seventy-year-olds showing up. But, because of the war, that year was different. We filled the auditorium with five hundred people, and it was amazing. Being a Southeast Asianist and against the war, I spoke up occasionally. Later, at a cocktail party, the dean of the College of Letters and Science, Leon Epstein, a big muckety-muck, who had been chairman of the Political Science Department and would later become president of the American Political Science Association, turned to me and said, "Scott, if we didn't need people like you and your ilk here . . ." His voice trailed off, and he never finished the threat, but what he was going to say was, "We would get rid of you." Epstein thought I was a clear and present danger to the department. That was the first time I realized that I had come under suspicion by the powers that be for my political involvement.

If I wanted to be charitable, which I generally don't want to be in this case because people like Epstein destroyed a lot of careers, I would point out that Wisconsin was growing like crazy when I arrived, and I came into the Political Science Department as one of eight assistant professors hired the same year. This was a huge, unswallowable phalanx. Before, junior hires had come in ones, twos, or threes, and they had been assimilated gradually, going to dinner with the senior faculty and so on. But my cohort came in a big clot. We were like a little society and had an esprit de corps. I wore blue jeans and flannel shirts, which wasn't the standard drill. So, our older colleagues feared we were ruining a wonderful craft and discipline.

When I got into trouble at Wisconsin, my good friend and colleague, Ed Friedman, said something that I've always remembered. Ed has actually said a lot of important things to me—I think he's the biggest influence on my intellectual life. Anyway, Ed told me, "You're going to have to start acting like a Jew. Every Jew knows that to make it professionally they have to be twice as good as a musician, twice as good as an accountant. You can overcome prejudice, but to do it you have to be a lot better than the *goyim* around you." Ed told me that if I wanted to get tenure at Wisconsin, I was going to have to be twice as good as anybody else, or they'd kill my ass. They wanted to get rid of me, and if I had given them an excuse, they would have done it. I was confronting people politically, and I decided I was not going to give that up because that's what really mattered to me. Yet I also decided that in every other respect I was going to be the best colleague they ever had. I started reading the work of my senior colleagues, went to lunch with them, and talked to them about their work. I was conscientious about doing all my department service, and blah, blah, blah . . . So, I knew that if they wanted to get me, they were going to have to do it based only on my politics, because, in every other respect, I did my level best to be a model colleague, even though I had to stifle my gagging impulse with some of those people.

Q: What was your interaction with students like? Many must have been highly mobilized against the Vietnam War.
A: Ed Friedman and I taught a course together on peasant revolution. It was a hugely popular course, as you can imagine, given the interest in this topic generated by the war. We had 350 students and took turns lecturing. But there were about eighty students who considered us insufficiently progressive. In fact, it turned out that three of the people who bombed the Army Math Research Center at Wisconsin took our course. We taught it in a big hall, and people were struggling for the microphone to denounce us. There were sixty or seventy students who spent all night after every lecture debating and preparing a critique of the lecture in four or five pages that they mimeographed and handed out at the start of the next class. It was as if it all mattered.

Q: In 1976 you left Wisconsin for Yale. Why did you leave? Were you unhappy at Wisconsin?
A: No. I loved Wisconsin. It had the Land Tenure Center, and I had wonderful colleagues like Ed Friedman. I would have been happy to stay there. When I got the offer from Yale, I left the decision to my wife, Louise. She chose Yale because all her relatives were on the East Coast, and she wanted to be closer to them, which was fine with me. I was happy to go to Yale

because there were lots of advantages, like having fewer students. It worked out fine.

When I got the offer from Yale, the chairman of my department said I had to give Wisconsin at least a chance to respond to the Yale offer. I did it, even though I thought it was a waste of time, because the decision was not about money. Well, I think Leon Epstein was still dean, and I forget how much Yale offered me, but whatever it was, Wisconsin's counteroffer was that amount minus a hundred dollars. I've never forgotten that.

From Wisconsin to Yale

Q: What was the transition from Wisconsin to Yale like?
A: I mentioned that when I went to Wisconsin I was part of a group of eight junior professors. But when I came to Yale, I came by myself, and I came with tenure. Also, I was busy getting the family set up and so on. Yale is a very forbidding place, and after a year or so I realized I didn't have any intellectual friends. I was going back and forth to work and seeing a few people, but I didn't really have an intellectual community. I was a lonely intellectual. To remedy this situation, I did something that is not normally my style. I sat down and said to myself, "Whom would I like to make an intellectual companion out of? Who are the people at Yale that seem intellectually interesting to me?" I figured out who these people were. Then I read their work, took them to lunch, and told them how great I thought their work was. Of these people, three or four have become very close friends.

Q: Who were these people? Who are the colleagues you have felt closest to at Yale?
A: Some have drifted away. But at that point, the people whom I decided I wanted to get to know included Helen Siu, an anthropologist who works on China; Bill Kelly, another anthropologist, who works on Japan; Bob Harms, a historian who works on Africa; Jonathan Spence, a historian who works on China; and Debbie Davis, a sociologist who also works on China. Later, I became close to Michael Dove, who's in forestry, environmental studies, and ecology, as well as Paul Freedman, a mediaevalist in history. I didn't think of it this way at the time, but I now recommend to colleagues that they make a self-conscious effort to define their invisible college: given what you are working on, who are the people, both at your institution and across the country and world, who are working on the kinds of things you like? In my case, my invisible college came to include people like Michael Adas, a super good historian. He and I don't know one another that well, but we have a tough collegial relationship in which we send each other manuscripts and the other hashes it up.

Q: It's interesting that you have not named a single political scientist.
A: I hung out with the political scientists at Yale whose work I read and who read my work. This includes Ian Shapiro, Rogers Smith, Margaret Keck, when she was here, and, more recently, Arun Agrawal. But, since 1991, when I and some colleagues started the Program in Agrarian Studies my intellectual life at Yale has not been centered in the Political Science Department. I like the department and have a warm feeling for it, but it's not my primary intellectual hub.

The Program in Agrarian Studies at Yale

Q: What is the purpose of the Agrarian Studies Program? How did it originate and what kinds of activities does it carry out?
A: The program brings together people interested in rural life, whether during the Tang dynasty in China, or in contemporary Asia or Africa. You name it. I like to think of the rationale for the program in the following way. If someone told me there was a political science talk around the corner, what are the odds I would enjoy the talk? The chances are probably one out of twenty, or one out of ten. But if someone told me there was a talk on peasants, farmers, or agriculture around the corner, I'm pretty sure I would be interested, and I might even have something to contribute. So, the Agrarian Studies Program is organized not around a theory, but around a *subject* that's relevant to lots of different disciplines. In a way that turned out to be simultaneously selfish and public-spirited, I created an intellectual circle and community that is like a seminar I am giving myself. That's the selfish part of it. But it also turns out that a lot of graduate students think the program is pretty cool, and a lot of colleagues have given a hand in putting it together. So, we've created a successful interdisciplinary program.

It's a little like my writing. Both in my writing and in Agrarian Studies I have somehow managed to keep rolling 7s and 11s. The dice seem to come up right more often than not. As long as the 7s keep coming up, I'm afraid to think too much about it. Somehow my instincts are working for me. If I get too clever and too self-conscious instead of just trying to have fun, then I'll screw it up.

Q: Could you discuss the nuts and bolts of the Agrarian Studies Program?
A: We have a joint graduate course on the comparative study of agrarian societies that three or four of us teach, and it's the largest course in the history of Yale's graduate programs. We've had up to fifty-five students enrolled at one time. Most of the students who take the course are interested in rural issues of one kind or another and feel orphaned by their

departments. The course meets every Monday for four hours, instead of the standard two hours. There is a lecture, and then we split up into small groups. So, it's double the amount of hours you would get in a normal course.

We also have eight post-docs who come every year. I spend lots of time every fall making sure I put them in touch with the faculty they need to do their best work. I'm like a marriage arranger, trying to figure out who ought to be matched. There is also a weekly colloquium, which is mostly attended by graduate students. The discussant at the colloquium is never a specialist on the speaker's subject—in fact, you're disqualified as a discussant if you know anything in depth about the subject.

When I started the Agrarian Studies Program, I went to see Lawrence Stone, a historian who ran the Davis Center for Historical Studies at Princeton, which is a good program. I said, "Is there anything you can tell me about how to run a good program?" He said, "Make sure you always have a social occasion after your major intellectual event." I took his advice, and, after the colloquium, which meets every Friday from 11 to 1, we have a free lunch. This fosters interaction across disciplines because it gives people who noticed that someone else said something clever during the colloquium the chance to sit down together afterward and make a connection.

By and large, graduate students are an unhappy, lonely lot, and if someone provides an intellectual event that also happens to be socially attractive, they will turn out in droves. There are even couples who have met in Agrarian Studies and gotten married. Scholars are not just brains in formaldehyde, they have creature needs as well. A graduate student once put this in a charming way. She said that coming to Agrarian Studies was like going to church: "You see all your friends from other disciplines, and people get dressed up for it." So our weekly colloquium acquired an event status.

Q: One group that seems absent from "church," however, is the political scientists. I have the impression that not many political science graduate students participate in the Agrarian Studies Program.
A: You're absolutely right. Some political scientists participate, but not many. The center of gravity is people from anthropology, history, and forestry and environmental studies, although we also get some people from sociology, the law school, public health, and occasionally from the natural sciences. This reflects the fact that not many graduate students in political science today are working on rural topics.

Q: Why are so few graduate students in political science working on rural issues?

A: The zeitgeist has left us. In 1975, lots of people in political science were working on rural issues, including Robert Bates. But the political science zeitgeist has migrated. Interest in rural issues has been renewed recently by people working on topics like indigenous rights, sustainable development, and environmental issues. But, work on rural issues today is done mainly by anthropologists and historians. These, of course, are the two place-based disciplines in which everyone's work is firmly grounded in a terrain, a context, even if it's an archive in the case of historians, or a global place in the case of anthropologists. By contrast, if you're a political scientist today, especially a formal, deductive kind of political scientist, you have a little tool kit of universal wrenches. They parachute you into Patagonia or Nepal, and you open your tool kit and put your wrenches to work. Some anthropologists also have universal tool kits. Take Claude Lévi-Strauss's idea about how to unpack myths, for example (Lévi-Strauss 1986).

Q: What is the difference between Lévi-Strauss's anthropological tool kit and the modern political scientist's universal wrenches?
A: There is no difference. But notice what happened to Lévi-Strauss: the formulaic part of his work has disappeared without a trace. By contrast, the work of someone like Clifford Geertz has endured. Geertz doesn't have a technique, and his work is idiosyncratic, a bit like mine, I suppose. If you were inclined to become a disciple of Geertz, it's hard to know exactly what you'd have to do, whereas if you wanted to become a disciple of Lévi-Strauss, you would try to master his techniques of mythical analysis.

Teaching

Q: You say that, like Clifford Geertz's work, yours is idiosyncratic and does not offer a packaged set of techniques for would-be disciples. Geertz has had few, if any, students. Do you have many students?
A: Because of the Agrarian Studies Program, I have tons of students, though not all are in political science. I learn a lot from students in other disciplines, like forestry and environmental studies, history, and anthropology, though advising these students is also a lot of work, and sometimes it's a thin line between how much it teaches me and how much it gobbles up my time. Also, for what it's worth, Rogers Smith, when he was the director of Graduate Studies for the Political Science Department, tabulated the number of graduate students that faculty members had advised in political science, and it turned out I was ranked number one. It surprised me.

It is really flattering to have people who want to work with you, because, after all, that's kind of why you're there. My problem is that I get too many

students now, and I don't think I do as well by each of them as I could
before. I have so many political science students partly because I get students who don't want to do the standard thing and see me as someone who
will protect them.

**Q: How do you feel about having so many students come to you for
protection?**
A: It's fine, although I worry about leading them into a blind alley in terms
of their own careers if it turns out the discipline is not headed my way. And I
think it's probably not.

**Q: Do you take steps to reduce the risk that your students will indeed
end up in a blind alley?**
A: I tell them, "You have to learn their stuff." If you don't like rational
choice research and you don't think it's the way political science ought to
be done, then you first have to make an effort to understand it and then do
your critique of it, rather than just disliking it from the outside. Be a mission boy turned bad, but know the catechism so you can't be dismissed as a
technophobe, which I can be dismissed as, I might add.

Q: Are you a technophobe?
A: No. But I don't propose to reformulate my work in algebraic terms.

**Q: Do you have an overall approach to training graduate students?
How should graduate students be trained?**
A: I don't have an overall pedagogical plan, and I think what each student
needs intellectually is likely to be different. I do, however, believe that for
those working on Southeast Asia, they have to have the language and a
great deal of local knowledge—history, literature, popular culture, art, religion. And, for what it is worth, I think that, even if you have a critical
intellectual position vis-à-vis the mainstream, you have to invest the time
to know carefully the intellectual foundations of the position you are criticizing. For example, if you want to criticize rational choice work, you have
to have a pretty thorough knowledge of it.

The Political Science Discipline
Between Art and Science

**Q: Through the prominent role you have played recently in the Pere-
stroika movement, you have been a strong critic of certain trends in
political science, such as the increasing emphasis on methodologi-**

cal rigor and the proliferation of rational choice theory.[7] Are you against rigor?

A: What passes for rigor? In political science, rigor has come to be defined as a narrow methodological rigor that, although you can't fault the technique, often does not get you anywhere because it is used to answer trivial questions. For example, my colleague at Yale, Don Green, whom I respect a lot because he's one of the brightest people I know, thinks political scientists should do experiments. He and Alan Gerber have done an experiment where two sets of voters were randomly selected, and one group was visited before the election by people from their neighborhood who asked them to vote, whereas the other was just sent letters asking them to vote (Gerber and Green 2000). Well, they can show that having someone visit voters and ask them to vote results in greater turnout than just sending a letter saying they should vote. That's a hard finding, a real scientific finding, and the experimental design was probably as good as you can get. Yet I don't think what they found is important at all. It's not an earth-shattering result. Don Green's response is that even if the result is not earth-shattering, at least it's solid. His premise is that if you get enough of these bricks, you finally get an edifice. I think you just get a pile of bricks.

More generally, the problem with methodological reductionism is that it looks like an achievement if someone shows a logical flaw in a step of reasoning and deduction. Contributions start to be defined as the refinement of tools, which is not, I think, why we're here. Behind that is the larger question of whether we're a real science or not, and behind that is the question of whether real sciences actually work according to the models of people like Popper (1959) and Hempel (1965, 1966).

Q: If political scientists should not aspire to be like natural scientists by carrying out experiments, then what should we aspire to?

A: That's a big question, and I'm not sure I have an answer to it. I'm not willing to say that we are just artists, so let's have fun. There are certain elementary canons of reasoning, found in classic treatises on syllogisms and logic, that need to be used and not violated. So, I don't think methodol-

7. In 2000, a scholar writing as "Mr. Perestroika" circulated an anonymous manifesto calling for reform of the *American Political Science Review* (*APSR*), the American Political Science Association (APSA), and the political science profession in general. Mr. Perestroika voiced concern that many leaders in the profession did not read or submit to the *APSR*, that the APSA's council and the *APSR*'s editorial board seemed to be chosen undemocratically by their predecessors, and that the *APSR* was focused on technical methods, rather than important substantive questions about politics. This scholar's frustration resonated with a large number of political scientists and generated much discussion and debate in the profession. On the Perestroika movement, see Eakin (2000) and Monroe (2005).

ogy is a waste of time. But political scientists are condemned to exist in a nether world between art, on the one hand, and an overblown, distorted image of natural science, on the other hand—we have penis envy when it comes to natural science. We cannot ever really be like the natural sciences, because we study the conduct of human subjects, which is amenable to self-reflection. Once you tell people what you have found out about their behavior they are free to change it and just piss in the soup. Take public opinion research, which was in its heyday when I was in graduate school in the 1960s. Murray Edelman, my old colleague at Wisconsin, liked to point out that by using surveys you might discover that people prefer X or Y, or that they believe the Supreme Court is doing a good job. But these are not stable opinions; they can change next week under slightly different circumstances. Also, there is not, in a simple way, an objective political and social reality "out there." This is an important insight from semiotics.[8] Geertz makes this point in his piece about the interpretation of winks and twitches (Geertz 1973, 3–30). John Dunn also has a nice piece about how you can never create a satisfactory explanation of people's behavior without providing a phenomenological account of what they themselves think they are doing (Dunn 1979).

Q: Despite these misgivings about the scientific aspirations of political science, do you think the field has accomplished anything in terms of producing knowledge?
A: You are asking me to think about the discipline and its role in the world, but the fact is, for some time, I have not thought about the discipline, partly because I decided it only had so much to teach me. I am embarrassed to say how long it has been since I read anything in the *American Political Science Review*—at least eight years. I still get it, because it arrives automatically if you are a member of the American Political Science Association (APSA). Every time I go to the annual meeting of APSA, which is a maximum of every four or five years, I renew my membership, but then I let it lapse. I throw the *American Political Science Review* straight from my mailbox into the trash. Still, if I behave like a responsible grown-up and ask, "What are the solid things I have learned or know because of being a political scientist and reading political science?" I would point to Weberian insights on rationality and crude forms of Marxism on material interests. I have certainly learned something from semiotics. For example, I had an epiphany when I was driving a few years ago. I saw a bumper sticker that said "America, love it or leave it," and I thought to myself, "It's only the readings I've done in semiotics that cause me to realize that a bumper sticker that says 'Amer-

8. Semiotics is a theory about the function of signs and symbols in language.

ica, love it or leave it' is a reply to an unstated bumper sticker that says, 'America, I hate it, and I'm leaving.' It's an assertion against a negative absence." Similarly, if you ever talk to someone from Allentown or Wilkes-Barre, Pennsylvania, and tell them what a shitty town they come from, they go ballistic. My wife came from Pittsburgh, and she did the same thing. The worse the place is, the more it has to be defended. Semiotics has taught me that every discourse is in a dialogue with other ways of seeing the world.

Q: What about comparative politics? Has the field of comparative politics generated cumulative knowledge?
A: Comparativists have learned some valuable things about presidential versus parliamentary government, the functioning of autocracies, the process of social movement formation, the consequences of electoral laws, and even ethnic conflict. None of this is cumulative in the strict scientific sense of covering laws, however, and much of this hard-won knowledge is carried, by its practitioners rather than its originators, as a naïve religious faith or template that can be plunked down rather unimaginatively in any situation without much knowledge of the context.

Q: You argue that the strong emphasis on methodological rigor in contemporary political science has led to a focus on trivial questions. What kinds of questions should we be asking in our research?
A: If you look at a whole bunch of dissertations, they can be divided into two categories: those that address a powerful and interesting question and those that don't. Most dissertations fall into the latter category, because they raise uninteresting questions that are not really worth asking in the first place. There are lots of dissertations on questions that I don't even want to know the answer to. I'd rather see a failed effort to tackle an important question than a successful effort to address a trivial one. Lindblom put this beautifully. According to Lindblom, a couple of Chicago brothers had tried to fly a plane before the Wright brothers. They failed, and their plane landed in the Chicago River. Lindblom's point was that the Wright brothers could not have done what they did without this previous noble failure. So, if you take a book like Ben Anderson's *Imagined Communities* (1991), it begins by asking, "Why is it that there is a tomb of the unknown Frenchman and the unknown American, but there is not a tomb of the unknown bourgeois and the unknown proletarian? Why do some collectivities inspire powerful sentiments and action, whereas others do not?" It's a fabulous question. *Imagined Communities* is a crazy book, but no one would ever claim it is about something of passing interest. Barrington Moore's *Social Origins of Dictatorship and Democracy* (1966) also poses an important question: How do we get different routes to the modern world? By contrast, a lot

of comparative politics today focuses on little things about central banks and democratic transitions. If I were convinced like Don Green that these little bricks were adding up to some great edifice, then I would have to climb down from my high horse. But I do not see any evidence of that.

Q: How can graduate students be taught to ask interesting and important questions?
A: It's not clear that this can be taught, but my colleague Arun Agrawal and I are trying. We are teaching a new course called "Creativity and Method in Comparative Research," which, rather than assuming a good idea and focusing on how you test it, as do most methodology courses, looks instead at the prior question of how you get a good idea in the first place. The first thing we assign is Karl Polanyi's *The Great Transformation* (1957), and we ask the students to write a research proposal for this book. We also have them read Tolstoy's *War and Peace* (1967) and ask them to derive three interesting propositions from it for a political scientist. Another week, the students are asked to observe something very carefully, say, a political discussion between two friends, or sessions of night court in New Haven, and write down what it says about political discourse.

We decided to put together this course because forty-seven graduate students sent a petition to the chairman of political science requesting a course on qualitative methods, which is offered at lots of other places. We got a bunch of syllabi for qualitative methods courses from other departments, but we decided we did not want to teach a course like that. Most of the material taught under the rubric of qualitative methods is critiques of positivism and hypothesis testing. You read things like Amartya Sen's "Rational Fools" (1977) and Hirshman's "The Search for Paradigms as a Hindrance to Understanding" (1970). We did not want to make it a methodology course in a narrow sense, because we felt we could do something more interesting.

The Problem of Hyper-Professionalism

Q: Besides the kinds of questions political scientists address, what other aspects of the discipline bother you?
A: Political science suffers from the problem of hyper-professionalism, by which I mean the proliferation of small coteries doing increasingly specialized work that appeals to narrower and narrower audiences. According to my colleague Douglas Rae, someone actually did a study of the average number of readers of a social science journal article, and it turns out to be less than three. Let's imagine they were off by a factor of three, and the average number of readers is really nine. This still means that the whole

business of peer-reviewed journals has no effect on the external world and is just a Rube Goldberg machine designed to get people tenure. The *Journal of Conflict Resolution* that Bruce Russett runs is an example. Nobody reads that. It has a small circulation, and the contributors massage each other. But publishing in refereed journals still gets people tenure, even if these publications are refereed by just a handful of people.

I have a critique along these lines of the *Social Science Citation Index*.[9] I actually do pretty well by its criteria, so this is not sour grapes. First, self-citations count. Second, there are junior professors who agree to cite one another to improve their chances of getting tenure. Third, critical citations count; citations that say, "This is a piece of shit and it's not worth the paper it's printed on" still give you one hit. Fourth, it privileges people who publish articles rather than books. Finally, it privileges people who write in the English language. The *Social Science Citation Index* is an Anglo-American operation that privileges people who are working on mainstream Anglo-American politics.

Q: What solutions do you propose to the problem of hyper-professionalism?

A: I would like to see a requirement that to make a new appointment in political science you have to prove to some other discipline that this person would be important to them too. That would be bracing. To get tenure in political science, what if you had to have another department say your work is of interest to them? In the run-up to tenure, what if you had to get people in two adjacent disciplines to read your stuff and say "This looks good"? And what if everybody who got tenure had to have a dual appointment in two disciplines, appointments that would cost each department something? In other words, the second department would not be allowed to just say, "Yeah, Snyder is fine with us, we are not against a joint appointment"; they would actually have to pay for part of Snyder's time. It would cost them real money. I have no idea how this would actually work out institutionally, but what I'm groping for is a way to constantly get information and judgments from outside, a way to have someone looking over the discipline's shoulder. The basic question is, how do you institutionalize a set of procedures that mitigate against hyper-professionalism?

I make the following argument to my colleagues. Given the contingencies in life and the political science discipline, neither you, nor I, nor anyone else knows for sure where political science is headed. Nobody knows what is going to be worthy and honorable work five or ten years from

9. The number of citations a scholar has in the *Social Science Citation Index* is a metric that many Political Science departments use in making decisions about hiring, salaries, tenure, and promotions.

now. A prudent and rational department, not knowing what the future will bring, would therefore place a whole series of bets in a lot of different fields, because light comes in through many windows. Now, in the case of a small department with only a handful of posts, maybe it makes sense to go for broke and gamble on one thing, the way Rochester did with rational choice theory. But then you win or lose with a single roll of the dice. Yale does not need to do that. We're big enough that we can and should place many prudent bets. My further argument is that rational choice people, if they are surrounded just by rational choice people, only become stupider, because they only hear their echo. Their methods are never challenged. If you want smart rational choice people, then you have to surround them with a challenging, Darwinian environment of natural selection that forces them to justify themselves every day. The best rational choice work will be produced in a department where scholars who do rational choice have to make a case for why their work is valuable. The same is true, of course, for people who don't do rational choice. In fact, the last thing I want is a Political Science Department that just has me and my kind of person in it.

Q: To continue with your Darwinian metaphor, should we strive for an infinite variety of species? Should we let a million flowers bloom? Or is there a limit to how much intellectual diversity can flourish under the roof of one discipline?

A: Ian Shapiro, the chair of Yale's department, has launched an inspired effort to reformulate Yale's hiring by focusing on six or seven perennial themes in political science, for example, distribution, the design of institutions, and so on. Ian's case, which I endorse, is "Tell us something interesting on any of these themes. We don't care if you're doing Kant and Hegel or rational choice work on the Cincinnati police force's race relations. We don't care what techniques you use." It's like what Deng Xiaoping said about China's switch toward more market-oriented economic policies: "We don't care if the cat is white or black, as long as it catches mice." Now, this approach to hiring is not oblivious to the fact that people have methodological commitments, but it forces them to make their case not by their methods, but by what they can actually show about these perennial themes in political science. In a perfect world, we would look at people who wanted a job and judge how interesting and powerful their minds are. And hopefully, that judgment would not be tied closely to the methods they use. But so many things get in the way of people's careers, personal problems and so forth, that hiring is an inexact science. If you were to bet every year on five new and creative people, chances are that three or four of them wouldn't work out. So, focusing on what job candidates have to say about perennial themes is probably the closest thing to a satisfying hiring strategy. But making a fetish out of methods of any kind, including making a fetish out of having no methods, would be a mistake.

Rational Choice Theory

Q: What is your overall assessment of the contribution of rational choice theory to political science?

A: Rational choice theory is a valuable, useful, and enlightening part of political science. I have found a focus on problems of collective action and transaction costs helpful in some of my own work, though it doesn't take you very far. What I object to is the universalistic, Leninist tendencies of some people who do rational choice. I also think rational choice theory has little to say about most human decisions. Even advocates of rational choice theory admit that massive, earth-shattering decisions, like whether or not to die for your country, are not rationally thought out. But they maintain that people do act rationally when making ordinary decisions. My reply to that is, "Bull shit!" Even when they make ordinary decisions, people are still in the grips of dreams, myths, and values whose origins are poorly understood. This is a point Fredric Jameson makes about the structure of advertisements (Jameson 1981). Most ads show you something you would like to be or have, but can't. For example, an ad will first show young, dashing people in a fast car, or a man holding a beautiful woman in his arms with a luxurious apartment in the background. Then you see a BMW or a bottle of Hennessy Cognac, and the suggestion subtly planted in your mind is, "You can't be young and dashing or have a beautiful woman and a posh apartment, but you can have the BMW or the Hennessy Cognac as a substitute." Jameson's point is that advertisements start with a utopia we believe in, whether its youth, beauty, success, or material possessions, and then use our desires to draw us to something else. This is even true for soap. You would think people buy soap because it gets them clean. Well, all soaps get you clean, but you choose a particular soap in the store because something about the packaging catches your eye. It has nothing to do with a rational decision.

The Future of Political Science

Q: You say that no one knows for sure how political science will evolve. Still, could you sketch a few plausible scenarios for the future of the discipline, especially in light of your concerns about hyper-professionalism and the narrowing of research questions?

A: I don't know where all this is headed. One version is that political science is just neoclassical economics ten or fifteen years to the rear. It's a plausible case, and there are many people who think political science is going to become like economics, but even more hyper-professional. I think two things will prevent that from happening. First, any discipline worth its salt produces its own internal critique dialectically. This has happened in economics with the movement in France for a post-autistic economics, which is an effort to build back into the discipline questions about consumer taste, the formation of the values that actors maximize, and traditional things that have been lost, like labor history. In political science, the people in rational choice imagine they are the new revolutionary vanguard, and, in fact, they are hegemonic in many contexts. Still, in many ways they are producing their own deep criticisms. My hunch, and this is just a guess because I don't believe in predictive science, is that rational choice will lay down a sedimentary layer, a layer of clay, that will mark its passing in the landscape. A lot of people will do it, and they will grow old together and eventually be superseded by new things. Like behavioralism, rational choice will leave a fairly thick sediment, a thicker sediment than I'm leaving.

The other thing that will prevent the transformation of political science into economics is an institutional limitation. In most places you have to teach undergraduates, and undergraduates are not taking political science courses in order to do rational choice theory. This can be seen in early warning signs like patterns of course enrollment. Any dean, vice-chancellor, or provost who allowed a department to become entirely rational choice would betray undergraduates, and most of them are unwilling to do it. There is an institutional responsibility that limits the reach of rational choice.

Q: You have been active in the Perestroika movement and will soon start a two-year term on the governing Council of the American Political Science Association (APSA). What role do you see yourself playing in the discipline?
A: On the one hand, I don't give a shit where political science is headed. They can wallow in whatever mire they want, and I can continue to do my stuff. On the other hand, I find myself, against my better judgment, getting involved in APSA on behalf of junior colleagues, even though the last thing I want to do is spend my declining years making revolution in the political science association because it takes time. As far as APSA is concerned, I have two roles, and only two roles. One role is to make the association more democratic, although I don't know if this ends up being in my interest or not. This requires changing APSA's procedures so that there are elections for the presidency and other offices. As it stands, APSA is probably the least democratic professional association I know, because, unlike the Association of Asian Studies or the American Sociological Association, for instance, APSA does not elect its officers.

Q: Why are you not sure it is in your interest to make APSA more democratic?
A: Because the rational choice people might win the elections, right? But that's okay because it will produce its own reaction. And, regardless, I'm going to try to make these changes no matter what, because it's something I believe I should do.

My other role in APSA, and here I disagree with some of the Perestroika people, concerns the status of the *American Political Science Review (APSR)* as the discipline's "flagship" venue. It seems to me there are only two options. You either keep the *APSR,* but change its whole complexion by making it catholic and open to a million breezes. I prefer that. The alternative, which is what has been done so far, is to create a new journal.[10] But the only way I'll be in favor of that is if they take away the label, *American Political Science Review,* because it gives the false impression that what is published there is the apex of professional excellence. If they want to remain arcane, let's give them a label that accurately describes the product, something like *The Review of Positive Political Science.*[11] It was very clever of the people who want to keep the *APSR* the way it is to try to divert Perestroika's energies by supporting the launching of a new journal. This could reduce the pressure for them to change the *APSR.* But I don't want to take the pressure off. Either they change, or else I am going to enjoy making them compete for an audience by taking away their misleading name so that the journal's label describes what is actually in it.

I'm not optimistic about how things will end up, though, because I've seen enough and read enough about Michel's Iron Law of Oligarchy.[12] I think I'm on the APSA Council as a token, and I'm under no illusions about the dent I'm going to make. On the other hand, this is all the more reason to be ferocious about what I would like to achieve. I consider it a waste of time, and rather than waste my time and be reasonable, I intend to be intelligently unreasonable and intractable. The problem is I don't have the time and energy to go around making coalitions. A really responsible person who wanted to reform the discipline would spend a lot of time on the e-mail network. I'm not going to do that, and I can't do that. I do have a little kitchen cabinet of people who have thought a lot more carefully than I about institutional issues involving APSA, and I plan to rely very heavily on them.

10. This new journal, *Perspectives on Politics,* first appeared in 2003.

11.The term *positive political science* here refers to work that uses formal, mathematical methodologies and rational choice theory.

12. The reference is to Robert Michels's idea that those in power use their power to stay in power. See Michels (1962).

Conclusion

Q: What advice can you offer students who are starting out in comparative politics?
A: I like to teach students who have been out of college for several years and come to graduate school with a passion for something they experienced in the world and want to work very hard to understand. For example, I have a graduate student who worked on the Burma-Thai border in refugee camps and then came to graduate school wanting to understand hill people and the development of the Burmese state. He basically wanted to put the themes that were his life for two years in a larger perspective. The disadvantage of teaching this kind of student is that sometimes they are quite rigid because they think they have already figured out everything. What you want ideally is someone who brings a set of questions they are passionate about yet is open to new ways of understanding these questions, which, by the way, doesn't describe what I was like as a student. But I have other students who think of scholarship as a career, as an 8-to-5 job. I have a colleague at Iowa State who says he has really good and very smart colleagues, but, for most of them, it is just a job. They're there 9 to 5, and they don't think about their work afterward. Here's what Ian Shapiro would say about the matter, "Look, you're never going to make any money in this racket. So if you're not having fun, why the hell are you in it in the first place? If it's just a career, a job, and you want to make money, then you're in the wrong place." There is something to be said for passion and fun. My advice is to make sure there is something you really want to understand, rather than just going to graduate school to get your union card.

Q: Do you see less passion in graduate students today?
A: Absolutely. We get a lot of people who are fresh out of college, did well in political science courses, liked their teachers, and think this is what they want to do for a career. By contrast, in the 1960s and 1970s, we would get people who had not done much more in the world, but were more interested in politics because they had been involved in antiwar struggles, for example. In my case, I was involved in student politics, the student rights movement, and other left-wing stuff. The first thing I did in graduate school was try to pass a student resolution against the Bay of Pigs, which the faculty went ape shit over and tried to stop, because they thought graduate students were professionals and should not take political positions. And when I worked with the National Student Association, the civil rights movement was in full swing. I was the international vice-president of the association, and I took part in a good number of civil rights marches. I was not at Selma, and I did not march with Dr. King. I just did stuff in

Maryland, Delaware, and the Washington, D.C. area. My point is that it's good if students have a reason for being in graduate school besides just getting smarter at understanding politics. We can give students the tools, skills, and readings, but we can't give them the passion. Unluckily, passion is not something graduate schools produce.

Q: Graduate school can actually have the opposite effect. It can beat the passion out of people.
A: That's right. You have to arrive with enough passion to sustain yourself. You're going to live with a dissertation for four or five years. And if it's not something you love, then it's not going to sustain you. You need to find something that will motivate you for four or five years

The other thing I would say is that politics is everywhere. For example, I recently took a train down to Washington, D.C., for a friend's seventy-fifth birthday party. The train died in Grand Central Station, and it wasn't clear when it was going to get under way again. So, they gave us the option of switching to another train that was going from New York to Washington. The other train was already crowded, and, to make matters worse, we boarded late because we came from our crapped-out train. The car was jam-packed. I was with my friend, who is seventy-five, and his sister, who is between seventy-five and eighty, and an elderly black woman was also standing nearby. So, all these old people were standing up while all these young people were just sitting there. It went on for ten or fifteen minutes, and I was really pissed off that nobody volunteered to give up their seat. So I stood up on the arms of some chairs and said, "I have a little announcement to make. At this end of the car there are at least two elderly women over seventy-five who have no place to sit, and I am wondering if any of you would be kind enough to give up your seats." Instantly, ten people were willing to do so. Well, if you had looked carefully you would have noticed that all these seated people were busy looking at their books as if they were genuinely unaware of what was going on around them. But they were not unaware, they were buried in their books as a way of isolating themselves from the situation. None of them wanted to make eye contact with someone to whom they should have given up their seat. But when they were summoned to their responsibilities, a large number responded instantly and got up. That's politics. So, if you're doing political science right, you're not just doing it when you're administering a questionnaire or reading a political science book. The world of politics is around you all the time, even in novels, and if you're doing political science right, you're doing it all the time, constantly asking why does this happen and why does that happen.

12

Alfred Stepan

*Democratic Governance and the Craft
of Case-Based Research*

Alfred Stepan is a leading comparative analyst of the military, state institutions, democratization, and democracy. His work on state autonomy and
capacity in Latin America defined him as a pioneering contributor to the
"new institutional" and "state-centered" approaches that gained prominence in comparative politics during the 1980s. Although Stepan started
his career as a Latin Americanist, his work later acquired a global scope,
drawing on cases from Europe and Asia, as well as South America.

Stepan's research initially focused on state institutions, especially the
military, and political regime change. In *The Military in Politics* (1971),
which analyzed the breakdown of democracy in Brazil in 1964, he challenged the prevailing view in comparative research that saw the military as
a force for achieving modernization and national integration. Because the
military in many instances was recruited unevenly from across a country,
he argued it could be a source of fragmentation, not unity. He also showed
that military coups did not necessarily emerge from inside the military.
Understanding the military's political behavior thus required a focus on the
broader context of civil-military relations. Stepan's finding that civilian
politicians were often complicit in military coups later emerged as a central
theme in *The Breakdown of Democratic Regimes* (1978), a volume he coedited
with Juan Linz. By emphasizing how the actions of democratically elected
incumbents contributed to the demise of democracy, this book challenged
prevailing explanations that highlighted the role of antidemocratic opposition groups in overthrowing democracies.

Stepan continued his research on state institutions in *The State and Society* (1978), which critiqued both pluralist and Marxist approaches for focusing insufficient attention on state elites. He formulated an alternative perspective, which he labeled the "organic-statist" tradition, that highlighted

This interview was conducted by Richard Snyder in Little Compton, Rhode Island, on
October 15–16, 2003.

the capacity of state actors to mold societal interests. *The State and Society,* which analyzed the Peruvian military's efforts to transform society in the 1970s, defined Stepan as an early and key contributor to the "new institutional" research that emphasized the potential autonomy of political institutions from economic, societal, and cultural forces.

In the 1980s and 1990s, as democracy expanded across Latin America and the globe, the focus of Stepan's work shifted to democratization. *Rethinking Military Politics* (1988a) argued that to achieve stable democracy, civilian elites in newly democratic regimes had to find ways to handle the problem of establishing civilian control over the armed forces. In contrast to much previous research, which had emphasized the role of civil society and social movements in democratization, Stepan highlighted the importance of *political* society—political parties, electoral systems, and institutions of civilian control over the armed forces—for achieving democracy. His coauthored book with Juan Linz, *Problems of Democratic Transition and Consolidation* (1996), was an ambitious cross-regional study of thirteen countries in South America, Southern Europe, and post-communist Europe. The book made important theoretical contributions by (1) introducing into the study of democratization a novel focus on "stateness" problems stemming from nationalist conflicts and (2) analyzing how the type of old non-democratic regime affected subsequent trajectories of democratization. The book also made an empirical contribution by incorporating post-communist European cases into a systematic comparative framework alongside the South American and Southern European cases that had been the focus of prior work on democratization.

Stepan's current research focuses on the impact of federal institutions on the prospects for democracy and peace in multinational societies. He is also working on a broad, comparative study of the relationship between democracy and religious identities.

Stepan was born in Chicago, Illinois, in 1936. He received his B.A. from the University of Notre Dame in 1958 and his Ph.D. in political science from Columbia University in 1969. He has taught at Yale University (1970–83), Oxford University (1996–99), and Columbia University (1983–93, 1999–present), where he was dean of the School of International and Public Affairs (SIPA) (1983–91). He was the first rector and president at Central European University in Budapest, Prague, and Warsaw (1993–96). Stepan was elected to the American Academy of Arts and Sciences in 1991.

Formative and Foundational Experiences

Q: You grew up in Chicago during the 1950s. Could you discuss your family background?

A: I grew up in a close, Catholic family of seven children and was the oldest son. My grandparents were all Irish, or Czech-German, first-generation, or immigrant, Americans. My father started a chemical business, a simple one making soaps, with about $500 during the Depression. It eventually became quite successful but when I was growing up he was very much in the building stage. He loved opera and was also one of the main early builders of the Lyric Opera of Chicago. He had great joie de vivre, and we talked a lot about how he was building both institutions. I suppose my career has also had an institution-building dimension that may have some relationship to all these conversations. He was particularly proud, probably because of his memories of the Depression, that he had been able to create jobs in his company, and to help bring opera back to Chicago. When he was ill, I would occasionally represent him back-stage at the Lyric Opera to congratulate the singers. He would always tell me, "Remember, opera singers aren't like other musicians. A violinist may have a million-dollar Stradivarius, but opera singers just have a tiny membrane in their throat to produce the emotion and sound. You can't congratulate an opera singer too much for what they have achieved." My father went to Notre Dame and was a trustee of the university. When he realized that no Jewish person had ever been given an honorary degree by Notre Dame, he helped arrange for his friend, the great tenor Richard Tucker, to get one. We received a phone call one New Year's Day at eleven o'clock in the evening—nobody ever called our house after ten because my father went to sleep early—and my father answered to give the person hell. It was Richard Tucker singing beautifully the Notre Dame fighting anthem, because Notre Dame had just won the national football championship.

My mother had an interest in politics, partly because her father was active in Democratic Party politics in Chicago. He had a press and published a Catholic newspaper and also many of the publications of Democratic Party organizations in Chicago. Since my father was a Republican, my mother was always nervous whenever the family got together, because she knew my father and her father were going to get into an argument about politics. My mother had been educated by nuns, some of whom were socialists, and she had a strong concern about social justice and a strong capacity for empathy. We visited Jane Addams's progressive Hull House and my mother would also occasionally deliberately drive me through some of Chicago's ghettos. The concentrated poverty I saw certainly gave me much to think about.

As an adolescent, I was interested in sports and learned boxing. I also read a lot, mainly novels. I liked theater and won some acting prizes. Drama, novels, and opera were my introductions to the life of the mind, spirit, and I suppose the love of the classroom, where I can create my own scripts.

Q: Do you have any political memories from childhood?

A: I learned a lot about democratic machine politics in Chicago from my grandfather. I also vividly remember the 1952 presidential campaign, and to my surprise, during the primaries, I took a position quite different from my father's and had to argue my corner. He supported Robert Taft, and I supported Adlai Stevenson. I also remember watching and reading about the McCarthy investigations. I was very surprised that what McCarthy was doing was acceptable to so many people.

Q: Did you have any interest in Latin America when you were growing up?

A: No, though I did visit Cuba in 1956, when I was in college; pre-Castro Cuba shocked me by the amount of open prostitution and gambling. It almost did not seem like a country. In 1957, I went to the World Youth Festival in Moscow, a trip that later got me into trouble with my draft board, because they questioned whether I was a good American citizen. After Russia, I went to Poland, which was fascinating. In Warsaw, I saw a Polish soldier walking down the street with a rifle, and when he passed in front of the cathedral, he dropped to his knees, very dramatically, and made a slow, genuine genuflection. I did not know the term *Gramscian hegemony* then, but from this and many other observations and conversations in Poland, I understood that there was no communist hegemony in that country.

Q: You received your undergraduate degree from Notre Dame in 1958. Why did you choose to go there and what did you study?

A: We were a very Catholic family and my father was a Notre Dame graduate. I considered applying to Yale but my family urged me, as the oldest of five boys, to set an example and go to a good Catholic university. I acceded to this wish and majored in English. Notre Dame for me was an environment that was conducive to thought, and to periods of solitude, in a campus with a lovely lake that froze for about three months in the winter. To this day I remember my solitary walks on this lake as periods of the almost surprising pleasure in thinking. There were no women students at Notre Dame then, and we had 10:00 p.m. curfews most nights. My friends dreaded me walking into their rooms at midnight, because, after my period of solitude, I would talk until three o'clock in the morning. Jerry Brady, who recently ran unsuccessfully for governor of Idaho, told me at our forty-fifth reunion, "You were terrible. You never paid any attention to time. You would just show up and talk and talk and talk."

Q: What were your plans when you graduated from Notre Dame? Did you know that you wanted to become an academic?

A: No. Notre Dame urged me to be one of their candidates to go to Oxford as a Rhodes scholar, but I never followed through because I did not think I would be eligible, since my draft board had said I could not leave the country until I had done my military service. They were suspicious of me because I had gone to Moscow to attend the youth festival. Eventually, I was told that if I somehow won a commission as an officer, I could leave the country for two years with the requirement that I serve three years of active duty when I came back. So, before I could go to Oxford, I first had to enroll in officer training. I took the Marine Corps Platoon Leaders' Course, a very brutal, Darwinian experience. Many candidates started the course but few finished. I finished. If I had been a more sensitive type, I guess I would have had a nervous breakdown.

Q: When you finally got there, what was Oxford like?
A: It was amazing, and I loved it. I took Philosophy, Politics, and Economics (PPE), which is a misnomer, because politics was barely covered. It was mostly history, political philosophy, and public economics. I was able to travel a lot, because classes only met for eight weeks followed by six-week breaks. And I had very gifted teachers, like the economists Paul Streeten and Thomas Balogh. Streeten was an Austrian Jew, and Balogh was a Hungarian Jew. Both were survivors of Hitler and never forgot it. Streeten was very calm, and Balogh was excitable and outrageously iconoclastic. They were known as "Buda" and "Pest." Streeten taught economic development theory and later became one of the most important economists who focused on human development, as opposed to merely economic development. Paul Streeten, Albert Hirschman, and I, many years later, helped Father Hesburgh, the president of Notre Dame and someone I have always admired, create the institutional design of the Kellogg Institute for International Studies at Notre Dame. Balogh, a left-wing Labour Party economist, loved to shock American students. The first essay I had to write for him was: "Why do Americans have such big tits on their cars?"

The students were fantastic. Besides meeting a beautiful, young Labour supporter named Nancy Leys, whom I would later marry, I also met Nigerians, a few black South Africans, an Iranian who was constantly talking about the CIA overthrow of Mossadegh,[1] and several Pakistanis and Indians, who remembered the horrendous slaughter of each other in the aftermath of the partition of India. The conversations among us were some of the most intense I have ever experienced. I also met Steven Lukes, who later became a prominent sociologist and lifelong friend.

1. Mohammed Mossadegh, prime minister of Iran, was overthrown in 1953 in a plot supported by the British and American intelligence agencies.

Q: What did you talk about?

A: Colonialism, Algeria, the newly emerging countries, the type of regimes these countries were going to have, socialism in developing countries, what had led so many people to kill each other in Pakistan and India, how many other countries would be the target of U.S. interventions like the one against Mossadegh in Iran, and the peculiar inequalities of the United States. Coming out of Eisenhower's America, I found these conversations eye-opening. Sometimes I was the only American in the room, and people would go at me and say, "Why is America doing this?" The sharp political debates and exchanges of opinion among people from different cultures, and trying to court Nancy, were the most important things about Oxford for me.

Q: Did you report immediately for duty in the Marine Corps after Oxford?

A: No. I had six months after Oxford before I had to report for duty. I used this time to travel. This was one of the most intense periods of my life. I chose six countries—Iran, Pakistan, India, Indonesia, Japan, and Vietnam—that interested me both politically and aesthetically and where I knew at least one key person. I read everything I could about each country beforehand: history, basic economics, basic geography, and literature. In Pakistan and India, I was deeply disturbed by vivid conversations about memories of communal violence. In West Pakistan, I was invited to stay at the home of a friend from Oxford. Staying in this Muslim household posed a real problem, though, because my friend, who, at the last minute was not able to be there, had a younger sister whom I was not permitted to see. This meant that his father, who was chief secretary of the civil service in East and West Pakistan, had to take me out of the house every day. I met all kinds of people and traveled lots of places with him, including to Chittagong in East Pakistan, where he went to oversee relief after thousands of people had died in a huge tidal wave. I saw hundreds and hundreds of people up in trees, and we could not do a thing about it. I noticed that virtually all the military officers I saw in East Pakistan were West Pakistanis.

India was extraordinary. The poverty was shattering for me as a human being, as it would be for anyone. Still, despite the poverty, the amount of human diversity and creativity was stunning. Even the poorest villages had marriage ceremonies with magnificent colors and a sense of community. Now, forty years later, I am finally beginning to write about India and will publish a book much of which is about how India, with its fifteen official languages, great poverty, and the world's third largest Muslim population, somehow has managed to create such an original and longstanding democracy (Stepan, Linz, and Yadav, forthcoming).

After India, I went to Indonesia, because I wanted to see another Muslim country and because I love big, exotic places. For some reason, I still don't understand why, I ended up seeing an eight-hour puppet show in the presidential palace and meeting President Sukarno briefly. I was enchanted with Indonesia, especially by the variation in Islam I observed. In contrast to what I had seen in other Islamic countries, women in Indonesia were not wearing scarves, and they were involved in the court system.

Finally, I went to Vietnam, because my three-year tour as a Marine was just two months away, and I was worried that, given the French defeat at Dien Bien Phu and America's sense that it was going to control the world, somehow we would end up getting involved there. The easiest people to meet were the French journalists. I met one in a Graham Greene-type situation at a decaying tennis club with a swimming pool you wouldn't dare jump into because the water was green. We had a drink, and he looked at me, almost anthropologically, and said, "Americans can't resist. You're going to be here." Unfortunately he was right.

Q: Could you discuss your experience in the Marine Corps?

A: I was an infantry platoon commander and, briefly, a company commander, which was an important experience for me sociologically. Many of the troops had lived incredibly close to poverty. They often had ended up in the Marine Corps because they were involved in a violent crime, and the judge had told the Marine recruiter, "This kid might be salvageable. Why don't you try to recruit him? Otherwise, I'll send him to jail for a few years." They saw "the street" almost as if it were a human being, a force that would suddenly grab you, pull you into something violent, and cause somebody to be killed or end up in jail.

Q: What were your future plans at this stage?

A: I was interested in going into public life in some way, perhaps electoral politics. Television was just emerging, and I thought maybe I could do that. I also thought about becoming a journalist, like Walter Lippmann; Lippmann was my role model, and I was fortunate to meet him during John F. Kennedy's inauguration. The Indian ambassador, B. K. Nehru, whose son had been a friend of mine at Oxford, invited me up to the inauguration from the Marine Corps Base at Quantico, Virginia. We had dinner one night with Lippmann and Joseph Alsop. We were all trying to figure out what the Kennedy phenomenon was going to be.

I also considered working for the State Department, but two experiences while I was in the Marine Corps changed my mind. During the Cuban Missile Crisis, my commander was given the job of preparing a diversionary attack on the city of Santiago de Cuba; although I did not know it at the time, the main attack was actually planned for the north, near Havana. He said, "You read Spanish, you've been to Oxford. I want you to read and interpret all the communications and intelligence reports and become the combat intelligence officer for our landing brigade. If we get the order to invade, we're going in first, and you'll help select the landing site." We were at sea, about twenty miles off Santiago de Cuba, for forty-eight days with the invasion force. Everybody was sure we were going into combat, and the amount of testosterone in the air was stunning and dangerous. We were in total radio silence, which meant that, as the combat intelligence officer, I had to be ferried by helicopter among the boats in the invasion fleet to brief all our units about any changes in our plans. The helicopter would drop me onto a pitching boat that would sometimes jerk up suddenly, driving my knees through my face. During the Missile Crisis, I read a great deal about American perceptions and misperceptions of Cuba and realized, to my horror, that we had in fact mobilized our nuclear weapons for a war that I felt never should have reached that point. My first paper in graduate school was about the role of mutually self-fulfilling prophecies in generating this near nuclear war.

About a year later, in September 1963, my commander received a request to prepare the execution part of a contingency plan to evacuate Americans from Vietnam, which I believed meant that Kennedy was seriously considering cutting U.S. involvement in Vietnam. We were also given orders to prepare for a contingency plan for landing the first U.S. combat unit in Vietnam, which eventually happened, but not for about another eighteen months with a different president. As in Cuba, we were again stationed offshore for over a month. Even at that time I was convinced the invasion would be a terrible mistake. For one thing, I had occasionally helped train Vietnamese officers in Okinawa, and my conversations with them were revealing. They would often ask, "How is your war going?" I would answer, "It's your war." And they would reply, "No, it's *your* war." It seemed absurd to me for the United States to be preparing to intervene in a country where the soldiers who came from that country were already saying it was not their war.

I decided that the U.S. government was so out of touch and so riddled with misconceptions that it made no sense for me to serve as a junior staffer in the State Department. I needed a base of autonomy if I was ever going to have any influence.

Q: But instead of going into academics when you left the Marine Corps, you worked as a journalist for a year. Why did you decide to postpone graduate school?
A: I had seen, and almost contributed to, so much violence that I wanted to learn more about the world, and eventually have my own influence on how the world was seen. Also, I had finally convinced Nancy to marry me, and because she had had a Fulbright fellowship, which entailed a visa restriction

before she could re-enter the United States, we could not go to the United States for a while. I went to *The Economist* in London and managed to talk them into taking a chance on me. *The Economist* makes its money on the Economist Intelligence Unit reports, which are written by people who have been in a particular country for five or ten years. But when you have been somewhere five or ten years, you know everyone, and are enmeshed in local networks. This means there are things you do not write about. So, *The Economist* has a need for stringers, whom they call special foreign correspondents, to possibly write such articles. In fact, the first article I wrote for them was about special investment deals Nkrumah was doing in Ghana.[2] The Economist Intelligence Unit permanent representative in Ghana would probably never have written that piece, because its title alone, which I believe was "Creeping Capitalism in Ghana," would have offended Nkrumah, who portrayed himself as the socialist leader of Africa. My article on Paraguay, which discussed among other things, women prisoners, who were actually interviewed by Nancy, was another such article. Partly because I had been at Oxford, partly because I had already been to a lot of countries, and partly because they thought my scheme might be good, *The Economist,* to my surprise said, "Fine," and I became one of their special correspondents. I received great help in my writing from one of their legendary editors, Barbara Smith, who to my good fortune had special interest in, and knowledge of, Latin America. I went first to Ghana and Nigeria, but I had told *The Economist* that my main interest was in Latin America and that was what I wanted to write about in preparation for becoming an academic. I was drawn to Latin America, partly by my experiences during the Cuban Missile Crisis.

Q: Did you speak Spanish or Portuguese?
A: I had taken Spanish in high school and college and spent time in Spain, but I did not speak it well. My knowledge of Portuguese was slight. Because I had studied with the Jesuits in high school, I had learned some Latin and could actually read Portuguese, but I could not speak at all when I arrived in Brazil. This is ironic, because on the airplane to Rio de Janeiro I happened to talk with a flight steward who saw me reading something by the Brazilian economist, Celso Furtado. I mentioned my role with *The Economist* and the steward asked me if I would like to meet some left-wing oppositionists. I said yes, and virtually the day we arrived, Nancy and I met some of them under very secret conditions. I rapidly understood that things were coming to a head and I had to cover this story at full speed and drop my plans for

2. Kwame Nkurmah (1909–72) was Ghana's first prime minister after the country gained its independence from Britain in 1957.

more leisurely learning of Portuguese. I was immediately plunged into one of the biggest things that happened in my career.

Before the military coup of March 31, 1964, occurred, which ushered in the first military regime in Brazil in the twentieth century, and the first of the four regimes that Guillermo O'Donnell later termed *bureaucratic authoritarian* (O'Donnell 1973), I filed a story with *The Economist,* called "Mend or End in Brazil." My story said a coup was probably going to happen, explained why it might happen, and said that it would not be a good thing for the Alliance for Progress,[3] if it did happen. The editors at *The Economist* held the story, no doubt thinking that I was not yet knowledgeable about Brazil. Six days later the coup took place. *The Economist* immediately published my story, hardly changing a word, and acknowledging in print that their special correspondent had filed it before the coup. I joke that this made my career, and might have ruined it. It made my career because *The Economist* published everything I sent them afterward. It could have ruined my career, because I was only twenty-seven, and maybe they should not have done so.

Q: Besides Brazil, what other Latin American countries did you cover while writing for *The Economist*?
A: I published stories on Argentina, Chile, Paraguay, Bolivia, Peru, and Venezuela. I covered the run-up to the 1964 presidential election in Chile. I immediately saw that, even though he had almost won the previous election in 1958, the leftist candidate, Salvador Allende, was not going to win in 1964, because, unlike 1958, the Center and the Center-Right parties had joined forces in support of Eduardo Frei, the candidate of the Christian Democratic Party. I wrote to *The Economist* and said, "I don't think Allende will be elected, and I am confident I can write an article about this that you can publish six months ahead of the elections."[4] I wanted to spend time with Allende while I was working on my story, and, as I have found in many countries, the way to spend time with politicians during a campaign is to follow them on long swings through the countryside for three or more days. Political leaders occasionally have time to kill as they travel from one stop to the next and will invite a reporter, or even an academic, into the back seat of their car for a long conversation. Even politicians get tired of talking only to other politicians and want to hear about the world. A successful interview is a transaction; it has to be interesting for both people. Someone like Salvador Allende would not wave you over several times in

3. The Alliance for Progress was a U.S. assistance program for Latin America begun in 1961 during the presidency of John F. Kennedy. It was created principally to counter the appeal of revolutionary politics, such as those adopted in Cuba.
4. Allende did lose in 1964, but won in 1970, when, as in 1958, the conservatives and the Christian Democrats ran separate candidates and split the anti-Allende vote.

three days for a one-hour conversation unless he was learning something every time. Allende asked me, "Where have you been?" I said, "I have just come from Argentina and from Brazil, where I covered the military coup. I went to Oxford, was a Marine, and I have been to Vietnam." He wanted to talk about the military coup in Brazil, because that was the big thing then, and he wanted to talk about Argentina. I offered him another opinion about what was happening in those countries, which made it interesting for him to talk to me.

I loved the intensity of writing for *The Economist*. I could go to any country in the world with a letter stating that *The Economist* was going to print my article in three weeks. I could ask to see the president, or major presidential candidates, early in my visit, and they would normally agree. Politicians wouldn't be politicians if they didn't believe that spending half an hour with them would make you see things closer to their view. That's why they are politicians. When other political leaders learned I was writing an article about their country for *The Economist* and had already spoken to their rival, they often let me know that I should get their viewpoint before I published my article. Thus, after going on a campaign swing with Allende, I went on a similar one with Eduardo Frei, who eventually won the 1964 presidential election.

Q: Since you found journalism so thrilling, why did you decide not to make a career out of it? Why did you still choose to become an academic instead?
A: Although I really enjoyed writing for *The Economist,* I would have liked to be able to spend more time filing each report. I would have been happier if I had had four or five months to write a report, but my comparative advantage was that I was able to crack a story in three weeks. But I wanted to be more systematic, and the weight of my thinking about Cuba, about Vietnam, and about how the United States had welcomed the military coup in Brazil with open arms made me see the need for contributions on a more fundamental level than journalism. I was ready to start my Ph.D.

Still, my experience as a journalist influences how I do some of my academic work, especially in terms of opening up new possibilities and audiences. I frequently take a week or so off and do something totally separate from my current research just to go to new places, see another country, have new experiences, and talk to new people. I don't reject the passions of the journalist. I also write an occasional column for the *Prague Syndicate*, which was founded by a group of thinkers and activists from post-communist Europe interested in getting many leading writers to give alternative perspectives on world affairs. My articles are published as part of their "Worldly Philosopher" series. The last column I wrote was on the prospects of democracy in Lebanon, Palestine, and Israel, and it was published in eighty-five countries in 103 different newspapers.

Training at Columbia

Q: You began your Ph.D. studies in political science at Columbia in the fall of 1964. Why did you choose Columbia?
A: Columbia offered me a International Fellows scholarship, and Albert Hirschman's work appealed to me. I liked the historical dimension of his research, the emphasis on "possibilism," and the fact that it was so well written and had a clean focus on the question at hand (Hirschman 1963).[5] I liked some of the work by the political historian Richard Neustadt, too. Also, Columbia was known for its focus on Latin America, especially Brazil. And as someone who liked opera and big, complex places, I knew I did not want to be in a small town and that Columbia would be interesting.

Q: Did you consider other graduate programs?
A: I considered Berkeley. I liked it, and they were very interested and supportive. I thought Stanford would be interesting, but when I visited they were in the middle of a war about behavioralism. I did not want to be in a warring environment. Also, my wife, Nancy, who was a science journalist, later she got a Ph.D. herself, felt she could find work in New York.

Q: What courses did you take at Columbia?
A: One day I saw some students I really liked running across campus, and I asked, "Where are you going?" They said, "To Linz!" I said, "Who's Linz?" They replied, "He's a young Spaniard." I said, "What does he teach about?" And they said, "Everything." So, I joined them. Juan Linz taught about the mega-thinkers in political sociology, Michels, Weber, Durkheim. He discussed their life stories and involvement in and perspectives on the politics of their countries. He wanted to show who they were, what they were writing about, and why. Later, when the German comparativist Otto Kirchheimer died, Linz took over his course on European politics, and, instead of covering the usual four countries, he discussed virtually every country in Europe. We learned about the Finnish Civil War after World War I, about the Spanish Civil War, and about the smaller European countries. If you took Linz's courses, you got an overview of every major political philosopher and every European country.

---

5. Hirschman had left Columbia for Harvard by the time Stepan arrived.

Linz had a style. He liked to teach from 10–12 or 11–1, because that way he knew he could lecture three hours by continuing into lunchtime. His normal teaching space was three hours. After class, he always went and sat at a roundtable for lunch, and if students joined him, as they often did, then he continued for another two hours. The conversation would always start as a continuation of the lecture, but it would usually develop into a discussion of contemporary political questions and the issues of social science they raised. People from sociology, history, economics, political science, and even some just off the street, would show up. We would argue about virtually everything. By then, it would be close to 4 o'clock, and a bunch of students would proceed to The West End, a local bar, to continue the conversation. That was called "Doing a Linz."

Soon, I was talking three hours a week with Linz. I told him I had just returned from Latin America and was interested in Brazil, and he asked, "Was the military coup in Brazil inevitable?" I answered, "Absolutely not. With ordinary competence by the chief executive, it would not have happened." So, we started discussing a *problématique* that would eventually evolve into our collaborative project on the breakdown of democratic regimes (Linz and Stepan 1978).

Q: Besides Linz, whom else did you take courses with at Columbia?
A: I took a course on India and Pakistan from a political scientist named Wayne Wilcox. He died at a relatively young age in an accident and is not well known now, but he was a very good observer. His course gave me a chance to think further about India and Pakistan. Columbia had good historians. I wanted to learn more about Latin America history, so I took a course with Lewis Hanke, a historian of colonial Latin America. I also spent time with the Argentine sociologist Gino Germani. In fact, my minor Ph.D. examination fields were actually Latin American history and Latin American sociology.

Overall, though, I tried to take the least amount of courses possible, so I would have time to think and write. I was publishing a lot, probably too much, in graduate school. I engaged in political arguments in *New Politics,* a socialist review, *The Nation,* and *The New Republic.* I also published a review of the literature on the military in *The Review of Politics* (Stepan 1965) and a critique of political development theory in the *Journal of International Affairs* (Stepan 1966). I also wrote, when asked, policy briefs for Senators Frank Church and Robert Kennedy.

Q: Linz was in the Sociology Department, and I find it curious that so far you have only mentioned one member of Columbia's Political Science Department, Wilcox.

A: Linz was a political sociologist and a close colleague of Stein Rokkan and Marty Lipset, also political sociologists. In Europe, I have more colleagues who are political sociologists than political scientists. The training in comparative politics at Columbia in the mid-1960s was not stellar. Still, Dankwart Rustow's class was very important. Rustow knew much more than most comparativists at American universities, because he was European and had lived in Turkey. He knew unusual things. Rustow was working then on his theory of how democracy emerges, and I liked the dynamic element of his work (Rustow 1970). I was attracted to Rustow's idea that democracy can emerge as a default option for parties that exhaust themselves fighting. Rustow would allow you to argue with him. I remember disagreeing with his argument that the problem of national unity had to be solved before a democracy could emerge. I did not think then, or now, that achieving national unity, particularly a nation-state, should be regarded as a prerequisite for democracy. I had been in India, which was a democracy but not a nation-state. Contra Rustow, I did not think Turkey, one of his main examples, had solved its problem of national unity democratically. The military were crushing Kurds. They also imposed national unity via a military-managed "secularism from above" that was forced on even moderate Muslims. Unfortunately, Rustow left Columbia after he got involved in the student riots of 1968 and was hit on the head while protesting against the police. He had little to do with Columbia afterward.

Q: **When you were a graduate student in the mid-1960s, the dominant approach in comparative politics was the structural-functional perspective of Gabriel Almond and his colleagues on the Social Science Research Council (SSRC) Committee on Comparative Politics. Where you exposed to this material?**
A: Linz, and even Rustow, felt a bit uneasy with the Almond project, as did I. It seemed too American, pluralist, and society centered. Linz and Rustow, and many of their students, including myself, had been places where you had to think about horrible civil wars, repressive regimes that structured many "societal" inputs, or statelessness. None of these serious problems seemed central to Almond's functionalist project. Nevertheless, I read almost all the Political Development SSRC series.[6] I was particularly influenced by Almond and Verba's *Civic Culture* (1963) and the volume comparing modernization in Japan and Turkey by Ward and Rustow (1964).

6. In the 1960s and 1970s, the Social Science Research Council's (SSRC) Committee on Comparative Politics, chaired initially by Gabriel Almond and later by Lucian Pye, published a nine-volume series, Studies in Political Development, with Princeton University Press.

Research: State Institutions, Regime Change, and National and Religious Identities
The Military and Politics in Brazil

Q: Turning to your dissertation, which was published as your first book, *The Military in Politics* (Stepan 1971), you wrote about the military's political role in Brazil. Why did you choose this question? Did you explore other possibilities?

A: I considered other topics. Everyone, the funding agencies and my advisors, said writing about the Brazilian military was impossible, because I would never get sufficient access to key military materials. So, I started to develop a dissertation prospectus on national integration in Brazil. I was influenced by the work of Karl Deutsch and proposed to look at communications across cities, postal flows, and things of that nature (Deutsch 1953, 1961). After three months, I decided that absolutely nothing was driving me to study this topic. Was national integration an important topic? Yes. But the years I had spent thinking about social science, politics, and big institutions had not prepared me to say anything exciting about national integration. By contrast, I had been involved in military organizations, and, as a journalist, I had seen the military coup coming in Brazil in 1964. I had published a review of the literature on the military (Stepan 1965). I was confident I had a distinctive understanding of what should, and could, be done in this research area. I decided to do my original topic anyway, without submitting a prospectus. I simply did my research and did a prospectus ex post facto.

Q: How did you get funding to go to Brazil and do your research, given that the funding agencies thought your project was too risky?

A: I accepted an offer from the RAND Corporation to work with Luigi Einaudi, who had sent me the draft of his book on the Peruvian military. This was by far the best book I had ever read on the military in Latin America, and I felt Luigi and I could work well together. His grandfather had been president of Italy and had written some fifty books, which probably immobilized Luigi, because he kept revising and rewriting his book, even though it had already been accepted by Harvard University Press. His book was a whole generation ahead of anything that had been written on the military in Latin America, but he never published it. RAND gave me a three-year research grant to write my book. Alex George at RAND was a very supportive presence.

Q: How did you proceed with your research? How did you surmount the difficulties of getting access to information about the Brazilian military?

A: First, unlike when I was writing for *The Economist,* I did the interviews very late in the process. I already knew that my topic was civil-military relations, because Brazilian political elites, since the fall of the empire in 1889, had always tolerated military involvement at a high level. The first thing I did was read all five constitutions of Brazil since 1891. Each one had a clause saying that the military should obey the president within the limits of the law and another clause saying that the military was responsible for maintaining the correct relationship among the executive, legislature, and judiciary. When I saw this second clause, I was flabbergasted, because the task of maintaining balance across the different branches of government in democracies is normally a judicial or political, not a military, responsibility. To understand these puzzling constitutional clauses, I read through the records of all the debates in the legislative subcommittees involved in drafting each constitution. This archival work took about three months. I focused on who the members of the subcommittees were, as well as the content of the various drafts that emerged from each subcommittee. I noticed that when military men were on the first subcommittee, the draft never had this clause. It was always inserted by the second subcommittee, where there were no active-duty military officers. The clause was inserted by civilian politicians. I even found congressional testimony by the military *against* the clause, which they feared was dangerous for the military as an institution because it would divide them. So, for sixty years, civilians, not the military, had written into the constitution an inappropriate judicial role for the armed forces. This was totally counterintuitive.

My hunch was that civilian politicians were embedding this role for the military in the constitution so they would have a basis for making public appeals to the military to carry out a coup d'état if, and when, the political elites wanted a coup. I thus embarked on a huge, time-consuming, content analysis of editorials published in the major Brazilian newspapers sixty days before each coup attempt. Prior to every successful coup, but not before unsuccessful coup attempts, the newspaper editorials expressed overwhelming support for military intervention. The editorials appealed directly to the constitution, saying, for example, "Article 354 of the constitution states that the military should obey the president within the limits of the law. The president is violating the law, and it is therefore unconstitutional to obey the president. Second, the constitution says the military has the obligation to maintain the correct balance among the judiciary, legislature, and executive. The president is violating this balance by intimidating the legislature. Therefore, it would be unconstitutional for the military to obey the president."

My findings cut against the grain of the existing literature on the military and politics, which saw military coups as emerging from inside the military. My study relocated the military's political behavior in the broader context of civil-military relations.

Q: The material you have described so far draws on public information from constitutions and newspapers. How did you get more sensitive information about the military itself?
A: Because of my experience as a journalist, I was used to figuring out how to get information from people, and, within a matter of weeks, had obtained a copy of the military's promotion book, which listed every single military officer. Every military has such a book, and officers look at it all the time to see who is above and below them in rank, who has been promoted, and why. The Brazilian promotion book proved especially useful, because it had a few lines after every person with letters of the alphabet indicating whether the person had won a certain medal, graduated first in his class, served in the Fôrça Expedicionária Brasileira[7] (FEB) in Italy, the only Latin American force to participate in Europe in World War II,[8] and a whole range of information that I turned into variables. I wanted to analyze who led the 1964 coup, and I studied the entire universe of 102 line generals on active duty in the Brazilian armed forces at that time. I had three confidential informants whom I considered credible and exceptionally well-informed, because they had been involved in the coup. They felt the coup had saved Brazil and thus were not going to give credit to somebody who had not in fact played a role. If two of my three informants said a general was a key organizer, I felt confident I had identified one of the coup plotters.

When I looked up the generals who led the coup in the promotion book, I noticed almost all had served in World War II and been to the Escola Superior de Guerra (ESG),[9] a new type of war college where 50 percent of the students and faculty were civilians, ranging from priests and journalists to politicians and businessmen. When I went through my data on the coup leaders, I found that 60 percent of the core group of ten active plotters had served in Italy with the FEB during World War II, 70 percent had been permanent staff members at the ESG, 100 percent graduated first in their class from one of the three major army schools, and 100 percent attended foreign military schools. Fifty percent of the core group had done all four of these things. Among the remaining ninety-two generals who were not plotters of the coup, only one had done all four of these things. I knew basic statistics, and I did something called a Z test, which showed that the probability of such a difference in proportions occurring by chance was one in a

7. Brazilian Expeditionary Force.
8. The FEB served alongside Allied Troops in Italy in 1944 and 1945.
9. Superior War College.

thousand. Now, that was really interesting. By identifying these key people, I was able to generate a powerful finding without even talking to anyone. I had a very robust correlation, but, as we always say in social science, correlation is not causation. I really had no idea what connection there was among variables like serving in World War II and a general's role in the coup of 1964 twenty years later. The only way to figure that out was by talking to the key actors.

Q: How did you approach the interviews with the Brazilian generals and what did you learn from them?
A: I began by saying I was writing a book about the coup of 1964 and had just noticed that they and a group of other people were involved in it. Each would respond, "Yes, and I'm very proud of my involvement. I'm going to write my memoirs about it." Then I pointed out that they and their colleagues who led the coup had all served together in the FEB in Italy during World War II and later attended the ESG. I said I was interested in that connection. Each one told me their story. They were given a terrific nationalist send off by President Vargas when they left for Europe in 1944. But when they got to Italy, they were humiliated, because they were put on the front line and quickly outflanked by the enemy. The Brazilian military unit, FEB, was asked to withdraw and submit to training by foreign troops before they were sent back to the front line. The officers who were a part of the FEB internalized these events as an absolutely humiliating experience, and they came home from Europe determined to build a strong army and a strong Brazil. They attributed Brazil's weakness partly to the lack of seriousness they saw among civilians about war and national power. Hence, they built a novel institution, the ESG, as a way to build stronger ties with civilian elites and get civilian opinion makers to start thinking about Brazil as a military power. In fact, the general who became the first president of the military regime, General Castello Branco, was the one who felt most humiliated by what had happened to the Brazilian troops in Italy.

Q: How did you get these soldiers to talk to you? After all, they were active officers in the Brazilian armed forces at a time when the military ruled the country, and you were a foreigner.
A: I told them I had been a Marine officer and a special correspondent for *The Economist*. I politely tried to impress upon them that I was writing a book about a part of history in which they had played a role, and I was going to write my book whether or not they chose to talk to me. In elite interviews, you have to send a subtle, credible message that the book will appear one way or the other. I said, "I'm writing a book. You're not going to

like all of it, but I have been published before, and I think this is going to be the most important book written on the Brazilian military." Then I said that all I wanted was the same information that Morris Janowitz had been given on American soldiers (Janowitz 1960). They knew Janowitz's book, because the Brazilian military had translated it into Portuguese. I showed them the copy from their military library and said, "These things are known about the American soldier. You say you're a world-class military. Can I just get the same information about the Brazilian soldier? Nothing more, nothing less. Then I can look at the information and you can look at it. It might be useful." They said, "Fine."

I followed the same strategy I had used with *The Economist*. I knew that once I talked to a few top people in the military, I would get access to a huge amount of information. In any large organization, there are always two or three top people who are key intellectuals. They write a lot, think a lot, and want to hear what you think and what you are doing. In my case, they wanted to know about the RAND Corporation. I was a complex enough figure to grab their interest.

When interviewing the Brazilian officers, I always tried to know almost more than they did. I'd ask five questions, the answers to four of which I already knew. If they said something that wasn't right, I would say, "Yes, but come to think of it, General, it was actually 1939," or "It wasn't in that battle of Italy, it was in the other one." They were impressed that I knew about their institution, because one of their key resentments was that they believed that nobody understood the military. I understood hierarchy, promotions, and ranks, could recognize important medals from twenty-five yards, and knew something about military history. How can you sustain a long conversation with key actors from an organization, whether it is the Catholic Church or the U.S. Senate, if you do not understand the history of their organization? So I had read about the Italian campaign and about a lot of material in which I had no direct interest. This made me a much more interesting person for the Brazilian officers to talk to. Some had gone to the American and French war colleges, so I looked into how those institutions operated. The Brazilians liked the fact that I knew about the military colleges of different countries and understood that their academy, the ESG, took a new and different approach. As a result, they gave me documents. One person asked if I would like to see the background memos on the creation of the ESG. I said, "Sure, of course I'd like to see the background memos." Once you have talked to somebody several times, you can say, "You know, there are three or four things in your documents that I can't quite understand." They would give their explanation, and then I would go ask someone else for their explanation of the same document. I can't stress enough that people who have been involved in creating history want to explain it.

Q: Your research also involved work in the military library. I imagine this was not the kind of place you could just walk into. How did you get access?

A: The library at the ESG was open to pensioners, and a lot of retired generals and colonels went there to read the newspapers and hang out. I went maybe ninety times. It wasn't as if I was sneaking in, but I was always prepared to be challenged and thrown out, which never happened. I have always been incredibly polite to librarians, and I've always worn a suit.

Q: Shifting from the empirical research to issues of theory, what literatures were you engaging and arguing against?

A: I was arguing against the idea that the military was the most modernizing, cohesive institution in Third World countries and, hence, was ideally suited to perform the task of nation building. My colleague at RAND, Guy Pauker, wrote in his study of Southeast Asia that ways had to be found to use the organizational strength of the military and their leadership potential as "temporary kernels" of national integration (Pauker 1959). John J. Johnson asserted that the armed forces in Latin America were a coherent group with the organizational strength and leadership to guarantee political continuity in their countries (Johnson 1964). Writing on Turkey, Dankwart Rustow said that, in comparison to other elites, the army is less parochial and has a national orientation (Rustow 1964). By contrast, I argued that in lots of places in the world, the military is highly selected from different regions, those regions have political connotations, and, hence, the armed forces can be a source of fragmentation, not unity. In the United States, the South was overrepresented in the army. In Nigeria, the Ibo tribe, partly because of its Christian religion and partly because of superior education, dominated the officer corps after 1961. Of the eighty Nigerian generals, nearly sixty were Ibos. Sudan and Pakistan had similar patterns of uneven regional recruitment. In Pakistan virtually all the field grade officers were from West Pakistan. This fact directly contributed to East Pakistan's war of independence that created Bangladesh. When we actually look at where the military comes from, we see that the prominent assertion in the literature that the armed forces represent national unity is bad social science. So, even though my first book is on Brazil, the first references it makes are to Nigeria, Sudan, Pakistan, and Indonesia.

Q: What do you regard as the main contributions of *The Military in Politics?*

A: A lot of new concepts came out of the research, including the distinction between the "military as government" and the "military as institution."

Many people did not understand that when there is a very complex set of promotion systems, a military government can generate tension with the military institution. This is why most coups are led by the military against the military. I created the concept of the *extrication coup,* which occurs because the military are terrified of dividing among themselves, since both sides are armed. If the "military as institution" perceives that the "military as government" is creating grave problems, then there will be an effort to build a coup coalition aimed at installing a caretaker government that holds elections.

One other thing I tried to accomplish in *The Military in Politics,* which is why I wrote an appendix on how to research a semi-closed institution, was to challenge the idea that topics like the military are not researchable, because the data either do not exist or are impossible to get. I wanted to show that new types of information could in fact be generated on something that seemed too difficult for social scientists to study. I also wanted to show that many of these data were even available to the public. What is more public than a constitutional provision or a newspaper editorial? An essential task of a good social scientist is to create new data and figure out strategies to get data, in order to research important, but until then, very under-researched, and thus often poorly theorized, political phenomena.

Q: How was the book received?
A: The Portuguese translation was a best-seller in Brazil. The book was censored, uncensored, reached number 1 or 2, and then was censored again, which was the absolutely best thing that could have happened for promoting the book. Everyone wanted to get a copy, academics, journalists, military officers, and politicians. It received serious academic reviews in many countries, as well as reviews in *The Washington Post* and *The Economist.* It was translated into Spanish, and pirated translations were published in Korean, Thai, and Indonesian. It was not bad for the start of a career.

Authoritarian Brazil

Q: Your second major academic publication, the edited volume *Authoritarian Brazil*, appeared in 1973 (Stepan 1973a). What were the origins of that book?
A: I had just been named director of Yale's Council on Latin America Studies, and I was convinced that the intensity of Brazil's authoritarian regime was an important theme. The conference on which the book was based was held in 1971, during the worst period of repression in Brazil. People were interested in whether the Brazilian case was a new kind of authoritarianism,

how it related to other authoritarian experiences, how it did, or did not, relate to the then dominant ideas of dependency theory,[10] and possible sources of contradiction and resistance.

With regard to selecting people for the project, I wanted leaders in the field who were among the most important people working on Latin America. I wanted a historian to set the context. So, I invited Tom Skidmore, who had written the standard history of modern Brazil (Skidmore 1967, 1973). I wanted a good economist, and I invited Al Fishlow, because he spoke Portuguese and had been audacious enough in the middle of the Brazilian economic "miracle" to point out, in a public debate in Brazil, the country's terrible performance on income inequality despite the economic "miracle" (Fishlow 1973). And I wanted Juan Linz, as a specialist on authoritarianism, to assess the chances that the political situation in Brazil would become institutionalized. Linz explored the different ways that authoritarian regimes had institutionalized themselves in the past—corporatism, fascism, one-party state—and, to our surprise, concluded that the Brazilian military could not institutionalize their rule (Linz 1973c).

Years later, I learned that the Brazilian military's top political strategist, General Golbery do Couto e Silva, had somehow managed to get an advance copy of Linz's chapter. As chief of staff in the president's office, Golbery was the theoretician of the process of *abertura* (political opening) that began in the mid-1970s. When I was working on the very early stages of the Brazilian transition to democracy, Golbery, in the first of five interviews with me, acknowledged in December 1974, that when he had finished reading Linz's paper, he said to himself in effect, "Linz's arguments are right; we cannot institutionalize. We better start an opening while we still have some power of initiative." He reiterated this to Elio Gaspari, a great Brazilian journalist who later wrote the meticulously documented five-volume historical classic on the Brazilian military regime.[11] Social science apparently had an impact on one of the key architects of the Brazilian military's extrication.

Q: Another contributor to *Authoritarian Brazil*, Fernando Henrique Cardoso, certainly had an impact on the "real" world, because he later became president of Brazil.[12]
A: Cardoso had been a good friend ever since 1965, when a mutual journalist friend brought him to dinner with Nancy and me at Columbia in order

10. Dependency theory emphasizes external determinants of the development prospects of poor countries.

11. The Linz paper is mentioned in Gaspari (2003, 437).

12. Cardoso served as president of Brazil for two terms during 1995–2002.

that we could exchange ideas about the Brazilian military. For *Authoritarian Brazil* I asked him to write about what type of political resistance was possible given the structure of Brazilian society (Cardoso 1973). His paper was not simple dependency theory, because it introduced dynamism and probed how cracks could emerge in the coercive apparatus. Cardoso said very clearly that a classic trade union-based socialist, or social democratic, led coalition was not possible in Brazil, because the size of the industrial workforce would never be large enough to sustain it. In the early industrializing countries of Western Europe, 35 percent of the workforce was probably in industry at one point. Because the industrial model had changed, the size of the industrial workforce in the late industrializing countries of Latin America tended to peak at just 15 to 18 percent. So, Cardoso argued, a viable, industrial-based, trade union social democratic movement was simply never going to exist in Latin America, but other types of progressive alliances were possible. That paper was one of Cardoso's first political works.

Q: Could you discuss your own chapter in *Authoritarian Brazil*, which focuses on what you called the "new professionalism" in the military (Stepan 1973b)?
A: I argued that the military was driven more deeply into politics when they focused on internal security threats and national development. This occurred because such a focus widened the scope of what the military had to know and study, leading them to think they had to know everything. As a result, they expanded their intelligence apparatus and were drawn into politics.

I was confronting Samuel Huntington's argument, which I called the "old professionalism," that as the military got more involved in their profession they removed themselves from politics (Huntington 1957). People were taking Huntington's argument and inappropriately applying it to places like Indonesia and Brazil, where the content of military professionalism was not external warfare, but internal warfare and national development. I was absolutely convinced that professionalization under such circumstances would have the exact opposite effect of increasing, not decreasing, the military's involvement in politics.

Q: What is the trick to organizing a successful edited volume?
A: Outstanding and flexible contributors, who share an interest in a common problem, and who look forward to discussing the problem with each other. You also have to be rough enough to drop a few people who do not write good papers. I have always dropped some writers from edited volumes, partly because I want the final product to be good enough to stay in

print. *Authoritarian Brazil* is still in print thirty years later. Also, I often bring people into edited volumes who were not involved at the start, because one of the original papers is just too weak or something new happens.

Q: *Authoritarian Brazil* also had a rather striking and intriguing cover. Did that help?
A: I always spend months, or longer, to find a cover I like. For the cover for *Problems of Democratic Transition and Consolidation,* I even commissioned a poster by a Polish acquaintance, Wiktor Sadowski, who had done some brilliant political posters during the Solidarity resistance period (Linz and Stepan 1996).With *Authoritarian Brazil,* after looking at artwork for months, I found a painting by the Spanish artist Juan Genovés that captured the conflict, tension, indeterminacy, and dynamism of the situation in Brazil. I loved it. It has two very powerful arrows pointing down, which represent the force of the state, with just the shadow of three persons running against the arrows. To me, that was a hopeful sign, because the persons running symbolized people moving against the state instead of being crushed by it. This cover had a highly political meaning, because the volume was published during the darkest period of the military regime, and we were trying to see if there were any ways out.

State and Society in Peru

Q: *The State and Society: Peru in Comparative Perspective* was published in 1978. Why did you shift from Brazil to Peru?
A: Working in Brazil was not an option for me at that time, because my first book, *The Military in Politics,* had been censored. People in Brazil respected my work, but they were not going to let me move around easily. I was also dangerous for my Brazilian friends.

Q: Because of its focus on state autonomy and capacity in relation to societal forces, *The State and Society* is seen as an early and key contribution to the social science literature that aimed to "bring the state back in" (Evans, Rueschemeyer, and Skocpol 1985; Stepan 1985). How did your theoretical interest in the state develop?
A: As a graduate student at Columbia and later as a professor at Yale, I was quite struck by the general absence of the state in much of the literature and ongoing research projects. Not just pluralism, but Marxism, too, took the state out of the analysis. Some of the most important books we read in graduate school were by David Truman (1951), Gabriel Almond and Sidney Verba (1963), and Arthur Bentley (1908), and I found myself asking, "What

are they talking about?" There was almost no state in these works; it was all interest groups. Bentley, who saw the state as essentially a "cash register" that neutrally recorded and dispensed money in response to societal demands, was the most extreme version. But I already knew that the state actively shaped society by blocking some demands. Even as a graduate student, I felt the pluralist approach was very strange.

Q: Why did the pluralist approach seem odd? What attuned you to the ability of states to mold societal forces and demands?
A: When I was reading the pluralists as a graduate student, many of my friends in Brazil were being censored and even arrested by the authoritarian regime. So, I was connected to a world where interest group activities were clearly being distorted by the state. Also, reflecting on the Vargas regime in Brazil in the 1930s and 1940s, I knew the government had created certain trade unions and blocked others. Later, in 1975, when I first met Lula,[13] the great Brazilian trade union leader, he said in effect that he did not think it was right that as an officially approved union they received lawyers, dentists, doctors, and vacation facilities from the government. It was not right because he knew there was a price for these special privileges: official unions could only call a strike if the strike had been declared legal by the state. He felt trade unionists were going to have to learn to live without these special benefits as the price for greater autonomy. Also, although most of the Marxist-inspired dependency theory literature in the 1970s gave the impression that foreign, multinational companies were running everything, I knew that twenty of the twenty-five biggest companies in Brazil were in fact state-owned. The state, though seldom autonomous, was structuring interest groups, social movements, and the economy.

I was also aware of an important line of thought rooted in Roman law that accords the state a far wider range of prerogatives than does the common law tradition. In *The State and Society,* I called this the "organic-statist" tradition, because it draws centrally on the metaphor of the state as an organism with a head and body. I had been reading organic thinkers since my exposure to Catholic social thought—St. Augustine, St. Thomas Aquinas—as an undergraduate at Notre Dame. These thinkers emphasized the state's role in integrating and molding society in order to reduce conflict. I did not like this vision, but I was acutely aware of its existence and influence. Vargas and many of the military regimes in Latin America during the 1960s and 1970s, including the Peruvian one, were constantly using organic metaphors.

13. "Lula" refers to Luiz Inácio Lula Da Silva, who was elected president of Brazil in 2002.

Q: Why did Peru seem like an appropriate case for exploring your interest in the role of the state?
A: I picked Peru because it was a major experiment where a military that embraced the new professionalism, which I had written about in *Authoritarian Brazil,* was trying to use the power of the state to transform society. The Peruvian military regime was engaged in some of the most audacious social experiments of the time. Peru thus seemed like a good case for addressing the questions, What is the state's capacity to carry out reform from above? What things can a state do, and not do? I tried to document and explain *variation* in the state's capacity to achieve its goals across different policy areas.

Q: Was it difficult shifting from Brazil to Peru and doing fieldwork in a new country where you had not previously done research?
A: Peru was not totally unfamiliar, because I had written about it when I was working for *The Economist.* I had been there a couple of times. Still, I never felt the same affinity for Peru that I felt for Brazil, probably because I deeply valued the broad set of colleagues, including great journalists, I found in Brazil. In Peru, the range of colleagues was narrower. Also, in Brazil, wonderful archives were open to me. This type of informal structure was not available in Peru. As a result, most of my research involved fieldwork in squatters' settlements and on sugar plantations. I spent a lot of time in squatters' settlements trying to address the question, how do you organize the unorganized?

Q: Your fieldwork in Brazil focused on elites, mainly military officers. By contrast, your fieldwork in Peru focused on non-elites, mainly urban squatters and rural workers. How did you approach the interviews with non-elites?
A: It wasn't hard to get interviews with the workers. They liked to talk, but they would only talk as a group. They didn't want the elected head talking to me alone, because they didn't necessarily trust him. We normally had a group meeting, and they would last forever. I had to watch what I drank, because I was always offered something alcoholic.

They were suspicious of the government and also of me. But they knew I had visited other sugar plantations, and they wanted to talk about how workers elsewhere were doing. In the case of the squatters, if they had heard about land conflicts in other countries, they wanted to see if I knew anything about those problems. There was always an exchange.

I loved doing that research, especially on the plantations. A plantation is a whole community unto itself. The struggle was somehow different in each place. I was able to use the Rashomon technique of pivoting among distinct vantage points on the same reality.[14] I would talk to people in the central government to see who they were trying to organize and what they thought would happen. Then I would talk to the workers and see what support they felt they were receiving or not receiving from the government and what they thought was going to happen. I went back to most of the big plantations three or four times over several years, and the difference between time one and time two, and time three and time four was fascinating. When the workers saw me coming again, they would say, "Remember the last conversation, when we said this would happen? Well, what happened was, boom, boom, boom . . ."

Q: How was *The State and Society* received?
A: Many social scientists like that book more than any other I have written. Still, because it focused on Peru, instead of, say, Brazil or Chile, the book may have had less impact than it could have. Also, Sandy Thatcher, the editor at Princeton University Press, wanted to publish the first half, which develops my theoretical ideas about the state, and the second half, which presents the empirical analysis of Peru, as separate, stand-alone books. I said no, because I am the type of comparativist who thinks it is terribly important to embed general theoretical arguments in an empirical context. I regret that decision in a way, because many more people would have read the theoretical part, but I understand why I took the position I did.

The Breakdown of Democratic Regimes

Q: In 1978, the same year *The State and Society* appeared, you also published an influential collaborative volume, *The Breakdown of Democratic Regimes,* coedited with Juan Linz.[15] Could you discuss the origins and goals of that project?
A: It grew out of the feeling that we were living through lots of breakdowns of democracies. Linz was born in Germany in the 1920s and then moved to Spain in the 1930s. The question of the breakdown of democracies was thus a major part of his life. For my part, I had been in Brazil during the military coup of 1964. So, we had both witnessed breakdowns of democratic regimes. Starting in the mid-1960s, we began talking about our different experiences. I was talking about Brazil, and Juan was talking about Germany. During this period, Juan was lecturing on Karl Dietrich Bracher's

14. The reference is to the movie, *Rashomon,* by the Japanese filmmaker Akira Kurosawa, which presents its central tale from the perspective of several different narrators.
15. See Chapter 6 for Linz's perspective on this project.

book on the collapse of the Weimar Republic (1955), which he considered, correctly, an absolutely major book.

The overall comparative argument of *The Breakdown of Democratic Regimes* is twofold. First, we presented extensive documentation that indicated that the breakdown of democracy was not inevitable in any of the twelve cases we studied. Second, in every one of these cases, we presented extensive documentation that indicated that democratic incumbents, the very people who should have been protecting democracy, contributed to the breakdown through their ambivalence about or violations of the law, their hesitation in using legitimate coercive force against antidemocratic groups, and their willingness to allow such groups to walk the streets wearing uniforms, something no democracy should allow. Much of the then existing literature on the breakdown of democracy focused on the power of antidemocratic opposition forces—the military, the fascists, the Nazis—to overthrow democracy, which generated a sense of inevitability about the outcome. But, as I had shown in *The Military in Politics* (Stepan 1971), there was a lot of civilian complicity with the military during the breakdown in Brazil, and the outcome was by no means inevitable. Linz and I were trying to introduce these other elements—the role of democratic incumbents and the non-inevitability of the outcome—into the analysis of the breakdown of democracies. We assembled a first-rate group of contributors who addressed this *problématique* from different angles, including Julio Cotler from Peru, Guillermo O'Donnell from Argentina, Erik Allardt from Finland, M. Rainer Lepsius from Germany, Paolo Farneti from Italy, and, when the breakdown happened in Chile in 1973, in the middle of our project, Arturo Valenzuela from Chile.

We had trouble publishing the volume, because the manuscript was 1,200 pages long. We submitted it first to Yale University Press. The press received two or three very good reviews, told us they would like to publish it but it was simply too long, and asked if we could shorten it greatly. So, I approached Henry Tom at Johns Hopkins University Press, and he came up with the imaginative, cost-cutting idea of binding what were essentially four paperbacks into a single hardback volume, which had four page ones in different places. More than a quarter of a century later, all four paperback volumes are still in print.

Work on Democratization and Democracy

Q: In the 1980s and 1990s, your work focused on democratization. One of your early publications on this issue was your chapter, "Paths toward Redemocratization" (Stepan 1986) in the O'Donnell, Schmitter, and

Whitehead volume *Transitions from Authoritarian Rule* (1986). Could
you discuss your contribution to that collaborative project?[16]
A: I originally wrote a different paper for that volume, which focused on
the tasks of the democratic opposition to authoritarian regimes. It was a
rather Dahlian piece in that it offered an abstract analysis of all the key
issues that had to be addressed by the democratic opposition, in an authoritarian regime, if they wanted to make a full transition to democracy. Some
of the scholars who participated in the O'Donnell, Schmitter, and Whitehead project came from countries where authoritarian regimes were still in
power, and they disliked my article intensely, arguing that they would be
jailed if they tried to carry out all the tasks I discussed. The editors of the
volume never said they would not publish my piece, but I got the feeling
they wanted me to do something else. I think it's a good piece, and I later
published it in the *Journal of Democracy*, but it probably was not dynamic
enough or sufficiently contextualized for the volume on transitions (Stepan
1990). The piece I wrote instead was on path dependence, and it looked
at how different types of authoritarian regimes set the context for subsequent processes of democratization (Stepan 1986). Because I believe in
what Hirschman calls "possibilism," I don't feel path dependence explains
everything or that you have to live with the weight of history forever. Still,
path dependence does shape the context. I was especially interested in the
conditions under which people who committed abuses under the old regime could be brought to trial. If the military is run by junior officers who
overthrow senior officers, and then get themselves into intense difficulties,
like the loss of a war, then such officers can be brought to trial quickly by a
successor civilian regime. This occurred in Greece and Argentina, where
colonels had overthrown the generals and then lost an international war.
By contrast, if the military enjoys a relatively high degree of acceptance
among societal elites and some important political parties, and does not
have to hand over power, then the officers can structure the rules under
which they leave in a way that makes it very difficult to hold trials later.
Chile in 1989 is an example.

Q: In 1988, you published *Rethinking Military Politics* (Stepan 1988a).
What were your objectives in that book?
A: One of the core ideas was that civilians in new democracies have to
decide how they are going to manage and control their own coercive apparatus. Like it or not, no democracy can exist without a coercive apparatus,
otherwise it would be impossible to maintain law, citizens could be killed
with impunity, and rights could be constantly violated. Therefore, if you

---

16. See Chapters 9 and 10 for O'Donnell and Schmitter's perspectives on this project.

are serious about democracy, you have to create a usable state, and a usable state requires a coercive apparatus. Still, I could not find a single decent article in the democracy literature on how civilians should control the coercive apparatus, especially intelligence and the police.

My first book (Stepan 1971) showed that one of the real factors in the breakdown of civilian rule was not only the military, but political society and civil society failures to take seriously the tasks of democratic governance of the coercive apparatus. In *Rethinking Military Politics,* I argued that civilians have to create their own schools and think tanks concerned with military issues, and they need to know a lot about military budgets and arms. They have to design force structures and develop and control the rules of engagement. Civilians should internalize control of the coercive apparatus deeply in their thinking about democracy.

Q: Your 1996 book with Juan Linz, *Problems of Democratic Transition and Consolidation,* covered thirteen countries across three regions of the world.[17] What were the roots of this ambitious comparative project?
A: In the penultimate paragraph of the preface to *The Breakdown of Democratic Regimes,* which Linz and I finished in 1977, we wrote that "high priority for further work along these lines should now be given to the analysis of the conditions that lead to the breakdown of authoritarian regimes, to the process of transition from authoritarian to democratic regimes, and especially to the political dynamics of the consolidation of postauthoritarian democracies" (Linz and Stepan 1978, xii). As soon as we wrote that, I told Linz, "You know what this means. That's our agenda. We have to write a book on that." The first step was creating, and co-teaching, what may have been one of the first courses on the problem of democratic transitions.

Q: But *Problems of Democratic Transition and Consolidation* was not published until 1996, eighteen years after the breakdown of democracy book. Why did it take so long?
A: Some problems merit a decade or two. To this day Juan thinks we rushed it. Also, we both were doing other writing. Between the two Linz-Stepan books, I also wrote *Rethinking Military Politics,* my contributions to *Bringing the State Back In* and to *Transitions from Authoritarian Rule,* my *World Politics* article with Cindy Skach on the parliamentarianism versus presidentialism debate, and edited *Democratizing Brazil* (Stepan 1985, 1986, 1988a, 1989; Stepan and Skach 1993). Big things also were happening in the world that had huge implications for the democratization literature, such as the Wall coming down in Berlin. Juan and I were colleagues at Yale, very good friends,

17. See Chapter 6 for Linz's perspective on this project.

and lived five miles from each other. But between the two Linz-Stepan books I moved to Columbia in 1983, then to Central Europe in 1992, and then to Oxford in 1996. As a result, we could not work on our book the whole time. We met in many countries around the world. We tried to accept invitations to the same conferences so that we could be in the same place at the same time. If Juan was in Paris and I was in Hungary, Juan would come to Hungary or I would go to Paris, and we would work for about three days.

Q: What do you consider the main contributions of *Problems of Democratic Transition and Consolidation?*
A: The idea that democracy is impossible without a "usable state" was a central concept, as was the idea of "political society." I had used the concept of political society in *Rethinking Military Politics* as a way to draw attention to political action, electoral systems, political parties, and a whole range of things that are distinct from civil society. Civil society—the church, women's groups, peasants' organizations—had been the celebrity of the democratization literature, but political society was under-theorized. And democracy is not possible without a political society. Our focus on the special theoretical and political problems multinational societies present for democracy is also crucial, as are the refinements we made to the categories for analyzing non-democratic regimes by elaborating the concepts of post-totalitarianism and sultanism.

Q: One criticism of the book is that its explanations are ad hoc, because new variables are introduced to account for particular cases, or different variables are emphasized across cases. Ultimately, then, the book develops a distinct explanation for every case, which makes it a work of analytic history, not social science. How do you respond to this criticism?
A: We in fact discuss each one of our variables for each case, but if "stateness" was not central, as it was not in Portugal, we said so very quickly. Where stateness was crucial, as it was in the USSR and Spain, it received great attention. The only country to combine our variables of "sultanism" and "totalitarianism" was Romania so, from a theoretical perspective, it merited special analysis of how this unique combination made the tasks of democratization distinctive. It is not unscientific to recognize historical specificity. But sure, the book could have been more rigorous. I accept this criticism and live with its implications. But there would have been opportunity costs. We were two senior scholars analyzing thirteen countries across three different geographical-cultural areas, a task that many said was impossible. Social science is a collective endeavor. Different people make different contributions that can be used and built on by others. Our actual

goal was to call attention to and elaborate major dilemmas and problems faced by democratizing countries. The book has been translated into about a dozen languages, including Indonesian, Chinese, and a private translation by reformers in Iran, so Linz and I are hopeful that hundreds of scholars and activists, in many different political contexts, are building and improving upon our work.

Q: You have been involved in three of the major studies of regime change published during the past twenty-five years: your volume with Linz on the breakdown of democratic regimes (Linz and Stepan 1978), the volume on transitions from authoritarianism by O'Donnell, Schmitter, and Whitehead (1986), and, most recently, your book with Linz (Linz and Stepan 1996). What linkages do you see across these three works?
A: The Linz-Stepan volume on breakdowns and the O'Donnell, Schmitter, and Whitehead volume on transitions are probably more similar today than when they were happening. Some participants in the O'Donnell, Schmitter, and Whitehead project felt that the Linz-Stepan volume on breakdowns had been overly voluntaristic, giving insufficient weight to structural forces. Ironically, that very criticism is now made against the O'Donnell, Schmitter, and Whitehead transitions volume.

Concerning the relationship between the transitions volume and the second Linz and Stepan book, *Problems of Democratic Transition and Consolidation,* we were writing in the 1990s, and, of course, the world was different. The O'Donnell, Schmitter, and Whitehead volume is only about Southern Europe and Latin America, because the transitions in communist Europe had not yet happened when their book was published in 1986. Our book includes post-communist Europe, which meant we had to discuss contrasting types of prior non-democratic regimes. The set of Southern European and Latin American cases analyzed in the transitions volume fit into just one of the four categories of non-democratic regimes that Linz and I used in our book: authoritarianism. None of these cases was totalitarian, post-totalitarian, or sultanistic. Because of the broader geographic scope of our book, we had to discuss a range of different types of non-democratic regimes. Also, problems of stateness and multinationalism were not really discussed in any of the Latin American or Southern European cases covered in the O'Donnell, Schmitter, and Whitehead volume, with the exception of a few pages on Spain. Despite the fact that Spain was in that volume, we, and I say "we" because I was one of the contributors, did not talk about the then under-theorized problems that multinationalism creates for democracy. So, the second chapter of *Problems of Democratic Transition and Consolidation* is called " 'Stateness,' Nationalism, and Democratization."

Current Research: Federalism and the "Twin Tolerations"

Q: Since the publication of *Problems of Democratic Transition and Consolidation,* you and Linz have been working on another big project, on federalism.[18] At first glance, the topic of federalism seems narrower than issues like democratization, which you and Linz addressed in your previous work. What excites you about federalism?

A: First, a strong majority of everyone who lives in a democracy in the modern world lives in a federal system. Also, the understanding of federalism in much of comparative politics has been skewed by the hegemony of a model based on the experience of the United States. Federalism was the central issue that William Riker, one of the most cited political scientists in the past forty years, wrote about. Riker argued that every federal system emerges from a bargain among groups with a high degree of autonomy, and even political independence, to pool their sovereignty. Linz and I call this pattern "coming together" federalism, and the United States, Switzerland, and Australia were indeed formed in this way. But those are the only clean instances of "coming together" federalism, and the most recent one, Australia, happened more than a hundred years ago. Since then, some countries—Spain, Belgium, and India—have become federal by a totally different route we call "holding together" federalism. These countries were de jure or de facto unitary states having trouble holding together because they contained more than one politically awakened national group in the territory of their state. The only way they could live together peacefully and democratically was to devolve power in order to hold the country together. This "holding together" style of forming a federation is exactly the opposite of the "coming together" version, because it emerges not by people with high degrees of political autonomy ceding power, but by people in a unitary state devolving it into a federation.

The consequences of this difference are huge. Political units with a high degree of autonomy that decide to "come together" in a federation only pool as much sovereignty as necessary. This means, for example, that they may withhold the right to pass comprehensive polity-wide social welfare legislation, because they want to do that in their own jurisdiction, or they might require multiple veto points that limit the power of the federal government. As a result, the three classic "coming together" federations, the United States, Switzerland, and Australia, all have three or four institutional veto points, a powerful upper chamber in addition to a powerful lower chamber, powerful subnational jurisdictions, which, in the United States,

18. Some of the many publications associated with this project to date are: Stepan, Linz, and Yadav (forthcoming). See also Stepan (1998, 1999, 2001a, 2004, 2005). Other works related to this project by Linz are found in Chapter 6 of this volume.

exert much control over social policy, and, in Switzerland and Australia, national referenda. The fact that all the classic "coming together" federations have three or four veto players is one reason why, on a whole series of indicators, they have the highest degree of inequality among the long-standing democracies. Switzerland and especially the United States have a high tolerance for inequality, which stems from the original federal bargain that created these institutional veto points. In comparison, Austria has only one electorally generated veto player, while Spain, Belgium, and Germany have two (Stepan 2004).

The "holding together" path to federalism is distinct, because it results in an asymmetrical federation where the constituent political units do not all have the same rights. For example, Quebec has special language and religious rights for French and Catholicism. By contrast, the "coming together" path leads to a symmetrical federation where every unit has identical rights and prerogatives, as seen in the equal amount of representation states have in the U.S. Senate. All the democracies in the world today with more than one awakened nationality—Canada, Spain, Belgium, and India—are asymmetrically federal.

Why is all of this important? It speaks to the question of how to have democracy and avoid civil war in countries where more than one politically awakened nation exists in the territory of the state when competitive electoral politics is initiated. Take Sri Lanka and Burma; there is no question that if these countries are to become peaceful democracies, they will have to be federal. Moreover, they will have to be asymmetrically federal. The person heading the peace negotiations in Sri Lanka once spent a year as a fellow at Oxford, and had heard that I was arguing that asymmetrical federalism is one of the only ways to help create a peaceful democracy in a multinational society. He asked if we could spend a day walking around and talking about constitutional designs that could help achieve peace in Sri Lanka. He told me, "Sri Lanka is a unitary state. But you are talking about asymmetrical federalism. What does this really mean? What are some examples?" I said "Spain is an example. Belgium is an example," and I explained these cases to him. He had been sending his people to study symmetrical federalism in the United States and Germany, and I told him he ought to send them to Belgium and Spain instead to study asymmetrical federalism. They would then understand why a unitary state should decentralize for reasons of peace and holding together a polity.

Similarly, I learned that the opposition to the military regime in Burma was being sold the idea of an American-type constitution with symmetrical federalism, giving every unit the same amount of representation in a powerful upper chamber. As a result, they had drafted a constitution that was one of the worst and most dangerous I had ever seen. In Burma, probably over 90 percent of the field grade officers come from the Burmese ethnic group, which comprises about 60 percent of the country's population. Under the constitution written by the opposition, the Burmese would get only 11 percent representation in the Senate, and, as in the United States, the Senate was designed to be just as powerful as the lower house. This meant that nationality groups with only 2 percent of the population were going to have the same level of representation as the Burmese, with 60 percent. Plus, there was going to be no national army, but each state could have its own army. Symmetrical federalism will never work in Burma (Reynolds et al. 2001).

Let me give a further example of why the menu of federal models available to political actors is important. I was recently asked on closed-circuit television with the entire Philippine Senate whether federalism was a feasible option. Someone from the floor said, "We are a unitary state. This means we can't create a federal system until every region is first given independence. Then we can ask them all to rejoin the federation by pooling their sovereignty. But wouldn't it be dangerous for every region of the Philippines to be given independence?" I was asked the same thing at a meeting with the General Staff of the Indonesian military, when Linz and I were invited to Indonesia in 1998 after the fall of Suharto. They were operating under the mistaken assumption that the American model of "coming together" was the only way to form a federation.

The big question we face is, what types of political regimes and constitutional arrangements help different nationalities live together peacefully? Linz and I believe that the idea that every nation should be a state, and that every state should be a nation, is one of the most pernicious in politics, because in many countries there exists more than one politically awakened group with a sense of its own nationhood. If you are committed to the idea of a French-style nation-state, this means fundamentally privileging the language, culture, and symbols of one of those nations above the rest. How can you do this in a politically robust multinational society? If it happens that the vast majority of the people in a state share one culture and language, then a nation-state can be democratic and inclusive, that is, democracy building and nation building can be reinforcing logics. But when you have two or three territorially concentrated national groups in a state, then democracy building and nation building are conflicting logics. How do you get around this problem? The first thing to recognize is that people can have multiple *and* complementary identities. Indeed, all federal systems operate on the basis of multiple identities and dual loyalties, because citizens in federations are necessarily involved with two different sovereigns, the central and the regional governments. Linz and I thus propose the concept of *state-nation* (as opposed to a *nation-state*) as a way to think about situations where citizens can have distinctive national identities *and* still identify with, and be loyal to, the polity-wide state.

Q: In addition to historical case studies and comparisons, your project on federalism draws heavily on survey research. Could you discuss how you are using surveys and why you find this tool fruitful for studying federalism?
A: Surveys are an especially appropriate way to explore the possibility of complementary and multiple identities. Linz and/or I have become actively involved in helping design good surveys in Spain, India, and Sri Lanka. Unfortunately, the questions on lots of surveys force dichotomous responses. For instance, a survey will ask, "Are you Catalan or are you Spanish?" However, a better way to ask the question is to give five options: (1) Are you only Catalan? (2) Are you more Catalan than Spanish? (3) Are you equally Catalan and Spanish? (4) Are you more Spanish than Catalan? (5) Are you only Spanish? We have data from dozens of Spanish surveys that pose the question this way, and the most frequently chosen response is "equally Catalan and Spanish." This is a very important finding, because most authors writing about nationalism think people should make choices about identities. It is the social scientists who treat multiple identities as a form of bigamy. But many human beings don't like to make these choices, and they don't necessarily have to make them. If you are a Croatian married to a Serbian and your child is both, the last thing you want is a world where you have to choose between one of these identities. Social science needs to work at understanding how people handle multiple identities, and especially how democratic governments can accept, and even nurture, multiple *and* complementary identities.

Q: What are your research plans after you finish the federalism project?
A: Linz and I are probably not done with federalism and inequality in the United States. Comparativists must increasingly examine the classic inequality outlier—the United States—and include it more systematically in our research. But my next project will be about the role of organized religion in politics. The social science thrust at the moment is to look at religious fundamentalism. Indeed, the National Academy of Sciences has already funded a major project on fundamentalism. But we should not just study fundamentalism. Every world religion, including Islam, is multi-vocal. Varieties of regimes across countries with the same dominant religion should be documented and analyzed. For example, I and Graeme Robertson showed that approximately 50 percent of Muslims who now live in non-Arab, Mus-

lim majority polities live in systems that are currently electorally competitive, a necessary but not sufficient condition for a democracy. In sharp
contrast, the figure in Arab Muslim majority polities from 1973 to 2003 was
zero percent (Stepan with Robertson 2003; Stepan and Robertson 2004).
Obviously, Islam itself, the common variable, cannot explain such variation. Every major religion, including Islam, contains many elements usable
by a non-democratic regime to justify itself, but also some elements potentially usable for building representative democracy. Instead of the separation of church and state, we actually need what I call "twin tolerations": religious leaders must give elected leaders sufficient space to carry out their
democratic tasks, and democratic leaders must give religious groups sufficient space for private worship, to participate in civil society, and, as long
as they do not violate other people's rights, to organize political parties
(Stepan 2000, 2001b). We need toleration of democracy by religious groups
and toleration of religion by elected leaders. These twin tolerations have to
be crafted and constructed politically.

The strict separation of church and state, which many people believe is
necessary for democracy, in fact exists almost nowhere in the democratic
world except France, and even there it has become less strict after 1958. Six
of the European Union (EU) countries—Denmark, Finland, Greece, England, Scotland, and, until recently, Sweden—have official, established
churches. Norway, which is not in the EU, also has an established church.
Germany still has a church tax. And in France, which passed a law in 1905
that rigorously separated church and state, the government began giving
money after 1958 to support Catholic schools, under the idea that every
citizen deserved a decent education. By 1961, 20 percent of the French
government's total education budget went to Catholic private schools. And
the last time I looked at my U.S. money, it said "In God We Trust." So, we
should not be telling all the non-democratic countries in the world that to
have democracy they need a complete separation of church and state, because that does not exist in virtually any of the world's longstanding democracies. Instead of focusing on the separation of church and state, or on
religious fundamentalism, we should focus on what I have called the "twin
tolerations."

The relationship between religion and democracy is arguably the most
urgent problem of our time. But if there is one thing that modern social
science has wanted to study even less than how coercive apparatuses can be
governed by the democratic state, it is the variety of patterns concerning
religion in democracies.

**Q: What explains this inattention to the relationship between religion
and democracy?**

A: The assumption of modernization theory was that spontaneous secular-ization would happen. Obviously this turned out to be a false assumption. We should have known it was false, because, historically, the way out of hundreds of years of religious wars was often not spontaneous seculariza-tion, but state treaties or complex political accommodations, such as India's form of secularism, which involves extensive state support to religions but is secular because of the "equal respect" and "equal distance" formula. Also, in some cases, people in the academy are afraid to talk about religion and politics. In many universities, few, or no, courses in comparative politics are taught that systematically examine the role of the world religions in democ-racies. As a result of this neglect, we do not have many categories to handle this topic, and the ones we do have are often empirically misleading.

The Research Process
Science

Q: Do you consider yourself a scientist?
A: Many colleagues think of science as offering law-like, universal rules. In fact, the work of most natural scientists is probabilistic. The idea often held by social scientists that science is universal and exact would actually make most natural scientists very uneasy. Moreover, we should expect even less predictability in the social world than in the material world. Molecules cannot speak and do not have a memory, whereas human beings can think about and remember the consequences of past actions, and, to some extent, they can learn. This means that just because something has happened a hundred times in a row, you cannot necessarily make it a social science law, because if human beings decide it is a miserable outcome and can think of ways to change it, the outcome can change. I feel quite at ease with this un-predictability. In fact, in *Problems of Democratic Transition and Consolidation,* Linz and I explicitly said we did not expect many of our observations to be true in a hundred years, because concepts of citizenship, participation, and identity change over time (Linz and Stepan 1996, xvii–xviii). What could be imposed in France in 1830 in the name of the nation-state would cause a riot if it were attempted in many places today. This does not mean you can't make powerful probabilistic statements about causal relationships, but knowledge in the social sciences is fundamentally context-dependent.

Interviews

Q: Your research often draws on interviews with key political actors as a major source of insight. What is the secret to doing a successful interview?

A: Every good interview with a key political actor is based on an exchange, and the exchange does not last unless it is interesting to both people. This means you need to know a lot before you do an interview so that the people being interviewed find the experience worth their time. Interviewing top people is actually much easier than most political scientists think. Politicians are never bored by the story of their own lives. If I say, "You have been involved in something historical, and I'm going to ask many other people about it. Can you tell me what happened from your side?" that is often the opening of a two-hour conversation, no matter how busy they are. If they are interested enough, they will talk a second time, often at their house, where they might walk over to a safe and say, "You know, if you really want to learn about this matter, you'd better read these documents, because they say what actually happened." Almost all the Brazilian generals who participated in the coup of 1964 had letters documenting their roles, and they showed me these documents. Also, the interview served not only as a way to learn their opinions, but also to open up a network. On my way out, I would ask, "Who else should I talk to?" They often would name six people, four whom I might dismiss, but two whom I had been dying to talk to. So, I would push a bit further and say, "Senator, General. Could you give me a small note of introduction, or could you phone?" Many would phone that very second. They would say, "I have this young person here. He is very serious, and he is here for . . ." I always said, "A long time." Then they would ask, "Could you possibly see him?" The other person almost never said no.

I like to do a series of interviews on both sides of a story. It's important, and I enjoy it.

Knowing a Country

Q: It is sometimes said that the best comparativists know one case very well. What role has your knowledge of Brazil played over the course of your career?
A: I have often gone back to Brazil. I've even gone back when a project on another country, frankly, was not panning out intellectually. In the mid-1980s, I spent two years working on a project on local popular participation in Cuba, until it finally dawned on me that there was never going to be any serious popular participation under Fidel Castro. Moreover, I was not getting the level of access I wanted. So, I said, "Scrub it." I was feeling bad, and my wife said, "Al, every time you have been to Brazil you have enjoyed it and learned something. You know Fernando Henrique Cardoso, you have talked to Lula, you have talked to the generals. Why don't you go down there and see how the whole re-democratization process is going?" I went

to Brazil, and, bang! I wrote *Rethinking Military Politics* (Stepan 1988a), and edited the successor volume to *Authoritarian Brazil,* called *Democratizing Brazil* (Stepan 1989). Going back to Brazil was energizing and helped me shift to a whole new stage of research.

Q: Do you keep up with events in Brazil?
A: When something is happening that I think is particularly important, I regularly read an online daily and a weekly newsletter on Brazilian politics by two of Brazil's best political observers. I read them as I would the sports page, because Brazilian politics is so interesting. That is often the first thing I look at after I wake up in the morning. And even though I am only supposed to teach two courses in the spring semester when I am at Columbia, I always teach three, because the third is a special one-credit course on Brazil. It is easy to do, because the course has a lot of guest speakers, and we always go out to dinner with them for three hours. If you have a base in a country, one way or another there is a means to keep in touch.

Over the past six years, India is the place I have paid the most attention to. This is partly because English is the language, partly because the press is terrific, partly because I know many different colleagues there and was asked to help design questions for a survey with 27,000 respondents, one of the world's largest census-based social science surveys ever, and partly because so much is at stake in India today involving religion, especially religious fundamentalism, and multinationalism. I also love the temple and mosque architecture. It's just a fascinating place.

Q: As we advance in our careers and lives, the accumulation of personal and professional obligations often makes it harder to spend time in the field. How have you managed to continue doing fieldwork over the course of your career?
A: I still get into a lot of airplanes to distant countries. I make it a priority. Also, e-mails back and forth to members of all my "invisible colleges" make it easier, as does being in places like Columbia, Yale, Central European University (CEU), or Oxford, because people pass through and visit. Even though you are not traveling to a particular country, a person from that country may stop by with a key set of problems for mutual discussion. For example, the person heading the peace negotiations in Sri Lanka came to Oxford, sent me his briefing papers, and then I went to Sri Lanka. That kind of interactive relationship is marvelous.

Fieldwork does not just happen in the field. I sometimes feel that some of my best fieldwork happens over a long dinner at my home, when someone is visiting and we have time for a four-hour conversation.

Reading

Q: What role does reading play in your research?
A: Once I get into a problem, I usually find a set of five or six people in the world, in four or five disciplines, who are widely seen as doing very important work on that issue, and I read what they have done. If I think the work is good and relevant, one way or another I am going to talk to that person. I send them something I have written, and, before you know it, one of us has invited the other to give a talk. I don't just read.

I have lots of friends and colleagues who are philosophers, economists, historians, sociologists, and anthropologists. I read their work, and we exchange documents and argue. In general, when I have defined a problem that interests me, then I chase it wherever I have to. If that means I have to learn about international law, medieval history, or anthropology, then that's what I do. A lot of people say, "Let's form an interdisciplinary group." That does not mean much to me. However, getting five people together who share a problem, and happen to be from different disciplines, excites me a lot. But, in the end, as Albert Hirschman once said, "The best interdisciplinary work is done under one skull."

Q: Do you read much political and social theory?
A: Lately, I have been reading political philosophers, like Charles Taylor, Seyla Benhabib, Amartya Sen, John Rawls, and Joseph Raz, a fair amount, because, as my research interests focus more on conflicts between multinationalism and democracy, or democracy and religion, I need to think about the relationship between individual rights and collective recognition. When an entire group of people has been denied the right to use their language, whether it is Russians in Estonia, Kurds in Turkey, or Catalans in Spain, their struggle to be able to articulate their interests using their language is often cast in terms of collective rights. A major counterargument to the assertion of collective rights is rooted in liberalism. So, I have been reading and thinking about political liberalism.

Writing

Q: You rarely publish your research as peer-reviewed journal articles. Why do you prefer to publish books and book chapters?
A: Peer-reviewed articles are a very important form of scholarly production, and I read journals like *World Politics* and *Comparative Politics* very carefully, and I occasionally publish peer-reviewed articles in such places as *World Politics*, the *Journal of Democracy*, and *Government and Opposition*. But you

are basically right, in my own research, I am often working with lots of countries and generating totally new types of information, and sometimes, especially when I collaborate with Linz, I end up with an eighty-page paper that is not yet a book, but is too long to publish as an article. I would not advise my students to try to build a career this way, but I do believe a good piece of work, however it is produced, will get read once it starts circulating. What are the ten articles that have had the most impact on our lives? Many may have come from a strange collection of places. Some, although they were circulating and were incredibly important, may never even have been published, because something wasn't quite solid enough. Invisible colleges thrive on the circulation of these kinds of works.

Take Linz's paper on presidentialism. A small piece of it was first published as an excursus in our volume on the breakdown of democratic regimes (Linz 1978, 71–74). Then it became a fugitive, but slowly changing paper for about sixteen years, until, finally, Arturo Valenzuela organized a conference at Georgetown University on presidential regimes where people were invited to criticize and comment on Linz's paper on presidentialism. They asked Linz, "By the way, have you ever published it? Is there something we can use?" So, Linz finally published it (Linz 1994).

In a sense, Linz is against finishing anything. He is quite happy just to keep working on a project. He didn't want to finish *Problems of Democratic Transition and Consolidation* (Linz and Stepan 1996) because he wanted to add a few more countries and have a bit more time with it. He asked me, "Do you think the book is getting better every time you come to my house and we work on it for three or four days?" I said, "Absolutely." Then he asked, "When we work on the book, is it fun?" I said, "Absolutely." Finally, he said, "Even though we haven't published the book, do you think our work is getting out and is useful in some way?" I answered, "Yes, somehow it is getting around and even getting translated." Then he said, "Well, why ever finish it?"

Collaboration

Q: Your work together with Juan Linz over the past thirty-five years is one of the most sustained and successful collaborations in modern social science. Could you discuss how this collaboration works?
A: First of all, we are close friends. If we are in the same country we may talk on the phone two or three times a week, even when we are not working on anything specific together. We share an interest in a whole range of problems, and we may call each other just to say, "Don't miss this article," or, "I just got this paper and sent it in the mail to you," or, "What's your take on this event in the news?"

When we meet, often at Juan and his wife, Rocío's, home to work we usually start around noon the first day and finish at 3 in the morning. We begin by talking about what is happening in the world and various other things, then we eat a late lunch and get going. The next day we get up around 8:00 a.m., have breakfast together, and then work the whole day. If it's a three-day meeting, we will work until 2 o'clock that night.

Q: When do your best ideas come?
A: Often between midnight and 3 in the morning.

Q: Why is that?
A: By that time, we have been talking about many things and have retrieved many books, either from Juan's home library, the Yale Library, or the suitcases of material I have lugged with me. We are very interested in the historical context, so we hunt in a bunch of books for exact references to an event. We are interested in censuses, so we may have to get out the 1930, 1940, and 1950 censuses. We always are on the lookout for historical maps. We often phone one of our colleagues somewhere in the world to talk, and maybe to see if a survey we all have been working on is advancing. If possible, we might suggest a new survey question that now seems to us a better way to explore a shared problem. One reference leads to another, and, all of a sudden, after we have been talking for hours about the maps, the censuses, the surveys, the competing histories, we say, "We need to think about this problem differently." Then we will get very excited and rush into it. We really enjoy this process, but it takes a long time to thrash through it. By 3:00 a.m., we might have as many as fifty books, articles, manuscripts, or surveys on the floor, because we both read them and then drop them there so we can refer to them later. There are so many books that we are stepping on them. Once in a while, maybe when we are sitting on the floor well past midnight going through some maps or a historical census, Linz will look over and say with a smile, "You know, they pay us for doing this."

Q: Do you write during your meetings?
A: We almost never write first drafts during the meetings themselves, but we rewrite things written afterward constantly. I take notes, and sometimes Juan will dictate something for his secretary or research assistant to type up later so we can both look at it. Lately, we are beginning to change our style. We have a research assistant, a graduate student finishing his doctoral dissertation, who writes things down on his computer if they sound interesting and then shows it to us. That's all new.

It's a slow process, which we don't mind. Look, the breakdown of democracy project started in the mid-1960s when Juan was already working through the German and Spanish cases and I was trying to begin to make sense of the Brazilian breakdown. We held a conference in Varna, Bulgaria, at the International Political Science Association (IPSA) meetings in 1970, and at Yale in about 1975. You could say that project took from 1965 to 1978 (Linz and Stepan 1978). But throughout that entire period, we rethought the classic cases, new cases of democratic breakdown were happening, and we were also working on other things.

Q: Do you and Linz have a clear division of labor? For example, do you divide up the cases?
A: It sounds strange, and it would probably be more efficient if we did it differently, but neither of us ever allows the other to be completely responsible for a particular case. Obviously, Juan is closer to the German, Spanish, and Italian material, and I am closer to the Brazilian, Indian, and post-communist material. Still, we both want to follow up our own thoughts on the other person's arguments. Juan is now reading a lot on India, and with one of my German graduate students I am working on the question of what mechanisms make German federalism inequality reducing and U.S. federalism inequality inducing. Whereas Juan's interests in Germany at the moment focus more on the nineteenth century and the question of why federalism emerged in Germany but not Italy. When we were writing *Problems of Democratic Transition and Consolidation* (Linz and Stepan 1996), Juan knew more about the Spanish and Portuguese cases, but I had been to, and taught in, both countries. I knew more about Brazil, Chile, and Argentina, but Juan had been to all those countries, too. I don't think he had been to Uruguay, but we worked together on the Yale dissertations on Uruguay by Luis González (1991) and Charles Gillespie (1991). I traveled to each of the post-communist countries we analyzed, and I talked with Juan about what I learned. He would quickly read anything I had written on these cases and then ask me very hard questions. Also, if we are interested in, say, eleven countries, then we both cover all eleven in our teaching, which means we inevitably have some students working on some of these cases. Linz and I would always call each other after our first class of the semester to see which new countries students were coming from. About five years before a transition from authoritarianism was possible somewhere, students from that country would start showing up in our classes. In the mid-1980s, Linz would call me excitedly and say, "I have two Koreans." And I'd say, "I have one." Five years earlier no Koreans dared take our classes, because South Korea had intelligence agents on American campuses. But something had changed. A similar pattern occurred with Hungarians, Poles, Taiwanese,

and then Indonesians. Many of these students already knew our work, and they had thought about how it might be relevant for their countries.

Q: Judging from your individual works, you and Linz have quite different writing styles. How do you reconcile these differences?
A: We have totally different writing styles. Juan feels comfortable with a two hundred-word sentence, whereas I feel comfortable with five eight-word sentences back-to-back, because that is how I wrote for *The Economist*. We can't have a half-Linzian and a half-Stepanian style book, so we forge a common style. It takes a while. A hidden partner is my wife Nancy. In our entire marriage, we have always read, and reread, everything the other has written. She has been particularly helpful in resolving some of the Linz-Stepan writing problems. When Juan and I have written fifteen or twenty pages, Juan will often read it aloud, and if I have written something he is uncomfortable with, he will ask me, "Why did we say this?" When you see the word *excursus,* borrowed from Simmel, in one of our books, it means the Linz-Stepan system had temporarily broken down. We have a couple of excursuses in some of our books, and in the end, they always focus on something that most scholars might think is tangential to our argument, but we had finally decided is a crucial aside.

Q: A lot of collaboration in the social sciences today is long distance, occurring mainly via e-mail and telephone. How important is the face-to-face interaction that you and Linz maintain?
A: It's hugely important, partly because we find documents and references together, which does not happen over the phone. I should add that Juan is efficiently well defended. He is not on e-mail, and does not even have an answering machine on his telephone! When we have a two- or three-day meeting, we have time to run to the library. If we are working on constitutions and focusing on what the preamble says, we may want to read eighteen constitutions to see whether they start out by saying "We the People . . ." or by saying "The Sovereign Republics of the following states . . ." So, we'll go to the library to get material on constitutions. Or if we are arguing about the impact of plebiscites and referendums, we'll go to the Yale library and find all the material on Swiss referendums, Australian referendums, and so on. We could not do that over the phone. But if we are involved in a three-day interactive meeting, which allows for a break at the library, we can follow these kinds of leads. Also, the best questions in our surveys on the four countries of South Asia emerged while working at Juan's house with Yogendra Yadav for four days in a process of collective exchanges, refinements, and radical reformulations. My e-mail exchanges with Yogendra never quite match this creativity—and fun.

Engagement with Public Affairs

Q: Could you discuss the role of normative values in your work?
A: My values are always involved in my decisions about what to study. I have always chosen to work on problems that affect a lot of people. I never understood the argument that social science should be value-free. Weber talks about "inconvenient facts," which refers to facts you discover that are inconvenient for your position (Weber 1946a, 147). Social scientists of course have an absolute obligation to report such inconvenient facts. However, the other part of Weber says you should only study problems that are worth being studied and that you should do it with passion and enthusiasm (Weber 1946a, 135). It is difficult to find a problem you care passionately about if you don't allow your values to influence your decision about what is important to study.

Q: You have been involved in advising political actors throughout your career. What do you get from engagement with public affairs and why do you do it?
A: I am not interested in policy analysis in the normal Washington sense. I have often been asked to get involved in politics as an advisor, and I have been sounded out by a couple of presidential administrations to serve on the National Security Council. But I do not find Washington a sufficiently interesting city for the long haul. It is a company town and the proximity to government is all too often agenda setting not only for the think tanks but for much of the university community, too.

I have always been much more interested in doing what I want by myself, rather than working for an administration. On the other hand, if people have a model in their heads that they see as normatively correct and a natural part of history, and if I think this model is causing problems in the world, then I feel obliged to write about it. This is why Linz and I have been so concerned to challenge the idea that every nation should be a state and every state should be a nation. I have even been willing to insert myself into complex situations when I feel I have an analytic edge, and think I can also learn something, and make a useful contribution. In this sense, my fieldwork and my political involvement feed on each other. I'm not a senator, and I don't work at the State Department, but if I can contribute something because I have an idea about a particular public problem, I am willing to commit myself, as I have often done for human rights issues.

For example, when I read the 1980 Chilean constitution, I said to myself, "Pinochet has introduced a guillotine moment." The constitution said Pinochet would be president for eight years, then the four commanders-in-chief—the heads of the military police, air force, army, and navy—would unanimously select a single name. That name would be the only one presented to the country, and, to be elected president, the candidate would need 50.1 percent of the vote. Americas Watch, the human rights organization, wanted to see if this election could possibly be fair and perhaps even won by the opposition. Because I had been in and out of Chile since 1964 and felt I could possibly talk to the military leadership and to the democratic opposition, I thought I had something to offer. So, when I arrived in Santiago as the head of the Americas Watch Mission, I set to work trying to get interviews with the heads of the air force and military police, whom I believed were ambivalent in their support for Pinochet. I understood that driving a wedge between the military as government, and the military as institution, would be crucial for a successful transition to democracy. I asked the question that hit precisely on this distinction. I asked the *commandante* of the air force, "What is worse for your country and the air force? The candidate that you nominate wins the election, but under great doubts domestically and internationally about the legitimacy of the vote, or the candidate that you nominate loses?" In a separate interview I posed the same question to the head of the military police. Both immediately shot back that it was more dangerous to have the candidate win under suspicion. Then I said, "Elections are complex things, would you create new rules, or would you use the traditional rules of Chilean elections?" They replied, "We'd use the traditional rules." Then I asked, "How many people are registered? How many people do you think would vote?" They said, "Seventy-five to 80 percent of the people." Then I told them, "Well, there is a problem, all the registration lists were burned after Allende was overthrown, so only about 20 percent of the people are actually registered. How long would it take to register the rest?" They said it would take six months. I said, "If you want legitimacy, then maybe you should not select the candidate until everyone has had the opportunity to register." They agreed. And you know what? Neither one voted to select a candidate for six months, until Chilean citizens had a chance to register.

The next key thing was to talk to people like Ricardo Lagos, a key opposition leader, who was worried about participating in the election.[19] Lagos said, "When do authoritarian regimes ever lose?" In essence, I answered, "They often lose, because they make mistakes. They just lost in Uruguay; they just lost in the Philippines; and they are in the process of losing in Taiwan and Korea. The guillotine moment is crucial. Pinochet is going to stick his head out just once, and only for a second. You have to chop it off at that precise moment. So, register people and get them ready to vote, but

19. Ricardo Lagos was elected president of Chile in 2000.

don't vote if you think the election is going to be fraudulent." So, this was a situation where I felt I could make a contribution (Stepan 1988b).

I'll give another example. I decided to accept an invitation to talk to the leaders of the minority ethnic groups of Burma, some of whom were the political-military leaders of the secessionist armies of their nationality group, because, as I mentioned earlier, I was concerned they were inappropriately being sold an American-type constitution. I told them, "Let's start by looking at countries where military governments ended in democracies. I'll go through about ten cases so we can think about the problem of democratizing in a country like yours, which is ruled by the military." My hidden agenda was to make them understand that no other country in the world had successfully democratized starting from a position where the opposition was as weak and the military had as few reasons to leave power, as in Burma. When they understood this, I tried to show them it was impossible, as their draft constitution proposed, to go from a situation where the Burmese ethnic group, with 60 percent of the population, dominated the military and the country's political institution, to one where they would get just 11 percent of the seats in the Senate and there would be no national army. The ethnic Burmese military had strong incentives not to accept this. After two days, the opposition leaders were discussing an asymmetrical federal system as a possibly more appropriate response to their needs (Reynolds et al. 2001).

Sometimes, when there is a major debate about a constitution, I am asked to give advice. In Ukraine I discussed presidential decree powers and the Spanish non-nation-state response to multinationalism. In India, the BJP[20] wanted to review the constitution and move from parliamentarism toward presidentialism. A group of friends involved in the discussion invited me, as an outsider who had written on the presidentialism versus parliamentarianism debate (Stepan and Skach 1993), to talk about these issues with a parliamentary working committee and to give a large public lecture. I thought it would be useful to discuss evidence from twenty or thirty countries. I also wanted to call their attention to the fact that no democratic country in the world had ever had more than eight political parties in a ruling coalition before India did. Now, India had twenty-three parties in the coalition, many of which were ethnically and territorially based. I posed the question, how would you handle such a large twenty-three-party coalition in a presidential system? There are incentives that often make parliamentarianism coalition requiring and coalition sustaining, whereas presidentialism, with its fixed term for the president, normally has fewer such incentives.

20. Bharatiya Janata Party.

Another useful invitation I accepted was to Iran, where I was asked to speak in a semipublic forum organized by reformers on "The Dialogue of Civilizations." After I arrived, it was clear that government officials at the Ministry of the Interior wanted to speak privately with me. This may sound threatening, because normally the people at the Ministry of the Interior in authoritarian regimes are hard-liners. But in Iran, which then was a diarchy, split between elected non-fundamentalists and unelected fundamentalist mullahs, the Ministry of the Interior was actually the key power base for the pro-democratic group interested in a democratic transition. They wanted me to look carefully at the Iranian constitution to see what possibilities it offered for pushing democratic reforms given that they then controlled the presidency and the parliament. When I realized what they wanted, I agreed.

Q: Is it true that you nearly ran for Congress?
A: Yes. I have always regarded public office as an honorable and very important profession. The difference between a good president and a bad president has an immense effect on the quality of life in this country. So, yes, I did consider running for public office.

I was on sabbatical from Yale in 1979 giving a seminar at Oxford with Stephen Lukes and Leszek Kolakowski on the theory and practice of socialism of all things, when I got a phone call from Chicago. They said, "I know this sounds strange, but a group of us would like you to run for Congress. Abner Mikva has just been appointed a federal judge and has resigned his seat for the 10th district. He's a Democrat who has won the last four elections, but only by the slightest of margins. A special election will be held soon to replace him, and we can't come up with any candidate. So, we've decided you're the candidate. Will you come talk to us?" I went to talk, with no commitment, to see what it was all about.

When I got to Chicago, I said, "What are you thinking? I'm the ultimate carpet bagger. I'm going to get defeated, and so will you." They said, "You went to high school in this district?" And I said "Yes." Then they asked, "How many relatives do you have in the district?" I said, "At least thirty." Then they said, "How many would have a fundraising party for you?" I said, "They're family. All of them would do it if I asked, even the ones who are Republicans." "Well," they said, "the Republicans may wish you were a carpet bagger, but anyone who can organize thirty fundraising parties in a week with their relatives is no carpet bagger." Then I said, "I have not lived here for many years." They immediately responded, "We don't count people who have been at college as being away. You've been at college." Finally, I said, "What the hell is really going on?" They replied, "Well, Al, we're about the most perfect '1/3, 1/3, 1/3' constituency in America." "What does that mean?" I asked. "We're 1/3 Catholic," they said. I told them, "I'm not the most orthodox or participatory Catholic." They said, "That doesn't matter. You went to Loyola Academy and Notre Dame. That means you'll get the Catholic vote." Then I asked, "What's the other 1/3?" They said, "WASP." "I'm not a WASP!" I told them. They responded, "You teach at Yale." Then I asked, "What's the last 1/3?" They said, "It's Jewish." I said, "What? I'm not Jewish!" And they told me, "Yes, but you're an intellectual."

The campaign had to start immediately, and it looked appealing, because if I won the first election in 1979, and the second in 1980, a Senate seat was going to be open in 1982. Charles Percy, one of the Illinois senators, had told me, "I hope you don't win. But whatever happens, I'm going to be stepping down."

Q: Why did you decide not to run?

A: The prospect of possibly becoming a senator was very interesting, but then I started thinking about how much money had to be raised in a short amount of time. I had some prominent backers who would have helped, but I still had to raise a lot of money myself in a matter of weeks. It became clear that one of the easiest ways would have been to appeal to "hot button" foreign policy issues of particular concern to Chicago's ethnic communities. But I had spent much of my life developing a more nuanced position on virtually all these foreign policy issues, which in a very short campaign, I doubted could be advanced winningly. Also, my wife had married me, Alfred Stepan, the individual, and if we had gone to Chicago, she would have been marrying Chicago politics. That would have been too big a jump. Still, at times I feel guilty not to have responded to this challenge and opportunity. Aristotle said only gods or beasts do not have to live in a polis. We are not living in a well-run polis.

Colleagues and Institutional Affiliations
Yale

Q: Your first academic job was at Yale, where you joined the Department of Political Science in 1970. At that time, Yale probably had the leading political science program in the country, with figures like Robert Dahl and Charles Lindblom. What was it like being an assistant professor at Yale?

A: It was a marvelous atmosphere. I never saw a bad fight in my thirteen years at Yale, and I heard very little backbiting. Bob Dahl deserves a lot of the credit for this supportive atmosphere. Dahl does not just write about pluralism, he *acts* pluralistically, and he is a very gentle and charming colleague. Nobody understood how he and Ed Lindblom could have such a good collegial relationship. Lindblom has an amazing tolerance for silence that was unnerving to some people. He would ask a really difficult question and then just be quiet. Dahl was the nicest, easiest person in the world, but Ed, whom we all respected, had a menacing silence about him.

Yale had a very good group of Latin Americanists: Sidney Mintz, a great anthropologist who worked on the Caribbean; Richard Morse, an incredibly funny and brilliant Brazilianist in the History Department; and probably the best two economists in the United States working on Latin America: Carlos Díaz-Alejandro, a Cuban economic historian who did great work on Argentina; and Albert Fishlow, a fellow Brazilianist. After six months at Yale I accepted an offer to be director of Yale's Council on Latin American Studies, even though everyone in the Political Science Department told me it was a bad move because I was not tenured and the administrative duties would get in the way of my research. I took this decision partly because I had done a quick study of centers for Latin American Studies at other universities and concluded that Yale had one of the most underperforming institutes given its intellectual resources and library. The council only had a $16,000 budget when I became director, but it had a $600,000 budget by the time I left. These resources meant I was able to run exciting research projects for the university, for me, for Yale's students, and for my colleagues from Latin America. This was a period when extremely repressive military regimes were taking power in Uruguay, Argentina, and Chile, and Yale became an occasional base for a number of scholars who had fled these countries. Also, many of my Yale colleagues in political science had, or developed, a strong interest in Latin America. At one point, five of us in the Political Science Department spoke or read Spanish or Portuguese. Bob Dahl had spent time in Chile; David Apter had learned Spanish because he became fascinated by the Allende experience and had gone to Chile and Argentina; Joseph LaPalombara learned Portuguese while I was at Yale because he became interested in studying the Peter Evans-like "triple alliances" among multinationals, state enterprises, and the national bourgeoisie (Evans 1979); and Juan Linz, of course, spoke Spanish. Guillermo O'Donnell, though formally a student, was a powerful intellectual and political presence. Whenever a visitor came from Latin America, there would be a lecture in the daytime, and in the evening almost everyone, the guest, Apter, Linz, Richard Morse, and all the graduate students, would gather at my home for drinks and informal conversation.

Columbia

Q: In 1983, you left Yale to become dean of Columbia's School of International and Public Affairs (SIPA). Why? What were the highlights of your tenure as dean?

A: The fundamental reason I left Yale was that my wife had published her second, very well-received book, on the history of science and medicine, and there simply were not enough opportunities in New Haven. We decided to let colleagues in big cities know we were moveable, by no means necessarily to the same university, but in the same town. Several universities were interested, and we decided on Columbia.

At Columbia I negotiated an offer in which I would continue to teach some courses every year as well as being dean. How can you run a school if you do not teach your students? When you teach, the students also have to debate with you as a more complex person than simply as the dean. I also negotiated twenty hours a week research support, and I was supposed to help generate, and fund, large research grants, revamp the curriculum, bring famous political actors to Columbia, and run some big conferences myself, all of which I did. SIPA gave me a base to bring George Soros closer to Columbia, and he helped us bring a whole series of important Central European academic dissidents to Columbia. I helped develop a joint program on human rights with the Law School, and a joint program with the Journalism School. My friend from Chicago, the brilliant and gentle Jay Pritzker,[21] agreed to become the chairman of our board, but only if I took him on one interesting trip a year, so in his travels with me, we had a six-hour one on one with Fidel Castro, a one on one with General Giap[22] in Hanoi, and a wild meeting with Lech Walesa in Gdansk.

The Central European University

Q: In 1993, you became the first rector and president of the Central European University (CEU) in Prague, Budapest, and later Warsaw. How did this opportunity arise and why did you decide to pursue it?
A: I had stepped down from my deanship at Columbia and was being sounded out by trustees of major universities in the United States that were searching for presidents. Not many people who had been deans were also members of the American Academy of Arts and Sciences, so that put me into a pool of potential university presidents. I did not pursue any of these possibilities because I knew that would have meant the absolute end of my life as a field-based comparativist. I got a phone call in Paraguay from the Hungarian political philosopher, János Kis, who was also the president of a major political party, and he said, "Al, we are finally ready to create the university in Central Europe you have been involved in exploring with us

21. Pritzker was a billionaire philanthropist who founded the Hyatt hotel chain.
22. The Vietnamese General Vo Nguyen Giap was the military leader of the Viet Minh guerrilla group under Ho Chi Minh's political leadership. He later commanded the North Vietnamese forces against the United States during the Vietnam War.

since 1991, and we want you to consider being our founding rector." I felt the opportunity to help launch CEU in the aftermath of the fall of the Berlin Wall was an important challenge. I also felt that my background and training had prepared me for it, and that this special university presidency was entirely consistent with my desire to remain a field-based comparativist with a deep interest in democratization. So, I went and talked with George Soros, who was funding the project. We talked for about eighteen hours, with no interruptions except for a brief sleep, one on one at his home in the Hamptons. It was a fascinating, but not an easy discussion. George is a brilliant person who is one of the most creative philanthropists of our era, but he hates institutions, hates long-term commitments, and does not like the word *knowledge,* because he thinks it is too static. I said, "George, even though you don't like it, if we are talking about starting a new university, then we are talking about institutions, long-term commitments, and knowledge. You will not consider it as much fun as working together against Pinochet."[23] Eventually, we agreed on a framework where I would serve as rector and president for a short, finite period in order to start the university.

Q: Post-Soviet Central Europe was surely a complex setting for launching such an institutional initiative. What were the main challenges you faced?

A: A major dilemma for existing universities in post-communist Europe concerned whom to appoint as professors in areas like political economy and political philosophy. Under the old communist system, political science was either not taught at all, because it was not trusted, or, if it was taught, anyone holding a university-level position in that field belonged to the *nomenklatura.*[24] The existing universities in Central Europe thus faced what I called the dilemma between "purge or petrification." Trying to purge professors in existing universities, in the key areas needed for democracy, would have meant going back to where communism had started in Prague in 1948. But keeping them meant "petrification." The only creative alternative was to try to launch a new private university. But since private universities were still quasi-illegal in Prague and Budapest, and we could not yet get recognition for our degrees, we decided to pursue the strategy of trying to get international recognition. We eventually obtained recognition agreements in the United Kingdom, Holland, and with the Regents of the State

23. Stepan had asked Soros to join the human rights group Americas Watch. He did and was a major supporter of the Americas Watch mission to Chile in 1988 for the presidential plebiscite that resulted in General Pinochet's defeat.
24. The term *nomenklatura* refers to the elite who were members of or sanctioned by the Communist Party.

of New York, for seven departments that could grant master's degrees, and in the case of our Nationalism program, led by Ernest Gellner, who had been born in Bohemia, recognition for a Ph.D. program. Getting us ready for accreditation was difficult. Some faculty members of CEU had never used a syllabus because they had taught in underground dissident universities. But it was impossible to get accreditation without syllabi. When I asked my colleagues for a syllabus, one wrote me angrily saying that even under high Stalinism, no one had interfered with his intellectual freedom as much as I had as rector.

Q: Administrative work and scholarship are often seen as standing in a zero-sum relationship. What were the intellectual payoffs of getting involved in helping build CEU?
A: The effect of administrative work on scholarship depends on how you are wired and what type of administrative work you are doing. I went from a new Ph.D. to full professor at Yale in six years and except for my initial six months, or later while I was on leave, I always ran an institution. This gave me a base to do many of the things I wanted to do as a scholar. CEU was the best base of all. The intellectual payoffs were immense. Many of my colleagues in Budapest and Prague had participated in the resistance movement against the old communist regimes, and I was able to talk to them at great length. Because I was traveling constantly across post-communist Europe to explore the possibility of opening branches of CEU in other countries, such as Russia, I also met all sorts of people who had been involved at various levels in the democratization process. I became attuned to a whole set of issues that the democratization literature had failed to address, especially the question of nationalism. As I said earlier, there was not a single chapter about nationalism in any of the three volumes of the O'Donnell, Schmitter, and Whitehead (1986) book on transitions from authoritarian regimes, an omission for which I am as culpable as anyone, because I was one of the contributors to that project. How can you think about the expansion of democracy in post-communist Europe without thinking about nationalism?

One of the intellectual highlights of being at CEU was the opportunity to interact with Ernest Gellner, the greatest student of nationalism in the modern era (Gellner 1983).[25] I supported Gellner in his effort to create a small doctoral and postdoctoral program on nationalism. We rapidly had a lively Center for the Study of Nationalism, with leading scholars of nationalism, like Benedict Anderson and Rogers Brubaker, serving as visiting professors. I told Ernest, "I have recently read all your work—well, not all of

---

25. For Stepan's thoughts on Gellner's theory of nationalism, see Stepan (1998).

it, because it's a huge amount—but everything that relates to nationalism, and, as far as I can tell, you have not written anything about democracy, have you? And, as you know, I write about democratization, but have never written about nationalism. You and I, as leaders of CEU, need to figure out what types of democracy can fit with what types of nationalism." He immediately agreed and proposed that we give a joint series of public lectures in Budapest and Prague on nationalism and democracy. I was to lecture on nationalism, first, and he would lecture on democracy, afterward. Ideally we would put together our lectures and write a common conclusion, making a small book. I was enchanted with the prospect. Gellner attended my set of lectures and sat in the front knocking his cane on the floor whenever he did not like something I said. The students were terrified and thought Gellner and I must be bitter adversaries. But he and I would always meet afterward at a restaurant and talk for hours. Tragically, Gellner died before he was able to give his lectures.

CEU was an extremely stimulating environment. In fact, the largest section of *Problems of Democratic Transition and Consolidation* (Linz and Stepan 1996) is about post-communist Europe and was written while I was rector. My ongoing work on multinational societies and democracy stems largely from my initial reflections about the problems facing many of the post-communist states.

Q: Besides Gellner, which other colleagues did you interact with?
A: László Bruszt, the prominent Hungarian sociologist who was writing a major work on the theory of "recombinant property" in East European capitalism with David Stark (Stark and Bruzst 1998), became my vice-rector and a close intellectual and personal friend. My exchanges with János Kis were important, because he was thinking about how creating new types of political regimes affected individual and collective rights, and he also was a political party leader. Wiktor Osiatynski, the brilliant Polish constitutionalist, who with Stephen Holmes and Jon Elster helped found the *East European Constitutional Review* in partnership with CEU and the University of Chicago law school, is a wonderful person whom Nancy and I love talking to when he passes by New York. I co-taught one of the first experimental courses for what was to become CEU with Pierre Hassner from Sciences Po in Paris. I discussed the specificities of Czech civil society issues with Jacques Rupnik, and of Polish political society issues with Aleksander Smolar, who is now a colleague on the *Journal of Democracy* editorial board. A lot of very interesting people from different parts of the world came a few weeks or months to help us get going, including Steven Lukes, Anne Phillips, Jean Cohen, Andrew Arato, Will Kymlika, John Hall, Benedict Anderson, Rogers Brubaker, and many others. Bronislaw Geremek, a world-class

medievalist from Poland, one of the main leaders of Solidarity, and a marvelous person, was always stimulating to talk to about a whole range of intellectual and political issues. Geremek and Ralf Dahrendorf became founding trustees of CEU when I finally convinced George Soros that both he, and I, needed a board. Discussing the future of CEU, and democracy, with Václav Havel in the presidential palace in Prague was certainly a highlight. And, of course, George Soros attended many of our meetings and was a great part of that whole experience.

Q: What were the students like at CEU?
A: They were often terrific, and I learned a lot from them. To our surprise, some of the best students were from Bulgaria and the worst from Czechoslovakia. Ironically, because the Bulgarians had been such good Communists, the Russians had stayed off their backs, which allowed them to develop one of the most internationally diverse and accessible central libraries in all of Eastern Europe. Also, the Bulgarians dutifully sent copies of each journal they published to every academic institute in Russia, and, in exchange, they received copies of all the Russian journals. Thus, some of our Bulgarian students knew more about good Russian sources than our Russian students did. In fact, it was actually easier for a Russian scholar to get access to the Russian-language journals in Bulgaria than in Russia. By contrast, although Czechoslovakia had a great university tradition, 1968 was a lobotomy that destroyed the library and put the *nomenklatura* in control of the university system.

The problems among the Yugoslavian students, between Muslims, Catholics, and Orthodox Christians, were intense. Once, a Serbian student in the new dorm that we built to encourage closer relationships among the students, put on a uniform and marched up and down the corridor with a sword, and fights nearly erupted every now and then. More than once, students from Muslim or Orthodox majority countries asked whether I thought it would be appropriate for them to attend my seminar on democracy. I said, "Of course it would be appropriate. Why do you think it might not be?" They replied, "I come from a Muslim or Orthodox country which people say lacks a democratic tradition." It broke my heart that they thought they should not sit in my course because they had been led to believe there were cultural prerequisites for democracy.

Oxford

Q: In 1996, you left CEU and went to Oxford. Why did you go to Oxford instead of returning to the United States? And why did you stay there for only three years?

A: I initially thought I would return to a U.S. university. It turned out, however, that the Gladstone Professorship of Government became open at All Souls College at Oxford, which I competed for, and received. Also, the Gladstone chair had previously been held by Samuel Finer, a very great scholar and raconteur, who had written a classic book on the military, *The Man on Horseback* (Finer 1962). Finer became one of my best dinner partners when I was a Ford Visiting Fellow at St. Antony's College. Plus, I inherited an office once held by Isaiah Berlin, overlooking a Christopher Wren quadrangle and the Old Bodlean. Nancy received an appointment as a senior fellow at the Wellcome Unit for the History of Medicine and later became a professor of modern history. So, we thought living in England would be fine and that going to Oxford would be a great experience.

A variety of things led us to go back to the United States earlier than expected. First, we started having grandchildren and they were living in Manhattan. We had loved raising our two children, Adam and Tanya, and looked forward to being closely involved with their children. Second, the Wellcome Unit was going through a difficult period that made it a less attractive place than Nancy had expected. Third, one of my key responsibilities was to teach the core course in comparative politics for the "taught" master's degree, but this turned out to have problems; I gave the core lectures, but there was a big final exam at the end of two years in which the questions were written by a different group of colleagues, and then graded by a third group of colleagues. This system made it awkward for me to spend an entire lecture on an emerging political science problem, on which most of the "invisible college" literature was either not yet published, or only recently published, and therefore not yet on the set reading list for the final examination. Fourth, government funding regulations punished Oxford if students did not hand in their Ph.D. thesis four years after getting their M.A. In many cases in comparative politics, it does not make intellectual sense to rush home from a great fieldwork experience. Many of my previous students—such as Evelyne Huber, the past president of the Comparative Politics Section of the American Political Science Association (APSA); Guillermo O'Donnell, the past president of the International Political Science Association (IPSA); the prize-winning duo Margaret Keck and Kathryn Sikkink; Nancy Bermeo, who has just left Princeton to join Oxford; and many others such as Cindy Skach now at Harvard, Scott Mainwaring, the director of the Kellogg Institute at Notre Dame, and Edward Gibson at Northwestern—took six or more years to get their degrees.

Still, there are many brilliant individual scholars at Oxford, and I have lots of very close friends there. It is one of the best places in the world for political philosophy, and I had colleagues like Ronald Dworkin and Joseph Raz. Archie Brown is one of the leaders in the field of Russian politics, and we ran a seminar together on problems of democracy in post-communist Europe. Laurence Whitehead and I ran a workshop on new approaches to democracy and I frequently met with Timothy Garton Ash. Dining with Ralf Dahrendorf and his colleagues and guests while he was warden of St. Antony's College was often a political and intellectual adventure. Plus Oxford has a wide variety of people working on Islamic, not just Middle Eastern, studies. For example, James Piscatori and I created a seminar in which we discussed where the "twin tolerations" did, and did not, work in the Islamic world.

Back to Columbia

Q: You left Oxford and returned to Columbia University in 1999. How had Columbia's department changed during the years you had been away in Europe?
A: When I left Columbia, the Political Science Department had great specialists on different parts of the world, but it was not as strong as it could have been in terms of scholars doing systematic comparative analysis. While I was away, a big effort was beginning to be made in that area. Also, the link between comparative politics and international relations had improved. Jack Snyder, whose work focuses on internal wars and statelessness, and thus stands at the intersection of international relations and comparative politics, was now a senior tenured colleague. Also Jean Cohen, whose pioneering work with Andrew Arato on civil society is of great interest to many of my students, had been awarded tenure and this facilitated new links between comparative politics and political theory (Cohen and Arato 1992). I share a lot of students with Jack and Jean. My links with American Studies are now also more organic because Ira Katznelson, who is a Dahlian presence and one of the best scholars of American political development, a branch of American Studies that comparativists should play a bigger role in, joined the department. Also, when I came back, Jon Elster, who is interested in constitutionalism and was a frequent visitor to CEU, had joined, as had Brian Barry, with whom I sparred over issues such as group rights. All of these changes, except for the loss of my immediate successor as dean of SIPA, John Ruggie, a close friend and a leader in "constructivism" in international relations, which is also of great interest to comparativists, were intellectual improvements over when I had been at Columbia as a student in the 1960s or a dean in the 1980s.

Teaching and Students

Q: Could you discuss the role teaching has played in your career and, more generally, your approach to teaching?

A: Teaching is a deeply rewarding part of my career and life. I find it perpetually rejuvenating to be in a profession where you open the door every six or twelve months and different people with new thoughts walk in. It's an exciting encounter.

I like the joint supervision of dissertations, because sometimes you have to tell a student the direction they are heading in is a dead end. As a result, you may have a bad or semi-broken relationship with them for four or five months, and it may be very useful for them to have someone else whom they can talk to during such periods. I am very direct in my comments to students. I will write "This is nonsense," "This is fantastic," or "Go with this and drop that." If we are close enough, and we share some perspectives on how social science works, they just take me with a grain of salt. But every once in a while I misjudge someone, and they do not know how to read me. Joint supervising also offers the advantage of having one person on the dissertation committee who is methodologically or substantively good on a topic and another who knows the relevant cases. Also, to be frank, most of the best comparativists fight to get the maximum amount of leave and when they get it are seldom at their university, or even in the country, so our students really need to have joint dissertation supervisors. At Yale, Columbia, CEU, and Oxford, I was part of the core team of advocates to make joint supervision not only possible, but the norm.

We professors do not pay enough attention to learning who our students are, to getting a sense of each student's unique package of capacities. Some of these capacities are almost physical and psychological. Will they feel sufficiently comfortable in difficult, even hostile, situations? Others are temperamental. Can they tolerate a quiet situation for a very long period of time? For example, Kenneth Sharpe can be quiet for a very, very long period of time, which allowed him to sit eighteen months in a small town in the Dominican Republic and do a terrific anthropological book (Sharpe 1977). Do they already have some strong hunches about politics? What are they, and how can they be developed in their research? Guillermo O'Donnell, the first graduate student I met at Yale, had been a student leader in Argentina, worked in the government, witnessed the breakdown of democracy firsthand, and had a taste for engaging in jugular issues in comparative politics. For example, he already had a strong instinct that Seymour Martin Lipset's (1959) idea that the wealthier a country is the easier it can achieve democracy was wrong for Argentina and probably many other countries as well (O'Donnell 1973). Brian Smith had been a Jesuit in Chile and had a profound institutional and theological sense of what the progressive wing of the Catholic Church could, and could not do, in helping progressive causes (Smith 1982). In the case of my dissertation on the breakdown of democracy in Brazil, I had seen the breakdown and knew I could talk to the military because I had been in the Marines. I had also been a boxer and a journalist and was confident that I had an aggressive enough style to make research opportunities possible. We all bring different things to the table.

I have supervised or co-supervised about thirty graduate students who have published their dissertations as a book. I feel profoundly that not one of these students could have written a better book if they had written one of the twenty-nine other books. Every student brought something distinctive to their research. One of our jobs as teachers is to listen carefully to students so we learn their temperament, help them believe in their own potential, and develop their own voice. Then you go along for the ride for four, five, or six years.

One trend I dislike about contemporary comparative politics is the idea of rapid dissertations. I am in favor of most, not all, comparativists, spending more time in the field. There is a limit to how much you can learn on the Internet or by just reading. It takes six years to really know Chinese, and if a twenty-three-year-old student who has only studied two years of Chinese walks into my office and says he or she wants to start a China-related Ph.D., what is the correct thing to do? I should say, with a smile, "Get out of my office and come back in five years. Go spend three years in China. Be a journalist, be a translator, whatever you have to do to survive and learn. Come back and get an M.A. in area studies; you should know Chinese history, language, economics, and anthropology, but you will find it very difficult to study them given the courses we will require once you are in our Ph.D. program in political science. You now have a unique opportunity to really learn the language, build a network of lifelong friends and colleagues in China, and develop cultural capital that will be useful for the rest of your career. Go have a great time for the next five years and I look forward to seeing you when you are ready for your political science Ph.D."

I also worry that modern political science increasingly expects beginning scholars to work on sets of, say, four or six countries. Very few young scholars can dominate that many cases, especially if they have never even lived in a single foreign country. I have recently seen dissertations on six or eight countries that are based almost entirely on secondary analysis, and terribly important books on these countries are sometimes missing from the list of references. We need a realistic sense of what someone can accomplish at different stages of a career and life. For a first book, it may make great sense to do research in a single country, enriching the study by reading carefully the secondary literature on several other countries. But unfortunately many young comparativists are increasingly being discouraged from spending a year or more in the field and concentrating on a single country for their dissertation book. For the second book, you can study a set of four countries. Later, when you are better known, and a member of two or three invisible colleges, you can tackle, say, twelve countries and look at every federal system, or every advanced welfare state in the world. This does not mean that senior scholars are better than junior scholars, simply that most of us can do different things at different stages in our careers.

Q: What qualities distinguish the best students?
A: They have worries. They bring deep concerns about a major problem to the table, along with the beginnings of actual insight. The best students almost always come to graduate school having internalized a major problem that they either saw in their own country or in a foreign country that they visited a lot. They are on to something, have hunches, and are willing to read extremely broadly. It helps if they have had a range of experiences and done a number of things. With very few exceptions, the best students I have worked with have been somewhat older or have lived in foreign countries, and have had four, five, or six years of different experiences before going to graduate school, experiences that inform how they look at things, define their questions, and design their research. For example, Kathryn Sikkink and Mimi Keck both worked with human rights organizations in Latin America before they went to graduate school. They acquired a profound sense of political conflict and cared deeply about the problems on which they wrote their dissertations (Sikkink 1991; Keck 1992). Take Graeme Robertson, a Scottish student with whom I recently coauthored an article on Islam and democracy (Stepan with Robertson 2003). After graduating from Oxford, he worked with the Scottish government on issues of economic development. Then he worked four years on Yugoslavia for the European Union and was dispatched regularly on fact-finding missions to Bosnia, Croatia, Macedonia, and Serbia. He is not writing his dissertation on Yugoslavia, but his sense of politics is informed by his experiences there, which also taught him important skills, like how to write crisply and be a very good briefer. When he decided to write his dissertation on workers' strikes in Russia, these prior experiences helped him learn to do research there very, very quickly. In the course of working on Russia, he realized he could get comparable Polish and Bulgarian data, and he wrote an article that will soon be published in *Comparative Politics* (Robertson 2004). Could he have moved so quickly ten years ago, straight out of college? I don't think so.

Q: Do you stay in touch with your students after they finish their degrees?
A: Advising is a lifelong commitment and mutual learning experience. You don't stop talking with your students after they finish the dissertation and get their first job. You talk with them about developing their next project,

getting tenure, and even getting into the American Academy of Arts and Sciences. I also talk with them to get their feedback on my work and for pure pleasure. It's not over until it's over, which means until one of you is dead. The intensity may taper off, but it remains a profound relationship. Students are a huge part of one's personal and professional life. We are in a very special profession that offers a continuous learning experience and many human rewards.

The Achievements and Future of Comparative Politics

Q: **What is your assessment of the achievements and failings of comparative politics since you were a graduate student forty years ago? What is your sense of the future development of the field?**
A: Forty years ago many very important countries, such as Korea or Indonesia, had excellent historians, but few, if any, modern political scientists. Now, many of these countries have large political science communities, all linked to the Internet, which makes the exchange of drafts, data, and comments on common problems easy and quick.

This is all to the good, but if we do not watch out there will be unfortunate unintended consequences. There is a growing tendency in dissertations in comparative politics to take existing data sets, do large-N comparative studies, and downgrade single-country case studies based on long-term field research of more than one year. For the comparative politics field, this may mean that young scholars neither master languages nor develop life-long networks of friends from foreign countries that often emerge out of the initial year in the field. Working in the field and developing your own data can also help teach the young scholar how to generate data of a sort that may not exist when she or he starts their research. If there is not good data on a critical question, there cannot be a sound basis for any large-N research, until someone, often driven by hypothesis-testing concerns, figures out how to generate such data, normally over many years, and in collaboration with other colleagues from various countries. You also do not know your own country, in a comparative sense, until you live and work in another country.

Deep exposure to a foreign country—case-based research, if you like—has in fact been crucial to the intellectual development of most important comparativists. Many of the concepts that have generated the most excitement and follow-on research in comparative politics came from scholars who were originally immersed in a particular contextual setting, developed a concept based on its explanatory power for that context, and then asked, "How far does this concept travel?" As further refinements are made by these scholars, and their supporters and critics, research becomes more cumulative. But, if Linz had not been deeply immersed in the history and politics of Spain, would we have his fine-grained concept of "authoritarianism" (Linz 1964)? What of Lijphart, Holland, and "consociational democracy" (Lijphart 1968a)? Sartori, Italy, and "polarized pluralism" (Sartori 1966)? Schmitter, Brazil, and "societal corporatism" (Schmitter 1971, 1974)? Putnam, Italy, and "social capital" (Putnam with Leonardi and Nanetti 1993)? O'Donnell, Argentina, and "bureaucratic authoritarianism" (O'Donnell 1973)? Evans, Brazil, the "triple alliance" and "embeddedness" (Evans 1979, 1995)? And it goes on. David Laitin's first works were deep country studies in Africa and later Spain about a problem: language and identity (Laitin 1977, 1986, 1989). Robert Bates wrote his first two books on Zambia (Bates 1971, 1976). Almost all of these scholars, of course, subsequently did many studies of sets of countries that they selected in relation to a common problem they had rigorously specified. Yet it is impressive how often these scholars still find their original country a source of new ideas in their continuing comparative inquiries. The questions these examples raise for comparative politics are of course: would these scholars have made these advances without their profound experience, knowledge, and anchoring in their original cases? And, would they, and the field, have advanced further if they had started with, and restricted themselves to, large Ns?

Conclusion

Q: What advice can you offer a student embarking on a career in political science?
A: For their morale and freedom, and also for the development of the field, it is good to think big. When I was writing my dissertation, I assumed I was writing a book, and I assumed I was going to send it to Princeton University Press the day I defended it as a dissertation, which I did. I even imagined how my footnotes were going to look. I tell students, "Don't internalize five people on a dissertation committee, and don't think you have to do the dreaded pro forma review of the literature, which no press is going to want to publish or the best scholars to read. Take a bold view, in a very few pages, about what is useful and not useful in the current literature for your problem and what your new contribution is going to be. Just get out there and get going."

If new, powerful quantitative methodologies and approaches appear, comparativists should certainly learn them. But, the work of David Collier and his collaborators on qualitative methodology is also of great importance (Brady and Collier 2004). However, students should not select their research questions on the basis of methodologies and techniques. Research should be problem-driven, not technique-driven. You are much more likely to sustain passion and enthusiasm for serious work if you really like the problem. Max Weber has a lovely statement about this in "Science as a Vocation": no scholarly work is worth pursuing unless it is "worth being known" and is pursued with "passionate devotion" (Weber 1946a, 135). Those are fine words. We do not hear enough today about passionate devotion and enthusiasm for research.

13

Adam Przeworski

Capitalism, Democracy, and Science

Adam Przeworski is a leading theorist of social democracy, democratization, and democracy, who has analyzed these issues in Western Europe, Latin America, and Eastern Europe as well as through studies of global scope. He is a methodological innovator, who has sought to apply formal and statistical methods in comparative politics, and he is one of the early proponents of rational choice theory.

Przeworski's research initially focused on social democracy, understood as an attempt to overcome the irrationality and injustice of capitalism without nationalizing the means of production. In *Capitalism and Social Democracy* (1985a) and the coauthored *Paper Stones* (1986), he argued that participating in the electoral process when the working class does not have a majority leads leftist parties to abandon socialism and adopt instead a reformist agenda within the parameters of capitalism. The argument, which was tested in the Western European setting, showed that, under certain circumstances, it was rational for workers to seek improvements within a capitalist system rather than the abolition of capitalism.

As authoritarian rule gave way to democracy in much of the South and East during the 1980s and 1990s, Przeworski turned to the questions of democratization and democracy, making several landmark contributions. In *Democracy and the Market* (1991), he offered the first application of game theory to the study of democratic transitions. In a coauthored article, "Modernization: Theories and Facts" (*World Politics* 1997), and book, *Democracy and Development* (2000), he analyzed statistically the causes and consequences of democracy across the globe. With regard to the *causes* of democracy, he made a major amendment to Seymour Martin Lipset's famous thesis about the impact of economic development on political re-

This interview was conducted by Gerardo Munck in New York, New York, on February 24, 2003.

gimes. Though Przeworski's data supported Lipset's argument that higher levels of economic development facilitated the stability of democracy, they challenged the view that increases in the level of development are associated with increased prospects of transitions to democracy. With regard to the *consequences* of democracy, Przeworski showed that, contrary to influential authors such as Samuel P. Huntington, democracies perform as well economically as do authoritarian regimes.

Continuing his interest in economic reform and policy making in democracies, Przeworski has analyzed neo-liberal economic reforms, the possibility of redistribution and independent national policy choices in the face of globalization, and the impact of democratic institutions on policy processes and outcomes. Relatedly, he has provided broad overviews of theories of the state and political economy in *The State and the Economy Under Capitalism* (1990) and *States and Markets* (2003).

Finally, Przeworski has had an important influence on methodological practices in comparative politics. He is the coauthor of a widely read book on methods, *The Logic of Comparative Social Inquiry* (1970). Because many of his works provide examples of how to apply different methods in analyzing complex substantive questions, his research has helped raise methodological standards in comparative politics.

Przeworski was born in Warsaw, Poland, in 1940. He received an M.A. in philosophy and sociology from Warsaw University in 1961 and a Ph.D. in political science from Northwestern University in 1966. He has taught at Washington University (1969–73), the University of Chicago (1973–95), and New York University (1995–present). He was elected to the American Academy of Arts and Sciences in 1991.

Intellectual Training and Formation:
From Poland to the United States

Q: How did you first become interested in studying politics? What impact did growing up in Poland have on your view of politics?

A: Given that I was born in May 1940, nine months after the Germans had invaded and occupied Poland, any political event, even a minor one, was immediately interpreted in terms of its consequences for one's private life. All the news was about the war. I remember my family listening to clandestine radio broadcasts from the BBC when I was three or four years old. After the war, there was a period of uncertainty, and then the Soviet Union basically took over. Again, any rumbling in the Soviet Union, any conflict between the Soviet Union and the United States, was immediately seen in terms of its consequences for our life. It was like this for me until I first left for the United States in 1961, right after the Berlin Wall went up. One's everyday life was permeated with international, macro-political events. Everything was political.

But I never thought of studying politics. In Europe at that time there really was no political science. What we had was a German and Central European tradition that was called, translating from German, "theory of the state and law." This included Carl Schmitt and Hans Kelsen, the kind of material that was taught normally at law schools. That was as much political science as there was. It was not a distinct academic discipline in Poland. So I never thought of studying politics per se.

Q: What did your parents do?
A: Both of my parents were physicians. My father, whom I never knew, was conscripted into the Polish army in 1939 and was eventually captured by Russians. He was killed in Katyn, in the massacre of Polish officers by the Russians, at about the time I was born. My mother could not work as a doctor under the Nazi occupation—she was baking cakes—but resumed her profession after the war.

Q: Where did you do your undergraduate studies and what did you study?
A: I entered the University of Warsaw in 1957 to study philosophy. In the European system at that time, you entered into a five-year program, and the first degree you received was a master's. I then discovered, as did many of my colleagues, that because I was in the Department of Philosophy and Sociology, I could get a double degree in philosophy and sociology if I took a few more courses. So, I ended up getting a master's in philosophy and sociology from Warsaw. Only later, when I came to the United States, to Northwestern University, did I study political science.

Q: What did you read at the University of Warsaw?
A: Before World War II, Poland had two very strong intellectual traditions in the social sciences. One was logical positivism. The so-called Vienna Circle was, in fact, a Vienna-Lwow-Warsaw Circle, and several eminent logicians were Polish.[1] That was a very strong tradition. The other tradition was a predominantly German idealist, right-wing historicist tradition.[2]

---

1. The Vienna Circle was a group of philosophers and scientists, organized in Vienna under Moritz Schlick, who met regularly from 1922 to 1932. Their approach to philosophy came to be known as logical positivism, which holds that philosophy should aspire to the same sort of rigor as science.
2. A historicist approach holds that concepts and facts can be understood only in relation to the context of a historical period.

After the war, although Marxism became an obvious new influence, positivism retained a strong presence. There was a debate in the journal *Philosophical Thought (Mysl Filozoficzna)* between Marxists and positivists, which the Marxists were losing. Then Stalinism took control of the country, and, in 1948, the debate was solved by so-called administrative measures. The journal was closed, and all the positivists were expelled from the university. Yet, unlike what happened in other Soviet-occupied countries, they were not killed but were sent to edit works of Plato, Aristotle, and so forth. With the end of Stalinization, in 1955 or so, the repression decreased, and the same debate resurged.

It was an excellent debate that was carried out in an atmosphere of true intellectual conflict and gave rise to very interesting developments. If you want to trace the real origin of analytical Marxism, it's in Poland in 1957.[3] Why? Basically, positivists were saying to Marxists: "What do you mean by 'long-term interests'? What are these things you call 'classes'? Why would classes pursue long-term interests?" And the Marxists, who were no longer protected by "administrative measures," had to find an answer to these questions. So I entered the university at a fascinating time of real ferment.

The program I entered reflected these broader trends. During Stalinism, the University of Warsaw's Department of Philosophy was closed and replaced by a Department of Dialectical Materialism. The Department of Sociology, which dated to the 1870s, was closed and replaced by a Department of Historical Materialism. Then, in 1957, the year I entered the university, these Departments of Dialectical Materialism and Historical Materialism were closed, and a new Department of Philosophy and Sociology, which reflected the influence of both positivists and Marxists, was opened. The program itself consisted of two years of mathematical logic and lots of philosophy of science. This was due to the influence of the positivists. It also included a very systematic and traditional Central European course in the history of philosophy taught by Marxists, people whose names you would recognize today: Leszek Kolakowski, Bronislaw Baczko. It was an excellent program.

Q: Why did you go to the United States in 1961 to pursue advanced studies at Northwestern University?
A: The story goes like this. First of all, Poland was a pretty closed country. So we all grew up in an atmosphere where we wanted to see other things, to get out. And by a complete accident, I met a Northwestern University professor, R. Barry Farrell, in Warsaw. He appeared at a meeting of a student

---

3. Analytical Marxism is a variant of Marxism that holds that Marxist theory should conform to "normal" scientific methods.

group where we would discuss regularly in English. He invited me for lunch and, out of the blue, asked if I wanted to go to the United States to study political science. I don't remember if I had the smarts to ask him what political science was: I did not know what it was. But even if he had asked me if I wanted to work on a ship sailing around the world, I would have said "yes." I was twenty years old, and I would have gone anywhere to do anything. I landed at Northwestern by pure accident.

Q: What did you study at Northwestern?

A: Northwestern at that time was one of the first "Behavioral departments" in the country. The faculty included Richard C. Snyder, who did international relations; Harold Guetzkow, the first person to start simulating international systems; and Kenneth Janda, one of the first people to do empirical, comparative research. Northwestern's Political Science Department had a certain mystique. But most of these people were not very good. To be frank, I learned next-to-nothing. I was too well educated to have learned much there. I remember that the opening course was a standard introduction to political science, with the first part dedicated to "what is science?" and the second part to "politics." I thought the teacher's knowledge about the philosophy of science was abysmal. I got myself in trouble several times because of that. I was not a disciplined graduate student since I read what I wanted rather than what I was told to read, basically a lot of "social Freudians."

To be fair, I took an interesting course on economic development from Karl de Schweinitz, an economic historian (Schweinitz 1964). And I took a course on research design from Donald Campbell, a psychologist.[4] That served me well the rest of my life. I have learned it is a very tricky business to design empirical studies. Those are the two courses from which I learned something in graduate school.

Q: Could you discuss your dissertation work?

A: I did two years of coursework at Northwestern. Then I passed my qualifying exams and went back to Poland with a dissertation topic on the impact of party systems on economic development. I took a job as a sociologist at the Polish Academy of Sciences. Since getting out of Poland was very difficult, both politically and financially, I never thought I would be able to defend my American thesis, so I was simultaneously writing a second dissertation in sociology, which I planned to defend in Poland. However, one

4. Donald T. Campbell is a scholar renowned for his work on research design. His works include Campbell and Stanley (1966), Cook and Campbell (1979), and Campbell (1988).

day the person who had invited me to study at Northwestern, Barry Farrell, wrote to say that Northwestern had agreed that I could defend my dissertation in Warsaw. Some American professors were visiting Warsaw, and Farrell told me that they could constitute a committee for my dissertation defense. So I had six months to finish my American thesis, which I did (Przeworski 1966).[5] To the best of my knowledge, it was the first empirical study of the relationship between political institutions and economic development.

Q: At this point, were you planning to work permanently in Poland?

A: I thought of staying in Poland. But in 1967 I was invited to the University of Pennsylvania for a semester. Since 1964, I had been involved in a collaborative international project called "International Studies of Values in Politics." It was a local politics project, based on surveys in the United States, Poland, Yugoslavia, and India, that was headed by a group of people at the University of Pennsylvania, notably the late Philip Jacob. We were at the stage of analyzing data, and I was invited to the University of Pennsylvania to teach a couple of courses and help with the data analysis. When I was in Pennsylvania, I got another invitation, to go to Washington University in St. Louis for a semester. I accepted this invitation, and then, during the spring of 1968, while I was at Washington University, there was a student demonstration in Warsaw that was very heavily repressed. There were many arrests, and my friends advised me not to go back.

Q: Why were you advised not to return to Poland? Were you in trouble with the government?

A: The year before I went to the University of Pennsylvania I had taught an introduction to sociology course at the University of Warsaw, and, after the government crackdown in 1968, some of my students became eminent dissidents. A Brazilian friend, who was a Communist in exile in Warsaw, Pedro Celso Cavalcanti, made a special trip to Berlin to call me and tell me not to come back, because twenty-eight of my forty students were in jail. I was also in trouble in Poland because, in 1963–64, I had participated in a little study group that researched who paid the cost of industrialization in Poland under Stalinism from 1948 to 1955. The clear conclusion was that the workers had paid the cost. Our study showed that the Communist Party, which claimed to rule the country as the crystallization of the dictatorship of the proletariat had actually exploited workers. Obviously, this

5. In addition to receiving a Ph.D. in political science from Northwestern University in 1966, Przeworski received a Ph.D. in sociology from the Polish Academy of Sciences in 1967.

was not something the Party liked. So, I could not go back to Poland. But I could not stay in the United States either, because I had visa problems. By complete accident, I ended up in Chile.

Q: Why Chile?
A: In Poland I had a Chilean student, Pablo Suarez, who eventually returned to Chile and invited me there to work. This was really the only opportunity that I had. I did not have any money, I did not have a job, I could not go back to Poland, and I could not stay in the United States. Eventually, this invitation did not work out. But I was still interested in going to Chile, and I accidentally met Gláucio Soares, who was then the director of FLACSO,[6] in Santiago. When he found out that I was interested in going to Chile, he invited me, and I went in the fall of 1968.

Q: Did you do research on Chile while you were there?
A: No, I didn't work on Chile at all. I was still working on the survey data project at the University of Pennsylvania. And I was writing a comparative politics methodology book with Henry Teune of Penn (Przeworski and Teune 1970). During that first stay of six months in Chile, my wife and I fell in love with the country. So I got a grant from the SSRC (Social Science Research Council) and we went back to Chile in 1970–71. By that time, I was actually working with a Chilean collaborator on the extensions of suffrage in Western Europe and Latin America. But I never completed that project. Indeed, I am doing it now. My wife, however, did write a doctoral dissertation on Chilean economic history.

Q: Eventually you were hired by Washington University.
A: Yes. I got a permanent position at Washington University in 1969. Then, in 1972, when I was spending a year in France, I got an offer from the University of Chicago. I went to Chicago in 1973 and stayed there twenty-two years.

Q: Were you ever a tenure-track assistant professor?
A: I think I was. But I didn't know the system very well, and tenure was almost automatic at that time. As a matter of fact, when I was going to Chile in 1972, I think, and I needed some travel money, I went to see the head of the Latin American Studies Committee at Washington University, the late sociologist Joseph Kahl, and asked him for money. He said, "Are you tenured or are you not tenured?" I asked, "What does that mean?" Well, it

6. Facultad Latinoamericana de Ciencias Sociales—Latin American Faculty in the Social Sciences.

turned out that I was not tenured. But I went to the University of Chicago with tenure.

Research on Social Democracy, Regime Change, and Development
Capitalism and Social Democracy

Q: The first substantive topic you worked on was social democracy. You published a series of articles and two books—*Capitalism and Social Democracy* (Przeworski 1985a) and *Paper Stones* (Przeworski and Sprague 1986)—on this topic. What motivated your interest in social democracy?

A: I was a Marxist, and I was trying to make political sense of social democracy. My question was, "Why was there no revolution in the West?" Marxism offered a theory that I thought was generally reasonable, which said that in industrialized countries there should be a revolution supported, if not led, by an organized working class. Yet the obvious observation was that there was no revolution and there probably would not be one. I was trying to figure out why not.

I was also very influenced by Chile and its history of socialism. I was living in Chile in 1970–71, the first year of Allende's government,[7] and this made me think about the feasibility of a strategy of gradual transformation of capitalist society. The Allende experience raised the question: Is it a viable strategy for socialists to compete in elections and enact reforms that have majority electoral support? This question led me to turn to Europe, to see what happened historically with the project to achieve socialist reforms in Europe.

My research agenda on social democracy evolved. Initially, around 1970, I was interested in studying the extension of the suffrage from the perspective of "the legalization of the working class," the title of a French book by an author whose name I do not remember. I was interested in why elites who enjoy voting rights are willing to extend these rights to others, and, in turn, why workers were willing to use these voting rights and work within the system rather than attempt to destroy it, a topic that recently became fashionable among economists. Eventually, my thinking evolved from a more narrow focus on the extension of the suffrage and the decision of early socialists to participate in electoral politics to a broader understanding of social democracy. In this broader perspective, I thought two questions needed to be answered. One concerned socialist parties and the electoral process: why did socialists decide to struggle for the suffrage and use it

7. Salvador Allende, Chile's president from 1970 to 1973, was head of a leftist coalition of parties that sought to introduce radical reforms through democratic means. He was overthrown in a military coup led by General Augusto Pinochet in September 1973.

for reformist goals? The second concerned economic strategy: why were the socialists willing not to nationalize the means of production once they had the power of government?

Q: What were the main conclusions you drew from this research?
A: The central thing I learned was that reformism was a rational strategy for workers. It was in the interest of workers to support capitalist democracy. An electoral victory of pure workers' parties was not historically feasible, because the assumption that manual workers in industry and transportation would one day become the overwhelming majority of the population in industrializing countries was mistaken. Hence, socialist parties could not win elections solely by representing workers; they could only win by acting as a catch-all, multi-class party. To achieve this, they had to broaden their appeal beyond the specific interests of workers.

The second thing I learned, working with Michael Wallerstein, was that workers face a trade-off between the goals of income distribution and economic growth and, under certain conditions, the optimal strategy for workers in the long run may be to limit their distributional claims (Przeworski and Wallerstein 1982). By exercising wage restraint, workers induce capitalists to invest, which causes the economy to grow. Hence, workers end up ahead. So, the social democratic strategy of class compromise had a rational basis.

Q: Were there any particular authors you were arguing against in your work on social democracy?
A: I was arguing against an entire socialist tradition—from Lenin to Trotsky, Lukacs, and Luxemburg—that saw social democrats as traitors. That was the main target of my polemic. More pointedly, there is a passage by Marx wrote from 1850 in *Class Struggles in France* that says that the combination of private property and universal suffrage is impossible (Marx 1952).[8] This phrase, which Marx repeats in other works, was my target. It was obvious that private property and universal suffrage could exist together, but it was far from clear why. The leftist tradition—radical socialism of every variety—said basically that the combination of private property and universal suffrage is possible because social democrats are "traitors." My view was that social democrats were not traitors. Rather, they did as well as they could under the circumstances. My position is captured in Engels's phrase that "ballots became paper stones," which I use as the title of one of my books (Przeworski and Sprague 1986). Engels came to hold the position that universal suffrage was in fact an effective instrument for advancing workers'

8. The passage from Marx's work is cited in Przeworski (1985a, 133).

interests and hence it was no longer necessary to build barricades, because ballots could be used to win office. The power of elected officers, in turn, could be used to transform capitalist societies.

Q: To a large extent, then, your research focused less on the origins of democracy, including why suffrage was granted and extended, than on the workings of capitalist democracy.

A: I did address the question, why is suffrage extended? My hypothesis was that the extension of the suffrage was a response to a revolutionary threat. Indeed, the extension of the suffrage was often preceded by violent mobilizations, for example, the mob climbing the fences of Hyde Park in London in 1867. I saw the suffrage as a conservative device, in the British sense, to calm down a revolutionary threat. But I did not think very much about how democracy itself comes about. I was bewildered by democracy. I did not grow up under democracy, so, for me, it was an alien object. Nothing about democracy was obvious. The question of how democracy works puzzled me. It still puzzles me.

Transitions to Democracy and the Stability of Democracy

Q: A second substantive area of your research involves transitions to, and the stability of, democracy.

A: I started thinking about transitions to democracy in a systematic way in 1979. I was an original member of the O'Donnell, Schmitter, and Whitehead project (O'Donnell, Schmitter, and Whitehead 1986).[9] We met for the first time in 1979 at the Woodrow Wilson Center in Washington, D.C. I really did not know what the whole project was about. Philippe Schmitter, a close friend, said, "Participate, you'll have something interesting to say," but it was extraordinarily painful for me to find something to say. Eventually I did write a paper (Przeworski 1986). But I really did not know which body of theory and experience was relevant to the question of transitions to democracy. I don't think anybody else did either.

In terms of theory, about three days into the meeting in Washington, it struck me that no one had mentioned either Barrington Moore (1966) or Seymour Martin Lipset (1959). Of the forty people in the room, at least thirty taught Moore and Lipset in their courses. I raised this point and said, "Isn't that strange?" I think we understood that the theories of Moore and Lipset were too deterministic. We were trying to strategize transitions to democracy, which meant that we thought some courses of action could succeed under particular conditions, whereas others could not. Contrary to

---

9. See Chapters 9 and 10 for O'Donnell's and Schmitter's perspectives on this project.

Moore, the prospects for democracy were not determined by what happened to agrarian class structure two centuries ago. Nor, contrary to Lipset,
were the prospects for democracy determined by the level of development.
In terms of cases, we looked at past instances of democratization. But we
were not certain whether they were relevant.

**Q: These meetings took place a good ten years before the collapse of
communism in Eastern Europe. When did you first sense that something big was going to happen in Eastern Europe?**
A: In June 1986. Now why? Well, in Poland in August 1980, there was a
strike followed by a massive mobilization. The Solidarity movement was
created in three weeks in September 1980. Sixteen million people became
members of the movement. It was the biggest explosion of a social movement in history. As a result, the whole system was on the brink. Then, on
December 13, 1981, Poland had what I saw as a Latin American style coup
d'etat, led by General Jaruzelski. I read that event through Marx's perspective on France in the 1848–51 period. Namely, I saw it as proof that the
Communist Party was incapable of ruling the country and had been driven
to seek protection through the military. At that time, I wrote a little piece
called "The Eighteenth Brumaire of General Jaruzelski."[10] For me, the question was whether the military could maintain the system when the party
had failed to. The military did so initially with a fair amount of repression.
Still, there was much popular unrest and intermittent strikes in the first part
of the 1980s. The military used a stop-and-go strategy: they would repress,
step back and seek reconciliation, and then they would repress and step
back again. July 22 was the national independence day of Communist Poland; that was when the Communists established control following World
War II. And the government would always declare an amnesty that day. The
joke in Poland in the early 1980s was: "What happened on July 22, 1982?
There was an amnesty. What will happen on July 22, 1983? There will be an
even larger amnesty." That is what everybody thought. But, by 1985, the
government saw that its strategy simply was not working, and it decided
not to arrest striking workers. I got a whiff that they might be giving up.

In June 1986, I was in Warsaw and I went for a walk, as I often did, with a
friend who was a prominent communist reformer, Jerzy Wiatr. He told me,
"We are beginning to think we can have elections at the local level to open
things up a bit." And I said, "If you have elections, you're going to lose," to

10. Marx wrote a book on France called *The Eighteenth Brumaire of Louis Napoleon* in which
he analyzed the process leading up to the establishment of a dictatorship led by Louis Bonaparte, Napoleon Bonaparte's nephew, in December 1851. The "Eighteenth Brumaire" refers
to November 9, 1799, in the French Revolutionary Calendar, the day the first Napoleon Bonaparte had made himself dictator by a coup d'etat.

which he replied, "You know, it doesn't matter so much *if* we win or lose, but *what* we will lose." And I thought, wow!

Q: What did he mean by "what we will lose"?

A: He meant whether the rulers were going to lose their lives, their jobs, or just elections. I thought this was strange. Gorbachev had come to power in Russia in 1985, and the Russians started talking about economic reforms. I don't know why, but after the conversation with my friend in Warsaw, I plunged into reading Russian economists' debates about economic reforms. One of my first strong intuitions was that there could be no end to these economic reforms once they started; it was a slippery slope. When you started doing what Gorbachev and his team of reformers were planning to do, namely introduce some sort of price mechanism, there was no way to justify the rest of the communist economic model. Once you take that first step, you have to go forward. It's like the bicycle theory: if you don't keep going, you fall. By 1987, I was persuaded that something important was underway in Eastern Europe.

I am staking a claim here. In 1984, Huntington, the great theorist of transitions to democracy, wrote an article saying that transition in Eastern Europe was not possible (Huntington 1984). In 1989, Juan Linz wrote something similar and published it in 1990 (Linz 1990c). In 1988, I was at a meeting in Brazil, and I talked about transitions to capitalism in Eastern Europe. I was shouted out of the room and accused of being a traitor, an idiot, a class enemy, and everything else.

Q: Your work on transitions to democracy was distinguished by its use of game theory to analyze strategic choices formally. Why did you turn to game theory at a time when it was not a common tool in the study of democratization?

A: I was extremely struck by the degree to which Polish Communists thought strategically. By the mid-1980s, I was going to Warsaw very often, and it was clear to me that the Communists were strategizing very carefully, even though they made a lot of mistakes. Indeed, whether you went to Spain in the mid-1970s or Poland in the mid-1980s, over drinks, people analyzed politics in strategic terms. This does not mean that everybody knew everything, that everybody could anticipate all the consequences of their choices. But I was struck from the beginning that people were thinking strategically. I started to think, "Maybe I'll put myself in their shoes, try to understand the situation strategically, model it, and then see what I come up with."

The decision to use game theory probably stems from my general methodological inclination to build a logically coherent argument and use formal tools to ascertain whether the argument is, in fact, logically coherent. That was why Philippe Schmitter invited me to participate in the Wilson Center project on transitions. When Philippe said, "You'll have something to say," it was because he thought I would probably think about transitions to democracy in different terms than he and Guillermo O'Donnell. José María Maravall, a close friend of mine, was recalling the Wilson Center conference recently, and he told me, "When you started talking, I thought you were from a different world. Then you went to the chalkboard and started drawing these boxes and arrows. I had no idea what it was all about." Now he uses game theory himself. So my use of game theory resulted from a combination of my methodological inclinations and my strong intuition that the political actors involved in transitions to democracy thought strategically.[11]

Q: What did your game-theoretic analysis of transitions to democracy add to the work by Guillermo O'Donnell and Philippe Schmitter (1986)?[12]

A: Let me answer in a roundabout way. I was at a conference in the mid-1970s with Fernando Henrique Cardoso, and he was doing one of his dependency theory things.[13] There were interests; then interests organized into classes and fractions; classes and fractions made alliances; and so on. I asked him, "How do you know that out of these classes and fractions, these alliances will emerge?" He replied, "Oh, Adam, you are asking for empty formalisms." Well, I did not think those were empty formalisms, because the way alliances emerge from a structure of interests is not obvious. It could be that only one alliance is feasible, that several are feasible, or that none is feasible. So, we need tools to find out what alliances are possible. I saw game theory as a tool to determine what kind of outcomes should be expected under particular conditions, under particular structures of interests.

Specifically, one of my discoveries was that if all the major actors involved in potential transitions to democracy have complete information about each other's preferences, then under the assumptions with which we described the situation, a transition would never occur. This means you have to start worrying about who knows what. Does the regime know about the opposition or does the opposition know about the regime? What

11. For Przeworski's reflections on the literature on transitions to democracy, see Przeworski (1997).

12. See especially Przeworski (1991, Ch. 2).

13. Cardoso is one of the founders of dependency theory, which emphasizes the importance of external determinants of the development prospects of poor countries. His most widely read book is *Dependency and Development in Latin America* (Cardoso and Faletto 1979).

difference does this make? To answer these questions, you need tools, formal tools. Philippe and Guillermo, in their *Tentative Conclusions about Uncertain Democracies* volume (O'Donnell and Schmitter 1986), sort of threw their hands up in the air and just said, "Things are uncertain in transitions to democracy." But these transitions were not as uncertain as they thought. There was more structure, and, hence, more information about regime transitions that they could have utilized.

Q: With whom were you talking concerning how to formalize your game-theoretic analysis of transitions to democracy? At that time there was no game-theoretic literature on transitions.
A: I was talking to nobody. I did not have interlocutors. Still, even though what I was proposing was novel, I think a lot of people were persuaded. They found some of the reasoning useful. In 1986, I published a piece in which I used ideas from Thomas Schelling's work to shed light on when supporters of the incumbent, authoritarian regime would start jumping ship (Przeworski 1986). People found that useful. Even Juan Linz found it useful. They were listening.

Q: Subsequently, your game-theoretic analysis of transitions was criticized for not being formal enough.[14] What is your assessment of these critiques?
A: My model was crude and rudimentary for three reasons. One, there was not as much game-theoretic work on politics twenty-five years ago. Two, my skills were not good enough to do it better. And three, I just wanted enough of a tool to understand, to my satisfaction, what was going on. I was not writing a game theory article. I knew that there were hard-liners, reformers, and the opposition, and that was good enough for me. I did not think I needed more.

Q: You followed up your game-theoretic research on transitions to democracy with statistical work on transitions to, and the stability of, democracy.[15]
A: By 1990 quite a few new democracies had emerged, and the question that appeared on the political and intellectual agenda was "consolidation," a term I do not like to use. I started asking the same question everybody else did, namely, "Now that we have these democracies, are they going to be successful? Are they going to survive or not?" I posed the general ques-

---

14. See, for example, Gates and Humes (1997, Ch. 5).
15. The main relevant works are Przeworski and Limongi (1997) and Przeworki et al. (2000, Ch. 2).

tion, "What are the conditions under which democracies survive and under which they die?"

The fact that we had many new democracies meant that we had enough cases of transition to democracy to start thinking statistically about democratization. Even though we never realized it, we used to be extremely Bayesian in our approach to studying democratization.[16] In 1979, we had only three cases of transitions to democracy on which to build our beliefs: Portugal, Greece, and Spain. As a result, every new case of transition to democracy changed our minds about the causes of democratization. Our beliefs were very unstable. Every case mattered, because there were so few. That was how we were learning about democratization. By the beginning of the 1990s, I started thinking there were enough cases of new democracies to begin developing statistics on them.

Q: One of the central findings of your research was that the level of economic development explains the survival of democracies, as Lipset had suggested in 1959, yet does not account for the emergence of democracies. Your thesis about this asymmetric pattern of causation has been questioned by several authors, who argue that even your own data do not support it.
A: There is no doubt that the probability that a democracy survives increases with per capita income. You can control it for everything from the kitchen sink to the grandmother's attic. That relationship will survive anything. It is monotonic and strong, unbelievably strong. I have no shred of doubt about that.

With regard to whether transitions to democracy are more likely as countries become more economically developed, let me say the following. When Fernando Limongi and I first studied this issue in our 1997 *World Politics* article (Przeworski and Limongi 1997), we did not find any significant relationship between transitions to democracy and the variables we considered. When we were writing the book—*Democracy and Development*—and refining the data, we found a little curvature in there, that is, we found some evidence of a relationship between economic development and transitions to democracy (Przeworski et al. 2000, Ch. 2). But we did not pay much attention to this relationship, partly because we could not pay attention to it statistically due to how we were estimating it. Then Boix and Stokes (2003) questioned our findings. Now there are a whole bunch of papers arguing that democratization becomes more likely as countries de-

---

16. Bayesian statistics analyzes data in light of the prior probability a researcher assigns to the occurrence of an event on the basis of existing knowledge and beliefs. This view is contrasted to a classical approach to statistical inference, which evaluates hypotheses concerning the relationship among variables against a null hypothesis that posits the lack of a relationship.

velop economically. But they all incorrectly specify the statistical model. It turns out that regime transitions do not follow a first-order Markov process:[17] the probabilities of transition depend on past history, not only on the current conditions. Once one introduces past regime history into any statistical specification, the relation between development and democratization vanishes (Przeworski 2004b). It is simply not true that as countries become more developed they are more likely to become democracies.

Q: Do you have a hunch about why the impact of income is not the same under democracy and authoritarianism? That is, why does the level of income have such a powerful effect on the survival of democracies but not on the survival of dictatorships?
A: I have hunches. I think democracy becomes more stable in more developed societies because as people become wealthier, too much is at stake in attempting to subvert democracy. Intense political mobilization is risky in general, and in wealthy democracies it is even more risky, because people have too much to lose. For example, if the American presidential election of 2000 had occurred in a country with one-third the income of the United States, it would have ended in a coup d'etat or a civil war, as it did in Costa Rica in 1948 under very similar circumstances. These outcomes did not occur because people in the United States have too much to lose. They eventually said, "We are going to be governed by a government that probably stole the election, has no legitimacy, and that we don't like. But so what? We will survive. We have our homes, our cars, and our TVs. So, why bother? There is too much at stake to go into the street and build barricades or whatever." This is why democracies survive in wealthy countries.

Q: But why doesn't the same mechanism work for dictatorships?
A: If I am correct that wealthy dictatorships are stable, the kind of mechanism I have just described may indeed be at work. Namely, when you become a Taiwan, South Korea, or maybe even an East Germany or a Spain during Franco's time, the system functions. People are eating, and turning against the system becomes dangerous. It is always dangerous, but maybe it becomes too risky because there is too much to lose. Now, rich dictatorships do eventually fall. But my claim is they do not fall because of the income level, they fall because of the accumulation of random hazards. For example, dictatorship fell in Taiwan not because the country became wealthy, but because it needed the support of democracies in its geopolitical struggle with China. Dictatorship fell in Spain, first, because the founding dictator

17. A process is a first-order Markov process when a current event depends solely on the most recent past event and is independent of all previous states.

finally died and, second, because Spain wanted to get into the European Community and could not get in as a dictatorship. Dictatorship fell in East Germany because dictatorship fell in the Soviet Union. Dictatorship fell in Venezuela in 1958—this was the fourth wealthiest dictatorship that ever fell—because the United States stopped supporting Jiménez.[18] Dictatorships eventually die. But they die for idiosyncratic reasons, not because they have become economically developed.

Q: You say that we have a pretty good understanding of why democracies break down, yet we still lack a good understanding of why dictatorships break down. Might part of the reason for this gap in knowledge be that people have spent far more time studying democracies than dictatorships?

A: Yes. We currently do not do a good job distinguishing one dictatorship from the next. This poses a problem for how I have been studying transitions to democracy. I have studied the question statistically by assuming that the fall of a dictatorship is equivalent to the emergence of a democracy. But very often dictatorships fall and are replaced by other dictatorships. So, we need to distinguish among dictatorships, allow for the possibility that the outcome of the fall of a dictatorship is another dictatorship, and then re-estimate the model. Then we will know more. At the moment, I am working on this issue with a former graduate student, Jennifer Gandhi. We wrote a paper together (Gandhi and Przeworski 2006), and she wrote a whole dissertation on the issue of institutions under dictatorship. For some reason, the literature decided a long time ago that institutions under dictatorship are merely window dressing. Ultimately, it is the individual or collective dictator who decides. Take Friedrich and Brzezinski. In the introduction to their book on dictatorship, they say, in effect, "We are not going to bother with constitutions and institutions. They don't matter" (Friedrich and Brzezinski 1956). The broader literature does much the same. There is a very good book by Paul Brooker (2000), sort of a review of the literature on dictatorship. However, the words *law* and *institutions* do not even appear in the index. Juan Linz has worried a lot about types of dictatorships (Linz 1964, 1975, 2000). The problem is that his classification is not operational. I cannot reproduce it. Juan knows, because all of history is stored in his brain. But I am a great believer in reproducible classifications, and I do not know what observables I would have to consider to reach the same conclusions Juan does.

So Jen Gandhi and I posed the question, "Is it true that institutions do

18. Marcos Evangelista Pérez Jiménez was the head of Venezuela's military dictatorship from December 1952 through January 1958.

not matter under dictatorship?" And we are finding consistently that institutions actually matter a lot under dictatorships. They affect all kinds of policies and outcomes. Dictatorships are by far the most understudied area in comparative politics. We need to start thinking about them.

Q: There is a notable contrast between your 1991 book, *Democracy and the Market*, and your 2000 coauthored book, *Democracy and Development*. In 1991, you critiqued Lipset and Barrington Moore for offering history without people, and you emphasized the importance of focusing on strategic actors. Yet your 2000 book could be characterized as correlations without people. There seems to have been a shift in perspective and a loss of a sense of politics in your work.
A: This is completely fair. The intent of the 2000 book was to clear up some of the mess in the empirical literature. We told ourselves, "Let us get the best facts we can, conduct robustness tests, and then decide what we should believe." We were programmatically repressing any theoretical findings, and we were deliberately saying, "We don't want to theorize, we don't want to hang these facts on our theoretical assumptions. We want to be purely inductive, purely frequentist." Let's first establish the facts, then we can think about how to explain them. I have recently published two pieces addressing why democracy survives in developed countries (Przeworski 2005; Benhabib and Przeworski, 2006). You have to write a very complicated model to figure that out. I think I now have a story that explains this. But addressing these kinds of questions and introducing micro-motivations and strategic decisions is a different task from what we proposed in the 2000 book. My idea was to see what the facts were that needed to be explained, then explain them. I get articles by economists all the time that say "Here is a stylized fact," and then propose a really complicated model to explain it. I frequently respond to such articles by saying, "There is no such fact." So, I did not want to write models until I knew what I wanted to explain.

The Determinants of Development

Q: Another major topic addressed in *Democracy and Development* concerns the political determinants of economic development.
A: I have had a lifelong interest in this question that goes back to Poland and my years as a graduate student at Northwestern. The communist regime in Poland legitimized itself by saying it was going to produce development. The Communists said they were offering a shortcut to modernity. In Poland, we had doubts about that claim. Was it true that dictatorship was necessary for economic development? Or was this just a propaganda line of

the communist regime? The same issue surfaced in the United States, where Karl de Schweinitz and Walter Galenson both published pieces in 1959 that basically said "We are democrats, but maybe we have to face the hard fact that in poor counties you need dictatorship to mobilize resources for development." That was the question I tackled in my dissertation, and it has been an issue I have thought about throughout my life.

After 1990, the broad question of the impact of political regimes on development became relevant again. We wanted to know not only whether the new democracies that had emerged were going to survive, but also what kind of economic results they were going to produce. American discourse on the matter had changed. Whereas the standard line had been that democracies were not good for development, now the official American propaganda line was that democracies would produce great development. Meanwhile, a literature had accumulated. I reviewed this literature with a former student of mine, Fernando Limongi (Przeworski and Limongi 1993), and found it bewildering. The most bewildering part was that no studies before 1988 showed that democracies grow faster, yet no studies after 1987 showed that dictatorships grow faster. And since a change in ideology had also occurred around 1982, I thought this pattern in the literature was peculiar. So I decided to study the question seriously, statistically, and with good data.

Q: What conclusions did you reach?
A: It is clear that democracy, at an aggregate level, does not affect the rate of growth of total income. Some people, Robert Barro (1997), for example, claim that if you measure democracy in continuous terms, you find a curvilinear relationship between democracy and development. But I think there is also a curvilinear relationship between dictatorship and development: non-democratic countries with medium levels of income also have high rates of growth. If you plot rates of growth by per capita income, you will see that they reach a maximum, and then start declining. So, economists like Barro are spotting a pattern that is independent of democracy. I think that regimes, at an aggregate level, have no impact on development.

The Holy Grail of this whole quest, and I am still active in it, is to find political institutions that are effective for development. This program has been unsuccessful so far. There is a literature that uses subjective measures of institutions, such as the security of property rights, independent judiciary, transparency, corruption, and so on. These measures all cover the recent period. If you do a cross-section, you find that these institutions correlate with economic growth. It always works. But when you try to reproduce these results using observables instead of subjective measures, you can never get any results. So even at this more disaggregated level, we still cannot find any effect of institutions on growth. There is a large literature that says "institutions matter," but then the question becomes "which institutions?" We do not know. Maybe institutions matter, but we really do not know which ones. I am still at it, collecting data that go farther back in history.

The Concept of Democracy

Q: In the statistical analysis in *Democracy and Development,* you use what you call a "minimalist conception" of democracy as a system in which rulers are selected without violence by competitive elections. Moreover, you have argued explicitly for such a minimalist conception (Przeworski 1999). Why have you adopted this view?
A: People have very high expectations of democracy. I start from an understanding of democracy as a system in which rulers are elected and subject to reelection, that is, they can be removed by a vote of a majority of citizens. I sought to understand, through inductive and deductive thinking, what is reasonable to expect from democracy. As we have discussed, statistical results show that we should not expect economic development from democracy. But should we expect that decisions will be rational, in a sort of eighteenth-century way? Again I say "no." Should we expect accountability? Well, we know that elections are a very dull instrument of accountability. They are certainly not sufficient to ensure accountability. Should we expect that democratic governments produce equality? Here the puzzle is still open. Why is it that democracies do not equalize incomes more? We should expect such equalization, but I don't think we see it. So, to the question, "What should we expect democratic governments to generate?" I respond: development no, rationality no, accountability little, equality perhaps.

What can we expect with some certainty from democracy? We should expect that people will neither kill each other nor be killed by governments. That is why I go back to Popper (1945) and Bobbio (1984, 156) and say, "Democracy is a system that keeps us from killing each other; and that's good enough." I came to this conception of democracy as a result of the 1973 coup against Allende in Chile. I realized how important democracy is and that any policy that may undermine democracy is irresponsible, because it may lead to mass murder. My minimalist view of democracy dates from that experience. We leftists had an ambivalent attitude about democracy. We used democracy if it advanced our goals and dismissed it if it did not advance our goals. But in 1973 I realized that democracy is a value to be defended above all else. That was a major transformation in my thinking.

Q: Currently, under the umbrella phrase the "quality of democracy," there seems to be a move away from a minimalist conception of democracy. Is this productive?
A: It is extremely productive. This question is related to the methodological controversy about dichotomous versus continuous measures of democracy (Collier and Adcock 1999). There are some countries we cannot think about as democratic, and comparing whether Pinochet was more democratic than Videla,[19] or whether Stalin was more democratic than Hitler, makes no sense. These regimes were clearly dictatorships, and they have a score of zero. Now, that does not mean we cannot say that one country is more democratic than another. Here I use pregnancy as an analogy. Somebody can be one month pregnant, two months pregnant, and so on. We can make distinctions. So I am extremely sympathetic toward endeavors to assess the quality of democracy.

The problem with such efforts is that it is very hard to devise satisfactory measures of the quality of democracy, and one has to be very careful doing it because this phrase, "quality of democracy," is becoming a geopolitical instrument of the U.S. government and of international financial institutions, which use it to force an institutional and political agenda on various countries. In this regard, there is an outburst of effort to rate "good governance." But, what does good governance mean from the point of view of the government of Kenya or Indonesia? It means that the U.S. government says, "We are going to give you hundreds of millions of dollars if you do this to your political system." And many of the people advocating such agendas have no idea what they are doing.

It might be different if such policy decisions were based on solid research, if we really knew what works and what doesn't. Then I would be hesitant, but sympathetic. But we don't know. Let's say we introduce an independent judiciary. What does an independent judiciary produce in Ecuador? I read a little piece on this topic, and the conclusion was that an independent judiciary makes judges cheaper to bribe. When judges lack independence from politicians, you have to bribe a politician, and that politician has to share the bribe with other politicians so they will back him up. But reforms that increase the independence of the judiciary may make it cheaper to bribe judges because foreign firms can just pick up one judge after another, thereby cutting out the politicians. We don't have an idea of what works and what doesn't. The debate about the quality of democracy has to be conducted with a greater understanding of its political consequences.

19. Jorge R. Videla was president of Argentina during 1976–81 in the context of a military regime.

What bothers me also is that many of these initiatives hide an ideological agenda. Take, for example, Freedom House's ranking of countries.[20] They rate countries according to whether people are free to do things. So the United States ranks close to the top. Americans are free to form political parties, they are free to vote. But they don't form political parties, and half the population doesn't vote, even in presidential elections. I find ideologically tainted and unconvincing this idea of freedom as an abstract potentiality divorced from the ability to exercise it. Rosa Luxemburg once said, "The problem is not to be free, but to act freely." In this spirit, we should be asking how many parties are there, what do they propose, how often do poor people compete and get elected, and the like? But that is not what Freedom House does. I see Freedom House as a product of American ideology.

Q: How would you go about studying the quality of democracy?
A: The first thing I would look at is the access of money to politics. This is what really differentiates democracies. When Lenin says, in a letter to Hungarian workers in 1919, "Bourgeois democracy is just a specific form of bourgeois dictatorship," he has the following mechanism in mind. Democracy is a universalistic system, like a game with abstract, universalistic rules. But the resources different groups bring into this system are unequal. Now, imagine a basketball game played between people who are seven feet tall and people who are short like me. The outcome is clear. We are playing this game of democratic politics between people who can spend a lot of money at it and people who cannot. I think there was a real grain of truth in the work by Miliband (1969) on the empirical Marxist theory of the state. Namely, when money enters politics, economic power gets transformed into political power, and political power in turn becomes instrumental to economic power. This is what we are witnessing in many countries. If I were to try to measure the quality of democracy, that's where I would hit first, on all the rules and practices that regulate the access of money to politics.

Research on Methodology

Q: In addition to your substantive projects, you have also written about methods, especially in the earlier years of your career. Why have you had this interest in writing about methods?
A: There are probably two reasons. First, several times I started tackling substantive problems only to discover that the available methods did not

20. Freedom House publishes two annual indexes of all countries in the world, one on political rights and another on civil liberties. The data can be accessed at http://freedomhouse.org/index.htm.

work, that they could not serve to answer the question. As a result, I got involved in methodological issues. I never did methodology for methodology's sake. But I do admit that I sometimes ended up writing methodological pieces without going back to the substantive problem. That was true of the book about systems analysis that I coauthored in 1974 (Cortés, Przeworski, and Sprague 1974), which grew out of a project on the extension of the suffrage. In that case, I never went back from the methodological issues to the substantive problem.

The second reason was that, when I left Poland, I did not want to study Poland, I did not know enough about the United States to study the United States, and I did not want to study Latin America because I was not a Latin American. So I had to figure out what I could do, and methods was one of those things. It was only in the early 1970s that I said to myself, "Why are you doing all this methodological stuff if what you really care about are substantive questions?" That was when I started doing substantive things again.

But I have continued flirting with methodological issues. I recently co-authored a piece with a former student, James Vreeland (Przeworski and Vreeland 2000). We wanted to know what impact the IMF (International Monetary Fund) has on economic growth. But when we started thinking about this problem, we concluded that there was really no statistical model that did what we wanted to do. So we ended up writing a methodological article as a byproduct of the substantive article (Przeworski and Vreeland 2002).

I have to admit that I find methodological work intellectually pleasing. I like working on methods because I like logical puzzles.

Q: Your best-known methodological work is your book with Henry Teune, *The Logic of Comparative Social Inquiry* (Przeworski and Teune 1970). What were the book's main contributions?
A: The book's main theoretical contribution, which originates from Polish sociology, is that comparative politics is not about comparing, but about testing hypotheses across countries. What we are involved in when we do "comparative research" is testing general hypotheses under different historical conditions.

Another contribution concerns the generation of data that are comparable across countries. We were focusing on surveys, and at the time people believed that you ensured comparability by translating, as accurately as possible, questionnaires from one language into another. We found that when you asked people if there were any conflicts in their community in the United States, they would say, "Yeah, there are three: over water, over schools, and over this road." But when you asked this question in India and translated the word *conflict* to the closest word in Hindi, people would say "No, no. In this community we live in peace, we don't kill each other." Why was this? Because in the Indian understanding there was nothing between the extremes of peace and harmony and mutual killing. The notion of limited, regulated conflict was not in their conceptual apparatus. I concluded that it did not work to translate questions literally, that there was no cross-national equivalence, which is the technical term we were concerned about. Teune and I developed what we thought was a clever way of controlling the meaning of different scales across countries.

Q: This book, published in 1970, is still used in many graduate courses. Given that the field of methodology is supposedly ever-changing, this is surprising.

A: Yes, the book is still being printed; it's still alive. Why is this so? I think it was a good book. We really set things straight. There are a lot of things in the book that I do not believe now. For example, the stuff on research design, about most similar and most different systems designs, was wrong. Still, I think the central thesis, that comparative research is fundamentally about testing hypotheses under different historical and geographical conditions, provides a tie to the general enterprise of social science. I also think we offered some useful advice regarding the specific pursuit of information under different historical and geographical conditions.

Q: If you were to rewrite *The Logic of Comparative Social Inquiry,* in what other ways would it be different?

A: That's easy to answer. I now believe that counterfactuals play the crucial role in comparative thinking. What we want to know in comparative research, in the social sciences in general, is what would have happened had a particular unit, say, a country, been observed in a different state of the causal variable, under a different "treatment." The trick is to find reasonable ways to inform such counterfactuals, to use what we can observe to inform the hypothetical states we do not observe. Take the impact of colonialism, the topic of a dissertation I am currently directing, by Sunny Kaniyathu. It is obvious that when Adam Smith thought that colonialism was ruinous for the colonized territories, he assumed that these territories would have developed had they not been colonized. Later, Marxists thought the same. In contrast, Marx and J. S. Mill thought colonialism was conducive to economic development because they assumed that otherwise these territories would have remained stagnant. Hence, the answers depend on the counterfactual one assumes. Which, then, are the correct counterfactuals? How do we choose among them? So, if I were to write a comparative methods book today, it would be selection bias driven.[21]

Q: Concerning selection bias, do you find King, Keohane, and Verba's (1994) discussion of the issue useful?
A: It is an excellent discussion, though, to my taste, the issue of counterfactuals is underemphasized. King knows what he is doing and understands the importance of the problem. But their formulation of the issues rushes too quickly to statistics, without going through philosophical problems entailed in counterfactual thinking.

Core Ideas and Their Reception

Q: What are your best ideas?
A: What good ideas do I think I've had? I think my idea of class compromise was a great idea. I like the way Wallerstein and I conceptualized the idea of structural dependence of the state on capital (Przeworski and Wallerstein 1982). I like the whole idea of electoral trade-off and the disintegration of the working class as it enters into electoral politics. But I am not sure it worked empirically. We expected much more of a decay of the socialist parties than we found in *Paper Stones* (Przeworski and Sprague 1986).

I think my understanding of democracy as a set of rules for processing conflicts in a peaceful way, that entail a particular kind of uncertainty, and that allow groups to make certain inter-temporal trade-offs, is a good one. I am very much attached to this idea of democracy enabling inter-temporal trade-offs.

From my methodological work, I think the idea that comparative politics is about testing hypotheses across countries is good.

Q: Have any of your works or ideas been unfairly neglected?
A: I have been lucky in that when I thought I had a good idea, it found echoes. Sometimes things I did not even think were particularly brilliant found echoes. These ideas were not strictly speaking original. You can always dig back somewhere and find somebody who said something like this. But for me they were original, and they were received as such.

I do think, however, that two of my methodological ideas were neglected. The idea that comparative research is testing general hypotheses under different historical conditions never took off (Przeworski and Teune 1970). Quite a few people do approach comparative politics in this way,

21. Selection bias is a systematic form of error that derives from the study of a nonrandom sample.

but open any comparative textbook, and you will find that the first or second sentence says that comparative politics is about comparing countries. Also, the suggestion about how to generate data that are comparable across countries has not been picked up, until the recent work by Gary King (King et al. 2004).

Q: Were any of your works fundamentally misinterpreted?
A: For some reason, the analysis of the process of economic reform in the fourth chapter of *Democracy and the Market* (Przeworski 1991) has been read as a sign of my support of radical neo-liberal reforms. This is an obvious misinterpretation.

The Research Process

Q: Turning to the research process, how do you formulate research questions? From where do you draw inspiration?
A: What typically happens is that I find that there is something I don't know, that we collectively don't know, or about which we collectively hold beliefs that are not mutually consistent. If I feel that the issues involved are politically important, then I am likely to start thinking about them. Basically, I get motivated by politically important problems that are intellectually puzzling. For me, research is a normatively and politically driven matter.

Q: Does reading political theory, the classics, inform your research?
A: Reading classics of political theory is extremely important to me. It is a source of hypotheses, historical information, and great ideas. I believe that few of the basic problems are new. If you read Aristotle, you will find the agenda of American political science pretty much laid out. Obviously, historical conditions have changed, and we can now ask all kinds of detailed questions that are not raised in the classics. Also, the classics often contain vague intuitions and lack formulations that can actually be researched. Still, they are an immensely important source of knowledge and intuition.

I interact with a group of political philosophers on a daily basis. I have been teaching a course for years with Bernard Manin, a historian of political thought and the author of a great book on the theory of representative government (Manin 1997). We teach this course together; he teaches about Rousseau and I do models, he talks about Condorcet and I do models. These authors are a very important source for me.

When I came to the United States in the 1960s, typically the same people taught political philosophy and comparative politics. In fact, most jobs in comparative politics were cast as jobs in political philosophy and comparative politics. The same person would teach "From Plato to NATO," as it was called then, and "Introduction to Comparative Government." That relationship between comparative politics and political theory has become disassociated. Today, we ignore political philosophy. Students of comparative politics are not introduced to big questions anymore, as vague as the intuition behind them may have been. The cost is that students are more and more narrow.

Q: You have characterized yourself as a "methodological opportunist" (Przeworski in Katzenstein et al. 1995, 16–21). Could you describe your general approach to methods?
A: I am averse to methodological controversies, which I distinguish from technical issues. Everyone wants to know about methodology of comparative politics, and I constantly get invited to engage in methodological controversies. David Laitin and Robert Bates, too, are running such things all the time. I avoid such controversies. I do think things have to be technically right. If you are doing theory, you have to do rigorous theory. If you are doing statistical analysis, you should be doing good statistical analysis. You need craftsmanship in both. I think craftsmanship is enormously important, but I don't have a methodological religion.

I don't think everything should be done with game theory, or statistics, or structural analysis, or stories. Methods are tools, and some methods are good for some questions and other methods are good for other questions. I am driven by substantive questions, and I try to answer them as well as possible. This leads me to use different methods.

There is another reason I do not think it is productive to get involved in abstract discussions about which is a good method and which is a bad method. As Kuhn (1962) suggested, people imitate exemplars rather than being persuaded by methodological preaching. I have always believed that good examples are more persuasive than abstract ideas. So, if I want to persuade people that something is a good method, I use it in my research.

Q: Yet you do seem to consider yourself a scientist.
A: Yes, I am a scientist. I believe that logical coherence and empirical falsifiability are essential criteria of science. What you say has to cohere logically, and it has to have observable consequences that can be shown to be true or false.

Models and Economics

Q: The tools of formal modeling and game theory figure prominently in your work. At what stage in the research process do you begin modeling? What are you trying to accomplish with your models?

A: What normally happens is that I start thinking about a causal chain. For example, consider a society with a particular per capita income, income distribution, and degree of inequality. This society also has political institutions that determine how decisions are made. One way to start to model the society is to focus on the decisive political actor and this actor's income location. That's a classic model. Then you might ask, "What will happen to this society over time if it starts off poor and unequal? Alternatively, what will happen to the society if it starts off poor and equal? How will income inequality and political institutions change in these different scenarios?" I immediately find that I cannot sort out this kind of problem without writing down symbols. I am not smart enough to think about this causal chain without formalizing it.

Many years ago my friend Jon Elster taught me that informal, deductive arguments do not work. Some people are geniuses; you give them assumptions, and they can tell you the conclusions. When you do the mathematical model to check their conclusions, you see that they are right. I have known people like this, but that sort of informal deduction is beyond my capacity. Mathematics, somebody once wrote, is a tool for the stupid. Smart people know what consequences are implied by the assumptions. But I find it too confusing. So I start writing down symbols quite early into the process. Very often these symbols never appear in print. I do it just to clear my mind. My daughter, who knows more mathematics than I, thinks I start modeling too early, that I don't think enough before I plunge into mathematics. She is probably right, because when you start formalizing there is a misfit between your intuition and the formalization, and the resulting model sometimes does not answer what you thought it would answer. But I have to formalize to clear my mind. I don't know how to think otherwise.

Q: Formal theorizing has not been part of the tool kit of comparativists until recently. How did you learn this way of thinking so early?
A: As a seventeen-year-old student in Poland, I was exposed to two years of tough, rigorous mathematical logic. I was taught to think deductively. That helped me when I came across Luce and Raiffa's book on game theory (1957). There was almost no training in formal theory when I was being educated as a political scientist. My greatest challenge has always been to keep up with my students. I always fear that I am just not capable of learning the new stuff. But my prior exposure to mathematical logic took away the fear of anything with symbols in it. In the end, keeping up is just a matter of time, of allocating the time to learn new things.

Q: In the process of formalization, of building a model, do you achieve new insights and reach surprising conclusions?

A: Sure. I have found lots of surprising deductive results. For example, when I was working on my model of transitions to democracy, I came to the conclusion that if the hard-liners and reformers inside the non-democratic regime and the opposition to the regime all know everything, there will be no transition. I did not see this until I wrote the model for it.

When you build a model you are not necessarily going to achieve results that are surprising in terms of your main intuition. Instead, the payoff very often comes in corollary, lateral conclusions that you did not think about. For example, I have been working on a model of the survival of democracy as a repeated conflict over wealth distribution (Przeworski 2005). I was trying to show that the probability that a democracy will survive increases at higher income levels. In the process, I discovered that poor countries cannot redistribute much income under democracy. That was completely surprising; I did not think about or anticipate it.

Modeling does produce surprises. But perhaps most often you just realize that your ideas are incoherent. I have been working with Jess Benhabib for more than a year on a model relating political accountability to economic growth, and the model just does not want to cohere. We fix one argument and immediately discover that it is inconsistent with another. I think we have it right now, but in the process we discovered that many published models of the "predatory state" are simply incoherent.

Q: In addition to using formal tools in theorizing, you often draw on the work of economists. When did you start reading economics?
A: Since about 1972. I was teaching a course on the Marxist theory of the state, a topic that had generated a great explosion of interest at the time. In 1969–70, there was an exchange between Miliband (1969, 1970) and Poulantzas (1969), and the literature was evolving every year as new works appeared. I came to the conclusion that the Marxist theory of the state made no sense, because Marxist economics made no sense. During this time there were several critiques of Marxist economics and several theorems that showed that Marx's claim about the declining rate of profit under capitalism was false. Elster, John Roemer, and I concluded that the economic model underlying Marxist theories of the state made no sense.[22]

That was when I decided to bite the bullet and learn some neoclassical economics. I was aided in the process by the fact that Michael Wallerstein, who had reached the same conclusion as I, was a student in my class. He went to the Economics Department and did their whole graduate program. He basically taught me the rudiments of neoclassical economics. Since then I have been reading more and more economics. Today I read more things by

22. For Przeworski's assessment of Marxist theories of the state, see rPrzeworski (1990).

economists than by political scientists, because a lot of economists do political science now. I recently published a textbook on political economy in which the main thesis is that you cannot do political economy unless you know economics (Przeworski 2003).

Statistics and Data

Q: What role do statistics play in your research?
A: Things end with statistics. I do not turn to statistics until after I have learned enough history and achieved a clear set of hypotheses with prima facie plausibility that follow logically from some assumptions. Then I turn to statistics to see if the hypotheses are true or false. But let me emphasize an important point: I do not regard my statistical observations as anonymous "data points." In *Democracy and Development,* we studied 130 countries (Przeworski et al. 2000). Yet I can tell at least a half-hour story of the history of a hundred of them. I really do believe that you have to know the history of these places before you do statistics.

Q: A distinctive aspect of your work is that you largely produce your own data sets, whereas economists and political scientists, too, tend to download from the Internet data sets created by somebody else. What are your criteria concerning data sets?
A: Economists are, by and large, careless about the data they use, especially the political data. I am a purist about data. First, I think data carry in themselves theoretical and sometimes ideological baggage. With regard to the data on political regimes that I used in my collaborative work on democracy and development, we first defined very explicitly what we meant by democracy and what we did not mean by democracy. Only then did we start to collect data. We discuss our methodology in some detail.[23]

Second, I very much believe that the data we generate should be reproducible by others on the basis of observations. Somebody who has the same information I do and who knows the rules I used to produce my data should be able to reach the same conclusions. Results have to be reproducible from observations and rules.

These are my main criteria regarding data sets. Some commonly used data sets do not meet these criteria. This is my quarrel with Freedom House, which I also find ideologically loaded. And this is my quarrel with the Polity data set.[24] Finally, data collection is an extremely messy operation, and, for this reason, you need to run all kinds of logical consistency checks. Very

23. See Alvarez et al. (1996) and Przeworski et al. (2000, Ch. 1).
24. The Polity project offers annual data on regime and authority characteristics of all countries of the world. The data can be accessed at www.cidcm.umd.edu/inscr/polity/.

often the data sets are structured in a manner that allows you to do this. For example, if you have "votes by party" and then "total number of votes," you can do a little check to see if the votes by party add up to the total number of votes. Surprisingly, these things often do not add up.

Q: In the 1960s, a surge of interest in generating data sets occurred in the social sciences. This interest subsequently faded, and now we are witnessing a strong renewed interest in data collection. What explains this cycle?
A: Your observation is correct that there was a major trend toward collecting aggregate data in the mid-1960s and early 1970s, that now there is a new trend in this direction, and that in the meantime not much attention was given to the issue. I really don't know why this is so. The mid-1960s was the age of factor analysis, and we had indicators of everything. That died out because it was not very informative. So perhaps the interest in data died out with factor analysis. The appearance of the Penn World Tables, widely used by growth economists since the mid-1980s, was an important occurrence. The Penn Tables gave us economic data at least. That convinced me to plunge back into the democracy and development stuff.

Narratives and Cases

Q: If one compares your book, *Democracy and Development* (Przeworski et al. 2000), to your books on social democracy (Przeworski 1985a; Przeworski and Sprague 1986), it seems you have moved away from using historical narratives in your research.
A: I do not think so. For my research on social democracy, I read a lot of writings and biographies of socialist leaders. I was trying to understand how these people saw the world, what choices they faced, and how they anticipated the consequences of their decisions. I thought that if I could put myself in their shoes, then maybe I could figure things out. So I read a lot of history. My method, to the extent I was aware of what I was doing, was almost a Weberian *verstehen* method.[25] I was attempting to see the structure of choices from the perspective of the protagonists. The things I wrote had a substantial narrative component.

Then, for the question I addressed in *Democracy and Development* I thought I needed statistics. But in my current work on development, I am back to reading biographies of dictators and novels about dictators, which are very informative. I would like to get into Park's shoes and Mobutu's

25. *Verstehen*, a German word, is usually translated as "interpretive understanding." See Weber (1949, 160).

shoes and see why one was a developmental leader and the other was a thief.[26] My hunch is that developmentalist dictators are those who loved their mothers. Obviously this is not something you will learn or be able to test with statistics, but when you read novels and biographies, the pattern becomes uncanny. Note, by the way, that if this is true, counterfactuals entail something we cannot observe, selection on unobservables.

Q: You do not write case studies, as this methodology is conventionally understood. Yet you have published various articles on Poland. What role does Poland play in your thinking?
A: Because Poland is the country I know, it is the case I used for trying out abstract ideas. It is not easy for me to think abstractly. So, I like to process abstract ideas through examples. Poland is the case I often used for this purpose. Also, when the rise of the Solidarity movement and the subsequent coup d'etat were happening in Poland, I got involved in studying Poland and writing some papers as political interventions. Otherwise, it plays no particular role. I have recently been to Latin America more than Poland.

Q: How do you learn about the countries that interest you?
A: I typically go to meetings abroad, where I have friends who grab me at the airport and eagerly say, "Do you know what's happening?" And they tell me all about what is happening. Then I go and sit for three days where people are delivering papers on Argentina, Kenya, Poland, or China, and I update. Conferences are a great way to do that. You are force-fed for three days, and you learn a lot. I learn by going to places and talking to people.

Q: Are there any countries you follow closely or on a regular basis?
A: To do comparative politics the way I do, that is, without a specific area focus, I have to keep up with and understand the complex realities of at least a few countries. For various reasons having to do with my personal history, I keep up with Argentina, Brazil, Mexico, Spain, France, Poland, South Korea, and Kenya. I visit these countries maybe once every two years, some more often. I also read about them systematically. And I have students there, who send me things that they and others write. When I go abroad, I never interview people formally. But I do talk to people, including government officials. Many former social science colleagues who participated in the Wilson Center project on transitions to democracy as well as some of my former students are in governments now, and I certainly talk to

---

26. General Park Chung Hee was the autocratic president of South Korea from 1961 to 1979. Mobutu Sese Seko was dictator of Zaire from 1965 until 1997.

them. We meet over dinner. That's how I keep up. But it's only keeping up, it's not the same as doing systematic research.

Q: You must have good language skills.
A: Polish is my native language. I can read and speak French and Spanish rather fluently, and I can get along in other romance and Slavic languages. I read novels in different languages. For example, I just finished a novel in Portuguese.

Nonacademic Writing

Q: Some of your writing has been aimed at a broad nonacademic audience. Do you make a conscious effort to produce more accessible versions of your work when you are attempting to reach a wider audience?
A: I almost always do. I very often write something technical for a smaller audience, and then, when I am really sure I have something, I write something less technical for a broader audience. I do try to write, from time to time, with the goal of making a political intervention. I wrote a piece in the *Journal of Democracy,* on neo-liberal fallacies, which had a lot of echo (Przeworski 1992). I wrote something for the *Boston Review* on democracy and the economy (Przeworski 1996). Another piece for the *Journal of Democracy,* on why democracies survive (Przeworski et al. 1996), as well as a collaborative volume, *Sustainable Democracy* (Przeworski et al. 1995), were intended as political interventions as much as anything else. Early on I wrote things on Poland that were deliberately politically aimed. I do see myself as a participant, even if marginal and ineffectual, in public life.

Colleagues, Collaborators, and Students

Q: At the start of your career, you worked briefly at the University of Pennsylvania and at Washington University. Then you spent more than twenty years at the University of Chicago, and now you teach at New York University (NYU). Which colleagues did you interact with most closely at these places?
A: At Washington University, I learned an amazing amount from John Sprague. I learned dynamic models and many other things from him. At Chicago, I was very close to Philippe Schmitter. We always disagreed about basic things, and whenever we were both on a student's committee, they always suffered immensely. But Philippe and I certainly talked a lot and were friends. He left Chicago in 1982.

Then something very rare occurred at Chicago: the crystallization of a group of people who were both personal friends and intellectual interlocutors. This group even had an institution, the Center for Ethics, Rationality, and Society, where "ethics" was Russell Hardin, "rationality" was Jon Elster, and I was "society." It also included Stephen Holmes, Bernard Manin, Pasquale Pasquino, and others. Almost everybody who was in this group at Chicago is now in New York City. We still meet every Monday in the fall, hosted by John Ferejohn. We talk for two hours and then have dinner. This is really the center of my intellectual life. We are probably somewhat exhausted with each other by now, because it has been a long time. But it is still thrilling and stimulating. I interact more with philosophers than anyone else. But I also have some economist friends at NYU from whom I learn a lot, in particular Jess Benhabib. And in the Political Science Department I talk to Neal Beck, who always finds something wrong with my presentation of statistical results.

Q: This rare moment at the University of Chicago ended when most of the group you were in moved to New York City. What was the reason for this exodus from Chicago?
A: We were not pushed. We all left mainly for purely personal reasons. Russell Hardin moved first. Then Jon Elster and subsequently I moved. Jon wanted to move to New York City for personal reasons. I did, too. My wife was working at the OECD in Paris, and for fourteen years I was commuting from Paris to Chicago. But then she got a job at the United Nations in New York, and this was a chance for us to live in the same city. Once Jon and I were here, that brought along Holmes, Manin, and Pasquino. They moved partly to be with us and partly because they were attracted by New York City. But it wasn't anything about Chicago that led us to leave.

I think we all regretted leaving Chicago, because we cherished that institution. Those were great days. It really was a place committed to the pursuit of ideas. You could walk into the office of the dean and say, "Look, I've been sitting on this project for five years. I'm sick and tired of it, and I'm close to finishing but I need some time off." The dean would just say, "Write me three pages telling me why you need time off." And you walked out with time off. The administration was willing to put the money behind the intellectual goals. Chicago was a unique institution. Anyone who was ever at Chicago was smitten and has romantic feelings about it.

Q: Another group with which you have been closely involved is the analytical Marxists. What was the basic agenda of this group?
A: It was dedicated to subjecting Marxism to the scrutiny of the methods of contemporary social science. The idea was to take Marxism and see how much and what part of it holds up when you apply the same standards of

inference and evidence applied to any other theory. Althusserian Marxism had this nice trick of having its own methodology, its own internal way of evaluating the validity of its theory.[27] We broke with this approach and said, "No, you have to evaluate Marxism the same way as any other theory. It is either coherent or incoherent, true or false." I joined the analytical Marxism group in 1979 or 1980—I think that was the group's second year—and I stayed until the mid-1990s, when Jon Elster and I left. I very much enjoyed it and learned a tremendous amount. But I eventually left because I thought we had accomplished our intellectual program. We produced important works that have lasted, including a reader by John Roemer, *Analytical Marxism* (Roemer 1986a), Elster's *Making Sense of Marx* (1985), my *Capitalism and Social Democracy* (Przeworski 1985a), Gerry Cohen's *Karl Marx's Theory of History: A Defense* (1978), and Roemer's *A General Theory of the Exploitation and Class* (1982). We ultimately found that not much of Marxism was left and there really wasn't much more to learn. So I left the analytical Marxism group mainly for intellectual reasons.

Q: During all the years you have worked at U.S. universities, have you been in touch with other Polish émigrés?
A: Only with friends from childhood, most of whom now live abroad. I never felt comfortable in the Polish culture, which is intensely nationalist, thoroughly Catholic, and highly intolerant. I was brought up as a Catholic, but at a very young age I revolted against both Catholicism and Polish nationalism.

Q: Some people find it strange that you did not follow the usual trajectory of academic émigrés coming from Poland, which is to abandon Marxism and even become virulently anti-Marxist. Instead, you became something of a Western Marxist. Why did you not reject Marxism?
A: Let me start by saying a little bit about Western Marxists. In 1978, at the International Sociological Association's (ISA) World Congress in Uppsala, Sweden, there was a big roundtable on development, and I presented a paper entitled "Capitalism: The Last Stage of Imperialism," which was basically turning upside down Lenin's famous argument that imperialism was the last stage of capitalism (Lenin 1939). I was arguing, supporting Karl Kautsky, that imperialism is just a way for capitalism to penetrate other countries. Once this penetration has been achieved, capitalism reproduces

27. Althusserian Marxism is a structuralist variant of Marxism that grew out of the work of French theorist Louis Althusser. The two classic texts are Althusser (1968) and Althusser and Balibar (1969). For an overview, see Benton (1984).

itself and, hence, imperialism is no longer necessary. A Russian participating in the panel became totally incensed and said, "Vladimir Illich Lenin said, 'Imperialism is the last stage of capitalism.' This guy says, 'Capitalism is the last stage of Imperialism.' *Ne vozmozhno,* which in Russian means, "you can't do that." There was general consternation in the room. A Polish Marxist friend took this guy apart and explained to him what I had and had not said. Finally, the Russian concluded that I was *isntij Markist,* or *"their* Marxist," by which he meant a Western Marxist.

I found myself in these kinds of situations not infrequently. I never thought of communism as an implementation of Marxism. I saw communism as a bureaucratic regime that betrayed the working class. I never had procommunist sympathies; I was a Marxist opponent of communism. As I mentioned earlier, this got me into trouble in Poland in the mid-1960s when I participated in a study group that criticized the Communist Party for oppressing workers. I found myself at the extreme opposite side of this coin, so to speak, when, in the early 1990s, I saw that neo-liberal economic policies were not, in fact, an application of neoclassical economic theory. There is no support in neoclassical economics for neo-liberalism. As you can see from these examples, I went to the sources and tried to distinguish theory from ideology. So, I was an anti-Communist and also a Marxist.

Q: You have coauthored many publications. Could you discuss the people with whom you have collaborated and why you seek out collaborators?
A: I'm a collaborator by nature, so there are quite a few. I collaborated with my colleague, Henry Teune, when I was at Penn (Przeworski and Teune 1970). I collaborated with John Sprague at Washington University. We wrote a book, joined by an old Chilean friend of mine, Fernando Cortés (Cortés, Przeworski, and Sprague 1974). John drove me crazy. He is the least disciplined person I know, and I am one of the most self-disciplined persons I know. Still, I had a lot to learn from John. So we wrote a second book (Przeworski and Sprague 1986). I collaborated on a book with Luiz Carlos Bresser Pereira and José Maria Maravall (Bresser Pereira, Maravall, and Przeworski 1993), both of whom had been ministers in their respective countries, and I learned from them how to think in policy terms. I am now writing some papers with an economist at NYU, Jess Benhabib, from whom I have learned how to think about economic growth (Benhabib and Przeworski, 2006). However, most of my collaborators were my graduate students. I think my main source of learning is teaching, and my main interlocutors throughout my life have been my graduate students. I have always run a sort of natural science laboratory with students who took courses from me, got interested either in things similar to what interested me or in some aspect of projects I was

working on, and we collaborated. I have continued to collaborate with some of them after they graduated. Working on *Democracy and Development* with my former students Mike Alvarez, Ze Cheibub, and Fernando Limongi was pure pleasure, on a personal as well as an intellectual level.

Collaborators straighten you out. It's more than one mind at the same time. For example, when I was working with Michael Wallerstein, I would be going on about something, and he would look at me with his characteristically sweet smile and say, "Are you certain this is true?" I would immediately realize that I was speaking nonsense. So, collaborators are good at tempering your enthusiasm. They are especially important when you do formal work. Everybody makes algebraic mistakes, and you need people to put things on the blackboard so the other person can check if it is true. Otherwise, you end up making mistakes. This is why formal work is so often co-authored. It is just too hard to do it alone. Finally, collaborators are useful because the amount of work is often too big for one person to handle. If you are collecting data, it's next to impossible to do it all by yourself. It's too time-consuming. I am now engaged in yet another massive data collection, again with a group of four graduate students. By and large, I just really love to collaborate.

Q: How do collaborative projects get started?

A: Typically, I start talking to somebody and find that they have ideas on the same topic or something original to tell me. And somebody, often it was I, would say, "Why don't we do it together?" With the project that resulted in *Democracy and Development* (Przeworski et al. 2000), I basically walked into class and said, "This is what I am about to do. If somebody wants to join, join." Essentially, you look for somebody with whom you get along personally and who you think is smart, hard-working, and disciplined. If people are undisciplined and don't do their part, you go crazy.

Q: How does the actual writing proceed when you collaborate?

A: In every collaboration, somebody does the first draft, then we talk about it. Somebody else does a rewrite, and then it goes back and forth, back and forth. Sometimes somebody writes one section, somebody else writes another section, then we merge it, and somebody rewrites it. And it typically goes through many rewrites. With *Democracy and Development,* I wrote the first and last drafts by myself, mainly because it was a book, and we were afraid that if different people drafted different chapters, the style would be uneven.

Q: You have trained many graduate students. What is your approach to teaching graduate students?

A: First, I do "train" them. I subject graduate students to a systematic program. Typically, a student says he or she wants to study with me. I ask them what they want to do. Then I ask what they know, and then I tell them, "Here is what you need to learn in order to do what you want to do." These days they usually need to learn some philosophy, some economics, and quite a lot of statistics. So my students get a systematic training by others.

In addition, I have always taught an introduction to something. For many, many years I taught a course called "Marxist Theories of the State," which evolved into "Theories of the State," and then into "Political Economy." I may not teach this course anymore, because I already published a textbook on the subject (Przeworski 2003). I don't think I can teach what I have already written. In any case, students generally take this introductory course. I also teach advanced courses, usually about whatever I am working on or about methodological aspects I think students should learn and cannot get from others. For example, I recently taught a course called "Statistical Methods of Comparative Research," which focused on selection bias.

I don't teach facts. My view is that students should learn facts by themselves, by reading history. But I do force all my foreign graduate students to take an American government course. And unless they are especially strong-headed and committed, I don't allow them to write about their own country for a long time.

Students acquire all these skills and then they formulate a research project. And I supervise them quite tightly. I usually run a doctoral seminar. One of the things I discovered a long time ago is that graduate students in the United States are left alone at the very time they most need interaction with their advisors and other students. In the United States, graduate students finish their coursework, defend their proposal, their funding typically ends, and then they are on their own precisely when they most need to speak to others, hear others, and learn new techniques they may need for their dissertations. So I have always kept some form of interaction framework for advanced students. I always encourage them to participate in seminars, talk to others, and present their work.

That's basically my model for training graduate students. I have been at this for a long time, and I think I know how to do it. I may have chaired more dissertations than anybody else in the discipline—the number is approaching fifty. I don't like teaching undergraduates, mainly because one has to motivate them—they have other preoccupations than learning in their lives—and there is little one can learn from them. But I love training graduate students.

Q: What is your view of the level of interest in politics among graduate students today?

A: The people who entered graduate school during the Vietnam era, the generation of the American cultural revolution, had gone through quite a lot in their lives. They had intense feelings about politics, culture, and society. They usually had done something else, often political organizing, and were going back to school to reflect on their experiences, often seen as failures. Very often they were not teachable, because they were mistrustful of "positivism" and hostile to rigorous method. This was very particularly characteristic of students from Latin America, who just knew that the United States was imperialist and did not think there was anything to learn here. But they deeply cared about politics; they studied politics because they wanted to change the world.

Today the situation is different. These kids, and they are kids, who are now in graduate school, by and large, have grown up in exceptionally peaceful, prosperous, and non-conflictive times. These students are smart, well educated, and eager to be taught. But they have no passions or interests. And it's not just the Americans. I get students from Bogazici or Bilkent, Turkey's elite private universities, and from Di Tella and San Andrés, Argentina's elite private universities, who are indistinguishable from the daughters of doctors from Iowa. These kids absorb education and all the skills easily, but when the moment arrives when they are supposed to start asking questions, they have nothing to ask. They want to be professionals, and they think of their task as writing articles and books, rather than saying something about the world, not to speak of changing it.

Q: What can be done to foster greater passion in graduate students today?
A: I don't know whether there is any kind of awakening experience. I certainly believe that Americans who study comparative politics in any form or fashion, even if it consists of doing models and statistics, should go somewhere and experience daily life abroad to see what it feels like. But I don't know whether that is sufficient.

The Achievements and Future of Comparative Politics
Findings and the Accumulation of Knowledge

Q: If you look at where the field of comparative politics was thirty years ago, when you were a young professor, and where we are now, what are the main things we have learned?
A: Let me preface my answer with one caveat. Some of the best research in comparative politics is done these days by economists, so I will include them in my answer. Daron Acemoglou and James Robinson, Alberto Alesina, Roland Benabou, Jess Benhabib, Torsten Persson and Guido Tabellini,

and many others do excellent work in comparative politics. They typically do not know enough about politics, but they address central questions and get answers. With that inclusion, yes, I think there has been a tremendous accumulation of knowledge.

What have we learned? Ever since Duverger's (1954) and Rae's (1967) seminal books, we have learned a lot about the consequences of electoral systems. Cox's book, *Making Votes Count* (1997), is the latest example of it. We know how the electoral systems interact with social cleavages to produce parties, how they affect the distributions of votes, and so on. We have learned a lot about coalition formation and cabinet formation; there is a formal and an empirical literature on these topics. We understand much more about the legislative process. We have learned a great deal very rapidly in the last few years about ethnic conflict and ethnic peace. We have learned that most of the time ethnic groups live together in peace, and perhaps we are beginning to understand some mechanisms that explain this finding. Finally, we understand much more about the processes of regime transitions. I could go on.

More broadly, one test of the advances we have made is that when a student raises a topic with me, most of the time I can say, "Read this, read that, here is the literature that says this and that." On various topics, the conclusions do not converge, but bodies of literature exist on a variety of topics.

Q: Are there any topics on which we have not made significant advances?

A: We still do not know why and when people with guns obey people without them: the determinants of civilian control over the military. We still do not understand political parties very well. This is truly an important topic, which we have neglected. We do not understand why parties come into existence, what mechanisms hold them together, and what the glue of party discipline is. Though we have learned a lot in general about authoritarianism, we know disastrously little about the structure of dictatorships. Perhaps most important, in spite of a flood of writing on this topic, we still do not understand how democracy can be compatible with poverty and inequality.

I also think we are not doing well with globalization. I have written a paper on it recently (Przeworski and Meseguer 2002), so I was forced to read the literature. I found it deeply unsatisfactory. In particular, the political consequences of globalization are poorly understood. I think the problem, in part, is that we need some kind of methodological breakthrough in this area of research. The methods that are currently used don't do well enough. The findings are disparate, and most are based on statistical methods that assume that observations of particular countries are independent. So it is hard to believe the statistical findings. This is a big, important topic. Somehow we have to start thinking differently and pay more attention to the sort of methods that would be appropriate for studying this issue.

Generally, to a large extent because of the availability of data, we know more about the OECD countries than about the less developed ones. But this gap is rapidly closing.

Q: Are there any other methodological problems holding back inquiry in comparative politics?
A: To elaborate on my prior answer, studying things in an interdependent world is an open methodological problem. We do not have answers yet. We have this notion of two-level games, for example (Putnam 1988; Evans, Jacobson, and Putnam 1993). But how do you estimate such models? How do you test what hypotheses say about conflicts within countries when these countries are interdependent? It is very hard. I think globalization is a big, open methodological issue in general.

Another central methodological issue concerns how to study things historically, how to study history. The new institutionalism contains a potential contradiction when it asserts simultaneously that institutions matter and that they are endogenous. If they are endogenous, then we need to sort out the effects of institutions and of the conditions under which they function. The central methodological problem in comparative politics is selection bias, and, while we do have methods for handling this problem, different methods are based on different assumptions and often generate disparate conclusions. This is true of statistical studies of the impact of institutions in general, but it becomes particularly prominent when we study history. If everything is path-dependent, then it makes no sense to speak of the impact of institutions. To identify their impact, we need to think more systematically about counterfactual histories in which different institutions would have existed under the same historical conditions.

Q: You emphasize the methodological difficulties of addressing complex questions in a rigorous fashion. Another reason why progress on such questions might not be made is that comparativists simply fail to pose big, interesting questions about politics in the first place.
A: What is it that we are not asking? Certainly, we are not asking, "What does all that we do know add up to?" But we also fail to ask several questions that are researchable with the methods we have. What determines the access of moneyed interests to politics? What is it about our democratic institutions that make people feel politically ineffective? Why is it that these institutions perpetuate misery and inequality?

There is a saying in my native language, "It is not the time to cry over roses when forests are burning." And as I talk to people in Argentina, France, Poland, or the United States, I hear that they are burning. People around the world are deeply dissatisfied with the functioning of democratic institutions, in the more as well as in the less developed countries. They see politicians as serving interests of the rich, of corporations. They cannot understand why democratic institutions seem impotent in reducing glaring and persistent inequalities. They feel that political parties do not serve as a mechanism of transmission of their values and interests. They perceive that important decisions are made by institutions, often international, over which no one has control.

The danger is that unless we keep asking such questions, we leave the answers to demagogues of different ideological stripes. I was struck on a visit to Argentina that the entire political discussion is polarized between neo-liberals, who believe "the market" is the demiurge of everything, and neo-populists, who believe the demiurge is "the people," in its eighteenth-century singular.

The entire structure of incentives of academia in the United States works against taking big intellectual and political risks. Graduate students and assistant professors learn to package their intellectual ambitions into articles publishable by a few journals and to shy away from anything that might look like a political stance. This professionalism does advance knowledge of narrowly formulated questions, but we do not have forums for spreading our knowledge outside academia; indeed, we do not talk about politics even among ourselves. It has been decades since professional journals—"professional" is what they are called—published essays on "What is wrong today with the United States, or with democracy?" or on "How to make the world better?" As far as I am concerned, we would be saying more if the *American Political Science Review* were simply closed.

Rational Choice Theory

Q: Given your remarks about training graduate students, it seems clear that you support the incorporation of game theory as a standard tool in comparative politics.
A: I send my students to take game theory courses because I think it is essential, a tool for everybody to have in their pocket, which does not mean that you pull it out in all circumstances. I once had a Chinese student whose father had participated in the Long March and later became a Chinese communist notable. He wrote a dissertation about the Chinese revolution based on intimate knowledge of the case and provincial archives that nobody could access before. He did an incredible amount of historical digging.

But he also had a game theory model. He was interviewed for several jobs in this country, and at one place he was told that he would have gotten the job if he had not used game theory. This was several years ago, and now, fortunately, that kind of bias is gone. One of the striking things about the job ads in comparative politics over the past two years is that they almost all call for applicants with broad comparative interests *and* methodological training. This is an evolution that is here to stay. It is a trend that is long overdue.

Q: Still, you have written works that are critical of rational choice and game theory (Przeworski 1985b).
A: Sometimes game theory is a useful tool, but other times it is not. I am skeptical about game theory in two ways.

First, I am quite willing to believe that sometimes people do not act strategically; I am not even going to say "rationally," because that is a narrow and very demanding notion. People are not always consequentialists, by which I mean they do not always do things because they look toward the future and see the consequence of their action. People very often have deep beliefs and will not admit anything that is inconsistent with those beliefs. They feel so passionate that they are going to do things regardless of the consequences. During the project on transitions to democracy, when we were trying to distinguish different strategic types within authoritarian regimes—"hard-liners," "reformers," and so on—Fernando Henrique Cardoso remarked, "But do not forget the stupid ones" (*tontos*). More generally, game theory starts with preferences, and we do not know what they are. It works, I think, when there are plausible reasons to impute motivations to particular classes of actors. It makes sense to impute motivations with regard to "consumers," who want to maximize consumption and leisure. Imputing motivations also works with "landlords and peasants," "unions and firms." But it fails with "individuals" or "voters": people have so many different motivations that no simple assumption can characterize all of them. In a nutshell, game theory works when it is accompanied by good sociology, when one can make reasonable inferences from positions in some structures of interdependence to motivations of actors who occupy these positions.

Second, game theory generates many equilibria and, consequently, it provides poor theories of history. Dynamic game models typically rely on ad hoc selection of equilibria. Again, sometimes they work and sometimes they do not.

Analytical Narratives and Comparative Historical Research

Q: One attempt to introduce game theory into comparative politics takes the form of analytical narratives, as proposed in the book by

Bates et al. (1998). Elster was quite critical of this book in his review in the *American Political Science Review* (Elster 2000). Do you share Elster's concerns?

A: I see *Analytical Narratives* as less path-breaking than its authors do, but I am sympathetic to the main intent of the analytical narratives project, which is that case studies should be theoretically informed and theoretically informing. I have nothing against studying cases. I think you can learn a lot by studying Poland or Argentina. But I want to know what general hypotheses are relevant to the particular case studies.

Let me add two further points. First, narrative does not necessarily have to take the form of game theory. Second, when you do case studies, you need to know where your case is located in the broader context of other cases. So, I say, "Do a regression before you do case studies. Then look at cases along the line first. After that, look at some outliers, because they may be illuminating about specific conditions." Here's an example. I think Guillermo O'Donnell's piece, "State and Alliances in Argentina" (1978c), is brilliant. I always give it to my students as *the* country study. Yet Argentina is a unique case. If one does, as I eventually did (Przeworski et al. 2000, 99–101), regressions of various kinds for the whole world, you find that Argentina is always standard deviations out. It had, by far, the largest number of regime transitions of all countries. And it had democracies that did not survive when the country was relatively wealthy. In fact, the wealthiest instances where democracy fell are Argentina in 1976, Argentina in 1966, and Argentina in 1962. Argentina was among the ten most developed countries in the world in 1900, but now it is in the doldrums. Argentina is the weirdest country in the world. What does all this mean? It means that when you theorize on the basis of Argentina you are going to get very little generality. This is why my first principle on political narratives is to locate the case in the broader context.

Concerning Elster's review of *Analytical Narratives,* I think he was critical for the wrong reasons. Elster has a way of weighing every criticism evenly. His typical critique of papers goes like this, "I have eleven points. Point number one is that on page three you made this mistake. Point number two is that everything you said is badly formulated. Point number three . . ." So, he has a laundry list approach. I am persuaded that he was right on many historical points; the contributors to *Analytical Narratives* did not get their history very right. But I do not think Elster grappled with their intent.

Q: Another approach to comparative politics that focuses centrally on cases and history is comparative historical analysis, which is often inspired by Barrington Moore's *Social Origins of Dictatorship and Democracy* (1966). What is your view of this literature?

A: What bothers me about Barrington Moore is the sense of action at a distance I get from his work. Moore's work has causes that are three centuries ago and consequences that are fifty years ago. What happened in between? I was never persuaded by *Social Origins of Dictatorship and Democracy*. It is a beautiful book: broad and erudite. But I was never persuaded by its analysis of causal mechanisms. More generally, I am typically not persuaded by macro-comparative historical sociology. As John Roemer observed in the "Introduction" to *Analytical Marxism* (Roemer 1986b), although we want to establish regularities at the macro-level, their explanation must by formulated at the micro-level: someone must be doing something to bring the macro-state about. Macro-comparative historical sociology fails to provide such causal mechanisms.

I do not find this literature very useful as a source of information either. One thing I discovered while trying to collect data is that we lack good political histories. In this regard, I found macro-historical sociology useless in terms of information. Much of the analysis happens at the level of mysterious actors. Macro-historical books provide very few dates, names, and places. They analyze collective actors, like peasants, landowners, and the bourgeoisie, who march through history without dates and places. From the factographic point of view, I find this literature uninformative.

Methodological Standards and Comparative Politics inside and outside the United States

Q: During the past decade, methodological issues have commanded much attention within comparative politics. What explains this change?
A: I have a rational choice explanation for this trend. I think Americanists in Political Science departments, who are more methodologically oriented, started pressuring people in other subdisciplines to beef up their methodological standards. In most departments the methodological development in comparative politics was pushed down the throat of area studies people. Americanists, because they were born and raised in the country they study, do not have to learn the language, history, and culture of other societies. So they could spend their time learning theory and methods. In turn, comparativists are often in the unenviable situation of having to learn both. You have to learn Turkish, the history of Turkey, and so on. And then you also have to learn the theory and methods that Americanists learn. But few comparativists did this, at least among those doing area studies work. At a certain point, I think Americanists revolted, because departments had double standards.

We had a tenure case once at the University of Chicago, concerning a person who did first-rate research on the Soviet Union. For two years this person sat in regular meetings of a local cell of the Communist Party and saw from the inside how it worked. This research was ethnographically impressive. But it had no question, no method, no conclusion. It was pure ethnography. When the tenure case came up, one of the people we asked for letters was an economist, who also studied the Soviet Union. And he wrote to us saying, "What is involved here is whether you want to have one standard or two. We economists abandoned this kind of ethnographic stuff, and we have one standard for everybody. But you may want to have two." He was not encouraging us one way or another. He was just saying, "This is what your decision is." I think this case illuminates what happened in Political Science departments across the country. Basically, Americanists said, "We want to have one standard."

Q: Is this healthy for comparative politics?
A: It is very healthy. I don't think we have coped with it institutionally, because having a single standard implies that comparativists have twice as much work to do as Americans who only study the United States. The changes are inevitable and beneficial, but costly.

Q: What are the implications of this imbalance for the future of comparative politics?
A: It will mean that, as in the past, foreigners educated in the United States will play a key role in the development of the field. If you look at the history of American comparative politics, you will find that many of the eminent comparativists are or were foreigners: Karl Deutsch, Guillermo O'Donnell, Leonard Binder, Juan Linz, Ari Zolberg—the list goes on.

Q: What about the contributions of Americans to comparative politics?
A: Well, let me say something that will shock and offend most of my area studies colleagues. I have strong feelings against studying foreign countries. When I lived in Poland and I saw foreigners, mostly Americans, come to Poland and study Poland, I thought these people did not have any idea what they were doing. They were framing their studies in terms of American ideological issues, and thus they did not address problems that we Poles, or Polish social scientists, saw as fundamental. They were just exporting American ideological fantasies.

I am extremely guarded about the American conception of comparative politics as a field where Americans go out and study other countries. Comparative politics is strange. When Americans study the United States they do American politics, and when Americans study Brazil, they do comparative politics. Now, I ask myself, "What do Brazilians do when they study

Brazil?" This is not to say that Americans have not done very good work on particular countries. One could go on citing and citing. Sometimes they did studies that were seen as important contributions in the countries they studied: Schmitter's work on corporatism in Brazil (1971) and Alfred Stepan's work on the military in Brazil (1971) are books that Brazilians see as fundamental contributions to the understanding of their country. But I suspect this kind of work is quite rare.

These days in particular, though it has been true for a very long time, U.S.-trained foreigners are much better at studying their countries than Americans will ever be. I had Argentine, Korean, Chinese, and Brazilian students, who are first-rate social scientists by every criterion. They went back to their country and did excellent work, better than most foreigners will ever be able to do. There is no reason why studying the world should be a monopoly of the United States. This does not mean that knowledge produced by Americans is of no use to people in other countries. But, at some point, we need to start thinking about the study of comparative politics as an enterprise in which we collaborate, exchange views, and perhaps provide some resources to people studying their own countries, rather than playing this parachuting game.

Conclusion

Q: **You have had a long, prolific career, yet you keep pushing yourself into new areas and learning new things. What keeps you going?**
A: To some extent, it is a question of tolerance for pain. Nowadays this is especially true for us older people. All these kids know things that you don't, and there are so many technical gimmicks around that you know you should be using but don't know how. You are never certain if you are still able to learn these things or if it surpasses your abilities. So, every time you plunge into something new, you feel the pain. But, obviously, I like what I am doing, and maybe I don't know how to do anything else. I guess I just like doing research. I also have strong political feelings, and a lot of my work is driven by that. I think of myself as making interventions in political debates, and I believe the quality of that intervention matters. So that is obviously part of the motivation to keep going.

Q: **What are your research plans for the years ahead?**
A: I only have medium-term plans now. The big thing that will keep me busy is what has kept me busy for a long time: democracy, development, and income distribution.

I am engaged in two projects and I am not yet clear how they are related. I want to examine democracy from the perspective of its founders. It is obvious to me that democracy is not what the "founders" in different countries intended and expected it to be. My question is "Why?" Was the original project unfeasible? Or did things take an accidental turn? As usual, I have a political motivation: I want to know why democracy has not generated more economic equality, more effective political participation, and a better balance between order and freedom. Are these shortcomings inherent in democracy and thus irremediable? What are the limits of democracy: how much equality, how much effective participation, and how much liberty can any democratic system generate at its best?

The second project entails collecting historical data. For various reasons, I have become persuaded that to make sense of recent developments, one has to go back farther in history than I have or we have. For example, as I already mentioned, the stability of the post-1950 political regimes appears to depend on their entire regime history. And if one wants to examine the impact of political institutions on development, one cannot jump centuries and assume that institutions never change. Hence, I want to return to the relation between political institutions and economic development by taking a longer view.

Q: What advice can you offer a young graduate student starting out today?
A: This turns out to be a very hard question for me to answer, for reasons that may have become apparent from what I lamented earlier. I think that our system of incentives, and the equilibrium culture that emerges from our institutional setup, promotes narrowly conceived thinking, entailing little risk, and saying nothing that may be politically controversial. Rewards lie with "professionalism." And a lot of students enter the graduate study of political science because, while they have some superficial interest in politics, they think academic jobs provide safe incomes and a good life. I would love to say, "Think big," "Take risks." But this would be cheap advice: I already have a safe job at a good university. So I do not give advice. I explain what I think the choices are and leave it to each to decide.

14

Robert H. Bates

Markets, Politics, and Choice

Robert H. Bates, an Africanist by training, has made major contributions to comparative politics and the political economy of development by elucidating the political origins of economic policies and challenging culturalist explanations of development. He is a leading proponent of the use of economic theories and tools, especially rational choice theory and deductive reasoning, in comparative politics.

In his first two books, Bates focused on the case of Zambia. *Unions, Parties, and Political Development* (1971) explored the failure of the government to implement a policy of industrial discipline. *Rural Responses to Industrialization* (1976), which analyzed the political and economic strategies of rural dwellers, explicitly used methodological individualism, rationality, and choice, all borrowed from neoclassical economics. His materialist focus cut against the then dominant culturalist explanations of development outcomes in Africa.

Markets and States in Tropical Africa (1981), Bates's most widely read work, established him as a leading thinker in development studies. He argued that African governments were captured by urban-based coalitions that favored policies harmful to agriculture and, hence, to economic development. As a result, economically irrational interventions by governments in rural markets were in fact politically rational. By showing how governments in developing countries reaped political advantages by distorting agricultural markets, he explained why they so often chose inefficient policies that impoverished their citizens.

In *Beyond the Miracle of the Market* (1989), Bates adopted a dual focus on political institutions and market forces in order to explain economic development. Drawing on the new institutional economics, he argued that institutions can compensate for the failure of markets and also help determine

This interview was conducted by Richard Snyder in Woodstock, Connecticut, on March 2, 2002.

which economic demands become politically effective. Focusing on rural property rights, pricing policies, and agrarian radicalism in Kenya, he explained why this country, in contrast to most African countries, had successfully nurtured its rural economy. The book thus illuminated the conditions under which political institutions can have positive economic consequences.

During the 1980s, Bates also published forceful statements of his rational choice approach, including *Essays on the Political Economy of Rural Africa* (1983) and the edited volume *Toward a Political Economy of Development* (1988).

The focus of Bates's research expanded beyond Africa in *Open-Economy Politics* (1997a), which analyzed the political economy of the world coffee trade. By studying an international institution, the International Coffee Organization (ICO), this book explored the interface between domestic politics and international political economy. Moreover, by blending formal, deductive models with rich, qualitative case studies of Brazil and Colombia, it exemplified the "analytic narrative" approach advocated by Bates and his collaborators in *Analytic Narratives* (1998).

Bates's current research focuses on the origins of violence, an issue he explores in *Prosperity and Violence* (2001), and in numerous journal articles.

Bates was born in Brooklyn, New York, in 1942. He received his B.A. from Haverford College in 1964 and his Ph.D. in political science from the Massachusetts Institute of Technology in 1969. He has taught at the California Institute of Technology (1969–84), Duke University (1985–93), and Harvard University (1993–present). He was president of the Comparative Politics Section of the American Political Science Association (APSA) in 1995–97 and vice-president of APSA (1989–90). Bates was elected to the American Academy of Arts and Sciences in 1991.

Intellectual Formation and Training

Q: How did you first become interested in politics and the study of politics?
A: My family was enormously politically engaged. My mother was a vehement Eleanor Roosevelt liberal and my father, a country doctor, was always talking about his view of things. Instead of family conversations at the dinner table, we had family combat over political issues, and it was fearsome. Part of the reason I got interested in politics was that I grew up with it so much, and I figured if I could learn enough about politics, maybe I could battle my way into the family conversation and steer it toward something really important and meaningful, like whether we loved each other! But maybe that's overpsychologizing things. In any event, my childhood was a mixture of Eleanor Roosevelt, civil rights, baseball, and politics.

Q: Why were you attuned to issues of civil rights?
A: Partly because some of my ancestors had been abolitionists, partly because of my love of the Brooklyn Dodgers and Jackie Robinson, and partly because it seemed like the right thing. My parents, especially my mother, had a rigidly moralistic, progressive stance. You did not argue with her, but as far as I was concerned, she was on the right side of 99 percent of the issues we cared about. So why argue?

Q: Did you have any interest in Africa at this early stage?
A: I was growing up in rural Connecticut having a very good time, eating lots of good food, and playing lots of baseball. However, my parents were not happy with how my education was going because I wasn't, so to speak, "putting out." So I switched from the local high school to the prep school, the Pomfret School, in the neighboring town. I went as a boarder, not a day student, because it was rough enough coming in as a local without revealing just how local you were. The school's administration decided we kids were spoiled, provincial, and didn't care about the rest of the world, all of which was true. To broaden our horizons, they set up a summer program in 1959, at the end of my junior year, that took us down to Mississippi, where we went to the college in Tupelo that several years later became the place where the Freedom Riders went. The summer we went there, the White Citizens' Councils, which had close ties to the Ku Klux Klan and the religious Right, were trying to take over the political system in Mississippi. These councils were local anti-black organizations resisting integration and mixing of the races. So, we students were exposed to some of the tension in the air at the time. After three or four weeks in Mississippi, we spent the rest of the summer in Africa traveling to Kenya, South Africa, and Ghana. That's how I got hooked.

Q: What were your impressions of Africa?
A: I decided that going to Africa was the most important thing I'd ever done in my life, and I wanted a career that would get me back to Africa as often as possible.

Q: It trumped baseball?
A: Yeah, and I wasn't that good at baseball anyway.

Q: A high school trip from Connecticut to Mississippi and Africa seems quite unusual, especially during the 1950s. Who put the program together?
A: The administration of the Pomfret School put it together. It was a very progressive administration for the time, though the students were not pro-

gressive in the least. The person who took me on that trip later became the administrator of several black colleges. He was very liberal, yet he had a realistic sense of where power was in the United States, which was in the hands of wealthy families. So he operated with the children of wealthy families to try and turn them around. The summer program was financed by Harold Hochschild, the father of Adam Hochschild, a classmate of mine.[1] Harold owned mines in Bolivia and Africa, and, in the context of the 1950s, he was pretty liberal. He was very sympathetic to the goals of the Pomfret School's administration. Adam never thought his father was liberal. He always saw him as a big rich capitalist, which was also true.

Q: You got your undergraduate degree at Haverford College. What did you study?
A: I was going to major in English literature, but the closer I got to the subject, the more I understood that "style points" were too important in that field for my taste. If you were really glib and could bullshit and write well, you could win a lot of arguments. But I wasn't sure that had anything to do with being right or wrong. I wanted something where you could draw inferences, reach conclusions, and make statements with truth value attached to them. That wasn't going to happen in English, and I became increasingly dissatisfied with the study of literature. It was too much style and too little substance.

I was shopping around for another major, and I discovered a wonderful professor, Harvey Glickman. Haverford had just received one of the first grants given to any college anywhere for African Studies; the grant was for a joint project with Lincoln College. Glickman was in charge of the project at Haverford, and, as a sophomore, I became his research assistant. He was writing a review of all the literature on Africa by political scientists in England and the United States. I got to read and take notes on all that stuff. This experience really got my education going, and it kept me involved with Africa, which was the name of the game. I wound up majoring in political science with a secondary concentration in economics. Haverford had a very good Economics Department.

Q: Did you learn much economics then?
A: Enough to know two things. One, I really liked economics. And, two, I read Samuelson's *Foundations of Economic Analysis* (1947) and realized I could never be a star in that field because I didn't have the mathematical skills.

---

1. Adam Hochschild is the author of a best-selling book about the horrors of the colonial rubber trade in the Belgian Congo (Hochschild 1998).

Q: Besides Samuelson's *Foundations,* do you recall other influential books from your undergraduate period?

A: Haverford had a very good program in the philosophy of science, and I was very much shaped by the work of Carl Hempel (1965) and John Stuart Mill (1874) on the logic of scientific inquiry. That material really clicked for me.

Q: You graduated from Haverford in 1964. Did you go straight to graduate school?

A: Yes. But the summer before my senior year at Haverford, the summer of 1963, was important. I had an internship at the State Department. It was part of a program run by Bobby Kennedy that basically let us get involved with whatever we wanted. There were about twenty of us, and we got into counterintelligence and Cuban Missile stuff. That was the summer the monks were burning themselves in Vietnam, and we interns were all over that. I worked on the Congo with Adlai Stevenson, the U.S. ambassador to the United Nations. At that time, the United States was backstabbing the United Nations' efforts in the Congo. I met my wife in that summer program, and a bunch of other interesting students participated in it, like the political scientist Peter Gourevitch, Larry Pressler, who later became a senator from South Dakota, and the historian Doris Kearns. It was a neat group, and the experience kept me involved with Africa because I was up to my ears in the Congo.

Q: After such a stimulating experience in Washington, D.C., why didn't you aim for a career as a policy maker?

A: Not a single person in that program decided to work for the State Department.

Q: That's curious. The effect of the program seems to have been exactly the opposite of what Bobby Kennedy intended.

A: Absolutely. The internship confirmed our beliefs that there was no time to use your head and analyze things if you worked for the State Department. You would end up stamping passports, working in a bureaucracy, and playing bureaucratic games.

Q: By the end of your State Department internship you had eliminated a government job as a career option. Did you know at this point that you were going into academics?

A: There was no doubt I was going into academics. First, academic jobs paid to go to Africa. What a great way to live. If someone had been selling tickets on the street, I would have gone to Africa that way. Also, I liked using my head, I liked academics, and I was comfortable in school. I couldn't think of anything else I wanted to do. I was headed for an academic job.

Graduate Studies at the Massachusetts Institute of Technology

Q: In the fall of 1964, you started graduate school in political science at MIT. Why did you choose to study there?
A: I wanted to go to a school that would teach political science as a social science. So I chose MIT over Harvard and found to my disappointment that they did not do much social science at MIT either. MIT had positioned its program as a methodologically rigorous one, and since the program was associated with MIT, I thought it was going to be scientific and rigorous. But it wasn't. Two or three people on the faculty thought in a rigorous way, but, overall, you could go through MIT's program slinging as much bullshit as you could in an English Department.

Q: Which faculty members were rigorous?
A: Ithiel de Sola Pool had a very careful and clear mind. His work was not methodologically driven, but his approach was rigorous. Pool was a major researcher. He was in communications, a field you had to take at MIT. In fact, when I first got to MIT, there was still no Political Science Department. You got your degree in "social science" or something like that. The whole MIT program in political science was built around the field of communications, which I don't think was a very good idea.

Q: Why was MIT's program built around the field of communications?
A: The people who created MIT's political science program were strongly influenced by the work of Harold Lasswell (Lasswell and Lerner 1965) and also by the voting studies of Paul Lazarsfeld, Bernard Berelson, and William McPhee (Lazarsfeld, Berelson, and Gaudet 1944; Berelson, Lazarsfeld, and McPhee 1954). Those studies were really about persuasion and communication. Lazarsfeld and Berelson did studies on voting because they could get funding for it, but they were really interested in studying marketing. Pool was a combination of Lasswell on one side, and Lazarsfeld and the Columbia Sociology Department, on the other.

Q: Besides Pool, Daniel Lerner was another major figure at MIT when you were there. Did you interact with Lerner?
A: Dan Lerner was a difficult man. He could be very nice or he could be very mean. It depended on how you struck him at the moment. He started out really mean to me. So I ran away from him. Later, he was nice to me, so I ended up sort of enjoying him.

Q: Did you have a mentor?
A: I avoided having a mentor. I was really uncomfortable with the idea. I basically went away to Africa, did my thing, and dropped a lot of dissertation pages on people's desks near the end.

Q: MIT does not sound like it was a warm and fuzzy experience.
A: Not at all. Remember, I came from a tiny little college, Haverford. At MIT there were very few other kids from liberal arts colleges. Many of the students in my program were mid-career people from the United States Agency for International Development (USAID) or the army and air force. They were not headed to academia.

One of the first times I was at MIT I was walking down what's called the "infinite corridor," and somebody was repairing it with a jackhammer. That image struck me as right. MIT was like an industrial plant. It did not have the feeling of a community of students, certainly not for the graduate students. So, no, MIT was not warm and fuzzy. It wasn't hostile either, but it was not a place where I could find a community or a mentor.

Q: Even though you did not have a mentor, did any members of the faculty influence you?
A: Myron Weiner was the person who influenced me the most and to whom I felt closest. Weiner had the ability to ask the right questions and follow the arguments. He remained totally unembarrassed by his lack of mathematical proficiency and wasn't snowed by methodology. If you had a question, a method, and an answer, he could evaluate whether you had answered the question. Weiner had a very clear and very sharp mind. I enjoyed watching him work.

Q: Lucian Pye was also at MIT. Did you interact with him?
A: Lucian was big, warm, and fuzzy, but I wanted more than warm and fuzzy. He had a big heart, but there was no way I was going to do the kind of work he did. It was so idiosyncratic. Lucian's work was very much in the Lasswell tradition, but it drew more on the personality theory side of Lasswell than on the communications and symbols side. It was something Lucian could do well, though probably not very many other people in the world could do that kind of work. Certainly not I. So I ducked out on him.

Q: With Pye, Weiner, and Lerner, MIT had some of the towering figures in the subfield of political development.
A: That's part of the reason I went to MIT—that and the methodology I was hoping to get. The political development group in the MIT department is interesting to analyze, and I teach about it in a lecture I call "Cambridge

against the COMINTERN." The subfield of political development emerged partly as a way to fight against the communist threat to capitalism in the Third World. The Center for International Studies at MIT was set up by its founder, Max Millikan, to keep the Third World from going the route of Nasser, Sukarno, or Mao Tse Tung. So, MIT had that ambiance to it in the 1960s. I would not say the scholars who worked on political development in the 1960s put the Third World under a microscope, because they tended to look through telescopes, not microscopes. But MIT was a key place where the study of development was happening.

Q: Weiner and especially Lerner and Pye emphasized cultural factors in their work, whereas your work has emphasized material factors. Was your materialist focus a reaction against the orthodoxy at MIT?
A: I don't know that *reaction* is the right word, though that often does happen to students in their relationship with their teachers. The reason I did not become a culturalist was that I did fieldwork. Fieldwork is the cure for bullshit. When you do fieldwork, you take your research problems from reality. You can only do the kind of work Pye and Lerner did if you're sitting in an office somewhere writing about a world you're not involved in. Lerner was working with large data sets and surveys, whereas Pye was interpreting people's biographies. In both cases, research was a clinical thing that was not anchored in the specifics of a micro-setting. I was much more comfortable with micro-settings.

Q: What methodological training did you get at MIT?
A: Tom Lehrer, the musician, was a very good statistician and a wonderful teacher. He taught all over the Boston area, including at MIT and Wellesley. When I got back to MIT from my fieldwork in Africa, Hayward Alker had moved there. I took as many courses with him as I could while I was writing my thesis to try to catch up with quantitative methods. But I was not well trained, and I knew it.

Q: When you were a student in the 1960s, several major works were published in comparative politics and comparative political sociology, including Seymour Martin Lipset's *Political Man* (1960a), Barrington Moore's *Social Origins of Dictatorship and Democracy* (1966), and Samuel Huntington's *Political Order in Changing Societies* (1968). Did these books have an impact on you?
A: Huntington's book is the one that really affected me. It was a great book, deep and thoughtful. Huntington had a real intuition about institutions and how they worked. The material on praetorianism is brilliant, and the stuff on the green revolution anticipates work I did on rural rebellion.

Again and again, the book gives good value. I regarded Huntington as a war criminal during Vietnam.[2] But later, when I worked in Uganda, I began to see the importance of political order as the fundamental premise for the possibility of a good life. Without order, there is no future. And if there is no future, then a lot of the things we want and need are not possible. I did not learn that until I was taught it in the field by people who had learned it directly. That's why I became much more supportive of Huntington's basic argument in *Political Order.*

Q: Did Lipset's *Political Man* have much impact on you?
A: Lipset was too cut and dry. He did not follow an unfolding question or problem. In *Political Man,* I felt Lipset had open and shut the case. With Huntington's *Political Order,* by contrast, I felt he had really opened something up and had more to offer. Every time I read *Political Order* it's like I'm seeing parts of it for the first time. The book re-creates itself in my mind every time I read it. It really stands up well.

I like Lipset when he is expositing somebody else's work and defining its position in the intellectual tradition. Lipset's introductory essays in books by Ostrogorski (Lipset 1964) and Michels (Lipset 1962) are good examples of this. When he's working on this kind of intellectual level, Lipset educates me every time.

Q: What other books had a strong impact on your intellectual formation?
A: One of the books I liked most was Durkheim's *Suicide* (1951). It's a wonderful example of the interaction of methods with the problem-driven mind. The book is not about methods for their own sake; it's about methods in the service of a really interesting question. I saw and liked that combination in Paul Lazarsfeld's work, too.

Q: Could you discuss your dissertation? What was the topic?
A: My dissertation focused on the Copperbelt in Zambia. It was a study of the relationship between the Mineworkers' Union and the United National Independence Party (UNIP), the governing party in Zambia. I chose to work in Zambia because I had been there before and felt my connections there were better than anywhere else, because of my relationship with the Hochshilds. Ironically, I ended up working on a mine owned by their competitors, the Anglo-American Corporation, which turned out to be a very good thing: they understood research and gave me good access to their

2. Huntington served as a State Department consultant during the Vietnam War.

records. My wife, Margaret, and I lived in a house trailer that we were able to park adjacent to the mine townships and formed a network of friends and acquaintances among the workers there. We visited, interviewed, and became part of their community. I still regard Mrs. Muluwe, Muhongo, and others as my coauthors and look back on them with fondness and gratitude. It was a lifetime experience.

We learned so much! There had been race riots in the town several months before we came, yet people could see *us* rather than the color of our skins, and we were taken in. We got to see the brutality that underlies political organizing: the intimidation factor, administered by the same people—members of the youth league—who became our friends.

Still, Zambia was at its height in those days. The mines were doing fine; the country was optimistic and proud. I feel a lot of nostalgia and heartache when I look back on those times.

Q: What did you get out of your dissertation research?
A: I got a good dissertation from the project and a pretty good book, one that has remained among the best histories of the politics of the Copperbelt at the time of independence (Bates 1971). But the book was too much shaped by the mindset of the field at that time—modernization theory—and insufficiently grounded on Marxism, which is the natural grounding for a study of labor. I regret that very much. The book looked at the organization of the party and the Union and attempted to explain the failure of the government to implement a policy of industrial discipline and wage restraint. The organizational analysis was quite good, but the premise was all wrong. I particularly remember Myron Weiner as, in his forthright and commonsense way, he peered over the chapters he had marked up and said, "Bob, I don't think that the government has failed to communicate. I think the workers simply disagree." I blushed from the roots of my hair when I heard that, recognizing how naïve I had been. This comment shaped me powerfully and in ways I did not recognize at the time.

Q: What was your interaction like with other graduate students at MIT?
A: When I came back to MIT in 1968, after three years away doing fieldwork in Zambia and studying social anthropology in England, MIT had changed. There were a lot more people who, like me, were preparing for careers in academics. The political science program had become a department and gotten its own budget lines. The department even had its own very elegant building. And we had a lot of students coming out of liberal arts colleges who wanted to be professors and were in the mainstream of political science. The whole complexion of the student body had changed, and there

were many more people with whom I felt comfortable, the main one being Peter Lange. After I came back from the field, I found MIT a much more congenial place, and I liked hanging out there and talking to people.

Student radicalism had broken out by the time I returned to MIT from Africa. I lived at Harvard while I was writing my thesis, because my wife was in graduate school there and they had better dorms than MIT. I used to go to the Students for a Democratic Society (SDS) meetings in Harvard's Memorial Hall. A lot of campus politics was going on at the time, and some of the MIT students were deeply involved. That felt sort of real to me, and being part of this community was certainly better than the alienating industrial environment I had encountered when I first got to MIT.

Q: What impact did the turbulence of the 1960s have on you? Were you engaged in political activities?
A: During a lot of that period, I was in graduate school just trying to survive. I was a study nerd grinding away. And I was off doing research in Zambia while lots of my colleagues were struggling against the Vietnam War and struggling for civil rights. My wife and I were in Africa when Martin Luther King Jr. was shot and the cities were filled with smoke. We were just coming home when Bobby Kennedy was shot. It all made America look like a very strange and dangerous place.

Q: Did you stay abreast of these events in the United States while you were in Africa?
A: You couldn't escape it. My wife and I were out in the boonies in Africa, but the people were tuned in. They had radios and they'd ask questions. We'd get grilled about the morning news because they'd heard it on BBC or Voice of America. They wanted to know whether your family was involved, which side of the issue you were on, and what you thought about it. Even in rural Africa, people were clued in about what was happening in our world.

Q: If you had not been away in Africa during this period, would you have played a more active political role?
A: To tell you the truth, I don't know what I would have done. I would have been involved in the civil rights movement, though I don't know how, maybe by doing freedom rides. On Vietnam, I had mixed feelings. I knew I'd get drafted, but I don't know if I would have gone or, instead, found a way to get out of the country. It was an issue I wasn't looking forward to confronting, particularly because we had a young child at the time. The idea of leaving her and my wife alone without any income seemed difficult.

Social Anthropology at Manchester

Q: While completing your Ph.D., you spent six months at Manchester University in England, which was famous for its Manchester School of Social Anthropology. Why did you go there?
A: I had a fellowship from the Ford Foundation, and part of the grant was for multidisciplinary training. I had been doing fieldwork in Zambia, and the Anthropology Department at Manchester had a major field site there. So, when I wanted to learn anthropology, it made sense to go to Manchester.

Q: Why did you want to learn anthropology?
A: The Ford Foundation grant wanted me to learn anthropology and I was damn interested in it. In its methodological sophistication, British social anthropology is very different from cultural anthropology as taught in the United States. In the 1960s, the anthropologists at Manchester were studying game theory and applying matrix algebra to understand social networks. Social anthropology tends to be very formalistic, providing typologies of kinship terms, but at Manchester, people like Clyde Mitchell and Bruce Kapferer viewed kinship as a strategy. They saw people manipulating kinship to their advantage by creating bonds with others in order to incur obligations and shape expectations. From this perspective, people were not trapped in norms, rather they used norms aggressively to skin the cat. Norms were dynamic and prone to manipulation. And when I was in the field, that's exactly what I saw.

Q: Why did the people at Manchester see norms this way, whereas the mainstream of social anthropology had a more static, formalistic understanding? Did the anthropologists at Manchester do more fieldwork?
A: I think that is the answer. Take the case of Victor Turner, who defected from Manchester and went to the University of Chicago. Turner had worked in the Ndembu region in northwestern Zambia. By the time he defected, he'd given up on fieldwork and gotten into the study of symbols and divination as a way to impress his students and colleagues at Chicago. He had basically stopped listening to the real world and started listening to academics.

Q: Did you have much interaction with Max Gluckman, the founder and leader of the Manchester School?
A: No, because he intimidated me. Gluckman was a yeller and screamer, so I lay low around him. I went to seminars to hear him do his thing, but I hid in the crowd and made sure he didn't see me. The person I had really gone

to work with was Clyde Mitchell, who was very gentle and nice. Mitchell was a sociologist, not an anthropologist. He started out in measurement and scaling and then moved to survey research. He also did a field study of a village, because you had to do a village study to make Gluckman happy. Mitchell eventually left Manchester for Oxford. A lot of people were disappointed because he never produced what people had hoped. But I think the stuff he produced was elegant and wonderful. I learned a ton from Mitchell and also from Bruce Kapferer, who did work on the mines in Zambia.

Q: Why did the people at Manchester have such a strong connection to Zambia?
A: First, Gluckman himself was South African, a South African Jew. He writes a lot about what it was like to be a Communist, a Jew, an anthropologist, and a white guy in South Africa—layers and layers of not belonging. Also, the mining companies gave money for research. They thought it would be useful to understand what they were up against in trying to create an industrial labor force and a modern society in Africa. That provided an opportunity for a young guy on the make like Gluckman. Having a field site in Zambia was a very valuable asset that allowed the Manchester department to attract top talent, people like Mitchell and Elizabeth Colson, another fine anthropologist.

Q: Overall, how did the experience at Manchester influence you?
A: It was a very powerful experience. I loved the debate and the sharpness of the ideas. For example, the Harvard sociologist George Homans, who had written a book about a medieval village outside Manchester (Homans 1941), debated Max Gluckman. What a ruckus! Another time, I was sitting in a seminar, and a guy in the back row emitted a show-stopping and brilliant argument proving the existence of God. That was Ivor Wilks, another Africanist. At Manchester, you could be a historian, a psychologist, an anthropologist, or a political scientist and just get in and knock ideas around. Every idea was taken on its own merits. If an idea worked, people talked about it; if it didn't, then out it went. It was wonderful.

Q: Manchester seems like it was the exact opposite of the infinite corridor at MIT.
A: MIT was cold silence. But Manchester was not warm and fuzzy; it was more intense than that. It was alive with a lot of smoking and drinking. Manchester was also extremely democratic. There was no deference to anybody, except Gluckman, whom everybody treated like a spoiled child. They were afraid of him because he was the chair. It was his department in the European sense. Still, overall the place was rebellious, contentious, and fun.

It was like the scrappy identity of the Oakland Raiders: anything you did outside the lines didn't count, the only thing that mattered was what you did between the lines during the game. At Manchester, you did not have to be patrician or upper class as long as you were smart, serious, and did good work.

Q: What is the secret to creating that kind of effervescent intellectual environment?
A: That's a very tough question that I've often wondered about. Besides Manchester, the only other place where I've experienced this kind of environment was Caltech, when I was a junior professor there in the 1970s. We almost achieved it at Duke for a four- or five-year period. But the intellectual intensity didn't sustain itself at Caltech, and at Duke, it glowed but didn't ignite.

It may be easier to generate a high-intensity environment in the business world. Enron had it, for better or worse. I was just reading *A Beautiful Mind* (Nasar 1999), about the economist John Nash, and Princeton achieved this kind of intensity for a while. Sustaining this kind of high-intensity environment is hard in the academic world, because it requires letting some people go. Tenure prevents that. Tenure is a lifetime marriage, but the intense stage of a marriage is the young part, not the older part. Still, I think I know how to create a high-intensity intellectual environment. One way is to make people cough up their resources after a couple of years. What happens in universities is that resources get decentralized and stay in people's hands far too long. When the intensity is over, the resources don't go back into the collective pot. The University of Chicago approximates the kind of model I have in mind. Each seminar series at Chicago has to compete for funding every few years. If they run out of steam, they're over. At Harvard, by contrast, JOSPOD—the Harvard-MIT Joint Seminar on Political Development—is still going after forty years!

Research: The Political Economy of Development in Africa and Beyond
Rural Responses to Industrialization

Q: Your dissertation and first book were on mineworkers in the urban communities of the Copperbelt in Zambia (Bates 1971). Yet most of your subsequent research, beginning with your second book, *Rural Responses to Industrialization* (Bates 1976), has been on rural Africa. Why did you shift from an urban-industrial to a rural focus?
A: I wanted to get into rural issues because the majority of Africa is rural. After completing my first book, I realized I'd only seen one part of Africa. I

wanted to see the life in the "bush," too. I also became interested in rural areas because of the Luapula people, who came from a region of Zambia that borders Zaire.[3] In the urban areas where I had done my dissertation fieldwork, immigrants from the Luapula region were specialists in violence and intimidation. The urban youth brigades, thugs, and political militants were all comprised of Luapula people. I wanted to see where these guys came from and why they were so violent, though I never did figure that out.

I financed the project that resulted in my second book through funding for migration studies offered by the National Institutes of Health (NIH). Myron Weiner, who had gotten NIH funding for his work on "sons of the soil" and migration in India (Weiner 1978), alerted me to this opportunity. NIH was willing to pay rather generously for me to get a Land Rover and go out to the bush. So, out I went.

The project was pitched as a rural-urban migration study, and migration certainly played a major part in the book. But the more I pieced the study together, the more I realized migration was only part of the story. Rural people were not just migrating to cities, they were also playing political strategies to get the cities to channel money to the countryside. There was pressure from the countryside, generated by electoral mobilization or through the formation of ethnic groups and secessionist movements, aimed at blackmailing the government into spending money on rural areas. The rural dwellers and their politicians were very good at this game. They had been dealt a lousy hand by nature, but they were extracting every bit of leverage they could from what God had dealt them. The rural politicians were very canny and shrewd.

Q: Why did you choose Kasumpa village as the focus for your study of Zambia's Luapula region?

A: Chance plays a large part in where you end up, and I ended up in Kasumpa village by chance. But Kasumpa was interesting because the villagers told me all kinds of stories about what they had done during Zambia's independence struggle.[4] They had heard about the Mau Mau movement in Kenya and thought it was a great idea to form their own Mau Mau. They wore animal clothes so others would know they could not be expected to act like people and would get out of their way to avoid being hurt. The villagers raised as much hell as they could to tie down the British and Rhodesian soldiers in the area, which they succeeded in doing for several weeks. If I'd been in any other village, I'd never have heard these same stories.

---

3. Zaire is known today as the Democratic Republic of Congo.

4. Zambia, formerly called Northern Rhodesia, achieved independence from the United Kingdom in 1964.

There is a guy named David Mulford who was a graduate student working in Zambia when the British were getting out. As the British were burning their secret files, they were all going across Mulford's desk, and he was taking notes on them. Mulford, who later opened a big banking company in London and eventually became undersecretary of the Treasury Department under George H. W. Bush, kept a box with all the notes from the British secret files under his bed. Whenever I did a project in Zambia, the first place I went was to Mulford, so I could look at his box of papers and see what the British secret service had said about the area I was working on. I came across a stack of files about Kasumpa village, and it turned out the villagers had told me the truth. They had not made up their stories. I had independent validation from Mulford's notes about how these people behaved and about the national importance of the politics in that part of the country. At that point, I knew I had a book. So I turned the study of migration from Kasumpa into a book.

Q: Around the time *Rural Responses to Industrialization* appeared, James Scott (1976) and Samuel Popkin (1979) also published books on peasants. Your book did not have as great an impact as theirs. Why not?
A: The Luapula book was actually published the same year and by the same press as Jim Scott's *The Moral Economy of the Peasant*. At that time, in the mid-1970s, comparative politics was focused on dependency theory and the Marxist critique of dependency theory. My book doesn't mention any of that and thus was far removed from the theory of the times. That's one reason the book was not taken up very strongly. It actually did have a big impact on Sam Popkin, though not on Jim Scott, because I don't think he read it.

Q: Why did your book not engage the prevailing theories of the times, for example, dependency theory?
A: Largely because I was teaching at Caltech then, and my colleagues and students were not paying much attention to what was going on in comparative politics. Comparative politics was not considered a cool thing to study at Caltech, because it was seen as a hotbed of radicalism and Marxism. In general, the field of comparative politics was denigrated by most other political scientists at the time.

Markets and States in Africa

Q: Your third and best-known book, *Markets and States in Tropical Africa* (Bates 1981), focused on the politics of agricultural policy in Africa. How did you formulate the research question for this book? What did you set out to achieve in writing it?

A: *Markets and States in Tropical Africa* resulted from a conversation with my friend, Thayer Scudder, an anthropologist at Caltech. We both had been reading Michael Lipton's book on urban bias (1977), and he peered across his desk from me and said, "What do we know about this in Africa?" The question stuck in my mind, and I found myself returning to it. Also, I needed to write a book that would take me beyond Zambia: that simply was too narrow a base from which to build a career. The book I had in mind was later published as *Essays on the Political Economy of Rural Africa* (Bates 1983), and I needed a last chapter for that book, one that would focus on the political economy of post-independence Africa.

Michael Lofchie at UCLA had been working on the politics of agriculture at the time—recall, this was the early 1970s and there were significant food shortages. He and I put together a course that brought a series of top scholars to UCLA to talk on this topic. Michael had secured funding to commission papers from these people, and we put together a very good volume on African agriculture (Bates and Lofchie 1980). In addition, these scholars helped me make contact with important policy centers in Tanzania, Ghana, Kenya, and other places, and I spent a summer gathering data on this subject. When I turned to writing this up, I found I was writing something that looked more like a short book than a long chapter. It took on a life of its own.

One of the things that made me realize I had a book was when I visited Elliott Berg at the World Bank. Elliott may have had a narrow view of economics, but he was extraordinarily generous to younger scholars. When he was starting out in academia, he focused on trade unions, and he had visited me in Zambia when I was doing my work on the Mineworkers' Union. He continued to work on Africa, and the World Bank, sensing a growing development crisis in Africa in the 1970s, commissioned him to do a policy review on Africa. When I looked him up, he was working out of a building the Bank had rented for this exercise, and we compared notes. It was immediately clear that quite independently we had arrived at the same conclusions: we were looking at the same elephant.

Berg's report (Berg 1981) remains a classic in development studies, and it ignited the pressures for policy reform, pressures that, after the debt crisis of the 1980s, culminated in structural adjustment.[5] My book seemed to explain why governments were choosing the policies that Berg's report criticized, and so his report and my book built on each other.

Q: In contrast to your first two books, *Markets and States* was far shorter and less laden with facts. What motivated your shift in style?

---

5. The term *structural adjustment* refers to policy reforms intended to diminish state intervention in the economy.

A: One reason the book came out so short was that my previous book had come out so long. I was whining about the lack of sales, and my editor said simply, "To sell more, write shorter." So I tried that, and it appears to have worked. In addition, I had terrific support from the University of California Press, which published the book. Sam Popkin was the series editor, and he has a terrific sense of how to present materials in a way that makes an impact. He flogged me toward clarity and precision, making sure I got the logic of the argument out in front and that the data—stories, figures, events, and the like—marshaled in service of the argument. And the Press, bless them, hired a wonderfully able copy editor, who took a crack at my style. I benefited enormously from that.

Q: What is your assessment of the reception of *Markets and States?* Why is it still widely read more than twenty years later?
A: I really do not know. It's short and brash, and that helps, because there is a good chance that the students will actually read it and react. I guess it's a pretty good book. Still, I think *Essays on the Political Economy of Rural Africa* is better. The last chapter takes a look back at *Markets and States* and, I think, gets closer to the truth (Bates 1983, 107–33). And there is some very neat stuff in the earlier chapters, including an anticipation of subgame perfection in Chapter 1 and some very serious economic history as well.[6] Also, *Essays* was the book that got Douglass North interested in me, which came at a very important time. Doug is a generous and enthusiastic man, and his affirmation of my work came at a time when I was getting pretty discouraged—social science was marginal to Caltech, comparative politics was marginal to the social sciences there, and African studies was marginal to comparative politics. Having Doug get excited about my work gave me a much needed boost.

Political Institutions and Economic Growth

Q: One criticism of *Markets and States* is that it underemphasizes the role of political institutions in shaping human behavior. Your next book, *Beyond the Miracle of the Market* (Bates 1989), focused centrally on political institutions to explain how Kenya achieved a high-growth economy in the 1960s and 1970s. Indeed, one observer described the 1989 book as "the mature, comparative institutional Bates" (Evans 1995, 35). Why did you decide to focus more centrally on institutions? Were you responding to criticisms of *Markets and States?*

6. *Subgame perfection* is an economics term used in game theory to describe an equilibrium such that players' strategies constitute a Nash equilibrium in every subgame of the original game.

A: Part of the reason I focused so much on political institutions in *Beyond the Miracle of the Market* was that I was really pissed that my previous book, *Markets and States,* was being used by the Reagan-Thatcher crowd to show that governments were bad because they created pure social cost. I did not want to be painted with that brush, because that was not my position. I wanted to look at political institutions and structures to show they could have positive economic consequences. Besides, a lot was happening intellectually at the time on the topic of industrial organization, much of it inspired by the thinking of Ronald Coase (1960) and Douglass North (North and Thomas 1973; North 1981). I wanted to sink my teeth into that material. It was fun.

Where I got myself into a trap regarding the impact of institutions on economic performance, a trap I still have not figured a way out of, is that, on one hand, institutions, especially in Africa, seem ephemeral. Yet, on the other hand, once you create them, institutions become constraints you cannot escape. Institutions operate both as independent and dependent variables. I want to make institutions endogenous, but once I make them endogenous I run the risk of saying they don't place constraints on people. I'm not yet sure how to deal with this problem. So I have paused on institutional thinking.

Q: Do you have any tentative thoughts about how to resolve this tension between the conflicting propositions that "institutions matter" and "institutions are endogenous"?
A: The answer may have to do with how institutions create vested interests by fixing certain costs. When an institution exists people tend to come up with investment programs in response to that institution. They don't want their investments destroyed as a result of changing this institution. So, they become a constituency with a vested interest in preserving the institution. This is partly what the literature on path dependence is talking about.[7] I especially want to look at some of the work on the new welfare state that my colleagues like Peter Hall (Hall and Soskice 2001) have been doing. I assume there is good material there because they are smart people and because some of the stuff that has come across my desk looks really good.

Q: What is your view on the notion of path dependence?
A: It's a way of talking about history and sounding like you are talking about social science. For some, talking about path dependence is just a lot of hand waving. For others, they actually show where history matters.

---

7. Broadly construed, path dependence refers to the notion that prior events constrain subsequent ones (David 1985; Arthur 1994; Pierson 2000).

When you have multiple equilibria, as do a lot of rational choice models, you always get a lot of path dependence. The question then becomes, are you looking at interesting equilibria and can you identify the mechanism that drives you down one path as opposed to another? It is easy for work that invokes path dependence to be very soft social science. But it can be very interesting if it's done right.

The Political Economy of Coffee

Q: Your next book, *Open-Economy Politics* (Bates 1997a), analyzed the world coffee trade. How did you become interested in this topic and decide to write a book about it?
A: I turned to research the international coffee trade after working in Uganda following the fall of Idi Amin (1971–79), and I had been deeply shaken by my encounter with violence. Through a contract between USAID and the University of California, Berkeley, I had been recruited to help change the marketing institutions in Uganda for export crops, coffee and cotton, in particular. I took with me Bob Hahn, who was then a graduate student at Caltech and was doing his thesis research on auctions.[8] We developed close working relationships with our colleagues in Uganda, and found them much buoyed by the overthrow of Amin and yet much troubled by the continuing violence brought on by the soldiers who flooded into the country during the operations that led to his overthrow.

The World Bank asked me to join a subsequent team and to implement the recommendations that Bob and I had proposed. When I met once again the people with whom we had been working, I was shaken by how they had changed—how their optimism had turned to despair, and how much energy had been drained from them by their day-to-day struggle to survive, physically and economically, in the chaos that engulfed them in the fighting.

Q: *Open-Economy Politics* was a departure from all your previous work because it focused on Latin America, especially Brazil and Colombia, not Africa. What motivated you to make this shift?
A: When I left Uganda the second time, I was burned out. In *Beyond the Miracle of the Market*, I had researched famine in the coffee zones of Kenya. I had now spent days trying to work in Uganda without being shot and watching people I knew and liked being dragged down, down, down. I wanted out of Africa. So I decided to trace the coffee market back to the

---

8. Hahn later set up the system of marketable permits for pollution, which was incorporated into national law by Congress and the Environmental Protection Agency.

place where the big economic forces came from: Latin America. The decision was fortuitous, because I ended up working in Colombia at the time of the peak of the drug wars. The leading presidential candidate was blown up the first year I was there. So, I learned that violence was not an Africa problem; it was a development problem. This is why I have been able to return to working in Africa and why I now study violence—it became emotionally possible for me to do those things.

Q: What are the main contributions of *Open-Economy Politics?*
A: The book succeeded at several levels. I was among the very first researchers given open access to the archives of the Federación Nacional de Cafeteros, which manages Colombia's coffee industry. Indeed, once I was given that access, I changed the nature of the project to take advantage of the opportunity and spend more summers in Colombia than I had originally intended. The book became a very serious study of the economic history of Colombia, particularly in the 1930s. It also contributes to the study of Brazil's economic history. I pieced together an account of the First Republic that is valid and important, and makes a contribution.

The book is also one of the first to actually model and measure the impact of an international institution. I came to understand the International Coffee Organization (ICO) sufficiently that I was able to calculate the impact of its rules on the foreign exchange earnings of member states, such as Uganda, which depend on coffee exports. And by winning a seat in the U.S. delegation to the ICO, I was able to spend a couple of weeks in London watching that institution at work: votes being traded, adjustments made in export quotas, and so forth. Indeed, I was even able to nudge an adjustment in the robusta coffee quotas in favor of Uganda, which made me feel pretty good. And I got to know the delegates to this institution well, and some of them are terrifically impressive people, especially those from Brazil and Colombia.

I think *Open-Economy Politics* is important, too, for putting the politics back in international political economy. Recent use of trade theory had taken institutions out, thereby taking out the politics of the process of adjustment to international markets. I felt this was wrongheaded. Countries adjust in different ways. I showed that, and subsequent work in the globalization field shows it as well. Without focusing on the politics, you cannot see how the costs and benefits of adjustment get allocated, and why some win and others lose when there are international shocks and commodity booms—or busts. Those who focus on factor price frontier theorems may get things right in the long run, but they will miss out on such short-term things as electoral changes, government changes, and political crises—and who wants to miss out on all that?

Lastly, I think I really broke new ground in comparative politics. The conclusion adumbrates what got more fully developed in *Analytic Narratives,* and it also urged a shift from comparisons by formal rules—for example, presidentialism versus parliamentary government—to comparisons by strategic properties—for example, the power to pivot and to agenda set (Bates et al. 1998). People like Roger Myerson and Daniel Diermeier have made greater progress on this line than I am able to make, and I think that once comparative politics amalgamates more with formal theory, this re-coding will serve us well.

All that said, I cannot say the book made the impact I had hoped for it. I do like to get things deeply researched and nailed down, but in the case of *Open-Economy Politics,* the substantive materials may have overwhelmed the analytic arguments. It gets read as a book on coffee rather than as one on social science.

Analytic Narratives

Q: In the mid-1990s, you were involved in a collaborative project that resulted in *Analytic Narratives* (Bates et al. 1998), which proposed a new agenda aimed at combining formal models, especially game theory, with historical case studies. How did this collaboration emerge?
A: I needed to get time to write up *Open-Economy Politics,* and I therefore applied to the Center for Advanced Study in the Behavioral Sciences. I had been there before, and to return, you must be part of a research group. Several of us wanted to work in political economy and at the intersection of economic history and development economics—Margaret Levi, Jean-Laurent Rosenthal, Phil Hoffman, Barry Weingast, and Avner Greif. So we applied together. Phil had to drop out at the last minute, but the rest of us worked on our individual projects in the morning and met to debate and discuss in the afternoons. Basically, we tried to figure out how our minds were working and how they should work—the strengths and limitations of the analytic habits we shared. We met, argued, discussed, argued, and met again—that year and for two years after. What you see in *Analytic Narratives* is the state of a debate that was and remains ongoing. Producing that book was very, very hard work for each of us.

Q: Besides crystallizing the debate among your group, what other objectives motivated you and your collaborators in writing *Analytic Narratives?*
A: The secret agenda in *Analytic Narratives* is to re-justify the case study. Case selection is an important part of research design, but, in contrast to the standard methodological advice that students get from King, Keohane, and

Verba's *Designing Social Inquiry* (1994), most of us don't pick our cases, our cases pick us.

Q: Our cases pick us? What does that mean?

A: That means I am always going to work in Africa. Likewise, my collaborator on *Analytic Narratives,* Jean-Laurent Rosenthal, is always going to work on the French Revolution. That's why he became a historian in the first place; he wanted to study the French Revolution. It's wrong to say that we are not allowed to be social scientists because we want to focus on cases that interest us. Given the high costs of doing qualitative, case-based work, which usually requires language training, the question is, how can we extract information of value from cases without having problems of bias and inefficiency in our estimates? But I don't think we should decide to work on things we are not interested in just because we need to get the case selection right. Sadly, my students all feel they need to come up with a research design for their dissertation that will pass the KKV test.[9] I tell them, "Are you really going to learn three languages and do in-depth work in four different countries?"

Of course, once you start to make causal inferences from cases, then you need to test those inferences to see what kind of error you are likely to have. I think we should follow the mental processes that KKV outline for testing hypotheses. But I don't want to begin by selecting cases just to get inferences. So, *Analytic Narratives* was essentially an attempt to move from the case to social science by extracting insights from the case that travel and can be tested systematically.

Q: What is your assessment of how *Analytic Narratives* has been received? Has it had the impact you hoped for?

A: It is difficult for me to judge how *Analytic Narratives* has been received. I don't place much weight on Jon Elster's review in the *American Political Science Review* (2000) because he is noted for negative reviews and he mainly reasserted arguments that he had been making in other forums; for all his seeming thoroughness, he does not much absorb the work of other people. More important, for me, has been the reception among economists and political scientists who seek to escape the limitations of large-N work—the endogeneity problems, the inability to discern causal mechanisms—by returning to case studies. The book provided a defense. I also like the impact it appears to have had in terms of promoting "antiphonal" research in which one side of the "chorus" launches a theme or interpretation, the other side

9. "KKV" refers to King, Keohane, and Verba (1994).

throws back discordant empirical material, and then the first side ventures out again—the process of revision is now incorporated into the process of research. Finally, I like the impact *Analytic Narratives* appears to have had on how people think about formal theory. We advocated thinking of formal theory as an empirical or inferential tool, seeing it in relation to induction rather than deduction. I think that is beginning to catch on.

The larger project is still in its infancy, however. I have yet to see dissertations that actually iterate between theory and observation—within-sample and then out-of-sample—as a way of closing in on a logically powerful and empirically verifiable account. Some senior scholars have done so, but not the young people. And it is the young who often provide the best measure.

Current Research

Q: Could you discuss your current research?
A: One thing I am working on now is the "African Dummy" (Nkurunziza and Bates 2003).[10] This term refers to the tendency of the African countries to comprise a large component of the unexplained variation in statistical equations that aim to explain why some countries are rich and others poor. What I am trying to do is get the African countries back on the regression line by revising our understanding of the economic growth process.

Q: What factors could help account for the African cases?
A: Things like political accountability and whether governments are restrained by the need for approval from electorates. The competitiveness of electoral systems and also political violence turn out to have an important impact on economic growth. In the face of instability and violence, capital runs away. Hence, African countries have lost the impetus of economic growth to capital flight. The study of Africa can make a contribution to the social sciences by helping us better understand the role of politics and political institutions in the growth process. Africa is a good place to study these things because it provides a Goldie Locks-sized set of countries, not too few to do statistical work, yet not too many to retain a sense of which countries are outliers.

My research project analyzes forty-six African countries over twenty-six years and looks at the relationships among three things: economic performance, political institutions, and political violence. A lot of the work I'm doing is econometric, partly because I've never done econometric work before.

10. The reference is to the dummy variables commonly used in statistical analysis.

Q: It does not sound like this project will involve fieldwork. It seems very macro in design.
A: It is, but I'm too old to live in a village. I lived in a village earlier in my career, and I'll always be informed by what I learned there. Still, I want to go back to Africa soon to keep from losing the sense of intuition I get by going there. This summer I'm slated to go to a policy research institute in Kenya and then to Uganda for a month. I definitely want to stay in touch.

Q: What will you do in Africa? Will you be doing interviews?
A: Not too much interviewing. Mainly I will take my own projects, a zip drive and notes, so I can write. I will try to see what others are working on and build research relationships with people. I'm trying to build research relationships between Harvard and the African institutions so some of their people can come over here and my students can go there. I will also just talk about what's going on. For example, I really want to find out what's happening in the elections in Kenya.

Q: Besides the African Dummy, what other projects are you currently working on?
A: I would like to start looking at public finance in order to understand what makes states financially sustainable. Why do some states become fountains of privilege that succeed in buying off warlords and demobilizing rival factions, whereas others do not? Why can some states afford to put an army in the field and defend themselves, whereas others, like Zaire, get picked apart? These are important, researchable questions about developing countries.

I am also working on violence. Rational choice theory has a difficult time explaining why people fight; most models suggest that people ought to negotiate and then settle up, thus avoiding the destruction of value. In political science, rational choice theory also has been best applied to the study of institutions; yet in fights, institutional constraints often do not bind. Both make the study of violence a fertile subject for this field. I began looking at it to understand what I saw in Uganda; and since that time, sadly, the topic has become of even greater relevance in Africa and, following September 11, in the world as a whole. To grasp the subject, I first started talking with Avner Greif. Having served with the Israeli armed forces in Lebanon, he knew what it was like to see ten-year-olds with AK-47s. While working together on *Analytic Narratives*, Greif and I began to build a model of stateless societies and societies with states. The paper took about a decade to get right, and we published it in 2002 (Bates, Greif, and Singh 2002). After returning from Uganda, I also began to read medieval history. I wanted to see how political order had been winnowed from the politics of families, lineages, and communities in agrarian societies that had been studied by historians. These two threads joined in *Prosperity and Violence* (Bates 2001), another short book like *Markets and States*.

Finally, I am studying conflict in Africa. Working with Karen Ferree, Smita Singh, Macartan Humphreys, Naunihal Singh, Matthew Hindman, and other graduate students, I have compiled a data set on conflict and political change in forty-six African countries during 1970–95. Catching up on my reading on Africa and building and analyzing this data set, I hope to have a lot to say about the origins of violence and its properties (Bates 2005). This project will take the form of a series of papers on the political determinants of economic growth. The papers will be published in the analytic volume of a four-volume study of Africa's growth performance in the second half of the twentieth century, which has been organized by the Africa Economic Research Consortium based in Nairobi. Twenty-seven teams of African researchers have combined on this project, and it has provided a royal road for my return to the study of Africa.

The Research Process
Science

Q: Do you think of yourself as a scientist?
A: Well, no. I have been around real scientists at MIT and Caltech, including the greatest scientists of my generation in physics and geology, and they are different from me. When I have a problem, I want an answer. If I have an answer, then I should be able to model it with a formal proof that connects assumptions to conclusions. I also want to see if my conclusions are right by testing them empirically. When I have those things down, I'm happy, and I consider myself a scientist. But that has happened only two or three times in my life.

Also, I'm not sure what a scientist is. Physical scientists disagree among themselves and come in many different stripes and sizes. People who refer to physical sciences to justify work in the social sciences don't know what they are doing. Instead of arguing about whether or not we are scientists, let's just do our work.

Q: Still, you seem to see a clear difference between physical scientists and social scientists. What sets the two apart?
A: Physical scientists really believe in testing. That's one thing that upsets me about my political science colleagues in rational choice and game theory. They like theory in and of itself, and they believe in a division of labor where it is somebody else's problem to test their theories. But I've been at lunches at Caltech where someone like Richard Feynman wandered in and

started talking about their ideas. They were always working on how to test ideas. What do we know? What would be the experiment? How can you get the equipment right to observe or measure the phenomenon? Those kinds of discussions don't come up a lot in the social sciences.

Q: Why not?
A: Because a lot of the theory people in the social sciences are not interested in testing. They are interested in theory for its own sake. It may also be that our theories are not very good.

Q: Some argue that because of the complexity and mutability of the social world, social scientists face far greater constraints than physical scientists on their ability to discover regularities and generalize. What do you think about this view?
A: The social and political world is an unruly, complicated beast. The trick is to find a way of carving into it by defining a tractable problem, one that allows control over observations and data yet is not so divorced from the big picture that the research is meaningless. Morris Fiorina made a great comment once about how much generality is possible and desirable in the social sciences. He said we should seek "as much as we can get." This doesn't mean you work at a general level. It means you do controlled observations and scale them up as far as you can.

Still, I don't think social scientists have achieved many powerful generalizations. The behavioral revolution was funny in this regard. It generated books with long lists of 457 propositions that were all true because they had been tested. But the propositions were not true in all times and places. So, what is general? What's general for me is the inductive side of game theory. If we can understand the kind of games people are playing, see the world from their viewpoint, and see the patterns that drive them to make decisions, then we have a very deep understanding of the situation. Noncooperative game theory and backward induction are tools for achieving this kind of understanding.

Formal Models and Rational Choice Theory

Q: What role do methodological tools play in your research?
A: Methods for their own sake have always bored me. What really interests me are questions and trying to answer them in a way that allows me to assess the quality of my answers. When methods are used in the service of questions and research problems, I can indeed get quite interested in them. But I never wanted to be a methodologist, and I never wanted to teach methods. I don't find methodology very interesting as a field. If you are a

mathematician or mathematically inclined, then methodology could be interesting. But answering questions is what interests me.

Q: Over the past twenty years, your work has increasingly used formal theory. Can you discuss how you use formalization in your work?
A: Formalization allows you to test the logical validity of your answer and see whether the conclusions flow in a compelling way from the premises. I'll give you a good example from my work. I did a paper with Da-Hsiang Lien on the origins of parliament (Bates and Lien 1985). It's a fun paper that I really like, and we have a really cool model in it. We argued that democracy results from a bargain between revenue-seeking governments and citizens over payment of taxes in exchange for policies that respond to citizens' preferences. For the argument to work, there had to be a condition in the utility functions that economists call separability, and the model had to be linear. The more I thought about separability, the less I liked it, because it basically required that actors' preferences over public goods were invariant with their private income. We know that is just not true, but it turned out to be a necessary condition for our argument about the origins of parliament to hold. I never would have figured that out unless we had tried to model the argument formally. Knowing that the condition of separability was necessary for our argument to be true, I no longer believed it was true, though I did not point a red flag to that in the paper.

Q: Where did your argument itself come from?
A: The argument came from trying to understand the origins of parliament. And it's a damn good argument. But if the condition of separability has to hold for the argument to be true, then I think the argument is false. I would have believed the argument had I not modeled it formally. So, formalization is a way of checking your argument and logic at a level to which you would not otherwise be driven.

Q: But formalization itself does not generate an argument.
A: No. No way.

Q: Where do arguments come from then?
A: Well, I don't know. That's the kind of thing that drives me nuts about Jim Scott and a former student of mine, Arun Agrawal, who are co-teaching a methodology course at Yale that is basically about where research questions come from. I told Jim, "If I could teach my students to be as creative as you are, I'd teach that course, too." But I don't think you can teach creativity. Arguments and ideas come from a sort of chemistry, not from methods.

You can derive new information from formal models by playing with them. And doing comparative statics on a model can help you move from ideas to empirical testing. If you wiggle this thing, then that thing ought to wiggle. And you can actually do tests by changing a component of the model and then running regressions to see if the coefficients are of the right sign and structure.

Of course, we're talking about an idealized research program here. In most work in comparative politics, including my own, the search for and testing of ideas is done much less formally, often by looking for apt comparisons and examples. It's very seat of the pants. Probably the closest I ever came to moving systematically from ideas to testing with comparative statics was in my book on coffee, *Open-Economy Politics* (Bates 1997a), where I compared Colombia in the 1930s with Colombia in the 1950s and 1970s. This cross-temporal comparison allowed me to turn off and on the element of party competition, which made it possible to test things by varying this one factor and seeing if the others followed in the ways predicted by my argument, while holding a lot of other things constant.

Q: Besides your paper with Lien on parliaments, are there other examples of how formalization has strengthened your work?
A: Not by the use of formalization, but by the influence of formal argument. What I like best about formal argument is the simplicity. Formal argument helps you take a very complex problem and find the simple core of it. Finding this inner structure of a problem provides a base from which I move back and forth in the process of developing a book. For example, in *Rural Responses to Industrialization* (Bates 1976), the core was the rural dweller out in the bush who could either stay, fight and grow cash crops, or migrate to the city. In *Markets and States* (Bates 1981), the core was the farmer who was purchasing goods in one market, selling them in another, and buying inputs and consumption goods in a third market. In *Open-Economy Politics* (Bates 1997a), the core was the structure of relative prices among different types of coffee. If the price of one type increased, consumers would substitute in another, which made it necessary in turn for economic actors to organize across the entire trade in order to operate successfully in the coffee market. I don't want to call these simple core stories "formalizations," because often they aren't formalized. But finding the simple structure at the core of a problem is a habit of mind that I picked up by reading formal work.

Q: Can you give examples of works by other scholars that also get to the heart of the matter in this way, either with or without formalization?
A: Elizabeth Colson's *Tradition and Contract* (1974) comes very close. She wrote it in the 1970s in reaction to the crisis at Berkeley where she was teaching. She was trying to demystify the dominant thinking then among

American students about non-capitalist, non-Western societies. Colson argued that much of the interaction in those societies was contractual, not communitarian. My colleague at Harvard, Elizabeth Perry, in *Shanghai on Strike* (Perry 1993), is also incredibly good at providing a clean, quiet sense of structure. She looked at how relationships within occupational communities prevented the creation of a working class, and she explored the problems this posed for the communist government in Shanghai. When you're reading her book, you always know where you are because it gives enough structure so you can wander away from the main theme and come back to it without getting lost.

Somebody else who came very close to finding the simple structure at the core of a problem was Jim Scott with his focus on peasant decisions in *The Moral Economy of the Peasant* (Scott 1976). He was not comfortable getting to the core, though, because he ran away from it as fast as he could. Still, his book has the kind of spirit I am talking about. One of the best books I've ever read that has a fair amount of formalization is Gary Cox's *Making Votes Count* (1997). It's an extraordinary, uncompromising book that reads almost like an eighteenth- or nineteenth-century treatise. Another set of works with a good formal core is the research on the American Congress and the role of the committee system by Keith Krehbiel (1991) and Ken Shepsle (1978). That literature is defined by formal argument, yet it also has a real political vitality.

Q: Game theory seems to be the tool for building formal models that you prefer. What is it about game theory that you find fruitful?
A: The reason I like game theory is that it gets you away from the assumption of the radically autonomous individual. Individuals are interdependent, for better or worse, and thus their fates are linked. Game theory helps us see the social part of human life. Also, I like game theory because it provides a sense of time and sequence. I find the apparatus of game theory to be a very natural way of thinking about the world. I should add here that the people who taught me the importance of rational choice theory were the people I did research on. These incredible villagers in Luapula were gaming the system for all they could get and doing a remarkably good job at it. They were not behaving at all in the way I had been prepared to think about villagers by Dan Lerner and other cultural theorists.

Q: Have you been drawn to evolutionary game theory (Maynard-Smith 1982; Weibull 1995; Young 1998)?
A: I've got to get into that more. Evolutionary game theory is appealing because it has been road tested and proven very useful in the biological sciences. But I haven't yet convinced myself that evolutionary mechanisms

are at work in politics. Maybe this is because I haven't seen a lot of losers in wars and politics who fail to reproduce themselves. The losers usually stick around for a while and continue the political struggle. In principle, I like evolutionary game theory and it is something I am paying attention to, but in practice, I'm not sure I could use it as much as I'd like to.

Q: An important growth area recently in the field of economics has been experimental economics, which uses social-psychological experiments to anchor assumptions about how people behave.[11] Have you paid attention to that work?

A: I'm so out of touch with that. It was just getting going at Caltech around the time I left, and it is now largely what the economists do at Caltech. Harvard hired Alvin Roth who does that. It strikes me that experimental work is going to have an enormous impact on economics and probably should have an enormous impact on political science. Experimental work shows that people often don't behave the way expected utility theory predicts, which means that a lot of our models are wrong. There are a lot of people in political science like myself, who are riding the rational choice hobbyhorse fairly hard, and really should be paying much closer attention to experimental economics.

Q: You have just suggested that recent developments in experimental economics may have shaken the foundations of rational choice theory as conventionally used in political science today. Recent events in the real world, like the terrorist attacks of September 11, can also be seen as challenges to theories of politics anchored in instrumental rationality. Can rational choice theory be reconciled with political behavior that seems driven more by passions and emotions than by choice?

A: If I had ever thought that rationality, on the one hand, and passion and emotion, on the other, were enemies, I would have had a very hard time being a rational choice theorist. The question is not "Are passions important?" It's "How do passions make a difference and how do people who feel passionately behave?" I feel passionate about the things I do, and the people I work with feel passionately about the things they do. That does not make us irrational, though it does make us intense as hell. And there are situations when rational choice theory just isn't going to work. Why do firemen go into a falling building? I can't explain that. God bless them. All I can do is salute like everybody else. There are points when you have to acknowledge that the intellectual games have come to an end, and you

---

11. For their work using laboratory experiments as a tool in empirical economic analysis, Daniel Kahneman and Vernon Smith received the Nobel Prize in Economics in 2002.

have to respect it and move on. There are creative moments when people just bear witness to what they are observing, and those are the turning points.

Q: Are there any examples of such turning points that you witnessed either from afar or up close in your fieldwork?
A: Not in my fieldwork, though there were things I certainly didn't understand. In Zambia, people made claims about what had happened during the anti-colonial liberation movement that involved the spirit world, mysticism, fogs coming to earth, and monsters. First, I had no way of checking whether or not these claims were true, because I wasn't there. Second, if these claims had turned out to be true, I wouldn't have had a clue about what the hell had happened. I wrote down these stories in my notes, and I began to understand witchcraft better than I thought I could. But I never figured out what to do with these stories.

Q: Have you ever thought about going back to those stories?
A: They are good stories, but I just don't know how one would use them. In any case, I got a lot of mileage out of the way I saw things, so I'm not sure I want to go back to those stories. It would be fun, but it would be accounting for Nth-order stuff, when I think I've already got the big stuff in pretty good shape. The creative moments people have are important, but, in the end, I've always looked for regularities, not idiosyncratic factors.

Fieldwork

Q: Fieldwork has played a central role in your research. What do you get out of field research?
A: I need to do fieldwork to know I'm not inventing stuff. For many of my colleagues, the world is what they read on a computer screen. They think that by sitting in Cambridge they are going to be able to understand Asia, and they don't know how much they are missing because they don't go there.

Q: What language skills did you acquire for fieldwork?
A: To do fieldwork, you must study languages. I have trouble learning to speak them, but I give it the old college try. Like everyone else, I studied French and German in school and passed examinations in them to get my Ph.D. Unfortunately, the French faculty thought that if we wanted to learn to speak the language, we should take a Berlitz course; they were going to teach us Molière, Villon, and Racine and have us write 1,500 words a week. Because of my own thick head—or tongue—and this background, even

though I am a member of the faculty of the University of Toulouse, I still cannot speak in French! As for German, enough said.

To work in Africa, I have several times learned—and subsequently forgotten—Swahili. The language I got deepest in, however, was Bemba, a complex, powerful, subtle, and fascinating language spoken in Zambia. When I go back to Zambia, I find myself sometimes saying words and expressions that I didn't even know I had known; Bemba really worked its way deep into my head. For my work in Latin America, I learned Spanish and Portuguese. I could read both well, and thus assimilate the archival material and secondary literature. I would be hard pressed to read a novel, however. Largely because of the amount of time I spent in Colombia, I could speak Spanish. Lack of practice has led to a considerable loss of facility. I wish I had had time to develop my Portuguese to the same level. I love the sound of that language and the music, and I would like to be able to do more in Portuguese-speaking countries. But I was not in Brazil long enough and I regret that.

Q: You once argued that doing rational choice theory right requires fieldwork. Could you discuss this issue?
A: Rational choice models are very thin and don't really mean anything until you embed them in a thicker world. People have passions, values, expectations, relationships, histories, and access to information that other people don't have. Until you have information about these variables you really can't say much, and rational choice theory does not provide information about these things. This information is provided by the context to which the model is being applied. I'll give an example. The equilibrium concept I use a lot is subgame perfection. Subgame perfection means that what is on the equilibrium path is determined by what you expect to happen if you go off the equilibrium path. The problem is that in the theory people never go off the equilibrium path and, hence, you can never actually observe such behavior because that history never happens. To understand why people don't go off the path, you have to find out their beliefs about what would happen if they were to go off. This means you have to interview people and find out, for example, what their mother told them about bad girls, or what the legend is about what happens to you if you go to that part of town as opposed to your own part of town. These are all beliefs about what happens to people if they go off the equilibrium path, and you are never going to find that out if you only follow the rational choice model. You have to go out to the field to find it out. Elizabeth Colson's *Tradition and Contract* (1974) provides a beautiful example of this. She writes about a village that is a tableau of Rousseauian bliss, with women feeding their neighbors' kids, sharing food, and guys buying each other beer. What she

discovered, however, is that this peaceful, nice behavior was actually driven by Hobbesian beliefs about reality. The villagers believed their neighbors were potentially their worst enemies and would kill them if they were not nice. The fieldworker is the only one who can see the beliefs that underlie this nice behavior.

Q: As we advance in our careers, we acquire more professional and personal responsibilities, which can make it harder to take long, extended trips to the field. Can you successfully go to the field for short periods, say, a couple of weeks?
A: I could not do a village study in two weeks, and I wouldn't do one in two weeks. In two weeks, I might try to find out all the papers written by the local law society, political society, and economic society and try to meet people. But it wouldn't be the same as real research. I'm a soaker and poker. I wouldn't go to the field for two weeks, except that it's better than not going at all.

Q: Fieldwork is not a formal requirement in most social science graduate programs, and limited funding opportunities and pressures to finish quickly can make it virtually impossible for graduate students to do fieldwork. Do you fear that fewer people in political science are doing fieldwork?
A: At Harvard it's not a problem because the area studies centers are so strong and well-endowed. There are lots of opportunities for people to go to the field. Even in economics, where they like students to get their degrees quickly, there is an emphasis on fieldwork. In applied and labor economics, they have always done a lot of fieldwork, and as microeconomics has grown in importance in development studies, economists want their students to get out to the field.

Area Expertise

Q: Do you consider yourself an Africanist?
A: I define myself as a political economist who works in Africa.[12] Africa is where I study, but I've known real Africanists, and they know a lot more about Africa than I. When I was working at Caltech, I would often go over to UCLA, which was next door, and hang out with the Africanists there. Those guys would know things I had no clue about, like who was the president of Algeria or the vice-president of Tanzania. I generally try to keep up

---

12. For a review and critique of Bates's work on the political economy of Africa, including a reply by Bates, see Stein and Wilson (1993).

with what's going on in Africa by staying on top of the press, but I never felt I had to be the arbiter of knowledge about my continent. I took ten years off from Africa in the 1980s and 1990s to write *Open-Economy Politics* (Bates 1997a), which focused on Brazil and Colombia. As a result, I lost track of the whole period of democratization and state collapse in Africa. I'm now reading my way through a library of books to catch up on democratization movements in Africa.

Comparative Analysis

Q: What role does comparative analysis play in your research? Do you use comparisons across cases to generate and test ideas?
A: It's strange. I work in comparative politics but do very little comparison. I've never believed that small-N comparisons are valid. When you do cross-case comparisons, so many other factors vary besides the one you're studying, and, as a result, you face a severe omitted variables problem. So, I always thought small-N comparative politics was a big lie. I prefer to analyze cross-temporal variation within a unit. By looking at changes in the same case over time, things can often be held constant, which makes the omitted variables problem go away. I know it's unfashionable and a little idiosyncratic, but I have always been drawn more to historical analysis of cases than to small-N comparative politics.

Q: Yet you use cross-case comparisons in your work. For example, the concluding chapter of *Markets and States in Tropical Africa* compares Kenya and the Ivory Coast with Ghana and Zambia. Also, *Open-Economy Politics* compares Colombia and Brazil.
A: Yes, the last chapter of *Markets and States* (Bates 1981) does draw some comparisons, but I mainly used the method of stylized fact, not comparison. All of Africa looks the same in that book. I agree on a set of facts about how agricultural prices are distorted and ask, how do you explain these facts? But I don't look at how, for example, the level of distortion of agricultural prices varies from case to case.

I think the coffee book on Colombia and Brazil (Bates 1997a) was the only time I tried to do carefully controlled comparison. I found it very difficult, because there's a lot of history and a lot of balls to keep up in the air. It is very hard to know what the right comparison is. Is the right comparison Colombia in 1950 with Brazil in 1950? Or is it Brazil during the First Republic of 1889–1930 and Colombia between 1910 and 1949, when it had an oligarchic democracy? I did the analysis of Colombia and Brazil the way any other comparative politics person would. That is, I looked first at Colombia and saw that the story about how public policy emerged in the coffee sector was linked with the country's party system. Then I went to Brazil, and the parallel story there turned out to center not on the party system, but on federalism. I had written a chapter on Colombia and a chapter on Brazil and then asked myself, "What's the comparison here?" The comparison hinged on political institutions that magnify or, alternatively, diminish the power of an interest group by determining its capacity to pivot and thereby make or break governments. Distinct institutions— the party system in Colombia and federalism in Brazil—were the common element that allowed me to compare across the two cases. One thing I realized as a result was that the most useful concepts for comparative research were based not on institutional facts, but on strategic opportunities. Hence, I concluded that comparative politics was probably going to move away from institutional description toward analytic formulations of how different institutions shape strategic opportunities, for example, how they affect the ability of political actors to pivot.

Collaboration

Q: What role has collaboration played in your research?
A: I enjoy collaborating with students, colleagues, and friends in Africa. Collaboration is fun. Well, it can be the best of times and the worst of times. I've had real problems with collaborators and they have had real problems with me; we are all busy people and collaboration can become a tug of war at times. But I learn a lot from collaboration, and I enjoy it. It's a lonely life being a scholar, and collaborating is a good way to cope with the loneliness. Also, I like working with students. It can get awkward, but now that I am who I am, I always try to make sure my name comes last in the collaboration so my student coauthors will get cited and not be seen as mere adjuncts. I learn as much from my student collaborators as they do from me.

Rural Studies

Q: With the exception of your first book, most of your books have focused on rural issues. Is Agrarian Studies something you feel passionate about?
A: No, not in the same way as someone like Jim Scott, who has a real romantic identification with pre-industrial societies. What I really liked about agrarian studies was that you could do anything with them. You could be an anthropologist or a historian, and you could do fieldwork or

modeling. Plus, rural studies lent itself to comparative work. The peasants in Russia lived a different life than the frontier men in the United States, and such differences offer a profound way of figuring out where the modern world came from. A focus on the rural sector is a nice way to frame a lot of the issues I care about in political economy and development.

Funding

Q: How have opportunities for funding shaped your professional trajectory?
A: First of all, I would not have gone through higher education if it had not been paid for. Africa is a very expensive ticket. It's a very poor place but very costly to work in. So, the funding the Ford Foundation put into area studies was crucial to me. Partly because of the high cost of doing research in Africa, I've always tried to be good at my disciplinary work so that I could be competitive for funding through the National Science Foundation, which has been very good to me throughout the years.

Q: Have you noticed any trends in the availability of funding for research in Africa and in general over the years?
A: There's less of it. Prior to September 11, the dominant attitude was that America had won the Cold War and could turn inward and not invest in area skills. Hopefully that will change. Also, the funding of the National Science Foundation and other sources was capped. So, funding is tighter.

Extra-Academic Engagement

Q: Over the course of your career, you have done a good amount of consulting, for example, to the World Bank. How does this activity relate to your research? Is consulting a source of new insights, ideas, and problems to study?
A: It can be. After I finished my fieldwork for *Rural Responses to Industrialization* (Bates 1976), I didn't want to go back to Africa for extended periods of time because I had a young daughter. So, I went to Africa for shorter periods doing consulting, and I wound up using a lot of that material. This is not the best way to do research, though, because you travel around in packs with other Americans, meet people largely like yourself, and don't get to see behind the scenes very much. A lot of time is spent working with teams of foreigners, rather than working with people from the country itself. Still, consulting got me over to Africa a lot, and I was able to build projects around contacts I'd made and things I'd learned. For example, in *Open-Economy Politics* (Bates 1997a) I was able to use material from consulting I'd

done in the coffee-producing areas of Kenya and Uganda. Overall, consulting is second best, but it does keep your hand in. Without the opportunities I've had for consulting, there would have been a lot of years I would not have made it to Africa at all.

Q: More broadly, is your research driven by a normative agenda?
A: There are two normative things I care about a lot. First, I want to mainstream Africa's experiences both within higher education in the United States and within the consciousness of young people in the United States (Bates, Mudimbe, and O'Barr 1993). Africa tends to be treated as something exotic, but Africa is part of our lives and world, and it shouldn't be considered the "other." With a flip of a coin you could have been born in Africa, and if you lived in Africa, you would behave the way Africans do, because it's the only reasonable way to behave under those circumstances. I want people to realize that if I brought somebody from my fieldwork into my classroom, within ten minutes they would be fully accepted because they are just as able as anybody else. The second thing I care a lot about and want to change is the idea that material wealth is not important. That notion is utter bullshit. I have had African students who could have been at Harvard and done just as well as any kid here if they had had the money. The only difference between the kids here at Harvard and the ones I work with in Africa is money: here they have it, there they don't.

Q: Who tells you that the material aspects of life are unimportant?
A: People with money, especially middle-class white kids. The belief that the material side of life is just a Western hang-up really bugs me. Only people who have no idea what it means to be poor and have never paid the price of being poor believe that nonsense. I want poor people to be wealthier, and I would like to make poverty go away. I don't know how to make Africa grow and become wealthy, but the fact that Africans are so poor upsets me. If I were better at being a George Soros, I'd be a George Soros, but that's not what I'm good at. The things I do best are teach and write, and that's how I try to make a difference. I've tried to move the institutions where I've taught—Caltech, Duke, and Harvard—to educate more about Africa and to educate more African students.

Q: Do your activities aimed at increasing awareness about Africa in American universities ever conflict with your disciplinary agenda as a political scientist?
A: No, because the only way to make Africa important in the United States is to be good at your discipline. Nobody thinks Africa is important. The only way to get a position at an upper-middle-class, American university

dominated by white males is to make them think hiring you is one of the best things they ever did.

Colleagues, Institutional Affiliations, and Students
The California Institute of Technology

Q: Your first job after completing your Ph.D. was at the California Institute of Technology, where you began teaching in 1969. How did you end up at Caltech?
A: When I started at Caltech, the university had no political scientists, zero. I was hired into the Department of Humanities and Social Sciences. I was told to apply by an anthropologist from Caltech whom I had met in Zambia, Thayer Scudder, and who became my best friend. One night in Zambia I came back to the rest house at the university where I was staying, and there was shouting and banging in the bathtub. The guy making the ruckus had been out in the field for three weeks and wanted a beer. I tossed a beer into the bathroom, and when he came out, it was Thayer Scudder. He and Elizabeth Colson had been studying the same group, the Tonga in the Gwembe Valley of Zambia, since 1957. They went out every two years and followed that group into the late 1990s. It's one of the best long-term anthropological studies ever done of any group anywhere. Ted was on the faculty at Caltech, and he said "We're starting a social science program. When you're done with your thesis, apply." It turned out I was the number two guy. The number one guy who they really wanted was Graham Allison, who had just written his great book on Cuba (Allison 1971). Allison decided to stay at Harvard, so they had to go to their second choice. Given that no other jobs were available, I was happy to go to Caltech, where I was the only political scientist at the whole damn school. I was delighted because I don't like being mentored anyhow. It was great!

They brought in a bunch of economists at the same time, including Roger Noll, Lance Davis, and Charlie Plott. The economists took control of everything, which is probably what they should have done. Then we began to build up in political science. We recruited John Ferejohn first. The next hire happened while I was away in the field. This was Morris Fiorina, a student from Rochester. So I came back to Caltech and discovered I had a new younger brother, and it was Moe. We stayed at three for a while and then hired Gary Miller and Bruce Cain the same year. Later we hired Douglas Rivers.

Q: You said there was no formal Political Science Department at Caltech. What was the graduate curriculum like?

A: To graduate from the social science division, to which political science belonged, students had to take exams on American politics and game theory. They also had to take microeconomics and econometrics. We taught no macroeconomics, because the economists thought it was nonsense. So, the political science curriculum was microeconomics, game theory, social choice, and American politics.

Q: Was there any training in comparative politics? Did you teach that?
A: They had never heard of comparative politics. I was teaching American politics all the time.

Q: That must have been difficult.
A: It was, but it was good. I learned a lot.

Q: Weren't you itching to teach your own material on Africa and developing countries?
A: Yes, and I got to do some of my stuff, but not very much. That happens at a lot of places. If you're a political scientist teaching in a business school, you don't teach your thing, you teach business. What you teach and what you do research on are often quite different. I used my teaching at Caltech as an opportunity to learn. Classes were very small, and you could take your time. You could also co-teach, and I worked with extremely bright people from different fields. But, in the end, you do want to teach your own field and produce students who are interested in and shaped by your work. That can be very satisfying, but I didn't get that at Caltech.

Q: You mentioned earlier that, after the Manchester School, Caltech was the second high-intensity intellectual environment you encountered. What made Caltech so exciting?
A: There was a feeling at Caltech that finally the mixture between economics and politics was taking place, right there. It was a combination of game theory and social choice theory. Economists were interested in politics, and political scientists were willing to train with and learn from economists. All of us political scientists joined the freshman class in math courses and worked our way through the required part of the undergraduate math curriculum. It was very interdisciplinary. History and anthropology were involved, too, but they were done on the side. The really hot part was the mixture of formal economic theory and politics.

In the late 1960s and early 1970s, students from the Rochester School led by William Riker had gotten jobs at Carnegie-Mellon and Washington University in St. Louis. When the Rochester School hit Caltech in the 1970s,[13] it took off and produced a whole new generation of students. Barry Weingast was the first. Gary Cox, Jeff Banks, and Randall Calvert came later.

Q: What role did you play in training these students?
A: I worked with them, usually as second banana because I lacked the formal training to really mentor them. The young economic theorists on the faculty were the ones with the formal training.

Q: So, what did the graduate students at Caltech learn from you?
A: They had to explain their work to me. I was sort of playing Myron Weiner to the formal theorists. I was learning formal theory, and I was also teaching the students how to communicate to the broader political science world in which they would have to find employment. If they could train at Caltech and learn how to articulate with, and survive in, the world of political science, then we would be a success. If we couldn't achieve this, we would all wind up with marginal jobs in lousy places.

The economist Roger Noll had the credibility with the graduate students to say, "You've got to work with Bates and make sure you understand what he is trying to tell you." The Caltech students needed to learn that the world was full of very bright people and very good work that wasn't the same kind of work they did. They tended to believe the only work worth doing was what they were doing. They were very arrogant. And if they showed themselves to be both arrogant and ignorant, they weren't going to get jobs. I was able to provide a sort of pre-professional socialization. Think of Richard Fenno and William Riker together in the same department at Rochester. Though I couldn't carry Fenno's jock strap up the capitol steps, I was fulfilling a bit of the Fenno role in relation to the microeconomists at Caltech. To give an example, I remember telling Barry Weingast, "When you hear the word *norm*, think *constraint*." This helped him see how to use the constrained maximazation framework, which was dominant in rational choice work at the time, in the context of the sociological literature on the American Congress. It was as if the penny dropped, and he began to see the political structures and institutions that the earlier behavioralist tradition had analyzed as things he could model. That's the kind of insight Riker had when he made his students train with Fenno. When things were going well at Caltech, that's the role I played.

Q: What exactly did you teach the Caltech students?
A: I taught them where the field was coming from: behavioral political

13. On the Rochester School, see Amadae and Bueno de Mesquita (1999).

science, social psychological approaches, political sociology, and political psychology.

Q: What was your impression of the behavioral material you were teaching? Did you admire this sort of work? After all, it was quite different from the economic theory you were being exposed to.
A: I thought some of those guys were really smart, and the more micro the work got, the more interesting it became. Homans's *The Human Group* (1950) is an awesome book. Merton's work is great. Stouffer et al.'s *The American Soldier* (1949) is one of the greatest pieces of research I've ever seen. The works of Lazarsfeld, Berelson, and McPhee are also great (Lazarsfeld, Berelson, and Gaudet 1944; Berelson, Lazarsfeld, and McPhee 1954; Katz and Lazarsfeld 1955), and I still teach them.

Q: What do you admire so much about these studies?
A: They show minds at work. These scholars have a problem they are trying to solve, and they really chase it down. The tradition of research that Lazarsfeld and Berelson started in the 1940s on voting behavior is one of the great cumulative research programs in the social sciences. They got deeper and deeper and more and more precise. They started in the 1940s with the Erie County study (Lazarsfeld, Berelson, and Gaudet 1944), which was really a failed project that didn't produce any results. They wanted to study the impact of a political campaign and the media on voters, but they couldn't find any impact, because the voters had already made up their minds. Then they shifted to doing panels of surveys and measuring how voting decisions were made. Later, they moved on to using sociometric techniques to trace the flow of communications. In contrast to the American voter school at Michigan, which just looked at electoral choice,[14] Lazarsfeld and his colleagues at Columbia looked at how campaigns influence voting decisions, at how electoral choice is processed through campaigns. By the time he was done, Lazarsfeld had a profound understanding of why people voted. I thought it was an enormously interesting research program, and this work had a big impact on some of my students at Caltech. The behavioralist work would be even more relevant today at Caltech, because economics is becoming more behavioral and doing lots of "social-psychological" experiments.

Q: Was there a downside to starting your career at Caltech?
A: Caltech was almost immune to anything having to do with the times, which was both a virtue and a danger. It was a virtue in that you could sit

14. The reference is to *The American Voter*, by Campbell et al. (1960).

things out, wait until the dust settled, and see what you made of them. It was a danger in the sense that you ran a real risk of losing your ability to find meaningful problems, or at least problems that others felt were meaningful.

But it really bothered me to leave Caltech and fit into a box. There were no departments at Caltech, only divisions. You found physicists in the biology and chemistry divisions. Similarly, you found social scientists working with historians. I really liked that there was no structure and that I could move around, across any field with something to offer. As we discussed earlier, I'd gone to a small, liberal arts college where I had done three fields: economics, politics, and literature.

Q: You were clearly out of the mainstream of comparative politics at Caltech. Did you make efforts to stay abreast of what was going on in the field at the time?
A: At one point, I decided to catch up with the Marxist-inspired work that was prominent in the field then. I read through *New Left Review* and looked at Perry Anderson's work (Anderson 1974a, 1974b). I found his work boring, so I mainly read reviews to try and get a feel for it. Then I read Barrington Moore and discovered there was actually some very good stuff in *Social Origins of Dictatorship and Democracy* (Moore 1966). But I was just checking it out, because it was not the kind of work I was engaged in. I found it too macro. Moore does have a nice research design, at least conceptually, but he does not execute case analyses in a controlled way. What I need is narrative, stories, and individuals making choices. I need institutions and things that really come alive. I have to be able to touch it. I don't need big, broad structural arguments. I want stories that allow me to see the problem from the point of view of the people making the choices. In Barrington Moore's work I have a sense of structure, but I don't have a sense of choice.

Duke and Harvard

Q: After sixteen years at Caltech, you moved to Duke University in 1985. What was Duke like?
A: Duke was terrific. The department was already a good one and had a configuration that could make it intellectually powerful: the comparativists— Allan Kornberg, the superb chair; Peter Lange, now provost at Duke; and Herbert Kitschelt—and the normative theorists—Michael Gillespie, Ruth Grant, Tom Spragens—embraced the movement toward empirical and analytic rigor. In many departments, those portions of the discipline block such a change. So change we did. We hired well, hired a lot, and produced a remarkable stream of absolutely first-rate graduate students who got jobs at the top universities in the field.

I had moved to Duke because Margaret, my wife, had been offered a job there as vice-provost. The provost, Philip Griffiths, was in the midst of radically upgrading the faculty and she plunged into the currents that he unleashed, seeking to turn his goals into sustainable arrangements. When Griffiths later left, then she, too, had to step aside. And it was time for us to move on.

I was sad to leave Duke; I loved it there—extremely bright students, great graduate students, and a small and devoted faculty, which has continued to get better. Leaving was also ironic, because Bob Keohane was just coming there from Harvard as I was leaving, and he and his wife, Nannerl, were people I liked and admired. Then John Aldrich, Mike Munger, and a slew of first-rate junior people came. It's a great department.

Q: When you left Duke in 1993, why did you choose Harvard over other places?
A: In choosing where to go, I balanced off career and personal considerations. I knew that realistically this could be our last move and I wanted to end up in a place I could think of as home. So Margaret and I came home—back to Boston, where we started our lives together, and rehabbed the house in Connecticut in which I had grown up, listening to so many debates about politics. We now use the place to keep my family together—we bring in my brothers and sister, their spouses and kids to eat and talk. We count ourselves lucky to have had such great lives.

Q: How has your experience at Harvard been?
A: Harvard has been less straightforward, but it seems now to be moving in directions that I feel are important. The backing for empirical and formal work has improved a lot. I had wanted to leave my mark by bringing African studies to Harvard, and that has happened, not because of me, but because of Harvard's president, Larry Summers, and the social historian Emmanuel Akyeampong. The highlight of the place for me, though, has been the flow of extraordinary students, both at the graduate and undergraduate levels. I enjoy watching "my" graduate students learn and grow as scholars and as people. They are performing feats of learning in graduate school that surpass anything I could have achieved at that point in my life. They are extraordinary.

The Rational Choice Revolution

Q: You were a leading figure in the movement that emerged in the 1980s and 1990s to bring rational choice theory and the formal methodologies used in economics and the study of American politics into

the field of comparative politics.[15] What are your reflections on the rational choice revolution in comparative politics? Did you self-consciously seek to play a central role in this transformation?

A: No. I felt I was on the margins of the profession, and I was happy being there. I mean, I was an Africanist. You don't become an Africanist to be mainstream. And going to a place like Caltech wasn't a mainstream thing to do. As long as I could get published and stay active in the profession, that was fine. I was perfectly happy doing what I was doing.

Q: How do you explain your arrival, and the arrival of rational choice theory, into the mainstream of comparative politics by the 1990s?
A: It happened to me. It just happened.

Q: When did you realize it had happened, that you had moved from the margins to the center of the field?
A: Things got really interesting in the early 1980s during the Popkin-Scott debate, because people knew I had been studying peasant decision making from a choice-theoretic perspective.[16] The Popkin-Scott debate about the behavior of peasants opened the possibility for talking about substantive problems in the realm of comparative politics in terms I was comfortable with and had been working in. That debate stayed around for a while, and it was the bridge that connected rational choice theory to a wider audience.

Q: Still, peasants were marginal actors from the standpoint of most political scientists. How did rational choice theory make the leap to becoming a widely accepted way to study the behavior of politicians?
A: Two things happened in the world that helped bring rational choice theory into the mainstream of American political science. First, the global wave of economic liberalization transformed even socialist economies into market economies. Second, and more important for political science, democratization happened across the world. As a result, people in comparative politics suddenly had to learn what the Americanists had been studying for thirty years. I was very lucky to have taught American politics at Caltech for much of that time and to have been comfortable with it. This helped me be influential with the growing number of students in comparative politics who wanted to understand the work that had been done in the American politics field.

15. See, for example, Bates (1988, 1997b).
16. The Scott-Popkin debate on "moral peasants" versus "rational peasants" generated great interest during the 1980s (Scott 1976; Popkin 1979). See the interview in Chapter 11 with James Scott.

The Comparative Politics Section of the American Political Science Association

Q: You served as president of the Comparative Politics Section of the American Political Science Association during 1995–97. What is your assessment of how the section has evolved since its founding in 1989?[17]
A: Peter Lange and the others who founded the section decided to make it entrepreneurial and contentious, not consensual. The section had a run under its first several presidents. I really loved it because people were raising hell and arguing about what was good comparative politics, what was bad comparative politics, and why. The comparative politics section was having a blast. Then various nameless figures decided they wanted to restore peace and order in the valley. As a result, all the debates are over, and nobody is yelling at each other anymore. That's really sad, because taking ideas, running with them to an extreme, and debating them is a great way to learn and grow. Since the comparative politics section was neutered about two-and-a-half years ago, it's become sort of boring.

Q: Your presidential letter in the section's newsletter concerning the status of area studies (Bates 1996) sparked quite a controversy.[18] **You argued for closer engagement between fieldwork and formal theory and, more generally, between area studies and the discipline of political science. Yet some saw your goal as trying to kill area studies in political science. What is your assessment of this controversy?**
A: I got a bum rap, dang it. Have you read the section's newsletter before I became president? Compared to my two predecessors as president, David Laitin and Ronald Rogowski, I was Mister Nice Guy. For example, Laitin proposed that all of comparative politics be moved to the History Department, keeping only formal theoretical work in political science.

Q: Why were you cast as the villain?
A: I don't know. Maybe because I was the third guy to speak up on the subject and for some reason it caught on. What I was trying to do was find complementarities, not rivalries, between area studies and formal theory. But the rivalries part got isolated, quoted, and passed on.

Q: Do you regret your intervention in this controversy?
A: No. What I regret is how the *Chronicle of Higher Education* reported the exchange (Shea 1997). I had it out with the *Chronicle*'s reporter over that. He

17. For the perspectives of Bates's predecessor and successor as president of the Comparative Politics Section of APSA, see the interviews with David Laitin and David Collier in Chapters 16 and 15.

18. See also Bates (1997c, 1997d).

had a story he wanted to write, and he interviewed a lot of Political Science departments, including Harvard's, to go over cases where he thought people had been denied promotion and tenure because they had done area studies work rather than formal theory. He finally found one case, in Michigan. But the woman had put everything except the kitchen sink into her case, sex discrimination, age discrimination, and so on. So, that case was clearly not about the issue of area studies versus formal theory. When he published the story, all the contentious material about the relationship between area studies and formal theory was put on the front page. The points I had made in my writings about moving toward synthesis, complementarities, and reconciliation were buried on the second page. When I met him at the American Political Science Association's annual meetings, I told him I thought he had really done a number on this.

Q: What is your view on how area studies have evolved in political science during the five years since this exchange? Are people who do area studies research more engaged now with the broader discipline?
A: In my own department at Harvard, the area studies people certainly do a wonderful job. I don't want to work with kids who don't know something. This means they have to do fieldwork and they have to know a time and a place really well. They can get that knowledge from people who have spent their entire lives working in an area, China, Russia or, in my case, Africa. But all my area studies colleagues at Harvard are also very open about getting their students trained so they can get good jobs and prosper in the field. So they push them to work with people like Gary King and Ken Shepsle. At Harvard, it's a very healthy balance. I can't say what it's like at other places.

Q: What are your thoughts about the Perestroika movement that emerged in 2000 calling for reform of the political science profession?[19]
A: I was on leave the year that was happening. It was an e-mail phenomenon, and I was off the Internet and never saw the traffic. So I missed a lot of that. Some of it sounded silly, some of it misinformed. One grievance concerned how elections are run for offices of the American Political Science

19. In 2000, a scholar writing as "Mr. Perestroika" circulated an anonymous manifesto calling for reform of the *American Political Science Review* (*APSR*), the American Political Science Association (APSA), and the political science profession in general. Mr. Perestroika voiced concern that many leaders in the profession did not read or submit to the *APSR*, that the APSA's council and the *APSR*'s editorial board were chosen undemocratically by their predecessors, and that the *APSR* was focused on technical methods, rather than important substantive questions about politics. This scholar's frustration resonated with a large number of political scientists and generated much discussion and debate in the profession. On the Perestroika movement, see Eakin (2000), Monroe (2005), and the interview in Chapter 11 with James Scott, a leading figure in this movement.

Association. But the only requirement to run against the slate proposed by the Association's Nominating Committee is enough signatures. I do not see that as a conspiracy of inside brokers. It's probably a good thing I wasn't around at the time, because the whole thing would have just pissed me off.

Students

Q: What is your approach to training graduate students?
A: First of all, they have to do fieldwork. I don't work with anybody who does not do fieldwork. Also, I like to have students explain to me what they are trying to do and then explain the point at which they get stuck, where something does not work out the way it's supposed to and they feel their research program might collapse. I find that's the most interesting place to start, because moments of failure are often very pregnant. Why didn't it work out? What was wrong with the original idea? Was it an unanticipated variable? Was the problem not right? What's missing? What can we learn from this apparent failure? How would you fix it? If you can turn the way they are thinking a little bit, or turn the problem over a little, you can help get students unstuck.

I was in San Diego last week talking to a bunch of graduate students, and one woman was very disappointed because her thesis had completely collapsed. There was a survey she couldn't do because the Palestinians had just done something, and she thought she had lost her whole research design. I listened for a moment and said, "I don't believe you. I don't think your thesis has collapsed. Let's put it up on the board and see what variation you have still got to work with." Just because she couldn't run a survey didn't mean her research had collapsed. She could still solve a problem.

Q: What qualities distinguish the best students?
A: It varies enormously from student to student. The main thing is passion: if they really care about what they are working on, they will do it well. But they have to make caring work *for* them, not against them. Sometimes they care so much about an issue or problem that scholarship seems a very detached way to get at it. But if they can see that scholarship will give them a voice or a position from which they can effectively address what they care about, then passion can be very powerful.

One book I almost always assign to students is Grant McConnell's *Public Power and American Democracy* (1966). It's a contentious book with a moral vision. McConnell is indignant about the privatization of the public domain and the way that power is used to transform public purposes into private advantage. The book gives you a reason to care, a reason to get pissed off and join the author in the joy of the chase. And McConnell knows what he is talking about, because he has a real knowledge of politics in the different substantive policy areas he studies. The book offers a very nice characterization of a problem and why we should care about it. It's an effective way of getting rational choice political scientists into politics.

The Achievements and Future of Comparative Politics

Q: Looking back over the thirty-five years you have been a political scientist, what has comparative politics accomplished? What have we learned?

A: We have a pretty good understanding of elections and campaigning. Our ability to make predictions is not great, but we understand pretty well how voters decide who they are going to support and how politicians decide how they are going to campaign. Certainly, migration looks the same the world over. I think you could explain migration anywhere without much difficulty. I'm hoping we will reach that point with the phenomenon of state breakdown.

Q: Why have we achieved a better understanding of elections and migration than state breakdown?

A: One reason is that a hell of a lot more research has been done on elections and migration. Political scientists have been studying voting systematically since at least the 1940s. And a pretty good set of studies exists on the determinants of migration in most parts of the world. But we only have something like eighty-one state breakdowns since 1950. That's not a lot of data.

But if you're looking for a repertoire of findings, like they have in physics, we do not have very many in the social sciences. Probably the only regularity we have in comparative politics is the Aristotle-Lipset hypothesis (Lipset 1959) that the wealthier a country gets, the more likely it is to be a democracy because of the expanding size of the middle class. Lipset came up with that hypothesis in the 1950s, then we went through the craziness of the democratic breakdowns of the 1960s and lost Brazil and Argentina. Then, with the third wave of democracy in the 1970s and 1980s, those cases and others snapped back onto the regression line. That's a fairly powerful regularity, and it's one of the few we have. In the future, we are likely to get cumulative results in research on varieties of electoral systems and institutions, work that advances the agenda set by Gary Cox and others at the University of California, San Diego.

Q: You have argued that scholars with area studies expertise should continuously strive to make contributions to the broader discipline of political science (Bates 1996). As you put it, they should be prepared to answer the question, "What has the study of your area contributed to the broader discipline?" (Bates 1997c, 169). So, what has the study of Africa, the area on which your research focuses, contributed to political science?

A: One of the all-time great contributions of African Studies concerns the anthropological understanding of government and societies. This partly stems from the fact that in Africa land is abundant and people are scarce, whereas in Asia, for example, people are abundant and land is scarce. When people are scarce, creating rights over people becomes a really important objective. This is one reason why Africa has had such dense anthropological coverage: because people are the scarce factor, all sorts of very complex relationships formed to extract the benefits of that scarce factor.

Regarding its contribution to political science, the study of Africa reveals very strikingly the political premise for the good life: without political order there is not much you can do. Also, I have increasingly realized that the study of Africa can help us better understand the relationship between politics and economic growth. The two outliers in the growth literature are Africa and Asia, and I think the quality of governance partly explains why, over the past forty years, the Asian countries performed far better than was expected, whereas the African countries performed far worse.

Frontiers of Research

Q: What is your overall assessment of the current state of comparative politics?

A: The field has gotten fairly boring. For example, research on the creation of market economies and the domestic impact of economic liberalization and trade opening has reached diminishing returns. A lot of students are being turned on to that topic now, but I don't know what is left to do. The same thing has happened with research on democratization. Not that it's all been answered, but the work that has been done still has not been digested. We need a panel or review article to take stock of what we know in these two areas. The shock to the discipline generated by the end of the Cold War, the collapse of communism, and the debt crisis has played out, and I don't see where a new sense of urgency will come from in comparative politics.

Q: Are there any research areas you find more promising than economic liberalization and democratization?

A: I think violence and state failure need to be looked at. Also, now that the second and third rounds of elections are occurring in many of the new democracies that emerged in the 1990s, the study of democratic institutions and varieties of institutions could yield a new stream of research. That's an area of research with variation, large Ns, and theory. So that could be where one frontier lies.

The other frontier is culture, especially the blending of rational choice theory and culture, because people manipulate culture and use it for political purposes. I don't think we understand how they do it. How do you mobilize people with symbols, rhetoric, arguments, similes, metaphors, and historical allusions? We know people do that, but how does it work? We don't understand why intellectuals are powerful. There are all sorts of things having to do with the role of debate, argument, and metaphor that we need to grasp in order to understand politics.

I just taught a course with Ken Shepsle called "The Economists Are Coming." We taught the new books on political economy by Persson and Tabellini (2000) and by Grossman and Helpman (2001). Part of what we are trying to do is write a review article on what political scientists should learn from economists and what economists should learn from political scientists. One thing the economists need to know, but clearly have no intuition about, concerns the role of debate and argument. On the other hand, when we look at our own work, we political scientists don't cover that either. We know a certain type of communication is important, but we don't do anything with that insight. We need to get a handle on discourse, language, metaphor, symbolism. The politics of interpretation and communication is really important (Bates, Figueiredo, and Weingast 1998).

Q: It is interesting that you are drawn now to these themes, because, as we discussed earlier, culture and communication were a central focus of the MIT program in the 1960s when you were a graduate student there.
A: Except that now we need to study culture the right way, that is, by building a theory about it that we test.

Conclusion

Q: What advice can you offer to graduate students in comparative politics?
A: The way to use graduate school is to take advantage of the fact that you can get help. If you have a hard time learning languages, then learn languages. If you have a hard time learning mathematics, then get as much training in mathematics as you can. I always felt that if people gave me the reading list I could read and learn what was available on my own, but I sure as hell was not going to understand statistics unless I got help with it. The

other advice I have is to go into the field and then come back and talk to people about it. It is important to process your fieldwork in discussion with other people. A lot of our students go off to Central Asia, for example, and then go to Washington to write up the dissertation. They mail in their thesis without having talked it through and worked it out with other people. That's a real loss. Finally, get to know your classmates well. They are going to be your best friends, hopefully, for the rest of your life.

15

David Collier

Critical Junctures, Concepts, and Methods

David Collier has made major contributions to comparative politics through his carefully conceptualized research on authoritarianism, democracy, and corporatism in Latin America. He has also been a leading figure in the field of methodology, publishing numerous influential works on concept analysis, as well as offering a new perspective on the relationship between qualitative and quantitative methods.

Collier's early work includes quantitative cross-national research on political regimes, corporatism, and social policy, as well as an exploration of the links between regime change and public policy toward squatter settlements in Peru, which was published as *Squatters and Oligarchs* (1976). In his edited volume *The New Authoritarianism in Latin America* (1979), a landmark study in the literature on national political regimes, Collier and collaborators explore alternative explanations for the rise of authoritarianism in Latin America in the 1960s and 1970s.

His most sweeping work on Latin America, the fruit of over a decade of research, is *Shaping the Political Arena* (1991), coauthored with Ruth Berins Collier. This book, one of the most ambitious and systematic studies of Latin American politics ever published, offers an in-depth analysis of eight countries across five decades. *Shaping the Political Arena* seeks to explain contrasting regime outcomes, such as military coups against democracies, as historical legacies of how labor was incorporated into national political institutions. In addition to making a fundamental contribution to the study of politics in Latin America, the book has had a significant influence on the broader field of comparative politics. Its theoretical framework of "critical junctures" is regarded as one of the most systematic, explicitly elaborated models in the historical institutionalist literature. Moreover, the book's careful, case-based comparative analysis is viewed as an exemplar of methodologically rigorous qualitative research.

This interview was conducted by Gerardo Munck in Berkeley, California, on July 8, 2003.

A second strand of Collier's work focuses on methodology. This research addresses issues of concept formation and measurement, emphasizing the procedures used in the comparative, largely qualitative, literature on democracy, authoritarianism, and corporatism. It also discusses the wide range of tools used by qualitative researchers, explores procedures for concept formation and evaluating measurement validity that apply to both qualitative and quantitative work, and examines commonalities and differences between qualitative and quantitative methods in part from the perspective of statistical theory. These latter themes are addressed especially in *Rethinking Social Inquiry* (2004), a volume coedited with Henry Brady.

Collier was born in Chicago in 1942. He received his B.A. from Harvard University in 1965 and his Ph.D. in political science from the University of Chicago in 1971. He has taught at Indiana University, Bloomington (1970–78), and at the University of California, Berkeley (1978–present). He was president of the Comparative Politics Section of the American Political Science Association (APSA) in 1997–99, vice-president of APSA in 2001–2, and founding president of the Qualitative Methods Section of APSA in 2002–3. He was elected to the American Academy of Arts and Sciences in 2004.

Training, Intellectual Influences, and Dissertation Research

Q: You grew up in Chicago and your parents were academics. How do you think these early years influenced your subsequent academic work?

A: Growing up in the community of the University of Chicago did place me in the midst of what was then, and remains today, one of the most stimulating social science communities in the world. Many of the major names in social science of that period—in the 1940s and 1950s—lived just down the block or around the corner. I come from a family of anthropologists, and my parents were both affiliated with the Anthropology Department at the university, though both also had employment elsewhere. Robert Redfield and Fred Eggan were close family friends, and on the basis of childhood associations, I later on found it easy to place in perspective Redfield's classic study of a Mexican village (1930) and Eggan's presidential address for the American Anthropological Association (1954), in which he explored the "method of controlled comparison" in anthropology. It is curious how this methodological agenda came back to the center of my attention many years later.

I went to the University of Chicago "Laboratory School," and classmates included Stephen Stigler—son of the eminent economist—who became a prominent statistician and went on to write his magisterial *History of Statistics;* and Michael Rothschild—whom I had known since nursery school and who later did innovative work on decision making under uncertainty. Mike was coauthor of one of the papers for which Joseph Stiglitz won the Nobel Prize, as well as the purveyor of numerous quips over the years—for example, "Economics is about that part of happiness that money can buy."

Q: **What are your first political memories?**
A: The 1950s were certainly complicated times politically. In the first half of the decade, various colleagues and friends of my parents were subject to damaging accusations of disloyalty during the McCarthy period, and I recall my father on more than one occasion testifying on their behalf to help them retain jobs and security clearance for classified work. These family friends included a student of my father's, John Murra, who had been in the Abraham Lincoln Brigade in the Spanish Civil War, and who went on to become a prominent ethnographer of the Andes. Murra later introduced the creative concept of the "vertical archipelago" for systems of cultivation in the Andes characterized by a strong integration of cultivation at different altitudes. This became a nice piece of inventive concept formation for me to think about.

Everyone in my parents' generation within the family was actively involved in the New Deal, in part following the lead of my paternal grandfather, John Collier Sr. Beginning in the 1910s, he had been a crusader for social reform and social justice in the United States, and he later became a member of Franklin Roosevelt's brain trust. However, by the 1950s I would say that we were simply devoted "Adlai Stevenson Democrats,"[1] frustrated by the blandness of the Eisenhower years.

Q: **How did you become interested in political science and comparative politics?**
A: In my undergraduate years at Harvard, beginning in the fall of 1959, it was pretty easy to be interested in politics. Momentum was building for John F. Kennedy's run for the presidency, many Harvard faculty were involved in the Kennedy campaign, and at Harvard there was a contagious sense of political excitement and political possibilities. One also remembers vividly certain terrifying and tragic moments: walking through Harvard Square at the height of the Cuban Missile Crisis; exactly where I was in Widner Library when we received the news of Kennedy's assassination; and then the vivid images in the days following the killing of Lee Harvey Oswald.

For one year I was an English major—I think due to my interest in poetry

1. Stevenson was the Democratic presidential candidate in 1952 and 1956.

and in writing—but I switched to government. Samuel Beer's Social Studies 2 introduced me to Max Weber, and H. Stuart Hughes's course on European intellectual history left me fascinated by the evolution of European thought over the nineteenth and twentieth centuries. But more than anything it was my first reading of Seymour Martin Lipset's *Political Man* (1960a) that showed me how big, fascinating questions, along with a variety of specific hypotheses about politics and political change, can be addressed through astute comparisons. I found the book breathtaking. The same academic term that I read Lipset's book, I also took my first statistics course. Although *Political Man* was not very statistical, the juxtaposition of the ideas about inference introduced through the statistics course, combined with the analytic power of Lipset's book, greatly extended my horizon, and was doubtless a key early step in sparking my interest in methodology.

Other memorable experiences at Harvard included Samuel Huntington's remarkable course on political development, which I took the same semester that he published his compelling *World Politics* article, "Political Development and Political Decay" (Huntington 1965), which in turn led to his book, *Political Order in Changing Societies* (Huntington 1968). It was an exciting course. Though Huntington was not a specialist on the Third World, he had a flair for coming up with engaging arguments and hypotheses. Another invaluable course on political change was Rupert Emerson's "From Empire to Nation," which provided a masterly overview of the decolonization in Asia and Africa (Emerson 1960). I recall a key visiting lecturer in that course—Aristide Zolberg—who later was Ruth Berins Collier's dissertation chair at Chicago, and has been a career-long friend and colleague. On the side of sociology, I was fascinated by the ideas about social structure conveyed by George Homans, whose book *English Villagers of the Thirteenth Century* (Homans 1941) provided a striking example of drawing interesting ideas about social structure out of archival materials, involving a society that had existed many centuries before. Homans's famous "quarter deck" speaking style made him a memorable lecturer. I also took a course on political sociology with Talcott Parsons.

Q: In 1965 you started graduate school in political science at the University of Chicago. Why did you select Chicago?
A: Political science at Chicago periodically loses large numbers of its faculty, and then goes through an exciting period of rebuilding. I had been told that the department was in the midst of precisely such a period of rebuilding, and this advice was on target. Susanne and Lloyd Rudolph and Aristide Zolberg had just arrived, and Leonard Binder had come a couple of years before, yielding a newly fortified comparative politics group. Theodore Lowi was just arriving from Cornell and, along with the vivid ideas spinning out

of his new work on "arenas of power" (Lowi 1964), he had a powerful instinct for mentoring graduate students long before that was a standard practice—and before we even had *mentoring* as a standard term. Building on my prior course with Talcott Parsons, I studied with David Easton and gained leverage moving from the details of politics and society to more generic analysis that went well beyond these details. Outside the Political Science Department, this was the period when the "Committee on New Nations," involving such faculty as Clifford Geertz and Edward Shils, was active at Chicago, exploring the large social science agendas opened by the proliferation of new nation-states in the Third World.

Nathan Leites—a close associate and collaborator of Harold Lasswell—had come to Chicago two years before, and he was a strong influence. Although I never took a formal course from him, sitting in on his brilliant seminars taught me a lot about careful, terse argumentation. In Leites's vocabulary, the most grave—and in his view, unfortunately common—defect of arguments in political science was that they are "banal." Students awaited this epithet with dread as they presented their own ideas in seminars. I believe that this concern of Leites remains highly relevant today—as one worries that some of the most technically elegant forms of analysis in political science yield findings that are, in fact, sometimes banal.

In addition to my work with these faculty members, I had the good fortune of receiving a NIMH Training Fellowship in Social Research at Chicago's National Opinion Research Center (NORC).[2] This training program in quantitative analysis and survey research offered what was certainly modest training in methodology by today's standards. We invested large amounts of time in carrying around long boxes of IBM cards, running them through counter sorters, and receiving instruction in how—if one had unbelievable levels of tenacity—it was possible to calculate correlations, and even do factor analysis, on what by now seem like ancient Monroe Calculators. Toward the end of the time at Chicago, Norman Nie and his entire SPSS group had arrived from Stanford University,[3] so attention shifted to lugging the boxes of IBM cards over to the campus computer center in the evening and then returning in the morning to pick up the printout. By today's standards, pretty slow turnaround!

Notwithstanding these headaches, by the norms of the time this program offered a fairly substantial level of methodological training, and again extended my intellectual horizon. Further, precisely the low-tech character of the program lent itself to teaching valuable skills and topics: for exam-

2. At the time the NIMH (National Institutes of Mental Health) was providing extensive basic training in the social sciences.

3. SPSS stands for Statistical Package for the Social Sciences, which was perhaps the first user-friendly computer-based statistical software for social scientists.

ple, an instinct for good comparisons, the vivid presentation of cross-tabulations, and an understanding of multi-variant relationships via the Lazarsfeld elaboration model[4]—an understanding that I believe too often does not come into sharp focus in today's methodological teaching. This NIMH-NORC experience was certainly another step toward the development of my subsequent work on methodology.

Q: What about your interest in Latin America?
A: As I noted, I come from a family of anthropologists, who have written books on Peru, Ecuador, and Mexico, and on the Americas more broadly. My father, grandfather, two uncles, and also cousins worked on Latin America. Traveling in Latin America, knowing those countries, studying them, and having a commitment to close collaboration with Latin American scholars—this was a family tradition. As a child and teenager, I had been with my family on two archaeological excavations in Latin America—my father was an archaeologist as well as an anthropologist. From these trips I had many vivid memories and impressions of Latin America, and hence the region was on my mind as a possible focus for my studies. Yet when I arrived in graduate school, Chicago had no Latin Americanist in political science, and although I audited a course from the historian Herbert Klein, it seemed implausible that I should write a dissertation on Latin America.

Then, at the end of my second year, Chicago hired Philippe Schmitter, who arrived from Berkeley amid the awe inspired by the fact that while in graduate school he had coauthored several publications with Ernst Haas (Haas and Schmitter 1964; Schmitter and Haas 1964)—who in turn later became a close colleague and friend of Ruth's and mine at Berkeley. Schmitter studied the region I wanted to study, and quite frankly, his brilliant analytic style and breathtaking framing of Latin American issues immediately made it obvious that I should work on Latin America. In his first term at Chicago, Schmitter taught a general course on Latin America, which among other things introduced ideas about non-pluralistic patterns of interest group politics that became central to his—and my own—later work on corporatism. Schmitter also anticipated by six years—clearly they were working on parallel, but at that time separate, tracks—Guillermo O'Donnell's famous book that sought to unravel the Argentine puzzle (O'Donnell 1973): a country at a high level of socioeconomic development, yet with

---

4. Lazarsfeld's elaboration model or formula, devised as a way of promoting causal analysis in non-experimental research, consists of a set of procedures for data analysis and causal inference that build up larger models from bivariate relationships by successively introducing control variables. That is, the principle behind the elaboration formula is to discover the explanations for an observed relationship between two phenomena (and variables) by means of introducing a third variable. See Kendall and Lazarsfeld (1950) and Lazarsfeld (1955).

patterns of regime crises quite divergent from what one would expect. This first course with Schmitter included myself, Ruth Berins, Karen Remmer—now the prominent Latin Americanist who teaches at Duke University—and a marvelous student from Brazil, Alexandre Barros, who was the first of many Brazilian students whom Schmitter brought to Chicago.

The following spring, Schmitter taught a course on comparative research methods, and this course was another factor in leading me to the kind of methodological work I have subsequently pursued. Schmitter had been strongly influenced by the intellectual ferment in comparative methodology at Berkeley in the 1960s, which included Haas's powerful use of typological methods and Ralph Retzlaff's foray into quantitative cross-national research. Retzlaff's work stimulated Schmitter to enter a period of exploring the potential for quantitative-comparative work on Latin America. That academic term my studies were agreeably disrupted by Ruth's and my marriage in March, but nonetheless this course gave me many ideas about methodology.

Q: What were some of the key books you read in graduate school at Chicago?

A: Let me respond narrowly by mentioning one line of analysis reflected in books—that came to be important to me—written around that time by researchers at Chicago. By then, scholars were reading a manuscript version of Schmitter's book on Brazil (1971). It produced a lot of excitement, not only among Latin Americanists, but also among scholars working on American politics. They saw it as giving a valuable new, non-pluralist perspective for looking at interest group politics. Besides Schmitter, three other faculty at Chicago, all of whom worked on the United States, were also concerned with this theme. One was Lowi, and another was Grant McConnell, who at that time was finishing his book *Private Power and American Democracy* (McConnell 1966). A central theme of McConnell's research focused on how interest groups are shaped by the wider systems of political power in which they are located. This can yield a system of group politics that is often highly noncompetitive, in which the group's role in representing its constituents becomes ambiguous—as does, indeed, the very definition of who those constituents are. This form of group politics is quite distinct from an image of interest groups involving the wide-ranging, competitive interaction among different groups, and with the state. With the publication of David Greenstone's book on labor politics (1969), and with the work of Lowi, McConnell, and Schmitter, it seemed that Chicago might develop a distinctive, non-pluralist school of analysis. But this did not coalesce: McConnell soon left for Santa Cruz, and Lowi went back to Cornell.

Nonetheless, this was an influential climate of discussion, and these issues later emerged in sharp relief in the Latin American field in research on corporatism. Within the framework of this discussion, we can define corporatism as a noncompetitive system of group politics, in which systems of private power, as in McConnell's framework, or of state power, as in Schmitter's subsequent work on state corporatism (Schmitter 1974, 1977), constrain competition among groups. In these contexts, the organized groups function only in part as "representatives" of their constituencies, in that they play a role of mediation between the larger system of power—whether private or public—and their presumed "constituents." This body of work—above all, that of McConnell and Schmitter—was enormously helpful in placing within a larger framework my subsequent thinking about different patterns of interest politics, as well as about different types of authoritarian regimes.

Q: What impact did the domestic situation in the United States, from the McCarthy period to the Vietnam War, have on you?
A: I commented before on the McCarthy period. Regarding the upheavals of the late 1960s, I was away from Chicago doing fieldwork during the most traumatic moments. I was not in Chicago during the tumultuous convention of the Democratic Party in the summer of 1968, and I missed the height of the protests over Vietnam and Cambodia that took place at the University of Chicago. So I was probably less wrapped up in the climate of the times within the United States than others who were in place at their home institutions during 1968–69.

However, I was also looking at these issues from Latin America, in part seeing them in the context of the hostility of the U.S. government toward the post-1968 military government in Peru. This hostility was triggered in part by the terms of the U.S. "Hickenlooper Amendment," which mandated a strong response to the expropriation of U.S. property abroad. But the reaction of many U.S. scholars working in Peru also reflected broader dismay that the United States did not respond more positively to this military government, which was after all trying to address problems that underlay the Peruvian political stalemate of the 1960s. This was a time when a great many U.S. researchers in Peru felt little sympathy for U.S. government policies on any level.

Q: Regarding your doctoral dissertation, your initial idea was to study the Peruvian congress.
A: I was intrigued by Lowi's ideas about arenas of power, according to which different political relationships crystallize around different types of public policies (Lowi 1964). And I had also been working with Duncan McRae, who was one of the first scholars to engage in the quantitative analysis of

legislative roll call voting. Given my interest in Latin America, I thought I could take Lowi's ideas about the different power relationships that crystallize around different public policies, and McRae's tools for analyzing legislative behavior, and apply them to the Peruvian congress. The mid-1960s had been an interesting period of political stalemate in Peru, with a legislature controlled by APRA[5] essentially blocking President Belaunde's reform program. It seemed that studying the legislature with some new empirical tools would be a productive enterprise.

The problem was that I arrived in Peru just a couple of days after the Velasco military coup in October 1968.[6] The legislative archive had been closed by the military government, this interesting political stalemate had been resolved by military force, and in the context of the dramatic regime change, the idea of studying the legislature had become impractical, and it seemed a lot less relevant. I ended up switching my dissertation topic.

Q: This is a graduate student's nightmare, to be in the field and suddenly have to rethink the topic of a dissertation. How did you pick a new topic?
A: Well, first of all, my research was supported by a Latin American Teaching Fellowship, a program administered by Tufts University. This fellowship paid for a full fifteen months in Peru, giving me time to adjust my topic. Also, the fellowship required that I teach a course during my stay, so it put me in touch with a spectrum of people who were invaluable in helping me find a new focus for my research. In the first months of my visit, I offered jointly with the Italian sociologist Giorgio Alberti an introductory statistics course at the Instituto de Estudios Peruanos (Institute of Peruvian Studies), the leading social science research center in Peru. This institute had carried out extensive studies of the squatter settlements of Lima, thereby strongly drawing them to my attention. A series of other circumstances also encouraged my focus on the squatter settlements. At the hotel where I was first staying, I encountered a fellow Harvard graduate who was part of an international aid group working on squatter settlements. Ruth and I went out to visit squatter settlements with him a couple of times at the beginning of the stay in Lima.

I also had the good fortune that a graduate student who was just returning to the United States gave me several key articles on squatter settlements that conveyed what was then the established image—that these communi-

5. Alianza Popular Revolucionaria Americana—the American Popular Revolutionary Alliance.

6. The coup led by General Juan Velasco Alvarado was particularly noteworthy because it inaugurated a left-leaning military regime that contrasted starkly to the right-wing military regimes that dominated much of South America in the 1960s and 1970s.

ties were formed as the residents illegally seized land and often valiantly fought off the police and other authorities, in order to secure precarious housing. These settlements, presumed to be illegal, were highly visible around the periphery of Lima, and their population at that time was roughly 1.5 million, approximately one-quarter of the city's population.

The idea that began to take shape in my study was motivated by a question posed to me by a Peruvian friend early in the research process. He asked how these settlements could possibly have been allowed to form, given the degree to which they appeared to be an affront to the system of private property. Until the 1968 military coup, private property had, after all, been a crucial foundation for the power of the Peruvian oligarchy, and the widespread violation of private property around the capital appeared to threaten this foundation. My dissertation and the subsequent book (Collier 1976) sought to address this puzzle.

Initially, I encountered a few hints that, although the squatters sometimes did valiantly fight off the police, many times there were various kinds of involvement by the government, political parties, and even landowners in encouraging settlement formation. The more I looked, the clearer it became that the settlements were embedded in a wider political and economic system that strongly supported their formation. Hence, I became strongly interested in the politics of squatter settlement formation.

Further, it increasingly appeared that this support for squatter settlement formation was linked to broader choices about cultivating the political support of the poor, about social policy, and about addressing concerns over political radicalization within the squatter settlement population. Thus, squatter settlement politics became a window through which I could analyze the evolving political relationships between the state and the poor, patterns of mobilization and control, populism, and a variety of topics that subsequently have come to have wide currency in the Latin American field, and far beyond. My dissertation thus came to focus on a game of squatters and elites, with some of the elites actually being members of the Peruvian oligarchy. Hence the title of my subsequent book, *Squatters and Oligarchs* (Collier 1976).

Q: How did you reconstruct the history of squatter settlement formation in Lima?
A: My most valuable source of data was a survey I carried out to reconstruct how squatter settlements were formed. From my experience as a training fellow at the National Opinion Research Center (NORC) in Chicago and my knowledge of what was called NORC's "Permanent Community Sample," I knew that surveys could be used not just to interview citizens, but also to generate data on a variety of institutional actors. Correspondingly, I did

a survey of eighty-five communities—involving both highly structured and open-ended questions, focused on early leaders in different squatter communities who had been involved in the actual episode of settlement formation. I did many of the interviews myself, and colleagues I knew through the Instituto de Estudios Peruanos helped me find skilled interviewers who, with careful supervision, applied the questionnaire in additional settlements.

A second principal source was an archive maintained by the Peruvian newspaper, *La Prensa,* which encompassed a remarkable collection of newspaper clippings and other kinds of data, including extensive information on squatter settlements. This kind of "hard copy" archive is difficult to imagine in today's world of computerized databases. I will always be grateful to my fellow graduate student, Liisa North, who secured my access to this archive. It had many hundreds of clippings and other information on squatter settlements and squatter settlement formation, and was invaluable to my research. I then connected my interviews, these data from the archive, and a wide spectrum of data from government housing offices and other sources to reconstruct the history of squatter settlement formation.

The picture that emerged showed a fascinating spectrum of different economic and political goals behind the promotion of squatter settlement formation, ranging from many direct interventions by the president and political parties seeking political support, to an initiative by a member of the economic elite seeking to launch a political career, to efforts by urban landowners to clear inner-city slums in order to develop the land as valuable real estate. These landowners would hire people to help organize the squatters for a land invasion, thereby clearing valuable inner-city land.

The answer to my friend's motivating question was thus that settlement formation was promoted by a complex network of political and economic relationships.

Q: It seems that you had a positive interaction with colleagues while conducting your fieldwork in Peru.
A: Yes. With regard to colleagues in Lima, two of whom I got to know through the Instituto de Estudios Peruanos in Lima were especially important. The leading Peruvian political sociologist Julio Cotler, and also Giorgio Alberti, became close colleagues and friends. My other great friend and collaborator was the Peruvian sociologist Sinesio López, who had long had a strong interest in the squatter settlements, and who provided an enormous amount of help in moving my research along.

I was also in touch with other Ph.D. students from the United States. Jane Jaquette was working on the politics of public policy formation, Liisa North was carrying out her interviewing of APRA leaders in all parts of the country that were centers of APRA strength, Edward Epstein was also working on APRA, and Howard Handelman was in the midst of the interviewing that led to his study of the peasant mobilization that swept the Peruvian Andes in the 1960s. Abraham Lowenthal was working in the Ford Foundation office in Lima, and he was then—as he has always been—a source of astute advice and commentary about research. All of these scholars have, in the intervening decades, made important contributions to the study of Latin American politics. Finally, in a subsequent visit to Lima I interacted extensively with Alfred Stepan, who became a friend and mentor throughout my career.

Q: Did you keep in touch with your dissertation committee as your research in Peru advanced?
A: I made no return trips to the United States, and at that time one could hardly send off an e-mail message, asking for suggestions about research plans. It was also a time when long-distance calls seemed incredibly expensive. I wrote my committee a letter about my new focus, and they wrote back, in principle approving the change. Also, Schmitter was in Argentina toward the end of my stay in Peru, and I went to Argentina and discussed the refocused dissertation with him.

I recall with amusement how Chicago handled the required formal oral exam on the dissertation prospectus. Not long after my return to Chicago, when the field research was already completed, I was invited to a faculty reception at Aristide Zolberg's home. Partway through the reception, Schmitter, Zolberg, and Ira Katznelson precipitously took me into a side room and retroactively conducted the oral exam on my prospectus. What can I say? At least I didn't have an opportunity to become anxious before the exam!

Q: Apart from your research on squatter settlements, what did you learn from observing the first fifteen months of the Velasco government in Peru?
A: This was a dramatic and fascinating period in Peruvian politics. Along with the research on my dissertation, living in Peru at that time played a key role in crystallizing my longer-term research interest in regimes and regime change. During these initial years, the military government was nationalist and populist. This was intriguing from a comparative perspective, because at that time military-authoritarian governments also held power in Argentina and Brazil, and they were following a development model that was internationalist and favorable to foreign capital.

In Peru, the military seized power to break the political stalemate of the 1960s and to implement what were widely perceived as needed reforms. Just days after coming to power, the new government nationalized the

Standard Oil holding that had been a source of great dispute and scandals. This occurred on October 9, the very day we arrived. I recall riding in a taxi from the airport, listening on our tiny portable radio to a curious voice that kept repeating a statement about the nationalization—a voice that, it turned out, was that of President Velasco. Several months later the government nationalized the sugar estates of the north coast, as well as large agricultural holdings in other parts of the country, thereby breaking the back of the Peruvian oligarchy and launching sweeping agrarian reform.

The government thus quickly addressed two parts of the reform agenda that had been stalled in the mid-1960s—involving the issues that had been the focus of the original version of my research project. An elaborate system of popular mobilization was also constructed, called SINAMOS.[7] Although SINAMOS fell far short of what it was intended to accomplish—a not atypical failure with such organizations—the idea of the explicit and very public involvement of the military in popular mobilization was intriguing, and again contrasted dramatically with the experience at that time with the military governments of Argentina and Brazil.

Overall, for my thinking and learning, the experience of being in Peru during this period heightened my interest in the contrasting approaches to policy making and problem solving that emerge under different sequences of national political regimes. A key part of this learning involved the recognition that not only had the democratic regime collapsed at the end of the 1960s, in the midst of dramatic policy failure, but within a few years the military's populist and nationalist initiatives also faltered. This provided the valuable lesson that a key element driving sequences of change in regimes and governments is often policy failure, an idea that would be of recurring concern in my subsequent research.

Research on Authoritarian Regimes and Critical Junctures

Q: You eventually turned your dissertation into a book (Collier 1976). What steps did that involve?
A: In the book version of the squatter settlement project, I went even further in focusing on the connections between regime change and the evolution of policy toward squatter settlements. After completing my fieldwork at the end of 1969, I went back to Peru several times over the next six years and tracked the ongoing evolution of squatter settlements. I gave a number of talks on the project, both in Peru and in the United States, and got further ideas. There is a delicate balance between going back to the field to

---

7. Sistema Nacional de Movilización Social—National System for the Support of Mobilization.

get enough fresh information to stimulate one's thinking and not getting so much new information that one ends up doing the whole project over again. I guess I came out reasonably well on that balance.

In looking at the connections between squatter settlement politics and broader patterns of change, I focused, for example, on a period of paternalistic authoritarianism under an antitrade union populist government, a period that we would now perhaps call neo-liberal, when elite actors sought to encourage autonomy and self-help among the squatters—an approach that anticipated by many years Hernando de Soto's well-known neo-liberal formulation in his book, *The Other Path* (de Soto 1989); a period of sweeping policy commitments during a democratic period of competitive party politics; and finally, in the post-1968 authoritarian period under Velasco, a new combination of elements, involving a focus on self-help and political control.

In this sense, I see the analysis as coming back to the themes that had motivated the initial framing of my dissertation, before I had to change the specific topic. Thus, I was concerned with how different political relationships crystallize around alternative public policies. I also see this analysis as a first step toward my continuing interesting in comparing political regimes, and sequences of regime change.

Q: How did your research interests evolve after your first project on Peru?

A: In the 1970s, I explored quantitative cross-national research as a tool for answering questions about political change. This phase of my work included one of my articles that I am most proud of, which analyzed the historical timing of the adoption of social security programs throughout the world (Collier and Messick 1975). That article, published in 1975, anticipated by many years the current proliferation of diffusion studies. I also wrote a quantitative cross-national article exploring the links between the timing of economic growth and regime characteristics in Latin America (Collier 1975)—taking some inspiration from Alexander Gerschenkron (1962).

Most crucially, it was during this period that Ruth Collier and I first received a National Science Foundation (NSF) grant to support an elaborate project collecting cross-national data on labor law. The Argentine lawyer Lila Milutín provided critical help in this effort. Obviously, labor law did not tell the whole story of state-labor relations in Latin America, but even at the level of formal, institutional data, important patterns emerged that led to our *American Political Science Review* article on corporatism that explored the dynamic interaction between inducements versus constraints in the evolution of state-labor relations (R. Collier and D. Collier 1979; see also

D. Collier and R. Collier 1977). That article, in turn, laid part of the foundation for our later book, *Shaping the Political Arena* (R. Collier and D. Collier
1991). Although *Shaping the Political Arena* centrally involved qualitative
comparison, our work during this period played an essential role in pushing us toward a wider comparative view of Latin American politics, as well
as generating important hypotheses that would be explored in our subsequent book.

The New Authoritarianism

**Q: In 1979, you published a widely read collaborative volume, *The New
Authoritarianism in Latin America* (Collier 1979). When did you first
encounter the book that was the focus of your volume, Guillermo
O'Donnell's *Modernization and Bureaucratic Authoritarianism* (1973)?**
A: In late 1972 I learned that this book on regime change by O'Donnell was
about to be published by Berkeley's Institute for International Studies.[8] A
central theme of his book is the relationship between the rise of authoritarianism in Argentina and Brazil in the 1960s and the difficulties associated
with a particular phase of industrial development, and this was the aspect
of his thesis that received the most attention. However, other elements
were also novel: his emphasis on the absolute, rather than the per capita,
size of the modern sector in explaining the rise of authoritarianism; and his
effort to move beyond conventional class categories to look specifically at
"social roles" as being critical to regime dynamics. Specifically, he emphasized the role of technocrats as a social category, and of the popular sector,
which encompassed both the working class, traditionally understood, and
important segments of the lower-middle class. The authoritarian coups in
Chile and Uruguay in 1973—the same year as the publication of O'Donnell's study—certainly caused many scholars to pay even more attention to
his book. At the same time, these new coups raised interesting problems for
certain parts of his argument.

**Q: How did you convene the group of scholars for the conference that
eventually led to *The New Authoritarianism?***
A: In the early to mid-1970s the Social Science Research Council (SSRC) was
supporting a working group on the "State and Public Policy in Latin America," with the goal of launching a more formalized, collaborative research
project. This initiative, which involved conversations among Albert Hirschman, Guillermo O'Donnell, Fernando Henrique Cardoso, Robert Kaufman,

---

8. See Chapter 9 for O'Donnell's discussion of *Modernization and Bureaucratic Authoritarianism*.

Julio Cotler, and myself, went through various false starts over a couple of years.

In the summer of 1975, Louis Wolf Goodman, the Latin American staff person at SSRC, phoned me and asked me to completely rethink the project, and to write a proposal that would provide a new, sharper focus for a collaborative effort. I had gotten to know Goodman a year before when I gave a talk on the squatters project at Yale, and ever since, Goodman has been a key professional colleague and friend.

I thought about Goodman's challenge for a while, and I decided it would be productive to do a project specifically centered on the arguments that O'Donnell had advanced in his book about the rise of a new form of authoritarianism. O'Donnell's thesis was an attractive focus because it raised extremely broad issues and sought to explain outcomes of enormous importance, at the same time that it pinpointed specific arguments and was formulated in such a way that it readily suggested intriguing rival explanations. My thinking in formulating the project benefited from consultations with Abraham Lowenthal and Robert Kaufman, as well as with Benjamin Most. He was a particularly talented graduate student at Indiana University, where I was a non-tenured faculty member, and from his own work on incremental budgeting he had astute instincts about the challenges of analyzing discontinuous patterns of change in regimes and in public policy.

Q: The participants in the project were a fairly diverse set of scholars, with some based in the United States and others in Latin America.[9] How was this group of participants selected?
A: Several of the participants were already involved in the prior SSRC working group, and that interaction was reinforced by the fact that in 1975 Albert Hirschman brought a number of Latin Americanist visitors to the Institute for Advanced Study in Princeton, where I was also affiliated. Hirschman strongly encouraged José Serra to bring his expertise as an economist to write specifically on a key part of the economic side of O'Donnell's arguments, and James Kurth was brought in because of his interesting focus on the timing and sectoral shifts in economic growth and their implications for political change.

Q: Edited volumes are usually little more than a collection of disparate papers. Hence, they often do not have much impact. This was clearly not the case with *The New Authoritarianism*. It had a large impact, and

9. The U.S.-based authors of the chapters of *The New Authoritarianism in Latin America* were David Collier, Albert Hirschman, Robert Kaufman, and James Kurth. The Latin American-based authors were Fernando Henrique Cardoso and José Serra, both from Brazil; Julio Cotler, from Peru; and Guillermo O'Donnell, from Argentina.

even though you had a range of authors with their own ideas, the volume held together as a coherent whole. What is the trick to pulling together that kind of edited volume?

A: The challenge is to work extremely hard, to engage in constructive but interventionist editing—including elements of what we now call "developmental editing"—and to do other things that add coherence. I included in the book my own summary of O'Donnell's framework, a summary that many people found illuminating in helping them grasp his complex arguments. This summary, along with an overview of my perspective on the wider debate, was published in *World Politics* (Collier 1978). I created a glossary that, while not aiming at the impossible goal of completely standardizing usage, made it clear how key terms were being used.

Another key element was the strong focus on O'Donnell's book, which as I just noted raised very broad issues, at the same time that it advanced very specific arguments. Indeed, I recall vividly that Guillermo was shocked at the conference that led to the volume, when he fully realized that the discussion among this set of people, some of whom were pretty eminent, was focused so specifically on his book. Further, my framing of the project—and obviously, the framing of O'Donnell's book—focused on an outcome, or dependent variable, that is, the rise of a new form of authoritarianism, on whose occurrence and dimensions the authors were in agreement. So the contributors to the volume had a well-delineated set of outcomes to explain, and that lent itself to coherence.

Shaping the Political Arena

Q: After *The New Authoritarianism in Latin America,* your next major work was *Shaping the Political Arena,* a broadly comparative study focused on the historical roots of divergent political regimes across eight Latin American countries in the twentieth century.[10] Could you discuss the genesis of this book, which you coauthored with your wife, Ruth Berins Collier? How did it link up with your previous work?

A: *Shaping the Political Arena* might be called a "prequel," as opposed to a sequel, in relation to *The New Authoritarianism*—an expression suggested by Jonathan Hartlyn. Thus, the outcomes that in *The New Authoritarianism* were analyzed within a relatively short time frame were explored in much greater historical depth in our subsequent volume. But more broadly, *Shaping the Political Arena* grew out of a convergence of research interests that Ruth and I had developed.

---

10. The eight countries are Argentina, Brazil, Chile, Colombia, Peru, Mexico, Uruguay, and Venezuela.

My Peru book had focused on regime change. In a short period of time, Peru had experienced a striking spectrum of regime alternatives, as I already noted. After my book on Peru, I had continued to develop my interest in comparing regimes in *The New Authoritarianism,* which sought to account for a broader picture in the pattern of coups, non-coups, and regime outcomes across Latin America in the 1960s and 1970s. So, in all of my prior work, I had been centrally concerned with the comparative analysis of political regimes, which was the outcome to be explained for *Shaping the Political Arena.*

Ruth provided some of the key independent variables. Her first book, which is a remarkable comparative study of the politics of decolonization and post-independence regime change in twenty-six countries of Sub-Saharan Africa, analyzed how different patterns in the introduction of elections and party politics in the period of decolonization were linked to different subsequent trajectories of change, and specifically to the emergence of one-party versus military regimes in the post-independence period (R. Collier 1982a). This work pointed to the value of developing hypotheses about how different forms of participation, mobilization, and control can lead to quite different trajectories of regime evolution. We had begun to explore together, in our work on corporatism starting in 1973–74, some related ideas about how state intervention—involving combinations of mobilization and control, that is, contrasting patterns of inducements and constraints—shaped labor movements in Latin America (D. Collier and R. Collier 1977; R. Collier and D. Collier 1979). These ideas ended up being a central theme in *Shaping the Political Arena.*

Another key source of the puzzle that motivated our book was found in the many single-country studies of party politics, the labor movement, and regime change in the cases we were studying. We were struck by the frequency with which excellent country studies converged in identifying a key period of state building, reform, and often popular mobilization as a formative episode in each country's political history. The rise of Perón in Argentina, the first Vargas period in the 1930s and 1940s in Brazil, and the Cárdenas era in the 1930s in Mexico are obvious examples. Scholars who write on Colombia argue that the 1930s were a turning point, and many experts see the first Ibáñez period—from 1927 to 1931—as a point of inflection in Chile's political history. For each of the eight cases we studied, country monographs highlighted as a crucial watershed the episode we came to designate as the "incorporation period," a period when the state assumed a new role in society, recognized organized labor as a legitimate actor, and, in highly varied ways, sought to institutionalize this role. The first footnote in the book provides an illustrative list of studies that treat these periods as a watershed. We thought it would be an interesting challenge to take what were often inevitably somewhat ad hoc claims about these presumably key transitions, made country by country, and place them in a comparative framework, focusing on the common and contrasting patterns that helped account for distinct starting points, and different trajectories of change.

In the literature on comparative-historical research, there is considerable debate on the use of primary versus secondary sources. Both are important, but we would defend the use of secondary sources on a variety of grounds, including the following: given the large literature for Latin America on topics such as labor movements, political parties, and regime change —spanning many decades in the twentieth century—it would be a great scholarly and intellectual loss if this rich "data set" were not used in comparative research. Careful research with secondary sources specifically meets this challenge. I should add, however, that between the two of us we had also spent time in most of these countries, and we did not merely know them through the secondary material.

Q: During the time you were working on this book there was a great interest in broad comparative-historical work. How did this intellectual context affect you?

A: As we began working on *Shaping the Political Arena*, we had just moved to Berkeley, and I cannot emphasize enough how important Berkeley was in convincing me that it was feasible to carry out a complex, comparative-historical project. Perhaps we can return to this theme later in the interview. Beyond the immediate influence of being at Berkeley, Theda Skocpol's *States and Social Revolutions* (1979) had just appeared and was the focus of much discussion. Cardoso and Faletto's *Dependency and Development* (1979)—sections of which I had read in Spanish in Lima in 1969—became available in English and was being widely used in graduate seminars. Barrington Moore's (1966) *Social Origins of Dictatorship and Democracy*, which I can remember debating in the 1960s, achieved new salience and received much attention in this intellectual environment. All this provided strong encouragement to pursue an ambitious comparative-historical study.

Q: Could you discuss the research process itself?

A: The comparative analysis for *Shaping the Political Arena* evolved in an iterative fashion as we learned more about the cases. We sought to be explicit about what we meant by a critical juncture and how it was to be identified, and about what we meant by the incorporation, aftermath, and heritage periods. The book has a glossary that explores how these categories can be applied across diverse national contexts and diverse historical periods. Further, Chapter 1 lays out what we called the "Critical Juncture

Framework," and I would like to think that it played a valuable role in helping to get the literature on this topic started within political science.

The central argument concerned the dialectical interplay between efforts to mobilize and/or control the labor movement in the incorporation period, and contrasting patterns of mobilization and control in the subsequent periods that we call the aftermath and the heritage of incorporation. These distinct phases, which James Mahoney (2000, 509) has subsequently labeled "reactive sequences," were demarcated by episodes of regime change, the collapse of governments, and policy failure—parallel to those that had originally struck me in Peru.

One of our key insights was that, through these sequences of change, for some cases a greater focus on control in the earlier period yielded more intense mobilization later on, whereas in other cases a greater emphasis on mobilization in the early period later yielded a greater capacity for control. These forces of mobilization and control played a key role in the period of social and economic crisis, and regime change, in the 1960s and 1970s.

We devoted close attention to considering rival explanations and weighing them vis-à-vis available evidence. We did not want to develop a lock-step argument, which claimed that the critical junctures set countries on consistent and unambiguous trajectories of change. Rather, we considered other explanations that potentially deflected these trajectories, or possibly reinforced them. We also tried to weigh carefully rival accounts, presented in country monographs, of historical episodes of major significance to our analysis. These included, for example, the question for Peru of President Leguía's relationship to the labor movement in the late 1910s and early 1920s, debates about the timing of the incorporation period in Argentina, and alternative interpretations of the 1964 coup in Brazil.

Given that we looked closely at these rival interpretations and tried to weigh the evidence with care, one of my regrets is that we did not include an appendix that explicitly discussed these rival explanations, and how we resolved them for the purpose of our analysis. Such an appendix would be a valuable addition to many works in the comparative-historical tradition.

Writing this book was a challenging undertaking, and it took much longer than we had intended. We worked on *Shaping the Political Arena* for ten years and got help along the way from a group of outstanding Berkeley graduate students, above all, James McGuire and Ronald Archer. Would I recommend that other scholars take on such a complex analysis? Well, it certainly would not be a good idea for assistant professors!

Q: What was the division of labor between you and Ruth Collier?
A: In discussing the division of labor, let me first report the insight of my Berkeley colleague Nelson Polsby. He observes that when he has coau-

thored research, both of the authors have done 75 percent of the work. That is a pretty good description of what happened with *Shaping the Political Arena*.

More specifically, I did the basic work on Argentina, Colombia, Peru, and Uruguay, and Ruth focused on Brazil, Chile, Mexico, and Venezuela. I had been interested in the Peru-Argentina pair for some time, specifically since my visit to Argentina while I was doing my dissertation research in Peru. There seemed to be many interesting parallels, as well as contrasts, between them. Both countries had a similar recurring dilemma concerning the banning of their labor-based party, APRA in Peru and the Peronists in Argentina, and appeared to have had parallel regime crises over several decades. Colombia and Uruguay also emerged in our comparisons as an interesting pair of cases, given the strong role of traditional parties and the specific role of these parties in the legitimation and institutionalization of the labor movement. Ruth from an early point became interested in the Mexico-Brazil comparison, and in fact published an article on that comparison early in the project (R. Collier 1982b). From there she expanded her focus to Venezuela and Chile.

Q: The book compares eight Latin American cases. Did you start out with those cases? Did you consider any non-Latin American countries?
A: We had originally planned to include Bolivia and Cuba, which in an earlier period were fascinating cases of labor populism. But it became clear that the eight cases we ended up with were enough of a challenge in terms of our time and energy. Regarding non-Latin American countries, in our initial effort to create a quantitative, cross-national data set on corporatism we scored various countries elsewhere in the world, but including them in the analysis seemed far beyond the scope of what we could possibly accomplish.

Q: Why didn't you publish a short article version of the arguments in *Shaping the Political Arena*?
A: Through the 1980s I either authored or coauthored with Ruth eleven conference papers that presented parts of the book. But we ended up not publishing any of these conference papers, because none adequately captured the overall argument. After we finished the book, we were invited to join an SSRC project with the idea of contributing a summary chapter on the book, but the project never took place. However, Ruth was more bold—and perhaps more talented—than I in writing such summaries. She published an early version of the Brazil-Mexico part of the argument in 1982, and wrote a brief summary of the book's argument in her 1993 article on the impact of internal and external factors on regime change in Latin Amer-

ica in the 1940s. She also introduced many of these ideas in her 1992 monograph on Mexico (R. Collier 1982b, 1993, 1992).

I should add that we did present concise summaries of the argument in
the initial "Overview" chapter, as well as in the concluding chapter. Furthermore, after the initial publication by Princeton University Press in 1991, the
University of Notre Dame Press reissued the book in 2002, with a splendid
introductory statement by Guillermo O'Donnell. For this edition, Ruth and
I wrote a three-page authors' note in which we do provide a very condensed
summary of the argument (R. Collier and D. Collier 2002). Yet I have been
somewhat hesitant about publishing a summary article of our book.

My hesitation about publishing a brief summary is partly connected
with the kind of empirical data employed in work of this type. The evidence
in major respects takes a narrative form—although, at least in our aspiration, a tightly constructed and analytically focused narrative. It simply
takes a lot of space to nail down the arguments for particular countries. In
our case, we covered a period spanning the first decade of the twentieth
century to the 1980s. So we ended up doing a long, elaborate analysis with a
strong grounding in narrative treatment, focused on the evolution of these
countries through what might variously be counted as five or six historical
phases. It would have been more convenient if the book could have been
shorter,[11] because that would have made the argument more accessible.

Q: How was *Shaping the Political Arena* received?

A: It received uniformly excellent reviews, and I think the book stimulated
many scholars to think about the critical juncture framework, to apply it in
their own research, and to work out different parts of our argument for
various countries. That is the kind of reception one wants to have. As mentioned before, I know that many scholars have liked Chapter 1, where we
lay out the critical juncture framework. I think they appreciate our clarity
in discussing critical junctures and path dependence,[12] and also our explicit engagement with rival explanations, through laying out a multivari-
ate perspective on critical junctures. More than a few works of comparative-
historical analysis are not attentive to rival explanations, and I think this is
essential. Indeed, one of the members of the committee that gave the APSA
Luebbert prize to the book specifically commended us for the methodological care with which the arguments were constructed.[13]

11. *Shaping the Political Arena* is 877 pages in length.
12. A critical juncture is a period of crucial change in the history of a given country or other
political unit that is hypothesized to leave a distinctive legacy. Path dependence refers to the
distinctive trajectories of change, within which the range of political alternatives is constrained
by the way the critical juncture occurred.
13. In 1993 *Shaping the Political Arena* was awarded the Gregory M. Luebbert prize for the

Yet there are always frustrations. In the minds of many scholars, the arguments of well-known books too often get reduced to a phrase or slogan. For Barrington Moore—and thus, indirectly, for Gerschenkron—it may be "No bourgeoisie, no democracy," which was only a small part of a vast comparative panorama. For O'Donnell, it is probably "the deepening hypothesis,"[14] which is only one element in a complex, multi-variate argument. In our case, it is "labor incorporation matters." One might speculate that this simplification is in part our punishment for writing an 877-page book. However, this is a standard experience even with shorter books, as with Moore's and O'Donnell's.

Research on Concepts and Methods

Q: After *Shaping the Political Arena,* you started to publish a stream of articles on concepts and methodology. When and why did you decide to focus on methods?
A: My interest in methodology had various sources, as I have already noted, beginning early in my career. The work I did at Indiana—in part with Ruth Collier—included a significant concern with concept analysis, in that both the research on corporatism and on bureaucratic authoritarianism explored the value of working with key concepts at a more disaggregated level. And I should note that the conceptual work on corporatism grew out of a quantitative project, whereas my efforts with the conceptualization of bureaucratic authoritarianism were connected with a line of research that was primarily qualitative. I see my work on concept formation as highly relevant to both traditions.

But it was the experience of coauthoring *Shaping the Political Arena* that decisively led to a sustained period of writing on methods. That book raised many methodological questions. How was one to make viable comparisons of incorporation periods? This required a conceptualization of these episodes that yielded a plausible sorting of cases—both across countries and over time. Yet this sorting was complex, because the whole point of the analysis was that these incorporation periods occurred in different ways. Thus, the analytic categories had to accommodate both similarities and crucial differences. In a world of scholarship sometimes too sharply divided between lumpers and splitters,[15] the book thus sought a middle ground.

"Best Book in Comparative Politics" by the APSA (American Political Science Association) Organized Section for Comparative Politics.

14. This refers to a phase of industrial growth in which countries begin to produce intermediate and capital goods.

15. Lumpers tend to assume that differences are not as important as broad similarities. In contrast, splitters tend to place more emphasis on the ways in which phenomena differ.

Further, it was essential to ask whether these analytic categories were crisply bounded. Alternatively, were they ideal types, which our historical cases approximated to varying degrees? Correspondingly, were we working at a categorical, nominal level of measurement, or were our categories ordinal? Obviously, if these descriptive claims are not addressed satisfactorily, explanatory claims are on shaky grounds. Further, one may ask to what extent the causal inferences are derived from the cross-tabulation of cases presented, in the case of *Shaping the Political Arena* in the summary tables, and to what degree they rely on our in-depth knowledge of cases, involving what Alexander George calls process tracing (George and McKeown 1985, 35). I increasingly came to think that the summary tables are crucial in setting up the problem, but the fine-grained, within-case analysis is the most important source of explanatory assessment.[16]

The experience of addressing these questions led me to conclude that comparative-historical research has a weak foundation if it is not attentive to issues of method. These questions therefore pushed me to explore further basic problems of concept formation, comparison, and measurement validity.

In earlier methodological writing, there had been an explosion of interest in the comparative method in the 1960s and early 1970s, but that tradition of writing had substantially lapsed. My initial attempt to revive this tradition was my article "The Comparative Method: Two Decades of Change," in which I sought in part to extend Arend Lijphart's (1971) inventive juxtaposition of the case-study method, the small-N comparative method, and the statistical method. I strongly emphasized, as I have ever since, the need for dialogue among these methods. I recall vividly first presenting this paper at a conference at the CUNY Graduate Center in New York, a conference that led to the edited volume in which the article appeared (Collier 1991).[17] Giovanni Sartori and Gabriel Almond were both in the audience, and their enthusiasm for my presentation strongly encouraged me to push ahead with this line of methodological writing.

Q: A major theme of your work on methodology is the analysis of concepts and concept formation. What are some of the main points you would highlight from this work?
A: I have been concerned with juxtaposing two traditions of concept analysis. One, which in political science is strongly identified with Giovanni Sartori, is invaluable for bringing analytic rigor to the research—whether qualitative or quantitative—of the individual scholar. This tradition focuses

16. Within-case, in contrast to cross-case, analysis considers a case over time or across subunits.

17. A more fully developed version of this article was published as Collier (1993).

on developing carefully defined concepts; addressing the problem of overlapping concepts and of confusions in the relationship between term and
meaning; achieving a sharp delineation of the crucial interaction between
the elements of meaning (i.e., the intension) and the range of cases that
appropriately correspond to the concept (i.e., the extension); and viewing
this interaction in terms of hierarchies of concepts—as in the Weberian
hierarchy in which authority is a specific type of domination, and charisma
is a specific type of authority (Sartori 1970). I should especially add that this
idea of hierarchies continues to be crucial to my work.

The other tradition is concerned with the complexities of concepts and
conceptual change across a wider community of scholars. This approach is
more centered on the recognition that the use of concepts is often confused
—and follows patterns that can be detected only with strong analytic tools.
Communication across different usages can be a major challenge; these
problems can seriously interfere with scholarship and with the accumulation of knowledge; and the problems can potentially—but not readily—be
resolved by "legislating" appropriate conceptual usage. Within political science, a key statement of this view is found in W. B. Gallie's (1956) idea of
"essentially contested concepts." I have sought to address this tradition as
well—indeed I am now involved in a project on Gallie's legacy—and my
thinking about the complexity of concepts is also strongly influenced by
what might be called the Berkeley School of cognitive linguistics, within
which Eleanor Rosch was a pioneer. George Lakoff's (1987) extension of
this tradition in his writing on concepts that are "radial," as opposed to
hierarchical, provided a stimulating contrast with Sartori's view of conceptual hierarchies. This branch of cognitive linguistics does not argue that the
use of concepts is necessarily confused; indeed, concepts routinely follow
highly regularized patterns. But this approach maintains that their internal
structure is complex, and that we must understand that complexity if we
are to work effectively with concepts.

I pursued these themes in a series of coauthored pieces. My *American
Political Science Review* article (Collier and Mahon, 1993), "Conceptual
Stretching Revisited," explores the interplay between these two traditions. I
had initially thought it was appropriate to view some concepts as "radial,"
and others not, but my subsequent work suggested that this is not a productive distinction, and that all concepts tend to have some radial elements. One example of a more productive avenue, closely related to the
idea of radial concepts, is the idea of "diminished subtypes"—as in illiberal
democracy—which I introduced in the article on "Democracy with Adjectives" (Collier and Levitsky 1997). These subtypes keep the analytic categories within the larger framework of debates about democracy, while recog-

nizing that within that framework, the cases being analyzed are not fully democratic. And crucially, these types and subtypes are not related to one another within the framework of a Sartori-type conceptual hierarchy, but rather a hierarchy of what may be thought of as part-whole relations.

Other articles sought to make strong connections between problems of concept formation and issues of measurement, offering a systematized understanding of the interaction between disputes about concepts and choices about measurement. One of these pieces explored the interaction between conceptual disputes over the idea of democracy and choices about whether the concept is operationalized in dichotomous or graded terms (Collier and Adcock 1999). A subsequent article sought to offer an integrated framework, addressed to both qualitative and quantitative research, for looking at the interaction among conceptual disputes, choices about measurement, and alternative conceptions of validity—again using as a running example different studies of democracy (Adcock and Collier 2001).

.Of course, the payoff of this kind of work with concepts is its contribution to improving substantive research. Much of political science is concerned with evaluating explanatory claims, yet if concepts and measures are muddled, this cannot be done in a coherent way. For example, my earlier concern with disaggregating key concepts—that is, authoritarianism and corporatism—sought to strengthen scholars' capacity to enter ideas connected with these concepts into explanatory claims. The "Democracy with Adjectives" piece similarly addressed the substantial conceptual confusion found in the literature on democratization. In this literature too many scholars are careless about definitions, and the literature has produced a startling proliferation of democratic subtypes—that is, democracy with adjectives. Such problems can paralyze efforts to assess the causes and consequences of democracy, and of different kinds of democracy. Subsequent articles also addressed issues that require central attention if causal inference is to be a viable enterprise: for example, choices about treating particular concepts in dichotomous or graded terms, as well as the need to offer a framework for establishing measurement validity in light of disputes over the meaning of concepts.

With regard to substantive payoff, I should add that articles on concept analysis written by former graduate students of mine have looked closely at how conceptual confusion can lead to problems in causal inference, including analyses focused on the concepts of institutionalization, peasant, and democracy (Levitsky 1998; Kurtz 2000; Elkins 2000). I would also note that concept analysis is now receiving more attention in political science, for example, in the work of the modeler at Rochester, James Johnson (2003).

Q: In 2004 you published an edited volume with Henry Brady, *Rethinking Social Inquiry*. What are the main arguments of that book?
A: In *Rethinking Social Inquiry* I seek—in joint authorship with Henry Brady and Jason Seawright, and in collaboration with other scholars—to offer a new view of the relationship between qualitative and quantitative methods. Let me spell out that idea in some detail.

Over the past two or three decades, the approach we call "mainstream quantitative methods"—based on regression analysis and econometric refinements on regression—has become hegemonic in some fields of political science. Simultaneously, alternative analytic tools identified with qualitative methods have been gaining importance. I have tried to play a strong role in supporting this latter development, and clearly quantitative and qualitative methods both require close attention. As the subtitle of our book puts it, in light of these *diverse tools* for political analysis—quantitative and qualitative—the challenge is to find *shared standards* for alternative approaches.

This search for shared standards vis-à-vis quantitative and qualitative approaches led us to explore the distinctive contribution of "statistical theory," understood as a broad set of tools for reasoning about evidence and inference. Whereas statistical theory might conventionally be thought of as providing the basic rationale for mainstream quantitative methods, in fact some statistical theorists are skeptical about quantitative causal inference based on observational, as opposed to experimental, data in the social sciences. In the analysis of observational data, these statistical theorists sometimes consider qualitative tools to be superior to quantitative tools for resolving certain kinds of analytic and methodological problems—or at the very least, they believe that qualitative methods make a contribution that is different in kind, but equal in importance.

A key goal in our book is to draw a parallel between "data-set observations," which are the empirical foundation of quantitative research, and what we call "causal-process observations," which are pieces of data that provide information about context and mechanism, and which contribute distinctive leverage in causal inference. In discussions of methodology, the idea of an "observation" has a very specific and special meaning.[18] We sought both to underscore the idea of an observation as the basic feature of a standard quantitative data set, and to link this idea to the insights that derive from qualitative data. Causal-process observations can be drawn from case-study research, from what Alexander George calls "process trac-

18. In a standard "rectangular data set," with rows corresponding to cases and columns corresponding to variables, by conventional usage an "observation" is a row in the data set, involving all of the values for a single case.

ing"—which I already mentioned in discussing *Shaping the Political Arena*— and from what Richard Fenno (1977, 884) calls "soaking and poking."[19]

This juxtaposition of the ideas of data-set observations and causal-process observations casts in a different light, for example, earlier debates on the "many variables, small-N" problem (Lijphart 1971), as well as more recent discussions of "increasing the number of observations" as a means of enhancing inferential leverage in social science research. With a focus on causal process observations, the idea of the "N," and of increasing the number of observations, takes on a different meaning—a meaning that points clearly to the strengths of qualitative research.

Q: Do you see *Rethinking Social Inquiry* as a defense of qualitative methods?
A: The book is not intended to defend qualitative methods. It explores strengths and weaknesses of both qualitative and quantitative approaches, and might better be understood as an effort to "level the playing field" in relation to these alternative sets of tools.

First and most fundamentally, we are concerned with trade-offs between qualitative and quantitative approaches. We disaggregate the qualitative-quantitative distinction into four closely interconnected dimensions—level of measurement, size of the N, whether statistical tests are employed, and whether the study is characterized by thin or thick analysis—the latter in the sense of employing detailed case knowledge. In relation to these dimensions, researchers encounter major trade-offs, with the analytic strengths of each tradition being balanced against weaknesses of the other tradition. Thus, by the definition of levels of measurement, a higher level of measurement provides more information about cases; but substantively rich typologies, utilizing case-based knowledge and categorical variables—that is, nominal scales, and thus a lower level of measurement—may provide insight of quite a different kind. Working with a large N can have enormous advantages, but it often comes at the cost of case knowledge. Statistical tests are a powerful analytic tool, but they depend on having good data and on meeting complex assumptions that underlie such tests—both of which may be hard to achieve. Thin analysis is closely connected with the second criterion, having the great advantage of permitting the examination of a large N. But, by definition, thin analysis lacks the close knowledge that is a great advantage of much qualitative research. Each approach has major strengths

19. George's process tracing is a method for identifying and testing causal mechanisms. Fenno's soaking (up information) and poking (into corners) refers to research that relies heavily on fieldwork, observation, and interviewing geared to obtaining an in-depth and close-up sense of the processes being studied.

and weaknesses, and, frankly, it is simply not appropriate for advocates of either tradition to make a special claim of analytic virtue.

Second, our goal in introducing the idea of causal process observations was in part to underscore the wider importance of a basic research procedure in qualitative analysis, but we also sought thereby to push qualitative researchers to situate their approach to causal inference in a more rigorous framework. For example, we tried to delineate carefully the differences between the two types of observations, and to encourage qualitative researchers to think carefully about the analytic consequences of introducing additional observations of each type, and also of introducing additional variables, within a given analysis (Collier, Brady, and Seawright 2004, 253 and 259).

Researchers should feel substantial humility in doing both quantitative and qualitative research. Producing meaningful and interpretable results from regression analysis can be just as hard as interpreting a case study. Quantitative methods do not have a special monopoly on analytic virtue, any more than case studies do. But I would emphasize that at this point in the evolution of political science, when I think the playing field is still not level, important parts of the discipline need to recognize more fully the limitations of quantitative methods.

Q: *Rethinking Social Inquiry* is in part a critique of King, Keohane, and Verba's *Designing Social Inquiry* (1994). How would you summarize their contribution and the relationship between the two volumes?

A: King, Keohane, and Verba's book has played an invaluable role in consolidating and legitimizing mainstream quantitative methods, the approach we have just been discussing, as well as stimulating an entirely new level of methodological debate and awareness among qualitative researchers. This is an enormous contribution. Still, we think the quantitative template that these authors seek to impose onto qualitative research has many problems, and it is hardly a panacea for the numerous challenges faced in qualitative work. To take one example, their idea of a "determinate research design" strikes us as misleading and unfortunate—even when applied to quantitative research. It implies a level of definite knowledge that we routinely do not achieve. We prefer to ask whether a research design is "interpretable" (Brady and Collier 2004, 292), a label that strikes us as far less rigid and much more helpful. Relatedly, I think many statisticians would feel that many aspects of King, Keohane, and Verba's advice about selection bias are not meaningful in a context in which analysts are not conducting their research in relation to a well-defined population. In comparative research, different combinations of cases routinely yield different findings, and if one assesses a given finding in relation to a larger N, there is no way of knowing if differences in findings reflect substantive differences among the cases, as opposed to selection bias, conventionally understood.

One of the insightful comments I have received about *Rethinking Social Inquiry* was from a Latin Americanist who commented that the book reminded him of my earlier volume, *The New Authoritarianism*. Indeed, my goal with both projects was to critically engage a prior book that had crystallized a debate at a high intellectual and scholarly level, was sharply focused in a way that gave tight structure to that scholarly debate, yet was broad enough to have many implications beyond the immediate arguments of the book. King, Keohane, and Verba's book plays this role in relation to *Rethinking Social Inquiry,* just as O'Donnell's book did in relation to *The New Authoritarianism.* The parallel extends to the fact that both of my books include a new—and many people feel extremely helpful—summary of the prior volume, as well as a glossary of terms intended to help establish a shared framework of discussion. And with both books, I engaged in energetic, interventionist editing of the component chapters, adding—I believe —greater coherence.

I emphasize this parallel between my two books for a specific reason. Some researchers believe that the best way to advance scholarship is to take audacious positions that claim a great deal, and that give the appearance of dramatically moving the discussion forward. I find this approach unappealing. I would rather be identified with research that is fair and balanced, that addresses issues of real analytic importance, but that does not pretend to accomplish things that, in fact, it does not accomplish.

Q: How is your research on methodology related to your substantive interests?
A: Methodological work is most useful when driven by substantive questions that scholars care about. So I have tried to keep my writing on methods closely linked to themes I have long been interested in: corporatism, regime change, democracy, and recent shifts in our conceptualization of democracy—from narrower, procedural issues of regime, to broader questions regarding the character of the state, the rule of law, and citizenship. These links can be seen in my piece on corporatism (Collier 1995), the "Democracy with Adjectives" article (Collier and Levitsky 1997), the "Democracies and Dichotomies" piece (Collier and Adcock 1999), and my *American Political Science Review* piece on measurement validity (Adcock and Collier 2001). Methodological work disconnected from substantive issues can get stale. Methodologists should stay close to areas where they have a sense of interesting research questions. Connecting methodological and substantive issues also specifically motivates other scholars to pay more attention to methodology. For example, *The New Authoritarianism* raised many method-

ological issues, and these issues captured researchers' attention because it was a book that I think was compelling in substantive terms.

Q: Are you currently involved in other projects on methodology?
A: Henry Brady and I continue to be strongly focused on basic themes raised in *Rethinking Social Inquiry.* One major theme, which Henry is pursuing, concerns the logical foundations of causal inference and the contributions of statistical theory to illuminating these foundations. I am continuing my work on conceptualization and measurement that we have just discussed. I continue to be interested in how we can most effectively take on complex concepts, recognize their complexity, and yet ground both qualitative and quantitative research in careful empirical work about which we can make at least reasonably sound claims concerning measurement validity. Dealing with these issues through an escape into a kind of operationalism is not the solution,[20] and I am trying to work further on finding better solutions.

In a closely related initiative, Jason Seawright and I are doing research that seeks to integrate four measurement traditions among which there is virtually no communication and no mutual recognition: axiomatic measurement theory, the pragmatic approach to measurement, structural equation modeling with latent variables, and what we are calling the case-based approach to measurement. We hope through this work to take steps toward placing conceptualization and measurement in comparative politics and political science on a sounder basis.

Science and Values

Q: Do you see yourself as a scientist?
A: *Science* is a label that carries a forceful positive valence in today's world of research funding, and for that reason one has to take it seriously. I consider it a significant transition for the Training Institute on Qualitative Research Methods of Arizona State University when it went beyond a modest National Science Foundation (NSF) seed-money grant to regular NSF funding.[21] There are substantial payoffs to doing work that others consider science, and to the extent that this imposes pressure to achieve more rigor in research, I think it is all for the good.

At the same time, within the natural sciences, "science" consists of such diverse practices that it is perhaps not a helpful label. It is more helpful to

20. Operationalism is the doctrine that the meaning of theoretical terms is located in the indicators employed to measure them.
21. This Training Institute runs an annual course on qualitative methods for graduate students. On the institute, see www.asu.edu/clas/polisci/cqrm/institute.html.

claim that certain lines of work in political science respond effectively and rigorously to specific challenges of research—as in the four dimensions of qualitative versus quantitative analysis discussed above. But to label the whole enterprise too definitively, and to insist that the whole enterprise is science—or should be science—well, I think it may be useful for fundraising or propaganda, but it is not very informative. The story has it that as a result of a log-roll among the authors of the King, Keohane, and Verba volume (1994), the subtitle ended up being "Scientific Inference in Qualitative Research." As you know, I think that volume makes a large contribution, but that it makes claims about rigor that cannot be sustained. To tout these claims as "science"—well, I think that is enough said.

Q: What roles do values and normative commitments play in your own research and in the research you consider important?
A: Scholars in comparative politics are routinely motivated by normative concerns when they study authoritarianism, human rights violations, inequality, poverty, and the collapse of the rule of law. The same is true in the international relations field for researchers who study the tragedies of war and other kinds of international conflict, and in the American politics field for analysts who focus, for example, on distortions in the U.S. system of elections and legislative representation, distortions that diminish democracy. Normative issues are always present, not only in the topics we study, but sometimes—more awkwardly—in the topics we fail to study. It is essential to emphasize that these normative sources of analytic agendas are fundamental in all political research. And these normative concerns should definitely not be seen as a departure from what we would routinely think of as rigorous analysis in the tradition of empirical political science. Of course, we will encounter disputes about the normative weighting of different issues and problems; and normative agendas should not lead to predictable research findings that merely serve to validate the normative commitments of the researcher. The "value-free social science" component arises in part when this empirical research can yield unexpected, and sometimes unwelcome, findings—in the sense of Max Weber's (1946a, 147) "inconvenient facts." But we cannot for a moment imagine that we are in an enterprise that is not normatively driven.

Colleagues, Collaborators, and Students
Colleagues

Q: You taught at Indiana University from 1970 until 1978. Who were the colleagues that influenced you most at Indiana? What kind of environment was it?

A: I must underscore my great debt for the support I received for both my substantive and methodological interests at Indiana. Eleanor and Vincent Ostrom founded their now famous Workshop in Political Theory and Policy Analysis in 1973, and Dina Zinnes and John Gillespie were engaged in mathematical modeling of international conflict. Simultaneously, Indiana had a robust areas studies tradition, and I will always be grateful—for example—for the friendship of the West Europeanist Alfred Diamant. Interestingly, given my emerging interests at the time, Diamant had written a book on corporatism in Austria (Diamant 1960).

During this period—both at Indiana and nationally—there was strong intellectual support for exploring the contributions of quantitative comparative research to understanding political change. For example, at Indiana Ronald Weber in political science was working on quantitative comparisons of state politics within the United States (Weber and Shaffer 1972), and in the Sociology Department Philips Cutright was engaged in quantitative cross-national research on development (Cutright 1963). These colleagues helped spark my interest in such comparisons.

Q: In 1978, you moved to Berkeley, where you have been ever since. What was Berkeley like? How did the colleagues you encountered influence your thinking?
A: Moving to Berkeley pushed me toward a strong interest in comparative-historical work. Reinhard Bendix, who had previously been in the Berkeley Sociology Department, had moved over to political science. In 1964 he had published *Nation Building and Citizenship* (Bendix 1964), which was extremely significant for my book with Ruth, *Shaping the Political Arena,* and just after Ruth and I arrived to Berkeley, his *Kings or People* (Bendix 1980) came out, and it was widely discussed in our department. In sociology, Neil Smelser had long been interested in historical analysis, as had Victoria Bonnell, who had studied with Barrington Moore at Harvard. The two of them coordinated a faculty seminar that gave substantial attention to issues of historical analysis, and it was in that seminar that I first read Theda Skocpol and Margaret Somers's invaluable article, "The Uses of Comparative History in Macrosocial Inquiry" (1980). At the Berkeley Institute of Industrial Relations, Clark Kerr was a towering presence, and he was coauthor of the classic study *Industrialism and Industrial Man,* which gave prominent attention to the incorporation of labor into national political institutions at a critical historical moment (Dunlop et al. 1960). Harold Wilensky's bold cross-national work on welfare states underscored the feasibility of broad comparisons.

On the conceptual side, Hanna Pitkin's compelling analysis of ideas such as representation, justice, reification, and utility set a high standard for careful conceptualization (Pitkin 1967). Ernst Haas's work was an intellectual anchor in efforts to rigorously conceptualize politics across a wide range of nations and historical periods, and Kenneth Jowitt's (1992) work on Leninism was a model for creative concept formation. I attended Jowitt's lectures on Leninism, and invited him to my methodology class to give his basic Leninism lecture as an exemplar of creative work with concepts.

Also, a few years after we arrived, Berkeley hired Gregory Luebbert in political science. Around the time *Shaping the Political Arena* was crystallizing as a book project, Luebbert was doing closely parallel historical work on Western Europe (Luebbert 1991). He was a key colleague. We began working on our books independently and did them in quite different styles. But, in certain substantive ways, the arguments are quite similar. There was cross-fertilization between the projects through many conversations with Luebbert, through joint seminars, and through extensive interaction with graduate students. Tragically, Luebbert died in the late 1980s in a whitewater boating accident. His manuscript was almost finished, and Giuseppe Di Palma made a crucial contribution in pulling it together. I had the bittersweet experience of writing a preface for the book with Seymour Martin Lipset, with whom Luebbert had worked at Stanford. Luebbert's death was an incredible loss for the discipline and for the Berkeley department, and I feel that we never regained that ground until we hired Paul Pierson from Harvard in 2004.

Overall, Berkeley was a setting where comparative-historical work was valued, and there was a sense that it was possible to do such work in a way that was conceptually innovative, analytically rigorous, and at the same time close to the cases. These criteria set a standard that we tried to meet in *Shaping the Political Arena.*

In discussing intellectual and institutional support for *Shaping the Political Arena,* let me mention two other debts, the first to Sanford Thatcher, then of Princeton University Press, which published our book, and now director of Penn State University Press. For several decades he has been the leading figure, in the world of publishing, in terms of support for the Latin American field, and dozens of scholars—including the Colliers—owe him a large debt for his dedication, patience, insight, and professionalism. In our electronic age, editors and book publishers still matter a lot. In addition, I also have a large debt for the intellectual support provided by the remarkable community of faculty, postdoctoral scholars, and graduate students at the Kellogg Institute for International Studies at the University of Notre Dame. During the past twenty years, Kellogg has played a singularly exciting role in supporting the kind of normatively informed and rigorous comparative social science that I care about.

Turning to the past ten years, I would underscore Berkeley's importance as the setting in which we ultimately wrote *Rethinking Social Inquiry.* In two successive years, Henry Brady and I jointly taught a methodology course in the late 1990s, which in turn pushed us to develop new perspectives on methods and on methodological debates. The Berkeley statistician David Freedman was a source both of broad ideas about the application of statistical theory and of meticulous help with editing—so meticulous that he once threatened to edit the menu at a restaurant where we were having dinner. In this setting, a number of graduate students were stimulated to pursue advanced training in statistics and methodology, and from among these students Jason Seawright ended up being coauthor of major portions of *Rethinking Social Inquiry.* Henry Brady has been a strong supporter of the Institute on Qualitative Research Methods, coming for two days every year to talk about our book and to address issues of causal inference, conceptualization, and measurement.

Collaborators

Q: You have done a lot of collaborative research. Why do you collaborate?
A: Well, I said before that in coauthoring with Ruth Collier, we both did 75 percent of the work. With that much effort going into the research, the result is likely to be of better quality. Correspondingly, the collaboration that went into not only *Shaping the Political Arena,* but also *The New Authoritarianism* and *Rethinking Social Inquiry,* produced something that was more than the sum of the parts. Further, I have had the good fortune of spending most of my academic career at Berkeley. We have extremely good students—and I dare say that Ruth and I are pretty well known in the department for pushing our students hard, so they come out of Berkeley with many newly acquired skills and talents. I have written extensively with graduate students: it makes my work better, and it launches them on a strong research trajectory.

Many scholars who are committed to collaborative research, and who do not have the good fortune of such good graduate students, may be more oriented toward writing with colleagues at other institutions, and this can work just as well. One of the striking features of academic life in the United States—as opposed, I think, to most other countries in the world—is that there are hundreds of universities and colleges where scholars can maintain an active research program, along with their teaching. This enriches scholarship for all of us, and for any given researcher it yields many opportunities for collaboration with scholars at other institutions.

In my experience, collaboration and coauthoring is a way to pool knowledge and combine different skills. For example, one contributor might know qualitative methods and the other might know quantitative methods. The quantitative person will argue, "No, you can't say it that way or everyone will know it's wrong." The qualitative person will say, "But that's not how qualitative researchers think about the problem. If you say it that way, they won't believe you at all." In working on *Rethinking Social Inquiry,* I was collaborating with scholars whose knowledge of statistical theory went far beyond mine. The statistician David Freedman, though not a coauthor, was a key intellectual contributor to the project. I once asked him what could motivate him to collaborate with someone like me, who does not have a broad knowledge of statistical theory. He responded that it is because I have "sechel"—Yiddish for "common sense," or "smarts." Perhaps it is a nice thing that at this late date in the evolution of the social sciences, a prominent statistician should think that common sense is important.

Students

Q: What is your approach to training graduate students, to their selection of dissertation topics, to coauthoring with them, and to supporting their professional development after their Ph.D.s?
A: Ruth Collier and I collaborate closely in training and mentoring students. Over the years we have routinely co-chaired dissertation committees, and we both work very, very hard at it. I should add that this question within your interview—indeed, an important part of this interview—should be seen as being as much about Ruth's work as about mine.

The way students pick a dissertation topic varies a lot. Some students go out on their own and select topics completely different from what Ruth and I do. We learn a lot from those dissertations. Other students focus on topics that are extensions of themes we have worked on. It varies a lot, and it is good to have both.

On coauthoring with graduate students, I do this extensively. It serves as a research apprenticeship, and gives them writing experience. I also have often given sustained, intensive feedback on graduate student articles that virtually amounts to coauthorship, but in situations where I want the student to get all the credit for the article. Hence, I am not listed as co-author. Regarding involvement in professional development after the Ph.D.—well, let me simply say that Ruth and I work very hard indeed in supporting the intellectual and professional development of our former students.

Institutional Initiatives
The Comparative Politics Section of the American Political Science Association

Q: During the past several years, you have been actively involved in several capacities in the American Political Science Association (APSA). I would first like to discuss your role in the Comparative Politics Section, of which you were president during 1997–99. What is your impression of the section?[22]

A: The field of American politics is well represented in APSA, scholars in international relations have the International Studies Association (ISA), and area studies associations are essential for some comparativists. But, until the Comparative Politics Section was started in 1989, comparativists had no overarching organization, giving the organized section a crucial role. Soon after it was launched, the section quickly became the largest organized section of APSA, by a wide margin. It has a fine newsletter that started at the University of Washington, prospered at UCLA, and is now prospering at Notre Dame. The section sponsors a large number of panels at the annual APSA meeting, for which immense numbers of applications are received, and the colleague who each year assumes the role of program organizer deserves a lot of credit. The section also gives four annual prizes— I was fortunate to have the opportunity to secure the endowment that supports the book and article prizes named after Gregory Luebbert. Overall, the section is a valuable and intellectually vital organization.

Q: What did you seek to accomplish as president of the Comparative Politics Section from 1997 to 1999?

A: I tried to ensure that the diverse interests of the membership were well represented. In appointing committees and taking initiatives, I sought balance among modelers, quantitative researchers, scholars engaged in qualitative comparative research, and those with strong, analytically grounded area studies backgrounds. I put a lot of effort into running a high-quality, eclectic, balanced section, and I thought it worked well. A broad constituency of first-rate scholars was willing to participate actively in the section.

I also sought to use my four letters from the president in the section's newsletter to raise issues I felt merited close attention, and my goals as section president may be summarized by noting ideas that I presented in these letters. I first revisited the earlier debate about the comparative method (Collier 1998a), emphasizing the interconnectedness among alternative

22. For the perspectives of two of Collier's predecessors as president of the Comparative Politics Section of APSA, see the interviews with Robert Bates and David Laitin in Chapters 14 and 16.

methodologies—a theme to which I have returned many times. Another letter was devoted to comparative-historical analysis and underscored the degree to which it has become a well-institutionalized current in the discipline, with a large number of exciting books having been published in the 1990s (Collier 1998b). I frankly think my letter on this latter topic helped to crystallize a new round of discussion focused on this approach. As with *Shaping the Political Arena,* this letter underscored my concern with the methodological underpinnings of comparative historical analysis and with achieving higher standards of analytic rigor in such studies.

In another letter I discussed the types of scholars, and the types of field research, that succeed in "extracting new ideas at close range," a phrase I adopted from the sociologist Alejandro Portes (Collier 1999a). I sometimes think we make too much of the deductive side of political analysis, and fail to recognize that a good deal of the most creative work comes from scholars who possess powerful analytic skills, and who are immersed in the reality of politics such that they "see" new political processes and structures in a novel way, based on deep experience with the cases they are studying. If they are really good at this kind of research, they may succeed in focusing our attention on "novel emergent processes," to use a phrase suggested by my Berkeley colleague Paul Rabinow, which will subsequently be the research focus for dozens of other scholars. To my mind, Guillermo O'Donnell's work is an exemplar of this approach.

Relatedly, I addressed the debate concerning the relationship between area studies and broader analytic agendas in the field of comparative politics. I argued in this letter that it had sometimes incorrectly been presumed that area studies had collapsed at the Social Science Research Council (SSRC) in the mid-1990s, when SSRC abolished its traditional area studies committees. In fact, at a key transition point in the evolution of SSRC, when the president of the Council Kenneth Prewitt played a lead role in eliminating these committees, he at the same time strongly underscored SSRC's commitment to area-based knowledge. I pointed out in my letter that at this juncture, SSRC funding for area-based dissertation research in fact was substantially increased.

In my final letter, I wrote about the challenge of building a disciplined, rigorous center in comparative politics (Collier 1999b), again underscoring the idea that between the area studies tradition, on the one hand, and research based on formal modeling and/or advanced quantitative methods, on the other, we must ensure ample room for qualitative-comparative research that is rigorous, and that should command full respect and prestige within the discipline. Many colleagues felt that I expressed those ideas in a way that was useful and productive for re-centering the Comparative Politics Section.

The Qualitative Methods Section of the American Political Science Association

Q: You have been the driving force behind the recent formation of the Qualitative Methods Section of the American Political Science Association (APSA).[23] What was your goal in starting this new section?
A: I have great admiration for my colleagues who created the Political Methodology Section of APSA, which has successfully institutionalized the subfield of quantitative methods. They have converted *Political Analysis*, which used to be an annual publication, into an important journal. Gary King played a key role in leading this initiative, Neal Beck did a splendid job as the first editor, and Robert Erikson has now taken on that role with impressive success. The degree to which they have successfully defined what it means to be a political science methodologist, and the criteria that must be met for scholars to be appointed in faculty positions that correspond to "methodology" in Political Science departments in the United States, are markers of a successful episode of academic institutionalization.

Yet I have been convinced for some time that the focus on methods in political science has been excessively tilted toward quantitative methods. This group of colleagues successfully appropriated the label *political methodology*, but their enterprise has almost entirely focused on quantitative methods. Not unrelatedly, for many years in quite a few departments, training in qualitative methods has not been available at all. Scholars who wanted to teach qualitative methods were not allowed to do so, or could do so only within the field of comparative politics, and not through what was accepted by their colleagues as a "real" course on methodology. For many years, I saw the need for a broader vision of methodology that was more eclectic, encompassing qualitative methods as well. We needed to do for qualitative methods what our quantitative colleagues had done for their branch of methodology. Qualitative methods are, in important respects, a foundation of the discipline—Andrew Bennett and collaborators have written a compelling article emphasizing this point (Bennett, Barth, and Rutherford 2003)—and this intellectual current needs to be strongly represented in our graduate teaching and, correspondingly, in the discipline and in APSA.

Q: Is this initiative in qualitative methods linked to other organizational efforts?
A: Yes. It is the result of a collective momentum that involves a number of people, and went through a series of steps. One should not seek to form a

---

23. Collier was the founding transitional president of the APSA Organized Section on Qualitative Methods.

new APSA organized section without a strong organizational, as well as intellectual, foundation. Part of our initiative began with my efforts to transform the earlier Committee on Conceptual and Terminological Analysis (COCTA)—which was closely identified with Giovanni Sartori. This committee was a "Related Group" within APSA, and it was Research Committee No. 1 within the International Political Science Association (IPSA). First we expanded the activities of this committee; then we renamed it, giving it the broader name of the Committee on Concepts and Methods. This remains today the Research Committee No. 1 of IPSA. Subsequently, we expanded this to be an Organized Section of APSA, gathering a thousand signatures in support of the new section, and our group quickly became one of the larger sections within the association. These efforts were reinforced by the initiatives of Alexander George, Andrew Bennett, Colin Elman, and myself in forming the Consortium for Qualitative Research Methods, which has sponsored a highly successful training institute at Arizona State University every January. This institute now draws eighty students annually, and it is taught by a rotating set of about twenty faculty who come from universities across the United States. I should reiterate that important legitimation for the institute was provided when it began to receive NSF funding.

Q: What are the potential gains from having a qualitative section of APSA?
A: If you wish to persuade the political science profession that a particular analytic or methodological perspective should be taken seriously, having a successful organized section is a valuable step. If the section is strikingly successful, as ours has been, it is a particularly good step. Almost immediately after the section's formation, it came to rank among the larger organized sections, and we have seen a surprising increase in our panel allocation at the annual APSA meeting. Having a large number of panels in turn serves as a vehicle for encouraging qualitative, comparative, and small-N research and is a valuable stimulus to scholars and graduate students who work in these areas. Our panels are extremely well attended: at the 2005 annual APSA meeting, we came in second among the forty-six divisions in our average panel attendance. We now award three prizes for outstanding contributions that either develop or apply qualitative methods—a book prize, an article prize, and a paper prize—and those play a valuable role in recognizing good work and calling attention to new developments in the field. We have an excellent newsletter, *Qualitative Methods,* with a strong editor, John Gerring, and I think a lot of good communication is taking place through the newsletter.

Q: What is the relationship between the Qualitative Methods Section and the Political Methodology Section of APSA?
A: I have good relations with many of the scholars who have played a leading role in the Political Methodology Section. We consulted with them extensively when we formed our section. At one point, we discussed the option of being part of their section. Various senior members of the already existing section thought this was not a good idea. When they first formed their group they were poorly institutionalized and felt they needed to do things on their own for a while, without anyone looking over their shoulder. I think the qualitative methods people today feel much the same way.

Let me underscore again a key point to which I already referred above: the inconvenience—one might say the irony—that they had preempted the name *political methodology*, committing them to a broader scope of methodological offerings than they in fact delivered. For a number of months when we were forming the new section, I resisted the label *qualitative methods*, feeling that this name framed our enterprise too narrowly. As I have already emphasized, I see major parts of my methodological work as being highly relevant to quantitative research. I thought about alternative terms such as *integrative methodology* or *eclectic methodology*, but those were hardly good names for an APSA organized section. In the end, given that the *political methodology* label had indeed been preempted, I acquiesced and accepted the name *qualitative methods*. For the purposes of this interview, it seems simpler to refer to qualitative methods, but what I have in mind is this more eclectic view of methodology, of the kind reflected in *Rethinking Social Inquiry*.

Related to this issue of labels, I think a small number of colleagues have thought that our initiative has been divisive, in that it appeared to separate out the qualitative component from the overall enterprise of methodology. To be perfectly frank, if any of these initiatives is to be called divisive, it is the original formation of the Political Methodology Section. The broad label was thereby appropriated, but by-and-large, only the quantitative aspect of methodology has been addressed.

Achieving coherence in work on an eclectic view of methodology that emphatically includes qualitative tools is necessarily going to be a gradual process. We are building a well-defined set of people who are reading and commenting on each other's work, gaining insights from one another, and publishing in leading journals. Another sign of progress is the greatly increased number of qualitative methods courses—or integrative methods courses—being taught in graduate programs across the country. Along the lines of the arguments in *Rethinking Social Inquiry*, it is also essential to have many qualitative methodologists who have strong training in statistical theory, which as I emphasized before can provide valuable underpinnings for both qualitative and quantitative methods. I think we are making progress, but we still have some distance to go. Yet looking at this in a longer perspective, at no point in the history of the political science discipline has the development of qualitative methods received the kind of systematic attention it is currently receiving.

Achievements and the Future of Comparative Politics

Q: Looking broadly at the field of comparative politics, has there been an accumulation of substantive knowledge over the past thirty or forty years?

A: Yes. I see entire bodies of valuable literature on political parties, party systems, and electoral regimes. We have enormous breadth and historical depth of knowledge about democracy and authoritarianism, and more broadly about the dynamics of different types of national political regimes. The growing literature on path dependence has provided new leverage in systematizing insights about continuities and discontinuities in political institutions, and the literature on ethnic conflict is impressive. The Mahoney and Rueschemeyer volume *Comparative Historical Analysis in the Social Sciences* (2003) provides a detailed account of long-term advances in research on social policy, revolution, and democracy and authoritarianism, and another chapter that was written for that volume, but unfortunately was dropped for lack of space, provides good insights into the cumulative expansion of our knowledge of European state building (Mazzuca 2001). Thus, in many areas, we know much more than we did a few decades ago.

Q: You have been a strong proponent of comparative-historical analysis. What, in your view, is the place of historically oriented work in political science, a discipline that is more focused on contemporary issues?

A: It is exciting to study the events that are unfolding in the present. But that kind of focus can sometimes involve a short-term perspective that is vulnerable to analytic mistakes. What is the purported comment of Mao on the legacy of the French Revolution? I understand that he said: "It is too early to tell." It is hard to identify the optimal time frame for good research, but sometimes the time frame is too short. For example, in the excellent and stimulating literature on democratic transitions that emerged two decades ago, some scholars hypothesized that the mode of transition would strongly influence subsequent regime dynamics. I think that idea has been substantially discredited, and a crucial problem may have been that analysts did not have a sufficiently clear historical framework for assessing what kind of transition is likely to leave a distinctive legacy.

I am convinced that macro-comparative analysis—often called comparative-historical analysis in political science and historical sociology
within that discipline—has a critical analytic contribution to make. The
concern with the micro-foundations of politics in the past decade or so is
an invaluable analytic advance. Yet it is equally important to understand
the macro-settings in which micro-foundations make a difference. I think
we have achieved enormous analytic gains in understanding these macro-
settings.

**Q: What is your view about how the ongoing methodological debates
in political science will unfold, and should unfold?**
A: One aspect of this picture is the continuing, and possibly expanding,
importance of mainstream quantitative methods. Parts of this tradition
exhibit a strong impulse toward the technification of analytic tools. In
many respects this technification has been productive, and has given us
new leverage in addressing a wide spectrum of substantive problems. Yet we
warned on the final page of *Rethinking Social Inquiry* that this technification
can go too far (Collier, Brady, and Seawright 2004, 266). It can become an
end in its own right and can cause scholars to lose sight of simpler tools that
may offer greater analytic leverage. Further, the complex training required
for using more advanced quantitative tools may absorb time and energy
that could otherwise be devoted to gaining essential substantive knowledge
of the topics under study.

The tradition of statistical theory on which we draw in our book, while
of course itself very technical, sometimes provides grounds for arguing that
simpler analytic solutions are better. Further, one of the most interesting
reviews of *Rethinking Social Inquiry*, "Beyond the Linear Frequentist Orthodoxy" (2006), written by the highly respected quantitative methodologist
Philip Schrodt, takes a far more harsh view of regression-based research
than we do in *Rethinking Social Inquiry*, and he also points to the potential
contribution of simpler tools. We need to recognize that the strong words
of caution in *Rethinking Social Inquiry*, focused on the elaborate tradition
of regression analysis and econometric refinements on regression, by no
means reflect an isolated position. These are very serious issues for the
future of comparative politics and political science.

This issue of balance among alternative methodological traditions is in-
sightfully addressed by Robert Keohane in his essay on "disciplinary schizophrenia" (Keohane 2003). He discusses the greater ease of professional cre-
dentialing in what he calls the "technical-specialization" track in graduate
training, focused on quantitative and formal research and on what is often
a quite narrow definition of the research question, as opposed to a much

broader track,[24] which is concerned with case-based, sometimes historical knowledge; with diverse methodologies; and with achieving rich substantive insights that cut across subfields of political science. Keohane argues that the technical-specialization track lends itself, to a greater degree, to a stream of articles in mainstream journals, giving scholars a readily definable record that, for example, yields a great advantage in tenure reviews. In contrast, scholars who pursue the broader track often follow a career trajectory in which it may take longer to develop an impressive professional record. Keohane sees this imbalance as reflecting a kind of disciplinary schizophrenia, and he speculates that political science may disadvantage itself, and inappropriately narrow the breadth of knowledge produced by the discipline, by shifting too far in the direction of the technical-specialization track.

Given these issues, where do we stand today? I think that faculty job recruitment in the field of political methodology still simply means mainstream quantitative methods. It is true that for searches in comparative politics and international relations, candidates with broad methodological skills that combine quantitative and qualitative tools are sometimes particularly welcome. I think this mix of skills should also be a requisite for political methodology positions in general—and specifically not just a mix of skills that, while appearing to incorporate and embrace qualitative methods, in fact marginalizes it.

Let me highlight one more point about how I think methodological debates should unfold. Generating meaningful regression coefficients and interpreting them appropriately can be just as hard as, if not harder than, making sense of a case study. It is time for important parts of the discipline to move beyond the view that quantitative methods have a special monopoly on analytic virtue. To the extent that this occurs it will be a welcome change, and it is a much needed change.

Conclusion

Q: To conclude, what advice can you offer graduate students entering the profession?
A: I would return to Keohane's discussion, just noted, of the tension between the narrower technical-specialization track in graduate training and the broader track, which encompasses a greater degree of case-based, often historical knowledge, diverse methodologies, and rich substantive insights

---

24. Keohane calls this the "contextual knowledge" track, but this description of the track follows his presentation.

that cut across subfields of political science. For students entering comparative politics and political science, pursuing the technical specialization track may be an attractive option because it appears to offer a more secure professional trajectory, and there is not the slightest doubt that scholars following this track have made major contributions.

Yet students should also recognize the professional opportunities associated with the broader track. Journals have become much more receptive to articles on qualitative methods, and many excellent journals welcome well-crafted articles based on small-N comparisons that may be focused on contemporary or on historical cases. Doctoral dissertations based on comparative-historical analysis are definitely feasible, and can lead reasonably promptly to a book. New organizational initiatives—such as the Institute on Qualitative Research Methods discussed above—have proved invaluable for creating networks of graduate students and younger scholars who share a commitment to maintaining a more eclectic version of our collective enterprise.

Hence, pursuing a broader line of work in graduate school is perfectly compatible with moving fairly quickly toward a strong professional record. This is obviously not to say that young scholars who follow the technical-specialization track are not making an important contribution. They definitely are. But we will be far better off if we address Keohane's concern with disciplinary schizophrenia through deliberate efforts—in graduate training, in hiring, and beyond—to maintain and protect multiple paths toward good scholarship.

16

David D. Laitin

*Culture, Rationality, and the Search
for Discipline*

David D. Laitin is one of the most influential scholars working on the relationship between culture and politics. Through his comparative and ethnographic research, he has challenged the dominant view in political science that culture affects politics yet politics does not affect culture. His work shows instead that culture both shapes and is in turn shaped by political choices.

Laitin advanced his research program on culture and politics by conducting fieldwork in a broad range of countries and by exploring the political issues involved in language use, religion, and the formation of national identities. In *Politics, Language, and Thought* (1977), he addressed the relationship between language and political action in Somalia. In *Hegemony and Culture* (1986), he turned to the link between religion and politics in the Yorubaland region of Nigeria, and, in *Language Repertoires and State Construction in Africa* (1992a), he offers a historical analysis that shows how the process of state formation affected the degree of linguistic heterogeneity in African countries. His subsequent work focused on the Catalan linguistic movement in Spain. And in *Identity in Formation* (1998a), he shifted his attention to the Russian-speaking zones of the former Soviet Union in order to analyze language choice in a context of rising nationalism.

Laitin's most recent work, carried out in collaboration with James Fearon, seeks to explain ethnic conflict and cooperation. It focuses on the origins and duration of civil wars, and combines game theory, statistical analysis, and historical narrative in an integrated whole. A core issue explored in this research is the extent to which violent conflict takes place within, not between, ethnic groups.

Laitin has also written various articles proposing a tripartite methodology that combines formal mathematical models with quantitative and

This interview was conducted by Gerardo Munck in Palo Alto, California, on November 18–19, 2001.

qualitative techniques. He has been a vocal advocate for an integrated political science discipline, one that makes self-conscious efforts both to synthesize its research findings and to focus on enduring questions about politics posed in the classic works of political theory.

Laitin was born in Brooklyn, New York, in 1945. He received his B.A. from Swarthmore College in 1967 and his Ph.D. in political science from the University of California, Berkeley, in 1974. He has taught at the University of California, San Diego (1975–87), the University of Chicago (1987–98), and Stanford University since 1999. He was president of the Comparative Politics Section of the American Political Science Association (APSA) in 1993–95, was vice-president of APSA in 2005–6, and was elected to the American Academy of Arts and Sciences in 1995.

Intellectual Formation and Training

Q: How did you get interested in the study of politics and decide to become a political scientist?
A: I come from a fairly political family in New York. My parents were World Federalists and active on civil rights issues. As a child, I remember coming home and seeing my mother, who was a schoolteacher, watching the McCarthy hearings on television. I was fascinated with my mother's fascination with it. Neither of my parents were Communists, but they hung around people who were. And the sense of fear that my mother's name might be raised was obvious. So, there was a feeling that politics was something exciting and worrisome.

I also recall how the Gold Coast colony became Ghana, an independent state, how Senator John F. Kennedy, my idol on the Senate floor, supported the Algerians in their war of independence and not the French. To me, all this represented the future. Africa was tied up with the civil rights movement, with liberation. It seemed these events were the most exciting things happening in the world.

A few years later, I was interviewing for college and the dean of admissions at Swarthmore asked me what I wanted to major in. I said "political science." I think it was the first time I ever used the term *political science* in my life. I had no idea what it was.

Living in New York I had a kind of political consciousness and felt a sense of excitement about the political world, a desire to know more about it. These factors led me to major in political science at Swarthmore. I should add that I'd never been abroad as a kid. The first time I experienced being abroad was when I joined the Peace Corps and went to Somalia in 1969. At that stage, my interest in things abroad was purely academic, not experiential. Africa was an imagined "other place" I wanted to know about.

Q: What was the undergraduate major like at Swarthmore?
A: Swarthmore was a breeding ground for political scientists in the 1960s. Among the students of that era were Robert Putnam, now at Harvard; Richard Mansbach, now at Iowa State; Jack Nagel, now at the University of Pennsylvania; Peter Katzenstein, now at Cornell; Margaret Levi, who was enrolled at Bryn Mawr but came to Swarthmore for a seminar; and Jeffrey Hart, now at Indiana University. Among the faculty were J. Roland Pennock, Kenneth Waltz, and Robert Keohane. This list includes four APSA presidents![1]

We received a pre-professional education in political science at Swarthmore. On Pennock's list of required readings in political theory in 1966 were Thomas Schelling's *Strategy of Conflict* (1960), Mancur Olson's *Logic of Collective Action* (1965), Karl Deutsch's *Nerves of Government* (1963), James Buchanan and Gordon Tulloch's *Calculus of Consent* (1962), as well as the classics in the canon. We were given no training in methods, but we were exposed to the classics as well as the work at the frontier of the discipline.

I should tell an anecdote that has become popular among my graduate students. For seminars at Swarthmore, we received our syllabi weekly, and they generally had a couple of pages of required and optional readings. I thought this was normal. When I went to graduate school and got my syllabi during the first week of classes, I was stricken with fear, as they were half again as demanding as Swarthmore's. It was only in week 2 that I found, to my relief, that at Berkeley, like most places, syllabi are handed out each semester. Well, after a trying first week, I had thirteen weeks to follow my own intellectual instincts!

Q: After Swarthmore, you went to graduate school in political science at Berkeley in 1967. What attracted you to Berkeley?
A: Virtually everyone at Swarthmore was going to graduate school because of the Vietnam War. Without a year of graduate school, we would be subject to the draft, so that wasn't really a choice. In terms of where to attend graduate school, I didn't have much of a choice either. I was nowhere near the top of my class. Peter Katzenstein, who was my roommate, was the star of the class. J. Roland Pennock, the chair of the Political Science Department, told me I shouldn't shoot as high as Harvard or Yale. As it turns out, the University of Chicago, where I subsequently became a professor, rejected me, and Stanford, where I now teach, also rejected me. Berkeley was the only school that gave me money. I think I got the fellowship from Berkeley because the guy who taught me political development at Swarthmore and who

1. Robert Keohane, Margaret Levi, Robert Putnam, and Kenneth Waltz were APSA presidents.

was my strongest advocate, a Japanologist named Donald C. Hellmann, had recently received his degree from Berkeley and was known there.

Q: Did you know about any of the professors at Berkeley?
A: I knew of the political theorist Sheldon Wolin, and I was especially looking forward to working with the international relations scholar and comparativist Ernst Haas. I had heard about Haas from Hellmann, so I knew what kind of an intellectual he was. I took Haas's and Wolin's courses my first semester, and thus got to work with two of the truly great intellectuals at Berkeley during the period. Eventually, I wrote my dissertation under Haas. I wanted to work with the political theorist Hanna Pitkin, but I thought she was at Wisconsin. So I was pleasantly surprised to learn she had just moved to Berkeley. Her interest in language philosophy complemented mine in language politics, and she became an invaluable second reader of my dissertation.

Q: From the names you have mentioned, it is clear you were not interested only in comparative politics. Indeed, you took a fair dose of political theory, and your dissertation was awarded the prize for the best dissertation in political theory from Berkeley.
A: At that point, the people at Berkeley who were called comparativists or behavioralists were at war with the political theorists. The conflicts were about the nature of the discipline, the free speech movement, the Third World College, and all the other things that were happening at Berkeley. It was a very deep divide, and the two sides were hardly talking to one another. Indeed, the two leading theorists, Wolin and John H. Schaar, eventually left Berkeley during my graduate period. In this polarized context, I tried successfully to keep both Ernie Haas and Hanna Pitkin on my committee. It was a wonderful achievement, because not only did they like the work I did, but they developed a great admiration for each other that they hadn't been able to develop before. This was my greatest achievement at Berkeley.

Q: What courses did you take?
A: From the moment I arrived on the Berkeley campus in the fall of 1967, I took courses around the university that interested me. Berkeley was an intellectual beehive, fantastically exciting. I took advantage of this opportunity, choosing courses always with an eye for what I wanted to write about and what I wanted to say.

Q: Did this include courses in comparative politics?
A: The training I had received at Swarthmore was excellent, but I never took a course in comparative politics. I took a course in political development

and the Soviet system, and one course in African history, but no regular course I can remember called comparative politics. When I went to Berkeley, again I don't think I ever took a course in comparative politics. I took a course on political development taught by Warren Ilchman and Norman Uphoff. I took a course on Africa with Carl Rosberg. I sat in on a lecture series by David Apter, right before he went to Yale. But he was mostly lecturing, as I recall, on Hobbes and the grand tradition of comparative theory rather than doing comparative politics. So, strictly speaking, I never really took a course in comparative politics.

At Berkeley, I also took courses outside political science, especially in sociology. I took William Kornhauser's course on comparative revolutions. That's when I first read Barrington Moore's *Social Origins* (1966). This book had a tremendous influence on me and shaped my ideas about what could be done in comparative politics. I also took Neil Smelser's social theory course and Ira Lapidus's course on the history of Islam. I sat in on two anthropology courses. But I took no economics courses. In the 1960s, when I was at Berkeley, the influence of sociology on political science was much greater than the influence of economics. And the courses I took reflected this trend.

Q: Can you discuss what Moore's book meant to you?
A: It was a shock to the whole liberal approach to development coming out of Almond and Coleman (1960) and the Princeton series,[2] that basically said what took 250 years to achieve in the West could be done in twenty-five years in the South and, more important, it could be done peacefully, through careful management of development. In contrast, Moore argued that unless there is revolution, social classes harmful to the development of democracy remain on the scene. Thus, Moore's chapter on India said that, even though the country had been democratic for twenty years, he was not sanguine about India's future, because it had not had a revolutionary break with its past. Moore's idea that the elimination of a social class through revolution was a necessary precondition for democracy stuck a knife blade into the liberal notion that great goals could be achieved peacefully. Through his historical analysis, Moore produced a shock, a normative shock that we had to take into account. Sam Huntington's book, *Political Order in Changing Societies* (1968), had a similar effect. As an undergraduate, I had read Huntington's earlier essay in *World Politics* (Huntington 1965), which became the basis of his book. But I think Moore's critique of the liberal approach to development was more powerful.

2. Princeton University Press published a nine-volume Studies in Political Development series between 1963 and 1978 that was edited by Lucian Pye, the chairman of the Committee on Comparative Politics of the Social Science Research Council (SSRC).

Q: What other authors did you read at the time?
A: During my undergraduate years, Robert Dahl was considered the leading political scientist. He was the king, the Midas. As freshmen, we read *Who Governs?* (Dahl 1961a), his critique of C. Wright Mills. We read *A Preface to Democratic Theory* (Dahl 1956), still a remarkable book, and his book on political oppositions (Dahl 1966a), which underlined his constant concern with studying democracy empirically. Dahl was also interesting because he was unwilling to accept that the United States was democratic just because we call it a democracy. Thus, he studied democracy in cities, in the workplace, and so on.

For people who did comparative politics and international relations, there's no doubt that Karl Deutsch was the leading figure at the time. As an undergraduate I read his papers on social mobilization and his famous work on nationalism and social communication (Deutsch 1953, 1961). But I was also tremendously influenced by Deutsch's magnificent set of essays, *The Nerves of Government* (Deutsch 1963). During my first year in graduate school, Ernie Haas was lecturing on *The Nerves of Government* and started to make fun of the sections on how to code and measure love. I remember defending Deutsch, because I thought he really had something. I argued that one of the important things we needed to know in order to understand the creation of political communities was how people thought about others like themselves. And we couldn't just ask them that directly, we needed to develop independent indicators of these sentiments, which was precisely what Deutsch had tried to do. Haas agreed and sort of backed down.

Both Deutsch and Dahl were part of the unbelievably exciting Yale department of the mid-1960s. Charles Lindblom, who had an enormous influence, was also in that department, as was Robert Lane, who was doing political psychology. Yale had Dahl, Deutsch, Lindblom, and Lane; it was really an unbelievable department.

Q: Were Seymour Martin Lipset and David Easton points of reference for you?
A: At Swarthmore, I had heard about Lipset's *Political Man* (1960a) as an important book, and I read it on my own in the summer after my junior year. I also read *The First New Nation* (Lipset 1963) in a course on political development. Lipset's work, like Dahl's, gave me a sense of an empirical project that could be done. At Berkeley, I became well acquainted with Lipset's work, but it was regarded more as sociology and wasn't read nearly as much as Dahl's and Deutsch's. Also, graduate students at Berkeley considered Lipset a political conservative. So there was a tendency to write off his books and not take them as seriously as we should have. Only much

later, when I was an assistant professor, did his research program with Stein Rokkan on cleavage structures (Lipset and Rokkan 1967b) become important to me.

Concerning Easton, I read two of his books on political theory at Swarthmore (Easton 1953, 1965b). Easton was never assigned at Berkeley. The first time I read Easton's work I thought it was brilliant. The notion of a political system, and inputs and outputs, made perfect sense to me. Then, when I got to the stage of wanting to do my own research, I realized that Easton's framework had little to offer empiricists. Like Talcott Parsons's framework, it was a gigantic superstructure that had no observable implications for the world and offered no help in doing what I thought was the most interesting thing to do: account for variation on dependent variables. It was an architectonically beautiful thing with no relevance to a real research project. So Easton quickly disappeared from my reading and my consciousness.

Q: Given the climate at Berkeley in the 1960s, I assume graduate students read a fair amount of Marxist literature.
A: The greatest Marxist influence when I was at Berkeley was Marcuse. Everyone was reading *One-Dimensional Man* (Marcuse 1964) and *Eros and Civilization* (Marcuse 1955). I read Marcuse for the first time when I got to Berkeley and then got interested in the Frankfurt School. I think the *New Left Review* was quite prominent in other departments. But I never read it at Berkeley. So the Frankfurt School had more of an influence on me than did the *New Left Review*. Later, I carefully read Perry Anderson's two great historical books (1974a, 1974b), which are similar to Moore's *Social Origins* and Anderson's essay on Gramsci (1977). In Haas's courses, I also was exposed to all the Marxist theorists of imperialism. So I got that not on the street, but in seminar.

Q: Were you involved in any protest activity against the war? What kind of political engagement did you have at Berkeley?
A: My public antiwar activities were quite limited. I participated in several demonstrations, including the attempted blockade of the Oakland induction center in October 1967. I was heavily involved in the presidential campaign of Eugene McCarthy in 1968. I did many days of precinct walking in diverse neighborhoods. But I have never been comfortable in public protest activities. I find the speeches boring and grossly exaggerated. I feel more repugnance than exhilaration in chanting political slogans. I never trusted the leadership of the protests. I therefore identified strongly with Norman Mailer when I read in his *Miami and the Siege of Chicago* (Mailer 1968) that, upon being carried to a paddy wagon, he put his fingers in a *V*

for victory, and muttered to himself something like "Heaven help us if we win." I often think that I study what Durkheim calls "collective effervescence" (Durkheim 1995) but avoid experiencing it myself.

Q: In terms of preparing yourself to carry out systematic empirical analysis, were there any courses you found especially useful?
A: At Berkeley there were no methodological courses that were required for people majoring in, or focusing on, comparative politics. As an undergraduate I had taken an excellent course in the philosophy of science by Hugh Lacey, a student of Michael Scriven. It helped me understand the logic of scientific explanation. At Berkeley I took no courses on methodology. But I should mention the importance of a seminar in international relations I took with Haas my first semester. Whatever we discussed, Haas would always ask, "What's the dependent variable?" I learned how to identify, even in muddled texts, a dependent variable and an independent variable, quicker than classmates of mine who knew a lot more than I about the subject matter.

Q: Where did you pick up this skill?
A: In Wolin's graduate seminar on philosophy of science I read Durkheim's *Rules of Sociological Method* (1982) and on my own his *Elementary Forms of Religious Life* (1995). I was very impressed with how he thought about cases and obsessed about isolating variables. For example, he would isolate the different implications for social behavior of the different aspects of religious life. There was something to this Durkheimian method. His *Rules of Sociological Method,* which was really the KKV of the early twentieth century,[3] strongly affected my way of thinking about the world. I felt as if he were doing science, and that's what I could do.

In Wolin's seminar, I also read Max Weber's *Methodology of the Social Sciences* (1949). Virtually the entire comparative faculty at Berkeley considered themselves Weberians, especially Reinhard Bendix, whom I did not get to know until I was an assistant professor at the University of California, San Diego. He visited there often, and he was an inspiration to me, especially when I began reading for my religion project in Yorubaland. He supported me as I worked through the theoretical ideas that drove the field research and were published in *World Politics* (Laitin 1978). Wolin used Weber's writings on method in part to deflate the scientific pretensions of his colleagues who claimed to be Weberians and positivists as well.

I can tell an anecdote about my methodological amateurism that relates

---

3. KKV refers to King, Keohane, and Verba (1994), the authors of a widely read book on methodology.

to Weber. As a graduate student, I could not read much of Weber's classic *Economy and Society* (1978). I found it a bore. With my newfound interest in comparative religion, however, his brilliance shone through his turgid prose (Weber 1951, 1958a, 1967). It was then that I encountered the concept of "elective affinity" that had long been a mantra for Berkeley comparativists wanting to claim causality but not having the evidence to demonstrate it. The independent variable, they would say, citing Weber, had an elective affinity with a certain value on the dependent variable. This term sounded important, but seemed to me an evasion. It was only years later, in reading Marianne Weber's biography on her husband (1975), that I found out the origin of this methodological concept. Weber was reading a love romance by Goethe, called *Elective Affinities,* and his wife heard him in his study laughing uproariously. It turns out that Goethe was using a discredited term in chemistry, one that evasively attempted to account for compounds, to mock extramarital lust. Weber must have been using this term as an insider's joke, and it fooled the Berkeley faculty two generations later. I felt justified in my suspicion of this concept. Good method for me has always been clear-headed thinking rather than appeal to abstruse terms.

Q: Are there any fellow graduate students you remember and have kept in touch with?
A: I probably learned the most from my generation of graduate students. These include Peter Katzenstein, who was my college roommate at Swarthmore; Margaret Levi, whom I met in a seminar at Swarthmore when she was a student at Bryn Mawr College; John Ruggie, who was in my class at Berkeley; and Peter Cowhey and Ian Lustick, who came to Berkeley a year or two after I did. We saw ourselves as a sort of generational movement, as teaching ourselves and remaking the discipline for ourselves. That intellectual interaction with my peers had an enormous impact. These people I've mentioned read almost everything I wrote before publication for the first decade of my career. It was an invisible college.

Q: Turning to your dissertation, could you discuss how you chose to study language politics in Somalia?
A: Much of the work on Africa at the time was driven by U.S. Cold War foreign policy agenda. But in my first year as a graduate student I read a fabulous article by Henry Bienen (1967) that got me thinking on a different track. Bienen's article described how he had gone to Tanganyika, which later became Tanzania, to study the Tanganyika African National Union (TANU), a party that was called a "mobilization party" in the literature, along with cases like the Communist Party of the Soviet Union (CPSU). But when Bienen arrived in the field, he couldn't find the party. There were no

party offices, nothing. He would go to small towns and ask where the party headquarters was, and there was nothing there. This may be a slight exaggeration, but that's my memory of it. Bienen realized that this comparison between TANU and the CPSU was an absurdity, that these African mobilization parties were mobilizational in name only. So it occurred to me that if I wanted to understand politics in Africa, I would have to find something about which Africans themselves were being political. I still had not been to Africa. But I knew I needed to focus on some issue that would allow me to observe real African politics, not imaginary issues driven by Cold War fantasies.

Now, in terms of how I decided to work on language politics in Somalia, I had read a lot of the Négritude literature that spoke about the importance of African languages and African culture. For me, these were the issues that made the idea of studying Africa exciting. I asked myself, "Why, five, six, seven years after independence, was the official language of virtually all African states still English or French? Why didn't they move into African languages?" Ali Mazrui had written a few essays on this question, and he argued that in cases like Nigeria, a country with four hundred different languages, the only language they could possibly agree on was the one they all knew equally poorly, English (Mazrui 1966). But that answer never satisfied me. I wondered why people were not pushing for their language. Then I read that there was a country somewhere on the east coast of Africa—Somalia—that had three official languages: Arabic, Italian, and English. So you had three official languages, even though virtually 100 percent of the people spoke Somali. It seemed exactly the opposite of what Mazrui argued: what they couldn't agree on was the one language they all spoke. That is, they couldn't even get Somali to be the official language of Somalia. I thought there had to be something political that explained this and that by studying Somalia I could get at the broader relationship between national cultures and states.

To make a long story very short, at the time, I had my emigration papers to Canada to avoid the draft. But my draft board—which had rejected my conscientious objector plea—indicated that if I went into the Peace Corps, they would not draft me right away. As it happened, I had already applied to the Peace Corps. Soon they called and asked if I would go to Somalia. I asked, "Are they going to teach me Somali?" and they said, "Yes." So I told them "We're going, my wife and I." That's how I went to Africa, learned Somali, and began working on my dissertation on Somalia.

Q: What did you get from your experience in Somalia?
A: We were in Somalia in 1969 for about nine months before we got thrown out because of a Soviet-backed military coup. But I had written to Ernie

Haas after about six or seven months in Somalia with an outline for a dissertation that turned out to be remarkably similar to my eventual dissertation and the book that came out of my dissertation (Laitin 1977). With only one year of graduate school under my belt and within six months of arriving in Somalia, I saw the entire project.

My job in the Peace Corps was to direct an English-language program at the National Teachers' Education College (NTEC) in Afgoy, Somalia. I was responsible for about fifty graduates from the Italian- and the Arabic-medium secondary schools in former Italian Somalia. They were designated to teach in Somali intermediate schools the following year through the English-language medium. My job, with a staff of five, was to give them intensive instruction to enable them to qualify as competent teachers of their subjects in English. The irony of this situation—inasmuch as both teachers and students would be perfectly fluent in Somali, and yet were compelled by the language situation to communicate in English—played well into my dissertation research.

I was getting far more from the experience than useful information for my dissertation. It was exhilarating for me to live abroad. I studied the Somali language and its poetry with my students. I went weekly to the market. I tried to pick up local gossip at the bus station and in the jitneys. My wife and I ran a kitchen in which we shared the embers of our charcoal-burning stoves. I tried to mimic locals in a way that would give me confidence that I knew what was driving their behavior. The greatest compliment my wife and I received came when we were spending the breaking of the Ramadan fast with our NTEC neighbors in their home city of Brava. The Bravanese speak Somali as their second language, and many were not fluent at all. Several of them mistook us for light-skinned Somalis (*reer Beenadeere*), and we quickly wrote home about our achievement.

Q: After the Peace Corps, did you come back to Berkeley?
A: I returned to Berkeley, completed my requirements, and was advanced to candidacy. Then I got a $1,500 grant from the Institute of International Studies (IIS) at Berkeley to go back to Somalia, where I spent another several months. There is actually a funny methodological story associated with this grant. Based on what I called the linguistic relativity argument in a paper I had written for Pitkin, I thought the use of different languages in political discussions would have substantive political and cultural implications. Thus, I built an experiment into my dissertation design. I would get Somali kids to do role-playing sessions in either English or Somali to see if there were any significant differences that could be tracked to the language they were asked to speak in. Well, Neil Smelser, who was on the board of IIS, didn't like the project, and he told Ernie Haas he didn't think it should be

funded. Ernie suggested that Smelser interview me, which he did. In this interview Smelser told me: "David, this is a very interesting project. But what happens to your career if these experiments do not go your way? What happens if language makes no difference? You will not have anything." I don't know how I had the guts, but I came back and said: "You mean, you don't believe in science? To me, it isn't science unless your experiments can be shown to be wrong." Smelser responded: "Yes, I do believe in science. But I also believe in the careers of the people we are funding." I said: "What if I told you that I have a library dissertation in my head that I could write instead if my linguistic experiment in Somalia falls apart on me." And I described a thesis that very closely resembled a book I wrote twenty years later, *Language Repertoires and State Construction in Africa* (Laitin 1992a). Smelser said, "Fine, I'll buy that." He approved my grant, and I got my $1,500 for fieldwork.

A Research Program on Language and Political Culture
From Somalia to Yorubaland to Catalonia to the Post-Soviet Republics

Q: In your research you have not only placed great emphasis on fieldwork, but you have also moved from one country to another, and even from one continent to another. You started out in the horn of Africa with Somalia, shifted to Yorubaland in Nigeria, then to Catalonia in Spain, and have focused most recently on the post-Soviet republics. This pattern is very rare for people in comparative politics who do fieldwork. Inasmuch as they continue doing fieldwork over the course of their careers, they tend to stay somewhat narrowly focused on the same country or region. Can you explain your reason for picking a research strategy that requires such a great breadth of knowledge about different places?

A: I've often argued that I'm the one who's very narrow. During all the years I've been doing political science research, I've largely focused on the same narrow set of questions, basically about the relationship between culture and politics, and the implications of cultural heterogeneity for politics. This is a very, very narrow set of questions. Whether my work was in Somalia, Nigeria, Catalonia, or the post-Soviet world, you can see the same questions asked repeatedly in several different ways.

I've often said to other comparativists that they overestimate the costs of equipping themselves for going to a new place and underestimate the costs of studying a new issue in the same place (Laitin 1994). So many people of my generation who were studying issues related to nationalism in Africa in the 1960s and early 1970s subsequently moved on to economic development issues, like dependency and structural adjustment, in the late

1970s and 1980s. My argument is that to make that kind of transition successfully you have to study economics and know macroeconomics pretty darn well, or you are just not going to be doing top-flight work. And it's not easy to learn the theoretical skills required to move from issues of nationalism to issues of economic growth and structural adjustment. In my case, because my topic remained stable, I have essentially worked on a single research program, and the research in each new field site has been driven by questions unanswered at the previous one. Such a strategy does not require the enormous capital expenditure needed to address fundamentally different questions. So I don't accept the premise of your question. I really haven't been all that broad.

Q: Could you spell out how your research program unfolded, how unanswered questions from one research project led to the selection of a new research site?
A: Let us start with my book on Yorubaland, *Hegemony and Culture* (Laitin 1986). When I finished the Somalia research, I thought I had something to say about one aspect of political culture, the relationship of language to political orientation. And I wondered if what I had found about the effects of language on how people think about and respond to political authority could be shown for other cultural subsystems. Might religion also influence how people respond to authority? I was using Clifford Geertz's terminology then and thus thought of language and religion as distinct cultural subsystems. Everybody I spoke with in Somalia said, "David, the big weakness of your work on Somalia is that you haven't really assessed the impact of Islam on how people think and act." I was told this again and again. And I answered these criticisms by pointing out there was no way I could address that question by looking at a country like Somalia, where everyone was a Muslim, because I would never be able to see any variation. So I started to wonder where I would be able to study the effect of Islam on African politics. I thought there had to be a place where people of the same culture had been influenced by Islam and by Christianity, and where the choice of Islam and Christianity was not systematically related to their political orientations. Then I would be able to trace out the implications of being Christian or Muslim for political orientations. From the course on African history I had taken as an undergraduate with Jean Herskovits, I knew there was a belt in West Africa with kingdoms that had been influenced by Islam and by Christianity at about the same time, and that people became converts for virtually the same reason, to participate in trade networks. I said, "I bet if I look at these cases I will be able to find cultures with 40 to 50 percent Muslims and 40 to 50 percent Christians for which the motivations for becoming Christians and Muslims occurred at the same time and for the

same reasons." I also thought I would find some towns where half the people joined the Muslim trading networks and half the people joined the Christian trading networks. Yorubaland, which was the place on which Herskovits had written her dissertation, met those criteria. I had remembered this from her lectures and started reading about Yorubaland. And I said, "This is the place to study." The link was very clear between my first and second studies, to see if religion would drive politics in the same way as language.

Q: After Yorubaland you moved on to Catalonia.
A: At that point I knew a good deal about the African cases of more or less failed language revivals and language movements. Tanzania was a success, Somalia eventually became a success. But basically most of the continent appeared to be institutionalizing either English or French. Yet I thought maybe you could have a case where a language revival comes much later, long after the full development of a national language. The question was: How do sudden breaks with a long-term pattern of linguistic hegemony occur? Yoruba was in the back of my mind. You can't think of Yoruba as dead, or Zulu as dead, or any of these languages as dead. They are maintained, as a kind of contradictory consciousness, available for a counter-hegemonic movement. Studying the Catalonian linguistic movement would allow me to develop the ideas about language and contradictory consciousness I had formulated in working on my Gramscian book, *Hegemony and Culture*. What I found in Catalonia, as I wrote in several articles, was what I called the marriage of the half-forgotten poets and the lonely philologists with a rising bourgeoisie, and the acceptance by the Andalusian immigrants to Catalonia of a regime that required them to be bilingual.[4]

My next move was to the post-Soviet cases. In 1988, as I was contemplating how I might consolidate the articles I'd been writing on Catalonia into a book, I was also doing research on the language laws in the fourteen non-Russian republics of the Soviet Union. The historic right of Russians to be monolingual was being challenged, and the Soviet Union itself was being challenged. For me, this was the most astonishing thing that I had ever witnessed in the field of *political linguistics,* a term I used to describe my specialization. I saw an opportunity to connect my research on culture to the most momentous political event of my lifetime. So I called up a bunch of old friends and asked, "Would I be considered a complete flake if I dropped everything and started studying Russian? I have to study this."

4. Laitin (1989, 1992b, 1995a), Laitin and Solé (1989), Laitin and Rodríguez Gómez (1992), and Laitin, Solé, and Kalyvas (1994).

Most of my friends said, "That's what tenure is for. Do it!" So I started learning Russian.[5]

Research Design

Q: Turning to methodological concerns, in *Designing Social Inquiry*, King, Keohane, and Verba (1994, 147, 205–6) refer to your study on Yorubaland as an example of how to gain control over key variables. Whom were you reading to help you think through these methodological issues? Or was your response to problems of research design intuitive?

A: Thoroughly intuitive. The funny thing about King, Keohane, and Verba's use of my study is that I had written a methodological appendix for both the Somalia book and the Yoruba book, and, in both cases, I had to fight to get the methodological material published. My publishers felt this focus on methods was breaking the continuity of the text and that I was just indulging my own fantasies of science, because no one else really believed in it. My wife, Delia, complained about my going to places that were not very great to live in. And I remember Ernie Haas wryly telling Delia and me that most of the people in political science understand her concerns and thus choose their places to do research by cuisine, but David chooses his cases by science. But the idea of isolating variables was intuitively obvious to me. I never took any methods courses of the type that are now inspired by King, Keohane, and Verba's *Designing Social Inquiry*.

Q: Still, by that point in time a number of widely discussed works on the methodology of comparative research had already appeared, including several chapters by Neil Smelser and his 1976 book (Smelser 1968, 1973, 1976), and Arend Lijphart's article in the *American Political Science Review* (1971).

A: That's true. I actually taught the Smelser book, using his chapter on how Tocqueville isolated variables through his comparison of the French *ancien régime* and American democracy. I don't think I had read Lijphart's papers on the comparative method until much later, in fact, until we were recruiting him at the University of California, San Diego.[6] So, yes, this kind of methodological material was in the air and available. But I never took a course on it. Let me put it this way, my mother has perfect pitch, and she can't understand how anyone could try to study matching pitches. It is just

---

5. This research resulted in Laitin (1998).
6. Lijphart joined the faculty of UCSD in 1978.

intuitive to her. And, to be honest, I find it almost unbearable to read the literature on case selection. Case selection is something I just feel in my bones. But, to come back to King, Keohane, and Verba's *Designing Social Inquiry,* I was in Estonia when I first saw the book. And when I saw they had given me credit for meeting their criteria of case selection, I had a quiet smile, because I finally had gotten a touch of recognition for something I actually didn't work to do. It just sort of came to me in an intuitive way.

Q: But your work has been far more explicit about methodological issues than a lot of the literature, and you have written extensively about your use of the comparative method.
A: I write about the methodology I use in my research very self-consciously, yet, when I read it from other people, my eyes just glaze over in boredom. That's a contradiction, it's a hard thing to reconcile. But all the methodology stuff I have written comes from trying to understand how best to account for some phenomenon in the world, and it's written not as a contribution to methodology, but as an attempt to sort out, to get a grasp on, some phenomenon that's ill understood. Take the chapter on methodology in my first Somalia book (Laitin 1977, 162–85), or the methodology appendix in *Hegemony and Culture* (Laitin 1986, 185–205), or the "National Revivals and Violence" article (Laitin 1995a). The discussion is self-consciously simple, focusing on how best to make inferences about the particular phenomenon I am interested in studying, on how not to violate basic rules of logic. I was never a pure methodologist. I was always trying to use elementary logic to make sure my inferences were reasonable.

Q: When you read King, Keohane, and Verba's *Designing Social Inquiry* (1994), did it merely confirm the ideas you already had? Or did it give you some new angles and insight?
A: The book was a breath of fresh air for me, as I said in my review of it (Laitin 1995b). It made me feel a little bit like Monsieur Jourdan in Molière's *Bourgeois Gentilhomme.* I had been doing methodology all my life, but I didn't know it. I was just writing about comparative politics. I really learned a lot from *Designing Social Inquiry.* I had done a good deal of statistical work, but I had always farmed it out, telling statistical consultants what I wanted. I had no feel for the peculiar rules or foundations of statistical work. In reading King, Keohane, and Verba, and especially Gary King's work—all I could of it—I gained a tremendous appreciation for the clarity of thinking that good statistical work forces on you, in a different way than formal theorizing. So, ironically, rather than teaching me about qualitative methods, which is the purpose of the book, it taught me some of the beauties of quantitative methods.

Q: When you were doing your research in Africa and later in Spain, others were doing quantitative research on political culture. Indeed, though you pursued your research program by moving from one research site to another and conducting field research in each place, you could have pursued another option: attempting to gain control over variables of interest through a large-N, quantitative study. Was that something you considered?

A: At that point in the development of the comparative field, the data available for questions I wanted to answer were pretty paltry. And I had a very strong intellectual disagreement with, say, a Gabriel Almond, a Sidney Verba, or a Ronald Inglehart, who were doing large, cross-national surveys (Almond and Verba 1963; Inglehart 1977). I couldn't believe they could get answers to the questions I was interested in. I thought their surveys were not addressing the kinds of concerns that needed to be addressed, and that the kind of processual things that interested me were best addressed with ethnographic methods. I didn't see the kind of things you can do with survey and quantitative research. I had an aversion to this sort of research and didn't show an interest in it until much later.

Fieldwork and Cases

Q: Your early experience in the field clearly had a formative influence, and you are one of the few senior comparativists who continues to go back regularly to the field. What does fieldwork do for you?

A: That's a hard question. People reach inspiration in different ways. I like living in a foreign place and reading newspapers every day. When I'm in a place foreign to me, I see the world in many different ways, with a clarity that I can never get from reading. I do not just mean traveling, but also living abroad, and I am not talking only about doing formal interviews, but even more so about doing regular things, like going to the market and watching people interact. When I do these things, I feel that I get an understanding of what's driving the political question I am interested in. I don't think it's the only way to get inspiration. But for me, it's the most powerful way.

I can give one example of this, which had some implications for my later work. When I was working on the Catalan normalization project, the drive by Catalonians to normalize the Catalan language, I was thinking in terms of the Gramscian perspective I had used in my previous book (Laitin 1986). I wanted to understand how a historic coalition of rural nationalists and the urban-based bourgeoisie was able to maintain itself and promote and preserve the Catalan language, even through the years of repression under Franco and also under the Bourbons, going back to the Law of the

New Foundation in 1716. Then, in 1984, after living in Barcelona for about two months, I saw the Sardana—the famous Catalan national dance—performed in front of the Church Sant Vicenç de Sarrià. It was 8 o'clock, stores were closing, and loads of people were coming home from work. There was a band that was hired to play the music, and the people started coming to the square with their briefcases, shopping bags, and all this personal stuff. Barcelona is a city of about three-and-a-half million people, a significant percentage of whom are thieves, as would be the case in any large town. Although you never see it in the Picasso paintings, when the people perform the Sardana they put their little bundles of possessions in the center and dance around them. So, they developed an urban dance that enabled them to protect their property the whole time they were dancing. And they have to count a fairly large number of steps in one direction, yet there was apparently no signal indicating when they have to switch to the other direction. I saw them counting their steps with their lips, though trying to hide it because you're not supposed to show it.

Thousands of tourists have seen the Sardana, it happens all the time, and the dance itself is relatively boring. But to me it was inspirational, and I asked myself a very simple question. "Here I am in the most bourgeois city I've ever lived in, with a commercial bourgeoisie that goes way, way back, which developed an urban form of culture in which they can protect their property while dancing. And they count! This is all they do. It's the fundamental commercial function to count." Then I asked, "Why are people who are so rational and so calculating pushing a linguistic movement that would increase their communicative capabilities by zero? You would think the Catalans would be on this gigantic learn English campaign, which would be tremendously more useful for their commercial dealings. Why are they pushing this language, Catalan, which, if successfully promoted, will allow them to communicate with no more people than they presently communicate with, and which will have no communicative payoff whatsoever? What are they doing with this language?"

And I just walked through the town for the next two or three days, sort of like a zombie, asking and re-asking that question to myself. Then I remembered that as an undergraduate I had read Tom Schelling's *Strategy of Conflict* (1960) and something about coordination games. I tried to recreate those games that I hadn't seen for almost twenty years. I hadn't seen anything like game theory since then. And I tried to redraw these game theory matrixes in my apartment, with no books, since this was not something I could get in a Catalan library. Also, there was nobody in Catalonia that I knew who could help me do this. I wrote some preliminary models that I would hate to look at again now, and sent them to Bob Bates, who wrote back and said, "You're a terrific anthropologist, David. Why don't you stick to writing anthropology?" But I felt there was something going on, that the language movement was an equilibrium that nobody really wanted, yet nobody could get out of. I had to figure out how they got themselves into this jam of promoting something they didn't really want. That's overstating it, but that's how I was thinking about the question.

That's what I get out of fieldwork and, incidentally, that's the origin of my interest in game theory. This insight from Barcelona pushed my research program for quite a while, in utterly new directions. Fieldwork has that excitement for me.

Q: To take this point a little further, what kind of work do you think you would have produced had you not done the fieldwork you did? What if your training had been different and you had put more emphasis from the outset on game theory and less on fieldwork?
A: I don't think my work would have been as good. I may have been quite adequate. I may have come up with good work. But I think what distinguishes my work is my ability to represent the basis of political life in the places I write about in a way that does not fundamentally violate the understanding of people who spend their lives in those places. And I am also able to portray these places in a way that speaks to theoretical issues in political science. So, I would say I have a comparative advantage in bringing insights from the field into theory. I don't think I ever would have gotten the successes that I've had if I had started out just in theory, because my skills are not as good in that area.

Q: What language skills have you acquired to carry out all this fieldwork?
A: My language abilities are not excellent, though I have developed conversational skills and an ability to read. I spoke Somali decently. I could get around and conduct preliminary interviews. As for Yoruba, although I studied hard, I could only carry on a basic conversation and read. For most of the sermons I listened to in churches or mosques, I had to have someone translate to me in English. In Catalonia, my Spanish was pretty good. I could read anything and conduct an interview in Spanish. I could easily read Catalan and understand it on television, but I couldn't speak it. With regard to Russian, I basically lived with a Russian-speaking family for seven-and-a-half months and developed pretty good conversational abilities and pretty good technical reading abilities. But for *Identity in Formation* (Laitin 1998a), I had the assistance of advanced graduate students who were doing complementary work in three other republics. These graduate students were all thoroughly fluent in Russian, and they helped me work through a great deal of Russian material that I never would have been able to grasp on

my own. I should add that I've always worked with local collaborators, and their help has been indispensable. So, in general, I was always able to pick up conversations in the street, read the newspapers, and get along. But I was never able to give a lecture, for example, except in Spanish. Spanish is the only language I was able to use to do professional work.

Q: In looking over your record of publications, it is striking that even as you moved from one place to another, you kept on writing about Somalia. Does the Somali case occupy a special place in your thinking?
A: There is no doubt that Somalia, the first foreign country I lived in, had an enormous impact on me. I keep up with it, I keep up with everything written on it. Somalia is a special place for me. I also keep up with, and keep writing about, Catalonia. I've done some papers in the past few years on what the European states will look like culturally as the process of European integration moves forward. Material I collected from Catalonia figures very strongly in those papers. And I keep up with Catalan politics as if it were my hometown, as I do with Somalia. I find it extremely difficult to shed myself of interest in a place where I've done fieldwork.

Q: Have you gone back to these places for visits?
A: I go back to Catalonia quite a bit. But I never returned to Yorubaland. And though I went back to Somalia two times after I finished my work there, I haven't been back in a long time, probably fifteen years. My style is more to set up shop in a place, rather than go for a quick visit. Even when I did some papers on India, I spent six weeks in the field. And when I did a small research project in Ghana, I spent a good amount of time there, too. I don't like to fly into a place for just a few days and then fly out. If you do that, I fear you would feel like you've only talked to taxi drivers.

Classics, Historical Analysis, and Normative Concerns

Q: What about the classics of social and political theory? Do you go back to any classic works for inspiration?
A: No. I read too slowly, and I have a terrible memory for a lot of things. But I am a junky for dissertations and work by young people. I read dissertations wherever I can find them. I get inspiration there rather than by going back to the classics.

Q: What role has historical analysis played in your work?
A: History plays a crucial role in all my books, especially in setting up the context that is necessary to understand the political phenomenon I exam-

ine. For example, in my work on Yorubaland, I offer a detailed historical narrative of the origins of Islamic and Christian evangelization there, addressing how it happened and how it was linked with imperialism. These questions constitute the historical foundation for the work. But the only book in which I offer a historical analysis in the sense that Alexander Gerschenkron (1962) or Ruth and David Collier (1991) do, that is, an analysis that focuses on a historical period or era as a variable, is *Language Repertoires and State Construction in Africa* (Laitin 1992a). In that book I argue that the historical era in which states consolidate has implications for the kinds of nations that form and, specifically, for the degree of national heterogeneity within a state. I thought this was an idea that would sell, because I took a historical era and specified its effect on a pretty important dependent variable. Yet I don't know of anyone who has picked up that idea.

Q: Has your research been guided by normative concerns?
A: I have been concerned primarily about the maintenance of cultural heterogeneity under conditions of individual freedom. Combining diversity with individual choice and freedom is a very hard mix. This normative concern has driven much of my research and underpins a lot of what I have written.

Core Ideas and Their Reception

Q: You said that you've worked in many places but on a fairly narrow set of questions about the political implications of cultural heterogeneity. Yet this issue is at the heart of fundamental debates about conflict resolution and the possibility of democracy in plural societies, debates that have been addressed by institutionalist scholars such as Arend Lijphart, in his work on consociationalism (1977, 1984), and more recently by Juan Linz and Alfred Stepan (forthcoming), in their work on democracy in multinational societies. Does this way of characterizing your research program and the link between your work and the larger literature make sense to you?
A: In retrospect, it seems that way. In fact, in the chapter on territorial integrity I wrote in Adam Przeworski's book, *Sustainable Democracy* (1995, Ch. 1), I did engage that literature in the way you're now articulating. But I saw myself then, and the institutionalists saw me then, as someone who was working on political culture, not on political institutions for managing conflict in heterogeneous societies. I had this illusion that people who worked on political culture would see that I was making a fundamental critique of the way they were going about it, and I hoped my findings and

data would have some influence on the course of future work on political culture. But I had zero impact on the profession. In fact, I did not even have a substantive footnote the first twelve or thirteen years of my career. This did not change until about 1987, when Aaron Wildavsky, who was president of the American Political Science Association at the time, wrote a presidential address on political culture, which was published in the *American Political Science Review* (Wildavsky 1987). It was no surprise that there was no citation to my work in Wildavsky's paper, because the only citation to my work that anyone ever made was "Somalia is on the east coast of Africa, see David Laitin." For some reason, I saw I could go after Wildavsky as a kind of response in the pages of the *American Political Science Review*. The editor at the time, Sam Patterson, had this outrageous policy whereby critiques of articles would only be accepted if the original author was willing to write a response. Wildavsky sat on my paper for nine or ten months, but finally decided to respond. So my piece was accepted (Laitin 1988). That was the first time my work ever hit a nerve in the profession. But, to return to your question, my piece wasn't used at all in the literature on consociationalism or accommodation in plural societies. It had an intellectual life of its own that was divorced from the literature you refer to.

Taking a step back, unlike others who were working on political culture at the time, I was trying to *analyze* culture, that is, to break it down into its constituent parts. I was arguing that you couldn't study this vast, generalized thing, called "a culture," but that you had to focus instead on the linguistic aspect of a culture, the religious aspect of a culture, the nature of family life, the demographic aspects of a culture, or the music and art that shaped high culture. These were all subsystems, and the relationships among them were open questions. You couldn't assume, as Talcott Parsons did, that these various subsystems were integrated into a homeostatic equilibrium. Now, other people had seen this. But I think I went further in actually doing empirical research—on the relationship between language and political action in Somalia, on the relationship between religion and political choice in Nigeria—that analyzed culture and did not take for granted that its different aspects were in equilibrium. The thing that really connected me to the political science profession, the vibrant part of the political science profession, was this idea I had that culture shouldn't be thought of as an exogenous limit on politics, but was in fact endogenous to politics.

Q: Were there specific authors you were arguing against?
A: I was going after Harry Eckstein from the very beginning. I was arguing against Eckstein's congruence theory, which posited a kind of direct map-

ping from one realm—culture—on to another—politics (Eckstein 1966). In contrast, I said there was no necessary connection between the cultural and other realms, between, say, religion and politics. Thus, whereas Eckstein thought there would be a natural and automatic adjustment between the two spheres, I thought their relationship could be politically altered, so that an aspect of cultural life, such as religion, might have no impact on politics. There was no necessary congruence, as Eckstein argued. Harry and I sort of became buddies. And he was a brilliant scientist who understood science far better than anyone in his generation.[7] But neither he nor his students ever responded to any of the things I wrote.

My views also went against Lijphart and also against almost everyone who had been writing on culture. Lijphart assumed, as did many democratic theorists of his generation, that ethnic or nationalist groups were impervious to change. He described and advocated consociational institutions that were built on expectations of stability in ethnic demography (Lijphart 1977, 1984). But those of us who had worked in Africa—or who had read the classic treatments of ethnicity by Aristide Zolberg (1965), Crawford Young (1976), and Nelson Kasfir (1979)—know that ethnicity was "situational" and ethnic demographies changed given new institutional structures. In several of his writings, Donald Horowitz (1985) captured this dynamic well. But it is only the current generation of comparativists—Kanchan Chandra, Daniel Posner, Steven Wilkinson, Elise Giuliano—who have more radically reexamined democratic theory with built-in assumptions that democratic institutions will alter the ethnic demography they were built to tame.

Q: Could you summarize your key ideas on culture?
A: The key ideas are that, under certain conditions, culture, and cultural subsystems, can have a profound influence on the way people act collectively and can be a guiding factor, but that the conditions under which this will occur are very narrow. Therefore, those anthropologists who say culture is everything and thus explains everything are thoroughly wrong. Culture viewed in that way explains nothing. To understand the conditions under which cultural subsystems might have an impact on politics requires, first, carefully isolating aspects of culture and, second, tracing those aspects to the political realm. In Somalia, I found that a key cultural element, the language people speak, had an impact on the way they thought about and responded to authority. This was a finding about the

7. Laitin offers a discussion of Eckstein's work in Laitin (1998b).

influence of culture on politics. In the Yoruba case, by contrast, I found that being a Muslim had *no* impact vis-à-vis being a Christian on how Yorubas acted in the political realm. Religion did have an impact on how Yorubas thought about responsibility, authority, and the mosque or church, yet there was no carryover to the political realm because world religion was not considered by the Yorubas themselves as an essential element of their cultural heritage. In short, the key idea driving my early work was that if you wanted to understand the impact of culture on politics you had to go step by step, and try to sort out the conditions under which you would expect culture to have an impact on the political realm. It was a research program aimed both at delimiting claims about culture and at setting claims about culture on a more scientific foundation.

Another key idea, one that came out in *Hegemony and Culture,* concerns the Janus-facedness of culture. By this I mean that even if we are studying the potential impact of culture on politics and focusing on the conditions under which culture influences politics, we still need to understand this relationship as endogenous, that is, to see how political choice itself could drive culture shift. We cannot treat culture merely as some exogenous factor. This is something that also comes through very clearly in my research on Spain. I show that you cannot just list ethnic groups and see whether or not they engage in conflict. Indeed, a great deal of the violence committed by ETA (Euskadi Ta Askatasuna—Basque Fatherland and Liberty), the Basque separatist movement, was designed to recruit supporters. So, we have to consider the effects of conflict itself on the formation of ethnic groups.

Q: Do you think the field has assimilated these ideas?
A: In some areas my ideas have had no impact at all. Take, for example, Alberto Alesina's work. He treats culture as an independent variable and measures culture with an ethnic heterogeneity index taken from Soviet Atlases of the 1960s. Or take Andrei Shleifer. I went to a talk by Shleifer in which he said ethnic heterogeneity is as exogenous as the distance of the capital city from the equator. But there are an increasing number of scholars who see themselves as constructivists and who try to endogenize culture in their models. I am part of this constructivist insurgency.

More generally, concerning the reception of my work in the social sciences, my research has been regarded as very good, very scientific, and very interesting. But I don't think it has had anywhere close to the impact, say, of a Samuel Huntington, or someone who had scores and scores of dissertations taking off from and trying to refine their ideas. There has been very little refinement of my ideas about how to study culture and its impact. My research is respected, but it hasn't been influential.

Q: Why do you think this is so?

A: One reason is that I never wrote a journal article summarizing my findings from the Somalia research. Articles penetrate. An article in the *American Political Science Review* penetrates into other people's research programs much more powerfully than a well-written book. Getting the essence of an argument with the best of your data out there is a crucial part of the scientific enterprise. I didn't understand this as a younger scholar. At that stage of my career, I believed my job was to write in the form with which I felt most comfortable; to say exactly what I had to say, no more, no less; and to pay less attention to packaging than to getting my research out as an integrated whole. I still would not advise anyone to do it much differently. Moreover, I have to confess that I never really cared that my work wasn't being read. I was considered by a lot of people in the elite networks of political science as someone who was dancing to his own tune and doing really interesting but bizarre research. I was perfectly happy about this. I was getting funding for my research. I was writing what I wanted to write. And I was getting promoted. I really didn't care much that my work wasn't having an impact on other people's research programs. Later on, especially when my polemic against Aaron Wildavsky got a lot of play, I became kind of cynical. It seemed as though you had to piss on giants in order to be heard. But, when I got closer to the people that live in the world of Caltech political science,[8] I realized how difficult and challenging it is to write an article for an *American Political Science Review* audience that says right up front exactly what you've found, why it's important, and why other people in the profession should take it into account. This is a great intellectual and professional enterprise that I didn't appreciate in the earlier part of my career.

It's interesting how ideas get picked up in science. In my article with James Fearon in the *American Political Science Review* (Fearon and Laitin 1996), the fundamental contribution was to show the role of in-group policing as an alternative to disputes that spiral rapidly beyond the two parties in conflict. We wrote at the beginning of the article that we aimed to explain cooperation, because cooperation, not violence, is the rule. One of the reviewers of the article challenged us to show how we knew that. Ada Finifter, the editor of the *American Political Science Review*, told us that we had better nail down this issue or else the article would not be accepted. So we went to a couple of data sources just to show the reviewer that the probability of violent interaction among dyads was close to nil. That table (Fearon and Laitin 1996, 717), which we would not have included in our article but for the prodding of the reviewer and the editor, became an obli-

8. Caltech political science is known for its use of advanced theoretical and methodological tools.

gatory cite for people writing articles that assume violence is rare. You never know which of your ideas will be picked up.

Q: In your earlier work you also drew heavily on authors who were hardly part of the mainstream of American political science. For example, in *Hegemony and Culture* you discuss Clifford Geertz, Abner Cohen, and Gramsci. Do you think the use of game theory in your more recent work has increased its visibility?

A: The shift to game theory, as we discussed earlier, was not done to enlarge my audience. It was done to explain what I had seen in Catalonia. But the use of game theory did make it easier to package my ideas in the form of an article. It was harder to do that for Gramsci, who is the theorist I drew on in *Hegemony and Culture,* or Benjamin Lee Whorf and Wittgenstein, who were the theorists of my first book. The use of game theory made it easier to employ the Caltech model of journal article writing. There is no doubt about that.

Research on Ethnic Conflict and Cooperation

Q: You are currently working with James Fearon on a project on ethnic conflict and cooperation.[9] How did this project get started? What are its basic features?

A: In the early 1990s, when I was at the University of Chicago, Jim Fearon came as an assistant professor with a degree from Berkeley. We felt we had a great deal in common, and we became good friends before we started an intellectual project. We spent many evenings talking about political science in general, international relations, Ernie Haas, Ken Waltz, and other memories of Berkeley. He had also lived in East Africa for a year, in Kenya, so we had a common interest in Africa. The discussions that led to our joint project were triggered by a paper I was writing on national revivals and violence (Laitin 1995a). Jim proposed that we answer a simple question: What, in general, causes ethnic violence? This basic question—what distinguishes countries that have had large-scale ethnic violence from those that have not?—has driven our research for eight years now.

Our 1996 *American Political Science Review* article is actually a theoretical paper that in a sense stood completely apart from the question driving us at the time (Fearon and Laitin 1996). In broad terms, I would characterize the book we are working on as follows. Substantively, we are analyzing the conditions under which civil wars erupt and are sustained, and we are also

9. Publications related to this project include Fearon and Laitin (1996, 2000, 2003) and Laitin (2000).

interested in the factors that explain the duration of civil wars. We will have a lot to say about that. Methodologically, we are combining formal game theory, statistics, and narrative in an integrated whole.

Q: Could we discuss the three components of this tripartite methodology, starting with the game theory part?
A: As Max Weber emphasized, to explain social phenomena requires putting oneself in the shoes of actors and understanding the reasons that account for their actions. One way to do this, following economists, is to see actors as engaging in optimizing behavior, and to show how actors make choices, from a range of options, on the basis of which choice would bring the highest expected utility. This is a core principle in game theory, to which one can add things such as the sequence of moves, the actors' beliefs, and so on. This aspect of our project is mainly Jim's responsibility.

Q: A key issue in game theory is the choice of how the game is modeled. And one can construct complex or simple games. What is your view on how to approach the design of the game?
A: Game theorists are divided on this issue. Jim was a student of Matthew Rabin in the Economics Department at Berkeley. Matt's view, which Jim finds very attractive and which also fits with my inclinations, is not to build the most complicated game. The purpose of theory is to simplify a complicated world, to capture the essential aspects of political interactions that drive the outcome of interest. The last thing you want, in the telling phrase of Jorge Luis Borges, is a map on a one-to-one scale.

To give an example, in one of our models we focus on why anyone would ever join a rebellion and put his life at risk. Jim develops a very simple model in which the potential rebel can either join the legitimate economy or the rebel economy. He uses the model to explore the conditions under which a rational actor will join the rebellion. It turns out that people are more likely to rebel if they live in a mountainous region or if the state's army is weak. Maybe this is something that students of insurgency already knew, but to understand it in terms of the rebels' calculations of being caught adds something.

Q: You seem to be defining the formal game theory aspect of your tripartite methodology in terms of the standard approach to modeling that uses rational choice assumptions. But you have also written about the virtues of evolutionary principles as opposed to the expected utility principle (Laitin 1999b). And many other alternatives, such as behavioral game theory, exist. What is the fruitfulness of pursuing some of these other approaches?

A: My view is that formal models in general, rather than specifically rational choice models, should be part of the tripartite methodology I am arguing for. Rational choice is a subset of a large set of formal models. Evolutionary principles have been used very effectively in game theory. There is also a literature associated with Herbert Simon's work on limited rationality (1957). Modeling is becoming much more diverse and, overall, the assumptions about the calculating abilities of humans have gradually been pared down.

From all this debate, I retain a fundamental insight: having to demonstrate what the conditions of equilibrium are imposes a healthy constraint on theorizing. Lacking this, there are no criteria for delineating what is a predicted or non-predicted response. I remember a paper that Neil Smelser gave at the seminar run by Gary Becker and James Coleman at the University of Chicago. Smelser argued that the Becker research program was going the same way as functionalism, which started out as a very powerful tool under Robert Merton, but after fifteen years began to see everything as functional and therefore explained nothing. As Becker and his disciples try to explain everything with rational choice theory, eventually the theory will be so weakened and so reduced in form that it will become a completely loose, anything-goes theory. I came back from that seminar thinking Smelser had made a really excellent point. But then I realized there is a difference between the functionalists and the formal modelers. The functionalists failed to establish precise criteria for what would constitute a functionalist explanation, and therefore they didn't have sufficient policing to keep their productive core. In contrast, formal modelers do have that kind of policing, because of their strict requirement that you have to show that certain behaviors constitute an equilibrium. There are sufficient constraints in the formal modeling approach to keep it above board and honest, and to sustain it as a positive research program.

Q: But isn't it possible to do this without a game-theoretic model?
A: Of course. Yet without the game theory modeling aspect, the tendency is to have something like Barrington Moore, where all the implications are there and presented in a way that is much more interesting to read than in game theory or formal modeling language, but the major insights are often buried in subtle half-sentences that are much harder to ferret out. The use of formal modeling makes it easier to capture the key insight. Also, because the fundamental assumptions are laid out explicitly in formal models, it is easier to see how some error of reasoning was made. It's possible to theorize without game theory or formal modeling, but formal modeling has several advantages.

Q: How does statistics figure into your current research on ethnic conflict?

A: If our model's predictions are consistent with our statistical findings, then we have some confidence that the theoretical model is correct. And the model, in turn, helps us attribute causal significance to statistical correlations. Our models also help explain why certain things do not hold. For example, Fearon and I are able to show statistically that there is no relationship between discriminatory policies by the state and rebellion. All this work on grievances as a cause of rebellion just isn't supported by our data. And with a simple model, you can suddenly understand why this takes place. It suddenly makes sense. To the extent that the state thinks a group can mount a successful rebellion, the state is less likely to provoke the group with discriminatory policies. So you are likely to get more discriminatory policies against groups that can't rebel than against groups that can. For this reason discriminatory policies in Romania, for example, are much more likely against the Roma than the Hungarians, because the Hungarians are potentially threatening, whereas the Roma are not. So you get this apparently ridiculous correlation, that discrimination isn't related to rebellion, which is nonetheless understandable in terms of an extremely simple model.

Q: Finally, could you say a few words about the narrative component of your project?

A: My book project with Fearon is not based on direct fieldwork. But it is based on an unbelievable amount of reading about the cases, that is, on field observations by others. We want to be able to tell narratives that are consistent with the formal model and with the statistical findings, and that also make sense of real cases. We want a book that is filled with systematic examination of places and cases, not just equilibrium predictions and R squares. And the important thing is that these three elements must work together. We have the formal models and the statistical results, as I've already discussed. We want the narrative aspect to be consistent with the formal models and the statistical data, while adding something important by connecting the models and statistical data to real people taking actions in real time. The narratives also help us get at sequencing and processes, thus adding confidence that we have identified a causal relationship.

Let me give an example of what I mean. I have tried to find the pathways of civil war initiation by reading about actual cases. One of the standard pathways in a lot of the Asian cases is what I call "sons of the soil" civil wars. In these cases, a large numbers of poor people are sent by the state to work in less well-populated areas of the countries that are "owned" by members of the minority. That's a pretty inflammatory situation, for a number of reasons, and it's one that I came across again and again in a whole number of Asian countries. Now, I got at this narrative inductively, by looking at the cases, but then the key is how to tell this narrative under the constraints of your model and your statistical findings. As soon as you say "sons of the soil," it sounds like a grievance story about the causes of civil war. The autochthonous groups are aggrieved that the state is sending impoverished people from the dominant ethnic group to farm a region "owned" by a minority group. This looks like a grievance story. So, one constraint on the narrative is given by the findings from our statistical data, which show that grievances don't drive civil wars. Another constraint is imposed by our game-theoretic model, which holds that states will know that minority groups will rebel if they send the poor populations from the majority group there. The narrative can't violate the rationality assumptions of your own models, and it can't violate what your statistical analysis is telling you. It's like sending a ship between Scylla and Charybdis: you have to tell a narrative that is consistent with the statistical and formal models, yet true to the case.

My "sons of the soil" narrative stressed the tactical disadvantage faced by the migrants amid everyday ethnic violence. Local police tended to support the autochthonous population, or if things got rough, they would disappear. The migrants demanded security, and the state could provide it only by stationing military units. Military convoys, however, were sitting ducks for the local population that was displaced by the resettlement schemes. If they were able to ambush a convoy, armies in weak states do not have the resources to ferret out the local rebels. The armies tend to bomb indiscriminately. This enhances recruitment by local insurgencies. Of course the local population has grievances, or else they wouldn't fight. But loads of peoples have grievances and don't fight. What distinguishes "sons of the soil" is the tactical advantage they face in attacking migrant settlements and challenging armies sent to protect them. This narrative is true to the case literature, and consistent with the formal and statistical models that constrain what can be held as causal in an insurgency narrative.

Q: This sounds similar to the "analytical narratives" program proposed by Bates and others (Bates et al. 1998). Do you identify with this program?

A: Yes and no. Some of the papers in the Bates et al. book are quite excellent. But I would make two criticisms. First, they advertised more than they delivered. This is a point Jon Elster (2000) has already made, though it bothered Elster far more than it bothered me. Second, they never took the next obvious step by testing their findings on cases other than those they studied. As Gary King and others would say, it all looks too much like curve fitting. In my view, after you've done your analytic narrative of an important case, you have to think of the kind of cases to which your model might apply, analyze what the equilibrium predictions are, and do a statistical test. The statistical part of this tripartite methodology is pretty much absent in the Bates et al. book. Also, Fearon and I have developed a new form of out-of-sample tests of the power of our models. We set up a random number generator to "choose" countries for us. We then present a graph showing how well our model does in predicting civil war onsets for each of the randomly chosen countries. This compels us to account for model failures, and even cases where we made the correct predictions for the wrong reasons. In sum, Fearon and I are more concerned with out-of-sample tests, both statistical and narrative, than the authors of *Analytic Narratives*.

Q: It seems virtually impossible that a single researcher would have the skills and energy to implement this tripartite methodology. Does this mean that this kind of research requires teamwork?
A: Given these methodological demands, I think there is going to be more and more collaboration. But, let me be clear, I also think that work which does not combine different methodologies is healthy, so long as those who choose to specialize in a single method are more aware of and constrained by the findings generated with other methods. The biggest failing in comparative politics is not that we are not all skilled in formal modeling, statistics, and case studies, which is impossible, but that we pay insufficient attention to what researchers using different methodologies are doing. I do not think we should love each other or even that we should admire each other. But anyone working with one methodology should be looking over her or his shoulder to see what is happening in the other two courts. They should be challenging findings that are contradicted by what they have found, and they should be trying to understand why we get different findings from different methods.

Q: Do you regret not having had these formal modeling and statistical skills and methods when you did your earlier work in Africa? Would your work have been different if you had had these skills?
A: There is an old Leo Durocher line, "Don't ever look back, someone might be chasing you." I had enormous fun doing my work in Somalia, Yorubaland, and Catalonia. And I've learned an immense amount from each of my projects. This is the great thing about research universities in America: they do everything they can to encourage faculty to keep learning. So, I was able to follow my research nose and learn new things. The amount I know now is so much more than when I got my Ph.D., and I still feel I have a lot to

learn. I am always wondering what I am going to learn next rather than thinking to myself, "Oh shit, if I had only learned this years ago I would have been able to do such and such a thing."

Colleagues, Institutional Initiatives, and Students
Colleagues

Q: Your first job was at the University of California, San Diego (UCSD), then you moved to the University of Chicago, and now you are at Stanford. What was it like working at these institutions?
A: UCSD was an amazing environment when I was there between 1975 and 1987, and it remains one. When I arrived, the Political Science Department had just been created. Sanford Lakoff was the chair, and he had come with Martin Shapiro, who didn't want to be chair, but was willing to come to UCSD if someone else were chair. I was part of the first group of junior appointments they made, and I joined UCSD in 1975 along with Susan Shirk and Sam Popkin. The department started out as a group of five—two full professors and three assistant professors. We became a committee of the whole, and I spent nearly my entire twelve years there in full-time recruitment. It was like being in a nonstop general seminar on political science. We grew, but the ethic remained the same: we read everything, argued about everything, and had to come to recruitment committee meetings with arguments about the quality of work in fields far from our own. That was a continuous education for me.

By about the time I left in 1987, the department we hired over those years had become one of the top ten Political Science departments in the country. By hiring Gary Cox and Mathew McCubbins the year I was chairman, we did something very few new departments are able to do: we hired the brightest, very top people in the generation after us, people who were asking the sort of questions we didn't ask and who did work that was foreign to many of us. So, we didn't replicate ourselves. And we made a correct assessment, at least from the point of view of the discipline, about who would be the stars of the next generation. Overall, I consider my experience at UCSD a fabulous educational period.

The University of Chicago, where I taught from 1987 to 1998, was the place I always considered the greatest intellectual center in the United States, and in many ways it still is. Chicago brought me a professional visibility that increased the number of political scientists who read what I wrote. It gave me a presence that made it obligatory for people who wanted to be up on things to read my work. And I got a lot more play in the profession, because Chicago was a place that virtually everyone in the profession came through at least once every year or two. So it was a great place for professional contacts.

My colleagues at Chicago—Adam Przeworski, Jon Elster, Stephen Holmes, Russell Hardin, Mark Hansen, Bill Sewell, Ronald Suny, and Jim Fearon—were fabulous and I learned enormously from them. Elster was developing his influential view on causal mechanisms (Elster 1999, Ch. 1), which were not part of my conceptual apparatus at the time. Elster's view was quite provocative. He argued that different mechanisms could be invoked to show how independent and dependent variables were linked. This represented a worrisome challenge to the scientific enterprise. At its most radical, Elster's view of mechanisms was one in which any mechanism could account for both a particular value on a dependent variable and its opposite. For example, consider the following two claims: (1) upon seeing an enemy AK-47, the mechanism of fear led the soldier to run away; (2) upon seeing an enemy AK-47, the mechanism of fear made the soldier far more alert, allowing him to freeze his body movements, and eventually shoot the enemy when he unknowingly closed in. If the same mechanism—fear—can lead people to act in opposite ways, it seems impossible to build a social theory where we can predict actions based on knowing values on independent variables. Elster's is a brilliant challenge to all of us trying to do explanatory social science.

Przeworski was a joy to work with. We interacted in many ways, but probably the most interesting interaction was sharing students. He demanded more than I ever did from students in terms of designing research projects that were clearly conceived and well specified. Adam is a genius for making hard problems seem simple by conceptualizing difficult relationships in clear ways. He also pays great attention both to specifying variables very sharply and also to linking them to the big questions we should all be asking. He demanded that invariably from his students and my students. It was a great joy working with him. Adam Przeworski is probably one of the brightest people we have in comparative political science.

Steve Holmes was another person I interacted with at Chicago. He is a brilliant political theorist who is deeply concerned about the world. Every conversation with him was a learning experience. In the early 1990s, we jointly taught a course on the collapse of the Soviet Union. Holmes felt that the Nazi experience had really changed social science in a number of ways, for example, through the development of the F-scale in psychology[10] and the whole set of approaches on understanding the sources of fascism. He argued that the collapse of the Soviet Union was equally world historic and

10. An F-scale is conventionally understood as a measure of authoritarianism.

would have a similarly profound effect on the social science agenda. So he said, "Let's teach a course on the future of social science after the collapse of the Soviet Union and try to identify the issues this historical watershed is likely to raise for the social sciences." He posed questions in very provocative ways like that.

At Chicago, I regularly attended the Rational Models in the Social Sciences faculty seminar led by Gary Becker and James Coleman. It was outrageously confrontational and intellectually exciting. When Coleman died, Becker asked me to co-chair the seminar, and I quickly agreed. This was the best introduction to Chicago-style economics one could ask for.

Being at Chicago was amazingly educational: it changed the way I thought about the world. Chicago was an intellectual cauldron that brought the kind of visibility that paid off for me.

Q: What about Stanford?
A: Stanford is a fascinating Political Science Department. The quality, person by person, of this department is really impressive. I moved here in 1999, and I am still getting acquainted with the place. So I don't have the same kind of historical view of it that I have of UCSD or Chicago. But I look forward to working with graduate students and colleagues, who I think are at the very top of their field. Whereas in Chicago my contacts were broadly cross-disciplinary, here at Stanford the people with whom I want to interact are mostly in the Political Science Department. I find it an exciting opportunity.

Overall, I have been very lucky to be associated with institutions where the research I do is supported in every possible way. The opportunities for independent research afforded by universities in the United States are unbelievable and unparalleled in the rest of the world. We live a very precious existence as university professors.

Q: Though you never taught at Yale, you have had some interaction with Juan Linz. Has Linz influenced you?
A: Juan Linz has had an enormous influence on me. I've read all his work in Spanish and in English, all that I can read. The stuff he's done on Spain, but not only on Spain, is unbelievably comprehensive and subtle. And he was immensely helpful to me and supported my research in a score of ways when I first started working on Spain and knew nothing. For example, he would call me up at eleven o'clock at night and say, "I don't have time to write to you, but here are some of my thoughts." And we would be on the phone for ninety minutes. He's wonderful.

I consider Linz part of the generation of Stein Rokkan, which included a number of people who developed an immense knowledge of European political history, of the pathways of state building and nation building. Along with Linz and Rokkan, I include in this group people like Perry Anderson, Ernst Haas, and Reinhard Bendix. There is no way I would ever have, or anyone in my generation will ever have, that kind of knowledge about the range of European and world cases. I try to make up for my weaknesses in this regard through my obsession with isolating variables and drawing inferences about variables. This is something Linz, like Rokkan, worries about less. In their work it is not uncommon to find scores and scores of variables and ten or fifteen cases. For example, if you look at the most recent book that Linz wrote with Al Stepan (Linz and Stepan 1996), they say early on that they are going to focus on something like four variables and eight conditions. But then they have a footnote that says they don't want to be constrained in the procrustean bed of what turns out be some twenty-five variables for a dozen cases, and that they will go and look at other factors whenever they feel such factors were important or influential. I think it's a wonderful book, a great achievement, and I've learned a lot from it. But scholars like Linz, Rokkan, and Stepan have never worried, as I do, about overdetermination and about empty cells with no cases in them.

There is also a second Juan Linz, the Linz who, especially during the Franco period, helped bring modern social science to Spain and taught a generation of Spanish sociologists how to collect and use survey data. This is the behavioralist Linz, whom I distinguish from the Rokkanian Linz. My admiration for Linz is enormous.

The Comparative Politics Section of the American Political Science Association

Q: I'd like to shift to another institution you were involved with, the Comparative Politics Section of the American Political Science Association (APSA). Could you discuss the formation of this group and your role as president of the section during 1993–95?[11]

A: The section's formation was an initiative of Sidney Tarrow and Peter Lange. Sid Tarrow argued that there was a need to forestall the fragmentation of the field of comparative politics by bringing all the comparativists together under one umbrella. Sid and Peter largely drew on their networks, which I was in. I was happy to join and went to the first business meeting.

Peter Lange was the first president. According to the group's constitution, a committee had to nominate two presidential candidates and then a president would be elected by a vote. In deciding who would be the second president, the committee nominated Ronald Rogowski and me, and there is

---

11. For the perspectives of Laitin's successors as president of the Comparative Politics Section of APSA, see the interviews with Robert Bates and David Collier in Chapters 14 and 15.

an interesting story associated with this process. Arend Lijphart said he would quit the section unless we changed the constitutional rule requiring that the president be chosen by a vote. Sid Tarrow giggled and said it was very amusing to see the world's leading authority on democracy quitting a professional organization because it was democratic. But Arend argued back that this was not a polity, this was a professional association, and it was demeaning to tell someone who had agreed to perform a professional service, "Sorry, you can't take on this role because you lost the election." In the end, we did vote, and Rogowski beat me by one vote. After that, we decided that subsequent presidents would be nominated and confirmed, rather than elected. I served as president after Rogowski.

When I came into the presidency, the organization was basically involved in setting up panels for APSA's annual meetings. We had a newsletter that included pleas for membership and a few news items. So the core idea behind the section at the time was the original Lange-Tarrow idea of constituting an umbrella organization so that comparativists would not go their separate ways and gather in area studies units. Ironically, Lange and Tarrow nonetheless went on to form the APSA's Western European Politics section.

One of my initiatives was to turn the presidential letter that was published in each issue of the newsletter into a polemic about the future of comparative politics. It was the right thing to do at the right time, because a lot of people were interested in broad issues concerning what the comparative politics subdiscipline was about. I addressed themes of broad interest such as how you develop a second project in the comparative field after you have published your dissertation work, how to do new fieldwork when you're an assistant professor with a small family, the relationship of fieldwork to formal theory, and whether hiring in comparative politics should be carried out along regional lines or according to topic.[12] These letters—I called them my William Safire-type polemics—created a buzz about the newsletter. Friends of mine, like David Collier and Ian Lustick, strongly opposed some of my positions. I told them, "That's great, write, go after me!" So we generated a debate, a serious debate, about significant issues.

I know a lot of people reading the newsletter got quite angry because they were losing out in defining what comparative politics was about. Indeed, I would say that a large percentage of the section's members felt the leadership at the time was mostly people who were analytic in perspective,

12. All back issues of the *APSA-CP: Newsletter of the American Political Science Association Organized Section in Comparative Politics* are available at www.nd.edu/apsacp/backissues.html.

overly sympathetic to game theory and statistical methods, and that these methods were being advanced at the expense of more traditional ways of doing comparative politics. We were seen by many as an out-of-touch insurgency set on scientizing the subdiscipline. To me that was not a problem, it was exciting. We were begging everyone to write in, criticize, and argue, because that would make the newsletter a forum where comparativists could discuss diverse ideas and advance diverse perspectives.

As president of the section, I also pushed for an initiative related to the replication of research. Gary King was on his great replication binge then (King 1995a, 1995b), and he sold me immediately on the idea. I thought it was important for the section to support the principle that journals require that the data we use in our articles be made available to the discipline under certain conditions of confidentiality. Not everyone agreed with me. For example, Tarrow and Robert Putnam felt the conditions of confidentiality should be much stronger than we initially proposed. We had exciting debates about what our position should be on how to make confidential interview material and other material of that sort available for replication.[13]

Overall, I felt that I was pushing the field to raise questions about our collective enterprise that had never been raised before. And I pushed for a newsletter in which the central issues that concerned us as a subdiscipline could be addressed forthrightly. The newsletter, as developed by Miriam Golden at UCLA,[14] turned out to be more exciting and published more substantive material than many of the journals. I am very proud of that development.

In the past couple of years, there was a kind of counterinsurgency within the Comparative Politics Section by people who felt we were representing one part of the subdiscipline at the expense of others. As I told Atul Kohli when his group won a couple of big battles concerning the direction of the section, the circulation of elites is something that happens to all organizations, and the ones who are circulated out always think it's too early. But I wished him good luck and told him I hoped that he and his group, to the extent that they gained authority in this section, would keep it as vibrant as I think we kept it. We haven't totally lost out, so there are still competitors in this organization. And I think the circulation of elites is a good thing. The section will die if we keep on trying to preserve the vision of a particular junta.

13. Part of this exchange was published in *APSA-CP: Newsletter of the American Political Science Association Organized Section in Comparative Politics* 7, no. 7 (Winter 1996) (www.nd.edu/apsacp/backissues.html).

14. Golden was editor of the newsletter of the Comparative Politics Section between 1995 and 2000.

Q: One interpretation of the letters you wrote as president of the Comparative Politics Section, though this was more the case with the letters of your successor, Robert Bates, was that they constituted an attack on area studies.[15] Was that a fair interpretation?

A: There is some truth to that view and, of course, some overstatement. The overstatement is that Bates and I are part of a generation of Africanists who had done fieldwork using African languages, respected fieldwork, and demanded that our students develop the skills and acquire the languages to do proper fieldwork. Moreover, both of us served on area studies committees at the Social Science Research Council (SSRC). So it amuses me that one of the big critics of our insurgency was Sam Huntington, someone who I don't believe has ever done any fieldwork. It is ironic that he is the one saying our generation hasn't gained a knowledge of places. I think our careers belie the label that's been put on us.

On the other hand, I did feel that area studies advocates and the SSRC were weighted too much against formal modeling and statistically oriented research. Indeed, I would say that two of the three parts of my vision of a tripartite methodology were being demeaned at places like the SSRC area studies committees. For example, I was on the SSRC committee on Africa, which was pretty much run by anthropologists and historians, whose primary belief was that unless you got deeper and deeper into a particular culture, you weren't doing serious work. As a member of the committee, I supported anthropologists and historians doing that kind of research, because I thought it was immensely worthwhile. But when grant proposals would come in that tried to understand causal mechanisms, along the lines of Bates's *Markets and States in Tropical Africa* (1981), those proposals were dismissed as very shallow and unworthy of the SSRC research committee. So, a very narrow group of scholars was putting an enormous number of constraints on the research agendas of young people. And the fact that almost all jobs in comparative politics were advertised in terms of regions and real estate meant that the regional mafias had a great deal of power.

I saw myself as trying to bring a balance among the three methodologies we discussed earlier, so that people doing area work would have to confront the findings of the theoreticians and statisticians. But I think it's reasonable that people operating within a traditional area studies mode of thinking would read my polemics as a direct threat to what they were doing, to what they considered the most important part of their enterprise.

15. See *APSA-CP: Newsletter of the American Political Science Association Organized Section in Comparative Politics,* available at www.nd.edu/apsacp/backissues.html.

The Laboratory in Comparative Ethnic Processes

Q: Another initiative you have been associated with is the Laboratory in Comparative Ethnic Processes (LiCEP). Could you discuss LiCEP's origins and mission?[16]
A: I'm glad you know about LiCEP. The basic idea for this group emerged in a conference organized with SSRC funds by Kanchan Chandra. She had written her dissertation on the political organization of the untouchables in northern India. Although Sam Huntington was the de jure chair of her committee, she was my de facto graduate student at Harvard while I was at Chicago. She got an SSRC grant to bring together people who were studying ethnicity and politics, and, in typical SSRC fashion, we had a meeting in Chicago with an interdisciplinary group. We discussed broad, deep questions from a variety of perspectives and addressed how researchers studying ethnicity from these perspectives did or did not speak to each other. It was the usual "big think." At the end of this interesting discussion, there was the inevitable question of where we wanted to go.

Maybe I was in an ornery mood, but I said that even though interdisciplinarity was a great thing, I didn't want any more of it. What we didn't have is disciplinarity, and I wanted to support disciplinarity. So, I said we couldn't work with the SSRC, because they have a total cult of interdisciplinarity. Moreover, I said I did not want to sit around and talk about the big ideas around our research. Rather, what I deeply needed, and thought the rest of us needed, was a kind of reverse engineering of our work. What this meant was that we would present not just our papers, but also the data that went into our papers, so that others could figure out for themselves if we had used the data correctly. This way other researchers would be able to look over our shoulders, as if we were in a laboratory.

Somebody said, "What about people who do fieldwork?" I responded that the most embarrassing thing about fieldwork is that we don't share our field notes, we don't share our interview notes. Issues of confidentiality would have to be dealt with, but I thought it would be great to share our field notes. This is something I needed when I was doing my dissertation. I had begged my dissertation advisors to read my field notes, because I felt as though there was no check on my research. So the idea with LiCEP was that field notes, quantitative data, and anything that went into research would be made available, and then we would meet to discuss each other's translation of raw data into scholarly research papers.

This proposal struck a chord. It promised something exciting that we couldn't get from our own universities because there wasn't a critical mass

16. For information on LiCEP, see www.duke.edu/web/licep/index.html#nav.

of people who cared about raw data on issues of ethnicity. So we started up this laboratory, basically with a set of Bob Bates's students from Harvard, a bunch of my students from Chicago, and a few other people who were working on issues of ethnicity—fifteen to eighteen individuals in all. We meet twice a year, and it was initially self-funded, with each university putting up enough money for a meeting. Later, we received a generous National Science Foundation (NSF) grant to continue meeting. We have also institutionalized ourselves, bringing in new members through open search procedures. Each meeting is planned by an ad hoc committee, whose membership changes biannually. And we each apply to the committee for time during our meetings to present our data and material.

These meetings are different from standard meetings. We have no epistemological debates, no real discussion of big findings. Rather, we discuss the mechanics of our work, whether the translation of our research from the data to the conclusions holds, what critical choices we are making in our specifications of our models, and so on. It's as if we are looking over each other's shoulders, acting like a superego constraint, which is what I long wanted. I always felt that when you presented a finished article you always tried to clean it up so none of the rough stuff showed, but you always felt embarrassed because you knew about all the stuff you were concealing. LiCEP is a laboratory of sympathetic but critical scholars with whom you can openly share the rough stuff. It's a very interesting group.

Graduate Students

Q: How do you approach the training of graduate students?
A: During the first fifteen years or so of my career, my philosophy was that graduate students should design a research program that fulfills their intellectual goals. I never wanted acolytes who fulfilled my research goals. I wanted students who were deeply curious about the world and who were able to figure out what they wanted to know about it. I would then try to get them the support they needed to carry out their projects. So I had graduate students working on the Green movement in the Federal Republic of Germany, the imagined economies in the republics of the former Soviet Union, and a range of other topics that were not part of my own research concerns. I was interested in bright students who would go after topics that were exciting to them.

In the past five or six years, I've changed somewhat, in part from watching Przeworski, and in part from reflecting on what's going on in the discipline. I've become increasingly concerned that students in comparative politics acquire a set of tools that allow them to do research that talks to the core of the discipline. I want my students to have basic formal and statistical training. If they want to do more than that, that's fine. But they should at least have the methodological skills to be able to read articles in the *American Political Science Review* and the *American Journal of Political Science,* and to understand what's going on in the discipline, what the major findings are. They should have the ability to be consumers of this literature. Also, in terms of my vision of a tripartite methodology, I think that students should be experts in one methodology and be able to work relatively well with one other. So, overall, I've become far more concerned with basic training in the last five years. And the results are very heartening. I have been the de facto or de jure dissertation advisor of many students, not only at Chicago and here at Stanford, but also at many other universities. And I have seen these students use an approach to comparative politics that reflects quite closely my vision of how things should develop. There is a new generation of young comparativists that is doing excellent work.

Achievements and the Future of Comparative Politics

Q: You have argued that political science is in a state of fragmentation and that this reduces the impact and prestige of political science.
A: We political scientists are institutionally embarrassed in some way about presenting our findings to our students and also to the wider world. With regard to our students, we currently teach them that we live under a broad umbrella and that political scientists have lots of opinions. But we do not give them a full account of what we know. I have argued that one way we could do this is by presenting our research findings through a standardized, introductory course in political science (Laitin 2004a). There is likely to be strong resistance to this idea and the broader notion of an integrated discipline. But if there were a Paul Samuelson,[17] who could write a text that integrates the field, and if you could then get twenty colleges to use it as a test, I believe this would set a standard for teaching political science that would spread rapidly through the discipline. Though ex ante this idea looks radical, ex post it would look obvious.

With regard to the wider world, we political scientists are insufficiently proud of our findings and thus do not make the wider scholarly community aware of them. This hurts us at the National Science Foundation (NSF), where economics and psychology get big budget jumps, and we don't. There is a view at the NSF that political science isn't producing new knowledge at the rate of economics, and I think that is partly a result of the way

17. The reference is to Paul Samuelson, winner of the Nobel Prize in economics in 1970 and author of *Economics: An Introductory Analysis,* first published in 1948 and currently in its sixteenth edition (Samuelson 1948). This textbook has dominated the college classrooms for two generations and is the best-selling economics textbook of all time.

we undersell ourselves. I was recently discussing with Gary King the idea that the APSA might hire two science writers to comb through leading journals and write press releases about the findings in political science and their significance. This kind of outreach should be seen as part of the enterprise of political science.

Q: The synthesis of political science you are proposing seems quite different from the one favored by rational choice theorists. Their idea of synthesis centers on the search for game-theoretic models that fit a broad range of settings or situations and that are integrated by the fact that all these models apply the same theoretical principles, the same theory of rational action.

A: Yes. William Riker's vision of the field was that there are a limited number of political principles, such as those associated with the issue of commitment. Once you know these principles, you can see how they work themselves out in national legislatures, in ethnic wars, and all over the place. So you have a general theory of commitment. Because we can find these principles at work in all sorts of political settings, the traditional fields like international relations, comparative politics, or American politics cease to be relevant. This is one vision of what the discipline is about and, I confess, it has its attractions.

But I think there is an essence to political science, which is worth nurturing, that is different from this Rikerian vision. This essence is found in the two thousand-year corpus of political theory that lays out the problems that have to be solved. These problems draw us together as political scientists. They are analogous to the great problems mathematicians strive to solve. And I don't think we would be intellectually happy if all we understood is the issue of commitment and its ramifications. That's not what drives us as political scientists. What drives us are the questions raised in the great political theory traditions: the question of order, the question of equality, the question of representation, and the question of citizenship. These big questions are the broad normative concerns that keep on setting and resetting the agenda of political science. These consequential outcomes constitute the essential foundations of what we are as a discipline.

Q: Your emphasis on synthesis seems at odds with the view, perhaps most clearly articulated by Mark Lichbach (1997), that what we need is not new attempts at synthesis, but a battle of paradigms among rationalists, structuralists, and culturalists.

A: I call that program the "IR-ization" of the field. I don't have reasoned arguments for my opposition to this view, but I do have some strong intuitions. When I listen to people in international relations (IR), I often hear them say, "I am going to get all the evidence I can for my theoretical school and present the strongest case I can for it." Realists do this, liberals or neo-liberals do this, and constructivists also do this. They do this instead of asking, why do we have wars? Or why do we have civil wars? This defense of schools leads to a kind of legal writing. Who cares if you mix liberalism with a culturalist account into some theoretical model? Who cares if you take variables from two different schools? Why should we compare schools?

With regard to the defense of schools, I often tell the anecdote about the time I did research for a paper on the decree of the New Foundation in eighteenth-century Spain. This decree stated that all *audiencia* (the king's court) material had to be presented in the Castilian language. For that research I asked myself a simple question: "Why did people comply with the king when they had never complied with most authorities in history?" I got a data set of *audiencia* material from the seventeenth and eighteenth centuries and found that the compliance with the king had occurred a generation before the decree. So the decree actually did nothing. Being a true comparativist doing fieldwork, I got completely consumed by reading the *audiencia* documents. One of the appeals to the king was from the University of Barcelona. The university authorities were representing the Philosophy Department, and the charter of the university said that the Philosophy Department had to have six members, three who were Thomists and three who were anti-Thomists. One of the Thomists had died, and the university had done a national search and found an excellent candidate who happened to be an anti-Thomist. The problem was that hiring this anti-Thomist would change the balance to four to two. So they asked the king for the right to make this appointment even though it would upset the balance.

I have always taken that as a fable for the IR field. Having a department of half Thomists and half anti-Thomists, or half rationalists and half culturalists, is not the way to go. It assumes there is no scientific learning, no discoveries that lead to new independent variables. If faculty members have property rights based on independent variables, what happens if the independent variables turn out to be inconsequential? They still have the property rights. To give an example of why this is problematic, consider astrology. Astrology must have seemed like a great idea at one time, and it had a big and obvious independent variable, the aligning of the planets. But this independent variable turned out not to explain anything about human life. What if faculty members had been given property rights over the right-hand variable, planetary alignments, even though it turned out to explain nothing on the left-hand side? Giving authority to people with commitments to right-hand side variables, that is, to independent variables, is the wrong way to go. Instead, departments and hires should be organized around the things that will remain on the agenda, no matter what happens to our thinking about the right-hand side variables, things such as our concern for democracy, equality, and so on. Organizing departments or hires on the basis of right-hand side variables seems to be a prescription against learning. This is a fairly strong statement, I know. Though I have some sympathy for the Rikerian vision, I have much less sympathy for the vision that sees the discipline in terms of paradigms and battles of paradigms.

Q: You seem to be agreeing with Donald Green and Ian Shapiro's (1994) advocacy of problem-driven research. Though their distinction between problem- and method-driven research can be interpreted in different ways, one thing they seem to be saying in *Pathologies of Rational Choice* is that we should focus on important dependent variables.
A: I think that's right, although Shapiro is quite critical of my view of how the field should develop. But we don't disagree as much as it sounds. Someone might argue that I've been pushing for a tripartite methodology that has rationalism as one of its parts. But I don't think that's the case. I see rational choice as just one part of a broad set of modes of formal analysis. Also, I agree with the real message of Green and Shapiro's book, which is that rational choice research needs to get a serious comparative statics program going in order to test the predictions of their models. I think the Green and Shapiro book was not as productive as it should have been, because it put people in a paradigm war mode.

Q: Concerning the big questions you see as central to political science and comparative politics, what are some of the things you consider important findings?
A: I present my views on this matter in my article in the most recent edition of *The State of the Discipline* (Laitin 2002; see also Laitin 2004b). In the study of the causes of civil wars, the field in which I currently work, we have found again and again that, no matter how you specify it, cultural differences are not in any way related to rebellion or civil war. Therefore, trying to separate peoples who are culturally different in order to make them less threatening to each other is an idea without merit. This is a significant finding that bears on important public issues. It prods us to find ways to treat conflict over cultural issues, much as we treat industrial conflict, as normal parts of society. We have learned a good deal about the relationship between cultural difference and civil war, things we didn't know before we started this research.

In the field of democracy, we have also learned a great deal. We've learned something about the effect of wealth on democracy that is more subtle than, though not inconsistent with, what Marty Lipset (1959) argued forty years ago. We have made progress understanding why wealthy democracies don't collapse, though we still lack a clear idea about the mechanism that links wealth to the lower likelihood of democratic breakdown. We also have interesting findings concerning the institutional basis for successful democracies, that is, about the kind of presidential institutions and the kind of parliamentary institutions that are most robust against perturbation or challenges. It is quite firmly established that parliamentary institutions are more robust against pressures for democratic breakdown than presidential ones. So, we have some good ideas about the institutional basis of democratic success.

We also know a good deal, from the research on OECD countries, about the conditions under which social democracy can survive in the face of globalization, and even in the face of the neo-liberal hegemony since the Reagan/Thatcher revolutions. The finding that social democracy is an equilibrium that exists and is likely to survive in a good number of countries is something of considerable importance to the world.

So, I see exciting findings across a range of areas. And I think we have good theories that explain why we have many of these findings. These findings also open up a lot of new and interesting research questions. We should be proud that we know these things, and we should teach them. Both the findings and the research opportunities should be presented to students. This will help generate the excitement our field deserves.

Q: Still, there is the methodological problem of knowing when we do, in fact, have a finding. After all, one reads study after study reaching very different conclusions about the same problem. What threshold should be reached before we call a conclusion an established finding?
A: Let me give an example. In the research that Fearon and I are doing, we find that linguistic fractionalization does not hold up as an explanation for the likelihood of civil war. At the same time, a group of researchers at the World Bank has come up with an ethno-linguistic fractionalization (ELF) measure and, on the basis of this measure, they conclude that it does help explain civil war. Well, in the old days we could have had a polemic and said they didn't do it right, we did. And the wider audience would not have known what to think: on the one hand, the World Bank people are saying this, and, on the other hand, Fearon and Laitin are saying that. Who knows? But now, with the sharing of data and the running of each other's specifications—that is, with the careful examination of the other lab's findings—we can better figure out who is right. Indeed, at a recent meeting of the two labs, I did some replications using their ELF variable and found that it wasn't doing what they said it was doing. There was something fundamentally wrong. And a graduate student at Harvard, Macartan Humphries,

did a theoretical analysis of their ELF and found it wanting. But the World Bank people didn't go off and say, "Let's have a big debate." Instead, they went back to the drawing board to see if they could get it right. I think there is a growing trend for political scientists to operate like labs, and if someone comes up with a finding that no other lab has, you can't just publish the finding and say, "Well, that's what our lab found." Every other lab is going to want to replicate the study, and, if they don't get the same results, they're going to go to the original lab and say, "I want to see you do this." So, I think there is going to be a lot more reconciliation of different findings than there has been in the past. Research in political science is beginning to work a lot more like natural science labs.

Q: In terms of the tripartite methodology you discussed earlier, there has been a fair amount of discussion within the field about the formal theory and qualitative aspects. This is certainly the case if you take the newsletter of the Comparative Politics Section of the American Political Science Association as a barometer. Yet the statistical, quantitative leg seems less developed and less integrated in current research on comparative politics. Do you agree?

A: That's a good point. The quantitative tradition in comparative politics goes back to Almond and Verba, and Inglehart. But the group that initially led the Comparative Politics Section, centered around Ronald Rogowski, Peter Lange, Bob Bates, and myself, felt the quantitative work coming out of the behavioral revolution was theoretically weak. It's hard for me to see what is theoretically at stake in the Almond, Verba, and Inglehart literature (Almond and Verba 1963; Inglehart 1977). So we tended not to take it as seriously as we might have. Yet I have no doubt that in the past ten years the quantitative literature in comparative politics has become increasingly linked with theoretically based research programs. The work on democracy and development by Przeworski is an obvious example (Przeworski et at. 2000), as is work on the OECD countries by people like Carles Boix (1998), Geoffrey Garrett (1998), Torben Iversen (1999), and David Soskice (Iversen, Pontusson, and Soskice 2000). There is also an increasing number of people using quantitative methods in research on violence and civil war. So, there is a new respect for econometrics.

Q: The examples you give are drawn mainly from the literature on Western Europe, where quantitative data sets are more readily available and more easily built. Do data problems pose a serious hurdle to extending the use of statistical methodology to other regions of the world?

A: It's true that this is a problem. However, we are beginning to get data sets on a wider group of countries that are sensitive to our theoretical interests.

We have data sets on civil wars, on democracy and civil rights, and so on. And the people in economics who do statistical work are moving ahead very quickly, taking advantage of these data sets. For example, Edward Miguel in the Berkeley Economics Department has used African rainfall data as an instrument for economic shocks, allowing for some excellent new econometric work on what triggers civil war.

Q: But it is a huge challenge to integrate quantitative research with work done using formal or qualitative methods. Indeed, there is still a huge disjuncture between the research done using these different methods.
A: Yes. Take democratic theory. You have theoretical findings, statistical findings, and narrative findings that are not commensurate. Przeworski's work is the best example. He published a book in 1991, *Democracy and the Market*, that was basically anti-structural. Then, in 2000, he published a book with his collaborators, *Democracy and Development*), that was completely structural. Both are very well-founded, but they seem to undermine each other. Another example is Ruth Collier's *Paths Toward Democracy* (1999). I liked this book, but it was blind to statistical methods. It would have been a much better book if it had been connected to the findings generated using other research methods. There is a lot of work waiting to be done to reconcile the findings from these different worlds.

I know of no area of comparative politics where the tripartite methodology is operating as I envision it. But I think it's a little premature to complain that these three methods have not been integrated well. I have no doubt we have a fantastic opportunity here.

Q: This discussion reminds me of the excitement generated by the research program formulated by Stein Rokkan and others in the 1960s (Rokkan et al. 1970). There was serious theorizing, deep knowledge of cases, and a push to generate large-N data sets. Still, after some very big projects, this program fizzled. Do you think this will happen again? Will we experience a period of euphoria, as a result of the challenges and opportunities you highlight, followed by disillusionment?
A: It's hard to say. You never know where the real advances are going to come from. This is a moment when statistical work is flourishing, and the advances in econometrics during the past fifteen years have allowed statistically oriented scholars to uncover a range of relationships that simply could not have been studied with the techniques of the 1960s. The payoff of these new techniques can be seen in economics. How long this momentum will last depends a lot on how much they find and what comes up in other fields. But if I were to make a prediction, I would say that within five

years we will have made all the progress we can on understanding micro-foundations. We will understand, for example, how the political Left is able to make a credible commitment to the Right that if they were to accede to democratic reform, the Left would not take advantage and confiscate the property of the Right. Commitment issues, reputation issues, and coordination issues, all having a role in understanding the micro-processes of democratization, civil war, and varieties of capitalism, should be well established. Then, the next generation, educated in micro-theory, will ask the same questions that motivated Moore, Lipset, Rokkan, and Linz: why were such issues as commitment resolved in the seventeenth century in England but not until the twentieth century in Spain? Built on new micro-foundations, there is going to be a return to macro-issues. People are going to want to know the broad patterns and whether the micro-foundations are linked to these broad patterns. This will be a new kind of macro-research, constructed on different, better micro-foundations than the one that Rokkan, Moore, and others were working on. Before this occurs, however, a good deal of formal micro- and statistical work has to be done, which will not compel, but will certainly invite, a return to the macro-level.

Conclusion

Q: To conclude, you mentioned a course you taught at Chicago with Steven Holmes on the impact of the collapse of the Soviet Union on the social sciences. Do you foresee the terrorist attacks of September 11 also having an important impact?
A: Yes, though this is thoroughly speculative, since we are talking about events that took place barely two months ago. Although democracy has been the largest area of research in comparative politics over the past ten years, I think September 11 is going to take democracy off the agenda. I think there will be a movement toward "order" as the primary dependent variable for the next decade. That's overstating it, but that's my prediction.

17

Theda Skocpol

States, Revolutions, and the Comparative Historical Imagination

Theda Skocpol has made major contributions to the study of revolutions, social policy, and civic participation. The impact of her work spans the disciplines of political science, sociology, and history. She is widely regarded as a leading figure in comparative historical analysis and American political development (APD).

Skocpol's best-known work is *States and Social Revolutions* (1979), a landmark book that offered a comparative analysis of revolutions in France, Russia, and China. She argued that revolutions resulted when peasant rebellions were launched against states weakened by the cross-pressure of external competition from rival states and internal resistance by landed elites to their efforts to extract revenue. By setting state actors and institutions at the center of analysis, she broke both with Marxist theories, that denied the possibility of state autonomy, and with behavioralist approaches, that focused on rebels and revolutionaries. Instead, she proposed a state-centered, structural perspective that explained revolutions not in terms of the purposive actions of revolutionaries, but in terms of the relationships between rulers and landed elites and between landed elites and peasants. Because of its explicit use of controlled comparisons, *States and Social Revolutions* set a new methodological standard for comparative historical research. The book is widely regarded as a classic of modern social science research.

Skocpol has played an important role building academic communities and defining research agendas. In her edited volume, *Vision and Method in Historical Sociology* (1984), she and her collaborators explored the analytic and methodological strategies of prominent historical sociologists. She thus bolstered the recognition of comparative historical analysis as a distinctive approach to social science research. In *Bringing the State Back In*

This interview was conducted by Richard Snyder in Cambridge, Massachusetts, on May 14, 2002.

(1985), coedited with Peter Evans and Dietrich Rueschemeyer, she further developed her state-centered approach. In the volume's introductory essay, Skocpol argued that states could act autonomously from societal groups and could also mold the goals, interests, alliances, and identities of these groups. *Bringing the State Back In* was seen as an agenda-setting book that offered an alternative to the pluralist approaches it criticized for failing to consider how state institutions affected political and societal actors.

The next stage of Skocpol's research focused on the historical origins of social policies and welfare states in the United States and Western Europe. This work culminated in *Protecting Soldiers and Mothers* (1992), which unearthed new historical evidence about American social policies that provided a basis for rejecting the conventional view that, compared to European countries, the United States was a laggard in the provision of social welfare. Skocpol showed instead that the United States was actually a precocious provider of benefits to Civil War veterans and later to mothers and children. Because it self-consciously set the United States in comparative perspective, contrasting the efforts of the American state to support women and children with the efforts of European states to support male wage-earners, *Protecting Soldiers and Mothers* bridged the fields of comparative and American politics.

Skocpol's current research focuses on civic engagement in the United States, analyzing how volunteer associations emerged and evolved over the past two hundred years. In *Diminished Democracy* (2003a), she aimed to explain the decline of civic participation in the United States in recent decades.

Since the mid-1990s, Skocpol has written and edited several books on contemporary social policy issues for a broad, nonacademic audience. *Boomerang* (1996) explored the causes of the failed health policy reform initiative during the Clinton administration. *The Missing Middle* (2000) called for universal social entitlements for American families.

Skocpol was born in Detroit, Michigan, in 1947. She received her B.A. from Michigan State University in 1969 and her Ph.D. in sociology from Harvard University in 1975. She has taught at Harvard University (1975–81, 1986–present) and the University of Chicago (1981–86). Skocpol was president of the Social Science History Association (1996) and the American Political Science Association (APSA) (2002–3). She was elected to the American Academy of Arts and Sciences in 1994.

Intellectual Formation and Training

Q: Where did you grow up and what were your parents' occupations?
A: I grew up in the heartland of the American Midwest, in Wyandotte, Michigan, an industrial city south of Detroit. My father was a high school

teacher of economics and business, and my mother was a substitute teacher. The life of high school teachers in Michigan in the 1960s was not easy because they were not paid well, faced increasing discipline problems among the students, and had lots of trouble with the local school boards. I admired my father, but I knew I did not want to become a teacher at the pre-college level.

Q: Given that your parents were both teachers, were there a lot of books in your home?
A: Yes, and I was definitely a bookworm. I was very studious and intellectual, traits that were not popular at the public high school I attended in Wyandotte, where about half the kids headed directly after graduation to work in the factories. Very few of those who went off to college left the immediate area.

Q: What kind of material did you read?
A: I read history, though I don't remember being particularly taken with that over anything else. I read about Gandhi in India and the civil rights movement in the United States. But I didn't think I was going to be a professor or a social scientist. I thought I was probably going to go to medical school. It was not until I was an undergraduate that I thought about being a social scientist.

Q: A major focus of your research has been civic participation and civic organizations. Were you actively involved in clubs or youth organizations when you were growing up?
A: I was involved in a few clubs. Since I wasn't a popular kid, I wasn't elected to anything. I was interested in drama, and I did plays in high school. I was in *Inherit the Wind* about Clarence Darrow and the Scopes Trial, though I did not have a starring role.

Q: You received your undergraduate degree from Michigan State University in 1969. Why did you choose Michigan State?
A: I wanted to get away from home, and college was the way to do it. My mother wanted me to go to a small liberal arts college to study home economics as she had. She did not think of me as having a career, because it was unusual then to think of girls having careers. My father was more supportive of the idea that I should pursue serious studies and go wherever they would take me. I persuaded him I should go to Michigan State, because the in-state tuition was cheap enough for my parents to afford and it also had an honors program. I was fortunate to study at Michigan State in the 1960s, because it was a state university on the make. Michigan State was conduct-

ing a national campaign to attract Merit Scholars and had instituted an Honors College program, partly to cater to the bright kids they were recruiting from all over the country. Because I went as a Merit Scholar, I ended up in the Honors College, which gave me access to small classes and allowed me a choice of excellent teachers in different programs. I got a superb education and met very bright and sophisticated students, many of whom were from the East or West Coast, not Michigan. So, Michigan State was both manageable for somebody from my background and also had about as cosmopolitan and elite a student body as you would find at many eastern colleges. Perhaps I would have done just fine at a place like Harvard, but I think going to Michigan State was an important confidence builder. I ended up with the highest grade point average in a class of about four thousand people and graduated feeling on top of things. Remember, this was a time when women were not encouraged to go on to further studies or a career, especially if they were married, as I was. Even at Michigan State, some professors encouraged me not to go to graduate school. But I was always a bull-headed person, and I wasn't about to take too much advice from anyone. I had the support of my husband, who always thought we would go to graduate school together.

Q: What courses at Michigan State had a strong impact on you?
A: I remember being intrigued as early as my freshman or sophomore year by a course on Russian politics that I took from Alfred G. Meyer, a political scientist and specialist on the Soviet Union. He was agitated about the behavioral revolution and was having an argument with a younger faculty member about behavioralism versus institutionalism and area studies. We undergraduates were mystified by this argument, and I found it intriguing. I was very puzzled, because both of them seemed to be talking about using empirical evidence to understand patterns of politics. I could not understand what the difference was. In any case, I became interested in the empirical study of politics, especially in how to understand changes in the Soviet regime. Later I took courses in African politics, though I ended up majoring in sociology.

Q: Why did you major in sociology?
A: Because it was the one social science that did not seem to exclude anything. Sociology gave me the freedom to study issues of power and class in the United States. And because the requirements were so flexible in sociology, I could also take courses in political science and anthropology, and I did. In my senior year, I took a very unusual, experimental honors course taught by William Hixson on all of American politics, from the Revolution to the Civil War to the twentieth century. Taking that course was probably

the first time I saw that studying long-term social change allows you to understand how a society moves through periods of major conflict that reconfigure the issues and essence of politics. My senior year I took another honors course where we read major works in social science, including Barrington Moore's *Social Origins of Dictatorship and Democracy* (1966). That book had an electrifying impact on me.

Q: What captivated you about Moore's book?
A: The scope of it; the fact that Moore was moving through the histories of six or seven nations across the globe and probing the causes and outcomes of revolutions. I thought he was a young radical. After all, this was 1968–69, and we were in the midst of the civil rights movement, which I was active in, and the antiwar movement. I was reading Moore's book as a very serious student, even as an activist, and I thought it was written by a young radical, because Moore was also writing very critical things about American foreign policy at the time.[1] But it was the book itself that entranced me. By the end of senior year, I had been accepted to graduate school in sociology at Harvard University. I set my sights on studying with Moore when I got to Harvard.

Q: Why had you decided to go to graduate school and train to become a professor?
A: My commitment to becoming a professor emerged because I liked college, I liked teaching, and I liked the idea of staying in a college environment.

Q: How did you know that you liked teaching? Your parents were both teachers, but had you done any teaching yourself?
A: I had an intense teaching experience as an undergraduate because I went to Mississippi to participate in a volunteer educational project working with African American college students. The 1960s was a period of agitation over civil rights, and I definitely wanted to get involved in that. I was a Methodist and participated in a Methodist youth group at Michigan State that organized students to go south each summer to teach freshmen entering Rust College, a historically black school in Holly Springs, Mississippi. I first went in the summer of 1966 and went again the next summer. Between those two summers I married a man from Michigan State, Bill Skocpol, whom I had met on the Methodist program in Mississippi. Ironically, we might not have met at Michigan State, because it had forty thousand students.

1. For example, after the Bay of Pigs invasion of Cuba in April 1961, Moore signed an open letter critical of U.S. foreign policy and wrote a memo pronouncing John F. Kennedy's New Frontier program a fraud. See Schlesinger (1965, 285–86).

Q: How did the experience in Mississippi change you?
A: It was the first time I saw extreme poverty. Even though we were dealing with African American college students, they mostly came from poor communities, and the immediate community of Holly Springs was very poor, especially for blacks. I was teaching youngsters who might not have had much chance to learn to read or write in any sophisticated way. I remember enjoying the teaching. My husband and I actually invited a few of the students we met in Mississippi up to Michigan State to visit us. This experience teaching in Mississippi was a way to get involved in large-scale social change, but without the danger. Basically, we stayed on the college campus, because the surrounding white community was pretty hostile to visiting northerners. I was very upset that I was not able to take part in civil rights demonstrations. Other people went, but I did not, because my parents would not give permission. This was a church-run project, and they would not allow their volunteers to go to marches unless the parents approved, and mine would not.

Q: How did these summer experiences in Mississippi link up with your formal education? Did you go back to Michigan State in the fall and select different courses or make new connections to the real world because of your experiences in the South?
A: I took a lot of courses from sociology professors who were teaching about power and stratification in the United States. One professor in particular, Harry Webb, a charismatic teacher, introduced me to the work of C. Wright Mills on the power elite (Mills 1956) and also his interpretations with Hans Gerth of the work of Max Weber (Gerth and Mills 1946). The work of C. Wright Mills made a big impression on me. I was excited by his willingness to think big about stratification and power in modern society, where it had come from, and how it was changing. I also studied with John and Ruth Useem, and with James McKee, all in sociology.

Q: Did you participate in antiwar protests as a student?
A: I was a passionate supporter of the antiwar movement, which was very large and active at Michigan State. It was also getting increasingly extreme. I did not join any of the violent groups, such as the Weather Underground, though I certainly participated in many mass demonstrations against the war. I was opposed to the Vietnam War because I thought it was the wrong war for the United States to be involved in. It was a civil war, and I thought we should not be there. I had taken courses on the Third World, and I understood that those countries had their own domestic politics. I certainly knew enough about the Vietnamese situation to see that we were picking up after the French and that we ought not to. I was also concerned about

the impact of the war on Americans. It was controversial among college students. All the young men, including the one I was living with and going to marry, were worried about being drafted. My husband went to great lengths to avoid being drafted, including getting married and teaching at a Catholic high school. These were visceral issues for young people at the time. It did not feel like a just war. Therefore it did not feel like a war worth dying in.

Graduate School at Harvard

Q: In the fall of 1969, you started graduate school in sociology at Harvard. Where else had you applied besides Harvard?
A: I applied and was accepted to quite a few other places, and I don't really remember all of them. I decided to go to Harvard because an honors student from Michigan State had gone there a year before me, which meant I would have at least one social tie when I arrived. Also, my husband Bill, whom I had married in 1967, was going to Harvard to study physics.

Q: You said your parents had mixed feelings about your decision to leave home to study at Michigan State for your undergraduate degree. Did they support your decision to go to graduate school?
A: My father did. My mother probably did not care much for the idea. I remember my grandmother, who was just a farm woman, telling me I should keep studying. She had not even finished high school, but she had a clear sense of a different future for me. The Danforth fellowship and National Science Foundation (NSF) fellowship that I won were important, because I don't know that my parents could have afforded to pay for me to go to graduate school.

Q: You mentioned that you had read Barrington Moore's *Social Origins of Dictatorship and Democracy* (1966) as an undergraduate and that you were hoping to study with him when you got to Harvard. What was your impression of Moore when you finally met him?
A: I believe it was my very first year at Harvard that I applied to get into Moore's seminar, a seminar on social theory, not comparative history. I quickly discovered that Barrington Moore was not a young radical, as I had imagined, but was much older and conservative, even authoritarian, in academic matters.[2] You had to write essays to get into his classes, and he picked and chose whom he would admit. I think I spent the first week in graduate school writing a paper trying to get into Moore's class.

---

2. Moore was born in 1913 and was in his mid-fifties at this time.

Q: Were you successful?
A: Yes, I was.

Q: What was the topic of your paper?
A: Moore told us to read and identify the testable hypotheses in Marx and Engels's "The Communist Manifesto." I'm not 100 percent sure, but it was an exercise of that type. I remember one of my best friends doing the paper and not getting into the seminar. Who knows why I got in, but I did. The seminar was on European social theory, and we read Mosca, Pareto, Tocqueville, Marx, Weber, and a very strange critical theorist, either Althusser or Lukacs, in French. Moore ran the class by what he called the "Socratic totalitarian method." He would go around the room and ask a question, a leading question, very close to the text of the reading. He would point at someone, that person would answer, and if he didn't like the answer then he would point at someone else. This was a very terrifying experience. It was so nerve racking that I used to take a drink of wine with several friends before we went to class. But that experience did not discourage me. The next year Moore again launched a seminar, a year-long seminar on comparative history. That's the one I really wanted to take. I applied and was accepted. It was probably the most important seminar I ever took.

Q: What was so important about that seminar?
A: It gave me the experience of actually doing comparative history. That is how Moore framed the seminar. For example, we were asked to compare France to England and think about the roots and results of revolutionary transformation in those countries. We worked our way through some of the great secondary sources he had used in *Social Origins* (Moore 1966) and discussed how to understand patterns of politics and make comparisons. We were learning comparative history by doing it.

Q: What kinds of papers did you write for this seminar?
A: Moore assigned the topics. I don't recall exactly, but they would be topics like "What are the causes of the rise to power of the Hohenzollern monarchy in Prussia?" Or he might pose a comparison, say, between English and German development.

Q: What was Moore looking for in his students?
A: He was certainly looking for people who would work hard and make original arguments. If you spent any time in a paper talking about other theories and why you disagreed with them, he would penalize that. He wanted you to analyze the history and use it to formulate social science hypotheses. And he demanded an essay with a clear thesis and rigorous

reasoning. It was a very traditional, almost an English tutorial style, educa-tion. Moore's seminars were very different from a graduate seminar that we would take or teach now. It was more like a practicum where you were working through secondary historical sources and analyzing them from a social scientific perspective. I think it's important for people who do com-parative and historical institutional work to find ways to convey the experi-ence of actually doing research and writing, as opposed to simply critiquing the work of others. In Moore's seminar we did not read, say, Reinhard Bendix, and critique him. Instead, we did the kind of work Reinhard Bendix did, as much as you can approximate that in a year-long seminar. Many of the students who were powerfully influenced by Moore's seminars pro-ceeded from that experience to define their own puzzles and do their own comparative historical work.[3]

Q: Besides Moore, which faculty members at Harvard had an important influence on you?
A: The Sociology Department at Harvard was in a wonderful phase at that time. People like Daniel Bell and Seymour Martin Lipset were producing major sociological works that were nationally debated. Talcott Parsons was fading in importance and at the end of his career when I arrived at Harvard. So, the great disputes between George Homans and Parsons were coming to their end.[4] I established a strong personal relationship with Homans, from whom I distilled a real distrust of grand theorizing, which was what Moore was teaching also. As far as Homans was concerned, empirical material and empirical tests of theory were what mattered. I learned from Homans that an explanation is a generalization about empirical regularities, it is not simply a series of abstract propositions or formal models. This distrust of grand theorizing, which in my graduate student years had developed in the context of disputes between empirical work and functionalist theory, has carried over into my work as a political scientist today, because I am still very skeptical of abstract modeling. The attempt to explain everything with grand theory often leads to an explanation of very little. That was a mes-sage I got in very different, but certainly overlapping, ways from both George Homans and Barrington Moore. I also studied political sociology with Marty Lipset, who was my personal favorite, because he is the sweetest

3. Students who took Moore's seminars around the time Skocpol did and went on to careers as comparative historical scholars include George Ross, Judith Vichniac, John Mollenkopf, David Plotke, and Victoria Bonnell. Ross and Vichniac contributed with Skocpol to a festschrift for Moore (Skocpol 1998).

4. Homans (1964) criticized Parsons's functionalist theory for providing an inadequate account of human action, one that artificially separated psychological and personality factors from the broader social system and thus failed to explain human behavior.

of these people. Lipset is a very kind man and a generous mentor. He was ahead of his time in his willingness to support women's careers. Lipset recommended women very generously and treated them just the same as the guys. He was willing to have an intellectual conversation with anyone. He was very important in my case, because he joined my thesis committee and softened some of the edges of Homans and Daniel Bell, who was the third member of my committee. Barrington Moore was not on my thesis committee, because I always had a very realistic sense of him. I found him a very intellectually stimulating professor, but I also found him ruthless. I never was afraid to disagree with him intellectually. In fact, my first article was a disagreement with his *Social Origins* (Skocpol 1973), and that did not cause any strain between us.[5] But Moore was not inclined to support people on the job market until their theses were entirely done, and he was a very severe task master. I wasn't sure I would survive that in terms of building my career. Also, Moore did not care at all about professional influence and power. I understood and respected that position, but I also needed to work around it. And that's what I did. I didn't have a break of any kind with Moore, and I think he respects the career success I have achieved. But I did not ask of him what I knew he was not going to give.

Q: Did you take classes with Daniel Bell?
A: Bell was a frightening and compelling figure. He is a brilliant intellectual, but is totally erratic. You never knew what he was going to say in class or when you went to see him in his office. I certainly did study with him, but I did not work closely with him. No one could work closely with Bell, because he zigs and zags and you can't follow him. Still, he had an important impact on me, because he was the one who encouraged me to do a broad, comparative dissertation on revolutions. It was unheard of at that time for a graduate student to write a thesis about a topic as vast as the French, Russian, and Chinese revolutions. We were expected to study statistics and find a focused, "doable" project. I took for granted that I would need to put aside the comparative historical things I was studying and enjoying in Barrington Moore's classes and find another kind of project for my dissertation.

Q: What were some of the other potential dissertation topics that you explored?
A: I thought about studying interlocking ties among the board members of corporations, because I was intrigued by methods of network analysis, which were being taught by Harrison White, a force in Harvard's Sociology

---

5. This and Skocpol's other articles on the topic of revolutions are collected in Skocpol (1994).

Department then. I may have considered writing on the New Deal, which I later came back to in my work. I spent time trying to come up with a topic on which I could use the statistical techniques I had learned. In fact, I had gotten the top grade in my statistics class. But I don't remember any of those topics going very far or exciting me. I was not getting anywhere with defining a thesis project.

Q: How did Daniel Bell help you break through this impasse and decide to write a comparative thesis on revolutions?
A: I had written a paper on the French, Russian, and Chinese revolutions for one of my graduate requirements, and I went to Daniel Bell's office to see him about the paper. I remember him looking up after he read the paper, and I think he asked me what I was writing my thesis on. I may have described these other topics, and he said "Well, this is a thesis in the best sense of the word. Why don't you do that?" I took his advice, or, rather, the permission it implied to do what I wanted to do, and I decided to write my thesis on the French, Russian, and Chinese revolutions. I wrote a prospectus and recruited a committee consisting of Homans, Lipset, and Bell. I was lucky because I had a series of professors who were prepared to think big and encourage that in their students. I do not think I would have had that experience at very many other places. I was very fortunate to have been in the Harvard Sociology Department at that time.

Q: Did you take any courses in the Government Department when you were a graduate student at Harvard?
A: I don't remember taking courses in government, which is odd given that I eventually ended up becoming a political scientist. It was probably fortunate that I was not in political science, though, because I didn't think of myself as a specialist in a particular area of the world. I wanted to be able to move freely between studying the United States and other countries. That would have been much harder in political science, because the divisions between American politics and comparative politics were much firmer in those days. Even though I didn't take courses in Harvard's Government Department, I certainly knew of Samuel Huntington's existence there, and I read his work and was influenced by it. Huntington was known as a supporter of the American war in Vietnam, so I was simply not prepared to study with him at that time.

Q: Which works did you know by Huntington?
A: *Political Order in Changing Societies* (Huntington 1968), which I greatly admired and still do. I found the chapter on revolutions very interesting, although I did not agree with it. In fact, I later argued against Huntington's

explanation of revolutions in my own work. Still, I liked the scope of Huntington's book and his willingness to think about modernization as a varied process. Even though their content was quite different, at the most general level what Huntington was doing in *Political Order in Changing Societies* was not very different from what Barrington Moore was doing in *Social Origins of Dictatorship and Democracy*. Both Huntington and Moore were interested in understanding varied patterns of modernization.

Q: Besides Huntington's and Moore's books, what other works had an important impact on you in graduate school?
A: The work of Immanuel Wallerstein had an enormous impact. I read his 1974 book, *The Modern World-System*, as a draft and found it fascinating. Very early in my graduate training I learned to see the analytic argument even in densely descriptive, historical work, and when I read Wallerstein's book I saw immediately that it was wrong. I started arguing with the book right away, playing it off against the work of Reinhard Bendix, Huntington, and Moore, and also against my own growing ideas about the role of the state and the transnational system of states as independent structures (Skocpol 1977). Still, I certainly was taken by the scope and boldness of Wallerstein's work as well as by his emphasis on transnational factors. I remember seeing him in operation at conferences at the time. He was a very charismatic figure in sociology in the mid-1970s, and his book was much debated at sociology conventions.

Q: What impact did interaction with other graduate students have on you while you were training at Harvard?
A: I learned a lot by participating with other students in study groups. We graduate students met regularly and read the latest work that was out. Whenever graduate students have to prepare for exams they form these kinds of study groups, and often they just go over materials in a rote way. But in our study groups we were setting our own agenda, going beyond what any of the professors were assigning and deciding for ourselves what we thought about things. That was partly because graduate students in the 1970s were not worried about getting jobs; we assumed jobs would be out there waiting for us, though we might have been mistaken about that. We were not even all that worried about being political dissidents.

Q: What were you worried about then?
A: Figuring out what we thought about things. We also worried about the structure of graduate programs. Many of us saw ourselves as radicals who were challenging the status quo. I certainly felt I was part of a powerful cohort of graduate students, about half of whom were women. Women

were more plentiful because my class entered during the Vietnam draft, when men could not get deferrals for graduate study.

Q: Were there any female role models on the Harvard faculty then?
A: No, though I remember Rose Coser, a leading sociologist and Lewis Coser's wife, was very encouraging and came to visit the Harvard Sociology Department as part of a delegation from the American Sociological Association (ASA) to look into gender issues. Agitation over the absence of women faculty members was beginning at that time.

Q: What sorts of intellectual issues were discussed in your graduate student study groups?
A: We argued about modernization theory and Marxist theory. Remember, this was a time when Marxist ideas were fashionable among young people. We were prepared to study European history to explore whether these theories were true. Students from the Third World, from Latin America and elsewhere, also participated in the study groups, and they discussed historical cases from their part of the world. So, many of us were learning to move back and forth between abstract theories about stratification and politics and the empirical patterns we saw as we read or heard about actual case histories.

I studied with really exciting people who went on to do wonderful things. Peter Evans was just a few years ahead of me. I didn't really know him then, but he was there. Harriet Friedman went on to do very interesting work. Claude Fischer, another fellow graduate student, was one of the few who was pro–Vietnam War. I definitely learned from students of Harrison White who worked on network analysis, such as Ronald Breiger and John Padgett. The study groups we formed allowed us to learn together even though we were working with different professors in different fields. The Harvard Sociology Department in the 1970s was conducive to this kind of learning, because the faculty included major people of different stripes, yet the department was small enough that all the students got to know one another.

Q: Let's turn to your dissertation, which formed the basis for your first book, *States and Social Revolutions* (Skocpol 1979). We have already discussed how you arrived at your topic, a comparative analysis of the French, Russian, and Chinese revolutions. I'd like to focus on the nuts and bolts of the research process. How did you implement your idea for a broadly comparative study of revolutions? Which of the three cases did you focus on first?
A: I didn't start with any particular case first. I had read about the French Revolution through the work I had done on Europe in Moore's seminars. I

knew a little bit about Russia from reading Moore's work (Moore 1950, 1954). And I had picked up the history of the Chinese Revolution in a seminar I took with Ezra Vogel early in graduate school. I am pretty sure the ideas that eventually developed into *States and Social Revolutions* came when I realized there were surprising similarities between the French and Chinese revolutions, especially regarding the types of regimes that were overthrown in these instances. These were two supposedly very different kinds of revolutions that happened in different parts of the world, and I had learned about them separately. I don't remember which one I learned about first, and I don't think it matters, because the "aha" moment was noticing the similarities between them.

Q: Besides reading about these historical cases, were you also reading about theories of revolution?
A: Yes. But I learned the history first. This created the possibility of a tension between the theories and the history I already knew. Comparative history also made it possible to see new patterns that I wanted to theorize. I had noticed analogies between France and China, and then I started thinking, "What kind of regimes did these countries have?" I realized there were a lot of similarities between the old regimes that were overthrown in France and China. Now, there were also big differences between the two cases. For example, the Chinese Revolution lasted almost forty years, from 1911 to 1949, whereas the French Revolution was much shorter. But I had learned in Barrington Moore's seminars that by noticing similar analytic processes across cases, you could find ways to compare historical sequences without taking the chronology literally.

Unlike many graduate students nowadays, who are told they have to read the social science literature, especially the current literature in the journals or in the most recent books, I didn't just read the literature. If I had only done that, I would have thought, "Oh well, there's Tilly's theory of revolution (1978), and there's Ted Gurr's theory of revolution (1970)." But because I had done a lot of empirical reading about revolutions before-hand, I had something to put those theories in tension with. The lesson of Moore's seminars was that it was okay to learn the history first and work with what I would now call analytic induction.[6] Analytic induction would not be approved by many methodologists today. But so what? Creativity comes from juxtaposing the unexpected. And that's what I did.

Q: Besides the three cases of successful revolution—France, Russia, and China—you also analyzed contrasting cases of failed revolutions, such

---

6. Analytic induction was first described as a method of data analysis in Znaniecki (1934).

as England, Japan, and Prussia/Germany. At what stage did you bring those other cases into the analysis?

A: I brought those cases in last. The first step was being intrigued by unexpected similarities between France and China. Then I brought Russia into the picture. Finally, when I was at the stage of writing the thesis, I tried to approximate a controlled comparison. So I looked for failed cases. I drew on what I had learned from Barrington Moore's seminars, because in those seminars we had worked our way through quite a lot of historical writing on the Prussian and English cases. As for Japan, I had become very intrigued about that case on my own through reading works that compared Japanese and Chinese development.

Q: Why were you concerned about constructing controlled comparisons? Barrington Moore's work does not devote much attention to this methodological issue.

A: You're right. When I was preparing for my exams as a graduate student, I came across the writings on comparative analysis by Arend Lijphart (1971), John Stuart Mill (1874), and Marc Bloch, who wrote a famous article on comparative history (Bloch 1967; see also Sewell 1967). I had learned statistical methods, and I remember being very taken by the analogy Lijphart drew between the statistical and the comparative methods. Without making controlled comparisons, I did not think I could establish whether a hypothesis could actually explain why an outcome did and did not happen. I picked up this idea in my basic statistical methods class and also in my work and conversations with George Homans.

Q: We discussed how you juxtaposed historical case material against existing theories of revolution as a way to generate new ideas about the causes and consequences of revolutions. Could you discuss other ways that you used historical evidence in the course of writing your dissertation?

A: I drew up questionnaires to organize and guide my use of secondary evidence. Using secondary evidence is tricky, because other scholars have done the research without your questionnaire in mind. The debates in different historical fields may be quite distinct and, as a result, historians may not cover the same things about France as they do about China or Russia. To get around this problem, I prepared systematic questionnaires of the kind of evidence I needed in order to address my hypotheses and also competing hypotheses. I got primary works whenever I could. I even went as far as to read Ph.D. theses. If I couldn't find the information I was looking for, I might never get it, because I was using secondary evidence. But at least I knew exactly what I was missing.

Q: How did you construct these questionnaires? What guided your choice of questions?

A: I had my own budding theory about the causes of revolutions: the break-down of the state was crucial; state breakdown could grow out of inter-national pressures and conflicts among classes; and the structure of peasant villages was very important in determining whether peasants would be able to rise up. I looked systematically for evidence of those things, whether or not the historians had been interested in them. I also had to search for evidence with which to test alternative explanations of revolution, such as a Marxist or "relative deprivation" hypothesis.[7] So, my questionnaires asked, for example, What is happening with class consciousness and orga-nization? What is happening to inflation and the price of bread? I tried to look systematically at both the positive cases of successful revolution and the control cases of no revolution to see what was going on in those areas. This technique helped ensure that my use of secondary evidence was guided by the theoretical issues I was exploring, rather than by what the historians happened to write about. As a result, although I did study the historical literatures in great detail, I did not spend very much time talking to actual historians. This got me into trouble later, after *States and Social Revolutions* was published, because each set of historians was prepared to say, "She hasn't got our case right." But I think it was important that I insulated myself from the historians while I was doing my research.

Q: What would have happened if you had consulted in real time with the historians?

A: I might have gotten bogged down in the hopeless quest to accurately describe each case according to historians' views. But that is not what com-parative history is about. Comparative history is about analytically inter-rogating cases and raising new questions.

Research: States, Revolutions, and Social Policy in Comparative Perspective
States and Social Revolutions

Q: Your first book, *States and Social Revolutions*, came out of your doc-toral dissertation. The book appeared four years after you completed the dissertation. What did the process of revising the thesis for publica-tion entail?

A: I could not even look at the thesis for months after I finished it. I had been hired as a faculty member by Harvard's Sociology Department before

---

7. For the argument that "relative deprivation" causes rebellion, see Gurr (1970).

my thesis was done, and I was nearly fired because my teaching load was preventing me from finishing the thesis. I had to finish the thesis to avoid getting fired by my own Ph.D. institution, which would have been disastrous. I have a quality of ruthlessness, and if I am up against the wall, I always find a way to pull through. I can take forever on a project, and many macro-social scientists do take forever on projects. But when it gets to a point where it has to get done, I get it done. And I did finish the thesis. But I felt like I had survived a near-death experience, so I put the thesis away for a while. I came back to it within a year, and an editor from Cambridge University Press, Walter Lippincott Jr., came by. He had read an article I published in *Comparative Studies in Society and History* that provided a précis of aspects of my argument (Skocpol 1976). Lippincott said my thesis would make a wonderful book. So, I went back to work on the thesis and did a lot with it. I added much more on the outcomes of revolutions in France, Russia, and China, which meant developing my sense of how the recentralization of state power worked in the three cases. I also tried to sharpen the causal argument about the outbreak of revolutions. To achieve this, I took the thesis chapters and reconfigured them. Overall, in the rewriting stage I thought much more about how I was conveying the argument.

Q: What specific steps did you take to clarify your argument?

A: I changed the order of the cases and did not present them in the same order in each chapter. For example, in Chapters 2 and 3, the chapters on state breakdown and peasant revolt, respectively, I had originally presented the cases in chronological order—France, Russia, and China. In revising the manuscript, I changed the order to bring out similarities and differences. I decided at the rewrite stage that this was perfectly legitimate, because pulling these cases out of their temporal context made it easier to compare the structural features that had led to state breakdown and allowed peasants to revolt or be mobilized in revolutionary ways. I was prepared to say both what the three cases had in common and also how they varied. I did not feel I had to choose between emphasizing similarities or differences across the cases, because, by then, it was a lot clearer to me exactly what I was arguing.

Q: Did simply changing the order in which you presented the cases help you see new patterns and potential explanations?

A: Yes. I remember I noticed new things about the process of state breakdown when I changed the order in which I was presenting the cases. In comparative work, people often think they have to narrate their cases according to time and chronology. You definitely don't have to do that, and, indeed, you probably shouldn't. It often works better to narrate the major lines of the causal process you are trying to understand. In *States and Social Revolutions,* this meant narrating state breakdown, peasant revolts, and finally the reconstitution of the state. When you are doing historical case analyses, the first time through you may not see very clearly what aspects of the case speak for or against your argument. Something I learned in the process of writing *States and Social Revolutions* is that when you are doing historical social science you are not simply doing description. You are trying to see whether a particular causal argument or process actually illuminates patterns found in the data. Frankly, when you are dealing with historians' work, you often notice patterns they did not see. I had that feeling many times. For example, I would be reading a work about the French Revolution by a quasi-Marxist historian who had ordered everything around the idea of class conflict. Well, I was interested in tracing the process of state breakdown, the events that led to the administrative collapse of the coercive apparatus, and how that opened opportunities for peasant revolts from below. As a result, I noticed patterns in the evidence that quasi-Marxist historians would report but not develop in their own arguments.

Q: Did you make many revisions to Chapter 1, the theoretical chapter, in the course of turning your thesis into a book?
A: I don't remember whether I changed it much. I spent a lot of time in the thesis trying to lay out the alternative theories and my own argument. So, the material in Chapter 1 was probably more developed in the thesis than anything else. Still, I probably did a better job in the revision of presenting my own theoretical perspective and arguments than I had done in the thesis. The introduction to my book was very different from many previous works of comparative historical analysis because I was trying to be a systematic social scientist.

Q: Your explicit discussion of methods and alternative explanations in the first chapter of *States and Social Revolutions* is one of the things that sets your book apart from Moore's *Social Origins of Dictatorship and Democracy.*
A: Moore is not against playing alternative hypotheses off against each other, but he certainly does not favor spending a lot of time talking about theories. In his books, he introduces competing hypotheses, but he does it in the narrative. I was attempting to put together what I had learned about methodology on the "straight" side of the sociology program with what I had learned in the student study groups and with Moore.

Q: The concluding chapter of *States and Social Revolutions* clearly defines a set of scope conditions that delimit the range of cases to which

you expect your argument to apply. Was that material in the thesis or did you add it during the revisions?

A: I was certainly much clearer in the conclusion of the book than in the dissertation about how far I wanted to go with my argument. I had even considered adding the Mexican Revolution as a case, and I did quite a lot of work on it. The Mexican Revolution fit the model in many ways, but I ended up not putting it in the book. First, I always do things in threes, and I already had three cases. That's just an idiosyncratic feature. Second, I felt that the Mexican case moved into a different kind of geopolitical circumstance, one that was outside the bounds of my model. So, in the book I clarified the international and regime conditions for my model that were implicit in the thesis.

Q: One of the main theoretical arguments in *States and Social Revolutions* was that the state could be an autonomous actor, one that was not captured by class and other societal forces. Do you recall how you arrived at this insight?

A: This idea must have come from thinking about Weber in tension with Marx. That was what sociologists were trained to do when I was a graduate student, play Marx and Weber against each other. C. Wright Mills, whom I had read as an undergraduate, combined the Weberian and Marxist traditions and made very strong arguments that bureaucracies and elites were independent of class power (Mills 1956). Also, Moore taught Mosca and Pareto, both of whom were elite theorists. And I had read Otto Hintze (1975) very early on. Charles Tilly's (1975) collection on the formation of national states in Western Europe was also influential in the development of my argument about the potential autonomy of the state, as was my critique of Moore's work (Skocpol 1973). It seemed to me that a lot of what Moore was describing could be better analyzed by positing the possibility of conditional state autonomy under different circumstances. What intrigued me was how much more variation could be explained across time and countries if, instead of taking just one macro-logic, like class structure, you took two or three intersecting logics and let them create different combinations. So, I played around with how class structures and modes of production interacted with geopolitics and also with different patterns of state formation. I was never interested in single-factor determinism, which seemed almost boring to me.

Q: What about the neo-Marxist debates of the late 1960s and early 1970s regarding the autonomy of the state (Miliband 1969, 1970; Poulantzas 1969)? Did those also influence your thinking about the relationship between states and social classes?

A: We read all the Marxist debates over the autonomy of the state in graduate student study groups, and I was very interested in them. But I was
prepared to go much further than the Marxists, because they debated state
autonomy, but, in the final analysis, they never really posited a basis for
state actors to act autonomously. I was working out the ideas about state
autonomy that were eventually published in *Bringing the State Back In* pretty
early on, mostly in the context of thinking about European monarchs and
agrarian bureaucracies for my work on revolutions (Skocpol 1985a).

**Q: What specific works served as models for what you were trying to
achieve in *States and Social Revolutions*?**
A: Barrington Moore's *Social Origins* (1966). I was also very taken by Charles
Tilly's work, especially his critique of Durkheim (1981). Perry Anderson's
Lineages of the Absolutist State (Anderson 1974a) and *Passages from Antiquity
to Feudalism* (Anderson 1974b), as well as Lipset's *Political Man* (1960a),
were also important. None of them seemed entirely right, which made
things exciting, because there was room for me. But these works were all
about big, important questions. They boldly interrogated history and made
comparisons. They made social science seem like something important that
could speak to the human condition.

**Q: Why do you think *States and Social Revolutions* made such a big
splash and has had such an enduring impact? After all, very few social science books are remembered, much less read, twenty years after
publication.**
A: Yes, and I am still earning substantial royalties every year on that book.
But I am probably the last person who knows the answer to your question. I
sensed the book was capturing imaginations when I first went on the job
market coming out of Harvard. I got a lot of interviews in Sociology departments where I presented the thesis of the book. My audience in these interviews consisted mainly of people who were studying contemporary American problems, but my argument about the structured processes that came
together in the French, Russian, and Chinese revolutions always created an
"aha" effect. In any good social science scholarship, you want people to
suddenly see something they never saw before; you want to create a gestalt
that allows them to see things in a new way. I was able to achieve this
by juxtaposing revolutions that people thought of as very, very different.
Maybe they thought the three revolutions were different because they happened in different times and places, or because the French Revolution was a
bourgeois revolution whereas the Russian and Chinese revolutions were
communist. Moreover, because I laid out the argument in a very plodding
way as a series of hypotheses concerning necessary and sufficient variables,

people who were used to statistical reasoning could appreciate my work. For example, I remember the sociologist Gerald Marwell at Wisconsin saying, "When I read this, I can see that it is social science."

Q: Social science as opposed to what?
A: As opposed to the standard comparative history, where the reaction of someone like Marwell would be, "I don't understand this," or "It's history, not social science." So, *States and Social Revolutions* straddled enough lines that it could be widely appreciated in the social sciences. A lot of historians got angry with the book, because they felt I was on their terrain without knowing the languages and without respecting the specificity of their cases. In the social sciences, however, the book gave people a way to think about revolutions beyond the three I studied. I had carefully bounded my argument, saying it was only about agrarian bureaucracies, not all types of regimes. But because the book offered a theoretical key—patterns of state breakdown and reconstitution—it provided a template people could use to analyze other kinds of revolutions, such as the Mexican and other Third World revolutions. When I first went on the job market, I presented my argument and people might ask, "What about Iraq?" I learned very early on to be cautious and deferential in my answers to this kind of question. I would respond, "Here is how I would think about that case, and here are the questions I would ask." In this way, I was able to show that my book provided a theoretical analysis that could help others formulate questions and hypotheses about their cases. Other scholars picked that up, and the fact that *States and Social Revolutions* became a template accounts for its impact. Not that it is above challenge or is the final word. That is never true of any book. But people were excited by it. Some picked up the hypotheses and took them to other instances of revolution; others picked up the comparative historical method and applied it to other kinds of phenomena.

Q: Did you know the book offered all these handles for other scholars to grab?
A: Of course not. I was just trying to make sense of an important subject, figure out the regularities across my cases, and work through an argument I was developing that seemed new. I did not expect my work to have a huge impact. Think about it for a minute. I was awash in hundreds of years of history, trying to master all the material I needed to master. I read hundreds and hundreds of books and articles to write *States and Social Revolutions*. When the book was published, it got a lot of favorable attention and won prizes, including the American Sociological Association's Award for a Distinguished Contribution to Scholarship, the major prize in sociology that usually goes to books by much more senior scholars. Quite a few macro-

sociological books, such as Wallerstein's *The Modern World System* (1974), were winning major prizes then.[8] My work hit a tide of rising respect for macroscopic research in sociology.

Q: Despite all the favorable attention it received, *States and Social Revolutions* also received sharp criticism. Which criticisms of the book do you find the most and least valid?
A: The criticism that my structural approach took actors out of history was the least valid. I just don't think that is right. My book was conceived partly as a critique of structural functionalism, and it is much more actor-centered than that type of work. The book does not put actors in total control of outcomes, because it analyzes how the interplay among actors produces unintended outcomes. Still, actors are all over the place in *States and Social Revolutions,* and their structured interaction is the source of conflicts and unintended outcomes. On the other hand, the book did not pay much attention to the role of ideology, and it could have done more of that.

Q: Why did you downplay the role of ideas?
A: Because I was arguing against theories that suggested revolutionary ideology alone was enough to cause a revolution. My exchange over this issue with William Sewell in response to his critique of the book was fruitful, and I acknowledged some ways I thought he was right about the role of ideology in revolutions (Sewell 1985; Skocpol 1985b).[9] I tried to incorporate ideology into my model in an article I wrote on the Iranian revolution, which happened right after *States and Social Revolutions* was published (Skocpol 1982).

Q: Another line of criticism against *States and Social Revolutions* came from country experts, who felt that you got "their" cases wrong.
A: The China experts were the most dismissive of the book.[10] There are several reasons for this. First, Chinese Studies are pretty insular because most of the experts invest so much in learning the language. Indeed, there is a separate tradition of China scholarship, and scholars of China often would not engage theories developed to deal with European patterns. Second, the fact that the Chinese revolution itself was still unfolding in some ways when I wrote *States and Social Revolutions* meant that the scholarship on China I could build on was highly polarized politically. As a result, what I had to say about the outcomes of revolution was less well established in

8. Wallerstein's book won the American Sociological Association's Sorokin Prize for a distinguished contribution in 1975.
9. Both pieces are reprinted in Skocpol (1994).
10. See, for example, the review by Perry (1980).

the Chinese case than in the other cases. I still don't think anything is fundamentally wrong with the thesis of the book, but there was not as mature a secondary literature to draw on for the case of China.

Q: *States and Social Revolutions* was also criticized by some historians.[11] What is your assessment of these criticisms?
A: The book was challenged by historians, but I was also invited to history meetings to defend it. One of my most vivid memories of dealing with historians is from Berkeley, where I gave a talk to the historians of France, Russia, and China. The talk was really a defense of my book before the entire History Department. Although I can't say that I could ever completely persuade historians, I did completely control that particular event because I convinced the assembled historians that I had read what all the specialists had written, knew the evidence and arguments in their books, and understood why I was using or rejecting it. I convinced them that I knew my history. One of my techniques for dealing with historians was to read across generations of historians. The history profession is extremely totalitarian in its interpretations during any given generation. Also, young historians stay off each other's turf and avoid working on the same problem. But if you read across generations, you get different perspectives.

Q: Was there a downside to having such a phenomenally successful and widely discussed first book?
A: Sure, because there was constant speculation, especially since I was a female, about whether I would be able to do it again. That was a big issue when I came up for tenure, both at Harvard and elsewhere. Would I do it again? The book was considered a home run, and it was. Soon after *States and Social Revolutions* was published, I got an offer at the University of Chicago, which was the leading Sociology Department. I definitely remember the seminar I gave there. It was electrifying. Several very powerful social scientists were at the talk, including James Coleman, Morris Janowitz, and William Julius Wilson. I knew they were considering me for a tenured position. And I rose to the occasion, as much by the way I handled questions as by the presentation itself. How one handles questions is important. If you are able to hear questions and engage in intellectual play with them, you can show that you have an approach capable of dealing with the unexpected. That's what I could do. I enjoyed comparative history and considered it a powerful intellectual tool. Also, I knew I had a theory. I was able both to demonstrate a thorough knowledge of my cases and to show how my model could approach other cases. From the time I sent the book to

11. See, for example, the review by Kiernan (1980).

the publisher in 1978 until it came out in 1979, I was traveling all the time giving invited talks. I was one of the most widely recognized young scholars.

Q: It must have been very exciting to get so much attention at such an early stage of your career.
A: I thought of myself as young. But I was at Harvard, where my junior faculty colleagues were also well known, so I may not have realized it was unusual for a young scholar to get so much attention. I was definitely out there presenting my work, and it was getting respectful interest and attention. People were debating it, and I was being attacked a lot, too. The old people were calling me a Marxist, and the young people were calling me a non-Marxist. There was controversy, which was a good thing on the whole. I have always felt better to be argued with than ignored.

Vision and Method

Q: After *States and Social Revolutions,* your next book was the 1984 edited volume, *Vision and Method in Historical Sociology* (Skocpol 1984). A distinctive feature of *Vision and Method* is that each chapter focuses on the work and career of a major scholar in historical sociology. Could you discuss the origins of the project that led to that volume? What were you aiming to achieve?
A: As a young faculty member, I felt comparative historical work had great potential, but that the field had become something of a preserve for isolated, grand old men. To realize the field's potential, deliberate efforts were needed to regularize and institutionalize what these older figures had done. This required clarifying the models for comparative historical work and establishing substantive and methodological literatures that people could debate about. Although I was still a young scholar, I already thought of myself as an agenda setter and institution builder. The reaction to *States and Social Revolutions* probably gave me confidence that I could do those things. I was aware of other models of institution building in historical sociology then. For example, Charles Tilly was approaching the task of institution building through methodology, moving more and more in the direction of quantitative studies of violence.[12] And Immanuel Wallerstein was laying out a grand theory and asking people to buy into it (Wallerstein 1974). Wallerstein's approach made me uncomfortable, and I felt that creating a grand theory and trying to get people to buy it was likely to lead into a cul de sac. Because I was teaching at Harvard, I was surrounded by very bright

12. See, for example, Tilly with Shorter (1974).

graduate and undergraduate students who wanted to make their own mark. So, instead of creating a "Skocpol theory," I tried to create the sense of an approach, an agenda of questions and friendly arguments about how best to tackle these questions. I also wanted to build a sense of "we" around comparative historical work. So I hatched the idea of running a conference and inviting younger historical comparative sociologists who were doing good, exciting work themselves, to present and critique the work of older, even classic figures. I also proposed to draw together a methodological bibliography on comparative and historical sociology. I was not sure the conference was going to succeed, because in some ways it was an academic exercise to write about the work of all these older scholars. But the conference turned out to be fascinating and electrifying. The younger comparative historical scholars got into all kinds of interesting, substantive discussions about the role of class relations and about class conflict versus geopolitics and political organization in explaining social change.

Q: *Vision and Method* focused on the work of nine major scholars.[13] How did you decide whom to include?
A: The scholars I included were the big names in historical sociology at that time, including a couple of other figures whom younger scholars were prepared to write on that I wanted to include. I think Fernand Braudel was considered, but Daniel Chirot wanted to write on Marc Bloch, so I included Bloch instead. Putting together the volume involved negotiating with the younger scholars who wrote the chapters.

Q: All the scholars on which *Vision and Method* focused worked mainly on Europe. Indeed, many *were* Europeans. Did you consider including non-European scholars or scholars whose work focused on non-European areas?
A: Like most sociologists then, my theoretical grounding was in Durkheim, Marx, and Weber. As a result, their work formed the terrain on which the rethinking of theoretical ideas was taking place. It would have been a step too far to have tried to bring in the development theorists who were working on the Third World.

Q: What is your overall assessment of *Vision and Method?* Did it accomplish what you set out to achieve?
A: I don't think the book was entirely successful. A valid criticism raised when I came up for tenure was that *Vision and Method* was too big an

13. Perry Anderson, Reinhard Bendix, Marc Bloch, S. N. Eisenstadt, Barrington Moore, Jr., Karl Polanyi, E. P. Thompson, Charles Tilly, and Immanuel Wallerstein.

investment in an exegetical edited book. I did it because I wanted to engage in an institution-building exercise, and that effort definitely succeeded. The conference itself and the process of bringing people together helped build the self-consciousness about an approach that I was trying to achieve.

Q: If you could do *Vision and Method* over again, what would you do differently?
A: I might just not do it. I think it's a nice book that has had a considerable impact. But, to my mind, it was not as important as *Bringing the State Back In* (Evans, Rueschemeyer, and Skocpol 1985), which was a fundamentally agenda-setting book.

Bringing the State Back In

Q: Could you discuss the origins of your collaborative volume with the sociologists Peter Evans and Dietrich Rueschemeyer, *Bringing the State Back In* (Evans, Rueschemeyer, and Skocpol 1985)?
A: Peter and Dietrich were both at Brown University, and they came to see me one day at Harvard with a proposal. They said the Social Science Research Council (SSRC) had these things called research planning committees and that maybe we should try to build one. It was Peter, I think, who really saw many of the convergent analytic possibilities around the work he had been doing on the state and economic development in Brazil (Evans 1979) and what I was doing on the state and politics. Our joint discussions went on, and on, and on. We had endless meetings where we would sit around and try to produce position papers to send to the SSRC. The SSRC responded favorably to our proposal for a research planning committee, but they asked us to raise money. We had ideas, but we did not have money. Not too far into the process we decided to hold a conference for the research planning committee. After the conference, we decided to pull together a book, *Bringing the State Back In*, which was the most structured and deliberately agenda-setting work I have ever done. We decided what to include and not include based on a conception about how states as actors and structures might affect important outcomes, like economic development, public policy, and democracy. We wanted to publish some of the essays presented at the conference but not others. This meant we had to say no to powerful people who were senior to us. We even rewrote several of the essays, sent them back to the authors, and said, "Here it is. Does this say what you had in mind?" We also recruited some new essays, because we wanted the book to lay out a theoretical frame of reference that crystallized questions and approaches across many different literatures. At the same time, we drew from the group of people who were invited to the conference and prepared

a hundred-page proposal that was accepted by the SSRC, leading to the formation of the Committee on States and Social Structures. The committee included the political scientists Peter Katzenstein, Steven Krasner, and Ira Katznelson. So, we were beginning to make our move into political science. By then I was also a political scientist, because I had recently moved to the University of Chicago, where I was in both the Sociology and Political Science departments. We held repeated meetings of the committee and published a newsletter. But I think *Bringing the State Back In* was the most influential product of that process. That book is still very cited.

Q: What was the chemistry like among you, Evans, and Rueschemeyer when you were working together on *Bringing the State Back In?*
A: Intense friendship. We met again and again and spent long periods talking about ideas that filtered into all our work, into Evans's work on state-society synergies and embedded autonomy (Evans 1995), my work in *Protecting Soldiers and Mothers* (Skocpol 1992), and Rueschemeyer's work on democratization (Rueschemeyer, Stephens, and Stephens 1992). Dietrich is senior to Peter and me, a generation older, and he is a wonderful intellectual. He combines a commanding knowledge of classical sociological theory with a passion for understanding substantive issues like democratization. Peter and I conferred constantly about how to push the project forward. But it was not a collaboration in which we were doing the same empirical project together. Rather, we collaborated around the common theoretical ideas implicit in the separate empirical projects we were pursuing and in the work of others whom we respected. We were trying to build awareness of these ideas across disciplinary boundaries in the social sciences. We wanted to further a certain style of research and line of theoretical argument in both political science and sociology. I think we gave people in comparative politics something on which to hook their more specialized studies, something that helped them see they were addressing issues of more general theoretical interest.

Q: One criticism of *Bringing the State Back In,* especially from rational choice scholars in political science, is that the "state" is an overly aggregated, even reified, concept. For example, I have heard that Robert Bates tells students that when he begins a project he always asks himself, "Which political actors am I going to talk to? Who am I going to take to lunch to start learning about the problem?" You can't take the state to lunch.
A: You certainly can take state officials out to lunch, and the fact that they are part of the same overall apparatus of authority relations and resource flows is what makes the organization to which they belong a state. There is

no need to reify the state to recognize this fact. Organizations are real; they are as real as power relations, flows of resources, and ideas in people's heads. In fact, a central argument in *Bringing the State Back In* was about the importance of disaggregating the state in organizational and concrete ways, following particular lines of policy making, and thinking through what state capacities meant. I actually don't believe there are as many contradictions as some people polemically claim between rational choice premises and what empirical historical institutionalists do. And *Bringing the State Back In* was not written as a polemic against rational choice theory.

Q: What was it a polemic against?
A: Reductionism of any kind, especially Marxist reductionism. But it is mostly a positive book, one that says, "Here are powerful ways of asking questions about the impacts of state actions and state structures that have proven fruitful in disparate literatures. If we think systematically about these ways of posing questions, we can draw inspiration for new applications or lines of analysis." It is that kind of agenda-setting book.

Q: Another criticism of *Bringing the State Back In* is that a large literature had already focused on the state, and thus it was not necessary to "bring the state back in."[14] How do you respond to this point?
A: Obviously, *Bringing the State Back In* built on many previous literatures that had treated state organizations and policy makers empirically or theoretically. That is acknowledged in the introductory chapter. What we did was highlight the agenda and concepts that many diverse literatures shared.

American Social Policy in Comparative Perspective

Q: During the 1980s, your work focused increasingly on the comparative study of welfare states and the historical analysis of social policy. This topic was quite a shift from your earlier focus on revolutions. What motivated this shift?
A: Soon after *States and Social Revolutions* appeared, I reached a point where I did not want to write about revolutions anymore. My strategy as a scholar is to define fruitful problems and use them to puzzle through theoretical issues, and I wanted to move on to new problems. I did not want to be an expert on revolutions, and I moved on pretty quickly after *States and Social Revolutions*. As early as 1980, I had already published an article on the New Deal (Skocpol 1980).

14. See, for example, Almond (1988).

Q: What interested you about the New Deal?

A: The New Deal was central to debates about the Marxist theory of the state. Faced with those theoretical disputes, I did my "Barrington Moore maneuver," which meant learning about the history of the New Deal. I wrote an early article with Kenneth Finegold, who had been a graduate student at Harvard, which worked through theoretical ideas about the autonomy of the state in the American context (Skocpol and Finegold 1982; see also Skocpol and Finegold 1990; Finegold and Skocpol 1995).

Q: How did your comparative historical background influence your approach to the study of American politics?

A: A lot of work on American politics takes for granted the overall context and just looks at one process, like voting, one type of organization, like interest groups or parties, or one part of the federal government. If you study American politics with a comparative historical background, you are much more likely to think big about the long-term trajectory of change and ask questions about policy making, politics, and institutional development that are informed by awareness of comparative variation. This is certainly true for my work. When I started working on the American welfare state, I was steeped in the comparative literature on the development of the European welfare states and the social democratic model, a model that was missing in the American case. I had those things in mind when I approached the American case (Skocpol and Orloff 1984; Skocpol and Weir 1985; Weir, Orloff, and Skocpol 1988).

Q: In 1992, you published *Protecting Soldiers and Mothers*, on the historical development of social policy in the United States. In the preface, you tell how you serendipitously discovered an old, forgotten book, Isaac Max Rubinow's *Social Insurance, With Special Reference to American Conditions* (1968), which portrayed pensions for Civil War veterans as a major social policy.[15] Finding Rubinow's book, in turn, helped you formulate your insight that the United States was, in fact, a precocious welfare state, not a laggard behind European countries as the conventional view suggested. How important was this chance discovery to *Protecting Soldiers and Mothers*? If you had not stumbled across Rubinow's book, would your own book have turned out very differently?

A: Yes, it might have turned out differently because there was nothing in the standard literature, either comparative or U.S.-specific, highlighting Civil War pensions as a major social policy. The process through which my

---

15. Rubinow's book was originally published in 1913.

argument in *Protecting Soldiers and Mothers* developed is a classic case of why one should be skeptical about received categories and open to surprise, to noticing new things. The historian Marc Bloch argued that comparative history makes it possible to notice things, startling similarities or differences, that you might not see otherwise (Bloch 1967). This, in turn, generates questions and theorizing. Even if you are only looking at one case, one history, noticing something that should not be there also stimulates questions and theorizing. Rubinow was saying, literally, that Civil War pensions were a major social policy that would soon cause the United States to overtake Europe in the public provision of social benefits. When I read this, it made me curious, because the mere empirical assertion that, in 1913, a lot of government social spending was going on that amounted to de facto old age pensions cut against the grain of the whole literature that saw the United States as a laggard in social provision. I was skeptical at first about Rubinow's claims, but I decided to look into the matter, because I had a hunch it might lead to something. When I realized that Rubinow was not wrong empirically, I connected his observation about Civil War pensions to the reading I had been doing on the early American state, especially Stephen Skowronek's work on the central role of patronage parties in nineteenth-century American politics (1982). I began to think there was an affinity between the Civil War pensions and the patronage parties, because I knew that Republicans had sponsored the pensions. This made me realize that Rubinow's observation was not a stray fact, but a fact I could explain with the theory I was developing about the logic of patronage politics. So, I was learning both from reading history and from an interpreter in his own time, Rubinow, who was seeing through different lenses than the ones we see through now.

Q: Tracking down a hunch generated by a chance discovery does not fit the conventional model of how science works. How would you respond to someone who dismissed the process of discovery and insight that led to *Protecting Soldiers and Mothers* as ad hoc, seat-of-the pants, and scientifically invalid?

A: The normal science model that innovation does not matter and that all we should do is test existing theories is the conceit of a very dull, overdeveloped field, one that is confident it already has all the questions and theories it requires and thus needs merely to play them out. It is understandable why an established group of people might think this, but it's a scholastic conceit. It is hopeless to approach things this way in the social sciences, because our questions and angles of vision change with changes in our and society's normative concerns. I think it is very important to test theories rigorously, but the sense of discovery is equally important. And in human terms, the sense of discovery is *more* important, otherwise we get bored with our work. I get very excited when I am discovering something. When I found Rubinow's book, I was already a tenured professor and did not feel the need to prove anything to anybody except myself. I was on to something new, and I was not going to let it go. So, I set to work to follow an intellectual lead wherever it would take me.

Q: One novel aspect of *Protecting Soldiers and Mothers* in relation to your earlier work, especially *Bringing the State Back In,* was your shift from a state-centered to what you called a "polity-centered" approach that emphasized more strongly the interaction between state and societal actors. Why did you make this shift?

A: It was mostly just a label change, because in all my work I look at the interaction of social groups with politics and states. The main purpose for this change was to hit people over the head with the fact that *Protecting Soldiers and Mothers* could not be dismissed as a book about bureaucratic action. The state-centric label had unfortunately led some people to dismiss work that used this label as a series of hypotheses about bureaucrats doing everything. Now, that was not what *Bringing the State Back In* said. In my introductory essay for that book, I argued that under certain resource and collective interaction conditions, bureaucrats, party leaders, and other officials in state or political organizations were potentially autonomous actors (Skocpol 1985a).[16] But I also argued that the impact of the state and political organizations could be seen in a different way, one that highlighted how states and institutions affect the goals, identities, and alliances of groups involved in politics. *Protecting Soldiers and Mothers* emphasized the latter set of ideas, which I called "Tocquevillian" in *Bringing the State Back In.* I think it was my Harvard colleague, Peter Hall, who sent me an e-mail that said, "What you're really talking about in *Protecting Soldiers and Mothers* is the structured polity approach." I decided to adopt the label, and I elaborated in the book's theoretical introduction the various things that a structured polity, or Tocquevillian, approach might mean. So, the switch to a polity-centered approach was a change of emphasis, one that was also tied to my shift from studying the outbreak of revolutions in a non-democratic context to studying politics in a democratic context.

Q: What is your assessment of the impact of *Protecting Soldiers and Mothers* compared to the impact of your first book, *States and Social Revolutions?*

---

16. Skocpol called this the "Weberian" perspective on the effects of states in contrast to the "Tocquevillian" perspective discussed here.

A: *States and Social Revolutions* had more of an impact because of its comparative scope and method. But *Protecting Soldiers and Mothers,* which is a comparatively informed national case study, is the better book. It is also my favorite.

Q: Why is *Protecting Soldiers and Mothers* your favorite book?
A: First, it interprets the history of my own country, and I am very much an American patriot. There is nothing particularly cosmopolitan about me. Also, *Protecting Soldiers and Mothers* is based on original, primary research. The book has discoveries about the role of women's associations in policy making that no one else had made before. Finally, I think the book is beautifully crafted. It took me a very long time to write, about eight years, and I achieved a level of power and gracefulness in the writing that I did not achieve in *States and Social Revolutions*. For all those reasons, it's my favorite book.

Q: Why did it take so long to write *Protecting Soldiers and Mothers?*
A: Because I thought I was writing a different book. I set out to write an analysis of the development of the entire American welfare state. I suddenly realized about three-quarters of the way through that I should limit the book to the period from the 1870s to the 1920s, because I had a powerful and original argument about this period.

Current Research on Civic Engagement

Q: Your current research focuses on long-run patterns in the transformation of civic participation in the United States. How did you become interested in this topic?
A: The way I always do, by deciding there were some puzzles, things I had noticed historically that did not fit the received theoretical wisdom. A central proposition that emerged from the debate that broke out in the 1990s about civic engagement in America was that volunteerism was local.[17] I was intensely suspicious of this idea, because I had seen evidence in my work on *Protecting Soldiers and Mothers* of vast, widespread voluntary federations that had the interesting property of mirroring the structure of the American state. I did not know how many large voluntary associations existed, so I assembled a team of students to find out by gathering empirical data on these associations. We wanted to know how many large membership associations formed, when they formed, and what they looked like. We made a startling discovery: volunteerism in the United States historically was very

17. See, for example, Joyce and Schambra (1996).

institutionalized in large federations that mimicked and paralleled the structure of the American state and fostered local activity. This pattern existed until the conjuncture of the Vietnam War and the civil rights struggles in the 1960s, when partisan polarization set in and radically transformed the old voluntary groups into professionally managed entities. I recently finished a pretty big book, *Diminished Democracy* (Skocpol 2003a), on the emergence of volunteer organizations in America and their radical transformation after 1965.[18] *Diminished Democracy* covers all of American history, though it is not as long or densely detailed as other books I have done. Now that I have mapped the rise and decline of a major structural feature of American society and politics, large voluntary associations, I am interested in explaining the radical juncture of transformation in the 1960s and 1970s. This juncture has all kinds of implications for American culture and politics.

Q: Will you do comparative research again in the future?
A: I might. The whole idea that voluntary associations mirrored the organization of the American state raises the question of whether civil society mirroring of the state has been true elsewhere. The impact of war on volunteer associations also raises comparative questions. So I may go back to comparative work. Whether or not I do, I will always be a comparatively informed Americanist.

Q: You have a fairly unique vantage point because you have worked for extensive periods in both the comparative and American politics fields. How do you see the linkage between the two fields? How can scholars in these fields best learn from each other?
A: American politics needs the breadth and temporal depth of vision that we have long seen in the best work in truly comparative politics, and the U.S. "case" should be compared to others in all kinds of research designs.

Q: To wrap up the discussion of your work, what are your best ideas and most important contributions?
A: It's hard for me to say, but I guess I have spelled out some of the ways that state actors and leaders of political organizations can have an independent impact on political outcomes. I have explored some of the ways that government institutions and political organizations can indirectly shape the goals, identities, interests, and alliances of political actors. Those are the core ideas I have worked out in the context of explaining revolutions, the development of social policies, and the emergence and transformation of

18. See also Fiorina and Skocpol (1999).

volunteer associations in America. I have also shown the feasibility and power of empirically grounded, analytically rigorous comparative historical research. I have provided examples of how to do it and ways forward that other people can use.

Q: Are there any works you feel have been neglected and that did not get the attention you hoped they would?
A: I have produced a lot of books and articles over my lifetime, and I'll produce a lot more. The major ones have gotten a lot of attention, and I am one of the most cited social scientists. So, I don't have any complaints. I suppose I would have liked *Boomerang* (Skocpol 1996) to have had greater commercial success. That book was a venture into trade publishing on a current policy episode, and because my publisher got sick, it came out a month too late, a month after Johnson and Broder's *The System* (1996), and that hurt it. Still, my books persist. I am very proud of the fact that many, many years after my major books came out people are still teaching them in courses and students are still e-mailing me and telling me they are excited by my work. The most important things I write are not written for the moment. Good comparative historical research should offer perspectives that endure, that do not disappear when the newspaper headlines change.

The Research Process
Science

Q: Do you consider yourself a scientist?
A: I absolutely do and always have. I have no patience whatsoever for post-modernism and the idea that we are not in the business of testing theoretical ideas against empirical evidence. I am not interested in philosophical arguments about whether or not the world is real. What interests me is formulating and testing hypotheses.

Q: The phenomena we want to study today may not exist in any meaningful way tomorrow. Is it possible to have a science of a social and political world that is unpredictable and changing in many ways?
A: The questions we ask can definitely come from pressing real-world issues and from normative concerns that will naturally change over time. Our angle of vision on the past is constantly changing, and that does not bother me. But once you have a question about a phenomenon that exists over a stretch of time and space, then it is important to look at variation and at hypotheses that address the variation. This requires systematic evidence that can either support or refute your hypotheses. This process of inquiry is partially inductive and partially deductive, and it certainly has to do with

science, though it is not an aspiration to model everything at the same time. It's social science.

Research Questions

Q: Your research tends to focus on big, humanly important questions like the causes and consequences of revolutions and the historical roots of national social policies. Why have you focused on such questions?
A: This focus stems from a combination of personal reasons and my understanding of the vocation of the scholar. In the United States, we are eventually given well-paid tenured jobs, and I don't think it is justified for us to engage in navel gazing. Our work has to engage issues that matter to the society. Sometimes highly technical scientific work is the best way to do this. But for many of us, myself included, it is important to have a sense of an audience beyond other specialists. An important part of the scholar's role is to go to a meeting of fellow citizens or undergraduate students, people who are not specialists, and talk about aspects of your work in a way they can understand. On a personal level, it's a lot more fun being a scholar when you are working on something you can imagine just might matter, like figuring out how revolutions happen, or understanding how the American welfare state developed. I believe that comparative historical work can provide a handle on possibilities for the future, and my research is very closely related to my politics, especially when I am studying my own society.

Part of the definition of an important research question is that it has both an academic side and a real world side (Skocpol 2003b). Some say that only puzzles that emerge from previous academic debates or theories should be pursued. I find this view extremely problematic, because if you limit your focus to puzzles generated by internal academic debates, you may well miss the most interesting things going on. New questions often come from real-world developments or from looking again at history and noticing something that no one else saw before. An important question should speak to a dual audience: you should be able to imagine explaining to your aunt why the problem matters and also giving an academic talk that says, "We should wonder about this issue, and if we figure it out, we gain leverage on a broader set of theoretical debates."

Q: But there may be problems we wish to study as social scientists that are difficult, if not impossible, to explain clearly to our aunts. Should we remove those sorts of problems from our research agendas?
A: I actually don't think there are things we social scientists study that cannot be explained to your aunt. People think they have to talk in jargon,

but they really don't. You do not have to be able to explain all the intricacies of the argument or academic debate to a nonacademic audience, but you should be able to tell people why they should care, and why *you* care, about the answer to the question on which you are working. The questions we ask should have this dimension.

Q: Should all social scientists focus on humanly important questions? Is there room for people who do "basic research," which may be several steps removed from the issues that matter to non-specialists?
A: Of course there is room for specialists who are developing techniques or sources of knowledge that may prove useful to other scholars. But it gets dangerous when you have schools of thought trying to take over whole sections of disciplines with the argument that it's okay to thumb your nose at issues of importance to nonacademics. Still, there is absolutely a place for statistical methodologists, for example, and they can do quite esoteric work and still make important contributions to the rest of us. Likewise, in the community of people doing comparative historical research, it's perfectly fine to have some who are puzzling about processes of institutional development and change in times and places far removed from the present. First, those questions are intrinsically interesting, and, second, people working on such issues may serendipitously produce ideas that will be a methodological or theoretical contribution that benefits the rest of us. I am not arguing for a purely pragmatic social science that only addresses pressing, contemporary public problems. I am arguing for variety, because we are a complex community, and I am very, very concerned about placing our bets as a discipline, or even an area within a discipline, on one horse. We need to find ways to build in pluralism, because that's where creativity comes from. Some of the most interesting work by young scholars is being done by people who are deliberately combining things their elders are fighting over. We need to preserve room for that.

Argument

Q: Two of your earliest articles were critiques of major works by Barrington Moore and Immanuel Wallerstein (Skocpol 1973, 1977). These critiques served to frame your own original arguments about revolutions and long-run processes of development. Is the technique of engaging and arguing with the work of other scholars something you do self-consciously?
A: I have always worked out what I was thinking by critiquing work done by others. What gets me excited is seeing that someone else is partly right and partly wrong. I have always regarded social science as a very argumentative

field. My major projects have always been launched with a sense of argument against a received wisdom or an interlocutor, especially somebody important whose work I respect. I don't like to argue with people whom I think are insignificant. And I prefer to argue with people who are mistaken yet also partly right, especially in identifying important issues and problems, raising the right questions, and setting the debate at an appropriately bold level. Both Moore and Wallerstein met these criteria.

Q: Is there a downside to this strategy of firing your mind by arguing with mistaken others?
A: Sure. If you get too carried away, you can argue against others at the expense of developing your own ideas. As I matured as a scholar and gained confidence, I focused more on developing my own ideas. Still, my latest round of research on civic engagement in America was partly driven by my conviction that a lot of the people studying social capital were wrong. I haven't stopped using arguments with mistaken others as a way to work out my own ideas. This makes things interesting. For example, as a graduate student, I felt I knew senior people like Wallerstein, Tilly, Perry Anderson, and Reinhard Bendix intellectually, because I was thoroughly versed in their work, even though I had never met them personally. When I finally did meet them in person, I knew their work and what I thought about it in detail. I had alternative interpretations; I was not just saying to them, "You were wrong about France." I had developed a different way of analyzing the range of cases these macro-comparativists were tackling.

Historical Analysis

Q: Historical analysis plays a fundamental role in your work. What do you enjoy about studying history?
A: I enjoy stories about individual lives and especially about how intended and unintended effects play out in social structures. I am interested in big patterns of change, in seeing and trying to make sense of them. And I find primary historical research addictive because of the fun of tracking things down.

Q: Do you do much archival work?
A: No. I mainly work with organizational and government documents. Tracking down historical data at the state and local levels on organizations in the United States, as I have, requires detective work to figure out where the data are and how to get them. I use any method I have to. For example, in my current research on African American fraternal groups I have gotten a lot of information from antique stores and off the Internet from E-bay.

Those are the places where I can find the information I want. I can't find it in libraries.

Q: What skills help you carry out broad-gauged comparative historical research?
A: From early on, I have had an ability to read large amounts of material and see patterns that were relevant to causal arguments. For example, I could read through a historical account of a pattern of change, and, especially when I was able to compare it across time or across cases, I could begin to formulate hypotheses about the institutional conditions that might be channeling events one way or another. People feel they need to work out a theory before they grapple with empirical material. But I have often generated my theoretical ideas by reading about historical processes of long-term change. The next step is to formulate these ideas more rigorously and bounce them off existing ideas and theories. Marc Bloch wrote a very nice essay on this process that said that by learning and comparing histories, you may able to form a hypothesis about what is going on (Bloch 1967). Bloch saw comparative history as a source of theoretical inspiration, and it certainly has been for me. Also, I have a strong ability not to get bogged down in details, to see the outline of the forest and not just the trees.

Q: Is an eye for irony an important skill for doing comparative historical research?
A: It certainly is for the kind of comparative history I do. I am interested in how history does not turn out as its makers intend. That's the structuralist side of my work. Unintended consequences are an extremely important reason for doing historical social science. To put this point in terms of today's disputes, so much work done by contemporary rational choice scholars is recycled functionalism that looks at an institution, asks whose interests it serves, and then assumes that those whose interests are served are the ones who designed the institution. Well, I don't think very many institutions are deliberately designed. I think they develop out of conflict in which actors may not achieve anything like what they set out to achieve. Unintended consequences are also an important part of what first got me interested in revolutions. To the degree they were made at all, revolutions completely frustrated the hopes of their makers. Alertness to the acerbic irony of history was something Barrington Moore taught in his seminars.

Q: You mentioned that you get a sense of efficacy from your historical work partly because you believe comparative historical research can illuminate future political possibilities. Can you give an example of this from your own work?

A: In my work on the development of American social policy, I have discovered that the United States has historically had broad social programs built across class lines that benefit constituencies with electoral clout. Those kinds of programs usually have longevity and the ability to grow over time to provide security for large numbers of people. This knowledge of historical patterns in American social policy can be used to imagine future policy options for either sustaining or deconstructing those programs. The fights you read about every day in the news over Social Security provide a good example. Those who want to privatize Social Security understand very well that in a democracy, and especially in American democracy, cross-class programs are more sustainable. Because they don't want government to have a strong social policy, they want to undo the cross-class support for programs of social provision by getting the middle class out of them. My historical work gives me a way to think about contemporary politics that goes beyond the obvious and informs my own political judgments when I talk to people who care about current policy choices.

Q: Although the present may closely resemble the past, it is never equivalent to the past, because some factors always change over time. How do you guard against the risk of misplaced analogies from the past?
A: The more contextually informed your research is, the more prepared you are to notice changes in the context that make a difference in the central process. This makes historical researchers better able to avoid overgeneralizations. Still, there is no perfect way to prevent mistaken analogies. The present and future are not fully determined, and they certainly are not in our control.

Social Theory

Q: What role has reading social and political theory played in your research?
A: It has played an enormous role. With regard to learning theory, I had an advantage starting my career as a sociologist rather than a political scientist. In political science, theory often means normative, philosophical reflections, whereas in sociology, when I was a student, theory meant the work of classical theorists like Marx, Weber, and Durkheim, who, although they definitely had normative interests, also claimed to be explaining empirical regularities. In sociology, a powerful link existed between the classical theorists and explanatory social science. From the very beginning, I was accustomed to respecting the art of macroscopic theorizing, and I learned to move comfortably between theoretical writings and empirical regularities.

Q: What was your take on Marxist theory, which was widely discussed when you were a student?
A: I was both intrigued and skeptical of Marxist ideas. I liked the Marxist commitment to analyzing conflict and conflictual processes in social change. Also, I found the idea of class politics an intriguing hypothesis, but I never quite believed it, because I did not think it adequately explained the variation in the world.

Q: Despite your skepticism of Marxist theory, some people, including a number of your senior colleagues at Harvard, pegged you as a Marxist in the early stages of your career. Why did this happen?
A: When I was a graduate student, I was certainly a supporter of the student movements against the Vietnam War. At that time, "Marxist" meant simply anybody who read Marxist theories, which I certainly did. Also, as a graduate student I allowed reporters from *The Harvard Crimson* to talk me into being photographed in front of a picture of Karl Marx.[19] They ran that photograph of me again and again and again, and that was terribly unfortunate, stupidity on my part. I finally succeeded in getting them to destroy the negative in return for an interview they wanted. I don't think anybody who has thought seriously about my work or my political positions would think I was a Marxist. I'm not. I'm a moderate to conservative social democrat, which means I believe in the use of democratic government to expand opportunity and mildly redistribute wealth in a capitalist society. I am fairly conservative on social values. My political position is well-known in Europe, but there is no label for it in the United States. New Deal liberalism would be close.

Quantitative Analysis and Data

Q: Could you discuss the role that quantitative, statistical analysis plays in your work?
A: I use statistical tools, or, more accurately, I team up with someone who uses statistical tools, when a crystallized hypothesis and appropriate data emerge from a larger project. I don't think statistics should determine the questions we ask, nor should statistics drive the data we gather. Still, when in the course of pursuing answers to questions we find data that are appropriately examined with statistical techniques, especially if we have hypotheses we want to test against powerful rivals, then we should take advantage of statistical methods. I did this in a statistical article in the *American Political*

---

19. *The Harvard Crimson* is an undergraduate newspaper at Harvard.

Science Review that tested propositions from *Protecting Soldiers and Mothers* (Skocpol et al. 1993). When I use statistical methods, I work with collaborators who can explain to me very clearly why the statistical method in question is appropriate for the kind of data and hypothesis we want to test.

Q: It is currently fashionable in political science to use "multi-method" research strategies that combine, for example, case studies and small-N comparisons with large-N, statistical analysis or mathematical models. Would *States and Social Revolutions* (Skocpol 1979) have been a better book if you had used statistical techniques instead of relying only on small-N comparisons?

A: No, because I was dealing with a type of phenomenon—revolution—that occurs very rarely in the world. The scholars who were studying revolutions using statistical methods were forced to dilute their conceptualization of revolutions into "violence" or "episodes of conflict in general," resulting in a meaningless mush. They lacked a sharp focus on major, relatively rare events and let the statistical tail wag the dog. Now, there may have been aspects of revolutions that I could have tested statistically. I'm not aware of any, but I do not rule out selective use of statistical analysis along the lines of Tilly's *The Vendée* (1964), which develops an overall argument about the structure of the French Revolution with implications for cross-local and cross-group variation and has enough data to test those implications statistically. Perhaps there might have been a way in *States and Social Revolutions* to have tested statistically which peasant villages were more likely to revolt than others, or to have mathematically modeled the process by which armies came undone. I was not aware of the data that would have enabled me to do those things. If I had come across the data, then it would have been entirely appropriate to have used those methods. Still, even if I had used statistical analysis or formal models in *States and Social Revolutions,* these analyses would only have formed one piece of a larger argument. They would not have been the larger argument itself.

States and Social Revolutions was criticized for not using random sampling. That's an absurd criticism. If I had randomly sampled all the polities of the world, I probably would not have ended up with any revolutions to study. *States and Social Revolutions* used the most powerful methodology it could have used to develop some hypotheses. Those hypotheses were subsequently extended to other cases and modified in the process. We now have powerful knowledge about what accounts for revolutions and their absence. This knowledge was developed not by leaping to the most general questions and most general data sets at the outset, but by studying bounded sets of cases to understand the vulnerability of different types of regimes to revolutions and other kinds of transformations.[20] Powerful generalizations can be achieved by linking theoretically the cumulative results of research on bounded sets of cases. Comparative politics at its best has done this in a number of different literatures.

Q: In *Protecting Soldiers and Mothers* and also in your current work on civic engagement, you have collected and analyzed lots of new data. How do you think quantitative data should be used in the social sciences?
A: I am frustrated by how data sets are currently being used in both sociology and political science. The advent of computers and powerful statistical techniques combined with a lot of pressure on graduate students to finish quickly, which was not true when I was in graduate school, has led many people to grab a canned data set, run a couple of tests on it, and wrap up. This is most unfortunate, because we need new, systematic data sets, and it takes time to build new data sets and make them usable.

Q: Indeed, building data sets is often a slow, tedious, and labor-intensive process. What intellectual rewards can be reaped from building an original data set?
A: It often allows you to address questions that cannot be addressed with canned data. For example, in my current work I am interested in the transformation of American civic participation and civic organizations in the post–World War II period. The canned data sets on which most scholars working in this area rely are national surveys with very vague and general questions about civic participation. These surveys usually specify neither the activities nor the organizations in which the respondents are participating, and they cover only the 1970s to the 1990s at best. Based on that data, you simply cannot get a handle on how civic participation is changing over the long run and who is doing the changing. I have set out to find new kinds of data about voluntary associations and how they are changing over time. I have also dug up more than a hundred years of data on Massachusetts state senators and what associations they list in their official biographies. These data are perfectly quantifiable if you are willing to spend months and months inputting them. When you finish, you end up with data on a comparable set of people and the very different kinds of associations with which they were affiliated over a long stretch of time. This makes it possible to pinpoint when changes occur and then start to hypothesize much more rigorously about why they occur. This exemplifies what I call question- or problem-driven research. First, you figure out what the ques-

20. See Goldstone (2003).

tion or problem is and what your theoretical ideas are about it, then you look for the kinds of data you need to refine and test your ideas. You may have to settle for lower-tech or incomplete data, and you may have to triangulate among various forms of data. But so what? If the question is important, then that's what you need to do. Besides, you may discover very rigorous kinds of new data. It is possible to get into ruts, and examples of that exist in many areas in the social sciences, where people get trapped in one mode of data collection and analysis. As a result, they miss the big questions and important ideas.

Q: What can be done to develop a stronger infrastructure of data in the social sciences?
A: I am convinced that, for better or worse, the availability of data influences patterns of research. When behavioralism initially emerged, a lot of excitement was generated by putting together social science data sets for the first time. It really was a period of enormous creativity. Here at Harvard I would like to achieve a stronger theoretical and methodological grounding for historical and institutional research by building data sets, archiving them, and making them available to others. A lot of historical institutional research depends on data about organizations and organizational configurations, but we have not been nearly as creative as we should about devising systematic ways to find, code, and make available such data. We need to be much clearer about the data requirements for historical institutional research. Over the next decade, as data collecting and self-conscious data sharing improve, we are going to see a real flowering of theoretical ideas in historical institutional research.

Fieldwork

Q: What role has fieldwork played in your research?
A: I don't do fieldwork, but I think it is very important because it is a source of surprise. Everybody I know who does fieldwork says they work out their hypotheses and theory, then they go to the field and half of what they had worked out beforehand goes out the window. They realize there are things going on that they should have been wondering about but never considered until they went to the field. I think we need to build time into graduate study and scholarly routines for fieldwork.

Q: Even though you say you do not do fieldwork, you actually did carry out interviews with key political actors while writing *Boomerang* (Skocpol 1996), your book on President Clinton's failed initiative to reform health care policy.

A: That was my one foray into fieldwork. It is the closest I have come to powerful political actors who are actually doing something in the political field I am studying. I moved back and forth from my historical sense of how American social policy worked to reading memos and talking to people who had been involved in a failed policy episode. But I did not do structured interviews. I was mainly looking at the documents, and I talked to people in the process. My historical work gave me a fresh angle. For example, I was able to suggest to Ira Magaziner, a senior policy advisor to President Clinton and a key architect of the health care proposal, some reasons why his policy had failed, and he said, "Gee, I wish we'd had you here to tell us that beforehand." It was fun. Although this sort of work is not my major comparative advantage, I may do it again. At this stage in my career, I feel very free to experiment with different combinations of techniques for gathering evidence.

Critics

Q: What is your approach to responding to critics of your work? How do you choose which critics to reply to?
A: I actually don't reply to critics very much.

Q: Well, you did reply to William Sewell's critique that *States and Social Revolutions* underemphasized interpretive analysis and the importance of ideas (Sewell 1985; Skocpol 1985b). You also responded to Elizabeth Nichols's methodological critique of the book (Nichols 1986; Skocpol 1986). Finally, you addressed rational choice and Marxist critiques of your work on revolutions in the concluding chapter of your book, *Social Revolutions in the Modern World* (Skocpol 1994, 301–44). What motivates you to reply to some critics? What do you get out of this process?
A: I am very selective about whom I respond to. I turn away ten requests to get involved in a debate for every one that I accept. I did the exchange with Nichols when I was very young. I was honored, and I did it. But by the time I got to the stage of writing the concluding essay in *Social Revolutions in the Modern World,* which is a tough polemic against Sewell, Michael Burawoy's Marxist approach, and the rational choice people, I knew it was the last thing I was ever going to write about revolutions. I decided to collect in that book the essays I had written on revolutions in the years since *States and Social Revolutions* and to review the field one last time. The critics to whom I responded were all tenured people, which was important to me, because I would not have used the tone I used in an argument with a younger scholar. They had all taken a very strong stand, using *States and Social Revolutions* as

a template to argue their cases. So, I took advantage of the opportunity to explain why I thought *States and Social Revolutions,* and the historical analytical literature on revolutions that grew out of it, were better than any of the alternatives they were proposing. I thought people would find it instructive to see what I had to say. But I chose to do that exercise in a book containing my own work. In fact, I even had to pay money to have Sewell's essay reprinted in my book, because I felt it was not fair to critique his work without having it in the book.

In general, I only reply to critics when I think it will clarify theoretical or methodological issues in a way that goes beyond quibbles. I'm not interested in quibbles. Older scholars often end up thinking they are misunderstood and misinterpreted, but I'm just not interested in that. I almost never write that I have been misunderstood or misinterpreted. The way I look at it, once something is published, it's in the eye of the beholder. Misinterpretation from one person's perspective is, from another person's perspective, just a creative way of either applying something or arguing with it.

Q: In addition to clarifying theoretical or methodological debates, do you have other motives for replying to certain critics? For instance, do you enjoy it?
A: Sure. I don't have any trouble arguing. I really did enjoy writing the concluding chapter for *Social Revolutions in the Modern World,* and I probably got a little too carried away. It was especially enjoyable because Sewell, with his call for interpretive case studies, and the rational choice people, with their call for abstract formal models, were coming at me from opposite directions. What I tried to do was show how comparative history, which Atul Kohli has aptly described as "between a rock and a soft place," solved some of the problems of both interpretivist and rational choice approaches. Comparative history allowed for theorizing, generalizations, causal analysis, and hypothesis testing in a way that purely interpretive case studies did not, yet it was also far more engaged with historical process and context than were the formal models advocated by rational choice theorists. I also included Burawoy's Marxist critique of my work on revolutions, because he's an old buddy and antagonist. He had written an outrageous essay that basically said "Be a Marxist, even if it's wrong" (Burawoy 1989). So, I fought back.

Collaboration

Q: Could you discuss the role collaboration plays in your work?
A: My big books are always solo-authored, but I have a habit of collaborating with graduate students or colleagues on articles and edited books. I have

approached my current project on civic participation in the United States as a series of collaborations with research teams that I put together. Organizing research teams is something I learned from my physicist husband and also from teaching at the University of Chicago, which is much more research team–oriented than Harvard. One of the enormous gains of my forcible ejection from Harvard for five years was that I spent time at a great university where collaborative intellectual life and working with teams of graduate students was much more the norm.[21] I greatly enjoy working with research teams.

Q: You mention that your collaborations tend to result in articles instead of books. What is your approach to writing articles?
A: It is a very disciplined exercise to boil down an argument into a journal-length piece, especially a complex argument of the kind I have always developed. Lately, I have become more committed to getting articles published in mainstream journals, because I think it's very important to create space in the journals for new styles of research. I am very proud of the article with Marshall Ganz on the nation of organizers that I published in the *American Political Science Review* (Skocpol, Ganz, and Munson 2000). I am also very proud of my recent coauthored article in the *American Journal of Political Science* (Crowley and Skocpol 2001).

Extra-Academic Engagement

Q: Do you consider yourself a public intellectual?
A: Yes. From time to time, I address nonacademic audiences on policy and political issues of the day. I am an explicit partisan and have written articles and books that take partisan stances using informed social science knowledge.[22] I draw a distinction between those works and my academic writings.

Q: How do you balance your roles as a public intellectual and a social scientist? Is it difficult to do both well?
A: I am not as effective a public intellectual as are those who specialize in it. It's easier today than it was twenty or thirty years ago for an academic-based scholar to get access to the media, and I was tempted a few years ago to focus more on playing a public intellectual role. I ultimately decided I did not want to spend my time cultivating media sources, hanging around Washington, D.C., and thinking only about very short-term policy and

---

21. As discussed below, Skocpol was denied tenure at Harvard in 1981 and taught at the University of Chicago from 1981 until returning to Harvard with tenure in 1986.
22. See, for example, Skocpol (2000) and Greenberg and Skocpol (1997).

political questions. I am so much more satisfied in my role as a teacher and scholar with distance and perspective on issues.

Q: Has being a part-time public intellectual enhanced your work as a social scientist?

A: Getting involved in contemporary debates on Social Security, welfare, and health care has certainly been a useful testing ground for some of my ideas about the development of social policy. But if I had made the kind of commitment necessary to be a major, publicly visible intellectual, I would have lost my ability to do serious scholarship. I do public intellectual activities on the side as a hobby.

Q: President Clinton invited you and other scholars to participate in discussions about social policy. Could you discuss that experience?

A: It was a lot of fun going to a White House dinner in 1993 and to Camp David in early 1995, seeing the Clintons in operation, and taking part in the give and take. It felt like a high-level intellectual seminar with an atmosphere of public purpose. But I never felt it was anything but what it was: a wonderful opportunity for a day.

Q: Would you participate in that sort of activity again if the opportunity arose?

A: I am not particularly interested in being invited to schmooze with the Bushes. But if there were Democrats in power, I would be interested. Senator Edward Kennedy asked me to take part in a discussion last year, and I did. Once in a while I have gone to Washington to meet with Democrats in Congress to discuss health care and American social policy, especially after my book *The Missing Middle* (Skocpol 2000) came out. I maintain my relationship with Stanley Greenberg.[23] We convened our group of moderate Democratic policy intellectuals after the September 11 attacks.[24] We decided that the call to patriotism should be broadened to include a critique of government giveaways to the rich and a new agenda for active government in social policy that builds on the patriotic solidarity of Americans.

Overall, I am a little too broad-gauged for most American politicians these days, who are very poll-driven and worry mainly about what they can find out from pollsters tomorrow. I enjoy talking to audiences that include

---

23. Greenberg served for many years as the principal polling advisor to the Democratic National Committee. He has also served as a polling advisor to President Bill Clinton, President Nelson Mandela, and Prime Minister Tony Blair.

24. This group of moderate Democratic policy intellectuals contributed to Greenberg and Skocpol (1997).

policy makers, hearing their questions, and seeing they are sometimes, though not always, interested in the broader perspective I offer. But I have no desire to stop being mainly an armchair scholar. Because I am a structuralist, I tend to focus on resource patterns and power relationships that play out behind people's backs. As a result, the message I offer policy makers is often one of unpleasant surprise.

Q: You say your research is too broad to appeal to poll-driven politicians who are focused on the very short term. Do comparative historical researchers have any advantages in terms of offering suggestions or advice to public officials?
A: There is a definite advantage to thinking about how policies play out over the long run. For example, the idea that to achieve an effective antipoverty policy you need to bridge groups rather than target the poor is not something that emerges from surveys and polls. You get that insight from understanding American politics over time. Powerful social science always has policy relevance.

Q: Have you ever aspired to hold public office?
A: Never. I don't want to be anything except what I am, a professor.

Colleagues, Institutional Affiliations, and Students
From Harvard to Chicago and Back to Harvard

Q: After finishing your Ph.D. at Harvard, you were a member of the sociology faculty from 1975 until 1981. Did you receive other job offers when you were first hired at Harvard?
A: I received quite a few offers, but not from major places. Harvard was the most important place from which I had an offer. I was hired at Harvard because they wanted women and because most of my professors thought I was safe since I was a known quantity to them.

Q: You were denied tenure at Harvard in 1981, a decision you disputed on the grounds of gender discrimination. After five years, Harvard found that your grievance had merit and offered you a tenured professorship, which you accepted.[25] Meanwhile, you taught at the University of Chicago as a tenured professor of sociology and political science. Could you discuss Harvard's decision to deny you tenure? What are your reflections about how things turned out for you?

25. On this incident, see Skocpol (1988).

A: I don't think I could have done anything to have made the original tenure decision at Harvard come out any different than it did. That was a fateful decision, both for the Harvard sociology department and for me. I chose to fight it, which consumed half a decade. I had a great time at Chicago, but I fought very hard to come back to Harvard. I am very proud of that fight. Still, it cost me the chance for institutional leadership. I gave up institutional leadership when I left the University of Chicago, and after I came back to Harvard the way that I did, I could not get a leadership position there. I think I would have had more chances for institutional leadership if I had had a more normal career. On the other hand, I would not have gone to Chicago, where I had a joint appointment in sociology and political science that opened up a whole new route for me.

Q: Can you discuss the five years you spent at the University of Chicago? What was this experience like?
A: It was both hard and wonderful. It was hard, because I was living like a graduate student. My husband lived in New Jersey, and every fall I would load up my car and drive off to Chicago to live alone in an apartment away from my husband. I lived a fairly lonely and complex life during that period, and, in many ways, I pulled into myself. But being at Chicago was also very exciting, because it is such a wonderful, intellectual place.

Q: Who were the colleagues at Chicago with whom you interacted most?
A: William Julius Wilson, Ira Katznelson, and I built a center together, eventually called the Center for the Study of Industrial Societies. It focused on politics and society in the United States and other industrial democracies. I also interacted with Morris Janowitz and Margaret Weir, who was a graduate student. I put together research teams that included some of my very best students. My colleagues in both sociology and political science were very respectful and pleased I was there. It was an intensely intellectual time. But when I went back to New Jersey in the summers, I pretty much lived alone, except for my husband. My life combined long periods of time on my own with the intense intellectuality of Chicago.

Q: Can you discuss your experiences at Harvard since you returned as a tenured professor of sociology in 1986?
A: On the whole, Harvard is a less collaborative place than Chicago. Harvard was very lonely when I first returned, because I was on my own in the Sociology Department and in big trouble because I had come back through a tenure case challenge. My colleagues in sociology tried to drive me out of

the department. So, I interacted mainly with graduate students. But, in recent years, since I joined the Department of Government in 1995, I have been quite happy. I have many colleagues whom I respect and enjoy. Until he left for Berkeley in 2004, Paul Pierson and I collaborated on teaching, building on our mutual interest in developing theoretical premises for historical institutional work (Pierson and Skocpol 2002). I have also had lots of interesting intellectual exchanges with Robert Putnam, especially since I began working on the topic of civic engagement.

Q: How has your relationship been with your Harvard colleagues who advocate rational choice theory, such as Kenneth Shepsle, James Alt, and Robert Bates?
A: On the whole, fine. There is a lot of mutual respect among my colleagues. I have quite a bit of affection for Morris Fiorina, who has since moved to Stanford, and also for Shepsle and Bates. I don't see some of my rational choice colleagues as often since they withdrew into the Center for Basic Research in the Social Sciences (CBRSS).[26] Harvard's Department of Government is big enough that we can have separate intellectual worlds, which is both good and bad. On one hand, there is not a lot of tension because there is room for everybody. On the other hand, I miss the earlier years of the Government Department, when people from different theoretical perspectives were attending the same seminars.

Q: What have you learned by interacting with colleagues like Shepsle and Bates?
A: It is very interesting to see how rational choice scholars model things. I don't agree with a lot of what they do, but at least they are clear. It's fun to think through what difference it would make if you brought history and a less functionalist sense of institutions to bear on the hypotheses that have been worked out in the rational choice literature on the U.S. Congress. Bates's work has always been interesting to me, because he has a strong sense of the organization of regimes and how they intersect with power and interests in society. Bates the polemicist is out on a limb that can't sustain itself, but I find his empirical work quite congenial.

Q: Since returning to Harvard, have you considered moving to a different university?

26. The Center for Basic Research in the Social Sciences (CBRSS) was an interdisciplinary center founded at Harvard in 1998 to develop and disseminate the tools of basic social scientific research. The center's affiliates included Harvard political scientists James Alt, Robert Bates, Gary King, and Kenneth Shepsle.

A: At various points, I have considered Yale, Princeton, and Stanford. But dual-career moves are hard to work out, and Harvard has become a pretty good place for me, finally.

Institution Building

Q: You have participated in a number of institution-building initiatives over the course of your career, for example, the Comparative and Historical Sociology Section of the American Sociological Association (ASA). What motivated you to get involved in such initiatives and what did you get out of them?

A: As a young faculty member, I was self-consciously committed, in a way that my teachers never had been, to building professional space for comparative historical research. In the 1970s and 1980s I worked with others to establish a comparative historical section of the American Sociological Association. We were explicitly trying to establish a label inside sociology for the methods and models of research we were using. We had a real sense of excitement about what we were doing, and I remember we had battles. We fought to keep comparative historical sociology from being defined either as Marxist or Weberian. I deliberately organized people politically to keep a sense of variety, a big tent.

It was a very propitious time to create institutions inside sociology, because there was no dominant methodology or theory. I have a structural analysis of how disciplinary institution building works. You form a section, get people to publish articles and books, and create a sense of a broad, exciting approach. Then departments will start hiring in that area. And that was exactly what happened. By the early 1980s, the sociology employment bulletins were running advertisements for people doing comparative historical work. My students at Harvard and Chicago were taking advantage of these new opportunities. I was a very self-conscious empire builder, not in the intellectual sense, but in the sense of trying to attract bright students. When I made the transition back to Harvard in the mid-1980s, I deliberately attended both the political science and sociology meetings so I could introduce students from one institution and discipline to students in the other. Building these kinds of ties is an important way to strengthen students' abilities to help each other in the job market and make intellectual connections.

Q: In addition to the Comparative and Historical Sociology Section of the ASA, another institutional initiative in which you participated was the SSRC's Committee on States and Social Structures, which emerged

in conjunction with your collaborative project with Peter Evans and Dietrich Rueschemeyer on *Bringing the State Back In* (Evans, Rueschemeyer, and Skocpol 1985). Yet this committee had a very short life and was never really institutionalized. What happened?

A: We were defunded. We had exciting ideas that crystallized what was going on in the field, but we were not able to raise a lot of money, and SSRC did not want to subsidize the committee, because they wanted to sponsor things that were getting their own money from foundations. Our committee did sponsor a few books, for example, a volume on states and social knowledge that Rueschemeyer and I edited (Rueschemeyer and Skocpol 1996), a book on Keynesian policy approaches edited by Peter Hall (1989), and a book on war and trade edited by Ira Katznelson and Martin Shefter (2002).

Q: Still, the Committee on States and Social Structures had a considerably weaker impact on the field than, say, the SSRC Committee on Comparative Politics that Gabriel Almond directed in the 1950s and early 1960s, which basically ran comparative politics for over a decade.

A: We probably could have pushed it further if we had wanted to, but I'm not sure we needed to. We were not trying to create a subdiscipline. Rather, we were trying to crystallize an agenda of questions and lines of analysis that were exciting and fruitful across different substantive literatures. *Bringing the State Back In* achieved that goal. After the years of discussion among us and the publication of *Bringing the State Back In*, there was really no need to pursue our agenda through projects we controlled directly, because, partly as a result of our efforts, asking about states as actors and considering how state actions and structures impact political and policy processes had already been woven into how work was done in political sociology and political science. I was very sorry that the SSRC cut the committee off, because it had a good newsletter with a huge circulation of about three thousand subscribers that cut across disciplinary boundaries. Still, I felt no desperate need to re-create it.

Q: You have also been actively involved in the American Political Science Association (APSA), serving as its president during 2002–3, a period when the discipline was responding to criticisms of APSA and its flagship journal, the *American Political Science Review* (*APSR*), made by the Perestroika movement.[27] What is your assessment of the issues

27. In 2000, a scholar writing as "Mr. Perestroika" circulated an anonymous manifesto calling for reform of the *American Political Science Review* (*APSR*), the American Political Science Association (APSA), and the political science profession in general. Mr. Perestroika voiced con-

raised by the Perestroika movement? What changes did you seek to bring to the APSA while you were its president?

A: Many political scientists, including me, agreed that the *APSR* had to open its pages to a wider variety of scholarship even before Perestroika emerged. Those reforms were well under way when I became president in 2002–3, and I simply supported them. I did not consider myself the president from any one faction—but the president of the *entire* APSA. I tried to foster and sustain pluralistic intellectual engagement and an inclusive style of governance. That was not hard, because the APSA is quite open and works well. My specific initiatives as president included (1) sponsoring a task force to look at how to foster excellent, pluralistic graduate education in political science; and (2) sponsoring a Task Force on Inequality and American Democracy, to examine what is happening to participation, governance, and public policy making in an era of rising economic inequality. I personally served on the latter task force. Both task forces worked well and issued important reports of which I am very proud.

Teaching

Q: Could you discuss the role teaching has played in your career?

A: Teaching has played a tremendous role. Harvard undergraduates are a great pleasure to teach. Every time I have to formulate what I have to say for lecture courses and seminars, I notice something new, especially about how things fit together in the big picture. Graduate students are especially important for me. I learn from graduate students, and I have always been fortunate to attract hardworking, excellent students. I collaborate with them, and the ones with whom I have collaborated most closely have always taught me things. I love to teach.

Q: What are the qualities of the best students?

A: The students I work with most closely are usually self-starters who work very, very hard. I have collaborated with students who bring quite different angles of vision to a project. I usually frame the research question in these collaborations, because I form teams to start investigating a topic. But if a student is prepared to propose new lines of argument, that's very welcome.

---

cern that many leaders in the profession did not read or submit to the *APSR*, that the APSA's governing council and the *APSR*'s editorial board were chosen undemocratically by their predecessors, and that the *APSR* was focused on technical methods, rather than important substantive questions about politics. This scholar's frustration resonated with a large number of political scientists and generated much discussion and debate in the profession. On the Perestroika movement, see Eakin (2000), Monroe (2005), and the interview in Chapter 11 with James Scott, a leading figure in this movement.

I have collaborated with students who were quantitative methodologists and taught me the value of those techniques. In my current project on civic engagement, which involves a lot of hunting down sources, I have been working with students who are good detectives.

Q: Do you encourage students to write big, ambitious dissertations?
A: Yes, but usually not out of the big research projects on which I am working. Most of my best students work with me on projects and then pursue dissertations on separate topics that they define themselves. This draws me into many, many different topics that range all over the map.

Q: Do you require students who want to work with you on their dissertations to also work with you on collaborative projects that you lead?
A: No. With some students, I just work with them on their dissertations. With others, I collaborate with them for a while and then they do their dissertations with someone else. It varies. In general, I interact with graduate students a lot in research workshops. When I went to the University of Chicago, I was introduced to their ongoing program of weekly faculty-student research workshops. When I came back to Harvard, I proposed the idea of organizing a similar program of research workshops, and now we have dozens in the Faculty of Arts and Sciences. And I practice what I preach: I am always attending and learning a lot from a research workshop. The most exciting of these for me was probably the one I started on Comparative Research on Political and Social Organizations (CROPSO) when I first came back to Harvard. That workshop, which ran for about five years, included comparativists and Americanists from political science as well as sociologists. It was a famous workshop, and a lot of things came out of it. In recent years, I have also enjoyed the American Politics Research Workshop.

Q: Do you have an overarching teaching philosophy or approach to training graduate students?
A: I am pretty hands-off on dissertations. But I am very hands-on in collaborative research with students. I participate in all aspects, and I expect students to do so, too. A lot of graduate teaching involves covering literatures or problems in a seminar setting, and my philosophy is to encourage lots of discussion and create structures where students work together in teams, because I think students learn a lot from each other.

The Achievements and Future of Comparative Politics

Q: What have we learned in comparative politics since you were a graduate student thirty years ago?

A: We have learned a tremendous amount. We have learned a lot about the conditions under which regime transformation from authoritarianism to democracy occurs. We have learned about the roots and results of revolutions. We know quite a bit about when ethnic conflicts emerge and how they are resolved. We have a tremendous accumulation of knowledge about the origins and development of Western welfare states and about efforts to retrench those welfare states. There are vast literatures on these topics, and hypotheses on these themes have been extended to additional cases and refined. We also understand much of what lies behind the variety of world politics. If you go back to the immediate postwar period, the field was dominated by broad, vacuous models that suggested every society traveled the same route. Those general models were wrong, and they have been replaced by solid, middle-level generalizations about various important outcomes.

Q: What kind of research programs lend themselves most readily to building cumulative, durable knowledge about politics?
A: There may not be any single pattern of cumulation of knowledge, because this process may depend on the nature of the phenomenon being studied. In his contribution to James Mahoney and Dietrich Rueschemeyer's volume, *Comparative Historical Analysis in the Social Sciences,* Jack Goldstone (2003) argues that in the study of revolutions, which is an inherently macro-phenomenon with a small number of cases, maybe a dozen or so, progress took the form of bounded generalizations about sets of cases that were eventually linked up with more general models. The literature on revolutions was developed mainly through comparative historical and small- to medium-N studies. By contrast, Edwin Amenta's (2003) contribution to that same volume argues that cumulation occurred very differently in the welfare state literature. In the study of welfare states, there were ways of formulating the dependent variable that proved amenable to both case-based and statistical research. Moreover, regardless of which methodology they employed, the scholars who worked on welfare states were totally willing to interact. They attended the same conferences and cross-fertilized a lot without wasting time arguing over techniques. That is a wonderful example of a literature that has cumulated through what I call "engaged pluralism." My guess is many more kinds of problems are amenable to this way of building cumulative knowledge. This is why it is terribly bad if we break into warring camps over theory and method. Instead, we need to foster problem-driven research by bringing together communities and networks of scholars that include people who mix methods and use different methods to work on the same problems. With regard to theory, it goes without saying that we need pluralism. There is only one literature where

the conceit has been maintained that buying into a single theory is the surest path to progress: rational choice theorizing about the U.S. Congress and the work that attempts to extend that theory to other legislatures. But even in that literature, when you look closely, it turns out that sharply contending theories exist among the rational choice people themselves. So, somebody like Eric Schickler comes along and blows all of them out of the water by bringing another method to bear—case-based comparative research (Schickler 2001). By rigorously analyzing forty cases of institutional change in the U.S. Congress, Schickler was able to resolve disputes and meld together contributions from different rational choice scholars who had been spinning their wheels arguing against each other. This example again shows the value of methodological and theoretical pluralism. I think the study of ethnic politics is ripe for a similar melding of approaches. Whether or not this melding happens will depend on the leading scholars demonstrating through their own person and work the comparative advantages of different approaches as well as a willingness to be pluralistic and tolerant. *Tolerant* is actually not the right word, because it implies passivity. The leading scholars should be engaged and open-minded; they need to meet and talk with one another. If they give in to the temptation to be Leninists, it will destroy creativity and block progress.

Q: Has the scholarly leadership in comparative politics been deficient?
A: There is a need for better leadership, and this leadership is emerging. I sense a new mood in the field. The rational choice movement is losing steam short of hegemony, which creates a situation where there is increasing recognition of the value of other approaches. Also, some of the people who don't do rational choice work are getting their act together. The closer we get to a balance among these groups, the better the conditions for people who want to cooperate across approaches.

Studies of intellectual development over the long run show that innovation often emerges in times and places where people come together and mix different ideas. The research of my late colleague in sociology at the University of Chicago, Joseph Ben-David, shows that competition made Western science innovative. The existence of a plurality of centers of research and, in the United States, the competitive, pluralistic university system have been engines of innovation. This means that in constructing social science graduate programs, the last thing we should try to do is create a theoretical or methodological orthodoxy. Instead, we should deliberately design graduate programs that build in strong practitioners of a variety of styles of research and thus expose students to the tensions among them. Students, in turn, have a responsibility to be active choosers. Graduate students today often complain to me that they are forced to do X, Y, or Z. I tell them, "You are not really forced to do as much as you think. Form study groups, and make different choices." The career pressures are strong, but they are not nearly as great as people imagine. I talk to a lot of graduate students who say they feel very confined. They seem to choose research questions out of a sense of duty, working on a particular topic because it is what they are expected to do to reach the next career stage. I am not sure enough people are following their noses and trusting their curiosity to lead them to a question that matters. There is too much emphasis on pursuing the next squiggle on the model, rather than standing back from the model and wondering how well it alerts us to important real-world problems.

Q: You emphasize the role of innovation as a motor of progress in the social sciences. Some would argue that an emphasis on creativity and innovation actually *prevents* progress by inhibiting the gradual accumulation of knowledge. A healthy discipline needs a critical mass of people doing incremental, normal science, not a lot of self-conscious mavericks striving to make big, paradigmatic breakthroughs. How do you respond to this line of thinking?

A: If we look at the natural sciences, which many people in political science today think they are trying to emulate, the ability to notice a startling new empirical pattern or recognize that the gestalt one has been applying is wrong, has been associated with fundamental moments of breakthrough. At the same time, it is true that if you have a promising theory, you need to follow through by systematically gathering evidence to test it. We obviously need both of these things. The question comes back not to what any individual does, but to how we can structure our discipline, our debates, our communities of learning, and our teaching so that we preserve the possibilities for innovation. I certainly do not want to give the impression that graduate students today should strive to be Barrington Moore; that was precisely what I was trying to get away from as a young scholar. Still, if you are a graduate student interested in, say, the operation of committees in Congress, you should expose yourself to a number of different approaches to researching the question. And you should be aware of serendipitous insights that can arise from juxtaposing these alternative approaches.

Q: Overall, what is your assessment of the current state of political science compared to sociology, the field in which you were trained and started your career?

A: Political science has been in a very exciting phase over the past decade. It has become more plural theoretically and methodologically, and it has grown and has more people in it. Politics in the real world constantly throws up all kinds of new puzzles and surprises—maybe too many at times.

I don't have as good a feel for sociology as a field, because my ties to it are attenuated. I have committed myself to political science. I do sense that comparative historical sociology is institutionalized, but I don't think there is anything particularly cutting-edge happening in sociology right now, and there may be more people looking at small questions. That is what some of my friends in sociology tell me. On the other hand, I am confident that political science will remain vital, pluralistic, and strong.

Q: What gives you such great confidence about the future of political science?
A: Political scientists study and engage the real world of political conflict, public policy making, and the operation of democratic and non-democratic governments. As a result, we have real-world audiences—journalists, politicians, and the general public—who want to hear what we have to say. This provides a powerful anchor for the discipline that protects against political science flying off into esoterics. I see excellent scholarship being done in political science, often by people who are talking to each other across theoretical and methodological divides and who are combining approaches. The question facing political science today is whether we can hold together as a discipline when we have so many different specialties and methodological and theoretical proclivities. Will we splinter? Until now, political science contained its conflicts in artificial boxes that separated the study of American politics and International Relations from comparative politics and divided normative from empirical research. Will we be able to move from that world to one defined by more fluid, cross-cutting fields and specializations without breaking apart?

Women and the Profession

Q: How have opportunities for women evolved over the past thirty years in comparative politics and in political science more generally?
A: There are a lot more women in political science than there used to be, though still not as many as in sociology. In comparative politics, women are now pretty important in the ranks of new Ph.D.s and young, tenured scholars. Opportunities for women have been opening up, and, as a result, the numbers are shifting toward a better gender balance.

Q: Do women in comparative politics today still face different challenges than men?
A: Yes, women still face problematic challenges regarding family issues and how they intersect with the timing of careers leading up to tenure decisions. But those same issues also impact many young men now. I suppose

many women would say that comparative politics and political science in general are both very male dominated. Still, there has been a welcome weakening of the tendency for women to segregate themselves into the study of gender questions and for men to fail to appreciate the importance of gender issues to the main literatures in the field. I see much more cross-fertilization in empirical research. For example, Michele Swers, whose thesis committee I chaired at Harvard, has just published a wonderful book on what difference female legislators make on policy making in the American Senate (Swers 2002). The book is quantitative, interview-based, and rigorous, and, although it happens to be about gender, it also explores the broader question of whether the identity of legislators makes a difference. Similarly, Mounira Charrad's wonderful book connects different patterns of policy making about families and women's rights to variation in state-building in Tunisia, Algeria, and Morocco (Charrad 2001). Mala Htun's work compares gender rights in Latin America under dictatorship and democracy (Htun 2003). These are all examples of splendid work that focuses on gender but also makes a broader contribution to social science, not to a segregated literature on women. Ironically, the fact that the gender revolution comes late to political science may mean that it comes better, because it seems to have resulted in less ghettoization of women. I hope that's true, because questions about gender and women illuminate the broad processes of politics. They are not something separate.

Conclusion

Q: What is your advice to students who are training to be political scientists?

A: Follow your nose, get passionate about something, and don't give that up. Don't let somebody tell you to study a problem or make a contribution in a particular way, when your instincts and curiosity point you toward something else. Remember why you came to graduate school in the first place, and make it work for you. Expose yourself to a variety of faculty and what they have to offer. Make space for yourself by diversifying; don't apprentice yourself to just one person or approach, but to several. Learning from several different people is a good way to create an original combination. And don't believe it if people tell you there is only one way to get a job. In my observation, the people who get the jobs care passionately about a topic and pursue it determinedly, usually with a combination of methods. This will continue to be true because, in the final analysis, most departments in most universities and colleges need people whose work is of interest to more than just fellow believers and specialists. Finally, have fun and care about what you are doing. If you don't feel that way, then you should do something else.

Appendix: Date and Location of the Interviews

Interviewee	Date of Interview	Location of Interview	Interviewer
Gabriel A. Almond	March 20, 2002	Palo Alto, CA	Munck
Robert H. Bates	March 2, 2002	Woodstock, CT	Snyder
David Collier	July 8, 2003	Berkeley, CA	Munck
Robert A. Dahl	March 4, 2002	New Haven, CT	Snyder
Samuel P. Huntington	May 31 and June 11, 2001	Cambridge, MA	Snyder
David D. Laitin	November 18–19, 2001	Palo Alto, CA	Munck
Arend Lijphart	August 5, 2003	San Diego, CA	Munck
Juan J. Linz	April 25–26, 2001	Hamden, CT	Snyder
Barrington Moore, Jr.	May 13, 2002	Cambridge, MA	Snyder
Guillermo O'Donnell	March 23, 2002	Palo Alto, CA	Munck
Adam Przeworski	February 24, 2003	New York, NY	Munck
James C. Scott	July 20 and 28, 2001	Durham, CT	Snyder
Philippe C. Schmitter	December 4–5, 2002	Notre Dame, IN	Munck
Theda Skocpol	May 14, 2002	Cambridge, MA	Snyder
Alfred Stepan	October 15–16, 2003	Little Compton, RI	Snyder

References

Acemoglu, Daron, and James A. Robinson. 2006. *Economic Origins of Dictatorship and Democracy.* New York: Cambridge University Press.

Achen, Christopher H. 1983. "Towards Theories of Data: The State of Political Methodology." In *Political Science: The State of the Discipline,* ed. Ada W. Finifter, 69–93. Washington, DC: American Political Science Association.

Adcock, Robert. 2003. "The Emergence of Political Science as a Discipline: History and the Study of Politics in America, 1875–1919." *History of Political Thought* 24, no. 3: 481–508.

———. 2005. "The Emigration of the 'Comparative Method': Transatlantic Exchange and Comparative Inquiry in the American Study of Politics, 1876–1903." Paper presented at the American Political Science Association (APSA) Annual Convention, Washington, DC, September 1–4, 2005.

Adcock, Robert, Mark Bevir, and Shannon Stimson, eds. 2007. *Modern Political Science: Anglo-American Exchanges Since 1870.* Princeton, NJ: Princeton University Press.

Adcock, Robert, and David Collier. 2001. "Measurement Validity: A Shared Standard for Qualitative and Quantitative Research." *American Political Science Review* 95, no. 3 (September): 529–46.

Alford, Robert R., and Roger Friedland. 1985. *Powers of Theory: Capitalism, the State, and Democracy.* New York: Cambridge University Press.

Allison, Graham T. 1971. *Essence of Decision: Explaining the Cuban Missile Crisis.* Boston: Little, Brown.

Almond, Gabriel A. 1945. "The Political Attitudes of Wealth." *Journal of Politics* 7, no. 3 (August): 213–55.

———. 1950. *The American People and Foreign Policy.* New York: Harcourt, Brace.

———. 1954. *The Appeals of Communism.* Princeton, NJ: Princeton University Press.

———. 1956. "Comparative Political Systems." *Journal of Politics* 18, no. 3 (August): 391–409.

———. 1960. "Introduction: A Functional Approach to Comparative Politics." In *The Politics of the Developing Areas,* ed. Gabriel A. Almond and James Coleman, 3–64. Princeton, NJ: Princeton University Press.

———. 1970. "Introduction: Propensities and Opportunities." In *Political Development: Essays in Heuristic Theory,* Gabriel A. Almond, 3–27. Boston: Little, Brown.

———. 1983. "Corporatism, Pluralism, and Professional Memory." *World Politics* 35, no. 2 (January): 245–60.

———. 1988. "The Return to the State." *American Political Science Review* 82, no. 3: 853–74.

———. 1990. *A Discipline Divided: Schools and Sects in Political Science.* Newbury Park, CA: Sage Publications.

———. 1991. "Capitalism and Democracy." *PS: Political Science & Politics* 26, no. 3: 467–74.

———. 1996. "Political Science: The History of the Discipline." In *The New Handbook of*

Political Science, ed. Robert Goodin and Hans-Dieter Klingemann, 50–96. Oxford: Oxford University Press.

———. 1997. "A Voice from the Chicago School." In *Comparative European Politics: The Story of a Profession,* ed. Hans Daalder, 54–67. New York: Pinter.

———. 1998. *Plutocracy and Politics in New York City.* Boulder, CO: Westview Press.

———. 2002. *Ventures in Political Science: Narratives and Reflections.* Boulder, CO: Lynne Rienner.

Almond, Gabriel A., R. Scott Appleby, and Emmanuel Sivan. 2003. *Strong Religion: The Rise of Fundamentalisms around the World.* Chicago: University of Chicago Press.

Almond, Gabriel A., and G. Bingham Powell Jr. 1966. *Comparative Politics: A Developmental Approach.* Boston: Little, Brown.

———. 1978. *Comparative Politics: Systems, Processes, and Policy.* Boston: Little, Brown.

Almond, Gabriel A., G. Bingham Powell Jr., Kaare Strøm, and Russell J. Dalton, eds. 2000. *Comparative Politics Today.* 7th ed. New York: Addison Wesley Longman.

Almond, Gabriel A., Taylor Cole, and Roy C. Macridis. 1955. "A Suggested Research Strategy in Western European Government and Politics." *American Political Science Review* 49, no. 4: 1042–49.

Almond, Gabriel A., and James S. Coleman, eds. 1960. *The Politics of the Developing Areas.* Princeton, NJ: Princeton University Press.

Almond, Gabriel A., Scott Flanagan, and Robert Mundt, eds. 1973. *Crisis, Choice, and Change: Historical Studies of Political Development.* Boston: Little, Brown.

Almond, Gabriel A., and Stephen J. Genco. 1977. "Clouds, Clocks, and the Study of Politics." *World Politics* 29, no. 4: 489–522.

Almond, Gabriel A., and Harold D. Lasswell. 1934. "Aggressive Behavior by Clients Toward Public Relief Administrators: A Configurative Analysis." *American Political Science Review* 28, no. 4 (August): 643–55.

Almond, Gabriel A., and Sidney Verba. 1963. *The Civic Culture: Political Attitudes and Democracy in Five Nations.* Princeton, NJ: Princeton University Press.

Alt, James E., and Kenneth A. Shepsle. 1990. "Editors' Introduction." In *Perspectives on Positive Political Economy,* ed. James E. Alt and Kenneth A. Shepsle, 1–5. New York: Cambridge University Press.

Althusius, Johannes. 1964. *The Politics of Johannes Althusius.* Boston: Beacon Press.

Althusser, Louis. 1968. *For Marx.* London: Verso/NLB.

Althusser, Louis, and Etienne Balibar. 1969. *Reading Capital.* London: Verso.

Alvarez, Michael, José Antonio Cheibub, Fernando Limongi, and Adam Przeworski. 1996. "Classifying Political Regimes." *Studies in Comparative International Development* 31, no. 2 (Summer): 1–36.

Amadae, S. M. 2003. *Rationalizing Capitalist Democracy: The Cold War Origins of Rational Choice Liberalism.* Chicago: University of Chicago Press.

Amadae, S. M., and Bruce Bueno de Mesquita. 1999. "The Rochester School: The Origins of Positive Political Economy." *Annual Review of Political Science* 2: 269–95.

Amenta, Edwin. 2003. "What We Know About the Development of Social Policy: Comparative and Historical Research in Comparative and Historical Perspective." In *Comparative Historical Analysis in the Social Sciences,* ed. James Mahoney and Dietrich Rueschemeyer, 91–130. New York: Cambridge University Press.

Anderson, Benedict O'G. 1991. *Imagined Communities: Reflections on the Origins and Spread of Nationalism.* New York: Verso.

Anderson, Perry. 1974a. *Passages from Antiquity to Feudalism.* London: New Left Books.

——. 1974b. *Lineages of the Absolutist State.* London: New Left Books.

——. 1977. "The Antinomies of Antonio Gramsci." *New Left Review* no. 100: 5–80.

Apter, David E. 1961. *The Political Kingdom in Uganda: A Study in Bureaucratic Nationalism.* Princeton, NJ: Princeton University Press.

——. 1965. *The Politics of Modernization.* Chicago: University of Chicago Press.

——. 1996. "Comparative Politics, Old and New." In *The New Handbook of Political Science,* ed. Robert Goodin and Hans-Dieter Klingemann, 372–97. Oxford: Oxford University Press.

Arendt, Hannah. 1951. *The Origins of Totalitarianism.* New York: Harcourt Brace.

Aristotle. 1946. *Politics.* Oxford: Clarendon Press.

Aron, Raymond. 1968. *Democracy and Totalitarianism.* London: Weidenfeld and Nicolson.

Arrow, Kenneth J. 1951. *Social Choice and Individual Values.* New York: Wiley.

Arthur, W. Brian. 1994. *Increasing Returns and Path Dependence in the Economy.* Ann Arbor: University of Michigan Press.

Baer, Michael A., Malcolm E. Jewell, and Lee Sigelman, eds. 1991. *Political Science in America: Oral Histories of a Discipline.* Lexington: University Press of Kentucky.

Banks, Arthur S., and Robert B. Textor. 1963. *A Cross-Polity Survey.* Cambridge: MIT Press.

Barro, Robert J. 1997. *Determinants of Economic Growth: A Cross-Country Empirical Study.* Cambridge: MIT Press.

Barry, Brian. 1970. *Sociologists, Economists and Democracy.* London: Collier-Macmillan.

——. 1975a. "Political Accommodation and Consociational Democracy." *British Journal of Political Science* 5, no. 4 (October): 477–505.

——. 1975b. "The Consociational Model and Its Dangers." *European Journal of Political Research* 3, no. 4 (December): 393–415.

Bartels, Larry M., and Henry E. Brady. 1993. "The State of Quantitative Political Methodology." In *Political Science: The State of the Discipline II,* ed. Ada W. Finifter, 121–59. Washington, DC: American Political Science Association.

Bates, Robert H. 1971. *Unions, Parties, and Political Development: A Study of Mineworkers in Zambia.* New Haven, CT: Yale University Press.

——. 1976. *Rural Responses to Industrialization: A Study of Village Zambia.* New Haven, CT: Yale University Press.

——. 1981. *Markets and States in Tropical Africa: The Political Basis of Agricultural Policies.* Berkeley: University of California Press.

——. 1983. *Essays on the Political Economy of Rural Africa.* Berkeley: University of California Press.

——, ed. 1988. *Toward a Political Economy of Development: A Rational Choice Perspective.* Berkeley: University of California Press.

——. 1989. *Beyond the Miracle of the Market: The Political Economy of Agrarian Development in Kenya.* New York: Cambridge University Press.

——. 1990. "Macropolitical Economy in the Field of Development." In *Perspectives on*

Positive Political Economy, ed. James Alt and Kenneth Shepsle, 31–56. New York: Cambridge University Press.

——. 1996. "Letter from the President: Area Studies and the Discipline." *APSA-CP: Newsletter of the APSA Organized Section in Comparative Politics* 7, no. 1 (Winter): 1–2.

——. 1997a. *Open-Economy Politics: The Political Economy of the World Coffee Trade.* Princeton, NJ: Princeton University Press.

——. 1997b. "Comparative Politics and Rational Choice: A Review Essay." *American Political Science Review* 91, no. 3 (September): 699–704.

——. 1997c. "Area Studies and the Discipline: A Useful Controversy?" *PS: Political Science & Politics* 30, no. 2 (June): 166–69.

——. 1997d. "Area Studies and Political Science: Rupture and Possible Synthesis." *Africa Today* 44, no. 2: 123–31.

——. 2001. *Prosperity and Violence.* New York: W. W. Norton.

——. 2003. [Review of Scott, *Seeing Like a State.*] *APSA-CP: Newsletter of the APSA Organized Section in Comparative Politics* 14, no. 2 (Summer): 25–26.

——. 2005. "Political Insecurity and State Failure in Contemporary Africa." *Working Paper* no. 115, Center for International Development, Harvard University.

Bates, Robert H., Rui J. P. de Figueiredo Jr., and Barry R. Weingast. 1998. "The Politics of Interpretation: Rationality, Culture, and Transition." *Politics and Society* 26, no. 2 (June): 221–56.

Bates, Robert H., Avner Greif, Margaret Levi, Jean-Laurent Rosenthal, and Barry Weingast. 1998. *Analytic Narratives.* Princeton, NJ: Princeton University Press.

Bates, Robert H., Avner Greif, and Smita Singh. 2002. "Organizing Violence." *Journal of Conflict Resolution* 46, no. 5 (October): 599–628.

Bates, Robert H., and Michael F. Lofchie, eds. 1980. *Agricultural Development in Africa: Issues of Public Policy.* New York: Praeger.

Bates, Robert H., and Da-Hsiang Donald Lien. 1985. "A Note on Taxation, Development, and Representative Government." *Politics and Society* 14, no. 1: 53–70.

Bates, Robert H., V. Y. Mudimbe, and Jean O'Barr, eds. 1993. *Africa and the Disciplines: The Contributions of Research in Africa to the Social Sciences and Humanities.* Chicago: University of Chicago Press.

Baum, W. C., G. N. Griffiths, R. Matthews, and D. Scherruble. 1976. "American Political Science before the Mirror: What our Journals Reveal about the Profession." *Journal of Politics* 38, no. 4 (November): 895–917.

Becker, Howard S. 1998. *Tricks of the Trade: How to Think about Your Research While You're Doing It.* Chicago: University of Chicago Press.

Bendix, Reinhard. 1956. *Work and Authority in Industry: Ideologies of Management in the Course of Industrialization.* New York: Wiley.

——. 1964. *Nation-Building and Citizenship: Studies of Our Changing Social Order.* New York: Wiley.

——. 1980. *Kings or People: Power and the Mandate to Rule.* Berkeley: University of California Press.

——. 1986. *From Berlin to Berkeley: German-Jewish Identities.* New Brunswick, NJ: Transaction Books.

——. 1990. "How I Became an American Sociologist." In *Authors of Their Own Lives:*

Intellectual Autobiographies by Twenty American Sociologists, ed. Bennett M. Berger, 452–75. Berkeley: University of California Press.

Benhabib, Jess, and Adam Przeworski. 2006. "The Political Economy of Redistribution Under Democracy." *Economic Theory* 29, no. 2 (October): 271–90.

Bennett, Andrew, Aharon Barth, and Ken Rutherford. 2003. "Do We Preach What We Practice? A Survey of Methods in Political Science Journals and Curricula." *PS: Political Science & Politics* 36, no. 3 (July): 373–78.

Bentley, Arthur. 1908. *Process of Government.* Chicago: University of Chicago Press.

Benton, Ted. 1984. *The Rise and Fall of Structural Marxism: Althusser and His Influence.* London: Palgrave Macmillan.

Berelson, Bernard R., Paul F. Lazarsfeld, and William N. McPhee. 1954. *Voting: A Study of Opinion Formation in a Presidential Campaign.* Chicago: University of Chicago Press.

Berg, Elliot. 1981. *Accelerated Development in Sub-Saharan Africa: An Agenda for Action.* Washington, DC: World Bank.

Berger, Bennett M., ed. 1990. *Authors of Their Own Lives: Intellectual Autobiographies of Twenty American Sociologists.* Berkeley: University of California Press.

Berger, Suzanne. 1981. "Introduction." In *Organizing Interests in Western Europe: Pluralism, Corporatism and the Transformation of Politics,* ed. Suzanne Berger, 1–23. New York: Cambridge University Press.

Bernhard, Michael. 2002. [Review of Moore's *Moral Purity and Persecution in History* and *Moral Aspects of Economic Growth and Other Essays.*] *Studies in Comparative International Development* 37, no. 1 (Spring): 116–20.

Bien, David D. 1960. *The Calas Affair.* Princeton, NJ: Princeton University Press.

Bienen, Henry. 1967. "What Does Political Development Mean in Africa?" *World Politics* 20, no. 1 (October): 128–41.

Binder, Leonard, James Coleman, Joseph LaPalombara, Lucian Pye, Sidney Verba, and Myron Weiner. 1971. *Crisis and Sequences in Political Development.* Princeton, NJ: Princeton University Press.

Bloch, Marc. 1961. *Feudal Society.* Chicago: University of Chicago Press.

——. 1967. "A Contribution towards a Comparative History of European Societies." In *Land and Work in Medieval Europe: Selected Papers by Marc Bloch,* Marc Bloch, 44–81. New York: Harper & Row.

Blondel, Jean. 1999. "Then and Now: Comparative Politics." *Political Studies* 47, no. 1: 152–60.

Bobbio, Norberto. 1984. *The Future of Democracy.* Minneapolis: University of Minnesota Press.

Bogaards, Matthijs. 2000. "The Uneasy Relationship Between Empirical and Normative Types in Consociational Theory." *Journal of Theoretical Politics* 12, no. 4: 395–423.

Boix, Carles. 1998. *Political Parties, Growth and Equality: Conservative and Social Democratic Economic Strategies in the World Economy.* New York: Cambridge University Press.

Boix, Carles, and Susan Stokes. 2003. "Endogenous Democratization." *World Politics* 55, no. 4 (July): 517–49.

Bracher, Karl Dietrich. 1952. "Auflösung einer Demokratie: Des Ende der Weimarer

Republik als Forschungsproblem." In *Faktoren der Machtbildung*, ed. Akadij Gurland, 39–98. Berlin: Duncker and Humblot.

——. 1955. *Die Aufösung der Weimarer Republik: eine Studie zum Probelm des Machtverfalls in der Demokratie*. Villingen/Schwarzwald: Ring-Verlag.

Brady, Henry E., and David Collier, eds. 2004. *Rethinking Social Inquiry: Diverse Tools, Shared Standards*. Lanham, MD: Rowman & Littlefield and the Berkeley Public Policy Press.

Bresser Pereira, Luiz Carlos, José María Maravall, and Adam Przeworski. 1993. *Economic Reform in New Democracies*. New York: Cambridge University Press.

Brooker, Paul. 2000. *Non-Democratic Regimes: Theory, Government and Politics*. New York: St. Martin's Press.

Bryce, James. 1921. *Modern Democracies*. New York: Macmillan.

Brzezinski, Zbigniew K. 1962. *Ideology and Power in Soviet Politics*. New York: Praeger.

Brzezinski, Zbigniew K., and Samuel P. Huntington. 1964. *Political Power: USA/USSR*. New York: Viking Press.

Buchanan, James, and Gordon Tulloch. 1962. *The Calculus of Consent*. Ann Arbor: University of Michigan Press.

Burawoy, Michael. 1989. "Two Methods in Search of Science: Skocpol versus Trotsky." *Theory and Society* 18: 759–805.

Camerer, Colin F., and Rebecca Morton. 2002. "Formal Theory Meets Data." In *Political Science: The State of the Discipline*, ed. Ira Katznelson and Helen V. Milner, 784–804. New York and Washington, DC: W. W. Norton and the American Political Science Association.

Campbell, Angus, Philip E. Converse, Warren E. Miller, and Donald E. Stokes. 1960. *The American Voter*. New York: Wiley.

Campbell, Donald Thomas. 1988. *Methodology and Epistemology for Social Science: Selected Papers*. Chicago: University of Chicago Press.

Campbell, Donald T., and Julian C. Stanley. 1966. *Experimental and Quasi-Experimental Designs for Research*. Boston: Houghton Mifflin.

Cardoso, Fernando H. 1973. "Associated-Dependent Development: Theoretical and Practical Implications." In *Authoritarian Brazil: Origins, Policies, and Future*, ed. Alfred Stepan, 142–78. New Haven, CT: Yale University Press.

Cardoso, Fernando H., and Enzo Faletto. 1979. *Dependency and Development in Latin America*. Berkeley: University of California Press.

Centers, Richard. 1949. *The Psychology of Social Classes: A Study of Class Consciousness*. Princeton, NJ: Princeton University Press.

Charrad, Mounira. 2001. *States and Women's Rights: The Making of Postcolonial Tunisia, Algeria, and Morocco*. Berkeley: University of California Press.

Chayanov, A. V. 1966. *The Theory of Peasant Economy*, ed. Daniel Thorner et al. Homewood, IL: R. D. Irwin.

Chehabi, H. E., and Juan J. Linz. 1998a. "A Theory of Sultanism I: A Type of Nondemocratic Rule." In *Sultanistic Regimes*, ed. H. E. Chehabi and Juan J. Linz, 3–25. Baltimore: Johns Hopkins University Press.

——, eds. 1998b. *Sultanistic Regimes*. Baltimore: Johns Hopkins University Press.

Chubb, Basil. 1970. *The Government and Politics of Ireland*. Stanford, CA: Stanford University Press.

Coase, Ronald. 1960. "The Problem of Social Cost." *Journal of Law and Economics* 3, no. 1 (October): 1–44.

Cohen, G. A. 1978. *Karl Marx's Theory of History: A Defense*. Princeton, NJ: Princeton University Press.

Cohen, Jean L., and Andrew Arato. 1992. *Civil Society and Political Theory*. Cambridge: MIT Press.

Coker, Francis W. 1934. *Recent Political Thought*. New York: D. Appleton-Century.

Coleman, James S. 1990a. "Columbia in the 1950s." In *Authors of Their Own Lives: Intellectual Autobiographies by Twenty American Sociologists*, ed. Bennett M. Berger, 75–103. Berkeley: University of California Press.

———. 1990b. *Foundations of Social Theory*. Cambridge, MA: Harvard University Press.

Collier, David. 1975. "Timing of Economic Growth and Regime Characteristics in Latin America." *Comparative Politics* 7, no. 3 (April): 331–59.

———. 1976. *Squatters and Oligarchs: Authoritarian Rule and Policy Change in Peru*. Baltimore: Johns Hopkins University Press.

———. 1978. "Industrial Modernization and Political Change: A Latin American Perspective." *World Politics* 30, no. 4: 593–614.

———, ed. 1979. *The New Authoritarianism in Latin America*. Princeton, NJ: Princeton University Press.

———. 1991. "The Comparative Method: Two Decades of Change." In *Comparative Political Dynamics: Global Research Perspectives,* ed. Dankwart A. Rustow and Kenneth Paul Erickson, 7–31. New York: HarperCollins.

———. 1993. "The Comparative Method." In *Political Science: The State of the Discipline II,* ed. Ada W. Finifter, 105–19. Washington, DC: American Political Science Association.

———. 1995. "Trajectory of a Concept: 'Corporatism' in the Study of Latin American Politics." In *Latin America in Comparative Perspective: New Approaches to Methods and Analysis,* ed. Peter H. Smith, 135–62. Boulder, CO: Westview Press.

———. 1998a. "Comparative Method in the 1990s." *APSA-CP: Newsletter of the APSA Organized Section in Comparative Politics* 9, no. 1 (Winter): 1–2, 4–5.

———. 1998b. "Comparative-Historical Analysis: Where Do We Stand?" *APSA-CP: Newsletter of the APSA Organized Section in Comparative Politics* 9, no. 2 (Summer): 1–2, 4–5.

———. 1999a. "Data, Field Work and Extracting New Ideas at Close Range." *APSA-CP: Newsletter of the APSA Organized Section in Comparative Politics* 10, no. 1 (Winter): 1–2, 4–6.

———. 1999b. "Building a Disciplined, Rigorous Center in Comparative Politics." *APSA-CP: Newsletter of the APSA Organized Section in Comparative Politics* 10, no. 2 (Summer): 1–2, 4.

Collier, David, and Robert N. Adcock. 1999. "Democracy and Dichotomies: A Pragmatic Approach to Choices About Concepts." *Annual Review of Political Science* 2: 537–65.

Collier, David, Henry E. Brady, and Jason Seawright. 2004. "Sources of Leverage in Causal Inference: Toward an Alternative View of Methodology." In *Rethinking Social Inquiry: Diverse Tools, Shared Standards,* ed. Henry E. Brady and David Collier, 229–66. Lanham, MD: Rowman & Littlefield Publishers and the Berkeley Public Policy Press.

Collier, David, and Ruth Berins Collier. 1977. "Who Does What, to Whom, and How: Toward a Comparative Analysis of Latin American Corporatism." In *Authoritarianism and Corporatism in Latin America,* ed. James M. Malloy, 489–512. Pittsburgh: University of Pittsburgh Press.

Collier, David, and Steven Levitsky. 1997. "Democracy With Adjectives: Conceptual Innovation in Comparative Research." *World Politics* 49, no. 3 (April): 430–51.

Collier, David, and James E. Mahon Jr. 1993. "Conceptual Stretching Revisited: Adapting Categories in Comparative Analysis." *American Political Science Review* 87, no. 4: 845–55.

Collier, David, and Richard Messick. 1975. "Prerequisites Versus Diffusion: Testing Alternative Explanations of Social Security Adoption." *American Political Science Review* 69, no. 4: 1299–1315.

Collier, Ruth Berins. 1982a. *Regimes in Tropical Africa: Changing Forms of Supremacy, 1945–75.* Berkeley: University of California Press.

———. 1982b. "Popular Sector Incorporation and Political Supremacy: Regime Evolution in Brazil and Mexico." In *Brazil and Mexico: Patterns of Late Development,* ed. Sylvia Ann Hewlett and Richard Weinhert, 57–109. Philadelphia: Institute for the Study of Human Issues.

———. 1992. *The Contradictory Alliance: State-Labor Relations and Regime Change in Mexico.* Berkeley: International and Area Studies Press.

———. 1993. "Combining Alternative Perspectives: Internal Trajectories Versus External Influences as Explanations of Latin American Politics in the 1940s." *Comparative Politics* 26, no. 1 (December): 1–30.

———. 1999. *Paths Toward Democracy: Working Class and Elites in Western Europe and South America.* New York: Cambridge University Press.

Collier, Ruth Berins, and David Collier. 1979. "Inducements versus Constraints: Disaggregating 'Corporatism.'" *American Political Science Review* 73, no. 4 (December): 967–86.

———. 1991. *Shaping the Political Arena: Critical Junctures, the Labor Movement, and Regime Dynamics in Latin America.* Princeton, NJ: Princeton University Press.

———. 2002. *Shaping the Political Arena: Critical Junctures, the Labor Movement, and the Regime Dynamics in Latin America.* Notre Dame, IN: University of Notre Dame Press.

Colomer, Josep M. 1991. "Transitions by Agreement: Modeling the Spanish Way." *American Political Science Review* 85, no. 4 (December): 1283–1302.

———. 1995. *Game Theory and the Transition to Democracy: The Spanish Model.* Aldershot, England: E. Elgar.

Colson, Elizabeth. 1974. *Tradition and Contract: The Problem of Order.* Chicago: Aldine Publishing.

Cook, Thomas D., and Donald T. Campbell. 1979. *Quasi-Experimentation: Design and Analysis Issues for Field Settings.* Boston: Houghton Mifflin.

Cortés, Fernando, Adam Przeworski, and John Sprague. 1974. *Systems Analysis for Social Scientists.* New York: Wiley Interscience.

Coser, Lewis A. 1956. *The Functions of Social Conflict.* Glencoe, IL: The Free Press.

———. 1984. *Refugee Scholars in America: Their Impact and Their Experiences.* New Haven, CT: Yale University Press.

Cox, Gary. 1997. *Making Votes Count: Strategic Coordination in the World's Electoral Systems*. New York: Cambridge University Press.

Crepaz, Markus M. L., and Arend Lijphart. 1995. "Linking and Integrating Corporatism and Consensus Democracy: Theory, Concepts and Evidence." *British Journal of Political Science* 25, no. 2 (April): 281–88.

Crick, Bernard. 1959. *The American Science of Politics: Its Origins and Conditions*. Berkeley: University of California Press.

Crowley, Jocelyn Elise, and Theda Skocpol. 2001. "The Rush to Organize: Explaining Associational Formation in the United States, 1860s–1920s." *American Journal of Political Science* 45, no. 4 (October): 813–29.

Cutright, Philips. 1963. "National Political Development: Its Measurement and Social Correlates." In *Politics and Social Life*, ed. Nelson W. Polsby, Robert A. Dentler, and Paul A. Smith, 569–81. Boston: Houghton Mifflin.

Daalder, Hans. 1993. "The Development of the Study of Comparative Politics." In *Comparative Politics: New Directions in Theory and Method*, ed. Hans Keman, 11–30. Amsterdam: VU University Press.

——, ed. 1997a. *Comparative European Politics: The Story of a Profession*. New York: Pinter.

——. 1997b. "A Smaller European's Opening Frontiers." In *Comparative European Politics: The Story of a Profession*, ed. Hans Daalder, 227–40. New York: Pinter.

Dahl, Robert A. 1940a. "Socialist Programs and Democratic Politics: An Analysis." Ph.D. dissertation, Department of Government, Yale University.

——. 1940b. "On the Theory of Democratic Socialism." *Plan Age* 6, nos. 9–10 (November–December): 325–56.

——. 1950. *Congress and Foreign Policy*. New York: W. W. Norton.

——. 1956. *A Preface to Democratic Theory*. Chicago: University of Chicago Press.

——. 1957. "The Concept of Power." *Behavioral Science* 2, no. 3 (July): 201–15.

——. 1961a. *Who Governs? Democracy and Power in an American City*. New Haven, CT: Yale University Press.

——. 1961b. "The Behavioral Approach to Political Science: Epitaph for a Monument to a Successful Protest." *American Political Science Research* 55, no. 4 (December): 763–72.

——. 1963. *Modern Political Analysis*. Englewood Cliffs, NJ: Prentice-Hall.

——, ed. 1966a. *Political Oppositions in Western Democracies*. New Haven, CT: Yale University Press.

——. 1966b. "Some Explanations." In *Political Oppositions in Western Democracies*, ed. Robert A. Dahl, 348–86. New Haven, CT: Yale University Press.

——. 1967. *Pluralist Democracy in the United States: Conflict and Consent*. Chicago: Rand McNally.

——. 1968. "Power." In *International Encyclopedia of the Social Sciences*, vol. 12: 405–15, ed. David Sills. New York: The Free Press.

——. 1971. *Polyarchy*. New Haven, CT: Yale University Press.

——, ed. 1973. *Regimes and Oppositions*. New Haven, CT: Yale University Press.

——. 1982. *Dilemmas of Pluralist Democracy*. New Haven, CT: Yale University Press.

——. 1985. *A Preface to Economic Democracy*. New Haven, CT: Yale University Press.

——. 1989. *Democracy and Its Critics*. New Haven, CT: Yale University Press.

——. 1993. "Why All Democratic Countries Have Mixed Economies." In *Democratic Community,* ed. John Chapman and Ian Shapiro, 259–82. New York: New York University Press.

——. 1997a. "From Personal History to Democratic Theory." In *Toward Democracy: A Journey, Reflections: 1940–1997,* vol. 1, Robert A. Dahl, 3–15. Berkeley: Institute of Governmental Studies Press, University of California, Berkeley.

——. 1997b. "A Brief Intellectual Autobiography." In *Comparative European Politics: The Story of a Profession,* ed. Hans Daalder, 68–78. New York: Pinter.

——. 1997c. "From Immigrants to Citizens: A New Yet Old Challenge to Democracies." In *Toward Democracy: A Journey, Reflections: 1940–1997,* vol. 1, Robert A. Dahl, 229–50. Berkeley: Institute of Governmental Studies Press, University of California, Berkeley.

——. 1998. *On Democracy.* New Haven, CT: Yale University Press.

——. 1999. "Can International Organizations be Democratic? A Skeptic's View." In *Democracy's Edges,* ed. Ian Shapiro and Casiano Hacker-Cordon, 19–36. New York: Cambridge University Press.

——. 2001a. "Political Equality in the Coming Century." In *Challenges to Democracy: Ideas, Involvement and Institutions,* ed. Keith Dowding, James Hughes, and Helen Margetts, 3–17. New York: Palgrave.

——. 2001b. "Is Postnational Democracy Possible?" In *Nation, Federalism, and Democracy: The EU, Italy, and the American Federal Experience,* ed. Sergio Fabbrini, 35–46. Bologna: Editrice Compositori.

——. 2001c. *How Democratic is the American Constitution?* New Haven, CT: Yale University Press.

——. 2005. *After the Gold Rush, Growing Up In Skagway.* Philadelphia, PA: XLibris.

——. 2006. "Reflections on Human Nature and Politics: From Genes to Political Institutions." In *The Art of Political Leadership: Essays in Honor of Fred I. Greenstein,* ed. Larry Berman, 3–16. Lanham, MD: Rowman & Littlefield.

Dahl, Robert A., Mason Haire, and Paul F. Lazarsfeld, eds. 1959. *Social Science Research on Business: Product and Potential.* New York: Columbia University Press.

Dahl, Robert A., and Charles E. Lindblom. 1953. *Politics, Economics, and Welfare: Planning and Politico-Economic Systems Resolved into Basic Social Processes.* New York: Harper & Row.

Dahl, Robert A., and Edward R. Tufte. 1973. *Size and Democracy.* Stanford, CA: Stanford University Press.

Dalton, Russell J. 1991. "Comparative Politics of the Industrial Democracies: From the Golden Age to Island Hopping." In *Political Science: Looking to the Future,* vol. 2: *Comparative Politics, Policy, and International Relations,* ed. William Crotty, 15–43. Evanston, IL: Northwestern University Press.

David, Paul A. 1985. "Clio and the Economics of QWERTY." *American Economic Review* 75, no. 2 (May): 332–37.

Dawidoff, Nicholas. 2003. *The Fly Swatter: Portrait of an Exceptional Character.* New York: Viking.

de Miguel, Amando. 1993. "The Lynx and the Stork." In *Politics, Society and Democracy: The Case of Spain,* ed. Richard Gunther, 3–10. Boulder, CO: Westview Press.

Dershowitz, Alan. 2001. *Letters to a Young Lawyer.* New York: Basic Books.

de Soto, Hernando. 1989. *The Other Path*. New York: Harper & Row.

Deutsch, Karl W. 1953. *Nationalism and Social Communication: An Inquiry into the Foundations of Nationality*. Cambridge: MIT Press.

———. 1961. "Social Mobilization and Political Development." *American Political Science Review* 51, no. 3 (September): 494–514.

———. 1963. *The Nerves of Government*. New York: The Free Press.

———. 1966. "The Theoretical Basis of Data Programs." In *Comparing Nations: The Use of Quantitative Data in Cross-National Research*, ed. Richard L. Merritt and Stein Rokkan, 27–55. New Haven, CT: Yale University Press.

———. 1968. *The Analysis of International Relations*. Englewood Cliffs, NJ: Prentice-Hall.

Deutsch, Karl W., Harold D. Lasswell, Richard L. Merritt, and Bruce M. Russett. 1966. "The Yale Political Data Program." In *Comparing Nations: The Use of Quantitative Data in Cross-National Research*, ed. Richard L. Merritt and Stein Rokkan, 81–94. New Haven, CT: Yale University Press.

Diamant, Alfred. 1960. *Austrian Catholics and the First Republic: Democracy, Capitalism, and the Social Order, 1918–1934*. Princeton, NJ: Princeton University Press.

Diamond, Larry. 1999. *Developing Democracy: Toward Consolidation*. Baltimore: Johns Hopkins University Press.

Diamond, Larry, Juan J. Linz, and Seymour Martin Lipset, eds. 1988–89. *Democracy in Developing Countries*. 3 vols. Boulder, CO: Lynne Rienner.

Di Tella, Torcuato. 1971–72. "La búsqueda de la fórmula política argentina." *Desarrollo Económico* (Buenos Aires) 11, nos. 42–44: 317–25.

Doggan, Mattei. 1996. "Political Science and the Other Social Sciences." In *The New Handbook of Political Science*, ed. Robert Goodin and Hans-Dieter Klingemann, 97–130. Oxford: Oxford University Press.

Domínguez, Jorge I. 2001. "Samuel Huntington and the Latin American State." In *The Other Mirror: Grand Theory through the Lens of Latin America*, ed. Miguel Angel Centeno and Fernando López-Alves, 219–39. Princeton, NJ: Princeton University Press.

Dos Santos, Theotônio. 1968. *Socialismo o fascismo: el dilema Latinoamericano*. Santiago, Chile: Editorial Prensa Latinoamericana.

———. 1977. "Socialismo y fascismo en América Latina hoy." *Revista Mexicana de Sociología* 39, no. 1: 173–90.

Downs, Anthony. 1957. *An Economic Theory of Democracy*. New York: Harper & Row.

Driver, Cecil. 1946. *Tory Radical: The Life of Richard Oastler*. New York: Oxford University Press.

Dryzek, John S., and Stephen T. Leonard. 1988. "History and Discipline in Political Science." *American Political Science Review* 82, no. 4 (December): 1245–60.

Duguit, Léon. 1919. *Law in the Modern State*. New York: B. W. Huebsch.

Dunlop, John T., Frederick H. Harbison, Clark Kerr, and Charles A. Myers. 1960. *Industrialism and Industrial Man: The Problems of Labor and Management in Economic Growth*. Cambridge, MA: Harvard University Press.

Dunn, John. 1979. "Practicing History and Social Science on 'Realist' Assumptions." In *Action and Interpretation: Studies in the Philosophy of the Social Sciences*, ed. Christopher Hookway and Philip Pettit, 145–75. Cambridge: Cambridge University Press.

Durkheim, Emile. 1951. *Suicide: A Study in Sociology*. Glencoe, IL: The Free Press.

——. 1982. *The Rules of Sociological Method, and Selected Texts on Sociology and its Method*. London: Macmillan.

——. 1995. *The Elementary Forms of Religious Life*. New York: The Free Press.

Duverger, Maurice. 1954. *Political Parties*. New York: Wiley.

Eakin, Emily. 2000. "Political Scientists are in a Revolution Instead of Watching." *New York Times*, November 4.

Easton, David. 1953. *The Political System: An Inquiry into the State of Political Science*. New York: Alfred A. Knopf.

——. 1965a. *A Framework for Political Analysis*. Englewood Cliffs, NJ: Prentice-Hall.

——. 1965b. *A System Analysis of Political Life*. New York: Wiley.

Easton, David, John G. Gunnell, and Luigi Graziano, eds. 1991. *The Development of Political Science: A Comparative Survey*. New York: Routledge.

Easton, David, John G. Gunnell, and Michael B. Stein, eds. 1995. *Regime and Discipline: Democracy and the Development of Political Science*. Ann Arbor: University of Michigan Press.

Eckstein, Harry. 1963. "A Perspective on Comparative Politics, Past and Present." In *Comparative Politics*, ed. Harry Eckstein and David Apter, 3–32. New York: The Free Press.

——. 1966. *Division and Cohesion in Democracy: A Study of Norway*. Princeton, NJ: Princeton University Press.

——. 1975. "Case Study and Theory in Political Science." In *Handbook of Political Science*, vol. 7: *Strategies of Inquiry*, ed. Fred I. Greenstein and Nelson W. Polsby, 79–137. Reading, MA: Addison-Wesley.

——. 1998. "Unfinished Business: Reflection on the Scope of Comparative Politics." *Comparative Political Studies* 31, no. 4: 505–34.

Eckstein, Harry, and David Apter, eds. 1963. *Comparative Politics: A Reader*. New York: The Free Press.

Eggan, Fred. 1954. "Social Anthropology and the Method of Controlled Comparison." *American Anthropologist* 56, no. 5: 743–63.

Eisenstadt, S. N. 1966. *Modernization: Protest and Change*. Englewood Cliffs, NJ: Prentice-Hall.

Eisermann, Gottfried. 1987. *Vilfredo Pareto: Ein Klassiker der Soziologie*. Tübingen, J. C. B. Mohr.

Elkins, Zachary. 2000. "Gradations of Democracy? Empirical Tests of Alternative Conceptualizations." *American Journal of Political Science* 44, no. 2 (April): 293–300.

Elliott, William Yandell. 1928. *The Pragmatic Revolt in Politics: Syndicalism, Fascism, and the Constitutional State*. New York: Macmillan.

Elster, Jon. 1982. "Marxism, Functionalism and Game Theory." *Theory and Society* 11, no. 4: 453–82.

——. 1985. *Making Sense of Marx*. New York: Cambridge University Press.

——. 1999. *Alchemies of the Mind: Studies in Rationality and the Emotions*. New York: Cambridge University Press.

——. 2000. "Rational Choice History: A Case of Excessive Ambition." *American Political Science Review* 94, no. 3 (September): 685–95.

Emerson, Rupert. 1960. *From Empire to Nation: The Rise of Self-Assertion of Asian and African Peoples*. Cambridge, MA: Harvard University Press.

España-Nájera, Annabella, Xavier Márquez, and Paul Vasquez. 2003. "Surveying the Field: Basic Graduate Training in Comparative Politics." *APSA-CP: Newsletter of the Organized Section in Comparative Politics of the American Political Science Association* 14, no. 1 (Winter): 28–34.

Evans, Peter. 1979. *Dependent Development: The Alliance of Multinational, State, and Local Capital in Brazil.* Princeton, NJ: Princeton University Press.

———. 1995. *Embedded Autonomy: States and Industrial Transformation.* Princeton, NJ: Princeton University Press.

Evans, Peter, Harold Jacobson, and Robert Putnam, eds. 1993. *Double-Edged Diplomacy: An Interactive Approach to International Politics.* Berkeley: University of California Press.

Evans, Peter, Dietrich Rueschemeyer, and Theda Skocpol, eds. 1985. *Bringing the State Back In.* New York: Cambridge University Press.

Fainsod, Merle, and Lincoln Gordon. 1941. *Government and the American Economy.* New York: W. W. Norton.

Farr, James. 1999. "John Dewey and American Political Science." *American Journal of Political Science* 43, no. 2: 520–41.

Farr, James, and Raymond Seidelman, eds. 1993. *Discipline and History: Political Science in the United States.* Ann Arbor: University of Michigan Press.

Fearon, James D., and David D. Laitin. 1996. "Explaining Interethnic Cooperation." *American Political Science Review* 90, no. 4: 715–35.

———. 2000. "Violence and the Social Construction of Ethnic Identities." *International Organization* 54, no. 4 (October): 845–77.

———. 2003. "Ethnicity, Insurgency, and Civil War." *American Political Science Review* 97, no. 1 (February): 75–90.

Fenno, Richard F. 1977. "U.S. House Members and Their Constituencies: An Exploration." *American Political Science Review* 71, no. 3 (September): 883–917.

Finegold, Kenneth, and Theda Skocpol. 1995. *State and Party in America's New Deal.* Madison: University of Wisconsin Press.

Finer, Herman. 1932. *The Theory and Practice of Modern Government.* 2 vols. London: Methuen.

Finer, Samuel E. 1962. *The Man on Horseback: The Role of the Military in Politics.* New York: Praeger.

Fiorina, Morris P., and Theda Skocpol, eds. 1999. *Civic Engagement in American Democracy.* Washington, DC: Brookings Institution Press and Russell Sage Foundation.

Fishlow, Albert. 1973. "Some Reflections on Post-1964 Brazilian Economic Policy." In *Authoritarian Brazil: Origins, Policies, and Future,* ed. Alfred Stepan, 69–118. New Haven, CT: Yale University Press.

Fishman, Robert M. 1990. *Working Class Organization and the Return to Democracy in Spain.* Ithaca, NY: Cornell University Press.

———. 2005. "On the Continuing Relevance of the Weberian Methodological Perspective (With Applications to the Spanish Case of Elections in the Aftermath of Terrorism)." *Working Paper* no. 317. Notre Dame, IN: Kellogg Institute for International Studies, University of Notre Dame.

Freeman, Edward. 1873. *Comparative Politics.* London: Macmillan.

Frenkel, Roberto, and Guillermo O'Donnell. 1979. "The 'Stabilization Programs' of the IMF and Their Internal Impacts." In *Capitalism and the State in U.S.-Latin American Relations,* ed. Richard Fagen, 171–216. Stanford, CA: Stanford University Press.

Frey, Frederick W. 1970. "Cross-cultural Survey Research in Political Science." In *The Methodology of Comparative Research,* ed. Robert T. Holt and John E. Turner, 173–294. New York: The Free Press.

Friedrich, Carl J. 1937. *Constitutional Government and Politics: Nature and Development.* New York: Harper.

———. 1963. *Man and His Government: An Empirical Theory of Politics.* New York: McGraw-Hill.

Friedrich, Carl J., and Zbigniew K. Brzezinski. 1956. *Totalitarian Dictatorship and Autocracy.* Cambridge, MA: Harvard University Press.

Friedrich, Carl J., Harold D. Lasswell, Herbert A. Simon, Ralph J. D. Braibanti, G. Lowell Field, and Dwight Waldo. 1953. "Research in Comparative Politics: Comments on the Seminar Report." *American Political Science Review* 47, no. 3 (September): 658–75.

Furtado, Celso. 1970. *Economic Development of Latin America.* Cambridge: Cambridge University Press.

Fustel de Coulanges, Numa Denis. 1882. *The Ancient City: A Study on the Religion, Laws, and Institutions of Greece and Rome.* 4th ed. Boston: Lee and Shepard.

Galenson, Walter. 1959. *Labor and Economic Development.* New York: Wiley.

Gallie, W. B. 1956. "Essentially Contested Concepts." *Proceedings of the Aristotelian Society* 51: 167–98.

Gandhi, Jennifer, and Adam Przeworski. 2006. "Cooperation, Cooptation, and Rebellion under Dictatorships." *Economics and Politics* 18, no. 1 (March): 1–26.

Garrett, Geoffrey. 1998. *Partisan Politics in the Global Economy.* New York: Cambridge University Press.

Gaspari, Elio. 2003. *O Sacerdote e o Feiticeiro: A Ditadura Derrotada.* São Paulo: Companhia das Letras.

Gates, Scott, and Brian D. Humes. 1997. *Games, Information, and Politics: Applying Game Theoretic Models to Political Science.* Ann Arbor: University of Michigan Press.

Gay, Peter. 1998. *My German Question: Growing Up in Nazi Berlin.* New Haven, CT: Yale University Press.

Geddes, Barbara. 1991. "How the Cases You Choose Affect the Answers You Get: Selection Bias in Comparative Politics." In *Political Analysis,* vol. 2, 1990, ed. James A. Stimson, 131–49. Ann Arbor: University of Michigan Press.

———. 2003. *Paradigms and Sand Castles: Theory Building and Research Design in Comparative Politics.* Ann Arbor: University of Michigan Press.

Geertz, Clifford. 1973. *The Interpretation of Cultures: Selected Essays.* New York: Basic Books.

Gellner, Ernest. 1983. *Nations and Nationalism.* Oxford: Blackwell.

George, Alexander L. 1979. "Case Studies and Theory Development: The Method of Structured, Focused Comparison." In *Diplomacy: New Approaches in History, Theory and Policy,* ed. Paul Gordon Lauren, 43–68. New York: The Free Press.

George, Alexander L., and Andrew Bennett. 2005. *Case Studies and Theory Development in the Social Sciences.* Cambridge: MIT Press.

George, Alexander L., and Timothy J. McKeown. 1985. "Case Studies and Theories of Organizational Decision Making." In *Advances in Information Processing in Organizations* 2, ed. Robert F. Coulam and Richard A. Smith, 21–58. Greenwich, CT.: JAI Press.

Gerber, Alan S., and Donald P. Green. 2000. "The Effects of Canvassing, Telephone Calls, and Direct Mail on Voter Turnout: A Field Experiment." *American Political Science Review* 94, no. 3 (September): 653–63.

Gerschenkron, Alexander. 1962. *Economic Backwardness in Historical Perspective.* Cambridge, MA: Harvard University Press.

———. 1966. *Bread and Democracy in Germany.* New York: H. Fertig.

———. 1968. *Continuity in History and Other Essays.* Cambridge, MA: Harvard University Press.

Gershman, Carl. 1997. "The Clash within Civilizations." *Journal of Democracy* 8, no. 4 (October): 165–70.

Gerth, H. H., and C. Wright Mills, eds. 1946. *From Max Weber: Essays in Sociology.* New York: Oxford University Press.

Gillespie, Charles Guy. 1991. *Negotiating Democracy: Politicians and Generals in Uruguay.* New York: Cambridge University Press.

Gilman, Nils. 2003. *Mandarins of the Future: Modernization Theory in Cold War America.* Baltimore: Johns Hopkins University Press.

Goldstone, Jack A. 2003. "Comparative Historical Analysis and Knowledge Accumulation in the Study of Revolutions." In *Comparative Historical Analysis in the Social Sciences,* ed. James Mahoney and Dietrich Rueschemeyer, 41–90. New York: Cambridge University Press.

Goldthorpe, John H. 2000. *On Sociology: Numbers, Narratives, and the Integration of Research and Theory.* Oxford: Oxford University Press.

González, Luis E. 1991. *Political Structures and Democracy in Uruguay.* Notre Dame, IN: University of Notre Dame Press.

Goodnow, Frank. 1900. *Politics and Administration.* New York: Macmillan.

Gramsci, Antonio. 1991. *Prison Notebooks.* New York: Columbia University Press.

Grann, David. 2004. "Mysterious Circumstances: The Strange Death of a Sherlock Holmes Fanatic." *The New Yorker* (December 13): 58–73.

Green, Donald P., and Ian Shapiro. 1994. *Pathologies of Rational Choice: A Critique of Applications in Political Science.* New Haven, CT: Yale University Press.

Greenberg, Stanley B., and Theda Skocpol, eds. 1997. *The New Majority: Toward a Popular Progressive Politics.* New Haven, CT: Yale University Press.

Greenstone, J. David. 1969. *Labor in American Politics.* New York: Knopf.

Grew, Raymond, ed. 1978. *Crises of Political Development in Europe and the United States.* Princeton, NJ: Princeton University Press.

Grofman, Bernard, and Arend Lijphart, eds. 1986. *Electoral Laws and Their Political Consequences.* New York: Agathon.

———. 2002. *The Evolution of Electoral and Party Systems in the Nordic Countries.* New York: Agathon.

Grofman, Bernard, Arend Lijphart, Robert McKay, and Howard Scarrow, eds. 1982. *Representation and Redistricting Issues.* Lexington, MA: Lexington Books.

Grossman, Gene M., and Elhanan Helpman. 2001. *Special Interest Politics.* Cambridge: MIT Press.

Guetzkow, Harold. 1950. "Long Range Research in International Relations." *The American Perspective* 4, no. 4: 421–40.

Gunnell, John. 1993. *The Descent of Political Theory: The Genealogy of an American Vocation.* Chicago: University of Chicago Press.

———. 2004. *Imagining the American Polity: Political Science and the Discourse of Democracy.* University Park: Pennsylvania State University Press.

Gurr, Ted. 1970. *Why Men Rebel.* Princeton, NJ: Princeton University Press.

Haas, Ernst B. 1958. *The Uniting of Europe: Political, Social, and Economic Forces, 1950–1957.* Stanford, CA: Stanford University Press.

Haas, Ernst B., and Philippe Schmitter. 1964. "Economics and Differential Patterns of Political Integration: Projections about Unity in Latin America." *International Organization* 18, no. 3: 705–37.

Hall, Peter A., ed. 1989. *The Political Power of Economic Ideas: Keynesianism across Nations.* Princeton, NJ: Princeton University Press.

Hall, Peter A., and David Soskice, eds. 2001. *Varieties of Capitalism: The Institutional Foundations of Comparative Advantage.* Oxford: Oxford University Press.

Hall, Peter A., and Rosemary Taylor. 1996. "Political Science and the Three New Institutionalisms." *Political Studies* 44, no. 5: 936–57.

Harrison, Lawrence E., and Samuel P. Huntington, eds. 2000. *Culture Matters: How Values Shape Human Progress.* New York: Basic Books.

Hartz, Louis. 1955. *The Liberal Tradition in America: An Interpretation of American Political Thought since the Revolution.* New York: Harcourt, Brace.

———. 1964. *The Founding of New Societies: Studies in the History of the United States, Latin America, South Africa, Canada, and Australia.* New York: Harcourt, Brace & World.

Heberle, Rudolf. 1945. *From Democracy to Nazism: A Regional Case Study on Political Parties.* Baton Rouge: Louisiana State University Press.

Heller, Hermann. 1934. *Staatslehre.* Leiden: A.W. Sijthoff's Uitgeversmaatsch appif N.V.

Hempel, Carl G. 1965. *Aspects of Scientific Explanation, and Other Essays in the Philosophy of Science.* New York: The Free Press.

———. 1966. *Philosophy of Natural Science.* Englewood Cliffs, NJ: Prentice-Hall.

Hermet, Guy. 2001. *Les populismes dans le monde: Une histoire sociologique XIXème–XXème siècle.* Paris: Fayard.

Hintze, Otto. 1975. *The Historical Essays of Otto Hintze,* ed. Felix Gilbert. New York: Oxford University Press.

Hirschman, Albert O. 1963. *Journeys Toward Progress: Studies of Economic Policy-Making in Latin America.* New York: Twentieth Century Fund.

———. 1970. "The Search for Paradigms as a Hindrance to Understanding." *World Politics* 22, no. 3 (April): 329–43.

———. 1971. "The Political Economy of Import-Substituting Industrialization in Latin America." In *A Bias For Hope: Essays on Development,* Albert O. Hirschman, 85–123. New Haven, CT: Yale University Press.

———. 1992. "In Defense of Possibilism." In *Rival Views of Market Society and Other Recent Essays,* Albert O. Hirschman, 171–75. Cambridge, MA: Harvard University Press.

———. 1995. *A Propensity to Self-Subversion.* Cambridge, MA: Harvard University Press.

Hochschild, Adam. 1998. *King Leopold's Ghost: A Story of Greed, Terror, and Heroism in Colonial Africa.* Boston: Houghton Mifflin.

Holcombe, Arthur Norman. 1930. *The Chinese Revolution: A Phase in the Regeneration of a World Power.* Cambridge, MA: Harvard University Press.

———. 1940. *The Middle Classes in American Politics.* New York: Russell & Russell.

———. 1948. *Human Rights in the Modern World.* New York: New York University Press.

Hollingsworth, J. Rogers, Philippe C. Schmitter, and Wolfgang Streeck, eds. 1994. *Governing Capitalist Economies: Performance and Control of Economic Sectors.* New York: Oxford University Press.

Holstein, Günther. 1950. *Historia de la Filosofía Política.* Madrid: Instituto de Estudios Políticos.

Holt, Robert T., and John M. Richardson Jr. 1970. "Competing Paradigms in Comparative Politics." In *The Methodology of Comparative Research,* ed. Robert T. Holt and John E. Turner, 21–71. New York: The Free Press.

Homans, George Caspar. 1941. *English Villagers of the Thirteenth Century.* Cambridge, MA.: Harvard University Press.

———. 1950. *The Human Group.* New York: Harcourt Brace.

———. 1964. "Bringing Men Back In." *American Sociological Review* 29, no. 5 (December): 809–18.

———. 1984. *Coming to My Senses: The Autobiography of a Sociologist.* New Brunswick: Transaction Books.

Horowitz, Donald L. 1985. *Ethnic Groups in Conflict.* Berkeley: University of California Press.

———. 1990. "Comparing Democratic Systems." *Journal of Democracy* 1, no. 4 (Fall): 73–79.

———. 2001. *The Deadly Ethnic Riot.* Berkeley: University of California Press.

Hoselitz, Berthold F. 1960. *Sociological Aspects of Economic Growth.* Glencoe, IL: The Free Press.

Htun, Mala. 2003. *Sex and the State: Abortion, Divorce, and the Family under Latin American Dictatorships and Democracies.* New York: Cambridge University Press.

Hudson, Helen. 1966. *Tell the Time to None.* New York: Dutton.

Huntington, Samuel P. 1950. "A Revised Theory of American Party Politics." *American Political Science Review* 44, no. 3 (September): 669–77.

———. 1951. "Clientelism: A Study in Administrative Politics." Ph.D. dissertation, Department of Government, Harvard University.

———. 1952. "The Marasmus of the ICC: The Commission, the Railroads, and the Public Interest." *Yale Law Journal* 61 (April): 467–509.

———. 1957. *The Soldier and the State: The Theory and Politics of Civil-Military Relations.* Cambridge, MA: Belknap Press of Harvard University Press.

———. 1961. *The Common Defense: Strategic Programs in National Politics.* New York: Columbia University Press.

———, ed. 1962. *Changing Patterns of Military Politics.* New York: The Free Press of Glencoe.

———. 1965. "Political Development and Political Decay." *World Politics* 17, no. 3: 378–414.

———. 1968. *Political Order in Changing Societies.* New Haven, CT: Yale University Press.

——. 1981a. "Reform and Stability in a Modernizing Multi-Ethnic Society." *Politikon* 8 (December): 8–26.

——. 1981b. *American Politics: The Promise of Disharmony.* Cambridge, MA: Harvard University Press.

——. 1982. "Reform and Stability in South Africa." *International Security* 6, no. 4 (Spring): 3–25.

——. 1984. "Will More Countries Become Democratic?" *Political Science Quarterly* 99, no. 2 (Summer): 193–218.

——. 1991. *The Third Wave: Democratization in the Late Twentieth Century.* Norman: University of Oklahoma Press.

——. 1996. *The Clash of Civilizations and the Remaking of World Order.* New York: Simon and Schuster.

——. 2004. *Who Are We? The Challenges to America's National Identity.* New York: Simon and Schuster.

Huntington, Samuel P., and Jorge I. Dominguez. 1975. "Political Development." In *Handbook of Political Science*, vol. 3: *Macropolitical Theory*, ed. Fred I. Greenstein and Nelson W. Polsby, 1–114. Reading, MA: Addison-Wesley.

Huntington, Samuel P., and Clement H. Moore, eds. 1970. *Authoritarian Politics in Modern Society: The Dynamics of Established One-Party Systems.* New York: Basic Books.

Huntington, Samuel P., and Joan Nelson. 1976. *No Easy Choice: Political Participation in Developing Countries.* Cambridge, MA: Harvard University Press.

Inglehart, Ronald. 1977. *The Silent Revolution: Changing Values and Political Styles among Western Publics.* Princeton, NJ: Princeton University Press.

——. 1990. *Culture Shift in Advanced Industrial Society.* Princeton, NJ: Princeton University Press.

——. 1997. *Modernization and Postmodernization: Cultural, Economic, and Political Change in 43 Societies.* Princeton, NJ: Princeton University Press.

——, ed. 2003. *Human Values and Social Change: Findings from the Values Surveys.* Boston: Brill.

Isaac, Jeffrey C. 2002. "Robert A. Dahl." In *American Political Scientists: A Dictionary.* 2nd ed., ed. Glenn H. Utter, and Charles Lockhart, 75–78. Westport, CT: Greenwood Press.

Iversen, Torben. 1999. *Contested Economic Institutions: The Politics of Macroeconomics and Wage Bargaining in Advanced Democracies.* New York: Cambridge University Press.

Iversen, Torben, Jonas Pontusson, and David Soskice, eds. 2000. *Unions, Employers, and Central Banks: Macroeconomic Coordination and Institutional Change in Social Market Economies.* New York: Cambridge University Press.

Jackall, Robert. 2001. "The Education of Barrington Moore, Jr." *International Journal of Politics, Culture and Society* 14, no. 2: 675–81.

Jackman, Robert W. 1985. "Cross-National Statistical Research and the Study of Comparative Politics." *American Journal of Political Science* 29, no. 1: 161–82.

——. 2001. "Cross-country Quantitative Studies of Political Development." *Revista de Ciencia Política* (Santiago, Chile) 21, no. 1: 60–76.

Jameson, Frederic. 1981. *The Political Unconscious: Narrative as a Socially Symbolic Act.* Ithaca, NY: Cornell University Press.

Janos, Andrew. 1986. *Politics and Paradigms: Changing Theories of Change in Social Science.* Stanford, CA: Stanford University Press.

Janowitz, Morris. 1960. *The Professional Soldier: A Social and Political Portrait.* Glencoe, IL: The Free Press.

Johnson, Haynes B., and David S. Broder. 1996. *The System: The American Way of Politics at the Breaking Point.* Boston: Little, Brown.

Johnson, James. 2003. "Conceptual Problems as Obstacles to Progress in Political Science: Four Decades of Political Culture Research." *Journal of Theoretical Politics* 15, no. 1 (January): 87–115.

Johnson, John J. 1964. *The Military and Society in Latin America.* Stanford, CA: Stanford University Press.

Jowitt, Kenneth. 1992. *New World Disorder: The Leninist Extinction.* Berkeley: University of California Press.

Joyce, Michael S., and William A. Schambra. 1996. "A New Civic Life." In *To Empower People: From State to Civil Society,* 2nd ed., ed. Michael Novak, 11–29. Washington, DC: AEI Press.

Kahin, George McT., Guy J. Pauker, and Lucian W. Pye. 1955. "Comparative Politics of Non-Western Countries." *American Political Science Review* 49, no. 4: 1022–41.

Kaplan, Robert D. 2001. "Looking the World in the Eye." *The Atlantic Monthly* 288, no. 5 (December): 68–82.

Karl, Terry Lynn. 1986. "Petroleum and Political Pacts: The Transition to Democracy in Venezuela." In *Transitions from Authoritarian Rule: Latin America,* ed. Guillermo O'Donnell, Philippe C. Schmitter, and Laurence Whitehead, 196–219. Baltimore: Johns Hopkins University Press.

Karl, Terry Lynn, and Philippe C. Schmitter. 1991. "Modes of Transition in Latin America, Southern and Eastern Europe." *International Social Science Journal* 128 (May): 269–84.

———. 1992. "The Types of Democracy Emerging in Southern and Eastern Europe and South and Central America." In *Bound to Change,* ed. Peter M. E. Volten, 55–68. New York: Institute for East-West Studies.

———. 1995. "From an Iron Curtain to a Paper Curtain: Grounding Transitologists or Students of Postcommunism?" *Slavic Review* 54, no. 4 (Winter): 965–78.

Kasfir, Nelson. 1979. "Explaining Ethnic Political Participation." *World Politics* 31, no. 3: 365–88.

Katz, Barry M. 1989. *Foreign Intelligence: Research and Analysis in the Office of Strategic Services, 1942–45.* Cambridge, MA: Harvard University Press.

Katz, Elihu, and Paul F. Lazarsfeld. 1955. *Personal Influence: The Part Played by People in the Flow of Mass Communications.* Glencoe, IL: The Free Press.

Katzenstein, Peter J., Peter B. Evans, James C. Scott, Susanne Hoeber Rudolph, Adam Przeworski, Theda Skocpol, and Atul Kohli. 1995. "The Role of Theory in Comparative Politics: A Symposium." *World Politics* 48, no. 1 (October): 1–49.

Katznelson, Ira. 2003. *Desolation and Enlightenment: Political Knowledge after Total War, Totalitarianism, and the Holocaust.* New York: Columbia University Press.

Katznelson, Ira, and Helen V. Milner, eds. 2002. *Political Science: The State of the Discipline.* New York and Washington, DC: W. W. Norton and the American Political Science Association.

Katznelson, Ira, and Martin Shefter, eds. 2002. *Shaped by War and Trade: International*

Influences on American Political Development. Princeton, NJ: Princeton University Press.

Keck, Margaret E. 1992. *The Workers' Party and Democratization in Brazil*. New Haven, CT: Yale University Press.

Keech, William, Robert Bates, and Peter Lange. 1991. "Political Economy within Nations." In *Political Science: Looking to the Future*, vol. 2: *Comparative Politics, Policy, and International Relations*, ed. William Crotty, 219–63. Evanston, IL: Northwestern University Press.

Keller, Suzanne I. 1963. *Beyond the Ruling Class: Strategic Elites in Modern Society*. New York: Random House.

Kelsen, Hans. 1929. *Vom Wesen und Wert der Demokratie*. Tübingen: Mohr.

Kendall, Patricia L., and Paul F. Lazarsfeld. 1950. "Problems of Survey Analysis." In *Continuities in Social Research: Studies in the Scope and Method of "The American Soldier,"* ed. Robert K. Merton and Paul F. Lazarsfeld, 133–96. New York: The Free Press.

Keohane, Robert. 2003. "Disciplinary Schizophrenia: Implications for Graduate Education in Political Science." *Qualitative Methods—Newsletter of the APSA Organized Section on Qualitative Methods* 1, no. 1 (Spring): 9–12.

Kiernan, V. G. 1980. [Review of Skocpol's *States and Social Revolutions*.] *English Historical Review* 95 (July): 638–41.

King, Gary. 1991. "On Political Methodology." *Political Analysis* 2: 1–30.

——. 1995a. "Replication, Replication." *PS: Political Science & Politics* 28, no. 3 (September): 444–52.

——. 1995b. "A Revised Proposal, Proposal." *PS: Political Science & Politics* 28, no. 3 (September): 494–99.

King, Gary, Robert O. Keohane, and Sidney Verba. 1994. *Designing Social Inquiry: Scientific Inference in Qualitative Research*. Princeton, NJ: Princeton University Press.

King, Gary, Christopher J. L. Murray, Joshua A. Salomon, and Ajay Tandon. 2004. "Enhancing the Validity and Cross-Cultural Comparability of Measurement in Survey Research." *American Political Science Review* 98, no. 1 (February): 191–207.

Klamer, Arjo. 1984. *The New Classical Macroeconomics: Conversations with the New Classical Economists and Their Opponents*. Brighton: Weatsheaf Books.

Krehbiel, Keith. 1991. *Information and Legislative Organization*. Ann Arbor: University of Michigan Press.

Kuhn, Thomas S. 1962. *The Structure of Scientific Revolutions*. Chicago: University of Chicago Press.

——. 1977. "The Essential Tension: Tradition and Innovation in Scientific Research." In *The Essential Tension: Selected Studies in Scientific Tradition and Change*, Thomas S. Kuhn, 225–39. Chicago: University of Chicago Press.

Kurtz, Marcus J. 2000. "Understanding Peasant Revolution: From Concept to Theory and Case." *Theory and Society* 29, no. 1 (February): 93–124.

Ladd, Everett Carl, Jr., and Seymour Martin Lipset. 1975. *The Divided Academy: Professors and Politics*. New York: McGraw-Hill.

Laitin, David D. 1977. *Politics, Language, and Thought: The Somali Experience*. Chicago: University of Chicago Press.

——. 1978. "Religion, Political Culture and the Weberian Tradition." *World Politics* 30, no. 4 (July): 563–92.

——. 1986. *Hegemony and Culture: Politics and Religious Change among the Yoruba.* Chicago: University of Chicago Press.

——. 1988. "Political Culture and Political Preferences." *American Political Science Review* 82, no. 2 (June): 589–93.

——. 1989. "Linguistic Revival: Politics and Culture in Catalonia." *Comparative Studies in Society and History* 31, no. 2 (April): 297–317.

——. 1992a. *Language Repertoires and State Construction in Africa.* New York: Cambridge University Press.

——. 1992b. "Language Normalization in Estonia and Catalonia." *Journal of Baltic Studies* 23, no. 2 (Summer): 149–66.

——. 1994. "Retooling in Comparative Research." *APSA-CP: Newsletter of the APSA Organized Section in Comparative Politics* 5, no. 2 (Summer): 1, 3, 23, 32.

——. 1995a. "National Revivals and Violence." *Archives Européennes de Sociologie* 36, no. 1: 3–43.

——. 1995b. "Disciplining Political Science." *American Political Science Review* 89, no. 2 (June): 454–56.

——. 1998a. *Identity in Formation: The Russian-speaking Populations in the Near Abroad.* Ithaca, NY: Cornell University Press.

——. 1998b. "Toward a Political Science Discipline: Authority Patterns Revisited." *Comparative Political Studies* 31, no. 4 (August): 423–43.

——. 1999a. [Review of Scott, *Seeing Like a State.*] *Journal of Interdisciplinary History* 30, no. 1 (Summer): 177–79.

——. 1999b. "Identity Choice Under Conditions of Uncertainty: Reflections of Selten's Dualist Methodology." In *Competition and Cooperation: Conversations with Nobelists about Economics and Political Science,* ed. James Alt, Margaret Levi, and Elinor Ostrom, 273–302. New York: Russell Sage Foundation.

——. 2000. "What is a Language Community?" *American Journal of Political Science* 44, no. 1: 142–55.

——. 2002. "Comparative Politics: The State of the Subdiscipline." In *Political Science: The State of the Discipline,* ed. Ira Katznelson and Helen V. Milner, 630–59. New York and Washington, DC: W. W. Norton and the American Political Science Association.

——. 2003. "The Perestroikan Challenge to Social Science." *Politics and Society* 31, no. 1 (March): 163–84.

——. 2004a. "The Political Science Discipline." In *The Evolution of Political Knowledge: Democracy, Autonomy, and Conflict in Comparative and International Politics,* ed. Edward Mansfield and Richard Sisson, 11–40. Columbus: Ohio State University Press.

——. 2004b. "Whither Political Science? Reflections on Professor Sartori's claim that 'American-type political science . . . is going nowhere. It is an ever growing giant with feet of clay.' " *PS: Political Science & Politics* 37, no. 4 (October): 789–91.

Laitin, David D., and Guadalupe Rodríguez Gómez. 1992. "Language, Ideology and the Press in Catalonia." *American Anthropologist* 94, no. 1 (March): 9–30.

Laitin, David D., and Carlotta Solé. 1989. "Catalan Elites and Language Normalization." *International Journal of Sociology and Social Policy* 9, no. 4 (October): 1–26.

Laitin, David D., Carlotta Solé, and Stathis N. Kalyvas. 1994. "Language and the Construction of States: The Case of Catalonia in Spain." *Politics & Society* 22, no. 1 (March): 5–29.

Lakoff, George. 1987. *Women, Fire, and Dangerous Things: What Categories Reveal about the Mind.* Chicago: University of Chicago Press.

Lane, Robert E. 1962. *Political Ideology: Why the American Common Man Believes What He Does.* New York: The Free Press.

Lanzalaco, Luca, and Philippe Schmitter. 1989. "Regions and the Organization of Business Interests." In *Regionalism, Business Interests and Public Policy*, ed. William D. Coleman and Henry J. Jacek, 201–30. London: Sage.

LaPalombara, Joseph. 1964. *Interest Groups in Italian Politics.* Princeton, NJ: Princeton University Press.

Lassman, Peter, and Ronald Speiers, eds. 1994. *Weber: Political Writings.* New York: Cambridge University Press.

Lasswell, Harold Dwight. 1936. *Politics: Who Gets What, When, How.* New York: McGraw-Hill.

Lasswell, Harold Dwight, and Abraham Kaplan. 1950. *Power and Society: A Framework for Political Inquiry.* New Haven, CT: Yale University Press.

Lasswell, Harold Dwight, and Daniel Lerner, eds. 1965. *World Revolutionary Elites: Studies in Coercive Ideological Movements.* Cambridge: MIT Press.

Laver, Michael. 1998. "Models of Government Formation." *Annual Review of Political Science* 1: 1–25.

Lazarsfeld, Paul F. 1955. "The Interpretation of Statistical Relations as a Research Operation." In *The Language of Social Research: A Reader in the Methodology of Social Research*, ed. Paul F. Lazarsfeld and Morris Rosenberg, 115–25. New York: The Free Press.

Lazarsfeld, Paul F., Bernard R. Berelson, and Hazel Gaudet. 1944. *The People's Choice: How the Voter Makes Up His Mind in a Presidential Campaign.* New York: Duell, Sloan and Pierce.

Lazarsfeld, Paul F., and Anthony R. Oberschall. 1965. "Max Weber and Empirical Social Research." *American Sociological Review* 30, no. 2 (April): 185–99.

Lchmbruch, Gerhard. 1967. *Proporzdemokratie: Politisches System und politische Kultur in der Schweiz und in Österreich.* Tübingen: J. C. B. Mohr.

Lehmbruch, Gerhard, and Philippe C. Schmitter, eds. 1982. *Patterns of Corporatist Policy-Making.* Beverly Hills, CA: Sage Publishers.

Lenin, V. I. 1939. *Imperialism: The Highest Stage of Capitalism.* New York: International Publishers.

Lévi-Strauss, Claude. 1986. "The Structural Study of Myth." In *Critical Theory Since 1965*, ed. Hazard Adams and Leroy Searle, 809–22. Tallahassee: University Presses of Florida.

Levitsky, Steven. 1998. "Institutionalization and Peronism: The Concept, the Case, and the Case for Unpacking the Concept." *Party Politics* 4, no. 1: 77–92.

Lichbach, Mark Irving. 1997. "Social Theory and Comparative Politics." *Comparative Politics: Rationality, Culture and Structure*, ed. Mark I. Lichbach and Alan S. Zuckerman, 239–76. New York: Cambridge University Press.

——. 2003. *Is Rational Choice Theory All of Social Science?* Ann Arbor: University of Michigan Press.

Lichbach, Mark Irving, and Alan S. Zuckerman, eds. 1997. *Comparative Politics: Rationality, Culture and Structure*. New York: Cambridge University Press.

Lieberson, Stanley. 1991. "Small N's and Big Conclusions: An Examination of the Reasoning in Comparative Studies Based on a Small Number of Cases." *Social Forces* 70, no. 2: 307–20.

Lijphart, Arend. 1966. *The Trauma of Decolonization: The Dutch and West New Guinea*. New Haven, CT: Yale University Press.

———. 1968a. *The Politics of Accommodation: Pluralism and Democracy in the Netherlands*. Berkeley: University of California Press.

———. 1968b. "Typologies of Democratic Systems." *Comparative Political Studies* 1, no. 1 (April): 3–44.

———. 1969. "Consociational Democracy." *World Politics* 21, no. 2 (January): 207–25.

———. 1971. "Comparative Politics and the Comparative Method." *American Political Science Review* 65, no. 3 (September): 682–93.

———. 1974a. "The Structure of the Theoretical Revolution in International Relations." *International Studies Quarterly* 18, no. 1 (March): 41–74.

———. 1974b. "International Relations Theory: Great Debates and Lesser Debates." *International Social Science Journal* 26, no. 1: 11–21.

———. 1975. "The Comparable-Cases Strategy in Comparative Research." *Comparative Political Studies* 8, no. 2: 158–77.

———. 1977. *Democracy in Plural Societies*. New Haven, CT: Yale University Press.

———. 1980. "The Structure of Inference." In *The Civic Culture Revisited*, ed. Gabriel Almond and Sidney Verba, 37–56. Boston: Little, Brown.

———. 1981. "Karl W. Deutsch and the New Paradigm in International Relations." In *From National Development to Global Community: Essays in Honor of Karl W. Deutsch*, ed. Richard L. Merritt and Bruce M. Russett, 233–51. London: Allen and Unwin.

———. 1984. *Democracies: Patterns of Majoritarian and Consensus Government in Twenty-One Countries*. New Haven, CT: Yale University Press.

———. 1985. *Power-Sharing in South Africa*. Berkeley: Institute of International Studies, University of California.

———. 1992. "Democratization and Constitutional Choices in Czechoslovakia, Hungary and Poland, 1989–91." *Journal of Theoretical Politics* 4, no. 2: 207–23.

———. 1994. *Electoral Systems and Party Systems: A Study of Twenty-Seven Democracies*. New York: Oxford University Press.

———. 1996a. "The Framework Document on Northern Ireland and the Theory of Power Sharing." *Government and Opposition* 31, no. 3 (Summer): 267–74.

———. 1996b. "The Puzzle of Indian Democracy: A Consociational Interpretation." *American Political Science Review* 90, no. 2 (June): 258–68.

———. 1997. "About Peripheries, Centres and Other Autobiographical Reflections." In *Comparative European Politics: The Story of a Profession*, ed. Hans Daalder, 241–52. New York: Pinter.

———. 1998. "South African Democracy: Majoritarian or Consociational?" *Democratization* 5, no. 4 (Winter): 144–50.

———. 1999a. *Patterns of Democracy: Government Forms and Performance in Thirty-Six Countries*. New Haven, CT: Yale University Press.

———. 1999b. "Australian Democracy: Modifying Majoritarianism." *Australian Journal of Political Science* 34, no. 3 (November): 313–26.

———. 2000. "Turnout." In *International Encyclopedia of Elections,* ed. Richard Rose, 314–22. Washington, DC: CQ Press.

———. 2003. "Majoritarianism and Democratic Performance in the Fifth Republic." *French Politics* 1, no. 2: 225–32.

———. 2004. "Constitutional Design for Divided Societies." *Journal of Democracy* 15, no. 2 (April): 96–109.

Lijphart, Arend, and Markus M. L. Crepaz. 1991. "Corporatism and Consensus Democracy in Eighteen Countries: Conceptual and Empirical Linkages." *British Journal of Political Science* 21, no. 2 (April): 235–46.

Lijphart, Arend, and Bernard Grofman, eds. 1984. *Choosing an Electoral System.* New York: Praeger.

Lindblom, Charles E. 1997. "Political Science in the 1940s and 1950s." In *American Academic Culture in Transformation: Fifty Years, Four Disciplines,* ed. Thomas Bender and Carl E. Schorske, 244–70. Princeton, NJ: Princeton University Press.

Linz, Juan J. 1959. "The Social Bases of West German Politics." Ph.D. dissertation, Columbia University.

———. 1964. "An Authoritarian Regime: Spain." In *Cleavages, Ideologies and Party System: Contributions to Comparative Political Sociology,* ed. Erik Allardt and Yrjö Littunen, 291–341. Helsinki: Westermarck Society.

———. 1966. "Michels e il suo contributo alla sociologia política." Introduction to *La sociologia del partito politico nella democrazia moderna,* Roberto Michels, 7–119. Bologna: Il Mulino.

———. 1967. "Cleavages and Consensus in West German Politics in the Early Fifties." In *Party Systems and Voter Alignments: Cross-National Perspectives,* ed. Seymour M. Lipset and Stein Rokkan, 283–321. New York: The Free Press.

———. 1970. "From Falange to Movimiento-Organización: The Spanish Single Party and the Franco Regime, 1936–1968." In *Authoritarian Politics in Modern Society: The Dynamics of Established One-Party Systems,* ed. Samuel P. Huntington and Clement H. Moore, 128–203. New York: Basic Books.

———. 1971. *Elites locales y cambio social en la Andalucía rural: Estudio socio-económico de Andalucía.* Madrid: Estudios del Instituto de Desarrollo Económico.

———. 1972. "Intellectual Roles in Sixteenth and Seventeenth Century Spain." *Daedalus* 101 (Summer): 59–108.

———. 1973a. "Opposition to and under an Authoritarian Regime." In *Regimes and Oppositions,* ed. Robert A. Dahl, 171–259. New Haven, CT: Yale University Press.

———. 1973b. "Early State-Building and Late Peripheral Nationalisms against the State: The Case of Spain." In *Building States and Nations,* vol. 2, ed. S. N. Eisenstadt and Stein Rokkan, 32–116. London: Sage.

———. 1973c. "The Future of an Authoritarian Situation or the Institutionalization of an Authoritarian Regime: The Case of Brazil." In *Authoritarian Brazil: Origins, Policies, and Future,* ed. Alfred Stepan, 233–54. Princeton, NJ: Princeton University Press.

———. 1975. "Totalitarianism and Authoritarian Regimes." In *Handbook of Political Science,* vol. 3: *Macropolitical Theory,* ed. Fred Greenstein and Nelson Polsby, 175–411. Reading, MA: Addison-Wesley.

——. 1976. "Some Notes Toward a Comparative Study of Fascism in Sociological Historical Perspective." In *Fascism: A Reader's Guide*, ed. Walter Laqueur, 3–121. Berkeley: University of California Press.

——. 1978. *The Breakdown of Democratic Regimes: Crisis, Breakdown, and Reequilibration*. Baltimore: Johns Hopkins University Press.

——. 1980. "Political Space and Fascism as a Late-Comer." In *Who Were the Fascists?* ed. Stein U. Larsen, Bernt Hagtvet, and J. P. Myklebust, 153–89. Bergen: Universitets Forlaget.

——. 1981. "Some Comparative Thoughts on the Transition to Democracy in Portugal and Spain." In *Portugal Since the Revolution: Economic and Political Perspectives*, ed. Jorge Braga de Macedo and Simon Serfaty, 25–45. Boulder, CO: Westview Press.

——. 1985a. "From Primordialism to Nationalism." In *New Nationalisms of the Developed West: Toward Explanation*, ed. Edward A. Tiryakian and Ronald Rogowski, 203–53. Boston: Allen and Unwin.

——. 1985b. "Democracy: Presidential or Parliamentary: Does It Make a Difference?" Unpublished manuscript.

——. 1986. *Conflicto en Euskadi*. Madrid: Espasa Calpe.

——. 1990a. "Perils of Presidentialism." *Journal of Democracy* 1, no. 1 (Winter): 51–69.

——. 1990b. "The Virtues of Parliamentarism." *Journal of Democracy* 1, no. 4 (Fall): 84–91.

——. 1990c. "Transition to Democracy." *Washington Quarterly* 13, no. 3 (Summer): 143–64.

——. 1992. "Types of Political Regimes and Respect for Human Rights: Historical and Cross-national Perspectives." In *Human Rights in Perspective: A Global Assessment*, ed. Asbjørn Eide and Bernt Hagtvet, 177–222. Cambridge, MA: Blackwell.

——. 1993. "Innovative Leadership in the Transition to Democracy and a New Democracy: The Case of Spain." In *Innovative Leadership in International Politics*, ed. Gabriel Sheffer, 141–86. Albany: State University of New York Press.

——. 1994. "Presidential or Parliamentary Democracy: Does It Make a Difference?" In *The Failure of Presidential Democracy*, vol. 1, ed. Juan J. Linz and Arturo Valenzuela, 3–87. Baltimore: Johns Hopkins University Press.

——. 1997a. "Between Nations and Disciplines: Personal Experience and Intellectual Understanding of Societies and Political Regimes." In *Comparative European Politics: The Story of a Profession*, ed. Hans Daalder, 101–14. London: Pinter.

——. 1997b. "Totalitarianism and Authoritarianism, My Recollections on the Development of Comparative Politics." In *Totalitarismus Eine Ideengeschichte des 20: Jahrhunderts*, ed. Alphons Söllner et al., 141–52. Berlin: Akademie Verlag.

——. 2000. *Totalitarian and Authoritarian Regimes*. Boulder, CO: Lynne Rienner.

——. 2001a. "Presidential Government." In *International Encyclopedia of the Social and Behavioral Sciences*, vol. 17, ed. Neil J. Smelser and Paul B. Bates, 12000–6. New York: Elsevier Science.

——. 2001b. "Nationalstaaten, Staatsnationen und Multinationale Staaten." In *Staat, Nation, Demokratie: Festschrift für Hans-Jürgen Puhle*, ed. Marcus Gräser et al., 27–37. Göttingen: Vandenhoeck und Ruprecht.

——. 2002. "Parties in Contemporary Democracies: Problems and Paradoxes." In

Political Parties: Old Concepts and New Challenges, ed. Richard Gunther, José Ramón Montero, and Juan J. Linz, 291–317. Oxford: Oxford University Press.

——. 2003a. "Faschismus und nicht demokratische Regime." In *Totalitarismus und
politische Religionen,* vol. III: *Deutungsgeschichte und Theorie,* ed. Hans Maier, 247–
325. Paderborn: Ferdinand Schöningh.

——. 2003b. *Fascismo, autoritarismo, totalitarismo: Connessioni e differenze.* Rome:
Ideazione.

——. 2006a. "Robert Michels and His Contribution to Political Sociology in Historical and Comparative Perspective." In *Robert Michels, Political Sociology, and the
Future of Democracy,* ed. H. E. Chehabi. New Brunswick, NJ: Transaction Publishers.

——. 2006b. *Robert Michels, Political Sociology, and the Future of Democracy,* ed. H. E.
Chehabi. New Brunswick, NJ: Transaction Publishers.

Linz, Juan J., and Amando de Miguel. 1966. *Los empresarios ante el poder público: El
liderazgo y los grupos de intereses en el empresariado español.* Madrid: Instituto de
Estudios Políticos.

——. 1968. "La élite funcionarial española ante la reform administrativa." *Anales de
Moral Social y Economica* 17: 199–249.

——. 1974. "Founders, Heirs and Managers of Spanish Firms." *International Studies of
Management and Organization* 4: 7–40.

Linz, Juan J., with Rocío de Terán. 1995. "La sociedad." In *Historia de España. España
actual: España y el Mundo 1939–1975,* ed. J. Andrés-Gallego et al., 117–231. Madrid: Gredos.

Linz, Juan J., and Seymour Martin Lipset. 1956. "The Social Bases of Political Diversity in Western Democracies." Stanford, CA: Center for Advanced Study in the
Behavioral Sciences, unpublished manuscript.

Linz, Juan J., Francisco Andrés Orizo, Manuel Gómez-Reino, and Darío Vila. 1982.
Informe sociológico sobre el cambio político en España 1975–1981. Madrid: Funda-
ción FOESSA, Euramérica.

Linz, Juan J., and Alfred Stepan, eds. 1978. *The Breakdown of Democratic Regimes.* 4
vols. Baltimore: Johns Hopkins University Press.

Linz, Juan J., and Alfred Stepan. 1996. *Problems of Democratic Transition and Consolidation: Southern Europe, South America, and Post-Communist Europe.* Baltimore:
Johns Hopkins University Press.

——. Forthcoming. *Federalism, Democracy, and Nation.*

Linz, Juan J., and Arturo Valenzuela, eds. 1994. *The Failure of Presidential Democracy.*
2 vols. Baltimore: Johns Hopkins University Press.

Lipset, Seymour Martin. 1950. *Agrarian Socialism.* Berkeley: University of California
Press.

——. 1959. "Some Social Requisites of Democracy: Economic Development and
Political Legitimacy." *American Political Science Review* 53, no. 1 (March): 69–
105.

——. 1960a. *Political Man: The Social Bases of Politics.* New York: Doubleday/Anchor
Books.

——. 1960b. "Party Systems and the Representation of Social Groups." *European
Journal of Sociology* 1, no. 1: 50–85.

——. 1962. "Michels' Theory of Political Parties." Introduction to *Political Parties:*

A Sociological Study of the Oligarchical Tendencies of Modern Democracy, Robert Michels, 15–39. New York: The Free Press.

———. 1963. *The First New Nation: The United States in Historical and Comparative Perspective.* New York: Basic Books.

———. 1964. "Ostrogorski and the Analytical Approach to the Comparative Study of Political Parties." Introduction to *Democracy and the Organization of Political Parties,* Moisei I. Ostrogorski, ix–lxv. New York: Doubleday.

———, ed. 1969. *Politics and the Social Sciences.* New York: Oxford University Press.

———. 1990. "The Centrality of Political Culture." *Journal of Democracy* 1, no. 4 (Fall): 80–83.

———. 1995. "Juan Linz: Student, Colleague, Friend." In *Politics, Society, and Democracy: Comparative Studies,* ed. H. E. Chehabi and Alfred Stepan, 1–11. Boulder, CO: Westview Press.

———. 1996. "Steady Work: An Academic Memoir." *Annual Review of Sociology* 22: 1–27.

Lipset, Seymour Martin, and Reinhard Bendix. 1966. "The Field of Political Sociology." In *Political Sociology,* ed. Lewis Coser, 26–47. New York: Harper & Row.

Lipset, Seymour Martin, Paul Lazarsfeld, Allen H. Barton, and Juan J. Linz. 1954. "The Psychology of Voting: An Analysis of Political Behavior." In *Handbook of Social Psychology,* vol. 2, ed. Gardner Lindzey, 1124–75. Reading, MA: Addison-Wesley.

Lipset, Seymour Martin, and Stein Rokkan, eds. 1967a. *Party Systems and Voter Alignments.* New York: The Free Press.

———. 1967b. "Cleavage Structures, Party Systems, and Voter Alignments: An Introduction." In *Party Systems and Voter Alignments: Cross-National Perspectives,* ed. Seymour M. Lipset and Stein Rokkan, 1–64. New York: The Free Press.

Lipset, Seymour Martin, Martin A. Trow, and James S. Coleman. 1956. *Union Democracy.* Glencoe, IL: The Free Press.

Lipton, Michael. 1977. *Why Poor People Stay Poor: Urban Bias in World Development.* Cambridge, MA: Harvard University Press.

Lowi, Theodore J. 1964. "American Business, Public Policy, Case Studies, and Political Theory." *World Politics* 16, no. 4: 677–715.

Luce, R. Duncan, and Howard Raiffa. 1957. *Games and Decisions: Introduction and Critical Survey.* New York: Wiley.

Luebbert, Gregory M. 1991. *Liberalism, Fascism, or Social Democracy: Social Classes and the Political Origins of Regimes in Interwar Europe.* New York: Oxford University Press.

Lustick, Ian S. 1997. "Lijphart, Lakatos, and Consociationalism." *World Politics* 50, no. 1 (October): 88–117.

Macridis, Roy. 1955. *The Study of Comparative Government.* Garden City, NJ: Doubleday.

Macridis, Roy, and Richard Cox. 1953. "Research in Comparative Politics. Seminar Report." *American Political Science Review* 47, no. 3 (September): 641–57.

Mahoney, James. 2000. "Path Dependence in Historical Sociology." *Theory and Society* 29, no. 4 (August): 507–48.

Mahoney, James, and Dietrich Rueschemeyer, eds. 2003. *Comparative Historical Analysis in the Social Sciences.* New York: Cambridge University Press.

Mailer, Norman. 1968. *Miami and the Siege of Chicago: An Informal History of the Republican and Democratic Conventions of 1968.* New York: Signet Books/New American Library.

Mainwaring, Scott. 1998. "Introduction: Juan Linz and the Study of Latin American Politics." In *Politics, Society and Democracy: Latin America,* ed. Scott Mainwaring and Arturo Valenzuela, 1–26. Boulder, CO: Westview Press.

Mainwaring, Scott, Guillermo O'Donnell, and J. Samuel Valenzuela, eds. 1992. *Issues in Democratic Consolidation: The New South American Democracies in Comparative Perspective.* South Bend, IN: University of Notre Dame Press.

Mainwaring, Scott, and Matthew S. Shugart, eds. 1997. *Presidentialism and Democracy in Latin America.* New York: Cambridge University Press.

Mainwaring, Scott, and Arturo Valenzuela, eds. 1998. *Politics, Society and Democracy: Latin America.* Boulder, CO: Westview Press.

Mair, Peter. 1996. "Comparative Politics: An Overview." In *The New Handbook of Political Science,* ed. Robert Goodin and Hans-Dieter Klingemann, 309–35. Oxford: Oxford University Press.

Malia, Martin. 2000. "Blood Rites, Must Violence Always Be the Midwife of History?" *Los Angeles Times Book Review,* May 28.

Malinowski, Bronislaw. 1931. "Culture." In *Encyclopaedia of the Social Sciences,* vol. 4, ed. Edwin R. A. Seligman and Alvin Johnson, 621–46. New York: Macmillan.

——. 1967. *A Diary in the Strict Sense of the Term.* London: Routledge and Kegan Paul.

Manin, Bernard. 1997. *The Principles of Representative Government.* New York: Cambridge University Press.

Mannheim, Karl. 1936. *Ideology and Utopia: An Introduction to the Sociology of Knowledge.* New York: Harcourt Brace Jovanovich.

Manoïlesco, Mihaïl. 1934. *Le Siècle du Corporatisme.* Paris: Alcan.

March, James G. 1955. "An Introduction to the Theory and Measurement of Influence." *American Political Science Review* 49, no. 2 (June): 431–51.

——. 1956. "Influence Measurement in Experimental and Semiexperimental Groups." *Sociometry* 19: 260–71.

——. 1957. "Measurement Concepts in the Theory of Influence." *Journal of Politics* 19, no. 2 (May): 202–26.

Marcuse, Herbert. 1955. *Eros and Civilization: A Philosophical Inquiry into Freud.* Boston: Beacon Press.

——. 1964. *One-Dimensional Man: Studies in the Ideology of Advanced Industrial Society.* Boston: Beacon Press.

——. 1968. "The Struggle Against Liberalism in the Totalitarian View of the State." In *Negations: Essays in Critical Theory,* Herbert Marcuse, 3–42. Boston: Beacon Press.

Martínez, Robert E. 1993. *Business and Democracy in Spain.* Westport, CT: Praeger.

Marty, Martin E., and R. Scott Appleby, eds. 1995. *Fundamentalisms Comprehended.* Chicago: University of Chicago Press.

Marx, Karl. 1930. *Capital.* 2 vols. New York: E. P. Dutton.

——. 1952. *Class Struggles in France, 1848 to 1850.* Moscow: Progress Publishers.

Maynard-Smith, John. 1982. *Evolution and the Theory of Games.* New York: Cambridge University Press.

Mayr, Ernst. 2001. *What Evolution Is.* New York: Basic Books.

Mazrui, Ali A. 1966. "The English Language and Political Consciousness in British Colonial Africa." *Journal of Modern African Studies* 4, no. 3: 295–311.

Mazzuca, Sebastián. 2001. "State, Regime, and Administration in Early Modern Europe: What Have We Learned?" Paper presented at the American Political Science Association (APSA) Annual Convention, San Francisco, August 30–September 2, 2001.

McClelland, David C. 1961. *The Achieving Society*. Princeton, NJ: Van Nostrand.

McCloskey, Donald N. 1983. "The Rhetoric of Economics." *Journal of Economic Literature* 21, no. 2 (June): 481–517.

———. 1986. *The Rhetoric of Economics*. Madison: University of Wisconsin Press.

———. 1990. *If You're So Smart: The Narrative of Economic Expertise*. Chicago: University of Chicago Press.

McConnell, Grant. 1966. *Private Power and American Democracy*. New York: Knopf.

McGuire, William J. 1997. "Creative Hypothesis Generating in Psychology: Some Useful Heuristics." *Annual Review of Psychology* 48: 1–30.

McManners, John. 2000. [Review of Moore's *Moral Purity and Persecution in History*.] *English Historical Review* 115, no. 464 (November): 1250–51.

Merelman, Richard M. 2003. *Pluralism at Yale: The Culture of Political Science in America*. Madison: University of Wisconsin Press.

Merriam, Charles Edward. 1921. "The Present State of the Study of Politics." *American Political Science Research* 15, no. 2 (May): 173–85.

———. 1925. *New Aspects of Politics*. Chicago: University of Chicago Press.

Merritt, Richard L., Bruce M. Russett, and Robert A. Dahl. 2001. "Karl Wolfgang Deutsch 1912–1992." In *Biographical Memoirs*, vol. 80, National Academy of Sciences. Washington, DC: National Academy Press.

Merton Robert K. 1968. *Social Theory and Social Structure*. 3rd ed. New York: The Free Press.

———. 1996a. "The Uses and Abuses of Classical Theory." In *Robert K. Merton: On Social Structure and Science*, ed. Piotr Sztompka, 23–33. Chicago: University of Chicago Press.

———. 1996b. "A Life of Learning." In *Robert K. Merton: On Social Structure and Science*, ed. Piotr Sztompka, 339–59. Chicago: University of Chicago Press.

Michels, Robert. 1962. *Political Parties: A Sociological Study of the Oligarchical Tendencies of Modern Democracy*. New York: The Free Press.

Migdal, Joel. 1983. "Studying the Politics of Development and Change: The State of the Art." In *Political Science: The State of the Discipline*, ed. Ada W. Finifter, 309–38. Washington, DC: American Political Science Association.

Miliband, Ralph. 1969. *The State in Capitalist Society*. New York: Basic Books.

———. 1970. "The Capitalist State: Reply to Nicos Poulantzas." *New Left Review* no. 59: 53–60.

Mill, John Stuart. 1874. *A System of Logic: Raciocinative and Inductive*. New York: Harper & Brothers Publishers.

Miller, Gary J. 1997. "The Impact of Economics on Contemporary Political Science." *Journal of Economic Literature* 35, no. 3: 1173–204.

Mills, C. Wright. 1956. *The Power Elite*. New York: Oxford University Press.

———. 1959. "On Intellectual Craftsmanship." In *The Sociological Imagination*, C. Wright Mills, 195–226. New York: Oxford University Press.

Mitchell, William C. 1969. "The Shape of Political Theory to Come: From Politi-
    cal Sociology to Political Economy." In *Politics and the Social Sciences*, ed. Sey-
    mour M. Lipset, 101–36. New York: Oxford University Press.
Monroe, Kristen Renwick, ed. 2005. *Perestroika! The Raucous Rebellion in Political
    Science*. New Haven, CT: Yale University Press.
Moore, Barrington, Jr.. 1941. "Social Stratification: A Study in Cultural Sociology."
    Ph.D. dissertation, Yale University.
——. 1942. "The Relation between Social Stratification and Social Control." *Sociome-
    try* 5, no. 3: 230–50.
——. 1945. "The Communist Party of the USA: An Analysis of a Social Movement."
    American Political Science Review 39, no. 1 (February): 31–41.
——. 1950. *Soviet Politics: The Dilemma of Power. The Role of Ideas in Social Change*.
    Cambridge, MA: Harvard University Press.
——. 1953. "The New Scholasticism and the Study of Politics." *World Politics* 6, no. 1
    (October): 122–38.
——. 1954. *Terror and Progress USSR: Some Sources of Change and Stability in the Soviet
    Dictatorship*. Cambridge, MA: Harvard University Press.
——. 1958. "Strategy in Social Science." In *Political Power and Social Theory: Six Studies*,
    Barrington Moore, Jr., 111–59. New York: Harper Torchbooks.
——. 1965. "Tolerance and the Scientific Outlook." In *A Critique of Pure Tolerance*,
    Robert Paul Wolff, Barrington Moore, Jr. and Herbert Marcuse, 53–79. Boston:
    Beacon Press.
——. 1966. *Social Origins of Dictatorship and Democracy: Lord and Peasant in the Making
    of the Modern World*. Boston: Beacon Press.
——. 1970. "Reply to Rothman." *American Political Science Review* 64, no. 1 (March):
    83–85.
——. 1972. *Reflections on the Causes of Human Misery and upon Certain Proposals to
    Eliminate Them*. Boston: Beacon Press.
——. 1978. *Injustice: The Social Bases of Obedience and Revolt*. White Plains, NY: M. E.
    Sharpe.
——. 1984. *Privacy: Studies in Social and Cultural History*. Armonk, NY: M. E. Sharpe.
——. 1998. *Moral Aspects of Economic Growth, and Other Essays*. Ithaca, NY: Cornell
    University Press.
——. 2000. *Moral Purity and Persecution in History*. Princeton, NJ: Princeton University
    Press.
——. 2001. "Ethnic and Religious Hostilities in Early Modern Port Cities." *Inter-
    national Journal of Politics, Culture, and Society* 14, no. 4 (Summer): 687–727.
Morton, Rebecca B. 1999. *Methods and Models: A Guide to the Empirical Analysis of
    Formal Models in Political Science*. New York: Cambridge University Press.
Mosca, Gaetano. 1939. *The Ruling Class*. New York: McGraw-Hill.
Moses, Jonathon, Benoît Rihoux, and Bernhard Kittel. 2005. "Mapping Political
    Methodology: Reflections on a European Perspective." *European Political Science*
    4, no. 1: 55–68.
Munck, Gerardo L. 2001. "Game Theory and Comparative Politics: New Perspectives
    and Old Concerns." *World Politics* 53, no. 2 (January): 173–204.
——. 2005. "Measuring Democratic Governance: Central Tasks and Basic Problems."

In *Measuring Empowerment: Cross-Disciplinary Perspectives,* ed. Deepa Narayan, 427–59. Washington, DC: World Bank.

Munck, Gerardo L., and Jay Verkuilen. 2002. "Conceptualizing and Measuring Democracy: Evaluating Alternative Indices." *Comparative Political Studies* 35, no. 1: 5–34.

Murray, Charles A. 1984. *Losing Ground: American Social Policy, 1950–1980.* New York: Basic Books.

Namier, Lewis Bernstein. 1930. *England in the Age of the American Revolution.* London: Macmillan.

Nasar, Sylvia. 1999. *A Beautiful Mind: A Biography of John Forbes Nash, Jr.* New York: Simon and Schuster.

Neumann, Franz. 1957. *The Democratic and the Authoritarian State.* Glencoe, IL: The Free Press.

Neumann, Sigmund. 1942. *Permanent Revolution: Totalitarianism in the Age of International Civil War.* New York: Harper.

New York Times. 2002. "David Riesman, Sociologist Whose 'Lonely Crowd' Became a Best Seller, Dies at 92." May 11.

Newton, Ronald. 1974. "Natural Corporatism and the Passing of Populism in Spanish America." *Review of Politics* 36, no. 1: 34–51.

Nichols, Elizabeth. 1986. "Skocpol on Revolution: Comparative Analysis vs. Historical Conjuncture." *Comparative Social Research* 9: 163–86.

Nkurunziza, Janvier D., and Robert H. Bates. 2003. "Political Institutions and Economic Growth in Africa." *Working Paper* no. 98, Center for International Development, Harvard University.

Nolle-Neumann, Elisabeth. 1995. "Juan Linz's Dissertation on West Germany: An Empirical Follow-up, Thirty Years Later." In *Politics, Society, and Democracy: Comparative Studies*, ed. H. E. Chehabi and Alfred Stepan, 13–41. Boulder, CO: Westview Press.

Norris, Pippa. 1997. "Towards a More Cosmopolitan Political Science?" *European Journal of Political Research* 30, no. 1 (Spring): 17–34.

——. 2004. "From the Civil Culture to the Afrobarometer." *APSA-CP: Newsletter of the APSA Organized Section in Comparative Politics* 15, no. 2: 6–11.

North, Douglass C. 1981. *Structure and Change in Economic History.* New York: Norton.

——. 1990. *Institutions, Institutional Change, and Economic Performance.* New York: Cambridge University Press.

North, Douglass C., and Robert Paul Thomas. 1973. *The Rise of the Western World.* New York: Cambridge University Press.

O'Donnell, Guillermo. 1973. *Modernization and Bureaucratic Authoritarianism: Studies in South American Politics.* Berkeley: Institute of International Studies, University of California.

——. 1978a. "Permanent Crisis and the Failure to Create a Democratic Regime: Argentina, 1955–66." In *The Breakdown of Democratic Regimes: Latin America,* ed. Juan J. Linz and Alfred Stepan, 138–77. Baltimore: Johns Hopkins University Press.

——. 1978b. "Reflections on the Patterns of Change in the Bureaucratic Authoritarian State." *Latin American Research Review* 12, no. 1 (Winter): 3–38.

——. 1978c. "State and Alliances in Argentina, 1956–1976." *Journal of Development Studies* 15, no. 1 (October): 3–33.

——. 1979a. "Tensions in the Bureaucratic-Authoritarian State and the Question of Democracy." In *The New Authoritarianism in Latin America,* ed. David Collier, 285–318. Princeton, NJ: Princeton University Press.

——. 1979b. "Notas para el estudio de procesos de democratización a partir del estado burocrático-autoritario." *Estudios CEDES* 2, no. 5 (Buenos Aires).

——. 1982. "Notas para el estudio de procesos de democratización política a partir del Estado Burocrático-Autoritario." *Desarrollo Económico* (Buenos Aires) 22, no. 86 (July–September): 231–47.

——. 1988. *Bureaucratic Authoritarianism: Argentina, 1966–1973, in Comparative Perspective.* Berkeley: University of California Press.

——. 1993. "On the State, Democratization and Some Conceptual Problems (A Latin American View with Glances at Some Post-Communist Countries)." *World Development* 21, no. 8 (August): 1355–70.

——. 1996. "Illusions about Consolidation." *Journal of Democracy* 7, no. 2 (April): 34–51.

——. 1999a. "Notes for the Study of Processes of Political Democratization in the Wake of the Bureaucratic-Authoritarian State." In *Counterpoints: Selected Essays on Authoritarianism and Democratization,* Guillermo O'Donnell, 109–29. Notre Dame, IN: University of Notre Dame Press.

——. 1999b. *Counterpoints: Selected Essays on Authoritarianism and Democratization.* Notre Dame, IN: University of Notre Dame Press.

——. 2001. "Democracy, Law, and Comparative Politics." *Studies in Comparative International Development* 36, no. 1 (Spring): 7–36.

——. 2004. "Human Development, Human Rights, and Democracy." In *The Quality of Democracy: Theory and Practice,* ed. Guillermo O'Donnell, Jorge Vargas Cullell, and Osvaldo Iazzetta, 9–92. Notre Dame, IN: University of Notre Dame Press.

O'Donnell, Guillermo, and Philippe C. Schmitter. 1986. *Transitions from Authoritarian Rule: Tentative Conclusions about Uncertain Democracies.* Baltimore: Johns Hopkins University Press.

O'Donnell, Guillermo, Philippe C. Schmitter, and Laurence Whitehead, eds. 1986. *Transitions from Authoritarian Rule: Prospects for Democracy.* 4 vols. Baltimore: Johns Hopkins University Press.

Offe, Claus, and Philippe C. Schmitter. 1998. *Democracy Promotion and Protection in Central and Eastern Europe and the Middle East and North Africa: A Comparative Study of International Actors and Factors of Democratization,* unpublished manuscript.

Olson, Mancur. 1965. *The Logic of Collective Action.* Cambridge, MA: Harvard University Press.

Orwell, George. 1950. *Shooting an Elephant and Other Essays.* New York: Harcourt, Brace.

Pareto, Vilfredo. 1963. *The Mind and Society: A Treatise on General Sociology.* 4 vols., ed. Arthur Livingston. New York: Dover.

Parsons, Talcott. 1951. *The Social System.* Glencoe, IL: The Free Press.

Parsons, Talcott, and Edward Shils. 1951. *Toward a General Theory of Action.* Cambridge, MA: Harvard University Press.

Pasquino, Gianfranco. 2005. "The Political Science of Giovanni Sartori." *European Political Science* 4, no. 1: 33–41.

Pauker, Guy. 1959. "Southeast Asia as a Problem Area in the Next Decade." *World Politics* 11, no. 3 (April): 325–45.

Payne, Stanley G. 1995. *A History of Fascism, 1914–1945.* Madison: University of Wisconsin Press.

Perry, Elizabeth J. 1980. [Review of Skocpol's *States and Social Revolutions.*] *Journal of Asian Studies*, 39, no. 3 (May): 533–35.

———. 1993. *Shanghai on Strike: The Politics of Chinese Labor.* Stanford, CA: Stanford University Press.

Persson, Torsten, and Guido Tabellini. 2000. *Political Economics: Explaining Economic Policy.* Cambridge: MIT Press.

———. 2003. *The Economic Effects of Constitutions: What Do The Data Say?* Cambridge: MIT Press.

Pierson, Paul. 2000. "Increasing Returns, Path Dependence, and the Study of Politics." *American Political Science Review* 94, no. 2 (June): 251–67.

Pierson, Paul, and Theda Skocpol. 2002. "Historical Institutionalism in Contemporary Political Science." In *Political Science: The State of the Discipline*, ed. Ira Katznelson and Helen V. Milner, 693–721. New York and Washington, DC: W. W. Norton and the American Political Science Association.

Pitkin, Hannah Fenichel. 1967. *The Concept of Representation.* Berkeley: University of California Press.

Plato. 1946. *The Republic.* New York: Oxford University Press.

Plumb, J. H. 1966. "How it Happened." *New York Times Book Review* 71 (October 9).

Polanyi, Karl. 1957. *The Great Transformation.* Boston: Beacon Press.

Popkin, Samuel L. 1979. *The Republic.* New York: Oxford University Press.

Plumb, J. H. 1966. "How it Happened." *New York Times Book Review* 71 (October 9).

Polanyi, Karl. 1957. *The Great Transformation.* Boston: Beacon Press.

Popkin, Samuel L. 1979. *The Rational Peasant: The Political Economy of Rural Society in Vietnam.* Berkeley: University of California Press.

Popper, Karl. 1945. *The Open Society and its Enemies.* London: Routledge & Kegan Paul.

———. 1959. *The Logic of Scientific Discovery.* New York: Basic Books.

———. 1972. "Of Clouds and Clocks: An Approach to the Problem of Rationality and the Freedom of Man." In *Objective Knowledge: An Evolutionary Approach,* Karl Popper, 206–55. Oxford: Clarendon Press.

Poulantzas, Nicos. 1969. "The Problem of the Capitalist State." *New Left Review* no. 58: 67–78.

Prebisch, Raúl. 1963. *Hacia una dinámica del desarrollo latinoamericano.* México: Fondo de Cultura Económica.

Przeworski, Adam. 1966. "Party System and Economic Development." Ph.D. dissertation, Northwestern University.

———. 1985a. *Capitalism and Social Democracy.* New York: Cambridge University Press.

———. 1985b. "Marxism and Rational Choice." *Politics and Society* 14, no. 4 (December): 379–409.

———. 1986. "Some Problems in the Study of the Transition to Democracy." In *Transitions from Authoritarian Rule: Comparative Perspectives,* ed. Guillermo O'Donnell,

Philippe Schmitter, and Laurence Whitehead, 47–63. Baltimore: Johns Hopkins University Press.

———. 1990. *The State and the Economy Under Capitalism.* New York: Harwood Academic Publishers.

———. 1991. *Democracy and the Market: Political and Economic Reforms in Eastern Europe and Latin America.* New York: Cambridge University Press.

———. 1992. "The Neoliberal Fallacy." *Journal of Democracy* 3, no. 3 (July): 45–59.

———. 1996. "A Better Democracy, A Better Economy." *Boston Review* 21, no. 2 (April–May).

———. 1997. "Democratization Revisited." *Items* (SSRC) 51, no. 1 (March): 6–11.

———. 1999. "Minimalist Conception of Democracy: A Defense." In *Democracy's Value,* ed. Ian Shapiro and Casiano Hacker-Cordón, 23–55. New York: Cambridge University Press.

———. 2003. *States and Markets: A Primer in Political Economy.* New York: Cambridge University Press.

———. 2004a. "Institutions Matter?" *Government and Opposition* 39, no. 4 (September): 527–40.

———. 2004b. "Economic Development and Transitions to Democracy: An Update." Unpublished manuscript, Department of Politics, New York University, March 1.

———. 2005. "Democracy as an Equilibrium." *Public Choice* 123, no. 3: 253–73.

Przeworski, Adam, et al. 1995. *Sustainable Democracy.* New York: Cambridge University Press.

Przeworski, Adam, Michael E. Alvarez, José Antonio Cheibub, and Fernando Limongi. 1996. "What Makes Democracies Endure?" *Journal of Democracy* 7, no. 1 (January): 39–55.

———. 2000. *Democracy and Development: Political Institutions and Well-Being in the World, 1950–1990.* New York: Cambridge University Press.

Przeworski, Adam, and Fernando Limongi. 1993. "Political Regimes and Economic Growth." *Journal of Economic Perspectives* 7, no. 3 (Summer): 51–69.

———. 1997. "Modernization: Theory and Facts." *World Politics* 49, no. 2: 155–83.

Przeworski, Adam, and Covadonga Meseguer. 2002. "Globalization and Democracy." Paper presented at the Seminar on Globalization and Inequality, Santa Fe Institute.

Przeworski, Adam, and John Sprague. 1986. *Paper Stones: A History of Electoral Socialism.* Chicago: University of Chicago Press.

Przeworski, Adam, and Henry Teune. 1970. *The Logic of Comparative Social Inquiry.* New York: Wiley.

Przeworski, Adam, and James Raymond Vreeland. 2000. "The Effect of IMF Programs on Economic Growth." *Journal of Development Economics* 62: 385–421.

———. 2002. "A Statistical Model of Bilateral Cooperation." *Political Analysis* 10, no. 2: 101–12.

Przeworski, Adam, and Michael Wallerstein. 1982. "The Structure of Class Conflict in Democratic Capitalist Societies." *American Political Science Review* 76, no. 2 (June): 215–38.

Putnam, Robert D. 1976. *The Comparative Study of Political Elites.* Englewood Cliffs, NJ: Prentice-Hall.

——. 1988. "Diplomacy and Domestic Politics: The Logic of Two-level Games." *International Organization* 42, no. 3: 427–60.

——. 2000. *Bowling Alone: The Collapse and Revival of American Community.* New York: Simon and Schuster.

Putnam, Robert D., with Robert Leonardi and Raffaella Y. Nanetti. 1993. *Making Democracy Work: Civic Traditions in Modern Italy.* Princeton, NJ: Princeton University Press.

Pye, Lucian W. 1958. "The Non-Western Political Process." *Journal of Politics* 20, no. 3: 468–86.

——. 1966. *Aspects of Political Development.* Boston: Little, Brown.

Pye, Lucian W., and Sidney Verba, eds. 1965. *Political Culture and Political Development.* Princeton, NJ: Princeton University Press.

Rae, Douglas W. 1967. *The Political Consequences of Electoral Laws.* New Haven, CT: Yale University Press.

Redfield, Robert. 1930. *Tepozlan: A Mexican Village.* Chicago: University of Chicago Press.

Reynolds, Andrew, Alfred Stepan, Zaw Oo, and Stephen Levine. 2001. "How Burma Could Democratize." *Journal of Democracy* 12, no. 4 (October): 95–108.

Ricci, David. 1984. *The Tragedy of Political Science: Politics, Scholarship, and Democracy.* New Haven, CT: Yale University Press.

Riesman, David. 1953. *The Lonely Crowd.* Garden City, NY: Doubleday.

Riker, William H. 1964. *Federalism: Origin, Operation, Significance.* Boston: Little, Brown.

——. 1975. "Federalism." In *Handbook of Political Science,* vol. 5, ed. Fred Greenstein and Nelson W. Polsby, 93–172. Reading, MA: Addison-Wesley.

——. 1977. "The Future of a Science of Politics." *American Behavioral Scientist* 21, no. 1: 11–38.

——. 1990. "Political Science and Rational Choice." In *Perspectives on Positive Political Economy,* ed. James E. Alt and Kenneth A. Shepsle, 163–81. New York: Cambridge University Press.

Rivista Italiana di Scienza Politica. 2003. A Special Issue with articles on Downs, Easton, S. E. Finer, Linz, Lipset, Verba. *Rivista Italiana di Scienza Politica* 33, no. 3 (December).

Robertson, Graeme B. 2004. "Leading Labor: Union, Politics and Protest in New Democracies." *Comparative Politics* 36, no. 3 (April): 253–72.

Rodrik, Dani, ed. 2003. *In Search of Prosperity: Analytic Narratives on Economic Growth.* Princeton, NJ: Princeton University Press.

Roemer, John. 1982. *A General Theory of Exploitation and Class.* Cambridge, MA: Harvard University Press.

——, ed. 1986a. *Analytical Marxism.* New York: Cambridge University Press.

——. 1986b. "Introduction." In *Analytical Marxism,* ed. John Roemer, 1–7. New York: Cambridge University Press.

Rogowski, Ronald. 1993. "Comparative Politics." In *Political Science: The State of the Discipline II,* ed. Ada W. Finifter, 431–50. Washington, DC: American Political Science Association.

——. 1995. "The Role of Theory and Anomaly in Social-Scientific Inference." *American Political Science Review* 89, no. 2 (June): 467–70.

Rokkan, Stein. 1970. "International Cooperation in Political Sociology." In *Mass Politics: Studies in Political Sociology,* ed. Erik Allardt and Stein Rokkan, 1–20. New York: The Free Press.

——. 1975. "Dimensions of State Formation and Nation-Building: A Possible Paradigm for Research on Variation within Europe." In *The Formation of National States in Western Europe,* ed. Charles Tilly, 562–600. Princeton, NJ: Princeton University Press.

Rokkan, Stein, with Angus Campbell, Per Torsvik, and Henry Valen. 1970. *Citizens, Elections, Parties: Approaches to the Comparative Study of the Processes of Development.* New York: David McKay.

Ross, Dorothy. 1991. *The Origins of American Social Science.* New York: Cambridge University Press.

Rothman, Stanley. 1970a. "Barrington Moore and the Dialectics of Revolution: An Essay Review." *American Political Science Review* 64, no. 1 (March): 61–82.

——. 1970b. *European Society and Politics.* Indianapolis, IN: Bobbs-Merrill.

Rubinow, Isaac Max. 1968. *Social Insurance, With Special Reference to American Conditions.* New York: Arno Press.

Rueschemeyer, Dietrich, and Theda Skocpol, eds. 1996. *States, Social Knowledge, and the Origins of Modern Social Policies.* New York and Princeton, NJ: Russell Sage Foundation and Princeton University Press.

Rueschemeyer, Dietrich, John D. Stephens, and Evelyne Huber Stephens. 1992. *Capitalist Development and Democracy.* Chicago: University of Chicago Press.

Russett, Bruce M., Hayward R. Alker Jr., Karl W. Deutsch, and Harold D. Lasswell. 1964. *World Handbook of Political and Social Indicators.* New Haven, CT: Yale University Press.

Rustow, Dankwart A. 1964. "The Military: Turkey." In *Political Modernization in Japan and Turkey,* ed. Robert E. Ward and Dankwart A. Rustow, 352–88. Princeton, NJ: Princeton University Press.

——. 1970. "Transitions to Democracy: Toward a Dynamic Model." *Comparative Politics* 2, no. 3 (April): 337–63.

Samuelson, Paul A. 1947. *Foundations of Economic Analysis.* Cambridge, MA: Harvard University Press.

——. 1948. *Economics: An Introductory Analysis.* New York: McGraw-Hill.

Sartori, Giovanni. 1966. "European Political Parties: The Case of Polarized Pluralism." In *Political Parties and Political Development,* ed. Joseph LaPalombara and Myron Weiner, 137–76. Princeton, NJ: Princeton University Press.

——. 1969. "From the Sociology of Politics to Political Sociology." In *Politics and the Social Sciences,* ed. Seymour M. Lipset, 65–100. New York: Oxford University Press.

——. 1970. "Concept Misformation in Comparative Politics." *American Political Science Review* 64, no. 4: 1033–53.

——. 1976. *Parties and Party Systems: A Framework for Analysis.* New York: Cambridge University Press.

——. 1987a. *The Theory of Democracy Revisited,* Part 1: *The Contemporary Debate.* Chatham, NJ: Chatham House Publishers.

——. 1987b. *The Theory of Democracy Revisited,* Part 2: *The Classical Issues.* Chatham, NJ: Chatham House Publishers.

——. 1997. *Comparative Constitutional Engineering: An Inquiry into Structures, Incentives, and Outcomes.* 2nd ed. New York: New York University Press.

Schelling, Thomas C. 1960. *The Strategy of Conflict.* Cambridge, MA: Harvard University Press.

Scheuch, Erwin K. 2003. "History and Visions in the Development of Data Services for the Social Sciences." *International Social Science Journal* 55, no. 3: 385–99.

Schickler, Eric. 2001. *Disjointed Pluralism: Institutional Innovation and the Development of the U.S. Congress.* Princeton, NJ: Princeton University Press.

Schlesinger, Arthur, Jr. 1965. *A Thousand Days: John F. Kennedy in the White House.* Boston: Houghton Mifflin.

Schluchter, Wolfgang. 1979. "Value-Neutrality and the Ethic of Responsibility." In *Max Weber's Vision of History: Ethics and Methods,* Guenther Roth and Wolfgang Schluchter, 65–116. Berkeley: University of California Press.

Schmidt, Steffen W., Laura Guasti, Carl H. Lande, and James C. Scott, eds. 1977. *Friends, Followers, and Factions: A Reader in Political Clientelism.* Berkeley: University of California Press.

Schmitter, Philippe C. 1968. "Development and Interest Politics in Brazil: 1930–1965." Ph.D. dissertation, Department of Political Science, University of California, Berkeley.

——. 1969. "New Strategies for the Comparative Analysis of Latin American Politics." *Latin American Research Review* 4, no. 2: 83–110.

——. 1971. *Interest Conflict and Political Change in Brazil.* Stanford, CA: Stanford University Press.

——. 1974. "Still the Century of Corporatism?" *Review of Politics* 36, no. 1: 85–131.

——. 1975. *Corporatism and Public Policy in Authoritarian Portugal.* Beverly Hills, CA: Sage Publications.

——. 1977. "Modes of Interest Intermediation and Models of Societal Change in Western Europe." *Comparative Political Studies* 10, no. 1 (April): 7–38.

——. 1978. "The Impact and Meaning of 'Non-Competitive, Non-Free and Insignificant' Elections in Authoritarian Portugal, 1933–1974." In *Elections without Choice,* ed. Guy Hermet, Richard Rose, and Alain Rouquié, 145–68. London: Macmillan.

——. 1979a. "The 'Regime d'Exception' That Became the Rule: Forty-eight Years of Authoritarian Domination in Portugal." In *Contemporary Portugal: The Revolution and its Antecedents,* ed. Lawrence S. Graham and Harry M. Makler, 3–46. Austin, TX: University of Austin Press.

——. 1979b. "Speculations About the Prospective Demise of Authoritarian Regimes and its Possible Consequences." *Working Papers* no. 60. Washington, DC: The Wilson Center, Latin American Program.

——. 1980. "The Social Origins, Economic Bases and Political Imperatives of Authoritarian Rule in Portugal." In *Who Were the Fascists?* ed. Stein Ugelvik Larsen, Bernt Hagtvet, and Jan P. Myklebust, 435–66. Bergen, Oslo, and Tromsø: Universitetsforlaget.

——. 1981. "Interest Intermediation and Regime Governability in Contemporary Western Europe and North America." In *Organizing Interests in Western Europe: Pluralism, Corporatism and the Transformation of Politics,* ed. Suzanne Berger, 287–327. New York: Cambridge University Press.

——. 1983. "Democratic Theory and Neo-Corporatist Practice." *Social Research* 50, no. 4 (Winter): 885–928.

——. 1985. "Neo-Corporatism and the State." In *The Political Economy of Corporatism*, ed. Wyn P. Grant, 32–62. London: Macmillan.

——. 1989. "Corporatism is Dead! Long Live Corporatism! Reflections on Andrew Shonfield's *Modern Capitalism.*" *Government and Opposition* 24, no. 1: 54–73.

——. 1990. "Sectors in Modern Capitalism: Modes of Governance and Variations in Performance." In *Labour Relations and Economic Performance*, ed. Renato Brunetta and Carlo Dell'aringa, 3–39. London: Macmillan.

——. 1993. "Comparative Politics." In *The Oxford Companion to the Politics of the World*, ed. Joel Krieger, 171–77. New York: Oxford University Press.

——. 1995. "Transitology: The Sciences or the Art of Democratization?" In *The Consolidation of Democracy in Latin America*, ed. Joseph Tulchin with Bernice Romero, 11–41. Boulder, CO: Lynne Rienner.

——. 1997a. "The Emerging Europolity and its Impact upon National Systems of Production." In *Contemporary Capitalism: The Embeddedness of Institutions*, ed. J. Rogers Hollingsworth and Robert Boyer, 395–430. New York: Cambridge University Press.

——. 1997b. "Autobiographical Reflections: Or How to Live With A Conceptual Albatross Around One's Neck." In *Comparative European Politics: The Story of a Profession*, ed. Hans Daalder, 287–97. New York: Pinter.

——. 1999. *Portugal: do autoritarismo à democracia*. Lisbon: Instituto de Ciências Sociais da Universidade de Lisboa.

——. 2000a. *How to Democratize the EU . . . and Why Bother?* Lanham, MD: Rowman & Littlefield Publishers.

——. 2000b. "Designing a Democracy for the Euro-Polity and Revising Democratic Theory in the Process." In *Designing Democratic Institutions*, ed. Ian Shapiro and Stephen Macedo, 224–50. New York: New York University Press.

——. 2002. "Seven (Disputable) Theses Concerning the Future of 'Transatlanticised' or 'Globalised' Political Science." *European Political Science* 1, no. 2 (Spring): 23–40.

——. 2003. "Democracy in Europe and Europe's Democratization." *Journal of Democracy* 14, no. 4 (October): 71–85.

Schmitter, Philippe C., and Imco Brouwer. 2000. "Analysis of Macro DPP Impact." Florence and Berlin: European University Institute and Humboldt-Universität zu Berlin.

Schmitter, Philippe C., and Nicolas Guilhot. 2000. "From Transition to Consolidation: Extending the Concept of Democratization and the Practice of Democracy." In *Democratic and Capitalist Transitions in Eastern Europe: Lessons for the Social Sciences*, ed. Michel Dobry, 131–46. Dordrecht: Kluwer Academic Publishers.

Schmitter, Philippe C., and Ernst B. Haas. 1964. *Mexico and Latin American Economic Integration*. Berkeley: University of California, Berkeley, Institute of International Studies.

Schmitter, Philippe C., and Patrick Hutchinson. 1999. "Se déplaçant au Moyen-Orient et en Afrique du Nord, ‹transitologues› et ‹consolidologues› sont-ils toujours assurés de voyager en toute sécurité?" *Annuaire de L'Afrique du Nord* (Paris) 38: 11–35.

Schmitter, Philippe C., and Terry Lynn Karl. 1991. "What Democracy is . . . and What it is Not." *Journal of Democracy* 2, no. 3 (Summer): 75–88.

———. 1994. "The Conceptual Travels of Transitologists and Consolidologists: How Far to the East Should They Attempt to Go?" *Slavic Review* 53, no. 1 (Spring): 173–85.

Schmitter, Philippe C., and Gerhard Lehmbruch, eds. 1979. *Trends Toward Corporatist Intermediation.* Beverly Hills, CA: Sage Publishers.

Schrodt, Philip A. 2006. "Beyond the Linear Frequentist Orthodoxy." *Political Analysis* 14, no. 3: 335–39.

Schumpeter, Joseph A. 1942. *Capitalism, Socialism and Democracy.* New York: Harper & Brothers.

Schweinitz, Karl de, Jr. 1959. "Industrialization, Labor Controls, and Democracy." *Industrial Development and Cultural Change* 7, no. 4: 385–404.

———. 1964. *Industrialization and Democracy.* New York: The Free Press of Glencoe.

Scott, James C. 1968. *Political Ideology in Malaysia: Reality and the Beliefs of an Elite.* New Haven, CT: Yale University Press.

———. 1969a. "The Analysis of Corruption in Developing Nations." *Comparative Studies in Society and History* 11, no. 3 (June): 315–41.

———. 1969b. "Corruption, Machine Politics, and Political Change." *American Political Science Review* 63, no. 4 (December): 1142–58.

———. 1972a. *Comparative Political Corruption.* Englewood Cliffs, NJ: Prentice-Hall.

———. 1972b. "Patron-Client Politics and Political Change in Southeast Asia." *American Political Science Review* 66, no. 1: 91–113.

———. 1976. *The Moral Economy of the Peasant: Rebellion and Subsistence in Southeast Asia.* New Haven, CT: Yale University Press.

———. 1977a. "Protest and Profanation: Agrarian Revolt and the Little Tradition, Part I." *Theory and Society* 4, no. 1 (Spring): 1–38.

———. 1977b. "Protest and Profanation: Agrarian Revolt and the Little Tradition, Part II." *Theory and Society* 4, no. 2 (Summer): 211–46.

———. 1985. *Weapons of the Weak: Everyday Forms of Peasant Resistance.* New Haven, CT: Yale University Press.

———. 1990. *Domination and the Arts of Resistance: Hidden Transcripts.* New Haven, CT: Yale University Press.

———. 1998. *Seeing Like a State: How Certain Schemes to Improve the Human Condition Have Failed.* New Haven, CT: Yale University Press.

Scott, James C., and Benedict J. Tria Kerkvliet, eds. 1986. *Everyday Forms of Peasant Resistance in South-East Asia.* London: Frank Cass.

Seidelman, Raymond M., and Edward J. Harpham. 1985. *Disenchanted Realists: Political Science and the American Crisis, 1884–1984.* Albany: State University of New York Press.

Sen, Amartya. 1977. "Rational Fools: A Critique of the Behavioral Foundations of Economic Theory." *Philosophy and Public Affairs* 6, no. 4: 317–44.

Sewell, William H., Jr. 1967. "Marc Bloch and the Logic of Comparative History." *History and Theory* 6, no. 2: 208–18.

——. 1985. "Ideologies and Social Revolutions: Reflections on the French Case." *Journal of Modern History* 57, no. 1: 57–85.

Sharpe, Kenneth E. 1977. *Peasant Politics: Struggle in a Dominican Village.* Baltimore: Johns Hopkins University Press.

Shea, Christopher. 1997. "Political Scientists Clash Over Value of Area Studies." *Chronicle of Higher Education* 43, no. 18, January 10.

Shepsle, Kenneth A. 1978. *The Giant Jigsaw Puzzle: Democratic Committee Assignments in the Modern House.* Chicago: University of Chicago Press.

Shugart, Matthew S., and John Carey. 1992. *Presidents and Assemblies.* New York: Cambridge University Press.

Sibley, Elbridge. 2001. *Social Science Research Council: The First Fifty Years.* New York: Social Science Research Council.

Sikkink, Kathryn. 1991. *Ideas and Institutions: Developmentalism in Brazil and Argentina.* Ithaca, NY: Cornell University Press.

Simmel, Georg. 1908. *Soziologie.* Berlin: Duncker & Humblot.

——. 1950. *The Sociology of Georg Simmel.* Glencoe, IL: The Free Press.

——. 1995. "Soziologie der Konkurrenz." In *Aufsätze und Abhandlungen, 1901–1908,* vol. 1, ed. Rüdiger Kramme, Angela Rammstedt, and Ottheim Rammstedt, 221–46. Frankfurt am Main: Suhrkamp.

Simon, Herbert A. 1957. *Models of Man.* New York: Wiley.

Skidmore, Thomas E. 1967. *Politics in Brazil, 1930–1964: An Experiment in Democracy.* New York: Oxford University Press.

——. 1973. "Politics and Economic Policy Making in Authoritarian Brazil, 1937–71." In *Authoritarian Brazil: Origins, Policies, and Future,* ed. Alfred Stepan, 3–46. New Haven, CT: Yale University Press.

Skocpol, Theda. 1973. "A Critical Review of Barrington Moore's *Social Origins of Dictatorship and Democracy." Politics and Society* 4, no. 1 (Fall): 1–35.

——. 1976. "France, Russia, China: A Structural Analysis of Social Revolutions." *Comparative Studies in Society and History* 18, no. 2 (April): 175–210.

——. 1977. "Wallerstein's World Capitalist System: A Theoretical and Historical Critique." *American Journal of Sociology* 82, no. 5: 1075–90.

——. 1979. *States and Social Revolutions: A Comparative Analysis of France, Russia, and China.* New York: Cambridge University Press.

——. 1980. "Political Responses to Capitalist Crisis: Neo-Marxist Theories of the State and the Case of the New Deal." *Politics and Society* 10, no. 2: 155–201.

——. 1982. "Rentier State and Shi'a Islam in the Iranian Revolution." *Theory and Society* 11, no. 3: 265–83.

——, ed. 1984. *Vision and Method in Historical Sociology.* New York: Cambridge University Press.

——. 1985a. "Bringing the State Back In: Strategies of Analysis in Current Research." In *Bringing the State Back In,* ed. Peter Evans, Dietrich Rueschemeyer, and Theda Skocpol, 3–37. New York: Cambridge University Press.

——. 1985b. "Cultural Idioms and Political Ideologies in the Revolutionary Reconstruction of State Power: A Rejoinder to Sewell." *Journal of Modern History* 57, no. 1: 86–96.

——. 1986. "Analyzing Causal Configurations in History: A Rejoinder to Nicholls." *Comparative Social Research* 9: 187–94.

——. 1988. "An 'Uppity Generation' and the Revitalization of Macroscopic Sociology: Reflections at Mid-Career by a Woman from the Sixties." *Theory and Society* 17, no. 5: 627–43.

——. 1992. *Protecting Soldiers and Mothers: The Political Origins of Social Policy in the United States.* Cambridge, MA: Harvard University Press.

——. 1994. *Social Revolutions in the Modern World.* New York: Cambridge University Press.

——. 1996. *Boomerang: Clinton's Health Security Effort and the Turn Against Government in U.S. Politics.* New York: W. W. Norton.

——, ed. 1998. *Democracy, Revolution, and History.* Ithaca, NY: Cornell University Press.

——. 2000. *The Missing Middle: Working Families and the Future of American Social Policy.* New York: W. W. Norton.

——. 2003a. *Diminished Democracy: From Membership to Management in American Civic Life.* Norman: University of Oklahoma Press.

——. 2003b. "Doubly Engaged Social Science: The Promise of Comparative Historical Analysis." In *Comparative Historical Analysis in the Social Sciences,* ed. James Mahoney and Dietrich Rueschemeyer, 407–28. New York: Cambridge University Press.

Skocpol, Theda, Marjorie Abend-Wein, Christopher Howard, and Susan Goodrich Lehmann. 1993. "Women's Associations and the Enactment of Mothers' Pensions in the United States." *American Political Science Review* 87, no. 3 (September): 686–701.

Skocpol, Theda, and Kenneth Finegold. 1982. "State Capacity and Economic Intervention in the Early New Deal." *Political Science Quarterly* 97, no. 2: 255–78.

——. 1990. "Explaining New Deal Labor Policy." *American Political Science Review* 84, no. 4 (December): 1297–1304.

Skocpol, Theda, Marshall Ganz, and Ziad Munson. 2000. "A Nation of Organizers: The Institutional Origins of Civic Voluntarism in the United States." *American Political Science Review* 94, no. 2 (September): 527–46.

Skocpol, Theda, and Ann Shola Orloff. 1984. "Why not Equal Protection?" *American Sociological Review* 49, no. 6: 726–50.

Skocpol, Theda, and Margaret Somers. 1980. "The Uses of Comparative History in Macrosocial Inquiry." *Comparative Studies in Society and History* 22, no. 2 (October): 174–97.

Skocpol, Theda, and Margaret Weir. 1985. "State Structures and the Possibilities for 'Keynesian' Reponses to the Great Depression in Sweden, Britain, and the United States." In *Bringing the State Back In,* ed. Peter Evans, Dietrich Rueschemeyer, and Theda Skocpol, 107–63. New York: Cambridge University Press.

Skowronek, Stephen. 1982. *Building a New American State: The Expansion of National Administrative Capacities, 1877–1920.* New York: Cambridge University Press.

Smelser, Neil J. 1968. "The Methodology of Comparative Analysis of Economic Activity." In *Essays in Sociological Explanation,* ed. Neil J. Smelser, 62–75. Englewood Cliffs, NJ: Prentice-Hall.

——. 1973. "The Methodology of Comparative Analysis." In *Comparative Research Methods,* ed. Donald P. Warwick and Samuel Osherson, 42–86. Englewood Cliffs, NJ: Prentice-Hall.

———. 1976. *Comparative Methods in the Social Sciences*. Englewood Cliffs, NJ: Prentice-Hall.

Smelser, Neil, and Richard Swedberg. 1994. "The Sociological Perspective on the Economy." In *Handbook of Economic Sociology,* ed. Neil Smelser and Richard Swedberg, 3–26. Princeton, NJ: Princeton University Press.

Smith, Brian. 1982. *The Church and Politics in Chile: Challenges to Modern Catholicism.* Princeton, NJ: Princeton University Press.

Sokoloff, Kenneth, and Stanley L. Engerman. 2000. "History Lessons: Institutions, Factor Endowments, and Paths of Development in the New World." *Journal of Economic Perspectives* 14, no. 3: 217–32.

Somit, Albert, and Joseph Tanenhaus. 1967. *The Development of American Political Science: From Burgess to Behavioralism.* Boston: Allyn & Bacon.

Stark, David, and László Bruzst. 1998. *Postsocialist Pathways: Transforming Politics and Property in East Central Europe.* New York: Cambridge University Press.

Stein, Howard, and Ernest J. Wilson, eds. 1993. "Robert Bates, Rational Choice and the Political Economy of Development in Africa." A special issue of *World Development* 21, no. 6: 1033–81.

Stepan, Alfred. 1965. "The Military's Role in Latin American Political Systems." *Review of Politics* 27, no. 4 (October): 564–68.

———. 1966. "Political Development Theory: The Latin American Experience." *Journal of International Affairs* 20, no. 2: 223–53.

———. 1971. *The Military in Politics: Changing Patterns in Brazil.* Princeton, NJ: Princeton University Press.

———, ed. 1973a. *Authoritarian Brazil: Origins, Policies, and Future.* New Haven, CT: Yale University Press.

———. 1973b. "The New Professionalism of Internal Warfare and Military Role Expansion." In *Authoritarian Brazil: Origins, Policies, and Future,* ed. Alfred Stepan, 47–68. New Haven, CT: Yale University Press.

———. 1978. *The State and Society: Peru in Comparative Perspective.* Princeton, NJ: Princeton University Press.

———. 1985. "State Power and the Strength of Civil Society in the Southern Cone of Latin America." In *Bringing the State Back In,* ed. Peter Evans, Dietrich Rueschemeyer, and Theda Skocpol, 317–43. New York: Cambridge University Press.

———. 1986. "Paths toward Redemocratization: Theoretical and Comparative Considerations." In *Transitions from Authoritarian Rule: Comparative Perspectives,* ed. Guillermo O'Donnell, Philippe Schmitter, and Laurence Whitehead, 64–84. Baltimore: Johns Hopkins University Press.

———. 1988a. *Rethinking Military Politics: Brazil and the Southern Cone.* Princeton, NJ: Princeton University Press.

———. 1988b. "The Last Days of Pinochet?" *New York Review of Books* 35, no. 9 (June 2).

———, ed. 1989. *Democratizing Brazil: Problems of Transition and Consolidation.* New York: Oxford University Press.

———. 1990. "On the Tasks of a Democratic Opposition." *Journal of Democracy* 1, no. 2 (Spring): 41–49.

———. 1998. "Modern Multinational Democracies: Transcending a Gellnerian Oxymoron." In *The State of the Nation: Ernest Gellner and the Theory of Nationalism,* ed. John A. Hall, 219–39. New York: Cambridge University Press.

——. 1999. "Federalism and Democracy: Beyond the U.S. Model." *Journal of Democracy* 10, no. 4 (October): 19–34.

——. 2000. "Religion, Democracy, and the 'Twin Tolerations.'" *Journal of Democracy* 11, no. 4 (October): 37–57.

——. 2001a. "Toward a New Comparative Politics of Federalism, (Multi)Nationalism, and Democracy: Beyond Rikerian Federalism." In *Arguing Comparative Politics,* Alfred Stepan, 315–61. New York: Oxford University Press.

——. 2001b. "The World's Religious Systems and Democracy: Crafting the 'Twin Tolerations.'" In *Arguing Comparative Politics,* Alfred Stepan, 213–53. New York: Oxford University Press.

——. 2004. "Electorally-Generated Veto Players in Unitary and Federal Systems." In *Federalism and Democracy in Latin America,* ed. Edward L. Gibson, 323–61. Baltimore: Johns Hopkins University Press.

——. 2005. "Ukraine: Improbable Democratic 'Nation State' but Possible Democratic 'State Nation'?" *Post-Soviet Affairs* 21, no. 4 (October–December): 279–308.

Stepan, Alfred, Juan J. Linz, and Yogendra Yadav. Forthcoming. *Non Nation-State Democracies.* Baltimore: Johns Hopkins University Press.

Stepan, Alfred, with Graeme B. Robertson. 2003. "An 'Arab' More than 'Muslim' Electoral Gap." *Journal of Democracy* 14, no. 3 (July): 30–44.

Stepan, Alfred, and Graeme B. Robertson. 2004. "Arab, Not Muslim Exceptionalism." *Journal of Democracy* 15, no. 4 (October): 140–46.

Stepan, Alfred, and Cindy Skach. 1993. "Constitutional Frameworks and Democratic Consolidation: Parliamentarism versus Presidentialism." *World Politics* 46, no. 1 (October): 1–22.

Stouffer, Samuel A., Arthur A. Lumsdaine, Marion Harper Lumsdaine, Robin M. Williams Jr., M. Brewster Smith, Irving L. Janis, Shirley A. Star, and Leonard S. Cottrell Jr. 1949. *The American Soldier.* Princeton, NJ: Princeton University Press.

Streeck, Wolfgang, and Philippe C. Schmitter, eds. 1985. *Private Interest Government: Beyond Market and State.* Beverly Hills, CA: Sage Publishers.

Summers, Robert, and Alan Heston. 1991. "The Penn World Table (Mark 5): An Expanded Set of International Comparisons, 1950–1988." *Quarterly Journal of Economics* 106, no. 2: 327–68.

Sumner, William Graham. 1959. *Folkways: A Study of the Sociological Importance of Usages, Manners, Customs, Mores, and Morals.* New York: Dover.

Sumner, William Graham, and Albert Galloway Keller. 1927. *The Science of Society.* 4 vols. New Haven, CT: Yale University Press.

Swedberg, Richard. 1990. *Economics and Sociology, Redefining Their Boundaries: Conversations with Economists and Sociologists.* Princeton, NJ: Princeton University Press.

——, ed. 1991. *Joseph A. Schumpeter: The Economics and Sociology of Capitalism.* Princeton, NJ: Princeton University Press.

Swers, Michele L. 2002. *The Difference Women Make: The Policy Impact of Women in Congress.* Chicago: University of Chicago Press.

Szanton, David L., ed. 2004. *Politics of Knowledge: Area Studies and the Disciplines.* Berkeley: University of California Press.

Sztompka, Piotr. 1996. "Introduction." In *Robert K. Merton: On Social Structure and Science,* ed. Piotr Sztompka, 1–20. Chicago: University of Chicago Press.

Taagepera, Rein, and Matthew Shugart. 1989. *Seats and Votes: The Effects and Determinants of Electoral Systems*. New Haven, CT: Yale University Press.

Tawney, R. H. 1954. "The Rise of the Gentry, 1558–1640." In *Essays in Economic History,* ed. E. M. Carus-Wilson, 173–214. London: Edward Arnold.

——. 1967. *The Agrarian Problem in the Sixteenth Century.* New York: Harper & Row.

Taylor, Charles Lewis, and Michael C. Hudson. 1972. *World Handbook of Political and Social Indicators II.* New Haven, CT: Yale University Press.

Taylor, Charles Lewis, and David A. Jodice. 1983. *World Handbook of Political and Social Indicators III.* New Haven, CT: Yale University Press.

Thelen, Kathleen. 1999. "Historical Institutionalism in Comparative Politics." *Annual Review of Political Science* 2: 369–404.

Thompson, E. P. 1964. *The Making of the English Working Class.* New York: Pantheon.

——. 1971. "The Moral Economy of the English Crowd in the Eighteenth Century." *Past and Present* 50 (February): 76–136.

Tilly, Charles. 1964. *The Vendée.* Cambridge, MA: Harvard University Press.

——, ed. 1975. *The Formation of National States in Western Europe.* Princeton, NJ: Princeton University Press.

——. 1978. *From Mobilization to Revolution.* Reading, MA: Addison-Wesley.

——. 1981. "Useless Durkheim." In *As Sociology Meets History,* Charles Tilly, 95–108. New York: Academic Press.

Tilly, Charles, with Edward Shorter. 1974. *Strikes in France, 1830–1968.* New York: Cambridge University Press.

Tocqueville, Alexis de. 1955. *The Old Régime and the French Revolution.* Garden City, NY: Doubleday.

——. 1969. *Democracy in America.* Garden City, NY: Anchor Books.

Tolstoy, Leo. 1967. *War and Peace.* New York: Modern Library.

Truman, David. 1951. *The Governmental Process.* New York: Alfred A. Knopf.

——. 1955. "The Impact of the Revolution in Behavioral Science on Political Science." In *Research Frontiers in Politics and Government: Brookings Lectures,* Stephen K. Bailey, Herbert A. Simon, Richard C. Snyder, Robert A. Dahl et al., 202–31. Washington, DC: Brookings Institute.

Turner, Henry Ashby. 1996. *Hitler's Thirty Days to Power: January 1933.* Reading, MA: Addison-Wesley.

United Nations Development Programme (UNDP). 2004. *Democracy in Latin America: Toward a Citizens' Democracy.* New York: UNDP.

Van Den Berghe, Pierre L. 1981. *The Ethnic Phenomenon.* New York: Elsevier.

Van Schendelen, M. P. C. M. 1984. "The Views of Arend Lijphart and Collected Criticisms." *Acta Politica* 19, no. 1 (January): 19–55.

Velasco Grajales, Jesús. 2004. "Seymour Martin Lipset: Life and Work." *Canadian Journal of Sociology* 29, no. 4 (Fall): 583–601.

Verba, Sidney, Norman H. Nie, and Jae-on Kim. 1978. *Participation and Political Equality: A Seven Nation Comparison.* New York: Cambridge University Press.

Verba, Sidney, and Lucian W. Pye, eds. 1978. *The Citizen and Politics: A Comparative Perspective.* Stamford, CT.: Greylock Press.

von Neumann, John, and Oskar Morgenstern. 1944. *The Theory of Games and Economic Behavior.* Princeton, NJ: Princeton University Press.

Waldo, Dwight. 1975. "Political Science: Tradition, Discipline, Profession, Science, and Enterprise." In *Handbook of Political Science,* vol. I: *Political Science: Scope and Theory,* ed. Fred I. Greenstein and Nelson W. Polsby, 1–130. Reading, MA: Addison-Wesley.

Wallerstein, Immanuel. 1974. *The Modern World-System: Capitalist Agriculture and the Origins of the European World-Economy in the Sixteenth Century.* New York: Academic Press.

Ward, Robert E., and Dankwart A. Rustow, eds. 1964. *Political Modernization in Japan and Turkey.* Princeton, NJ: Princeton University Press.

Weber, Marianne. 1975. *Max Weber: A Biography.* New York: Wiley.

Weber, Max. 1921. *Gesammelte Politische Schriften.* Munich: Drei Masken Verlag.

——. 1946a. "Science as a Vocation." In *From Max Weber: Essays in Sociology,* ed. Hans H. Gerth and C. Wright Mills, 129–56. New York: Oxford University Press.

——. 1946b. "Politics as a Vocation." In *From Max Weber: Essays in Sociology,* ed. Hans H. Gerth and C. Wright Mills, 77–128. New York: Oxford University Press.

——. 1949. *The Methodology of the Social Sciences,* ed. Edward A. Shils and Henry A. Finch. New York: The Free Press.

——. 1951. *The Religion of China: Confucianism and Taoism.* Glencoe, IL: The Free Press.

——. 1958a. *The Religion of India: The Sociology of Hinduism and Buddhism.* Glencoe, IL: The Free Press.

——. 1958b. *The Rational and Social Foundations of Music.* Carbondale: Southern Illinois University Press.

——. 1958c. *The Protestant Ethic and the Spirit of Capitalism.* New York: Scribner.

——. 1967. *Ancient Judaism.* New York: The Free Press.

——. 1978. *Economy and Society: An Outline of Interpretive Sociology.* Berkeley: University of California Press.

Weber, Ronald E., and William R. Shaffer. 1972. "Public Opinion and American State Policy-Making." *Midwest Journal of Political Science* 16, no. 4 (November): 683–99.

Weibull, Jörgen W. 1995. *Evolutionary Game Theory.* Cambridge: MIT Press.

Weiner, Myron. 1978. *Sons of the Soil: Migration and Ethnic Conflict in India.* Princeton, NJ: Princeton University Press.

Weingast, Barry R. 2002. "Rational Choice Institutionalism." In *Political Science: The State of the Discipline,* ed. Ira Katznelson and Helen V. Milner, 660–92. New York and Washington, DC: W. W. Norton and the American Political Science Association.

Weir, Margaret, Ann Shola Orloff, and Theda Skocpol, eds. 1988. *The Politics of Social Policy in the United States.* Princeton, NJ: Princeton University Press.

Whitehead, Lawrence. 1986. "International Aspects of Democratization." In *Transitions from Authoritarian Rule: Comparative Perspectives,* ed. Guillermo O'Donnell, Philippe Schmitter, and Laurence Whitehead, 3–46. Baltimore: Johns Hopkins University Press.

Wiarda, Howard J. 1974. "Corporatism and Development in the Iberic-Latin World: Persistent Strains and New Variations." *Review of Politics* 36, no. 1: 3–33.

——, ed. 2002. *New Directions in Comparative Politics.* 3rd ed. Boulder, CO: Westview Press.

Wildavsky, Aaron. 1987. "Choosing Preferences by Constructing Institutions: A Cultural Theory of Preference Formation." *American Political Science Review* 81, no. 1: 3–22.

Wolf, Eric R. 1969. *Peasant Wars of the Twentieth Century.* New York: Harper & Row.

Wolpert, Lewis, and Alison Richards. 1988. *A Passion for Science.* Oxford: Oxford University Press.

Worcester, Kenton W. 2001. *Social Science Research Council, 1923–1998.* New York: Social Science Research Council.

Xiaotong, Fei. 1953. *China's Gentry: Essays in Rural-Urban Relations.* Chicago: University of Chicago Press.

Young, Crawford. 1976. *The Politics of Cultural Pluralism.* Madison: University of Wisconsin Press.

Young, H. Peyton. 1998. *Individual Strategy and Social Structure: An Evolutionary Theory of Institutions.* Princeton, NJ: Princeton University Press.

Zagorin, Perez. 1990. *Ways of Lying: Dissimulation, Persecution, and Conformity in Early Modern Europe.* Cambridge, MA: Harvard University Press.

Zakaria, Fareed. 2003. *The Future of Freedom: Illiberal Democracy at Home and Abroad.* New York: W. W. Norton.

Znaniecki, Florian. 1934. *The Method of Sociology.* New York: Farrar & Rinehart.

Zolberg, Aristide R. 1965. *Creating Political Order: The Party-States of West Africa.* Chicago: Rand McNally Publishers.

Zuckerman, Alan S. 1991. *Doing Political Science: An Introduction to Political Analysis.* Boulder, CO: Westview Press.

Name Index

A glossary containing additional information about most of the individuals in this index is available online at www.brown.edu/polisci/people/snyder/.

Subject Index

Almond, Gabriel A., 5, 6, 11, 27n35, 41n12, 43, 44, 45, 48n34, 128–29, 141, 155, 158, 179, 227, 228, 229, 241, 244–45, 255, 269, 270, 313, 333, 346, 355, 405, 415, 579, 605, 617, 646, 700; biographic information, 63–64; *The Civic Culture*, 45, 64, 80, 128–29, 229, 405, 415–16, 617, 646; on classical social theory, 66, 75; on collaborators, 65–66, 73, 74–75, 80, 85; on colleagues, 68–69, 72, 73–74; comparative politics, 82–84; on concept formation, 77–78; on country cases, 75, 82; on craft and methods, 76–82; *Crisis, Choice, and Change*, 64, 72, 78–79, 80, 82; dissertation, 67; education, 65–67; on field research, 75, 77–78; formative experiences, 64–65, 68; and Great Depression of 1929, 64–66; institutional affiliations, 68–69, 73–74; institutional roles, 69–71, 74; intellectual influences, 66; on language skills and training, 66, 68, 75; mentors, 73; parents, 65, 77; on political theory, 75; *The Politics of the Developing Areas*, 44, 63–64, 70–71, 76–77, 227, 270, 355, 605; research, future, 85; on research and real world events, 81–82; on science and normative values, 70–71, 81–82; on students, 73–75; on teaching, 75; traveling, 84; war time experience, 68; writings, favorite, 81; young scholars, advice to, 84

American Academy of Arts and Sciences, election to, 64, 114, 151, 211, 235, 274, 352, 393, 457, 505, 557, 602, 650

American Council of Learned Societies (ACLS), 316

American Historical Association (AHA), 35

American Political Science Association (APSA), 35, 382, 388–89, 550–51, 700–701; presidents of, 64, 114, 211, 235, 650, 700–701

    Comparative Politics Section, 52, 549–50, 592–93, 635–36; presidents of, 505, 557, 602

    Political Methodology Section, 51n43, 594, 596–97

    Qualitative Methods Section, 56n60, 557, 594–97

American Political Science Review (APSR), 149, 382, 389, 497, 641, 700–701

American politics, 220, 676–81. *See also under* comparative politics

American Sociological Association (ASA), 388; Comparative and Historical Sociology Section, 699

analytic narratives. *See under* methods

anthropology. *See under* comparative politics

area studies. *See under* comparative politics

Arizona State University, 586, 595

authoritarianism. *See under* concepts; theories

Bates, Robert H., 5, 8, 10, 14, 15, 16, 19, 365, 379, 454, 482, 499, 618–19, 630, 638, 640, 646, 675, 698; on African Studies, 527, 537–38, 540, 553; *Analytic Narratives*, 505, 525–27; on area studies, 549–550, 553; biographic information, 504–5; on collaborators, 520, 525; on colleagues, 542, 544, 546–47; on comparative politics, 522, 524–25, 526, 534, 537, 543, 545–46, 552–54; on country cases, 525–26; on craft and methods, 530–39; dissertation, 512–13; education, 507–17; on field research, 511, 528, 535–37; formative experiences, 505–7; influences, intellectual, 508, 511–12; institutional affiliations, 542–47; institutional roles, 549–50; on language skills and training, 535–36; *Markets and States in Tropical Africa*, 504, 519–21, 532, 538; mentors, 510; on normative values and research, 541–42; parents, 505–6; policy recommendations and consulting, 523, 540–41; on rational choice theory and formal models, 525, 527, 528, 530, 531–35, 536–37, 547–48; research, 520, 525, 527–29, 539; on research and real world events, 511, 548; on research questions, 511, 530–31; on science, 529–30; on students, 529, 539, 544–45, 547, 551–52; on teaching, 543–45, 551–52; and Vietnam War, 512, 514; work in government, 508; young scholars, advice to, 554–55

behavioralism. *See under* theoretical approaches

Berkeley. *See* University of California, Berkeley

Brooklyn College, 64, 68

Brown University, 674

Bryn Mawr College, 603, 609

California Institute of Technology (Caltech), 517, 519, 529–30, 542–46, 625, 626
Carnegie Foundation, 73
Carnegie-Mellon University, 543
case studies. *See under* methods
Center for Advanced Study in the Behavioral Sciences, 43n16, 74, 76, 79, 123, 140, 143, 157, 169, 170, 265, 525
Central European University (CEU), 443–47
Chicago. *See* University of Chicago
civil-military relations. *See under* theories
Civil Rights Movement, 6, 8, 48, 390–91, 506, 514, 651, 653–54, 681
class analysis. *See* theoretical approaches, Marxism
classics. *See* social theory, classical
collaborative research. *See under names of interviewees*
Collier, David, 5, 8, 17–18, 56, 273, 287, 454, 621, 636; biographic information, 556–57; on collaborators, 569–71, 582, 586, 590–91; on colleagues, 561, 571, 588–90; comparative politics, 594, 597–600; on concept formation, 578–81; dissertation, 563–69; education, graduate, 558–63; on field research, 564–69; formative experiences, 557–58, 561; institutional affiliations, 587–88; institutional roles, 592–97; mentors, 567; on methodology, 578–87, 598–99; *The New Authoritarianism in Latin America,* 273, 287, 556, 570–73, 585, 590; parents, 557–58, 561; on research, 572–73, 575–76, 586, 590–91; *Rethinking Social Inquiry,* 557, 582–85, 586, 590, 591, 596, 598; on science and normative values, 586–87; *Shaping the Political Arena,* 17–18, 556, 570, 572–79, 583, 588, 589, 590, 593, 621; on students, 571, 575, 581, 590, 591; on teaching, 591; traveling, 561; and Vietnam War, 563; young scholars, advice to, 599–600
Columbia University, 35, 155–56, 158, 177–78, 202–3, 216, 403–5, 442–43, 449, 509, 545
Committee on Comparative Politics (SSRC). *See* Social Science Research Council (SSRC) Committee on Comparative Politics
Committee on Political Behavior (SSRC). *See* Social Science Research Council (SSRC) Committee on Political Behavior
Committee on Political Sociology (ISA and IPSA), 46n29, 161, 192
comparative historical analysis. *See under* theoretical approaches
comparative methods. *See under* methods

comparative politics: in pre-1920, 33–41; in 1920s to 1940s, 41–43, 116, 144–45, 227; in 1950s and 1960s, 43–48, 227, 229; in 1970s and 1980s, 47–52; in 1990s and 2000s, 52–58; achievements of field, 29, 144–45, 200–201, 227–28, 269–71, 300–301, 344–46, 383–84, 453–54, 494–95, 552–53, 597–98, 644–45, 702–4; and American politics, 41–43, 51–52, 53, 54, 55, 69, 122, 231–32, 270, 343, 346, 347–48, 500–502, 544, 548, 677, 681, 696, 706; and anthropology, 44, 70, 76, 89–90, 230, 310, 372–73, 378, 379, 432, 513, 515–16, 543, 557, 605, 618–19, 652; and area studies, 46, 50, 52, 57, 67, 202–3, 346–47, 500, 501–2, 537–38, 540, 549–50, 552–53, 592, 593, 636, 638, 652; and economics, 33, 36, 53, 57, 65, 75, 76, 205–7, 228, 301–2, 353, 360, 387–88, 396, 484–85, 493, 494–95, 504, 507, 522, 524–25, 534, 537, 543, 545–46, 554, 605, 613, 634, 641, 647, 651; in Europe, 46, 193–94, 266, 347, 458; future of field, 82–84, 131–34, 146–48, 202–7, 231–32, 271–72, 301–4, 347–50, 387–88, 497–502, 553–54, 597–99, 645–48, 704–6; graduate training in, 1–3, 9–11, 13–14, 16, 20–21, 27–29, 30–31, 146–47, 198, 226–27, 232, 349, 380, 383–84, 390–91, 451, 453, 493–94, 497, 501–2, 503, 526, 594, 598–600, 638–41, 705–6; and history, 35–36, 88, 89, 104, 184–85, 275, 301, 378, 379, 396, 404, 493, 543, 549, 651, 671, 685; and International Relations, 211, 228, 231, 239, 241, 247, 307, 309–10, 349–50, 449, 606, 608, 642–43, 706; and Perestroika movement, 55, 351, 380, 381n7, 388, 389, 550–51, 700–701; and psychology, 44, 70, 76, 228, 301, 358, 545, 606, 641; shortcomings of field, 9–11, 13–14, 20–22, 27–30, 145–46, 201–2, 228–31, 301, 345–49, 495–97, 641–44; and sociology, 33, 36, 44, 53, 70, 76, 80, 88–89, 151, 153, 173, 228, 301, 309, 404, 458, 498, 559, 605, 606, 652–55, 660, 672–73, 675, 687, 705–6; term, first use of, 42n13. *See also* concepts; methods; political science; theoretical approaches; theories
concept formation. *See under* methods
concepts: authoritarianism, 150, 161–63, 182, 454; bureaucratic authoritarianism, 273, 284, 298, 454; civil society, 422, 680–81; consociationalism, 245; corporatism, 22, 23, 305, 316, 319, 333–34, 454; democracy, 114, 127–28, 131, 145–46, 295–96, 338, 475–77; democracy, consensus, 249; democracy, consociational, 234, 247, 454; democracy, delegative,

dissertation, 157; education, 152–58; on fascism, 168–69; on federalism, 171–72, 174, 184; on field research, 186–88; formative experiences, 151–54; influences, intellectual, 153–54; institutional affiliations, 153–54, 158, 192–94; on language skills and training, 157; mentors, 153, 155–58; on nationalism, 170–171, 180, 183; non-democatic regimes, life under, 153; on normative biases, 169–70, 188–189; opportunities missed, 191–92; parents, 152; policy recommendations and advice to politicians, 194; political institutions, 167–68; political leadership, 162–65, 201–2; presidentialism, 151, 166–67, 180–81; *Problems of Democratic Transition and Consolidation,* 151, 169–170, 195, 393, 421–23, 433, 435, 446, 635; on rational choice theory, 203–7; on research, 194–95; on research and real world events, 178; on research questions, 178–81; on science, 172–78, 205; "Spain: An Authoritarian Regime," 161–63, 193; on structural functionalism, 159–61; on students, 196–200; on survey research, 185–86; on teaching, 195–98; war time experience, 152; writings or ideas, best, 170–71; young scholars, advice to, 158, 188, 198–99

London School of Economics, 116

Manchester University, 515–17
Marxism. *See under* theoretical approaches
Massachusetts Institute of Technology (MIT), 15, 509–11, 513–14
McCarthyism, 140, 395, 558, 602
methods, 37, 45–46, 50–52, 54, 56–57; analytic narratives, 498–99, 525–27, 630–31; case, critical, 314; case, deviant, 243, 245, 258; case studies, 258, 525–26, 499; comparative methods, 222–23, 263–64, 478, 479, 538–39, 579, 615–16, 663; of concept formation, 155, 182–84, 579–81; counterfactual analysis, 479–80, 496; of data collection, 412, 478–79, 485–86, 690–91; deductive methods, 482–84; experimental methods, 381, 534; factor analysis, 249, 258, 486; formal methods, 123–24, 482–84, 525, 527, 530–35, 628; multi-methods, 627–31, 689; qualitative methods, 384, 582–85; quantitative methods and statistics, 121, 222, 495–96, 582–84, 598, 688–91; and survey research, 129, 185–86, 427; and typologics, 76–77, 161–62
Michigan State University, 651–55
MIT. (*See* Massachusetts Institute of Technology

modernization theory. *See under* theoretical approaches
Moore, Jr., Barrington, 5, 6–7, 12, 15–16, 17, 18–19, 21, 29, 57, 71–72, 128, 164, 222–23, 277, 303, 359, 365, 383, 465–66, 473, 499–500, 511, 546, 574, 578, 588, 605, 628, 648, 653, 655–658, 660, 661, 662, 663, 666, 667, 668, 673n13, 677, 684–85, 686, 705; on area studies, 96, biographic information, 86–87; on classical social theory, 103–4; on collaborators, 107–8; on colleagues, 92–94; on country cases, 96; on craft and methods, 95, 97, 104–7; on critics, 95, 100, 101; dissertation, 90; education, 87–90; on field research, 106–7; formative experiences, 87–88; on historical analysis, 104–6; influences, intellectual, 89, 97–99; institutional affiliations, 92–94; institutional roles, 110–11; on language skills and training, 88, 105; mentors, 88, 89–90; opportunities missed, 108–9; parents, 87, 102; research, 107–8; on research and real world events, 102–3; on science and normative values, 102–3; *Social Origins of Dictatorship and Democracy,* 7, 15, 17, 19, 57, 71–72, 86, 88, 90, 91, 95, 96–101, 103, 105, 107, 108, 110, 128, 277, 359, 365, 383, 465–66, 499–500, 511, 546, 574, 605, 607, 628, 653, 655, 656, 658, 660, 666, 667, 668; on students, 110; on teaching, 109–11; traveling, 108; war time experience, 90–92; work in government, 90–92; writings, 100–103; young scholars, advice to, 111

National Academy of Sciences, election to, 64, 114
nationalism. *See under* theories
National Science Foundation (NSF), 51n43, 540, 569, 586, 640, 641, 655
New School for Social Research, 154
New York University, 267, 457, 488–89
Northwestern University, 15, 43, 69–70, 457, 458, 459–61
Notre Dame, *See under* University of Notre Dame

O'Donnell, Guillermo, 5, 7–8, 18, 50, 144, 167, 306, 320, 323–24, 326, 327, 328, 329, 335, 339–40, 340, 347, 401, 419, 420, 423, 442, 448, 450, 454, 465, 468–69, 499, 501, 561, 570–72, 577, 578, 585, 593; biographic information, 273–74; on classical social theory, 299–300; on collaborators, 290–91; on colleagues, 278, 280–81; comparative politics,

totalitarianism. *See under* concepts; theories
Tufts University, 564
typologies. *See under* methods

University of Buenos Aires, 274, 275
University of California, Berkeley, 15, 235, 246–
47, 264–65, 279, 306, 309–12, 403, 557, 574,
588–90, 602, 626, 671
University of California, Los Angeles, 520, 537,
592
University of California, San Diego, 235, 247,
267, 602, 632
University of Chicago, 14, 41, 64–65, 67, 73, 76,
89, 92–93, 211–12, 306, 341–43, 457, 462–63,
488–89, 517, 557, 559–61, 602, 603, 632–34,
671, 694, 697, 702; Chicago School, 41, 43,
43n16
University of Geneva, 319
University of Indiana. *See* Indiana University at
Bloomington
University of Leiden, 235, 247, 265–66
University of Madrid, 152–53
University of Michigan, 51n43, 279, 545
University of Notre Dame, 274, 282, 394–95,
396, 589, 592
University of Pennsylvania, 461, 488
University of Rochester, 53n49, 386, 543–44
University of Warsaw, 457, 458–59, 461

University of Washington, 115, 592
University of Wisconsin at Madison, 358, 374–
76

Vietnam War, 6, 8, 9, 48, 223, 310, 314, 358–59,
374–75, 390, 398–99, 494, 512, 514, 563, 603,
654–55, 659, 661, 681, 688

Washington University, 457, 461, 462, 488, 543
welfare state. *See under* theories
Williams College, 87–88, 353–54
women in comparative politics and social sciences, 660–61, 696–97, 706–7
Woodrow Wilson Center, 180, 288–90, 323, 465
World Values Survey, 55, 227
World War II, 5, 6, 7, 42, 48, 68, 73, 82, 90, 116,
120–21, 137, 138, 178, 229, 235–37, 244, 306,
353, 356, 408–9, 457–58. *See also under names
of interviewees*

Yale University, 43n16, 64, 73–74, 156, 211, 240,
274, 358, 375–76; Department of Political Science, 121–22, 240–42, 276–77, 377, 386, 441–
42, 606; Department of Sociology, 89; Institute of International Studies, 68–69; Program in Agrarian Studies, 365, 377–79; Yale
Political Data Program, 46

Gerardo L. Munck, Argentinian by birth, teaches in the School of International Relations at the University of Southern California, and does research on political regimes and democracy, methodology, and Latin America. He is editor of *Regimes and Democracy in Latin America* (Oxford, 2007) and author of *Authoritarianism and Democratization. Soldiers and Workers in Argentina, 1976–83* (Penn State, 1998). His articles include (with Richard Snyder) "Debating the Direction of Comparative Politics," *Comparative Political Studies* (2007); "Democratic Politics in Latin America," *Annual Review of Political Science* 7 (2004); (with Jay Verkuilen) "Conceptualizing and Measuring Democracy," *Comparative Political Studies* (February 2002); "The Regime Question," *World Politics* (October 2001); "Game Theory and Comparative Politics," *World Politics* (January 2001).

Richard Snyder is associate professor of political science at Brown University. He studies the political economy of development, political regimes, and Latin America. His publications include *Politics after Neoliberalism: Reregulation in Mexico* (Cambridge University Press, 2001) and three edited volumes on the political economy of rural Mexico (Center for U.S.-Mexican Studies, University of California, San Diego, 1998–2000). Among Snyder's articles are "Does Lootable Wealth Breed Disorder? A Political Economy of Extraction Framework," *Comparative Political Studies* (October 2006); "Diamonds, Blood, and Taxes: A Revenue-Centered Framework for Explaining Political Order," *Journal of Conflict Resolution* (August 2005, with Ravi Bhavnani); "The Value of a Vote: Malapportionment in Comparative Perspective," *British Journal of Political Science* (October 2001, with David Samuels); and "Scaling Down: The Subnational Comparative Method," *Studies in Comparative International Development* (Spring 2001).